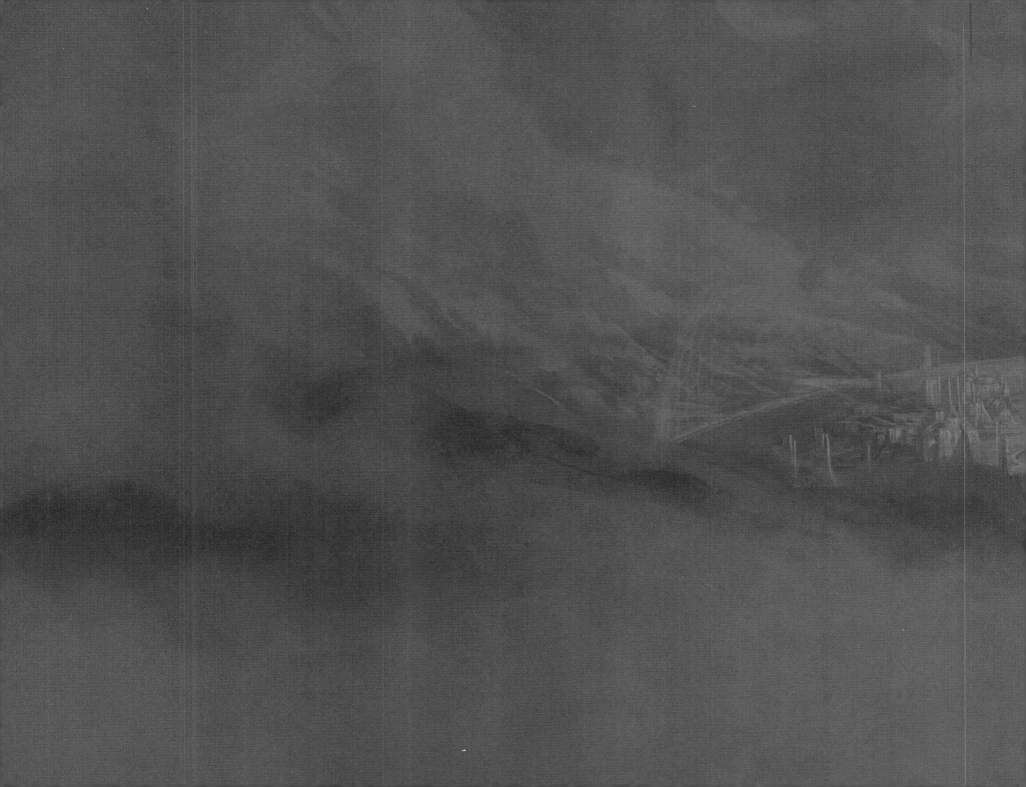

LINE DEVELOPMENT

JACK NORRIS
BENN GRAYBEATON

RULES DEVELOPMENT

BENN GRAYBEATON

DEVELOPED FROM THE ORIGINAL
2D20 SYSTEM DESIGN BY JAY LITTLE,
FOR MUTANT CHRONICLES

WRITING

RICHARD AUGUST
JENNIFER BAUGHMAN
JASON BRICK
DARREN BULMER
MARK CARROLL
CHRIS LITES
BRYAN C.P. STEELE
JONATHAN M. THOMPSON
PETER WRIGHT

EDITING AND PROOFING

BRIAN CASEY
VIRGINIA PAGE
ARIC WIEDER

LITERARY CONSULTANT

SCOTT TRACY GRIFFIN

GLOSSARY AND INDEX

VIRGINIA PAGE

ART DIRECTION

SAM WEBB
KATYA THOMAS

COVER ART

BJÖRN BARENDS

LOGO DESIGN

MICHAL E CROSS

GRAPHIC DESIGN

CHRIS WEBB

CHARACTER SHEET

FRANCESCA BAERALD

INTERNAL ART

NATE ABELL
CHRIS ADAMAK
DAREN BADER
BJORN BARENDS
GIORGIO BARONI
TOMA FEIZO GAS
CHAIM GARCIA
MICHELE GIORGI
RODRIGO GONZALES
JACK KAISER
SOREN MEDING
ROLF MOHR
CRISTI PICU
JEFF PORTER
PAOLO PUGGIONI
CHRISTIAN QUINOT
MARTIN SOBR
STEVE STARK

CARTOGRAPHY

FRANCESCA BAERALD
N.R. BHARATHAE

PUBLISHING DIRECTOR

CHRIS BIRCH

HEAD OF RPG DEVELOPMENT

SAM WEBB

PRODUCTION MANAGER

STEVE DALDRY, PETER GROCHULSKI

PUBLISHING ASSISTANT

VIRGINIA PAGE

SOCIAL MEDIA MANAGER

SALWA AZAR

COMMUNITY SUPPORT

LLOYD GYAN

WITH THANKS TO

JAMES SULLOS
CATHY WILBANKS
TYLER WILBANKS

Modiphius Entertainment Ltd, 2nd Floor,
39 Harwood Road, London, SW6 4QP, England
Produced by: Standartų Spaustuvė, UAB, 39
Dariaus ir Girėno, Str., LT-02189 Vilnius, Lithuania

INFO@MODIPHIUS.COM   WWW.MODIPHIUS.COM

Modiphius Entertainment Product Number: MUH051392
ISBN: 978-1-912743-11-7

CONTENTS

CONTINENTS

1

Most people I know around my age or a bit older started their foray into speculative fiction with Tolkien. This isn't universal, but I find it rather common. Many younger folks took the dive with Harry Potter.

For me? I started on Mars. I first encountered Edgar Rice Burroughs' **John Carter** series in a bookstore as a kid. I'd gotten good grades and my grandmother had taken me to the bookstore to get some reading material. She was a teacher and, unlike some teachers and authority figures, her philosophy towards getting me comics or "weird" fiction was "whatever, as long as he's reading." So, when I did well in school or helped around the house to a significant degree, I basically got a line of credit usable for reading material. It wasn't a lot, but it was enough to keep me reading, which was, of course, the goal.

I doubt you're reading this, grandma, but I love you and can't thank you enough for that. It's a big part of the reason I'm here writing this.

Even with as encouraging as grandma was about me reading almost anything that wasn't outright inappropriate for a kid whose age was in the single digits, I was a bit unsure grandma would let me buy a novel with a mostly naked man and woman on it, but it certainly drew my eye. However, even beyond Michael Whelan's wondrous cover, the title got me: A Princess of Mars. I remember thinking, why was it "A" Princess of Mars. Were there more than one? What made this one so special? Who was that guy on the cover if the woman was the princess? Who were those scary looking four-armed green creatures around them? Wasn't Mars all red and stuff?

I really wasn't sure of a lot of things about that book, but I knew one thing: I really wanted to find these things out. So, I asked for the book and got it. I really can't recall if I had to beg or cajole my way past that cover or not, but I do remember what happened once I managed to secure a copy. I took the book home and read the whole thing that night.

And I loved it. Carter was a cowboy and a soldier and he was on another planet and in love with a princess! He had an awesome alien dog and four-armed green buddy who was fifteen feet tall! They had flying ships and fought giant apes! My kid brain could barely contain how amazing it all was.

So, as soon as I could, I got the next Carter book I could find. And the next. And the next. I didn't read them all in order, not at first. It was literally whatever I could get and I started them as soon as I got a new one. I was pretty frustrated when I found out there were only eleven books, or that Burroughs wasn't around to write any more. But even so, I fell in love with Barsoom.

Then after Carter came Pellucidar. And Carson of Venus. Those were cool too. Not as cool as Carter, but I loved them too. Tarzan left me a bit less impressed for some reason I can't completely recall, so I finally ended up looking outside Burroughs to other fantastic settings and stories. During this time, I'd also been reading superhero comics and the occasional monster-oriented book, but as far as science-fiction fantasy went? Carter and Burroughs were my first forays.

Of course, a few months later I read The Hobbit and then Lord of the Rings, found my way from there to Howard's Conan and Kull, Zelazny's Jack of Shadows, and on to other heroes and their stories. Appreciation for all these works also pushed me to comics outside of superheroes, such as Warlord and Arion, Lord of Atlantis. A short time later I discovered roleplaying games as well. Fast forward a few decades and now here I am, writing my own books and working with games that let players transport themselves to amazing places where they can be the heroes of their own tales of daring and adventure, at least for a few hours at a time. I've worked on a lot of books in many settings and genres, including those involving many creations and characters I grew to love as a fan.

But it all started on Mars. On my beloved Barsoom. So, when the fine folks at Modiphius asked me to develop **John Carter of Mars** for them? I eagerly accepted. And so now, like Carter himself, to Mars I return.

Hopefully you'll take this trip with me. I think you'll have fun.

Jack Norris
September 2018

CHAPTER 1: WELCOME TO BARSOOM

> *With scarcely a parting glance I turned my eyes again toward Mars, lifted my hands toward his lurid rays, and waited...*
> – John Carter *Gods of Mars*

Welcome to the ***John Carter of Mars Roleplaying Game***. Within the pages of this book you will be introduced to the world of Mars as imagined by Edgar Rice Burroughs, creator of the Barsoom novels, as well as a version of Modiphius Entertainment's 2d20 Roleplaying Game System customized for fast-paced pulp-inspired action. Before we dive into either the setting or system full force, let's briefly cover a few things.

While it is possible, even likely, that many reading this book are familiar with John Carter, Barsoom, Edgar Rice Burroughs, planetary romance, roleplaying games, and other concepts featured in this text, we are not going to take any chances. In brief, we are going to cover various topics that will hopefully enrich the enjoyment of this book both as a text and game.

WHO WAS EDGAR RICE BURROUGHS?

Edgar Rice Burroughs (September 1, 1875 – March 19, 1950) was easily one of the leading pulp writers and fantasists of his day. Son of a US Army major and businessman, Burroughs' own poor health kept him from military service. In an effort to support himself, a young Burroughs turned to writing fiction and soon found he was able to support himself writing pulp adventure tales featuring various heroes. In addition to John Carter and the Barsoom series, Burroughs created various other worlds and heroes, from the Venusian explorer Carson Napier to David Innes, explorer of the Hollow Earth realm known

as Pellucidar. In addition, he wrote various one-off novels and shorter series, most nominally set in the same bizarre and wonderful setting, with heroes and supporting cast from one work occasionally mentioning or even interacting with those in other tales. In addition to his writing, Burroughs worked as a war correspondent during World War II.

Burroughs' most famous creation was that of Lord Greystoke, more commonly known as Tarzan. Burroughs wrote twenty-four novels featuring the jungle-dwelling "lord of the apes" and countless movies and TV shows later featured the character. Tarzan even lent his name to Tarzana, Burroughs' California ranch home that eventually gave rise to a community of the same name.

However, if Burroughs' most famous creation was Tarzan, then his second most famous, and generally more complex and engaging hero, was John Carter. Carter was one of the earliest interplanetary heroes, undertaking adventures beyond the confines of Earth and finding purpose, adventure, and love on the wondrous world of Mars, or Barsoom as Burroughs' Martians called it.

At the time of his death in 1950, Burroughs had written nearly eighty novels featuring numerous memorable characters. His creations have featured in comics, television, and movies. Many modern creators credit Burroughs and his work as being incredibly influential on their lives and creations. The list of such creators includes author Ray Bradbury and filmmaker James Cameron.

JOHN CARTER AND THE BARSOOM NOVELS

In John Carter and his Barsoom novels, Burroughs explored not just a distant jungle as with Tarzan, but a whole new planet. Beginning with *A Princess of Mars*, first published in serial format in 1912, the series explores the life of one John Carter, Virginian gentleman, soldier, and wanderer. In the eleven books featuring Carter and other heroes of the dying Martian world its denizens called Barsoom, Burroughs tackled a variety of themes and ideas, many far more advanced than the "pulp adventure novel" format of the Barsoom books suggested. In *A Princess of Mars*, we see a brave and competent hero struggle with social customs and romance in ways that counterbalance his otherwise hypercompetent presentation. In *Gods of Mars* and *Warlord of Mars* Burroughs and Carter both confront the issue of fanatical and destructive religious beliefs. Throughout the series, complex politics, cultural clashes, and other problems plague the heroes. In many ways a stranger on his own Earth, Carter finds love, family, and friendship on Mars.

Many elements Burroughs introduced into Carter's personality made him remarkable compared to other science fiction fantasy heroes of his day. He misunderstood social cues and customs, he waxed philosophical about the pressure of false belief and fanaticism, championed the use of compassion with man and beast, downplayed his own bravery, recognized skill and talent in his enemies, and otherwise exhibited a deeper personality than many of his contemporaries. Where some heroes of various adventure tales would leave a string of

bodies in their wake while wading single-handedly through a sea of foes, Carter made allies. Sure, he killed foes by the dozens, even the hundreds, but the friends he made were far more notable. Across Barsoom and beyond, Carter befriended individuals of varying skin tones, genders, backgrounds, and outlooks. Even though the Barsoom stories are products of their times in many ways, they also showcase Burroughs' ability to craft a hero who looked past cultural and racial differences in ways that shamed many of his contemporaries. His best friend was a four-armed green skinned warrior whose culture laughed at love and friendship. He never wavered in his love or loyalty to his beloved Dejah Thoris, fighting across Barsoom and beyond to be with her. Carter was flawed and in many ways a bit backwards, but that imperfection mixed with sincerity and genuine goodness made him one of the classic science fiction fantasy heroes of the early 20th Century.

The plots of the Barsoom stories are often deceptively simple: a threat steals away John Carter from his loved ones, most often his lovely wife Dejah Thoris. While resolving these conflicts, Carter meets new allies and fights various villains, from false goddesses to corrupt warlords to synthetic monsters. Carter triumphs for a time, sometimes he aids another hero in their own quest, and then things grow calm until a new threat arises. Such is the way of not just the Barsoom stories, but many of Burroughs' works, especially in his long-running series that grew popular with the readers of his day.

What readers may not always immediately notice is how often some deeper argument or idea creeps into these simple plots that Burroughs relied on to keep selling his work to an audience who had come to expect a certain type of story. Repeatedly, Burroughs buried questions about blind obedience to harmful ideologies and how one should repay love and loyalty in these otherwise straightforward stories about a displaced Earthman fighting monsters and marauders on another world. Thus, the stories of John Carter and other tales of Barsoom became not just pulp science fantasy, nor period-flavored science fiction, but something much more.

RATIONALISM, ROMANTICISM, AND PULP ROLEPLAYING

John Carter of Mars is a roleplaying game that adapts Edgar Rice Burroughs' rationalist, romantic pulp tales of Barsoom. Heroes fight enemies born of lust, ignorance, and tyranny to save their friends, loved ones, and those cultures and places they call home. False gods, lying priests, deceitful nobles, treacherous assassins, and many other cruel adversaries are the biggest threats. These are the types of stories that will feature in the game sessions and campaigns of *John Carter of Mars*, using a modified version of the 2d20 system also used in such games as *Conan: Adventures in a Land Undreamed Of* and *Mutant Chronicles*.

While the people of Barsoom can be almost heartlessly pragmatic and even a bit emotionally stunted at times, it's generally a temporary and fixable condition. There are no "evil" races on Mars. Some beliefs are shocking to Earthling sensibilities, and cultural differences can certainly lead to comedic or tragic misunderstandings (a common Burroughs theme), but there are no Tolkien-style orcs or similar cultures. Even the largely villainous groups have individuals who eventually see that oppression and cruelty is a hollow and ultimately poor substitute for love and loyalty.

The animals and nature of Barsoom also echo this idea. There aren't really "evil" animals or beasts on the planet. Just hungry, territorial, or savage ones. Barsoom is dangerous, and survival is often difficult, but it's not an evil or arbitrary place.

Characters can forge new alliances, tame savage beasts, and make some bumbling outworlder one of the most powerful people on the planet through a combination of action and alliances. Decisive action tempered with sense and compassion is the best way to cut through cultural misunderstandings, defeat false beliefs, and make creatures loyal to you.

These are the sorts of stories Burroughs told with Carter and Barsoom. These are the sorts of themes *John Carter of Mars* seeks to bring to your gaming table.

GLOSSARY

The world of *John Carter of Mars* is literally its own world! It has its own cultures, language, history, flora, and fauna. Much of this will be detailed extensively in chapters devoted to these various topics. However, there are some commonly used terms.

* **Airship.** Flying craft that sail using Barsoomian eighth ray technology.

* **Banth.** Lion-like predator of Barsoom. Known for its ferocity.

* **Barsoom.** Mars, the name given to the planet by its natives.

* **Calot.** Ten-legged lizard-dogs that serve as pets and guards on Barsoom. Commonly kept by green Martians.

* **Cluros.** The furthest of Barsoom's two moons. Known as Deimos on Earth.

* **Dejah Thoris.** Princess of Helium and the titular character of *A Princess of Mars*, Burroughs' first Barsoom story. Wife and lover of John Carter.

* **Earthborn.** The term this book gives to human characters from Earth. Also known as Earthlings or Jasoomians.

* **First Born.** Also known as black Martians. They are physically near-perfect and possess secret technology and knowledge. The oldest humanoid race on Barsoom.

* **Green Martian.** Four armed, green-skinned denizens of Barsoom. Fierce warriors organized into various tribes and hordes.

* **Helium.** One of the great kingdoms of Barsoom. Centered around the cities of Greater and Lesser Helium, it is home to Dejah Thoris and her family and eventually John Carter.

* **Jasoom.** The name given to Earth by the people of Barsoom.

* **Jed.** A leader of a city. Usually serves under a jeddak.

* **Jeddak.** A leader of a kingdom. Also used by the green Martians for a head of a horde.

* **John Carter.** Earthborn soldier and gentlemen. Transported to Barsoom where he becomes a famous hero and warlord. Main character in the Edgar Rice Burroughs Barsoom series.

* **Kadabra.** Capital city of the Kingdom of the Okar. Protected by a great device known as the Guardian.

* **Okar.** Also known as yellow Martians. They were once a powerful culture on Barsoom, but now dwell in isolated cities in the arctic polar wastes.

* **Omean Sea.** Lost sea of Barsoom that exists below the planet's surface. Initially known to and accessible only by the First Born.

* **Red Martians.** The dominant race of modern Barsoom. Copper-skinned and athletically built, they are the most common race on Barsoom.

* **River Iss.** Sole remaining river on Barsoom. Traveling down the river to its end is believed to begin one's journey into the afterlife.

* **Tharks.** One of the most well-known of the green Martian hordes.

* **Thoat.** A riding beast common on Barsoom.

* **Thuria.** The nearest moon of Mars, known as Phobos on Earth. Erroneously believed to be the home of the First Born by other races.

* **Valley Dor.** A great valley located at the end of the River Iss. Believed to be the location of the Barsoomian afterlife. In reality, a terrifying place of monsters dominated by white Martian theocrats.

* **White Apes.** Mostly hairless massive white primates native to Barsoom. Unlike the Earth primates they bear some resemblance to, they are fearsome carnivores and one of Barsoom's deadliest predators.

* **White Martians.** An ancient race of white-skinned Martians. Now only exists in small hidden groups, such as the Holy Therns or Orovars.

* **Zodanga.** Another red Martian kingdom and one of Helium's chief rivals in the early Barsoom stories. Eventually conquered and becomes part of the Kingdom of Helium.

THE MEASURES OF MARS

In an effort to lend atmosphere and style to the text, the majority of measurements in this book will be given in Barsoom standards. Instead of the Earth foot or meter, we record things in the Barsoomian ad or sofad. When months and years, or ords and teeans, are mentioned, they will not be the standard Earth versions but their longer Martian counterparts.

Of course, we realize this is confusing to those not familiar with these systems of time, weight, and distance. And while these measurements will be revisited later in this text, we see no reason to leave readers dwelling in confusion one moment longer and so present:

BARSOOMIAN DISTANCES

	MEASURE	IMPERIAL	METRIC
Sofad	10 sofs	11.694 inches	0.2967 m
Ad	10 sofads	9.7 feet	2.97 m
Haad	200 ads	1,949.05 feet	594.07 m
Karad	100 haads	36.92 miles	59.407 m

BARSOOMIAN TIME

The Barsoom day is slightly longer than an Earth day at 24 hours and 37 minutes long. Their day starts at the equivalent to our 6:00am, and is divided into 10 equal parts. Each of these is then again divided in 50 shorter parts, and so on as explained below:

	MEASURE	EARTH EQUIVALENT
Tal		.89 seconds
Xat	200 tals	2 minutes, 57.7 seconds
Zode	50 xats	2 hours, 28 minutes, 4.8 seconds
Padan	10 zodes	1 Barsoomian day
Teean	67 padans	1 Barsoomian month
Ord	10 teeans	1 Barsoomian year

GETTING READY TO PLAY

As noted earlier, *John Carter of Mars* is primarily a game, specifically a roleplaying game. In it, most players take the role of a heroic character adventuring in the world of Barsoom. With the help of another player known as the narrator, they undertake various quests, adventures, and play their characters through a number of scenarios across multiple game sessions throughout a whole campaign. Player characters can come from various races and professions on Barsoom. They can even be Earthborn characters transported to the planet much like John Carter himself.

Unlike other players, narrators take the role of not one character, but many. They direct the other characters that the player character heroes encounter, and plot and direct the encounters and adventures which drive sessions and, ultimately, campaigns forward.

During play, player characters will gain experience and become more skilled and effective. They will also gain fame and renown, allowing them to influence the world. Characters may lead nations, command armies or vast airships, and otherwise make major changes to the setting — perhaps changes Burroughs himself never imagined!

NEW TO ROLEPLAYING?

If you have had prior experience with roleplaying games, you can safely skip ahead to the next section. If this is your first experience with tabletop roleplaying games, by all means continue reading. Ultimately, roleplaying games are about stretching the imagination to have fun, while providing a framework within which the participants can imagine they are heroic adventurers in a bygone age of savage and exotic wonder. The rules present a system to help everyone agree on what happens, encouraging players' imaginations to work together to make sure that the experience is as fair as it is exciting.

WHAT YOU WILL NEED

To get the most out of these rules and begin your adventures in *John Carter*, it's strongly recommended that you assemble the following before beginning:

PLAYERS

You will need at least two players, one to be a narrator and another to play a character. Most gaming groups have multiple players playing their own characters, but even two is enough to get started. Generally, a group of three to six players is standard. More players are possible but with more players, each player gets less time in the spotlight.

PLAYER CHARACTERS

Also called PCs or player heroes. With the exception of the narrator, every player needs their own character. This is the player's icon, avatar, or representative in the game. By playing these characters, players interact with the setting, go on adventures, and otherwise play the game. Creating a character is covered in the next chapter and a number of pre-generated characters are included for players who just want to grab a character and go.

Each character will need to have their various statistics recorded, either on a sheet of blank paper or on a character sheet provided in this book. Character sheets can be photocopied out of this book or downloaded at modiphius.com and printed for use.

DICE

John Carter uses two common types of dice: twenty-sided dice (abbreviated as d20) and six-sided dice (abbreviated as d6). These dice can be easily found in most hobby or gaming stores or ordered from various retailers online. In addition, various apps for phones and computers can simulate dice rolls.

Groups should have at least two d20s for the narrator and two d20s for the players and at least a half dozen d6s for the group. As these dice, especially the d20s, will be used frequently for various challenges, tests, and conflicts during play, it is recommended that, if possible, the group should have a few more dice than the minimums on hand.

COUNTERS

Players will need something to keep track of various resources during play, particularly each player character's Momentum and Luck, two valuable resources during play. Tracking these can be as simple as making marks on scrap paper, though many groups find it useful to use poker chips, glass beads, extra dice, or similar objects to track various resources.

Narrators will need some similar way to track their own special resource, called Threat. Narrators may find it particularly useful to use physical markers to track Threat. Threat enhances the actions of various dangerous creatures, villains, and other hazards the player characters will face during play and can be increased by players in exchange for resources of their own. Watching the pool of Threat points increase and decrease during play gives a sense of rising and falling tension that many groups appreciate.

PAPER AND PENCILS

Paper and pencils are not strictly necessary, but they are useful for drawing maps, making notes, tracking various game effects, and passing secret messages between players and the narrator if necessary. It's possible to keep track of all of this with tablets, smartphones, or laptops, but electronic devices at the game table can be distracting and should only be used with the gamemaster's consent and are subject to technical difficulties and power supply limitations.

ERAS OF PLAY

The races of Barsoom live for centuries and lead lives that require them to focus on the present instead of dwelling on past events or future possibilities. Months or even years may pass between significant events, during which time things do not change much. This is illustrated in Burroughs' work, as Carter and other characters often spend long periods of time between events detailed in the novels. Even during some stories weeks, months, or even a year or more will be done away with in a few lines of text, with time passing in leaps and bounds before returning to some crisis or significant action. In a **John Carter of Mars** campaign, similarly long periods of time may pass and it is of limited utility to adhere to a strict timeline. It will often be important to know the general political landscape and where things lie in relation to certain events, but exact time-keeping and strict timelines are less vital than in some settings.

Despite this, there are significant periods, events, and developments in the Barsoom novels. Most of these revolve around the actions of John Carter and his allies. Depending on exactly when a campaign, adventure, or game session is set, certain kingdoms may be rising or falling. Certain figures may be alive, dead (or believed so), unborn, or even off planet. Certain races, customs, and beliefs are very different based on which general era of Carter's time on Barsoom the action is set.

John Carter of Mars addresses these temporal changes not with a strict timeline, but with three distinct eras of play. These eras are named for Carter himself and relate to various events in the Barsoom novels. These eras are:

✳ The Dotar Sojat era

✳ The Prince of Helium era

✳ The Jeddak of Jeddaks era

Whenever history, events, or other elements of the setting are specific to a certain era, they will be marked with an icon corresponding to the era where these things are relevant.

THE DOTAR SOJAT ERA

Named for Carter's name among the Tharks, this era begins around the time John Carter arrives on Barsoom at the beginning of *A Princess of Mars* and covers the majority of the first book, when he lives with the Tharks, meets Dejah Thoris, and has his earliest adventures on Mars.

During this period, many nations of Barsoom are in constant conflict. Helium, Zodanga, and other red Martian kingdoms are regularly at war with each other, as are the green Martians and red Martians. The First Born and Okar are mostly unknown save for the occasional raid or covert action, and those who know of them believe the First Born "Black Pirates" come from the Martian moons. Belief in the Barsoomian afterlife, the Valley Dor, and the River Iss are nigh-universal, with only the First Born and Holy Therns knowing these tales are manufactured to manipulate and misdirect.

During this time John Carter is relatively unknown outside a handful of groups such as the Tharks and their soon-to-be jeddak, Tars Tarkas. The Earthborn hero has had little impact on Barsoomian culture or traditions at this time. Because Carter is a stranger during this time, most of what holds true for this era also applies for some time before Carter's arrival. Thus, while this era begins technically in 1866 with Carter's arrival on Barsoom and lasts only about a year, events and information relevant to this period can be used for games set before this time as well.

THE PRINCE OF HELIUM ERA

This period covers a large time period in the first three Barsoom novels, *A Princess of Mars*, *Gods of Mars*, and *Warlord of Mars*. During this period Carter marries Dejah Thoris and becomes a prince of Helium. Dejah lays the egg that will eventually become Carthoris, the couple's first child. For about nine Earth years Carter has mostly undocumented adventures and experiences, during which time Helium rises to prominence and the Thark horde and other neighboring nations develop good relations with Carter's adopted nation. At the end of this period of prosperity the atmosphere plant, which supplies much of Barsoom's breathable air, malfunctions and is restarted by Carter in an act that leaves him stranded back on Earth with the world of Barsoom believing him dead.

For ten more Earth years, Carter seeks to return to his beloved wife and adopted world. During this time, his son grows to manhood and then disappears into the Valley Dor. Dejah Thoris grieves for Carter's loss for years until she too disappears. Eventually, the Thark Jeddak Tars Tarkas journeys to the Valley Dor in time to meet Carter, who finally "died" on Earth only to return to Barsoom. During these adventures, chronicled in *Gods of Mars* and *Warlord of Mars*, Carter discovers and defeats both the Holy Therns and the First Born false goddess Issus. They are the main forces behind belief in a Barsoomian afterlife which, in truth, leads those who follow it to slavery and death. Shortly thereafter, Carter defeats the Okar Jeddak Salensus Oll and creates a great alliance of leaders of various kingdoms and races.

This era is rife for adventure, with Carter either occupied with the affairs of Helium and his family, or lost and believed dead. His son Carthoris is a promising young prince, but he quickly disappears himself. Player heroes during this time can carve out their own legends and even raise their own kingdoms without having to worry about how Carter and his fellows feel about their actions. Campaigns set early in this era may also see characters becoming early allies or followers of Carter, a valuable position as the hero becomes more well known.

During this time Carter is either a relatively well-known living figure in the regions around Helium or a great hero believed to have died saving Barsoom. The green Martians, particularly the Tharks, are beginning to understand the value of kindness and friendship, but tension between various races and kingdoms still run high in most places. This period covers about twenty years Earth time, from 1867 to 1888. The beliefs of the Barsoomian afterlife, the Valley Dor, and the River Iss are still nigh-universal until the very end of this period, when the lies behind them are revealed and the truth begins to spread.

THE JEDDAK OF JEDDAKS ERA

This period covers the later novels in the Barsoom series, when Carter is well-established as the great unifying warlord of Mars whose allies include various kingdoms and groups of red Martians, green Martians, Okar, and First Born. During this time, new heroes such as Ulysses Paxton appear, and younger heroes such as Carthoris and Thuvia of Ptarth have their own grand adventures.

During this era, much of the conflict and adventure involves remote locales, hidden threats, forbidden science, and other dangers which threaten the general peace and prosperity of Helium and its many allies. Active wars are less common than smaller conflicts, but only constant vigilance and regular heroism keeps the fragile peace. The old beliefs and rivalries that once limited Barsoom are largely gone or on the decline, leaving a bright future that must be nurtured and protected.

This era is the default "modern day" for *John Carter of Mars*. It begins in the late 1880s by Earth's calendar, but extends well beyond, covering the days or World War I and later. During this time, Carter is a great hero, famous across Barsoom. His allies, children, and followers are themselves great champions and famous luminaries. This era can be a bit daunting for players seeking to carve out major roles and grand reputations for their own heroes, but this is balanced by the ability to interact with the characters of the Barsoom novels and the possibility of *John Carter* campaigns set in this time ushering in a grand new era, defined by the players and their characters' adventures.

SECTION 1

CHAPTER 2:
CREATING YOUR CHARACTER

CHAPTER 3:
TALENTS

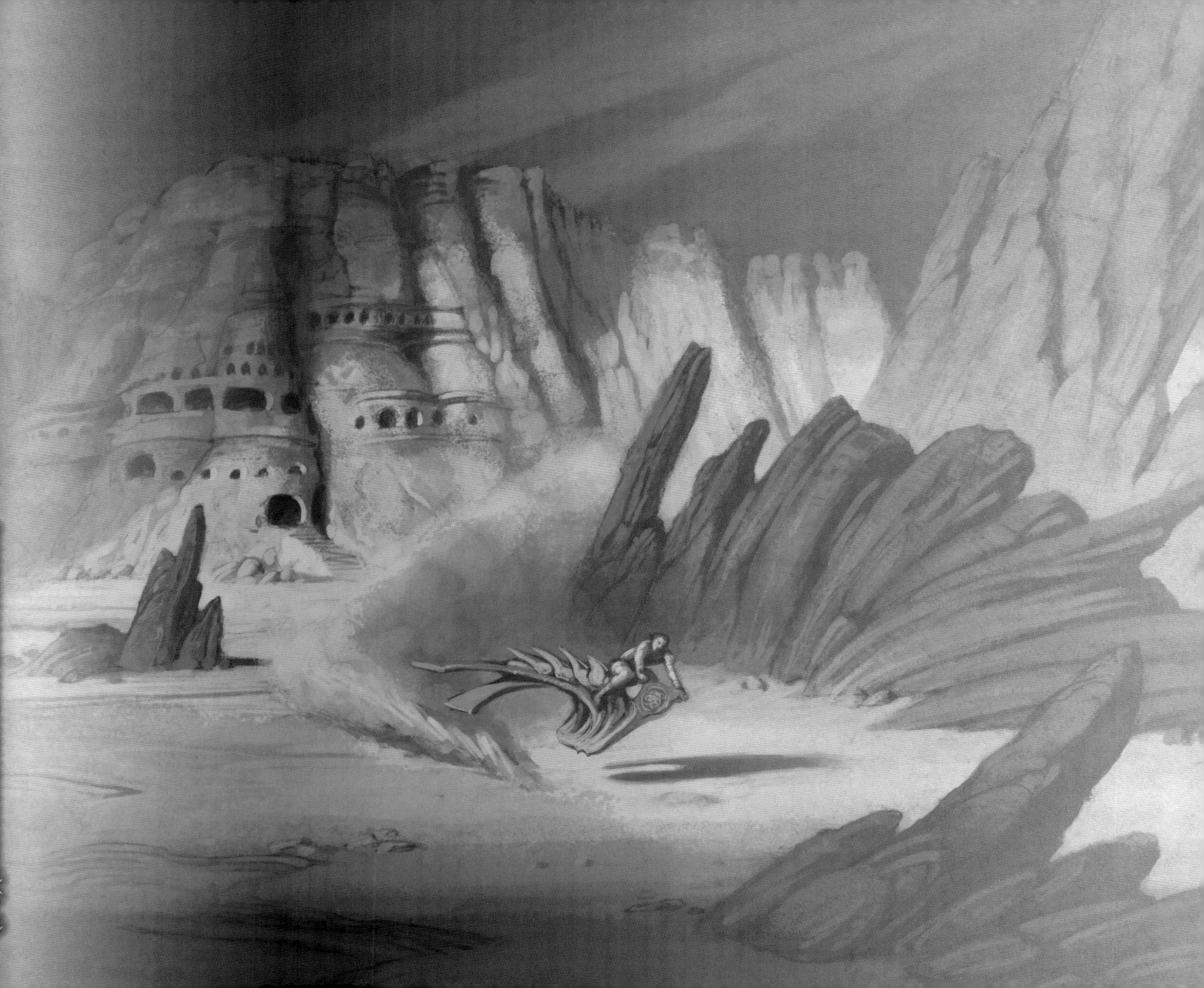

CHAPTER 2: CREATING YOUR ADVENTURER

In that little party there was not one who would desert another; yet we were of different countries, different colors, different races, different religions--and one of us was of a different world.
– John Carter, *The Gods of Mars*

This chapter details character generation, walking players through the steps to create their own adventurers in *John Carter of Mars*. There are nine steps to character generation — one for each of the mysterious Martian rays!

* **Step One:**
  General Concept

* **Step Two:**
  Starting Attributes

* **Step Three:**
  Selecting Your Race

* **Step Four:**
  Select Archetype

* **Step Five:**
  Select Descriptor

* **Step Six:**
  Talents

* **Step Seven:**
  Starting Renown and Equipment

* **Step Eight:**
  Choose a Flaw

* **Step Nine:**
  Name and Finalize Concepts and Attributes

STEP ONE:
GENERAL CONCEPT

The first step in creating a player character is to decide what general sort of character to create. Then either select a concept from the list in this section or create your own. In fact, keeping the concept intentionally vague to start is a good way to begin, as it allows the character to change and adapt going forward.

Some sample concepts include:

* **Wandering Princess:** A noble of your people in search of adventure or seeking some artifact or resource that will help your people.

* **Reformed Assassin:** Member of a dreaded Barsoomian assassins guild, you are an ex-killer for hire seeking peace or redemption thanks to your past deeds.

* **Airship Raider:** A privateer or pirate, you fly the Martian skies in search of profit or adventure.

* **Adventuring Scientist:** You study Martian science and seek to rediscover lost technologies and make bold new discoveries.

* **Panthan Warrior:** A Martian soldier for hire, you seek glory and riches on the battlefields of Barsoom.

* **Lost Explorer:** You come from far away, perhaps even another world, to explore the wonders of Barsoom.

This basic concept will refine and change throughout character generation, but it provides a framework to start the process. Once you have a concept you're happy with, move on to the next step.

PLAYING
JOHN CARTER AND FRIENDS

In addition to making their own characters, players may play John Carter, Tars Tarkas, Dejah Thoris, and other important characters from Edgar Rice Burroughs' Barsoom novels. There are two ways to do this:

Use this chapter to create your own versions of Carter, Tars, Dejah, and others, perhaps using the optional rules for playing more advanced and powerful characters.

Use the statistics provided in *Chapter 15: Champions of Barsoom* later in this book. These statistics may be modified slightly to represent characters at various stages of their lives or during different eras of play.

Either approach works, but it is recommended all players use the same approach to avoid creating characters of different and potentially unbalancing capabilities.

STEP TWO:
STARTING ATTRIBUTES

Each character in *John Carter of Mars* has a number of attributes. These are used to determine a character's general aptitudes and abilities, forming the core of most mechanical tests and die rolls in the game.

Unlike some games, attributes in *John Carter* are deliberately abstract and result-focussed. They focus more on how a character accomplishes something and less on the exact physical or mental abilities used to accomplish the task. All player characters have a set of attributes rated from 4 to 12. A rating of 4 indicates the minimum that any important character would have, representing the low value for a bystander or unimportant supporting character.

1–2	**Well Below Average,** suggesting permanent illness or infirmity.
3	**Average.**
4	**Average.** The starting default for all player character abilities.
5–6	**Above Average,** suggesting considerable skill and natural aptitude.
7–8	**Exceptional,** suggesting great skill and natural aptitude.
9–10	**Fantastic,** matching those of the greatest heroes of Barsoom.
11–12	**Legendary,** noteworthy even among the great heroes of Barsoom.

There are six attributes representing a character's capabilities. The attributes are **Cunning**, **Daring**, **Empathy**, **Might**, **Passion**, and **Reason**.

Cunning: Used whenever a character wants to weaken another. Cunning is used for all attacks, insults, and thefts. Cunning is used with Might to scuttle a ship or bash down a door and used with Reason to shoot a rifle.

Daring: Comes into play whenever a character is at risk and movement is important. Daring covers movement, piloting, and defense actions of all sorts. Daring is often used with Cunning to strike with a sword or with Empathy to avoid a blow.

Empathy: Used whenever a character seeks to understand or heal another. Empathy is used to heal all types of impairments and to understand what your senses might be telling you about a person. Empathy is used with Reason to spot a character up to no good.

Might: Used to apply force to inanimate objects. It is used outside of combat to lift, bend, and break items. Might is used with Daring to pick up an unconscious character and carry them to safety.

Passion: Governs any attempt to lead, love, or entertain. It is used whenever another character needs to be convinced to attempt an action. Passion is used with Empathy to lead troops into battle or to woo a lover, and with Cunning to seduce or insult.

Reason: Supports any action that applies the mind or senses to work out a problem. It is used with Cunning to sabotage an enemy flier or device, and with Empathy to understand a foe's battle plans.

A starting player character starts with 4 for each of their attributes. This will be modified by the character's race, descriptor, and archetype in coming steps. Furthermore, each player gets 2 extra attribute points to distribute along their character's abilities. Attributes cannot be raised higher than 12. Also, if the campaign is focused on more experienced heroes, *see Advanced Characters on page 29.*

STEP THREE:
SELECTING YOUR RACE

The next step in character generation is to select the race to which your character belongs. A character's race in *John Carter of Mars* informs much of how they play, including attributes. By default, most Martian cultures are racially homogenous and there are many common traits in different cultures dominated by the same race. Races available for player characters are:

✳ Green Martians

✳ Red Martians

✳ Earthborn (Jasoomian)

✳ First Born (black Martians)

✳ Okar (yellow Martians)

Red Martians are the most common race, followed by the green. Earthborn are the rarest, canonically only including a handful of individuals. Mixed heritage characters are also possible in some cases and will be discussed later in the chapter.

In some campaigns, narrators and other players may agree to limit the races available, usually due to the time period and general concept for the campaign. In such cases, agree before selecting which races are available for new characters.

The following pages describe the various races in more detail, including their general knowledge of Barsoom, common abilities, and other considerations. These are not designed to be all-inclusive descriptions, but to provide basic information to get you prepped and ready to play quickly. More information on the various races and their cultures can be found later in this book. Generally, tests associated with a race's general knowledge are automatic or easier than those outside what they commonly know and understand.

The Afterlife and the Truth of Issus

One commonly shared belief of nearly all Martians is that, upon reaching the end of their lives, everyone takes a journey down the River Iss to the Valley Dor, where the Martian afterlife is located. In truth, the myth of Iss is a lie perpetuated by the living "goddess" Issus and spread by the Holy Therns. The true Valley Dor is a hellish place of plant men and other threats that devour those who venture there seeking peace. During the early days of John Carter's time on Barsoom, all red and green Martians and Okar believe the following:

You are aware of the Barsoomian afterlife and will one day take your trip down the River Iss to the Valley Dor. All other views are heresy and those who return from the Valley still living are cursed. However, it is rare that your people live long enough to make this journey, so it generally matters less to you than those of other races.

After John Carter and his allies destroy Issus and reveal the truth of this myth, the knowledge of the red and green Martians and the Okar changes to:

After the death of Issus and the truths revealed by John Carter, you have heard the legends of Iss and Dor are lies spread by the First Born and their puppets the Holy Therns. Whether you believe this or not is up to you, but again it matters less to the green hordes in the wastes than some other cultures.

Earthborn characters know of this myth whatever they are told by natives of Barsoom, and what they believe is up to them. First Born characters know that most of these stories are lies spread by their own people. Before her death, most worship and obey Issus herself as a living goddess. However, it is ultimately also the First Born who destroy Issus after Carter and his allies reveal her flaws and extreme cruelty.

Martian Telepathy

Communication among individuals on Barsoom is partially telepathic and all the Barsoomian sentient races have some degree of telepathic ability. This psychic communication melds with spoken language, creating a form of communication that is largely vocal, but incorporates direct and even unsubtle mental communications. This makes lying and hiding emotions on Barsoom difficult, encouraging the already direct and forthright manner common to most cultures.

The telepathic elements of communication can be developed and learned by non-Barsoomians, but they will always be somewhat resistant and removed from telepathic contact compared to natives of the Red Planet. This means that Earthborn, and possibly other races, are more able to lie and deceive. Holy Therns and some other races and individuals who have developed their mental capabilities find an easier time lying, cheating, and deceiving others.

A character's personal knowledge and experience always trumps their general level of racial knowledge. If a green Martian is taught to fly an airship, they can do so even if his fellow horde members cannot. If a red Martian visits a lost city, he knows of his experiences there, even if his fellow red Martians remain ignorant of its existence.

Example: *Toras Ral is a red Martian player character from the Kingdom of Ptarth. Looking at the entry for red Martians, he knows of the customs of his home nation, their rulers, and has a general knowledge of his people's allies and rivals. However, he knows little of the remote areas of Barsoom. If he is trying to recognize Thuvan Dihn, Jeddak of Ptarth, he likely doesn't even need to roll any dice. If he is trying to act appropriately in audience with his jeddak, the difficulty of such a test would be reduced due to his general knowledge. However, if he finds himself trying to decipher the customs of a faraway Okar diplomat, he will find this test more difficult, at least until he gains personal knowledge through play to add to his race's common knowledge.*

RED MARTIANS

The most common race on Barsoom, red Martians populate most of the kingdoms and cities on the surface of Barsoom. The race came about through interbreeding between the First Born, Okar, and the white-skinned Orovar. This makes them the youngest of the human-seeming races, though they have expanded to cover most of the planet. Red Martian societies all follow the same general customs and traditions, though they can vary widely in belief and outlook based on their personal histories and their individual rulers.

Red Martians are masters of the air. They are not the only race to use airships, but their navies rule the skies and their airships are not an uncommon sight even over the wastelands. It is a rare red Martian who cannot at least operate a personal flier, and many have experience with larger craft as well.

The typical red Martian is copper-skinned and athletic of build. They are generally the same height as Earthborn humans. They have little or no body hair and few grow facial hair. They rarely wear much in the way of clothing, favoring harnesses, jewelry, and cloaks to other coverings. Like all the Barsoomian races, the red Martians are oviparous, laying eggs that over several years gestate until a partially grown youth emerges. Like most races on Barsoom, red Martians are extremely long-lived. Barring death by injury or accident, they will live for centuries.

ATTRIBUTE BONUSES

Add +2 to one of the following attributes: Daring, Empathy, Passion, or Reason. Add +1 to any two others.

WHAT YOU KNOW

✳ You speak and read common Barsoomian.

✳ You know of your nation and its neighbors.

✳ You have likely heard of the great cities of Helium and Zodanga, even if you don't hail from there.

✳ You know of the threats, politics, and customs of your home kingdom.

✳ You know the basics of airship operation and red Martian science.

WHAT YOU DON'T KNOW

✳ The customs of people in hidden places and remote locales.

WHAT YOU CAN DO

✳ You know the basics of self-defense, including the use of blades and firearms.

✳ You can operate basic machinery and use medicines and machines common to red Martian culture.

✳ You can fly most vehicles under normal conditions and ride trained mounts.

GREEN MARTIANS

Hailing from the Tharks, Warhoons, or one of the other hordes that dwell in the wastelands and wilds of Barsoom, the green Martians are definitely the most visually distinct of the races. Tall and six-limbed, the tusked and antennaed green Martians live in great hordes ruled by their strongest warriors. Many warriors do not even earn their full names and identity within the horde until they have killed another in duel or open combat. Green culture is notoriously grim, finding dark humor in the death and misfortune of others and valuing only individual achievement and the good of the horde. However, this changes over time as alliances and friendships with those outside their horde teaches some green Martians to value these concepts.

The typical green Martian is between one to one-and-a-half ads (10 to 15 feet) tall and has green skin of varying hues. Their bodies are powerful and long-limbed, with large eyes and tusks that jut up from their lower jaw. Their exact garb and armaments vary somewhat by the warband or horde to which they belong, but it is rarely more than a harness, loincloth, jewelry, ornaments and perhaps a furred or feather trimmed cloak.

Like all the Barsoomian races, the green Martians are oviparous, laying eggs in great creches that gestate for years until they are harvested and taken to the horde camps where the hatchlings are given to adults who raise them. Also like most races on Barsoom, green Martians are extremely long-lived. However, their violent lifestyle means few live long before dying at the hands of an enemy or wild beast.

ATTRIBUTE BONUSES
Subtract -1 from Empathy or Reason. Add +2 to Might. Add +1 each to two of the following: Cunning, Daring, or Passion.

RACIAL TALENT
FOUR-ARMED FOR WAR (GRADE 1)
Your warlike, combative culture and four arms give you an edge in combat, allowing you to attack with multiple weapons or steady your rifle with ease.

* **Circumstance:** When attacking with melee weapons or using a rifle.

* **Effect:** When you generate Momentum while attacking with a melee weapon or rifle, gain an extra Momentum.

WHAT YOU KNOW
* You speak and read common Barsoomian.

* Your horde, its leaders, and customs.

* The wastelands and wilds your people wander, including the location of various birthing creches where the eggs of the young are kept.

* General knowledge of your enemies, including their leaders and their major settlements.

* You know the basics of green Martian medicinal salves and treatment.

WHAT YOU DON'T KNOW
* The identity of your mother or father. If you do know this, you risk the ire of your horde by breaking one of the sacred customs.

* How to operate or repair an airship.

WHAT YOU CAN DO
* You are trained in the ways of battle, including the use of rifles, blades, and spears.

* You can ride and care for thoats, calots, and other beasts used by your horde.

* You can hunt and forage.

* You can more easily intimidate other races.

OKAR

The ancestors of the yellow-skinned Okar once ruled a much larger area of Barsoom than their descendants do today. Where once great Okar kingdoms dwelled in cities across the surface, now the Okar live in the far north in domed cities protected from the frozen climate. The existence of the Okar is not exactly a secret, but many of their fortresses and kingdoms are unwelcoming to visitors and details about them are scarce outside their lands. Travelers are often turned away, enslaved, or imprisoned by the Okar to maintain their security and as a show of superiority and force.

Okar resemble the red Martians closely except in two important details; their yellow skin and the dark beards of their men. Okar dress much as red Martians do inside their cities with little clothing, favoring harnesses and jewelry. However, in the arctic areas outside their cities they don practical and protective thick furs, cloaks, and other garb. Only a foolish Okar would venture outside their city unarmed, and within the city many carry sword, dagger, and various other weapons as well. While skill at arms varies among individuals, one of the greatest swordsmen on Barsoom was found in the Okar capital of Kadabra until his death at the hands of the Earthman, John Carter.

Like other Martians, Okar lay eggs. They can interbreed with red Martians and First Born and presumably other non-green humanoid races as well. In fact, it was such interbreeding with the First Born that gave rise to the red Martian race millennia ago.

ATTRIBUTE BONUSES
Add +1 each to Cunning and Daring. Then add +1 each to two of the following: Empathy, Might or Reason.

WHAT YOU KNOW
* You speak and read common Barsoomian.

* You know of your nation and its neighbors, including the ancient history of the Okar who once ruled much of Barsoom.

* You know how to survive in the frozen lands near your home.

* You know the creatures and perils of the frozen wastes, particularly the deadly apts.

* You know the basics of Okar science, including the magnetic science used by Kadabra's Guardian.

WHAT YOU DON'T KNOW
* You don't know much of the lands far from your arctic home.

* You aren't skilled in surviving in extreme heat or other foreign climes.

WHAT YOU CAN DO
* You know the basics of self-defense, including the use of blades and firearms.

* You can operate basic machinery and use medicines and machines common to Okar culture.

* You can fly most vehicles under normal conditions and ride trained mounts.

* You are adept at arctic survival and navigating in such climes.

* You are unhindered by wearing heavy furs and clothing, especially in harsh weather.

With the death of Okar Jeddak Salensus Oll, a new age of communication and friendship begins between the Okar nations, Helium, and other allies under the Warlord, John Carter. Since then, Okarians have become a friendlier and more common sight in other parts of Barsoom.

Earthborn

You hail not from Barsoom, but Jasoom, the blue planet seen on clear Martian nights. Your spirit and consciousness have somehow been transplanted here to Barsoom, the planet your people know as Mars. You arrive naked and unknown to this harsh planet. A lifetime in the higher gravity of Earth gives you surprising strength and agility compared to others of your size and build. Earthborn characters are noteworthy on Barsoom both for their power and ignorance, though if they are lucky, they will survive long enough to overcome the latter.

Earthborn characters can be from any culture or ethnicity native to Earth, from Virginia of the United States to the Australian Outback. They will look somewhat strange and alien regardless of their Earthborn background—an African American is not "black" like a First Born, nor is a Native American "red" like a red Martian. Only rare white Martians somewhat resemble the Caucasians of Earth, but even then, there are often notable differences, such as the hairlessness of the Holy Therns. These differences can be disguised with effort, just as John Carter at times poses as a red Martian, Okar, or Thern, but it takes effort and success is not guaranteed.

Unlike all the races of Barsoom, humans give birth to live young. They are also capable of mating with the red Martians, and presumably the races that can interbreed with them.

Note that it is presumed that any human who comes to Barsoom will somehow gain the longevity that John Carter attributes to himself, through some natural ability, Martian science, or some other phenomenon. Likewise, it is presumed that any Earthborn character knows the basics of personal combat and that their Barsoomian-based body is free of any disability that would make survival unlikely.

ATTRIBUTE BONUSES

Add +3 to Might. Add +1 each to any two other attributes and subtract -1 from any one remaining attribute.

RACIAL TALENTS

LEAPS AND BOUNDS (GRADE 2)

Your Earthborn muscles allow you leap great distances and perform great feats of strength while on Barsoom.

* **Circumstance:** When moving on Barsoom and planets with similar gravity.

* **Effect:** You may close one range category automatically, ignoring any obstacles or intervening terrain as long as you have clearance and space to leap between your starting point and destination. You may spend 1 Momentum to move an additional range category.

In addition, all Earthborn characters also gain seven grades worth of talents instead of the usual five (*see Step Six*). At least two of these seven grades must involve your character's Might attribute in some way. These talents vary based on exactly how the character learns to best channel and use their Earthborn strength and muscle power. For example, many Earthborn characters with combat training gain talents that allow them to do additional damage or use Might more effectively while attacking. An Earthborn character can choose to have 1 talent include the abilities of the other talent as per the normal talent rules (*see Designing Talents on page 38*).

As noted later in this chapter, Earthborn lack certain starting abilities the native races of Barsoom possess, including starting renown and the ability to select a piece of core equipment. Since Earthborn are so heavily focused on talents, players unfamiliar with the talent systems should usually avoid these characters.

WHAT YOU KNOW

✴ You speak at least one Earth language, possibly more.

✴ You are familiar with your native culture and others you've interacted with.

✴ You know the skills and knowledge of your Earth profession and education.

WHAT YOU DON'T KNOW

✴ The Barsoomian language.

✴ Any details of Barsoomian culture, customs, and history.

✴ The beasts and other dangers of Barsoom.

✴ How to fly an airship.

✴ Anything much about Barsoom, especially if it causes you problems until you know better!

WHAT YOU CAN DO

✴ Defend yourself, even if only using your Earthborn strength.

✴ Perform tasks that have some clear Earth analog, such as riding or shooting a firearm.

✴ Quickly learn the ways of this strange new world after being shown or taught.

✴ You can resist telepathy.

CHARACTERS AND DISABILITY

The default presumption in *John Carter* is that player character heroes are relatively healthy and able-bodied because that's how they are presented in the novels and because Martian science seems capable of curing nearly any manner of severe injury or illness given time. Even Earthborn characters who were disabled on Earth, such as Ulysses Paxton of the later *John Carter* novels, have physical disabilities removed through Martian science.

If a player wishes to play a character with a disability they may, but this disability only limits them as much as strict logic demands and they desire. This is pulp planetary romance and there is more than enough room for blind swordswomen who navigate the landscape as well as a sighted person or five-limbed green Martians who have learned to compensate for severe injury. Extreme disabilities may provide the basis of a character's flaw (*see Step Seven*), but this is optional and up to the player.

Mental illnesses are dealt with in much the same way, with the "madness" some villains display being in fact megalomaniacal narcissistic tendencies and a desire to harm others for their own amusement rather than any real-world mental illness. A player character with a mental illness can take this as a flaw if the player desires, but there is no requirement to do so.

As always, be mindful of your fellow players. If playing a character with a particular problem, flaw, or ailment is going to upset another player, do not do it. When in doubt, ask. You might think it is cool to play a terminal cancer patient given a new lease on life on Barsoom, but it is possible a fellow player who just lost a loved one to that disease may feel differently.

MIXED HERITAGE

It is possible to play a character whose parents hail from different races. In fact, Carthoris of Helium, son of John Carter and Dejah Thoris, is just such a character. To play such a character, decide which culture he follows predominantly. Use that to determine what a character knows and can do generally.

For characters of mixed Martian heritage, use the attribute bonuses for red Martians — they were the original hybrid race on Barsoom and many with mixed ethnicity tend to develop along similar lines. Then take the talent, if any, from the parent race they most favor. They also gain the What Do You Know and What Can You Do knowledge of whatever culture they were raised in. In fact, Okar and First Born hybrids are red Martians by all appearances. Note that the green Martians don't seem to be able to breed with the other races of Barsoom.

For Earthborn-Martian hybrids, the result is somewhat more dramatic. These mixed heritage characters get the attributes of their Martian parent, except that if Might isn't one of the attributes with a bonus, they *must* substitute one of their existing racial attribute bonuses for an equivalent Might bonus. They also gain the Leaps and Bounds talent of their Earthborn parent. They gain the What You Know and What You Can Do knowledge likely to be that of their Martian parent. They gain the core equipment and starting renown of a Barsoomian native character. However, they only receive four grades of additional starting talents instead of the usual five (*see Step Five*) and must purchase at least 1 grade of talents that are based on the character's Might attribute.

Narrators may veto the playing of mixed Earthborn-Martian characters. By the canon of the Burroughs' novels, none were active during the Dotar Sojat era, and only Carthoris is seen in the other novels. Such characters, if they appear, are likely more suitable for generational campaigns, where an existing Earthborn player character falls in love with a Martian character and has a child who eventually becomes a player character in their own right.

FIRST BORN

Your people are believed to be the first race of Barsoom. You spawned from the Tree of Life and your people ruled Barsoom before the other races arose and many First Born still consider themselves the secret masters of the world. Most First Born are allied with Issus, the living goddess-tyrant, who rules her kingdom from her secret stronghold. Interacting with other races mostly as raiders and spies, First Born are known for their arrogance and devotion to perfection: weakness is the worst sin an individual can commit. Travelers and adventurers encountering the First Born are often at risk of death or enslavement, especially if they encounter Issus herself. Some races, therefore, view the First Born as mythic monsters who serve a death goddess, rather than living beings, and many First Born find this useful when dealing with and manipulating other races.

First Born are onyx-skinned and most are physically "perfect" in their proportions and physique. They are generally the same height as Earthborn humans, though many are somewhat taller than average to match their perfect physiques. They have dark hair and eyes to match their skin. They tend towards the harnesses and cloaks favored by other races, but most First Born favor more jewels and ornaments than the average red or Okar. In battle they prefer swords, pistols, and other armaments similar to those used by red Martian and Okar warriors. Like other Barsoomians, they are oviparous, and can interbreed with most other races of Barsoom, much like the Okar with whom they birthed the first red Martians.

All First Born are trained in combat and intrigue as a matter of survival, though proficiency in these crafts varies greatly between individuals. They know the basics of both airship and submersible operations, the latter being a rarity on Barsoom. The Holy Therns will respond more positively to the First Born than they do other races, presuming they are allies, co-conspirators, or even agents of a superior power.

Like all Martians, the First Born lay eggs. They also live for centuries, with a lifespan of a thousand years being far from uncommon. Like red Martians, they have little to no hair besides the black hair that adorns their heads.

ATTRIBUTE BONUSES

Subtract -1 from Empathy. Add +2 to Cunning and +1 to Daring. Add 1 to two of the following: Might, Passion, or Reason.

WHAT YOU KNOW

✳ You speak and read common Barsoomian.

✳ You know the secret strongholds of your people and their neighbors.

✳ You know the history of the First Born, and that yours is the first race of Barsoom.

✳ You know the basics of First Born science, including airship and submersible operation.

✳ You know the truth of the myths of Issus, including knowledge that Holy Therns are mere pawns of Issus.

WHAT YOU DON'T KNOW

✳ You are not aware of sciences and customs of the "lesser" races. Your ways are clearly superior!

WHAT YOU CAN DO

✳ You know the basics of self-defense, including the use of blades and firearms.

✳ You can operate basic machinery and use medicines and machines common to First Born culture.

✳ You can control most vehicles under normal conditions, including submersibles.

✳ You understand intrigue and deceptions better than most Barsoomians.

Upon the death of Issus and the revelations that the religion based around her was a lie, most on Barsoom realize the First Born are simply another race of Martians, albeit an ancient one. Some First Born, such as those ruled by Xodar, have allied themselves with other races and nations. Others live as raiders and warlords, seeking profit and power across Barsoom.

STEP FOUR:
SELECT ARCHETYPE

Next, select a general archetype for the character. These archetypes are designed to be relatively broad and cover a wide range of concepts from various races and cultures. Each provides certain attribute bonuses and a suggested free grade 1 talent. Advanced players can substitute another talent that makes sense for a character of that archetype, but you can also just take the selected talent, finish character generation, and jump right into playing your character.

Also included with each archetype is a common list of What You Know and What You Can Do as a member of that archetype, as well as suggestions for what sort of core equipment you might favor (*see Step Six*). Note that Earthborn characters have the Earth-bound equivalent of Barsoom-based knowledge and skills at character generation, and quickly pick up the Martian equivalents of their Earthborn skills and abilities.

Example: Lily Porter is an aviator and explorer who finds herself on Barsoom after her plane crashes in a remote corner of Earth. Looking at what an explorer knows and can do, she and the narrator both note that, when she first arrives, Lily is unfamiliar with Barsoomian beasts, terrain, and various hazards, but that she can often squeak by with her extensive knowledge of traveling in hazardous Earth terrain and dealing with dangerous animals such as tigers and venomous snakes. After a short time on Barsoom, Lily begins to pick up the general knowledge and aptitudes of a Barsoomian explorer, and far faster than she would learn things like Martian science or medicine.

AIRSHIP OFFICER

You are most at home on the deck of a Martian airship. From piloting to navigation, you know how to crew and even command ships of various sizes, from personal fliers to the huge flagships of the great navies of Helium, Zodanga, and other nations.

ATTRIBUTE BONUSES
+2 each to Daring and Reason

SUGGESTED TALENT
AIRSHIP PILOT (GRADE 1)
You can crew and command airships, flying them with skill beyond most pilots.

✳ **Circumstance:** When crewing or commanding an airship.

✳ **Effect:** When crewing or commanding an airship, you may roll 1 bonus d20.

WHAT YOU KNOW
✳ The basic engineering and scientific principles behind Martian airships.

✳ Tactics and strategies of airship combat.

✳ Barsoom's most famous navies and their most prominent ships and commanders.

WHAT YOU CAN DO
✳ Fly anything that floats on Martian rays.

✳ Command, navigate, and repair most types of airship.

✳ Fight close quarters and with ship-based weapons.

ASSASSIN

Also known as a "gorthan", you are a hired killer, taking the lives of others for pay. You are likely a member of an assassins' guild, though freelance killers-for-hire also exist on Barsoom. Many assassins cling to their own code of honor, but some are merely heartless killers.

ATTRIBUTE BONUSES
+2 each to Cunning and Might

SUGGESTED TALENT
EASY TARGET (GRADE 1)
Lesser targets are no challenge to your deadly skills as an assassin.

✳ **Circumstance:** Targeting a minion.

✳ **Effect:** You can automatically kill a target minion with typical assassination methods (melee, strangulation, poison, etc.)

WHAT YOU KNOW
✳ Familiarity with various methods of assassination, including poison, sniping, and close-quarters killing.

✳ How to analyze a target or assassination location for weaknesses.

✳ Barsoom's most famous assassins and their guilds.

WHAT YOU CAN DO
✳ Come and go unseen.

✳ Kill quickly and efficiently, especially the unprepared or weakened.

✳ Disguise yourself — useful to get close to your targets!

BEASTMASTER

While many on Barsoom use fliers and airships for long-range transport, everyone makes use of trained or domesticated animals. From thoats and calots to tamed apts and banths, you are a master of beasts. You know their ways, their behavior, and their temperament. More often than not, they heed your wishes and, when they do not, you know how best to bring them down.

ATTRIBUTE BONUSES
+2 each to Might and Empathy

SUGGESTED TALENT
CALL OF THE WILD (GRADE 1)
Lesser beasts heed your call. They bend to your will and follow your commands.

- ✴ **Circumstance:** Commanding or controlling an animal.

- ✴ **Effect:** You may automatically control the actions of 1 minion beast for the rest of the scene. You may control additional minion-class beasts for 1 Momentum per additional beast. If attempting to use this talent on an exceptionally loyal beast bonded to another, you may only control the beast for one turn.

WHAT YOU KNOW
- ✴ The habits, habitats, strengths, and weakness of the beasts of Barsoom.

- ✴ Various training methods and uses for various types of domesticated and tamed beasts.

WHAT YOU CAN DO
- ✴ Fight savagely for your survival against beast and Martian alike, often with your beast companions by your side.

- ✴ Train beasts of all sorts, though you likely have your favorites or a special rapport with some types of beast.

- ✴ Track and set traps for beasts.

- ✴ Treat the wounds and common ailments of beasts.

DUELIST

You are extraordinarily skilled with the sword, able to defeat several lesser foes at once. Your superior reflexes and ability with blades can be transferred to other weapons and even unarmed combat. While many archetypes are skilled in practical combat, your mastery of theory and artistry of martial combat are usually beyond them.

ATTRIBUTE BONUSES
+2 each to Cunning and Daring

SUGGESTED TALENT
FEARSOME FENCER (GRADE 1)
Your reputation and talent with a blade unnerves and even terrifies many opponents, making it easier for you to disarm and dispatch them.

- ✴ **Circumstance:** When holding a sword or other melee weapon.

- ✴ **Effect:** When fighting in accordance with Martian honor, you can disarm a character for 1 Momentum less than normal.

WHAT YOU KNOW
- ✴ The art of the blade, including common defenses, attacks, and theories of swordplay.

- ✴ How to size up a fellow swordfighter to get a rough idea of their skill.

- ✴ Barsoom's most famous duelists and duels.

WHAT YOU CAN DO
- ✴ Defend against and disarm lesser foes with ease.

- ✴ Attack an equal or superior opponent skillfully and with a high chance of success.

- ✴ Judge a sword or other dueling weapon's quality, testing balance, edge, and durability quickly and accurately.

ENVOY

Politics is the life blood of the nations and cultures of Barsoom. While many jeddaks rule by force of arms or personality, their retinues and families are filled with individuals skilled at politics and negotiation. It is common for princes, princesses, or majordomos to negotiate treaties, alliances, and even political marriages for the great nations and city-states of Barsoom.

ATTRIBUTE BONUSES
+2 each to Empathy and Passion

SUGGESTED TALENT
PASSIONATE ORATOR (GRADE 1)
Your unwavering loyalty and love for your people moves others to aid you. Even when dealing with the sworn enemies of your nation, culture, or group, you can often gain concessions or create opportunities with your words.

* **Circumstance:** When speaking to convince an audience.

* **Effect:** You may reroll the result of any failed die roll in a Passion-based attempt to convince or charm others.

WHAT YOU KNOW
* The history, customs, and politics of your own people.
* The basic customs and major figures of your nation's chief allies and enemies.
* The history of the great nations, guilds, and organizations of Barsoom, especially those with political significance.

WHAT YOU CAN DO
* Negotiate, lead, and charm others.
* Spot political plots and ploys and craft effective counters to them.
* Inspire others to aid you and your people, forming temporary and permanent alliances.

EXPLORER

You are driven to explore the lost and remote corners of Barsoom, and possibly beyond. Regardless of where you began, or from what land you hail, you long ago realized your destiny lay among the secret places, ruins, and forgotten locations. You make a valuable scout and may even serve as a first contact negotiator in a pinch, though you're usually more concerned with survival and discovery than diplomacy. Explorers tend to be hardy, quick-witted, and adaptable — or quite dead.

ATTRIBUTE BONUSES
+2 each to Daring and Empathy

SUGGESTED TALENT
FIND THE WAY (GRADE 1)
You can find safe paths and hidden places with ease. You are also more likely to bypass and survive hazards like dangerous terrain, ancient traps, and other deadly obstacles.

* **Circumstance:** When travelling in wastes, ruins, and wilderness areas.

* **Effect:** When facing an environmental danger (falls, traps, etc.), you roll 1 less combat dice than normal.

WHAT YOU KNOW
* The flora and fauna of Barsoom.
* How to evade predators in the wild.
* The locations of ruins, oddities, and occasionally even wonders.

WHAT YOU CAN DO
* Navigate the wastes with or without equipment.
* Travel the wilderness finding shelter, food, and water as you go.
* Use both fliers and mounts in rough terrain to travel and explore.

FUGITIVE

You escaped from captivity and you are not going back. Maybe you were a slave, a hostage, or a prisoner, but you have spent too long locked up, beaten down, or forced to toil against your will. You may need to hide your true identity to avoid capture, or perhaps you only need to discover a place where you can live free. As a fugitive, you may come from nearly any background, but it is your status as a renegade, prisoner, or outsider that defines much of you.

ATTRIBUTE BONUSES
+2 each to Cunning and Passion

SUGGESTED TALENT:
NO CHAINS CAN HOLD ME (GRADE 1)
Able foes may capture you, but holding you is another matter. You are adept at escaping from all manner of prisons, bonds, and confinement.

* **Circumstance:** When attempting to escape from captivity.

* **Effect:** Roll 1 bonus d20 with any action based on escaping from imprisonment or restraints.

WHAT YOU KNOW
* How to scrounge simple weapons, tools, disguises, and sustenance.
* General background, culture, and tactics of your former captors.
* At least a few valuable secrets learned from a fellow prisoner, careless guard, etc.

WHAT YOU CAN DO
* Evade pursuit and elude capture.
* Fight like a cornered banth when required.
* Plan and execute escapes and infiltrations.

Gladiator

Arena games and arms-based competitions are common across Barsoom. Many warlords, especially the more tyrannical ones, love to pit captives, slaves, and their favorite gladiators against beasts and each other for the amusement of their subjects. You are one of the elite gladiators of these contests, tempered by rigorous training and regular battle. Regardless of what you were before, you were reborn in the arena and there you found your true destiny.

ATTRIBUTE BONUSES
+2 each to Might and Passion

SUGGESTED TALENT
ARE YOU NOT ENTERTAINED (GRADE 1)
You can read the crowd, making them love you with well-placed taunts or sword strokes alike.
* **Circumstance:** When fighting in front of a crowd or audience.

* **Effect:** You may spend 1 Momentum during a fight to sway a crowd or audience of onlookers to your side. The exact effects of this vary with each situation, but they should cheer you on, attempt to aid you, briefly distract your opponent, or otherwise act favorably.

WHAT YOU KNOW
* The arenas and battle-based games of Barsoom.

* The strengths and weaknesses of all manner of melee weapons and environments.

* The beasts and dangers of Barsoom, especially those pitted against fighters in area combat.

WHAT YOU CAN DO
* Fight like a savage banth for freedom, glory, and your life.

* Read a crowd's emotional state and act to exploit it.

* Spot and exploit weaknesses in others during personal combat.

Guide

You are adept at moving and guiding others across the harsh Martian landscape. You are a keen hunter and forager who may serve your nation as a scout or may work for those in need. You are a capable fighter, though you prefer skirmishing and small unit actions to large battles.

ATTRIBUTE BONUSES
+2 each to Might and Reason

SUGGESTED TALENT
LIVE OFF THE LAND (GRADE 1)
The wilderness opens up to you like an old friend, revealing bounties and secrets.
* **Circumstance:** When surviving in the wild.

* **Effect:** You may automatically forage or scrounge enough to eat and drink and can locate or construct basic shelter. For each Momentum spent you may also locate enough sustenance and shelter for a number of extra people equal to your Reason.

WHAT YOU KNOW
* The wild areas of Barsoom, especially those near your home or areas where you have spent considerable time.

* How to hunt, forage, and identify harmful plants and natural hazards.

* The basics of animal behavior, especially as it pertains to tracking, hunting, or avoiding them in the wild.

WHAT YOU CAN DO
* Fight alone or as part of a small group, especially against wild creatures or in natural environments.

* Track, scrounge, and forage in even the most inhospitable regions.

* Map and navigate various territories, quickly and accurately marking important landmarks, ruins, and settlements.

Healer

While Martian medicine is potent and accessible, it is not perfect and does not come from nothingness. As a dedicated and trained expert in the healing arts, you can mend wounds, create healing salves and compounds, and perform acts of precise and life-saving surgery. Your exact methods and training may vary based on your culture, but they are effective and welcomed by the sick and injured.

ATTRIBUTE BONUSES
+2 each to Passion and Reason.

SUGGESTED TALENT
SHOW ME WHERE IT HURTS (GRADE 1)
Your healing arts are wondrous, capable of quickly and efficiently healing wounds using Martian science.
* **Circumstance:** When healing a character with Wound afflictions.

* **Effect:** Your treatment tests for Wounds afflictions are Average (D1) instead of the normal Challenging (D2). Also, any Momentum costs to remove additional afflictions are reduced by 1 Momentum.

WHAT YOU KNOW
* Extensive knowledge of Martian medicine and the healing arts of your culture, including the manufacture and use of healing salves and other medicines.

* Chemicals and extracts with both medicinal and toxic properties.

* The weaknesses and capabilities of the Martian body and any other beings you have studied or examined.

WHAT YOU CAN DO
* Diagnose and heal injury and illness.

* Comfort a patient and analyze his symptoms and behavior for possible causes.

* Operate and even create medical technology, including medicines.

PANTHAN

A mercenary, you sell your sword across Barsoom. Working alone or with various mercenary companies, you share the skill at arms of the soldiers in various standing armies, but have learned to often make do with fewer resources and a looser command structure. This archetype can include Earthborn soldiers of fortune who somehow find their way to Barsoom.

ATTRIBUTE BONUSES
+2 each to Daring and Might

SUGGESTED TALENT
WHO DARES WINS (GRADE 1)
Striking swiftly and fiercely will often compensate for small numbers or other tactical disadvantages. You learned long ago to hit hard, fast, and put foes down without hesitation.
* **Circumstance:** When using a particular type of weapon.
* **Effect:** Pick a category of weapon (sword, pistol, spear, etc.), you inflict an additional 1 ☙ of damage and add 1 to the total damage rolled on successful attacks with that weapon.

Note: You can use additional grades of this talent to apply this effect to other weapons (one per grade).

WHAT YOU KNOW
* The most popular mercenary companies and those nations and organizations that frequently hire them.
* Tactics and strategy, especially small-unit and guerilla tactics.
* History of military conflicts on Barsoom, especially those making extensive use of mercenaries.

WHAT YOU CAN DO
* Fight with common military weapons, such as the sword, firearms, and dagger.
* Negotiate basic contracts and agreements, especially for mercenary work.
* Plan small scale assaults and military operations, even with minimal resources.

ROGUE

You are a rake and a troublemaker. You may be a raider or a brigand, or just someone who prefers to take the easy way out whenever possible. Your heart might be in the right place, or maybe not, but your tactics and methods are often of questionable integrity and honor. This doesn't often win you many friends, though those you have tend to accept and even appreciate your ways.

ATTRIBUTE BONUSES
+2 each to Cunning and Empathy

SUGGESTED TALENT
RAKE AT THE MOUTH OF ISS (GRADE 1)
You are able to con or charm the jewels off a princess and slip the sword from a guardsman's sheath before he realizes what is happening. Your approach may be subtle or direct but, either way, it tends to be effective.
* **Circumstance:** When stealing from others.
* **Effect:** When attempting to steal or acquire an object by subterfuge or stealth, you may reroll one failed die.

WHAT YOU KNOW
* Methods of subterfuge, thievery, and various criminal or underhanded enterprises.
* The rich, powerful, and influential individuals in your nation or home culture, especially those you can convince or con into making your life easier.
* The shady and hidden corners in various places you have lived or worked, and where to find such locales in new lands.

WHAT YOU CAN DO
* Deceive, seduce, and mislead. Outright lying is difficult and rare on Barsoom, but you are adept at pushing the truth as far as it will go.
* Fight like a mad calot when cornered, caught, or when you have no other choice.
* Sneak, hide, steal, and escape from even improbable fates with a combination of skill and luck.

SCIENTIST

You are a scientist or scholar, studying Barsoomian science both ancient and modern. Many scientists seem somewhat eccentric by normal social standards, but this is not a requirement for heeding this calling.

ATTRIBUTE BONUSES
+2 each to Empathy and Reason

SUGGESTED TALENT
WEALTH OF KNOWLEDGE (GRADE 1)
You possess a wealth of scientific knowledge, both theoretical and practical.
* **Circumstance:** When researching a scientific phenomenon or device.
* **Effect:** You may reroll any single failed die in a science-related Reason test.

WHAT YOU KNOW
* Fundamentals of Barsoomian science and technology, including the nine rays and other common principles.
* Intimate familiarity with the science and discoveries of your own culture, as well as a passing familiarity with the science of all other cultures known to you.
* Legends of lost technology and scientific discoveries from ages past.
* Barsoom's most famous scientists and researchers, their reputations, history, and well-known discoveries.

WHAT YOU CAN DO
* Skillfully analyze and research scientific phenomena.
* Determine a scientific device or artificial creature's basic purpose and at least the theoretical basis of its creation. Thorough examination of a subject may tell you much more.

SOLDIER

You are a member of one of Barsoom's national armies, a veteran of many battles. You are skilled with arms, tactics, and accustomed to military life. Depending on your rank, you may lead entire armies into battle, but even as a foot soldier you are familiar with the basics of leadership.

ATTRIBUTE BONUSES
+2 to Daring and Passion

SUGGESTED TALENT
BATTLE VALOR (GRADE 1)
You are a true warrior and steadfast soldier, at home in the chaos and carnage of war and always willing to meet your fate with sword and pistol in hand.
- ✳ **Circumstance:** When suffering Fear damage in combat.
- ✳ **Effect:** You may ignore the first 2 points of stress inflicted to your Fear stress track taken during combat. You suffer Fear damage normally after this during a combat scene or from other situations.

WHAT YOU KNOW
- ✳ The command structure, traditions, and capabilities of your army.
- ✳ The basic structure and capabilities of your nation's usual military rivals.
- ✳ Combat strategy and tactics, especially those you have drilled or used effectively in battle alongside your fellow soldiers.

WHAT YOU CAN DO
- ✳ Fight skillfully with the arms of your military, usually sword, firearms, and dagger.
- ✳ Lead troops into battle and effectively follow battle plans and orders.
- ✳ Train others in battle formations, the use of weapons, and basic tactics.

SPY

The politics of Barsoom are often deadly and direct, but that doesn't mean there is no place for espionage. Spies, scouts, and other covert operatives are invaluable in protecting state secrets, uncovering and foiling the plans of rival nations, and rooting out threats to important leaders, locations, and operations. By necessity, spies are experts in close combat, disguise, and infiltration.

ATTRIBUTE BONUSES
+2 each to Cunning and Reason

SUGGESTED TALENT
MASTER OF DISGUISE (GRADE 1)
You are a master of disguise, transforming yourself completely and effectively. It is possible even your closest friends have never seen your real face.
- ✳ **Circumstance:** When disguising yourself.
- ✳ **Effect:** Spend 1 Momentum to leave a scene. Then spend 1 Momentum to replace any minion-type character in a scene, revealing you were actually in disguise all along.

WHAT YOU KNOW
- ✳ The major threats to your nation or organization, including enough knowledge of their culture and customs to infiltrate them.
- ✳ Various methods of disguise and surveillance.
- ✳ Ciphers, codes, and technology used to protect and discover information.

WHAT YOU CAN DO
- ✳ Fight in close quarters effectively, especially with swords, daggers, pistols, and even your bare hands.
- ✳ Disguise yourself effectively, including masking your race, if possible. Green Martians are nigh impossible for other races to duplicate, nor can they effectively duplicate other races.
- ✳ Infiltrate guarded and secret locations.

CREATING UNIQUE ARCHETYPES

Each archetype provides 4 total ranks of attribute bonuses and a grade 1 talent. The bonuses are usually +2 bonuses to two different attributes. Using these guidelines, narrators and players can create their own archetypes. They can also modify existing ones slightly. For example, perhaps your scientist favors Passion and Reason over Empathy and Reason.

WHY NOT SKILLS?

Competency is presumed in *John Carter*. A character is presumed to have the skills and abilities that it makes sense for them to possess. Exceptional skills are covered under talents, but basic skills are a function of character concept, background, and common sense.

If a character would not have the skill for a particular task, it will either be deemed impossible (they cannot attempt it) or more difficult (the test becomes harder).

Narrators and players wishing more guidance on what skills a character has can have each player write down or highlight four or five parts of the character's concept that suggest or describe certain skills. Those skills can be attempted without increased difficulty. For example, John Carter displays skills with swordsmanship, riding, shooting, and athletics. He can attempt those actions without penalty or increased difficulty. He might also be able to attempt other actions without penalty as well, but he can always pick up a sword or gun and attack, ride, or perform some athletic feat without increased difficulty.

STEP FIVE:
SELECT DESCRIPTOR

Characters in *John Carter* are larger than life, dramatic, and tend to be boldly presented. There is usually one adjective or description that sums up their character, how they deal with conflicts and problems, and what many characters seem to think of them. In character generation, this term is called a character's descriptor and it affects what attributes a character favors.

Each character should select a descriptor from the list below that best describes their character and emphasizes the attributes they favor. There are fifteen descriptors, one for each possible combination of two favored attributes.

If a player wishes, they can rename their descriptor if they want another word to describe their character, such as changing Romantic to Lovable or Brash to Reckless. However, make a careful note the attribute bonuses granted to avoid confusion during the next step in character generation.

* **Bold:** +1 each to **Cunning** and **Daring**
* **Courageous:** +1 each to **Daring** and **Empathy**
* **Fierce:** +1 each to **Daring** and **Might**
* **Brash:** +1 each to **Daring** and **Passion**
* **Canny:** +1 each to **Daring** and **Reason**
* **Charming:** +1 each to **Cunning** and **Empathy**
* **Driven:** +1 each to **Cunning** and **Might**
* **Dashing:** +1 each to **Cunning** and **Passion**
* **Brilliant:** +1 each to **Cunning** and **Reason**
* **Stalwart:** +1 to each to **Empathy** and **Might**
* **Romantic:** +1 each to **Empathy** and **Passion**
* **Thoughtful:** +1 each to **Empathy** and **Reason**
* **Savage:** +1 each to **Might** and **Passion**
* **Disciplined:** +1 each to **Might** and **Reason**
* **Devoted:** +1 each to **Passion** and **Reason**

STEP SIX:
TALENTS

Characters, especially player characters, have talents. Talents represent those unique or developed abilities that make a character special. Talents may represent a skill, natural aptitude, or even an arcane power or psychic talent.

At their core, talents are ways for characters to accomplish special actions normally requiring Momentum. In some cases, they can also allow a character to use Momentum in ways not normally allowed. The following section discusses building talents as well as providing example talents to take for your player characters.

Player characters start with five grades of talents, in addition to the talents already provided by your race and archetype; these can be designed by the player to fit some specific need or selected from *Chapter 3: Talents*.

Each talent must also be justified by your character concept and race. If your green Martian warrior has never been on an airship, he can't take a talent that makes him an expert pilot, at least not at character generation.

Several example talents and rules for designing your own talents are found in the next chapter.

STEP SEVEN:
Starting Renown and Equipment

Once you have talents selected, it is time to assign your starting renown and equipment. Renown is part of character advancement, representing your character's fame and notoriety. All characters except Earthborn receive some starting renown to purchase titles, allies, contacts, or other advantages at the beginning of play. Player characters tend to be important figures in their respective homelands and cultures, and their starting renown reflects that. Starting renown is the same as renown earned during play. The rules and effects of renown are found in *Chapter 6: Growing Your Legend*.

Aside from Earthborn, all starting player characters get 10 renown. Being strangers to Barsoom, Earthborn PCs start with zero renown.

Starting characters also have access to some equipment based on their culture and concept. This includes weapons, and also other devices and gear commonly used by the people of Barsoom. Again, Earthborn don't fare so well.

Core Equipment

While most characters carry various pieces of equipment, many player characters have some core equipment. Core equipment represents an item or type of item that a character always has available and can always easily replace if stolen or lost. For example, a swordsman may never go anywhere without his sword and, should he somehow lose it, he always seems to secure a replacement. Likewise, a scout is rarely without his field glasses or a strong rope.

Core equipment is essentially a specialized talent. For each grade of it, with each grade costing 5xp, the characters get one piece of equipment designated as core equipment. Possession of some specialized or very useful items may require more than 1 grade.

During play, if a narrator takes away a piece of core equipment, they must pay the character 2

Momentum. If the player wants to prevent this, or reacquire the item in the same scene, they must pay 3 Momentum. However, if they wait until the end of the scene, or later, they may regain the item for 1 Momentum. This can happen even in the most unlikely circumstances: a dead enemy may have a similar item on them, or the original may be found discarded nearby. The narrator does not need to disarm the player in combat to remove the item; the Momentum payment is enough and assumes that fate intervenes to deprive the character of his gear.

Note that the item needn't always be the exact same item as before, but it is functionally the same. Thus, a character with a cavalry sabre may find a Zodangan sword to replace the blade they lost, and it functions the same way.

With one exception, all starting player characters may start with 1 grade worth of core equipment, representing a common weapon, item, or object they are rarely without. Earthborn characters begin with no core equipment, coming unknown and unarmed to the savage world of Barsoom.

Additional pieces of core equipment can be purchased during character generation or play. All core equipment has a rank which indicates the cost in talent grades to possess the item. For most items, this is 1, but larger goods such as fliers, ancient artifacts, and some mounts or animal companions may cost more.

OPTIONAL RULE:
No Core Equipment

If the narrator approves and it fits a character's concept, they may refuse any core equipment at character generation. If they do so, they will either receive an extra starting renown or an extra grade 1 talent of their choosing. This option allows for increased character customization, but it creates another choice during character generation, potentially slowing down the process.

STEP EIGHT:
Choose a Flaw

Each player character hero, no matter how strong, beautiful, brilliant, reliable, or charming, has a flaw. This flaw informs not just how a player character hero acts, but also the challenges they regularly face. Flaws may represent psychological flaws, social constraints, or just plain bad luck that tends to manifest in a particular way around a character.

Mechanically, flaws are essentially "anti-talents". Usually these are an event or class of events that cost the character some Momentum or damage unless they engage in the stated activity. Usually this is 3 Momentum, though flaws that come up in play more often cost less Momentum and those which are less frequently relevant cost more Momentum when they do surface.

If a character cannot afford to spend Momentum when their flaw surfaces, they take damage instead. This is usually Confusion damage but, if the player and narrator agree, it may be taken as other types, though it is rare that a flaw causes Injury damage.

The following flaws can be used, or serve as a basis for player-created flaws.

HEROIC FURY
Your courage is complemented by hot-blooded righteousness. When faced with an act of wrongdoing or oppression, every turn you spend not acting to stop it causes you to lose 2 Momentum.

OVERPROTECTIVE
When someone in your charge becomes injured as a result of your action (or lack thereof), lose 5 Momentum from your pool. If you cannot lose 5 Momentum, take the excess in fear damage.

SELF-SACRIFICING
Strong and loyal, you value the lives of friends over your own. During a scene where an ally, other player character, or an innocent's life is in mortal peril, the narrator can ask you to take the place of that character, or lose 3 Momentum. This danger doesn't need to be immediate: you could offer to

take the place of another as a hostage or prisoner. If your attempt is rebuked or refused, you don't lose Momentum, provided you attempt to take their place to the best of your ability.

SOFT-HEARTED

If you leave another character to suffer or cause undue suffering, you lose 3 Momentum. This flaw is viewed as particularly egregious among the green Martians and similarly hard-hearted cultures.

TARGET OF OPPORTUNITY

When encountering an enemy or rival in conflict or otherwise, the narrator can declare that you must spend 3 Momentum or be separated from your fellow party members. This can be through being kidnapped, a sudden change in scenery, the rival insisting they continue a conversation in private quarters, etc.

STEP NINE: NAME AND FINALIZE CONCEPT AND ATTRIBUTES

You might already have a name for your character, but if you don't now is the time to select one. Pay attention to the naming conventions of certain cultures. For example, Tharks adopt full names recalling warriors they kill in battle, while red Martians often take names that invoke their parents or grandparents in some way. Here are guidelines for naming characters of various races:

RED MARTIANS

Red Martian names tend towards a first and last name consisting of one or two syllables. Alliteration is common, such as with Kantos Kan, but names also often share common traits with a parent or ancestor, such as Kantos' son, Djor Kantos. Sample red Martian names include Mors Kajak, Kulan Tith, and Saran Tal. Nobility and adventurous travelers sometimes use only their first name and their homeland, such as with Thuvia of Ptarth.

GREEN MARTIANS

Green Martians often gain names given to them by superiors in their clan or horde and can be granted an additional or new name by killing another warrior in personal combat. Thus, a green Martian given the name of Molat would use this name, but after he killed a rival warrior named Garok could go by the name Molat Garok. In some cases, killing two esteemed warriors might result in a new name consisting of those of both slain rivals. Sample green Martian names include Tars Tarkas, Sola, and Thar Ban.

OKAR

Okar names are similar to red Martian names, though they seem to use singular names a bit more frequently, in the case of Okar officers and officials such as Solan and Sorav. Generally, only Okarian names use double "L" in a name, such as Salensus Oll. "Ll" is also used in place names occasionally and such places may appear in place of a last name, such as Solak of Illall. Sample Okarian names include: Solan, Sorav, and Talu.

FIRST BORN

Some First Born have surnames and others do not. Often, high-ranking First Born such as dators, raiders and pirates, don't bother with surnames. They use their title and first name instead, such as Dator Xodar, or they simply use their first name. The First Born sometimes use double "S" in their names, such as with the goddess Issus. This is hardly done outside of First Born culture. Sample First Born names include Xodar, Thurid, Ban-Tor, and Yersted.

EARTHBORN

Earthborn characters either use the name given to them on Earth or adopt names given to them by their allies and comrades on Barsoom. In many cases, Earthborn characters will have both such names, such as John Carter, also known as Dotar Sojat among the green Martian Tharks.

WHAT'S IN A NAME?

If you are stuck for a name, check out various examples throughout this book and in the Barsoom novels. There are literally dozens of names in Burroughs' novels and many of them can be altered or adapted to create appropriate sounding names for new characters.

This is also the time to refine and finalize your character's concept. This includes discussing with other players how your character relates to the world and other player characters. This may result in subtle or significant changes to your concept, or may answer outstanding questions about your character. For example, you might decide that, given multiple player characters are red Martians from Helium and, given their alliance with Helium, you will be a Thark warrior instead of hailing from a different green Martian horde.

Finally, you need to assign any remaining bonuses from earlier steps. Once those are assigned, record the character's stress tracks, to represent how durable they are to certain types of damage. There are three stress tracks based on pairings of attributes: Fear (Daring and Passion), Injury (Cunning and Might), and Confusion (Empathy and Reason). Each stress track is equal to the highest of the two relevant attributes.

Example: Peter's Okar Swordsmaster has the following attributes: Cunning 7, Daring 7, Empathy 6, Might 5, Passion 4, and Reason 7. Taking the highest attributes for Fear (Daring and Passion), Injury (Cunning and Might), and Confusion (Empathy and Reason) he records that, at start, his character has Fear 7, Injury 7, and Confusion 7, creating an equally durable, courageous, and strong-minded character. He also names his character at this point, electing to call him Dolan Ath, modeling the name in Martian style after both his character's master, Solan, and his favorite Musketeer, Athos.

Once your character is named and concept is finalized, you're ready to begin a life of adventure and dramatic peril in the world of Barsoom!

Sometimes a campaign will require a player character or characters who are more powerful than a usual starting character. This may be because the character is being added to an existing campaign where the other characters are already quite advanced, or simply because the narrator wants to begin with more powerful characters. In such cases, the narrator can grant the player characters an amount of experience and renown (*see Chapter 6: Growing Your Legend*) to spend during creation to buy new talents, increase attributes, and buy various accolades. To add characters to an existing campaign that match existing characters, simply provide them with between 90 and 100 percent of those characters' experience and renown. To create generally more powerful player characters, consult the following table:

ONE OF THE MASSES
- ✳ Increase one attribute by: +1

A HERO OF SOME RENOWN
- ✳ Increase two attributes by: +1

A HERO TO YOUR PEOPLE
- ✳ Increase one attribute by: +2
- ✳ Increase one attribute by: +1

A HERO ACROSS THE LAND
- ✳ Increase one attribute by: +2
- ✳ Increase two attributes by: +1

A HERO OF MARS
- ✳ Increase two attributes by: +2
- ✳ Increase two attributes by: +1

A HERO OF MANY WORLDS
- ✳ Increase one attribute by: +3
- ✳ Increase two attributes by: +2
- ✳ Increase one attribute by: +1

CHARACTER GENERATION WALKTHROUGH

The following example walks through the process of character generation, detailing the creation of Kantos Than, a dwar of Lesser Helium.

Example: Mark is making his character for Jen's upcoming **John Carter of Mars** game. He knows the campaign will begin in Helium during the Prince of Helium era, specifically, the time when John Carter is believed dead. He opens his rulebook to the section on character generation and starts going through the steps.

EXAMPLE STEP ONE: GENERAL CONCEPT
First comes concept. This is easy, as he's already sure he wants to play a dashing officer in the vein of Kantos Kan, perhaps even a distant relation of the famed airship commander and ally of the great John Carter.

EXAMPLE STEP TWO: STARTING ATTRIBUTES
The second step is also easy. He records 4 in each of his starting attributes, Cunning, Daring, Empathy, Might, Passion, and Reason. He also notes he has 2 bonus attribute points to spend as well, but he elects to save those for after he's selected his race and other aspects of his character.

EXAMPLE STEP THREE: SELECTING YOUR RACE
The third step, selecting his character's race is also simple. As he plans to be inspired by and possibly related to Kantos Kan, he elects to be a red Martian, the same race as his role model. Being a red Martian gives him +2 to one of the following attributes: Daring, Empathy, Passion, or Reason and +1 to the others. Seeing his character as a dashing romantic type, he takes +2 in Passion, and +1 in Empathy and Reason. He notes these increases in attributes and moves on to the next step, selecting his archetype.

EXAMPLE STEP FOUR: ARCHETYPE
Mark gives some thought to simply mimicking Kantos Kan and taking Airship Officer as his archetype. However, he wants to do something a bit different. Instead he decides his character is a guardsman in Lesser Helium, commonly assigned to ground-based patrols and assignments. Looking over the archetypes he thinks Soldier makes

the most sense for his character. This archetype provides him with a +2 bonus to both Daring and Passion making Mark's character very focused in those areas so far. For his archetype's free grade 1 talent, he elects to take the suggested one, Battle Valor — Mark sees his character as very brave and virtually fearless in battle.

EXAMPLE STEP FIVE: DESCRIPTOR
After archetype, it's time to pick a descriptor. This one word helps present a snapshot of the character's personality and provides two attribute bonuses as well. Looking over the various descriptors, he decides that Dashing best describes how he sees his character: young, courageous, and with a bit of flair. Dashing grants him +1 to Cunning and Passion. With race, archetype, and descriptor in place his attributes are: Cunning 5, Daring 6, Empathy 5, Might 4, Passion 9, Reason 5. His Passion is very high, as is Daring. Everything else is at or near average for most characters. Considering this, he elects to assign his 2 bonus attribute points now, increasing Might to 5 and Daring even further to 7. Mark's Dashing Red Martian Soldier might not be very balanced in his attributes, but he will have notable strengths and weaknesses to keep things interesting.

EXAMPLE STEP SIX: TALENTS
Next come talents, and Mark gets 5 grades' worth of talents to give his character. Looking over the examples he selects 2 grade 1 ready-made talents: Daring Rider and Cut Them Down. He also creates his own grade 2 talent, Passionate Swordsmaster, which allows him to substitute Passion for one of his attributes when attacking with a sword and lets him do 1 additional die of damage and 1 bonus point of damage with a sword attack — effectively combining two grade 1 talents into a single talent. With such a high Daring already, an attribute commonly used with attacks, Mark's soldier is sure to be deadly with a blade! For his final talent grade, he decides to shore up one of his character's weaknesses and creates a grade 1 talent, Surprisingly Strong, which lets him reroll any one failed die in a Might-based test.

EXAMPLE STEP SEVEN: RENOWN AND CORE EQUIPMENT

Next comes starting renown and core equipment. Core equipment is easy: Mark figures his character is rarely without his sword. While this could be any blade, he decides it's an ornate Helium-style saber that was given to him by his cousin, Kantos Kan. Since he knows Jen won't be worrying too much about non- core equipment in the campaign, he makes a note to check that out later and moves on.

Given his choice of core equipment, Mark finds spending most of his starting renown quite easy: he definitely wants Kantos Kan as an ally. Looking at the renown rules in *Chapter 6*, he decides Kantos is a 6 renown ally, being both exceptional and politically connected by this era in the game, with several airships and many Helium Navy personnel that he can call on to help in assisting his "favorite cousin." Deciding he could use a friend with knowledge of strange places and bizarre scientific phenomena that he is sure the campaign will feature, Mark then purchases another 2 renown ally in the form of a young scientist of Helium he befriended when guarding a scientific expedition a few years ago. The scientist, a charming young woman named Adara, isn't particularly well connected politically, but she is brilliant and no slouch with a pistol. For his remaining 2 renown, Mark purchases the title of padwar, defining it as his character's rank in the Army of Helium.

EXAMPLE STEP EIGHT: FLAW

Next comes the character's flaw. Mark decides that his soldier's fearless and somewhat reckless nature also makes him somewhat impatient and quick to jump into danger. He creates a flaw called Hot-Blooded and, working with the narrator, it is defined as costing him 3 Momentum if he waits too long or is overcautious in a dangerous situation or potential battle. This flaw will encourage Mark to play his character as impulsive and quick to jump into the fray, and cost him valuable Momentum when he denies this important part of his nature.

EXAMPLE STEP NINE: NAME, FINALISE CONCEPT AND ATTRIBUTES

With everything done but his character name, Mark decides that he wants a family name similar to Kantos Kan. He decides on the name Kantos Than, suggesting his relation to the famed Helium officer. After a brief discussion with the narrator about the beginnings of the campaign, he decides Kantos Than is assigned to Lesser Helium as a leader in a company of advance scouts and skirmishers. His chief duty recently is escorting important dignitaries and scientists through hostile territories.

With that done, Mark is ready to adventure on Barsoom, as Kantos Than, Dashing Red Martian Soldier who is fearless, skilled with a blade, and filled with youthful daring and passion!

With all this done, Mark only needs to record Kantos Than's stress tracks. Mark's high Daring and Passion give his character a Fear of 9 — he's very hard to scare. His Confusion and Injury are more moderate, both at 5. That's not bad, it just means he's far more likely to fall to distraction, mental assault, or physical injury than Fear. He considers changing one of his talents to something that will let him move some Confusion or Injury damage to his potent fear tracker, but decides he would rather play for a while and decide if that's something he would like to alter with experience later.

SAMPLE PLAYER CHARACTERS

These ready-made characters were created using the process detailed in this chapter. They can be used by players who wish to grab a character and jump right into the game, or as inspiration for creating characters. If desired, these characters can be easily modified by changing their race or substituting new talents with others from this chapter or new ones created by the players.

COURAGEOUS EARTHBORN EXPLORER

"I was on a solo flight across the Atlantic when the engine failed. As the ocean rushed to fill my vision I saw the Red Planet in the sky, and it grew in my consciousness. I blacked out shortly after and, when I awoke, I was here. Sometimes I wonder if I am here at all, or if my dead body lies in the deep oceans of my homeworld. But I suppose it doesn't matter if Barsoom is real or some strange purgatory or afterlife. It is a new world to explore."

You were always restless. While your family and friends were content to stay home, you sought strange new locales, lost cities, and new challenges. Your luck finally ran out on Earth, but a strange twist of fate sent you to Barsoom. Now you must survive on the wonderful, but deadly, Red Planet.

ATTRIBUTES

DARING	CUNNING	EMPATHY
8	5	6

MIGHT	PASSION	REASON
7	5	5

STRESS TRACKERS

CONFUSION	FEAR	INJURY
6	8	7

TALENTS

BARTITSU (GRADE 1)
You know a few tricks in personal combat, mostly due to training back home in various forms of unarmed self-defense.

* **Circumstance:** When fighting unarmed.

* **Effect:** You gain 1 extra Momentum whenever you spend Momentum while engaged in unarmed combat.

FIND THE WAY (GRADE 1)
You can find safe paths and hidden places with ease. You are also more likely to bypass and survive hazards like dangerous terrain, ancient traps, and other deadly obstacles.

* **Circumstance:** When travelling in wastes, ruins, and wilderness areas.

* **Effect:** When facing an environmental danger (falls, traps, etc.), you roll 1 less 🎲 than normal.

STEADY NOW (GRADE 1)
You are a skilled markswoman, especially when you take a moment to aim.

* **Circumstance:** When using a move action before making an attack with a firearm.

* **Effect:** Use a move action before you make an attack with a firearm, you don't move but your attack gains an extra d20 for the attack test.

IF IT HAS WINGS (GRADE 2)
You're a skilled pilot, capable of flying any manner of aircraft in even the most hazardous conditions.

* **Circumstance:** When piloting aircraft, airships, and other flying craft.

* **Effect:** You gain a bonus of 1d20 to any piloting-related tests and can reduce environmental-based difficulties while piloting by 1.

LEAPS AND BOUNDS (GRADE 2)
Your Earthborn muscles allow you to leap great distances and perform great feats of strength while on Barsoom.

* **Circumstance:** When moving on Barsoom and planets with similar gravity.

* **Effect:** You may close one range category automatically, ignoring obstacles and terrain if you have clearance and space to leap to your destination. You may spend 1 Momentum to move an additional range category.

MIGHTY ATHLETE (GRADE 2)
You've quickly learned to use your enhanced strength to more easily traverse obstacles.

* **Circumstance:** When performing athletic tasks.

* **Effect:** You may use Might in any test based on athletic skills (jumping, running, catching, etc…) and may reduce the difficulty of such test by 1.

FLAW
CURIOSITY KILLED THE BANTH
Lose 3 Momentum when you fail to take an opportunity to explore a new mystery, unknown location, or strange new culture.

RENOWN AND ACCOLADES
RENOWN: 0

BOLD EARTHBORN SOLDIER

"I served with Her Majesty's Army as one of her 'Black Lions'. While I wouldn't claim it was a wholly pleasant experience free of prejudice, I found camaraderie and purpose during those days. It was during the end of the Great War to End All Wars that I was wounded, I believed, mortally so. In a bloody haze, I stumbled into an ancient circle of stones. As I lay there, I looked up at distant Mars and wondered what sort of beings could be watching me. I soon found out…"

As a Sikh soldier in the Indian Army, you were no stranger to battle or being an outsider. Here on Barsoom, you find your training and the newfound strength granted by Mars' lesser gravity and atmosphere gives you all the tools you need to survive and protect those in need.

ATTRIBUTES

DARING	CUNNING	EMPATHY
8	4	5

MIGHT	PASSION	REASON
8	7	4

STRESS TRACKERS

CONFUSION	FEAR	INJURY
6	8	5

TALENTS

BLACK LION OF JASOOM (GRADE 1)
Your training, experience, and courage are sure to make you a legend on this strange new world.

* **Circumstance:** When performing a **Daring +** action.

* **Effect:** When you gain more than 2 Momentum on a test, gain an additional Momentum.

CUT THEM ALL DOWN (GRADE 3)
Your skill with a sword is such that no lesser foe can hope to stand against you.

* **Circumstance:** When wielding a sword or other bladed weapon.

* **Effect:** You automatically defeat 2 minions as part of your action. You may spend additional Momentum to defeat more at the cost of 1 Momentum per additional minion. You also gain a bonus d20 to attack tests with a sword.

LEAPS AND BOUNDS (GRADE 2)
Your Earthborn muscles allow you to leap great distances and perform great feats of strength while on Barsoom.

* **Circumstance:** When moving on Barsoom and planets with similar gravity.

* **Effect:** You may close one range category automatically, ignoring any obstacles or intervening terrain as long as you have clearance and space to leap between your starting point and destination. You may spend 1 Momentum to move an additional range category.

MIGHTY THEWS (GRADE 2)
Your muscles give strength to your blows that few can match.

* **Circumstance:** When wielding a muscle-powered weapon such as a sword, spear, or your fists.

* **Effect:** Spend 1 Momentum to reroll any 🎲 that inflict no damage on an attack. You may only do this once per attack.

UNCOMMON KINDNESS (GRADE 1)
You understand that mercy keeps ferocity from becoming tyranny.

* **Circumstance:** When a minion is defeated.

* **Effect:** After combat one defeated minion can be "set free". This can be used to have the minion accomplish limited goals, such as delivering a message to a nearby ally or having them find food, and will be executed to the best of the minion's ability. The kindness of the character will be well remembered by the minion.

FLAW
CODE OF HONOR
You lose 3 Momentum if you break your word, refuse to defend the innocent from harm, or otherwise act dishonorably.

RENOWN AND ACCOLADES
RENOWN: 0

CANNY RED MARTIAN ENVOY

"I serve my nation with my words, seeking allies against our many enemies. My family's position helps lend power and authority to my negotiations. However, when words fail, I have my pistol and sword."

A noble of Barsoom, you serve your family and nation as a diplomat and stateswoman. Unfortunately, your position makes you a regular target for kidnapping and assassination, requiring you to be skilled at self-defense. Despite trying to be a woman of peace, you are always ready for war: such is life on Barsoom.

ATTRIBUTES

DARING 7 | CUNNING 5 | EMPATHY 6
MIGHT 4 | PASSION 8 | REASON 6

STRESS TRACKERS

CONFUSION 6 | FEAR 8 | INJURY 5

TALENTS

PASSIONATE ORATOR (GRADE 1)
Your unwavering loyalty and love for your people moves others to aid you. Even when dealing with the sworn enemies of your nation, culture, or group, you can often gain concessions or create opportunities with your words.

* **Circumstance:** When speaking to convince an audience.

* **Effect:** You may reroll the result of any failed die roll in a Passion-based attempt to convince or charm others.

EN GARDE (GRADE 2)
You are adept at using and defending against blades, the common weapon of duelists, soldiers, and assassins.

* **Circumstance**: When defending with a sword or blade.

* **Effect:** You may reroll the result of any failed die roll in a defense test when defending against swords or blades. You may also ignore the first point of damage from swords or blades in a scene.

SPEAK FROM THE HEART (GRADE 2)
Your words can soften hearts, win over allies, and confuse your foes.

* **Circumstance:** When speaking or negotiating.

* **Effect:** You may use Passion in all spoken-action tests or social-based contests. When inflicting damage in social-based attacks, you roll an extra 1 🎲 of damage and may always opt to do 2 Confusion damage when an effect is rolled (5-6) on such tests.

ONE DIPLOMAT TO ANOTHER (GRADE 1)
You are skilled at understanding the agendas and motivations of people like yourself.

* **Circumstance:** When attempting to learn a diplomat's agenda

* **Effect:** When you attempt to discover the agenda of another character, on a successful test, you gain 1 Momentum to ask a clarifying question of the narrator as per the Obtain Information Momentum spend.

FLAW
SEEK A BETTER PATH
You lose 3 Momentum if you attack or ambush another without first attempting to negotiate or otherwise win them over to your side.

CORE EQUIPMENT:
Symbol of your Royal House: This weapon deals 2 🎲 base damage with the Psychic quality.

RENOWN AND ACCOLADES
RENOWN: 10
* **Title:** Chieftain (8 renown)

* **Ally:** Loyal Servant and Bodyguard (2 renown)

STALWART RED MARTIAN DUELIST

"This isn't just a sword, it's an extension of myself. It reflects what I truly am. And what I am right now is severely irritated you would dare attempt to harm those under my protection. So arm yourself and let us be about it…"

Few can match your skill with a blade. Though technically a member of your nation's military, your special talent for personal combat means you spend most of your time serving as bodyguard, escort, or champion for important dignitaries.

ATTRIBUTES

DARING	CUNNING	EMPATHY
8	6	7

MIGHT	PASSION	REASON
5	5	5

STRESS TRACKERS

CONFUSION	FEAR	INJURY
7	8	6

TALENTS

BODYGUARD (GRADE 1)
You are skilled at protecting a subject in your charge from harm.

✳ **Circumstance:** When protecting another.

✳ **Effect:** At the beginning of a combat name a character you intend to protect. If they are adjacent, you may choose to defend them from any physical attacks. If they are within Near range, you may spend 1 Momentum to move adjacent to them and defend them, provided there is an unobstructed path between you and your charge.

PEERLESS SWORDMASTER (GRADE 3)
You are one of the greatest swordfighters in your nation, if not all of Barsoom.

✳ **Circumstance:** When using a sword or similar melee weapon (daggers, sabers, etc.) in accordance with Martian honor.

✳ **Effect:** You gain a bonus d20 to attack tests while sword fighting and whenever you generate at least 2 Momentum with a test involving a sword or similar weapon, you gain an additional Momentum. In addition, your blade gains the Fearsome quality.

SENSITIVE DEFENDER (GRADE 1)
Your keen perception and ability to read the moods and expressions of others serves you well in battle.

✳ **Circumstance:** When defending against any opponent you can clearly observe.

✳ **Effect:** You may always use Empathy to defend against an attack by an opponent you can clearly observe.

A MATTER OF HONOR (GRADE 1)
You are bound by honor and consider it of great importance when challenging another.

✳ **Circumstance:** When you spend a Spoken action to issue a formal challenge to any narrator character that is not a minion.

✳ **Effect:** One minion attending the challenged narrator character is automatically considered defeated, so long as you maintain the correct standards of Martian Honor. Should you break the standards of Martian Honor (narrator has the final say) the minion is no longer considered defeated and may act as normal.

FLAW
LOYAL TO THE SWORD
You lose 3 Momentum if you opt to use a firearm, spear, or other non-sword like weapon unless honor demands it.

CORE EQUIPMENT:
Sword

RENOWN AND ACCOLADES
RENOWN: 10
✳ **Title:** Teedwar (8 renown)
✳ **Ally:** Your old swordmaster (2 renown)

CHARMING OKAR SPY

"There are many ways of keeping one's people safe. The soldier does so with pistol and sword. The scientist with his texts and tests. I protect my people with lies, deceptions, and the occasional blade in the dark. Some may think me underhand or cowardly, but I ask you… how many brave warriors would walk into enemy territory lightly armed and alone?"

You are a loyal Okar trained in espionage and covert operations. Using various dyes and other props, you can color your skin and shave your beard to pose as red Martian, First Born, or even Holy Thern. Your missions often carry you far from home, but you may also be called on to root out dissidents, traitors, and malcontents among your own people as well.

ATTRIBUTES

DARING 5 · CUNNING 8 · EMPATHY 5
MIGHT 5 · PASSION 4 · REASON 7

STRESS TRACKERS

CONFUSION 7 · FEAR 5 · INJURY 8

TALENTS

CUNNING BLADE (GRADE 1)
You are adept at using your wits and cunning in battle, finding the perfect opening or opportunity.

* **Circumstance:** When using a sword or dagger.

* **Effect:** When you gain at least 2 Momentum with a Cunning-based action involving a sword or dagger, you gain 1 additional Momentum.

FITTING IN (GRADE 2)
You are adept at convincing others to consider you one of their own. With proper skin paints and disguises you walk the cities and hallways of Barsoom without drawing attention or seeming out of place.

* **Circumstance:** When convincing others you belong.

* **Effect:** Add a bonus d20 with tests to convince others you belong in a place or group. You may pose as a member of any race or culture with the same basic language and physical form without fear of casual discovery.

MASTER OF DISGUISE (GRADE 1)
You are a master of disguise, transforming yourself completely and effectively. It is possible even your closest friends have never seen your real face.

* **Circumstance:** When disguising yourself.

* **Effect:** Spend 1 Momentum to leave a scene. Then in the next scene, spend 1 Momentum to replace any minion-type character in the scene, revealing you were disguised as them all along.

STATE SECRETS (GRADE 2)
Few secrets, ciphers, or enemy battle plans escape your scrutiny and understanding.

* **Circumstance:** When discovering important secrets or plans.

* **Effect:** When using Reason to understand, search for, uncover, or decipher coded messages, secret plans, or similar intelligence, gain 2 bonus d20.

FLAW

SECRETS AND LIES
When operating covertly in foreign territory, the narrator may tell you to spend 3 Momentum or face a challenge to your cover identity or mission. This does not automatically result in your capture or discovery, but can make things more difficult for a time.

CORE EQUIPMENT:
Dagger

RENOWN AND ACCOLADES
RENOWN: 10

* **Title:** Dwar (5 renown)
* **Ally:** Gain allies equal to 5 renown (*see page 86*), representing fellow agents or others who may know your true identity.

DRIVEN FIRST BORN AIRSHIP OFFICER

"I am captain and dator to my crew; they would fly into certain death if I ordered it, though there's no reason or profit in such suicidal endeavors. Instead, we seek profit and power by sword and gun, sailing on the ninth ray across Barsoom…"

A raider and pirate at heart, you are not closely connected to the politics or ideology of your people, preferring the freedom of the open sky and regular raiding. You were recently lost or separated from your crew and ship due to calamity and are seeking to reclaim it or a suitable replacement. With luck and skill, you will soon be commanding from the deck of an airship once more.

ATTRIBUTES

DARING	CUNNING	EMPATHY
7	7	3

MIGHT	PASSION	REASON
6	5	6

STRESS TRACKERS

CONFUSION	FEAR	INJURY
6	7	7

TALENTS

AIRSHIP PILOT (GRADE 1)
You can crew and command airships, flying them with skill beyond most pilots.

* **Circumstance:** When crewing or commanding an airship.

* **Effect:** When crewing or commanding an airship, you may roll an extra d20.

NO QUARTER (GRADE 2)
You are merciless in battle, striking suddenly and without pause or restraint.

* **Circumstance:** When attacking in combat.

* **Effect:** You may reroll the result of any 1 🎲.

CRUEL BEAUTY (GRADE 2)
Your deadly nature and natural charms cause many to underestimate or favor you when they should not.

* **Circumstance:** When deceiving or charming another person.

* **Effect:** You may reroll any failed die on an attempt to deceive, charm, or seduce another. In tests against those you have previously charmed or seduced, gain an additional d20.

I'VE HEARD OF YOU, I'M NOT IMPRESSED (GRADE 1)
You have met many people on your travels and have the ability to learn about them from first impressions.

* **Circumstance:** When being introduced to any new narrator character that is not a minion.

* **Effect:** When you are introduced to a new narrator character, you gain a bonus d20 on the first test you make to interact with them. You must spend the first 1-2 Momentum gained on the test to learn information about the narrator character, as per the Obtain Information Momentum spend.

FLAW
A PIRATE'S LIFE
You bristle under authoritarian abuses and allow no challenges to your leadership. If harassed or bullied by those in power or if someone challenges your leadership you lose 3 Momentum unless you challenge or confront them.

CORE EQUIPMENT:
Pistol (usually hidden)

RENOWN AND ACCOLADES
RENOWN: 10
* **Title:** Dator (10 renown)

"These cities and settlements are not like it is in the deep wilds, in the heart of the dead sea bottoms and other such places. The wilderness is a thriving, angry thing with a spirit of its own. That spirit wishes to harm you if you are foolish or do not respect its dangers. Even most of my horde cannot walk the ways safely. So, pay attention and follow me…"

While you cannot claim to be the greatest warrior of your people, you are undoubtedly among their best hunters and trackers. Your skills serve you well as a scout and guide for warbands and hordes navigating the wildest areas, and years of hunting and survival have made you a skilled fighter. Your skills have saved the lives of many, including the chieftain of a local band and a red scout from nearby Helium whose comradery you have earned despite the differences of your respective people.

ATTRIBUTES

DARING	CUNNING	EMPATHY
5	5	4

MIGHT	PASSION	REASON
8	4	7

STRESS TRACKERS

CONFUSION	FEAR	INJURY
7	5	8

TALENTS

FOUR-ARMED FOR WAR (GRADE 1)
Your warlike, combative culture and four arms give you an edge in combat, allowing you to attack with multiple weapons or steady your rifle with ease.

✳ **Circumstance:** When attacking with melee weapons or using a rifle.

✳ **Effect:** When you generate Momentum when attacking with a melee weapon or rifle, gain an extra Momentum.

CALCULATED SHOT (GRADE 2)
You are a skilled shot, able to naturally calculate wind, distance, and other factors to help you find the target.

✳ **Circumstance:** When attacking with a firearm.

✳ **Effect:** You may always use Reason to attack with a firearm in ranged combat and inflict an additional 1 🎲 of damage in successful ranged attacks.

SKILLED INFILTRATOR (GRADE 1)
You are quiet and patient when you stalk your prey, crouching mere meters from those who would seek you out.

✳ **Circumstance:** When infiltrating a location.

✳ **Effect:** You automatically avoid all minion-type enemies when infiltrating or sneaking into an area. Only non-minion characters have any hope of discovering you.

WILD HUNTER (GRADE 2)
Though you are a formidable force in any battle, you are particularly skilled at stalking and bringing down banths, wild thoats, and other dangerous beasts of Barsoom.

✳ **Circumstance:** When tracking, stalking, or fighting wild beasts.

✳ **Effect:** You gain a bonus d20 when tracking, stalking, or fighting wild beasts.

FLAW

OUT OF MY ELEMENT
When in a city or other civilized environment, the narrator may declare you have become disoriented, lost, or have stumbled into somewhere you shouldn't be unless you pay 3 Momentum. These situations are never immediately deadly, but they can be dangerous.

CORE EQUIPMENT:
Green Martian Rifle

RENOWN AND ACCOLADES
RENOWN: 10

✳ **Title:** Padwar of the Thark Horde (2 renown)

✳ **Ally:** Green Martian war chieftain and his band of warriors (6 renown)

✳ **Ally:** Red Martian scout from Helium (2 renown)

CHAPTER 3: TALENTS

Talents are an important part of **John Carter of Mars** characters. They represent exceptional abilities that allow characters to perform great feats at a high level of competence.

WHAT ARE TALENTS?

In other role-playing games characters have skills, perks, and advantages. **John Carter** presumes a level of hyper-competency in characters that avoids the need for such mechanics. If your character would logically know how to fly an airship, they can. If they don't know and someone takes the time to teach them? Now they can.

Talents are more than skills or learned abilities. They are a core element that makes a character who they are. They allow characters to regularly bend the rules in their favor or boost their chances of success with certain actions. They represent mastery of skills, natural abilities, and other elements that take a character from "I can do that" to "I can do that with style, and far better than others."

USING TALENTS

For ease of play and to avoid confusion, you can only use one talent at a time. If you have two talents that affect your character's ability to swing a sword, you can only use one at a time. You combine similar effects into a single talent (*see Multiple Effect Talents later in this chapter*).

Note that using a talent to change an attribute used before an action begins and talents that augment die rolls and tests are still allowed. Some talents don't engage directly with a single contest, but allow characters to bend the rules by always using particular attributes for certain actions or similar effects.

Example: The Thark marksman Haldus Hark has three talents relating to shooting firearms, particularly his trusty rifle. He has one talent, Keen Marksman, which allows him to always use Reason when using a rifle, even when the attribute would not seem appropriate. He has a second talent, Suppressing Fire, that makes him harder to hit with ranged weapons when he too is armed with a firearm. When he wants to use both these talents in rapid succession in a gun battle, he's allowed because they don't engage with a single action. The first alters the attribute used before any actions occur and the second deals with defense actions.

However, if Hark has a third talent, that also boosts his defense or made him harder to hit? He could not use that and Suppressing Fire on the same attack action.

Multiple talents cannot be used if both of their effects would impact a single test or the same action.

Example: Okar spy Vunn Horek has two talents that relate to his skill with a pistol, Deadly Pistoleer and Expert Aim. Deadly Pistoleer allows him to roll 2 additional combat dice when he makes a successful attack with a pistol. Expert Aim lets him add 2d20 to a test involving shooting on a turn where he doesn't also move. As both these talents directly relate to the same action, shooting, he can only use one of these each time he makes a test involving shooting his weapon.

Note that you can merge such effects into a single talent if desired, especially if it's easier for you to keep track of or allows creation of a talent with a particularly narrow scope (*see Designing Talents*), but it's not required.

Example: Verna Mal, a First Born assassin, is particularly adept with using a dagger in close combat. She has a talent, Mistress of the Knife, that gives her a bonus d20 on both attacking and defending when wielding a dagger. While attack and defense are two separate actions, she can use her talent on both attack and defense when using her signature knives and daggers. However, if she also has a talent, A Knife in the Dark, giving her a bonus to attack and damage on an unsuspecting foe, she must decide which of the two talents to use when attacking—though she could use A Knife in the Dark for an attack action and Mistress of the Knife for defense if she is attacked immediately after.

DESIGNING TALENTS

Talents are designed based around two things: Momentum value and scope. A grade 1 talent is roughly equivalent to spending 1 Momentum on a roll and generally covers an action or type of action that is fairly narrow (attacking with a sword, scientific research, riding a thoat, etc…). The same holds true of grade 2 and above talents, except that they represent a higher Momentum spend. If a talent covers a very wide area, it will be treated as being higher grade. If its use is exceptionally narrow, it may be treated as lower grade. Ultimately the narrator must approve the cost of any designed talents.

The following list of talent abilities based on grade covers their most common uses.

Each grade of talent can let you…

- Add a d20 to a particular type of action.
- Always use a particular attribute for a type of action, regardless of the details of the situation.
- Move an extra range if not blocked or hindered from moving.
- Roll an extra 🎲 to the damage dealt.
- Dispatch an additional minion on a successful attack.
- Avoid dangers and bad situations while traveling through an area.
- Get a "yes or no" answer to a single question about a particular scene or situation.

For grade 2 of a talent you can…
- Send a weapon or device flying as part of an attack or defense.
- Gain an additional specified movement or Spoken action.
- Automatically remove another's affliction.
- Ignore the effects of an affliction for a scene. It doesn't go away, you just ignore its effects.

For grade 3 of a talent you can…
- Move up to two additional ranges between you and the target, if not blocked or hindered from moving.
- Automatically repair or recover a device or piece of equipment.

For grade 4 of a talent you can…
- Gain an additional specified Conflict action.
- Automatically remove 2 afflictions from another.
- Automatically remove an affliction from yourself.

In addition, a talent can do anything Momentum can do on a 1 grade = 1 Momentum basis. Note that the circumstance a particular talent covers is by default a fairly narrow, relatively specific action, but usually one that comes up fairly often in play. Thus, it can't just be "an attack" but needs to be "attacking with a sword" or "shooting a firearm." Likewise, it shouldn't be too narrow like "lunging forward with a cavalry saber." It won't be "when commanding the crew of this one ship" or "when commanding anyone" but circumstances like "when commanding airships" or "when commanding the Armies of Helium."

If desired, narrators may allow broader talents, charging extra grades for them. They may also allow more potent talents to be purchased at a lower grade by limiting their circumstance. To a limited degree this is even encouraged as it helps create some fun variations of talents among characters. However, if a talent is always or never coming up, it runs the risk of unbalancing play. Thus, narrators can veto a particular talent if necessary and help players come up with a more suitable one.

Example: Peter wants to make an Okar duelist who studied under the great Solan of Kadabra, Switchmaster of the Guardian of the North and swordsmaster extraordinaire. He first wants to take a talent that gives him a bonus d20 to use "when attacking and defending with a weapon" for grade 1. The narrator, Jack, informs him that's too broad a circumstance and too potent an effect for a grade 1 talent. After a bit of discussion, Jack and Peter come up with the Okar Swordmaster talent, which grants a bonus d20 when attacking or defending with a sword. The talent is grade 2 (1 grade each for the bonus die on attack and defense).

Example: Jennifer wants her red Martian noble to possess a particular affinity with banths, much like Thuvia of Ptarth. She wishes to take a grade 2 talent giving her a bonus d20 when attempting to command or calm banths and being able to always use Cunning as

one of her attributes in all such tests. The narrator, Jack, knows that while banths will be present in the campaign, they won't show up all that often. He informs Jennifer that she can have that talent as grade 1 instead of grade 2 — 2 grades worth of abilities, but reduced by 1 for how rarely it will come up in play.

The following talents are ready to be selected by player characters during character generation. They can also serve as examples for player-designed talents. Some talents are similar to others, but with minor changes in when they apply or how they are used. These talents may be easily changed as needed. For example, Expert Rifleman (grade 1) and Deadly Pistoleer (grade 2) are both talents that do extra damage 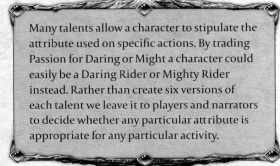 with a particular weapon. If desired, a player might make a grade 2 talent that uses the Deadly Pistoleer effect but for a rifle instead, calling it something like Deadly Rifleman. Conversely, another player might take the Expert Rifleman effect and wish to use it for pistols or other weapon, renaming it Expert Pistoleer or some other appropriate title.

GRADE 1 TALENTS

ACROBATIC DODGE
You're always moving and have a knack for recognizing opportunities to escape an aggressive enemy.

* **Circumstance:** When successful in defending against a physical attack.

* **Effect:** After dodging any physical attack you can move anywhere within Near range.

CUT THEM DOWN
Your skill with a sword is such that no lesser foe can hope to stand against you.

* **Circumstance:** When wielding a sword.

* **Effect:** You automatically defeat 1 minion as part of your action. You may spend additional Momentum to defeat more at the cost of 1 Momentum per additional minion.

PASSIONATE RIDER
You ride with your heart as much as your hands on the reins. You treat your beast as a loyal and valued companion and it always performs its best for you.

* **Circumstance:** When riding a thoat or other beast.

* **Effect:** You may substitute your Passion for any roll to ride, guide, or control a thoat or other riding beast.

Many talents allow a character to stipulate the attribute used on specific actions. By trading Passion for Daring or Might a character could easily be a Daring Rider or Mighty Rider instead. Rather than create six versions of each talent we leave it to players and narrators to decide whether any particular attribute is appropriate for any particular activity.

EXPERT RIFLEMAN
With a long gun in your hand, there are few who can match your ability to place a shot where it will do the most damage.

* **Circumstance:** When you hit with a rifle.

* **Effect:** Roll an extra 1 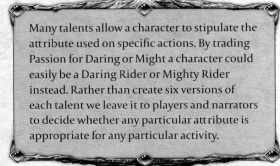 of damage on a successful attack.

EYE FOR DANGER
You are skilled at seeing if a foe — or even an ally — is carrying any concealed armaments.

* **Circumstance:** When looking at another character.

* **Effect:** You may ask the narrator if a particular character is armed, even if they don't appear to be. They must answer you truthfully. This talent cannot detect poisons, only weapons.

KEEN MARKSMAN
You are a careful and discerning shooter whose ability to think clearly and calculate a target's distance and speed improves your shooting.

* **Circumstance:** When using firearms.

* **Effect:** You may always use Reason when shooting a firearm.

SKILLED INFILTRATOR
You are quiet and patient when you stalk your prey. You are capable of crouching mere meters from those who would seek you out.

* **Circumstance:** When infiltrating a location.

* **Effect:** You automatically avoid all minion-type enemies when infiltrating or sneaking into an area. Only non-minion characters have any hope of spotting you.

GRADE 2 TALENTS

EXPERT AIM
When you take a moment to aim, you rarely miss even the most challenging targets.

* **Circumstance:** When shooting but not moving.

* **Effect:** You gain a bonus 2d20 when attacking with a firearm provided you don't move during this turn.

JUST A SCRATCH
Either due to high pain tolerance or years of experience with injury, you can shrug off the effects of most minor flesh wounds and shallow cuts.

* **Circumstance:** When suffering a Wounds affliction.

* **Effect:** You can ignore the effects of 1 Wounds affliction for the scene. It doesn't go away, but you suffer no negative effects. This affliction does not count against a character's total afflictions for blacking out.

WITTY REPARTEE

Your tongue is as quick and lithe as your blade! You are always able to slip in a comment or call out important information to your allies even during the tensest situations.

- ✳ **Circumstance:** When performing an action.

- ✳ **Effect:** You may always take an additional Spoken action as part of an attack, defense, or other action.

SKILLED PHYSICIAN

You are a skilled healer and physician, able to tend minor wounds and comfort patients quickly and efficiently. Your treatments always provide some benefit, no matter how challenging the injury.

- ✳ **Circumstance:** When healing another's afflictions.

- ✳ **Effect:** You may use a Conflict action to automatically remove 1 affliction from any character you treat, no test is required. You may perform a test to heal additional afflictions if you desire as part of the action.

DEADLY PISTOLEER

Your skill with a pistol is well-known and justly feared. Your shots always strike for maximum force and damage, often killing a lesser foe instantly.

- ✳ **Circumstance:** When you successfully attack someone with a pistol.

- ✳ **Effect:** Roll an extra 2 🎲 of damage on a successful attack.

SUPPRESSING FIRE

You are adept at keeping enemy marksmen ducking and firing off only wild shots.

- ✳ **Circumstance:** When both you and your opponents are armed with firearms or ranged weapons.

- ✳ **Effect:** The difficulty to attack you with firearms and ranged weapons while you are similarly armed is increased by 2. You must be able to shoot back at your attackers to gain this benefit.

GRADE 3 TALENTS

FIXED

You can fix even the most damaged of equipment, often with minimal tools and in record time. Unlike simple jury rigs and patches, your repairs are permanent — at least until you break it again.

- ✳ **Circumstance:** When repairing a device.

- ✳ **Effect:** Take a Conflict action and automatically repair one device or piece of equipment. This repair is permanent, lasting until the device is damaged again.

DISARMING PARRY

You can disarm an opponent's blade even as he closes to attack. With a twist and a flick of your wrist you can turn a deadly armed attacker into an unarmed target.

- ✳ **Circumstance:** When defending at Immediate range against a physical attack.

- ✳ **Effect:** Roll 1 bonus d20 for a defend action against an Immediate range physical attack. If successful, you automatically disarm your opponent unless he pays 2 Momentum.

FROM EVERY CHANDELIER

You're used to grabbing onto the smallest of rails or ledges. When traversing perilous landscapes, you seldom come to harm.

- ✳ **Circumstance:** When traversing a danger.

- ✳ **Effect:** When taking damage from a danger, you can reduce the damage by 3 🎲. This can reduce damage to 0.

GRADE 4 TALENTS

FLURRY OF BLOWS

Your whole body is a weapon and when you are armed the effect is even deadlier. You land two blows for every one your foes manage, quickly cutting them down to size.

- ✳ **Circumstance:** When making a physical attack based Conflict action in Immediate range.

- ✳ **Effect:** Take an extra physical attack based Conflict action at any target in Immediate range.

CAN'T I JUST USE TALENTS TO ATTACK WITH MY BEST ATTRIBUTES?

A common question among players is, "Can't I just pick a talent that lets me use a generally non-offensive attribute like Empathy or Reason to attack, take that attribute at a really high rank, and have a powerful fighter with strong abilities to do other things as well?"

The answer to this is "Yes, yes you can." It's not even "cheating". It's definitely intended as an option for character generation and advancement. You can absolutely take an Empathic Swordplay talent for your character and use Empathy when skewering enemies with a sword.

However, you should realize two things first. One: you still need a reason for the talent and why it works. This can be as simple as saying "I am adept at sensing my opponent's emotions, particularly their anxiety, anger, and fear. This means I can more easily sense when and how they will act in combat." In fact, that's a great reason, and it tells everyone something more about your character.

Two: you need to realize that in taking such a talent, you're surrendering a talent selection to optimizing your character in this way. You may be limiting your character somewhat. This isn't wrong, far from it. Many characters will have similar talents to excel at certain tests. Just remember that a character who doesn't do this probably has a more versatile range of talents, and possibly attributes. They may be inferior to you in some ways, but they can often act more effectively if injured or otherwise hindered in ways that affect their few strong attributes.

PAIN DOES NOT HURT

You are remarkably resistant to injury and possess superior focus and force of will. You can ignore injuries that would disable lesser individuals.

✳ **Circumstance:** When taking an affliction.

✳ **Effect:** Use a Conflict action to remove any one affliction. You cannot remove more than three afflictions in a single scene and must take a Conflict action to remove each one.

MULTIPLE EFFECT TALENTS

Some talents allow for multiple effects, usually those relating to two or more lower-graded talents combining as a single higher-graded talent. There is mechanically little difference between these talents and a single higher-graded talent. The grade of such a talent is equal to the combined grades of the included effects. Thus, a talent that provides a 1 Momentum effect and a 2 Momentum effect would be a grade 3 talent.

*Example: Korr Magis, a red Martian panthan and skilled close combatant, wishes to create a multiple effect talent that lets him deal deadly and accurate blows when wielding his sword. His player decides these effects translate into bonus dice for sword-based attacks and bonus combat dice for successful attacks. He wants 2d20 bonus dice for his sword attacks and wishes to roll an additional combat die on such attacks. Bought separately the 2d20 bonus would be a grade 2 talent, equal to spending 2 Momentum and costing 10xp to create. The extra damage would be a grade 1 talent, equal to spending 1 Momentum and costing 5xp to create. Combined into a single talent the ability to take a 2d20 bonus and roll an additional combat die when attacking with a sword is a grade 3 talent equivalent to spending 3 Momentum. It costs 15xp (10xp + 5xp) for Korr Magis to acquire this talent. He names this talent **Deadly Bladework**.*

The significance of multiple effect talents comes with how talents work winthin the rules. For ease and speed of play, a character can only bring one talent into play on a single die roll, conflict, or other test. Thus, if you have a talent that adds to your damage in combat and another that increases your chances to hit, you can only use one at a time. This rule keeps combat scenes and other times when the rules are actively used in play from becoming bogged down with lots of "Wait, but then I bring this talent into play!" or "Wait, I forgot I can also use these two talents here."

Characters can create multiple effect talents during character generation or buy them during play. If you want to merge two talents into a new talent, you repurchase them with experience as you advance and the combination is considered a new talent. By default, you receive no discount and pay no extra cost for "merging" lower grade talents into higher grade one, though narrators can, of course, decide to offer "buy back" discounts if they want.

*Example: In addition to his grade 3 **Deadly Bladework** talent, Korr Magis also possesses a grade 4 talent (costing 20xp) called **Flurry of Blows**, that lets him make an additional Conflict action at any target in Immediate range. He cannot combine **Deadly Bladework** and **Flurry of Blows** when fighting with a sword, he must use one or the other. He wishes to combine these talents into a new talent, **Flurry of Deadly Steel** that allows for both two Conflict actions with a sword from one talent, and for each action to have the additional*

die bonuses and damage from the other talent. This new combined talent costs the total of the two talents or 35xp (15xp + 20xp, respectively) and is considered a grade 7 talent (grades 3 + 4). **Flurry of Deadly Steel** is costly and Korr's player gets no discount for it despite having talents that individually duplicate its overall effect. However, this is a formidable ability! Should Korr later wish to add additional effects to this talent each effect will need to be purchased again.

Combining talent effects can be costly in terms of experience, but it can result in very powerful talents that make characters incredibly formidable and effective in their chosen areas of expertise. Generally, the advantage of being able to combine talents offsets the cost of having to purchase them again. If a narrator believes this is not the case with a particular talent, they can offer a discounts on a case by case basis.

The following multiple-effect talents are ready to be selected by player characters during character generation. They can also serve as examples for player-designed talents.

MULTIPLE EFFECT TALENTS

EMPATHIC RIDER (GRADE 2)
You understand your mounts and treat them with a kindness rare on Barsoom. As a result, your beasts perform amazingly well.

✳ **Circumstance:** When riding a beast.

✳ **Effect:** You may always use your Empathy when riding or controlling a living mount. You also may reroll any one failed d20 for riding tests.

PERCEPTIVE SCIENTIST (GRADE 2)
Your scientific analysis is so keen you even glean insight from failure and your successes are even more impressive.

✳ **Circumstance:** When analyzing a scientific device or theory.

✳ **Effect:** Roll a bonus d20 when analyzing scientific devices and theories. The narrator must answer one "yes or no" question about the device or theory regardless of the result of this roll.

DILIGENT SWORDMASTER (GRADE 3)
Your training and discipline when studying the sword makes you a terror to your enemies. You may also give on the spot guidance or instruction to your pupils, allies, and any who heed your advice.

✳ **Circumstance:** When using a sword in combat.

✳ **Effect:** You may re-roll any single d20 with attack or defense actions when using a sword in battle. You can spend 1 Momentum to grant this effect to any nearby ally you can clearly see and communicate with.

FEARSOME MIGHT (GRADE 3)
Even among the stalwart men and women of Barsoom you inspire fear. Lesser foes flee from you and even respected opponents are reluctant to let you get too close.

✳ **Circumstance:** Might-based actions.

✳ **Effect:** You gain a 2d20 bonus in any Might-based action. In addition, any 1 minion retreats or flees from your presence. You may spend additional Momentum to intimidate more lesser foes at the cost of 1 Momentum per additional minion.

YOU WILL REGRET THAT (GRADE 4)
Injury often doesn't slow or discourage you, it only spurs your desire for retribution. If a foe injures you, you push past the pain and unleash your vengeance upon them.

✳ **Circumstance:** After being wounded by another.

✳ **Effect:** Ignore the effects of an affliction for the rest of the scene. Also, for the rest of the scene gain a bonus d20 to attack and roll an extra die of damage against the person or creature who caused this affliction. You can only use this for one affliction and one target at a time.

CUNNING LOTHARIO (GRADE 4)
You are a master of seduction not out of any romantic inclination but simply as a means to an end.

✳ **Circumstance:** When using seduction to gain access to riches or equipment.

✳ **Effect:** You can always use Cunning to make seduction tests for the purposes of gaining property. After a successful test, the Cunning Lothario automatically gains 2 Momentum and can use 2 Momentum (repeatable) to gain any 1 piece of equipment that could normally be purchased as core equipment.

WHY NOT JUST ONE MEGA-TALENT?

Experienced gamers are likely looking at the rules on using only one talent at a time and thinking "Why don't I just make one talent for everything?" The reason for this is a bit complex.

Yes, you should consider creating logical multiple effect talents for your characters, either during creation or later during play. Such talents help define characters and can often form the basis of their reputation with others. A swordsman with a potent multiple effect Swordmaster of Helium talent that involves many aspects of swordplay may become widely known for their skills.

However, as talents need to work together organically on a single type of action or situation, it's often not sensible to lump everything into a single talent. For example, attack and defense are separate tests in a contest. A talent that rolls several attack and defense abilities into a single talent is both unwieldy and unnecessary.

Likewise, talents are focused on a single type or category of action as part of their scope. If your talents involve different scopes, they work poorly together and can become confusing and hard to manage.

Narrators can always veto talents they find are excessive or which bog down play.

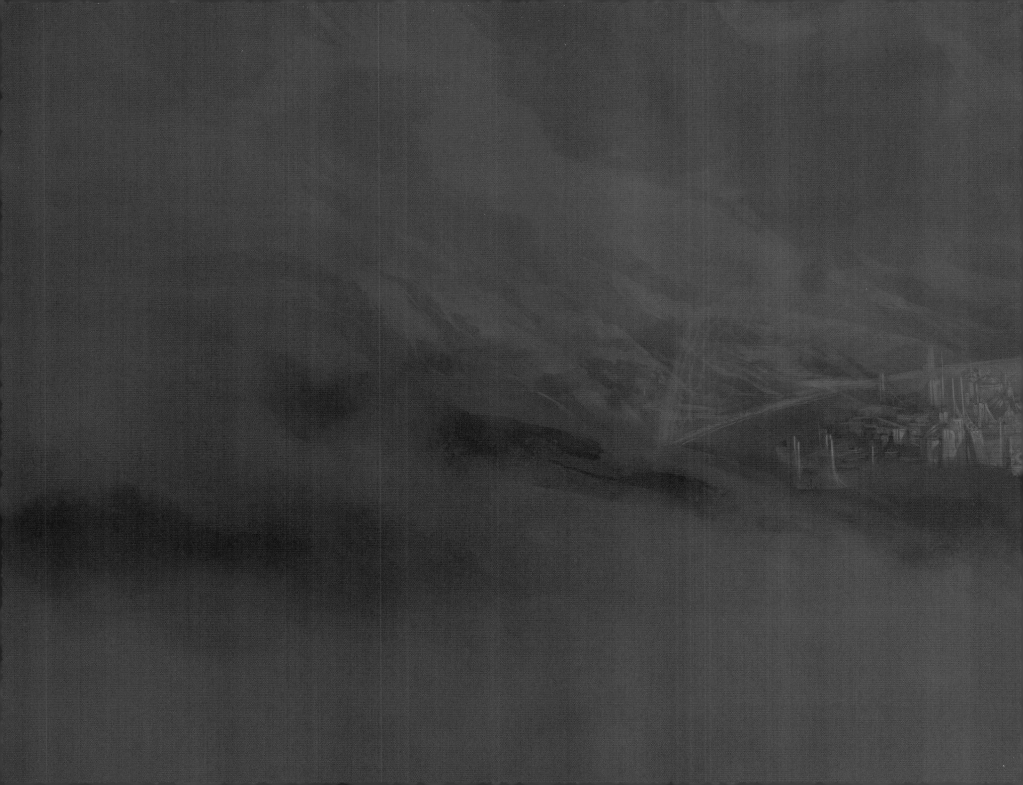

SECTION 2

> *For what, pray, is the pleasure of doing an easy thing?*
>
> — John Carter, *The Gods of Mars*

This chapter covers the basic rules of *John Carter*.

The participants in a game of *John Carter* take on certain roles. The majority are **players**, the actual people sitting around the table in a living room, or even playing online together. Each player controls a single character — normally referred to as a player character, to distinguish those characters from the many narrator-controlled characters that populate the game world. Players make the decisions that influence and direct their characters, deciding what a character does in a given situation, how the character reacts to a threat, etc.

The **narrator** is responsible for everything else. The narrator controls every other character, making decisions for them and determining their actions and responses. He is also responsible for setting scenes, establishing environments, and determining unfolding events. The narrator must interpret how the rules apply to a given situation. This includes ruling on the difficulty of tests, and ruling on outcomes when unusual situations or disagreements arise.

The narrator is not an adversary to the players. Playing this game is a much greater experience for everyone if the narrator is an enthusiastic supporter of the player characters and their exploits, seeking to make those characters' lives as dramatic, exciting, and challenging as possible.

DICE AND DICE ROLLS

Two types of dice are used to resolve the actions any character (player or narrator) may attempt and the situations they may face.

TWENTY-SIDED DIE (D20)

The first, and most commonly used dice type is a twenty-sided die, abbreviated throughout as a d20. These d20s are used for resolving attribute tests and for rolling on certain large tables. More often than not, multiple d20s are required, noted as Xd20, where X is the number of dice to be rolled. The most common roll is the 2d20 roll.

COMBAT DIE 🎲

The combat die, or 🎲, is a six-sided die (d6) rolled to determine damage and other special effects. When rolling a 🎲, ignore any results of 3 or 4. Results of 1 and 2 have their normal values. Results of 5 or 6 are referred to as effects. Specially-made *John Carter* combat dice replace the 1 and 2 sides with success icons, and the effect icon (the Barsoom symbol) for the 5 and 6 faces, with the 3 and 4 faces left blank. An effect adds 1 to the total, and triggers certain abilities, such as weapon qualities and other special conditions.

= 1 Damage	
= 2 Damage	
= No result	
= No result	
= 1 Damage + Effect	
= 1 Damage + Effect	

Most of the time, more than one 🎲 is rolled together and the results totaled.

Multiple combat dice are noted as X 🎲, where X is the number of combat dice rolled.

In most circumstances, multiple dice of any given type are rolled at once. Collectively these dice are referred to as the dice pool (or the pool).

ROUNDING NUMBERS

Whenever you need to divide the result of a die roll, a value in the game, or some other number, the players and narrator alike should always round up.

RE-ROLLING DICE

Many circumstances allow a player or narrator to re-roll one or more dice. When a talent, ability, item, or circumstance grants a re-roll, the player or narrator chooses which die to re-roll, and rolls it (or another die of the same kind). This re-rolled result replaces the original result entirely. The new results always stand, even if they're the same as, or worse than, the original results.

Some situations allow for a specific number of dice to be re-rolled, while others allow all dice in a pool to be re-rolled. In this latter instance, the player or narrator chooses how many dice to re-roll from those rolled, up to the number of dice listed (if any). Note that, in most cases, re-rolling is optional. The player or narrator does not have to re-roll any die if the original result is acceptable.

ATTRIBUTES

A collection of six attributes defines each character: **Cunning**, **Daring**, **Empathy**, **Might**, **Passion** and **Reason**. These attributes indicate a character's inherent abilities and their physical and mental limitations. Most attributes for player characters have values from 4 to 12, with 4 to 5 representing an average person, and 6 or higher showing heroic prowess. The higher the attribute, the greater the ability (*these are described in detail on page 12 of Chapter 2 Creating Your Adventurer*).

ATTRIBUTE TESTS

In situations where a character attempts a task and the outcome is unknown or uncertain, the character attempts an **attribute test**, sometimes just called a test.

As noted, an attribute test is required when a character attempts a task and the outcome is in doubt, where there are consequences for failure, or when the character is distracted or threatened. Outside of these circumstances, it's easier to assume that the character simply succeeds: player characters are heroic individuals, unlikely to fail at routine tasks.

The **target number** (TN) of a test is equal to the total of the two attributes that govern the activity (*see attribute definitions on page 12*). When asked to perform an attribute test, the player usually rolls 2d20. Each die roll equal to or less than that test's target number scores a single success. The greater the number of successes scored, across the entire dice pool, the better the test's result.

Additionally, the weaker of the character's attributes used in the test creates the possibility to score extra successes: each d20 result equal to or less than the character's weaker attribute scores *two* successes instead of one.

Example: *Zala Zors has a* **Daring** *of 7 and a* **Might** *of 4. She attempts to endure the dangerous heat of a forced march through the southern deserts. The narrator calls for her player to attempt a* **Daring** *+* **Might** *test. Zala's* **Daring** *7 +* **Might** *4 = 11 meaning her target number for this attempt is 11. A roll of 2d20 results in a 2 and a 9. Both succeed, as they are under Zala's target number of 11. The 2 is also under her* **Might** *of 4, so she gains an additional success on this test, for a total of 3 successes.*

Attribute tests are assigned a **difficulty rating**, a value ranging from Simple (difficulty 0, or D0) to Epic (D5) and beyond. The difficulty rating determines the minimum number of successes required to succeed at the test. Most of the time, tests are Average (D1). *The different difficulty ratings are shown on the test difficulty table on page 49.*

Difficulty ratings are often modified by steps. A test can become harder, such as an Average (D1) test becoming a Challenging (D2) test, or it can become easier, such as Daunting (D3) being reduced to Challenging (D2). Many factors can cause difficulties to increase or decrease by steps, such as environmental or situational conditions, character abilities (talents), and other modifiers.

The more d20s rolled during a test the higher the chances of success. There are a variety of ways by which players and the narrator may obtain additional d20s to roll during an attribute test, and these are described later in this section. **However, a character is never allowed more than three bonus d20s on an attribute test (5d20 in total).**

Successes in excess of the difficulty become Momentum, which can be spent to gain additional benefits and bonuses.

Example: *From the prior example, the narrator determined that Zala needed two successes on her test, thus making it a Challenging (D2) test. Since Zala scored a total of three successes, she has one success above the needed minimum. Zala Zors therefore gains 1 Momentum (added to the Momentum pool) which she (or another player) may spend later.*

COMPLICATIONS

Even when a plan succeeds, everything doesn't always go smoothly. Characters are likely to face new problems and unexpected complications, despite everything going according to plan.

Whenever a result of 20 is rolled on any d20 in an attribute test, the narrator immediately creates an impediment or problem — called a **complication** — that is applied to the situation or the specific character that made the roll. One complication is created for each 20 rolled.

Complications are an inconvenient change of circumstances. A complication can present an obstacle to further progress, requiring a new approach (like a route of escape being blocked), a loss of personal resources (such as using up ammunition or medical supplies), or something that hinders the character temporarily (a dropped weapon, a social *faux pas*, or a stuck door). It does not represent an injury to the character, and is merely a temporary setback.

The important thing to remember is that a complication is an inconvenience, not a benefit nor a catastrophe. They make things more difficult, more interesting, but they do not seriously harm important characters or eliminate important opportunities. Complications are independent of success or failure, and it is entirely possible to succeed at an attribute test while simultaneously generating a complication. The complication should only take effect immediately after the attribute test's results have been applied. A character may become vulnerable when fighting but, if the attribute test succeeded, the attack still connects before the character suffers the complication.

When rolling multiple 20s, the character may suffer multiple complications. These can be resolved separately, or the narrator may choose to group them together into a bigger problem. If the target number for a test is 20 or greater, any roll of 20 is considered both a success and a complication.

Example: Zala Zors' companion, Haran Phel, is crossing the desert with her. Haran's player rolls for a similar test, getting two successes, but one of the dice results is a 20. Haran still succeeds in his test, but the narrator determines that he will also suffer a complication. The narrator decides that Haran hurts his ankle trying to cross a rocky area in the desert. It doesn't do any damage, but it is awkward and causes him to walk more tenderly. The forced march does not harm Haran (because he succeeded the test), but he has a nagging ache and a bit of a limp (the 20 caused a complication). The narrator announces to Haran's player that any physical actions he attempts while suffering from the limp will have an additional level of difficulty.

THREAT AS COMPLICATION

If a suitable complication is not easy to determine, the narrator can choose to add 2 points of Threat to the Threat pool instead. Threat is a narrator resource, discussed in more detail on page 56 of this chapter and in *Chapter 9: Narrating Barsoom*. If a narrator character suffers a complication, the players may choose to have the narrator remove 2 points of Threat from the pool. If multiple complications are generated, then those effects are resolved individually at the narrator's discretion, so some could be turned into Threat while others have an immediate effect. The players and narrator should agree together to determine what works best for them and the adventure.

Players may request that the narrator take the Threat instead of applying a complication (and similarly, the narrator can make the same request of his players for narrator characters), essentially buying off a complication.

TEST DIFFICULTY

As already noted, the difficulty of an attribute test is a value from Simple (D0) to Epic (D5). This value is the minimum number of successes necessary to succeed at the test attempted. A Simple (D0) test requires no successes, and is the default difficulty for any test that a character can simply succeed at without any particular effort. A test with a difficulty of Epic (D5) is a virtually impossible task that only the most skilled and driven character can overcome.

The levels of difficulty, and examples of tasks for each level, are described on the table opposite.

DIFFICULTY ZERO TESTS

Some circumstances — as well as particular talents, items, and abilities — can reduce the difficulty of an attribute test, thus reducing the test's difficulty to Simple (D0). At other times, a test may be so easy and basic that it is not required in the first place. These are also Simple (D0) tests. If a test is Simple (D0), it is automatically successful with 0 successes, requires no effort whatsoever, and carries no risk of complications (see above). However, if a test is made, it can generate no Momentum — even bonus Momentum from talents, gear, or particularly advantageous situations.

In circumstances where something significant is at stake, or during a dramatic sequence of events, the narrator may require an attribute test even for a Simple (D0) task, representing a potentially unexpected outcome, even when all seems predictable and safe. This test takes the normal amount of time and generates Momentum as normal (since 0 successes are required to pass the test, every success generated is Momentum). Such a test also comes with the risk of complications.

SIMPLE (D0) *0 Successes*
* Opening a slightly stuck door.
* Researching a widely known subject.
* Hitting a stationary ranged target during rifle practice.

AVERAGE (D1) *1 Success*
* Overcoming a simple lock.
* Researching a specialist subject.
* Shooting an enemy within a weapon's range.

CHALLENGING (D2) *2 Successes*
* Overcoming a complex lock.
* Researching basic historical information.
* Shooting an enemy within a weapon's range in bad light.

DAUNTING (D3) *3 Successes*
* Overcoming a complex lock in a hurry.
* Researching obscure information.
* Shooting an enemy at Far range in poor light.

DIRE (D4) *4 Successes*
* Overcoming a complex lock in a hurry, without the proper tools.
* Researching historical information in a deserted ruin.
* Shooting an enemy at Far range, in poor light and heavy rain.

EPIC (D5) *5 Successes*
* Overcoming a complex lock in a hurry, without the proper tools, and in the middle of a battle.
* Researching historical information from the Time of Seas.
* Shooting an enemy at Too Far range in poor light and heavy rain.

SETTING THE DIFFICULTY

The narrator determines the difficulty level of a given test. Attribute tests in combat often have specific difficulty ratings, but these are baselines, and the narrator should feel free to alter any difficulties based on the situation at hand.

The narrator may often assume an attribute test starts at a difficulty of Average (D1). This represents fairly typical conditions for a task that isn't a guaranteed success, but is still quite straightforward to accomplish. If there are no other factors influencing a particular test, the narrator should leave the test at Average (D1).

However, a number of factors can make an attribute test more or less difficult. The narrator should consider whether a given factor influences a particular attribute test.

Example: Trying to patch up a severe wound might be a Challenging (D2) test normally, but trying to do it in the back of a wagon driven at full speed might increase the difficulty to Daunting (D3).

The differences between the difficulty levels can be quite significant, and the highest difficulties can be extremely challenging, or even impossible. The narrator should keep this in mind when determining the difficulty of tests.

The following page gives a summary of a number of common sources of difficulty modifiers. Note that not all of these are likely to influence a given attribute test: some are more applicable than others depending on circumstances around the test.

OPPOSED TESTS

At times, rather than overcoming the challenges and difficulties posed by circumstances, a character may instead be forced to best an opponent directly (e.g. striking a defensive foe) or indirectly (multiple characters attempting to reach an object all at once). These situations are called **opposed tests**.

When two characters are in direct opposition to one another, each character involved in the task performs an attribute test related to that action. The character who gains the greatest quantity of Momentum succeeds, in achieving the goal or

DIFFICULTY MODIFIERS

COMBINATIONS:
If there are multiple elements that individually are not enough to warrant a penalty, the combination of conditions can increase difficulty by one step.

LIGHTING:
Dark conditions impose higher difficulties to observation tests and other tests reliant on sight. A bright, moonlit night may increase difficulty by one step, a cloudy night by two steps, and complete darkness by three steps. Extremely bright light, or moving from an area of darkness into bright light (or vice versa) can increase difficulty. Bright light can impose similar difficulty increases to stealth tests.

DIFFICULT TERRAIN:
Slippery floors, sheer surfaces, deep snow, dense foliage, heaps of refuse, or even dense crowds all make movement-related tests more difficult. At the narrator's discretion, awkward terrain conditions can increase the difficulty of movement-related tests, or even require a test where none would normally be required.

DISRUPTION OR DISTRACTION:
The interference of hostile creatures or characters may increase difficulty, depending on the severity of the interference.

DISTANCE:
If an attribute test is applicable at a distance, every range category beyond Near increases difficulty by one step.

EQUIPMENT:
A character performing a task without the proper tools increases the difficulty by one step. In some cases, performing an attribute test outside of a proper environment (a workshop, laboratory, archive, etc.) may increase the difficulty by one step. If failed, the test can be redone later in that environment.

FOREIGN LANGUAGE:
Any social test when a character does not speak the language fluently has the difficulty increased by one step.

NOISE:
Loud noises can hinder a character's attempts to be heard or to hear other noises. Moderate noise (such as a crowd) increases difficulty by one step. Loud noise (an angry mob, a battle) increases difficulty by two steps.

POOR WEATHER:
A character exposed to severe weather (wind, rain, snow, fog, etc.) may face an increase in difficulty by one step.

RANDOM MOTION:
Strong winds, turbulence, and the like are often enough to hinder a test. Attribute tests relying on concentration or a controlled environment increase difficulty by one step when used in an unstable environment, such as a ship in turbulent air.

SOCIAL FACTORS:
Social tests when interacting with a character who does not trust you, who is of a rival faction, or who thinks you have committed a slight or social *faux pas*, increase in difficulty by one or more steps, at the narrator's discretion.

UNFAMILIARITY OR COMPLEXITY:
Performing complex or specialized tasks, or tasks in which the character has little experience, increases the difficulty. This is subject to narrator's discretion and varies by situation and conditions. For example, a village healer may have little experience with Zodangan poisons, while a Heliumite scientist may struggle when confronted with a text dealing with advanced fluid mechanics.

preventing the opponent from doing so. The Momentum gained by the victor is reduced by 1 point for each point of Momentum gained by the loser. In the case of a tie, the player character wins, unless the narrator spends 1 point of Threat. If two player characters or two narrator characters are tied, the narrator should randomly determine what breaks the tie, perhaps by comparing the related attributes or simply rolling a die.

There are two roles in an opposed test, the **acting character** and the **defender**. An acting character is any character who is taking an action on their turn which is being impacted by the defending character. Defenders are limited in how they can spend Momentum after succeeding on a test. *See Counterstrike on page 54.* The acting character is not limited and can spend Momentum as they see fit.

*Example: Volan Von is in hot pursuit, through the night time back alleys of Zodanga, of a rival spy who has stolen important artifacts from him. This sort of sustained pursuit is an opposed test. Volan's **Daring + Empathy** gives him a TN 10. The narrator determines that the spy's **Daring + Might** also gives him a TN of 10. Due to the chaotic nature of the alleys, darkness, and Volan's relative unfamiliarity with the area, it is a Challenging (D2) chase (the narrator combines the smaller complications into one step). Normally, the spy would have an easier time of it but, since he's constantly looking backwards to see where Volan is at, as well as lugging Volan's heavy satchel, the difficulty is the same Challenging (D2).*

Each of them rolls. Through a combination of spent Momentum and other talents, Volan rolls 5d20, and gets results of 17, 1, 10, 10, and 12. The narrator throws the spy 2 points of Threat to add 2d20 to his roll (to make it a bit suspenseful), so the Zodangan spy rolls 4d20, with results of 10, 20, 8, and 6.

Volan gets a total of four successes (10, 10, and two from the 1). The spy is less fortunate, with only three successes (10, 8 and 6) and a complication. Both of them achieve their goal and do not trip, get lost, etc. But Volan is the clear winner of the opposed test. After the difficulty is met, Volan has 2 Momentum and the spy 1 Momentum from their individual tests. The spy's one Momentum is subtracted from Volan's two Momentum, giving Volan a total of one Momentum. Volan is now free to use the remaining Momentum

The narrator determines that the complication results in the spy inadvertently running down an alley and finding that the end has been bricked up recently… putting him in a dead-end, with the very person he stole from blocking the only way out.

The narrator asks Volan what he is going to do. Volan pulls a long knife from his belt and closes in on the trapped spy …

If there are no other factors involved, the difficulty of the opposed test is Simple (D0), or Average (D1) if making an attack or defending. However, some situations may mean that it is possible for one or both sides to simply fail without offering any opposition. These situations apply a difficulty to the tests attempted by the characters involved. If a character fails the test, the opposed test is automatically lost. If both characters fail, then neither achieves anything.

If either side has some circumstance which would make its test more challenging for them than for its opponent, then that side's difficulty increases as usual. As noted above, if one side fails the test outright and the other does not, then the failing character loses the opposed test.

Characters may spend Momentum or Luck points (*see Luck on page 68*), pay into the Threat pool (*see Threat on page 56*), or use any other means of gaining successes or extra Momentum to boost their chances on an opposed test.

Characters may also spend Momentum to perform a Counterstrike or seize the initiative (*see pages 54 and 57 for details*).

Voluntary Failure

There are situations where a player may feel it will be better or more dramatic to fail, rather than to get bonus dice by using Momentum or Luck, or adding to the Threat pool. This might be when an attribute test contradicts what a character might know, or where the difficulty level makes success unlikely. In such cases, the character may risk gaining complications when there is little-to-no chance of success.

A player may choose to have their character fail an attribute test, so long as there are meaningful consequences for failure (if being pursued, attempting to perform a complex task under pressure, avoiding an attack, etc.) and the narrator agrees to it. To voluntarily fail an attribute test, the player "pays" the narrator one point of Threat, as opposed to the 2+ Threat points potentially added by complications. In exchange, the character immediately gains one point of Luck (up to the normal maximum allowed). A character may *never* choose voluntary failure for a Simple (D0) attribute test.

Luck points are discussed on page 68 of this chapter.

Success at Cost

There will be times when a failed attribute test may cause an interesting scene to grind to a halt, or the consequences of failure may not be particularly noteworthy. In such situations, the narrator may permit a character to succeed despite a failed attribute test, but at some additional cost.

In these cases, the character succeeds at the attempted task, but fails to prevent some additional problem from arising as well. The character immediately suffers 1 to 3 complications. It is up to the narrator to adjudicate the cost, but the guideline is one complication for most tests, and two complications for tests above Daunting (D3). These complications are in addition to any generated by the test itself.

Example: *If the character rolls a 20 on a failed Average (D1) test, and the narrator permits the character to succeed despite the failure, then the roll counts as generating two complications, one for the roll of 20 and one for being allowed to succeed at cost.*

As normal with complications, the narrator determines the specific effect, including adding to Threat if appropriate.

Any success at cost is gained without Momentum, from any source, even bonus Momentum. The character only achieves the most basic level of success.

Attribute Challenges

Attribute challenges are protracted tests that can be performed with multiple Conflict actions over multiple rounds. They represent detailed or complex actions that can't be confined to a simple roll, such as repairing a device or solving a complex puzzle. Each attribute challenge has both a difficulty and a threshold. Difficulty is the target difficulty that must be reached each round the test is attempted. Threshold is the total Momentum that must be accumulated to succeed in the complete test. For example, a difficulty 2, threshold 6 challenge requires a character to succeed on a number of difficulty 2 tests until they have accumulated a total of 6 Momentum. Failing a roll for an attribute challenge twice before the threshold is reached fails the test and brings whatever consequences of failure the action involves.

Example: *Captured by raiders and having just managed to escape his cell, Kale Singh seeks to sneak out of the villains' camp. The narrator runs this as an attribute challenge, informing Kale's player he will need to make a difficulty 2, threshold 8 challenge using* **Cunning + Empathy** *to sneak through the camp while avoiding patrols and not alerting any guard beasts. The first turn Kale succeeds on his test, generating 3 Momentum. He fails the next test. On the third test he succeeds and generates another 2 Momentum, but sadly fails the fourth test. The narrator says that, with 5 Momentum out of a necessary 8, he is more than half way through the raider's camp before a guard spots him and raises the alarm, summoning more raiders to prevent his escape. Kale must now decide to run, fight, or surrender, but sneaking out is no longer an option.*

Improving the Odds

While succeeding at most common tasks is a straightforward matter, even the most skilled character cannot succeed at difficult tasks without effort, opportunity, or assistance. To truly triumph, a character needs to find some other way of improving the odds.

There are a number of ways to succeed at difficulties beyond those granted by the default 2d20 roll and most provide additional d20s for an attribute test. Extra dice allow a character to score more successes and succeed at higher difficulties, or simply generate more Momentum. However, these extra dice always come at some sort of cost. The "payment option" a character chooses depends entirely upon what the player is willing and able to pay.

There are five different ways to improve the odds of success. These are described below and can be combined as desired. Regardless of the methods used, a character can never roll more than three additional d20s on any attribute test, limiting the total number of dice rolled to 5d20.

Create Opportunity

The Momentum spend, Create Opportunity (*see page 54*), is a straightforward and effective way of obtaining additional dice. Each point of Momentum spent adds a single bonus d20 to an attribute test. This is simple and easy, but it requires that the player characters have Momentum to spend.

Adding Threat

If there is insufficient Momentum available to spend on Create Opportunity, then a player has the option of adding to Threat. The end result is the same: each point of Threat the narrator gains is a single bonus d20 to an attribute test. This can be done at any time, but gives the narrator greater resources to empower narrator characters, or otherwise complicate the player characters' adventures.

In the narrator's case, when buying bonus d20s for narrator characters, these latter two options are identical. The narrator spends points of Threat to add bonus dice to a narrator character's attribute test.

Using Luck

From time to time, characters can turn to **Luck** to aid them. Each player character has a limited supply of Luck points that can be spent in a variety of advantageous ways. One of those ways is the addition of bonus dice. A single Luck point adds one bonus d20 to an attribute test. However, this bonus d20 is unlike other bonus d20s because it is "pre-rolled." Bonus d20s bought using Luck points are automatically assumed to have rolled a result of 1: when Luck is spent the player should place a d20 with a result of 1 displayed. For Challenging (D2) or Average (D1) tests this is usually enough to succeed: remember results under the character's weakest attribute count as two successes

If the character scores enough successes with d20s bought with Luck, the player may choose not to roll any other dice, and thus not risk potential complications. **Players can spend multiple Luck points on a single test, but these must be spent before any dice are rolled.** Dice bought with Luck count as part of the d20 pool, so if one or more Luck points are spent, the maximum number of dice is still limited to 5d20.

Teamwork and Assistance

Assistance differs from the other ways of improving the odds, because it does not add bonus dice directly, but allows other characters to contribute their efforts and skill to a test.

A number of tasks can benefit from the assistance of others. If the situation, time, and narrator allow, several characters can work together as a team when attempting to perform a task. When more than one character is involved in a task, a character is designated as the leader and the other characters are designated assistants. The narrator may decide that only a certain number of characters can assist — confined space may limit the number of people able to work together, for example — or can apply other limitations.

In order to assist with an attribute test, you must describe how your character is assisting the test's leader. If the narrator approves, each participating assistant rolls one d20 using the character's own attributes to determine if any successes are scored, with additional successes from Luck or other talents applied. The leader makes his attribute test as normal. Assistants may not use any means to roll additional dice, though the leader may use Momentum, Threat, Luck, or other methods of gaining extra d20s. Because assistant characters roll their own dice, they do not count towards the limit of three bonus d20s applied to a single test. However, any character providing assistance cannot do anything else while helping, because it takes time, concentration, and effort.

If the leader scores at least one success on the roll, any successes generated by the assistants are added to the leader's successes. If the leader does not generate any successes, then any successes from the assistants are lost and the effort fails utterly due to poor leadership and coordination.

Characters providing assistance do not have to use the same attributes as the leader: sometimes assistance is best provided with the contribution of outside knowledge and different training. Ultimately, the narrator decides whether a particular approach can be used to assist, and may require a player to explain how any assistance would work.

MOMENTUM

When the number of successes scored on an attribute test is greater than the difficulty rating, the excess becomes Momentum. Momentum can be spent immediately to perform the given task more effectively, or it can be saved and applied to actions taken later.

Beyond serving as a reward for characters that succeed spectacularly well, Momentum represents the raw heroism or villainy of a character. Players are encouraged to be creative in their uses of Momentum, allowing them to build new successes upon the foundation of past victories. The narrator may require that players describe how they take advantage of Momentum that they have saved up but this shouldn't be a bludgeon to force a style of play. The purpose of any description is to add to the gaming experience, not penalize the shy.

MOMENTUM AND NARRATIVE

Momentum evokes the heroic, scientific romance of Barsoom and John Carter. Carter often finds that one success leads to another, allowing him to achieve incredible, sometimes next-to-impossible feats. However, Carter also finds himself trapped by circumstance, an indicator that Threat is ever-present, a force challenging him to his utmost as he strives to succeed.

GENERATING MOMENTUM

As already noted, successes scored beyond the difficulty rating of an attribute test become Momentum. Each success scored above that minimum threshold becomes a single point of Momentum. Characters can spend Momentum to achieve greater effects, obtain useful bonuses, or make future actions easier for themselves or their teammates. Momentum is never generated with a failed test, only when there are excess successes beyond those required by the difficulty.

Example: Haran Phel is trying to scale a cliff quickly in pursuit of an assassin. The test is Challenging (D2) and Phel generates four successes with his roll, two more successes than he needed for the test. These extra successes translate into 2 Momentum, one for each extra success.

Upon succeeding at an attribute test, the player should take note of the amount of Momentum generated. Those points can then be used while the character resolves the current test, or saved for future use as described later. Importantly, the player does not have to determine what the Momentum will be used for at this point. A player determines what Momentum is used for only when it is spent.

Some talents, items, and circumstances grant bonus Momentum, which is added to the total Momentum generated by a successful attribute test. The bonus Momentum doesn't come into existence until after the test is successful.

SPENDING MOMENTUM

Often, a character will spend some or all of the Momentum generated to benefit the test currently being attempted.

Example: A character attacking an opponent may spend Momentum to increase the amounr of damage inflicted.

As noted before, the player does not have to declare what Momentum is being used for until it is spent, and does not need to spend Momentum in advance to obtain effects later.

Continuing from the prior example, an attacking character doesn't need to spend Momentum to increase the amount of damage inflicted until after the damage roll.

Momentum spends can be made as soon as the need for them becomes apparent. Momentum is *always* useful; there is no chance of wasting Momentum by spending it on a benefit that isn't needed.

Most Momentum spends can only be used once on any given attribute test or effect. In action scenes (*described later in the Action Scenes section*), a character can only use Momentum once in any round. However, some Momentum spends are described as **repeatable**. This means they can be used as frequently as the character has the desire and Momentum to spend.

Once the character's test is resolved (or in an action scene, at the end of the turn), any unspent Momentum is lost. However, characters have the option to save Momentum for later use if they wish.

SAVING MOMENTUM

As noted above, players have the option of saving Momentum rather than letting unspent Momentum go to waste. This saved Momentum goes into a personal pool. This pool represents the benefits of success, new opportunities created by their daring actions, good fortune favoring the bold and heroic, and even good old fashioned dramatic license.

The maximum amount of Momentum that can be saved in a pool is equal to the owning character's lowest attribute. Any points of excess Momentum are discarded. With the narrator's permission, players can contribute Momentum to a fellow player's pool, but the total still cannot exceed the character's lowest attribute.

During any successful attribute test, the owner may draw as many points from their Momentum pool as desired, adding those points to any points generated on the attribute test. The player may subsequently spend that Momentum as desired, just if it had been generated from the attribute test. As normal, Momentum is only spent as needed; a character does not have to use Momentum from the pool until it is actually needed, and it does not need to be all used at once, though all points of Momentum spent on a specific roll must be spent when it is made.

At the end of each scene, or full round in an action scene, each character looses 1 Momentum from their pool, representing the cooling of tempers, the waning of enthusiasm, and loss of energy.

Momentum Outside of Tests

Some Momentum spends are not tied to a specific test and can be used freely as they are required.

Players can spend points from their Momentum pools at any time, as long as the narrator deems that its use is justified and reasonable for the circumstance. Some Momentum spends have restrictions on how or when they can be used, but those are specific to those individual spends.

Momentum spends that are used in this way can also be paid for with Threat, which will be described later. A single point of Threat paid to the narrator provides the same benefits as a single point of Momentum being spent. When paying for a Momentum spend, you can pay partly in Threat and partly in Momentum if you desire.

Narrator Characters and Momentum

Unlike player characters, narrator characters do not have the option of saving Momentum into a pool. Instead, any narrator character that concludes a test with Momentum left over can add a certain amount of Momentum to the Threat pool depending on their narrator character classification. Each point of Momentum becomes one point of Threat. Villain class characters can add to the Threat pool up to their lowest attribute. Monsters can add Threat to the pool based on their menace rating. Minions can only ever add 1 Threat.

Narrator characters can spend from the Threat pool just as player characters draw from their Momentum pools. The Threat pool is described on *page 14* and in *Chapter 12: Narrating Barsoom*.

Common Uses for Momentum

The most common uses for Momentum are listed below. Players are also encouraged to be creative in their use of Momentum. An exceptional success should spur a player to think outside of the box in terms of how that superb performance can be reflected, in the result of the immediate test, or in how the outcome of that test impacts what happens next.

Regardless of how it is used, the benefits of Momentum spends must make sense from the perspective of the characters, and the narrator can veto Momentum spends that do not support events during in the course of play. Players should not use Momentum spends to take advantage of information their characters would not know, and they should not use Momentum to create events or circumstances that are distracting (or annoying) to other players.

Repeatable spends can be made as many times as desired, so long as the Momentum is available. **Often repeatable** spends are based on the circumstances and are subject to the narrator's discretion, meaning that in some situations they are repeatable and others they might not be. Most uses of Momentum are also immediate, and any Momentum earned can be spent as soon as it is earned to generate an effect. Momentum cannot be used to alter the dice result of a test that generated it.

Example: Kale Singh is scaling the side of a tower to reach a kidnapped companion. His test to climb the sheer wall generates 4 Momentum. Kale can use his Momentum immediately, either to make it harder to scale the tower for the Okar warriors climbing up after him, climb quicker himself or some other similar great effect, or to notice important details about the tower and its surroundings. However, he cannot spend this Momentum to retroactively add more dice to the test he just made: that opportunity has gone.

The use of Momentum in combat (and other dramatic conflicts) are explored in detail under *Actions and Attacks page 64*.

CREATE OPPORTUNITY
(REPEATABLE)

The most straightforward use of Momentum is to add an additional d20 to an attribute test, with each point of Momentum spent granting a single bonus d20. The decision to purchase these bonus dice must be made *before* any dice are rolled on that test. As noted, no more than three bonus d20s may be added to a single attribute test.

CREATE OBSTACLE
(REPEATABLE)

A character can choose to make things more difficult for a rival, adversary, or opponent by creating problems, distractions, or more direct opposition. This increases the difficulty of a single attribute test for that rival by one step per 2 points of Momentum spent. It costs two points of Momentum to increase the difficulty of a test by one step, four points of Momentum for a second step, and six points of Momentum for the third step. No individual test can have its difficulty increased by more than three steps in this way. The increase is only for a single test, regardless of whether that test is passed or failed. The decision to increase a test's difficulty must be made before any dice are rolled.

COUNTERSTRIKE

A character can spend 3 Momentum after they have defended during an opposed test. This grants the defender an immediate Conflict action. The character can perform any action as if it were their turn, but cannot save or donate any Momentum gained during this action. The character taking the Counterstrike can only use a Conflict action against the character who initiated the original opposed test but can use the Counterstrike to move, speak, or make regular tests that are not opposed.

Characters defend against a Counterstrike as normal but cannot Counterstrike against a Counterstrike. Once the Counterstrike has been defended against and resolved, initiative passes to the next character.

OBTAIN INFORMATION
(REPEATABLE)

Momentum allows a character to learn more about a situation. Each point of Momentum spent can be used to ask the narrator a single question about the current situation, item, object, structure, creature, or character present in (or relevant to) the scene at hand. The narrator must answer this question truthfully, but the narrator does not have to give complete information. A partial or brief answer that leaves room for further questions is a common response. The information provided must be relevant to the attribute test being attempted, and it must be the kind of information that a character might uncover while performing the attribute test. A character shooting a rifle might discern general details about a scene, a swordsman might rip away part of a disguise in a fight, a character in mid jump might leap over a discovery, etc. The more Momentum spent, the more in-depth the information uncovered.

IMPROVE QUALITY OF SUCCESS
(OFTEN REPEATABLE)

Momentum allows a character to succeed stylishly and to immediately capitalize upon or follow up on a success. The effects and cost of this are broadly left to the narrator's discretion, but examples are described later. Some uses of this type of Momentum spend may be repeatable, such as inflicting more damage or helping a patient recover from serious injuries.

INCREASE SCOPE OF SUCCESS
(OFTEN REPEATABLE)

With Momentum, a character can affect additional targets, increase the area affected by a successful test, or otherwise improve an accomplishment. The precise effects and cost are left to the narrator. Under some circumstances, this spend may be repeatable, such as a swordsman cutting down multiple weak foes.

REDUCE TIME REQUIRED

The narrator reduces the amount of in-game time that a task requires to complete. A task that should take a whole day or several zodes may now only take a single zode, for example. The precise effects and cost are left to the narrator's discretion. In some cases, multiple uses of Momentum may be allowed to reduce further the time of a lengthy action.

MOMENTUM SPEND	EFFECT
Create Opportunity	For each Momentum spend, roll an additional d20 for test. You must spend Momentum before you roll.
Create Obstacle	For each 2 Momentum spent, increase difficulty of another character's action by 1. Cannot increase difficulty more than 3 steps.
Counterstrike	Spend 3 Momentum after defending in an opposed test to immediately take a Conflict action against the other character in an opposed test. You cannot Counterstrike a Counterstrike.
Obtain Information	Spend 1 Momentum to ask 1 simple question about a character, situation, or scene. Narrator must answer truthfully.
Increase Quality of Success	Make effect of success more dramatic or useful. Cost often varies with type and amount increase.
Increase Scope of Success	Make effect of success affect more characters or a wider area. Cost often varies depending on how much the scope increases.
Reduce Time Required	Reduce normal time needed to accomplish a task. Cost varies based on circumstances and length of time reduced.

THREAT

USING THREAT

In most cases, Threat is used in a similar way to Momentum, both by narrator characters and player characters. When a character uses Momentum on a test, they can spend Threat instead.

Example: Jack is running a game of **John Carter** *and wishes to give his main antagonist, a villainous jeddak, a boost to an attack. He spends 2 Threat to give the villain a bonus of 2d20 on their next attack as the evil jeddak takes aim at one of the player characters and presses the trigger of his pistol…*

Threat is also used identically to Momentum if a particular talent requires a Momentum spend. The major difference in Threat is not how it's used, but where it comes from and how it is generated.

THE THREAT POOL

Threat comes from the Threat pool and all narrator characters draw from Threat instead of a personal Momentum pool. Threat is generally spent the same as Momentum from the pool, it is simply shared by all narrator characters. When Threat is spent, the pool is reduced by the amount spent until more Threat is generated and added to the Threat pool.

Example: Jack needs 2 Momentum to fuel a talent of a villainous henchman in his campaign. The henchman, being a narrator character, does not have their own Momentum pool and instead uses Threat as Momentum. As the Threat pool currently has six Threat in it, Jack removes two and uses them as Momentum for the henchman's talent. The current Threat pool is now four (6 minus the 2 used as Momentum).

Threat is also spent to win ties on tests. Normally a player character wins ties in a contest but a narrator may spend 1 Threat to have a narrator character win instead. Advice on how to best use the Threat pool is found in *Chapter 12*, including some special uses for Threat only narrators may use, such as using it to create additional characters or dangers for the player characters to face.

GENERATING THREAT

There are many ways to generate Threat. The narrator begins each session with a Threat pool equal to the total number of Luck points (*see Luck on page 68*) of all the player characters. If a player uses Threat as Momentum for their characters, this amount is also added to the narrator's Threat pool. The narrator may also add 2 points of Threat to the Threat pool instead of creating a complication.

LOSING THREAT

Threat is used as it is spent from the Threat pool. It is also lost when a narrator character suffers a complication and the player whose character caused the complication decides to remove 2 Threat from the pool instead.

OPTIONAL RULE:
GIVING ALLIES MOMENTUM

While all narrator characters draw from the Threat pool, in some cases player characters might wish to give some narrator character allies a boost when the narrator is disinclined to do so because Threat is needed to help the actions of antagonists. If this happens, narrators may consider using this optional rule: player characters may gift Momentum to narrator characters by paying 1 extra Momentum over the amount given to the target character. This Momentum does not increase the Threat pool and cannot be used by other narrator characters. Narrator characters cannot receive more Momentum than the value of their lowest attribute.

This rule is optional because, while a useful way to simulate player characters inspiring and leading allied narrator characters to victory and glory, it also increases bookkeeping. It should only be used by groups ready to track individual Momentum for characters. This option also eliminates any possibility that narrator allies performing exceptionally well in a scene will increase the Threat pool as a side effect. Whether this is a "bug" or "feature" depends on how individual narrators view scenes where narrator characters temporarily move into the spotlight through their actions.

A narrator might also link this ability to talents, only allowing characters who possess a Momentum-sharing talent to gift Momentum. Such a talent would typically allow 1 Momentum to be gifted to an ally per grade of the talent, though limitations on usage might reduce the overall grade cost.

This option is much easier to control, though narrators who use it should take care to make sure player characters receive ample opportunities to use such a talent. Otherwise, it's a waste of grades that could be used elsewhere.

ACTION SCENES

Armed combat and violent encounters are the most dangerous and engaging part of adventuring in Barsoom. Amidst the din and chaos of combat, it is vitally important for players and narrator alike to clearly understand what is happening, so they can make important decisions about what characters will attempt. These dramatic encounters are called **action scenes**, and this section addresses the way they are handled, introducing the use of zones for movement and range purposes, the structure of turns and actions, the actions characters can undertake, and the ways characters are harmed or recover from harm.

TURN SEQUENCE

In an action scene, the passage of time is compressed and structured into individual rounds and turns. Every round, any character present in the scene has an opportunity to act. This opportunity is known as the character's turn. Each round encompasses several characters' turns and, once all characters have taken a turn, that round concludes and a new round begins.

Rounds have no specific or fixed duration. They do not represent a specific, consistent length of time but rather a snapshot of the intense activity occurring over a period of time. In a furious clash between small groups of warriors, a round may represent a few seconds. A battle across a massive castle may require rounds comprising a minute or more, as the combatants jockey for position within the environment. A battle between ships in the skies of Barsoom may track several minutes of time between rounds as vessels maneuver for position.

Regardless of how much time a round may represent, each character takes a single turn during each round. During a character's turn, the character has a number of options in the form of different actions to perform. During a round, a character can perform each of the following: a single Conflict action, a Movement action, and any number of Spoken actions. The character may exchange a Conflict action for a Movement action and/or a Movement action for a Spoken action. Outside of the character's turn, a character can defend in an opposed test and make a Counterstrike if they can pay the Momentum but no other actions are allowed.

TURN ORDER

During a round, the order in which characters act is important, as actions may change based on what transpires with each turn, creating new opportunities for action and forcing re-evaluation of plans based on the outcome of prior actions. Normally, a player character acts first each round. This character begins the turn and must resolve all the actions they wish to make before another character can act. Play then passes to a new player character, who performs all their actions for the turn. Once all the player characters have taken their turns, all the narrator characters take their turns.

After all player and narrator characters have taken their actions in a round, that round is over. One point of Momentum is removed from each player's Momentum pool and a new round begins.

DETERMINING TURN ORDER

There are four methods of determining turn order. None are better than any others; they simply appeal to different groups and play styles.

1. **Narrator determines order:** The narrator determines who goes first, second, etc. in the turn based on what makes the most sense in the current situation. If the scene continues after this turn, the player character who went last in the turn goes first next turn.

2. **Players determine order:** The players vote or otherwise choose who goes first among them and then the active player chooses who goes next. If the scene continues after this turn, the player who went last has the option of going first next turn.

3. **Attribute determines order:** The narrator picks an attribute that is important to the current scene and characters take turn in descending order based on attribute values. For added flair, narrators can announce this by labeling the scene with the attribute ("This is a time for Daring action" or "In this encounter Might makes right!") but this isn't required.

4. **Randomly determined order:** Each player rolls a d20 for their character and they take their turns in descending order based on the die result, starting with the player who rolled the highest. Narrators may allow characters to spend Momentum to roll extra d20s, but this may be of limited utility as typically all the player characters go before the narrator.

Once a method of determining turn order is chosen the narrator and players should stick with it. If their chosen method isn't working out, it is recommended they change it at the start of a new adventure or arc in the campaign when all current players are present to avoid confusion.

SEIZING INITIATIVE

At the start of the round before anyone has acted, or at any time immediately after a player character has finished acting (and before another player character has begun to act this turn), the narrator can spend 1 point of Threat to interrupt the player characters' turns. This allows a narrator character to immediately take a turn.

The narrator character's actions are resolved normally, and once finished, the turn order passes back to the player characters, unless additional points of Threat are spent to allow other narrator characters to take their actions before the player characters. Any narrator characters acting out of order like this do not get to act again that round.

INDECISION

If the players spend too much time deliberating and discussing their choices during an action scene rather than taking action, the narrator can add 1 point of Threat to the Threat pool as a warning that the player characters are wasting time and giving the initiative to their opponents.

If the players' deliberation continues, the narrator can add additional Threat points, warning the players this is happening, until the narrator chooses to spend the Threat, allowing any narrator characters to act first.

SURPRISE AND AMBUSHES

Sometimes, one group of combatants may try to surprise or ambush another group. If one group has sufficient time to hide, set up an ambush, or otherwise prepare themselves to attack an unwitting foe, then they may attempt an opposed test (*see page 49*) to gain an advantage. Each side nominates a leader to attempt an attribute test (*see below*). Other members of the group may assist this test as normal, as they either contribute to preparations or simply provide extra eyes and ears.

Under most circumstances, the ambushing side attempts a **Cunning + Empathy** test which the ambushed side opposes by attempting an **Empathy + Reason** test. However, the players and narrator are free to suggest alternative ways to secure surprise. Perhaps a sudden attack during a negotiation could be handled by **Cunning + Passion**, opposed by **Empathy + Reason**. The feasibility of these is up to the narrator.

If the group attempting to gain surprise succeeds at the opposed test, every character on that side gains 1 Momentum and acts immediately at the start of combat. Narrator characters do not need to spend Threat to gain this, nor should the narrator spend Threat to override this.

If the player characters attempting to gain surprise fail at the opposed test, they may choose to add two points to Threat or spend one Luck point (for the whole group) to gain surprise instead.

MOVEMENT, RANGE, AND ABSTRACT ZONES

In battle, knowing where everyone is, is of vital importance and determining both absolute position (where you are on the battlefield) and relative position (how far you are from a given friend or foe) is important. Rather than track everything in precise distances, this matter is handled using abstract **zones**.

An environment represents the battlefield as a whole. This may be a building, a city street, an area of wilderness, or the deck of an airship. An environment is divided into a number of zones based on the terrain features present in the area. A building may treat individual rooms as distinct zones, using the internal walls as natural divisions for range and movement. A city street may focus zones around features like shop stalls, the fronts of buildings, alleyways, and so forth.

Zones can be defined in three dimensions, so the narrator may choose to map multiple floors of a building connected by stairs, ramps, or ladders. A relatively simple battlefield may consist of three to five significant zones, while complex environments may have many. More zones are typically better than fewer, as they provide greater movement options and tactical opportunities, but this takes more planning on the part of the narrator.

Because zones are of no fixed size, they can vary to accommodate the narrator's needs for a given scene, and to represent other factors. For example, a battle in a twisting canyon may be divided into many small zones amongst the rocks, and a couple of larger zones representing long stretches of clear ground. The larger size of the zone helps convey quick movement and easy target acquisition in open areas. However, zones should not be too complex to describe quickly: in most situations, a few seconds should be all that's needed to describe

zones and their relative positions, or to sketch out a rough map on paper. This does not prevent the narrator coming up with elaborate environments. Locations that will be used frequently, or those that are especially important to key moments in an adventure or a campaign, might require additional time to map.

Individual zones can have terrain effects defined when the narrator creates them. This may be as simple as declaring them to be difficult terrain, but the narrator is welcome to devise other terrain items such as interactive objects, dangers to overcome, or even terrain that changes under particular circumstances. Some zones may be defined more by the absence of terrain than its presence, and a few empty zones between obstacles enhances some environments.

Narrators that desire concrete values rather than abstract ranges are encouraged to set specific sizes and shapes for individual zones, effectively turning them into a large grid.

CHARACTERS AND ZONES

To help players visualize their characters' positions in an encounter, and to manage action scenes effectively, it is important to keep track of where characters are at any given moment. This should be relatively easy in most cases. As zones are defined by the terrain and surroundings, tracking a character can be a matter of simple description. An enemy might be "behind the bar" or "standing in front of the high altar." This has the advantage of relying on natural language and intuitive concepts, rather than game terms. It likewise avoids the need to track distances without miniatures when there are a lot of characters present.

Larger or particularly complex scenes can be tricky to track purely by memory, so the narrator may wish to use something extra to show everyone's position in a scene. If you're already using a sketched map, then marking character positions in pencil is one approach, as is using tokens or miniatures, and then moving them around as required.

MINIATURES

John Carter doesn't require the use of miniatures, but miniatures can add to everyone's enjoyment and understanding of the action. The narrator may often employ sketch maps or even pre-made map tiles in order to depict an area and denote different zones. In these cases, counters or markers representing each character can be a useful reminder of where everyone is. Miniatures are, of course, a more elaborate form of counters or markers for this purpose. Modiphius manufactures a range of high quality *John Carter* miniatures for the game.

DISTANCES

Movement and ranged attacks need some sense of distance to make them meaningful. In combat, the relative proximity of zones determines this distance. To keep things simple and fluid, range is measured with four categories and one state. Most conflicts take place at **Near** and **Immediate** ranges. It is both noteworthy and significant when characters are **Far** or **Too Far** as many interactions with them require other actions to set up.

✳ The state of **Immediate** is when an object or character is within arm's length of the acting character. Characters enter Immediate range to interact with objects manually, to attack in close combat, and to perform any other actions where they may need to touch the target or subject of their action. Immediate isn't a specific range, but rather is something that the player can declare when the character is moving. That is, when a character moves into or within a zone, the player may freely declare that the character is moving into Immediate contact with an object or another character.

✳ **Near:** Not immediately adjacent to but close enough to reach a target fairly easily. Characters can shoot at, speak with, and generally interact with anyone Near. Some creatures are big and fast enough to be able to treat Near as Immediate for making melee attacks. Generally, characters who are not being hindered, blocked, or obstructed can move into Immediate state to attack a target in melee while they are already Near.

✳ **Away:** Away distances place a target apart from others. This includes both long distance and closer places that can only be reached by dramatic actions such as leaping and climbing. Thus, the other side of a small valley might be Away, but so would a high cliff or a nearby airship with fifty sofads of Martian sky between it and a character.

✳ **Far:** Reachable only by the most long-distance attacks or methods of interaction. Most firearms have a range of Far, and this generally covers the furthest a character can see.

✳ **Too Far:** Targets that are Too Far may be visible or otherwise detectable, but they are beyond the ability to interact with physically. Communication requires special technology.

DISTANCE AND COMMUNICATION

Characters often want to communicate during an action scene. Calls for help, battle-cries, derisive slurs, and other dialogue abound in action scenes adding tactics and flavor. In most cases, characters can converse normally with anyone Near to them. They're considered close enough to one another to be heard and to make themselves understood without raising their voices.

A character can communicate with someone at Far range but only by shouting, rather than talking. At greater distances, a character can shout to draw attention, but conveying any depth of meaning, or understanding anything beyond basic instructions or information, is unlikely.

DISTANCE AND PERCEPTION

The further away something is, the harder it is to notice. In game terms, this means that characters and objects in distant zones are harder to observe or identify than those nearby. A character increases the difficulty of tests by one step when trying to notice creatures and objects at Away range, by two steps when dealing with creatures and objects at Far range, and by three steps when trying to discern things at Too Far. A creature that isn't trying to avoid notice requires a Simple (D0) test under normal circumstances. A creature attempting to hide makes the test more challenging by making the test an opposed test. Creatures or objects that are particularly noticeable — a flier, roaring beasts, or a fast-moving or brightly-colored object — may reduce the difficulty.

OTHER SENSES

Broadly speaking, sight and hearing define the majority of character perception and are the senses dealt with most frequently here. However, at times, other senses come into play. Naturally, a character's sense of touch is limited to the Immediate state. The sense of smell is most effective for character within the Immediate state, and tests made to smell something at a greater distance increase in difficulty by one step, plus one step for each range category beyond Near.

Non-human characters and creatures may have different limits and capabilities when using their senses.

Example: A white ape is able to discern details by scent that a human cannot, but its eyesight may be somewhat less acute by comparison.

Such creatures often have talents to reduce the difficulty of all tests related to their best sense.

Movement and Terrain

Under normal circumstances, moving around does not need an attribute test. Moving to anywhere within Near range is only a Free action. Moving to anywhere within Away range takes a Movement action. Moving to anywhere within Far range takes a Conflict action, which adds +1 to the difficulty of all tests until the start of the character's next turn, including tests to traverse difficult terrain.

However, movement in some circumstances may require a test to be made. This is an attribute test, typically using **Daring** for characters and creatures, though unusual terrain may require **Might** or **Reason**. A situation may allow multiple variations depending on how the character attempts to traverse the terrain. If movement requires an attribute test with a difficulty of Average (D1) or higher,

then it cannot be performed as a Free action even if the movement is only within Near range. **Under no circumstances can an attribute test be attempted as a Free action.**

Circumstances that require a test are one of three types: obstacles, hindrances, and dangers.

Obstacles

Obstacles exist at the places where two zones meet, impairing efforts to move between those zones. Not every zone intersection must include an obstacle, however. Climbable walls and fences, ladders, and similar barriers can all be obstacles. Attempting to bypass an obstacle requires an attribute test, normally with an Average (D1) difficulty. Particularly large obstacles may increase this, while straight-

forward and simple obstructions might reduce this to Simple (D0), or no challenge whatsoever to move across. Failing this test prevents the character from moving across the obstacle. Some obstacles may only require a test in a single direction, or may require different difficulties in different directions.

Example: A slope that is more difficult to ascend than to descend would have differing difficulties based on the character's direction of travel.

Some obstacles are impassable, preventing any movement between zones the obstacle borders. The internal walls of a building are a good example, as they cannot be climbed over. There should normally be a way around an obstacle, such as a doorway, or a weak point where sufficient force could break through.

EXAMPLE TERRAIN AND DANGERS

Generally, when a character takes a move action while in, or crossing, particular terrain, a penalty is taken to all actions during the turn that would be hindered. The exception is defensive actions. It is assumed that, where possible, characters are taking cover; there are no specific rules for cover, and there are no terrain penalties applied to defending characters.

TERRAIN	DIFFICULTY / DIFFICULTY INCREASE
City street or Martian sands	0
The rocky wastes	1
Spires and mountainside	2
Any terrain during a sandstorm	3

DANGER	DAMAGE
One floor fall	1
Two floor fall	2
Three floor fall	3
Hard Martian sand / beach of small rocks	n/a
Needle-like spines	+1
Cooling lava	+2
Next to bubbling lava	+4
Into the caldera of an active volcano	+10

HINDRANCES

Hindrances affect entire zones, slowing movement within them. A character moving within or through a hindered zone must either give up a portion of that movement (moving one fewer zone than normal with an action) or attempt a test, with failure meaning that the character stops moving within the hindering terrain. The test is normally Average (D1), but some terrain may require a more difficult test. Less-troublesome hindrances may only require a Simple (D0) test. Areas of quicksand or broken ground can be considered hindrances.

DANGERS

Dangers function in the same way as obstacles or hindrances, but with one significant difference: they cause damage after a failed test. In addition to being difficult, each danger has a rating equal to the number of combat dice the danger rolls if a character fails to cross it safely.

Example: Jack has created a danger for an upcoming adventure in the form of an area of loose sand where vibrations can set off explosive gas pockets hidden below the surface. He decides that walking carefully (or running so quickly you outrace the explosions) is a Challenging (D2) test with a danger rating of 3. If a character fails to overcome the danger, they will take 3 🎲 of damage — equal to the rating of the danger.

FALLING

A rather common form of danger is falling. The distance a character falls determines how much damage is inflicted. Falling inflicts damage to the Injury stress tracker. Falling a Near distance inflicts 1 🎲. Falling an Away distance inflicts 2 🎲. Falling a Far distance inflicts 4 🎲. Falling a Too Far distance inflicts 8 🎲 in Injury. A falling character may suffer different damage should they fall on something other than the usual hard sand of Barsoom.

Characters who reasonably have some way to lessen their fall can attempt an Average (D1) **Might + Daring** test (plus 1 for every category of range beyond Near). Success avoids 1 🎲 of damage. Momentum can be spent to reduce the damage further at the cost of 2 Momentum per combat die not rolled.

OTHER FORMS OF MOVEMENT

In general, different forms of movement are treated the same. Each is a means of crossing particular types of terrain or obstacles.

CLIMBING

Climbing is any movement where a character traverses a steep slope or sheer vertical surface. These are normally obstacles such as walls, cliffs, and similar barriers, but some situations may have whole zones where climbing is the only way to move around. Climbing movement requires a test using **Daring + Might**. The more challenging the climb, the higher the difficulty. A rough cliff face with plentiful handholds has a difficulty of Challenging (D2), as does a moderately steep slope that requires some effort to climb. Attempting to climb a vertical surface without tools like rope, hooks, and so forth increases the difficulty by one step. Attempting to climb upside down across a horizontal surface, such as a ceiling, increases the difficulty by two steps.

JUMPING

Jumping is any movement across a gap or space, a controlled drop down to a space below, or movement in an attempt to reach something above. Jumping also uses **Daring + Might**, and it can be used in a variety of ways. Jumping across a small gap or over a small barrier counting as an obstacle is an Average (D1) **Daring + Might** test. Jumping down from a height uses the same rules as falling but reduces the difficulty of the attribute test by one step to Simple (D0). Jumping up to grasp something within the character's Immediate range is an Average (D1) **Daring + Might** test, increasing in difficulty to reflect the height jumped.

SWIMMING

Swimming is movement through a body of water and is defined in game terms as one or more zones of hindering terrain (creating the hindered condition on the character, described on *page 61*). Swimming is the only way to traverse zones filled with water, using **Daring + Might** for tests. The rougher the water being crossed, the greater the difficulty, with calm water requiring an Average (D1) **Daring + Might** test to cross quickly. Treading water requires a Simple (D0) **Daring + Might** test.

FLIGHT

Flight is movement through the air. Only creatures specifically noted as capable of flight are able to fly. A creature capable of flight can move freely through any zone (above the ground), including through zones that are normally inaccessible. Flying creatures don't suffer the effects of difficult terrain, though tall structures (such as the tops of buildings) can serve as obstacles, and strong winds can be hindrances. Particularly stormy weather might well count as a danger, as strong winds and lightning are risks for high-flying creatures.

OTHER ZONE ITEMS

Other than terrain, there are other things that might be present in a zone. A zone can contain a variety of objects that the characters can interact with. These are described below.

INTERACTIVE OBJECTS

Interactive objects are any object or terrain feature that a character could conceivably alter or use. Doors and windows are a common example, as are light sources, traps, and the like. Interacting with these objects may take time and effort depending on the circumstances. A Free action can be used to interact with an object, as long as it does not require an attribute test to do so.

Actions and Attacks

There are four forms of actions in use during an action scene: Spoken actions, Movement actions, Conflict actions and Free actions. As part of a normal turn, a character can preform a single Conflict action, a Movement action, a Spoken action, and a number of Free actions (if the narrator considers them relevant and appropriate). The character may exchange a Conflict action for a Movement action and/or a Movement action for any number of Spoken actions.

Outside of the turn sequence, a character can attempt Counterstrikes after an opposed test. Actions can be taken in any order, but all actions must be declared before each is resolved, and the narrator has the final decision as to whether a particular combination of actions is possible.

Spoken Action

A Spoken action is any use of simple speech requiring little or no effort to accomplish. A Spoken action never includes an attribute test where dice are rolled. If speech of any kind requires an attribute test, it is a Conflict action. In a character's turn, they can say a short comment to one character or a single sentence to multiple characters. The narrator has full discretion as to when a Spoken action becomes a Conflict action even if no test is needed. It's a Spoken action that allows a character to make a memorable quip as they strike an opponent.

Movement Actions

A character can move to any point within Away range as a Movement action. *John Carter* is a world of derring-do and acrobatic motion. As such, characters are rarely in a position where they cannot move. Movement actions include everything from climbing to piloting a flier. Movement actions do not require attribute tests unless there is a danger to avoid and they often add a swashbuckling element to a Conflict action. It is the Movement action

that allows a character to swing on a chandelier as they attack an opponent.

Conflict Actions

Conflict actions are the focus of action scenes and take up most of a character's attention and effort. Most Conflict actions require an attribute test. A character can normally perform one Conflict action per turn, but there are ways a character can perform a second Conflict action. Regardless of the method used, however, a character cannot take more than two Conflict actions each turn.

The following list describes the various ways characters can gain an extra Conflict action per turn.

* **Luck Points.** A player may spend a Luck point to allow the character to perform an additional Conflict action.

* **Swift Action Momentum Spend.** By spending 2 points of Momentum from a prior attribute test the character immediately gains an additional Conflict action. The difficulty of any test connected to the extra Conflict action increases by one step.

* **Talent**. A grade 4 talent (*see Chapter 3: Talents page 38*) will allow a character to perform an additional Conflict action of one specific type without spending Momentum or paying Luck points.

Free Actions

A Free action is used to accomplish a minor activity within a turn that does not warrant the use of a Conflict, Spoken or Movement action. These are things such as moving anywhere within Near range as long as there is no obstruction to your movement, pushing open an unlocked door or picking up an object.

The use of a Free action should never involve an attribute test, if an attribute test would be called for a Conflict or Movement action must be used.

Making an Attack

There are multiple ways a character can attack a target. Weapons merely scratch the surface of the variety of ways a creative character could harm another. A character might engage in ferocious arguing, make barbed jests, or wield weapons of extravagant super science. Regardless of the method used, the process for attacking remains the same.

* The attacker declares their Conflict action, nominating a single target within range.

* The attacker attempts an opposed test determined by the type of attack. This is an Average (D1) attribute test using **Cunning** plus another attribute which varies based on the exact circumstances. For most melee-based combat, **Cunning + Daring** is the default, while **Cunning + Reason** is more common in shooting-based attacks. Insults often use **Cunning** and **Passion**, or **Might** in the case of threats and intimidation.

* If the attack is made beyond its usual range then the difficulty increases by 1 for every range outside the weapon's normal use. For melee weapons this is Immediate, for pistols this is Near, and for rifles, Away. Melee weapons used at ranges outside Immediate are thrown at their target.

* The defending character commonly resists with **Daring** and another attribute appropriate to the defensive action, such as **Passion** for bravely meeting a sword thrust or **Empathy** to sense where an attack is directed so it can be avoided. Insults and social conflicts typically use **Passion** or **Empathy** to defend. This may vary depending on the situation or a character's talents.

* Attack combinations are determined by the narrator, and the narrator may change any of these combinations as the situation warrants.

* If the attack hits, then the attack inflicts damage (*as described in Damage and Recovery, see page 65*). If the attack misses, then nothing happens.

SELECTING THE PROPER ATTRIBUTES

The rules for actions and conflicts often suggest particular attribute combinations for use in attack and defense when engaged in melee, ranged, or social conflicts. The default suggestions (**Cunning + Daring** for melee attacks, etc.) are there to keep things moving and balanced. However, they are not set in stone.

Depending on the exact situation, it might be more appropriate to defend against a sword thrust with **Daring** and **Passion** or engage in a social action with **Might** and **Cunning**. Narrators should be open to interesting combinations of attributes for various actions and players should feel free to suggest them. A character who wishes to "take it on the chin" might even defend against an attack with **Might**, describing it as striking him but with no effect. Or a brilliant character might be able to use **Reason** to strike an opponent they have been watching closely for weaknesses. Narrators are encouraged to allow such variations as long as they don't slow down play or result in characters only using the same one or two attributes for every test.

Players who wish to regularly use an atypical attribute for a type of action should consider acquiring a talent which allows them to regularly substitute one attribute for another in certain types of actions.

Remember to treat each attack and defend test separately before successes are compared. In many cases, the attacker and defender may not have the same difficulty for their respective tests.

*Example: Jane Porter is shooting with a rifle at a Warhoon raider who is charging her companions with weapons drawn. Her target is in range and the narrator informs Jane's player she will need to use **Reason** and **Cunning** for this attack. The target is at Away*

*range, so there's no increased difficulty for distance, however there is a large amount of smoke and dust in the air from a recent airship crash. The narrator rules this increases the difficulty of Jane's attack by 1. The Warhoon is defending with **Daring** and **Reason** as it attempts to see the path of Jane's shot, but has nothing to increase the difficulty of his action. Jane generates 4 successes on her (D2) test while the Warhoon generates only 2 on his (D1) test. Despite the tough shot, Jane hits the Warhoon!*

ACTION SCENE MOMENTUM SPENDS

Momentum is a key tactical resource during action scenes. When a character generates Momentum in an action scene, it can help in many ways to overcome enemies, empower allies, and bolster the effectiveness of actions.

The following provides a number of options for a character generating 1 or more points of Momentum in combat. These are in addition to the normal uses of Momentum and any others that players or narrator create. Momentum lists are never exhaustive and both players and narrators should be creative in making new spends as needed.

Many of these options are primarily focused upon boosting attribute tests made when attacking. However, many can be used creatively for all manner of combat attribute tests.

MOMENTUM SPENDS

When fighting a foe:

* **Roll extra damage.** After succeeding on an attack, but before you roll for damage, you can spend Momentum to roll extra combat dice. Each point of Momentum spent provides 1 bonus 🎲. (E.g. spend 3 Momentum to roll 4 🎲 damage rather than the usual 1 🎲)

* **Send their weapon flying.** Three points of Momentum can send an enemy's weapon flying to where an ally might get it. Two points might knock it to your enemy's feet.

* **Dispatch a minion narrator character.** Every extra point of Momentum spent when fighting minions will dispatch an additional minion.

When moving during an action scene:

* Spend 1 Momentum to move an additional range between the character and a target if not hindered or blocked by another character or obstacle.

* Spend 3 Momentum to move an additional range between you and a target, ignoring any obstacles (characters in your way can still attempt to stop you).

OPTIONAL RULE: SIMPLIFIED ACTIONS

While each action in *John Carter of Mars* serves a purpose, the terminology and rules can be a bit daunting for new players. Instead of breaking actions into Conflict, Movement, and Spoken actions, if desired the following simplified actions can be used:

* All characters can move (up to Away range), and take one action (like attacking or using a device, or moving further than Away).

* Characters may speak and perform other short actions for free, provided this makes sense and the narrator doesn't think it would take too much effort.

* Characters may spend 5 Momentum for a bonus action, once per turn.

Simplified actions speed play, but at the cost of some tactical finesse and dramatic movement during conflicts. Narrators should consult their players to see if the trade-off is acceptable to everyone.

DAMAGE AND RECOVERY

The following section describes the three types of damage that characters can inflict and suffer: Confusion, Fear and Injury.

When a character is successfully hit by an attack during combat, the attack inflicts an amount of damage. Some environmental effects can also inflict damage, such as falling from a great height, being set on fire, or encountering something terrifying.

Damage is always resolved in the same way, regardless of the type of damage inflicted. Each weapon and event determines damage based on several factors:

✳ **Basic Damage:** Each source of damage inflicts a minimum of 1 🎲 of damage. Some sources will have a higher basic damage; this is usually noted in the text.

✳ **Momentum:** A player can spend Momentum when making an attack to add more damage. Each Momentum spent adds 1 🎲 to the damage. In addition to this, minion-class creatures can be killed instantly for 1 Momentum. Both of these Momentum spends are repeatable.

✳ **Qualities:** Weapons often have qualities that inflict damage in specific ways when an effect is rolled on the combat dice. *(See page 71.)*

Once these factors have all been accounted for, the player making the attack should roll the pool of combat dice. This is called the **damage roll**, and the final total is the amount of damage inflicted.

STRESS AND AFFLICTIONS

A character can only withstand so much damage of any one type before being unable to fight further.

Each damage type has a stress track. Each stress track is related to two of a characters attributes. The higher of these two attributes is the maximum stress that can be lost from that stress track.

Stress is the representation of the effect damage has on a character. For each point of damage scored on the damage roll, a point of stress is added to one of the three stress tracks. This rep-

resents the character suffering minor injuries, or becoming weary and fatigued.

Stress can be recovered quickly, under normal circumstances only requiring a little rest. However, if a large amount of stress is gained at once or a stress track is filled, then the character suffers afflictions.

Afflictions represent long-term effects and can be extremely problematic. Each stress track has a related affliction, and imposes a penalty on certain attribute tests. The two attributes affected are the two related to that particular affliction's stress track. Each affliction suffered increases the difficulty of a test using either of these attributes by 1. This penalty is cumulative, increasing with each affliction suffered.

Afflictions are suffered when:

✳ 5 or more damage is inflicted at once.
✳ The target's stress track is filled.
✳ The target takes damage with a stress track that is already full.

If more than of these circumstances happens at once, an affliction is suffered for each case.

Example: Kale Singh takes 5 damage and applies it to his Injury stress track, which fills his stress track. Kale suffers 2 Wound afflictions, one for the 5 damage applied at once and the second for the stress track being filled.

At the narrator's choice, stress inflicted in multiples of 5 can also cause additional afflictions, with 10 stress added causing 2 afflictions etc.

A character suffering from four afflictions of the same type is incapacitated. They are unable to take any actions or defend against an attack without spending a point of Luck. A character suffering with five or more afflictions of the same type is blacked out. They are unable to take any actions at all, even by spending Luck (for Wounds this is death; for Trauma it might be an irreparable loss of confidence; for Madness it might be insanity). Afflictions are more difficult to recover from than stress.

Narrator characters are less able to withstand afflictions. Minion-class characters are dis-

patched as soon as they suffer any damage, and Monster-class characters have a menace rating, indicating how many afflictions of any type they can withstand before being dispatched.

INFLICTING DAMAGE

The damage roll determines the amount of damage inflicted by a successful attack. The attribute combination used when defending against an attack determines the type of damage inflicted.

When damage is inflicted and a character gains stress, they consult the damage types table to decide which stress track is affected, based on the attributes they used to defend against the attack. If more than one stress track is applicable, the player chooses which stress track to apply the damage to.

Example: Kale Singh is struck by a sword. He defended against the attack with Cunning + Might. Cunning and Might are both related to the Injury stress track. Since he failed to defend against the attack, the stress he suffers is added to the Injury stress track.

ATTRIBUTE USED TO DEFEND	DAMAGE TYPE / STRESS TRACK
Empathy or Reason	Confusion
Daring or Passion	Fear
Cunning or Might	Injury

DAMAGE TYPES

The three types of damage are described on the following page. Under each damage type, several useful details are listed; 'Relevant attributes' are the attributes used to calculate maximum stress and those affected by that damage types affliction. 'Affliction' names the affliction suffered when that damage types stress track is full, and 'recover with' gives the attribute test used to remove stress from that stress track.

CONFUSION

RELEVANT ATTRIBUTES: EMPATHY OR REASON
AFFLICTIONS: MADNESS
RECOVER WITH: EMPATHY + REASON

Damage inflicted upon the mind is Confusion. It might be caused by complex tasks, impossible timelines, psychic attacks or even the fog of war. Confusion represents a character's determination, and their ability to handle pressure, control emotions, and resist the hardships of life. Characters whose current Confusion is high are weary, less certain, and less able to cope with challenging situations. A character's maximum stress for Confusion is equal to the highest value of a character's Empathy or Reason.

AFFLICTIONS

If a sufficient amount of Confusion is inflicted, the afflictions are called Madness. Madness increases the difficulty of attribute tests using Empathy or Reason. A character suffering 4 Madness is barely coherent, overwhelmed by fears and doubts. A character suffering 5 Madness counts as **blacked out** and is either catatonic or fleeing as best they can.

RECOVERING CONFUSION

When attempting to recover their Confusion during battle or treat their Madness naturally, characters should use an **Empathy + Reason** attribute test. The same test is used to assist an ally in recovering from Confusion or Madness.

FEAR

RELEVANT ATTRIBUTES: DARING OR PASSION
AFFLICTIONS: TRAUMA
RECOVER WITH: DARING + REASON

Damage inflicted upon the will is Fear. It might be caused by fear, doubt, panic, despair, and sudden shocks, such as a near miss with a blade. Fear represents a character's bravery, willingness to take risks, and their ability to work through the risks inherent in a life of adventure. Characters whose current Fear is high are scared, easily frightened and less able to cope with challenging situations. A character's maximum stress for Fear is equal to the highest attribute between Daring and Passion.

AFFLICTIONS

If a sufficient amount of Fear is inflicted, the affliction is called Trauma. Traumas increase the difficulty of attribute tests using Daring or Passion. A character suffering 4 Traumas is barely coherent, overwhelmed by fears and doubts. A character suffering 5 Traumas counts as **blacked out** and is either catatonic or fleeing as best they can.

RECOVERING FEAR

When attempting to recover their Fear during battle or treat their Traumas naturally, characters should use a **Daring + Reason** attribute test. Characters attempting to assist with the Traumas or Fear of an ally should generally use **Daring + Reason**.

INJURY

RELEVANT ATTRIBUTES: CUNNING OR MIGHT
AFFLICTIONS: WOUNDS
RECOVER WITH*: MIGHT + REASON
** Treating another character always uses **Empathy + Reason** unless you have a talent which says otherwise.*

Damage inflicted upon the body is Injury. Blades, radium bullets, or exposure to dangerous substances (such as acids) might cause damage. Injury represents a character's endurance, stamina, and ability to ignore minor injuries such as cuts, scratches, bruises, and abrasions. It also represents the ability to avoid serious injuries. A character with high Injury is tired and unable to avoid serious harm. A character's maximum stress for Injury is equal to the highest attribute between Cunning and Might.

AFFLICTIONS

If a sufficient amount of Injury is inflicted, the afflictions are called Wounds. Wounds increase the difficulty of attribute tests using Cunning or Might. Characters suffering 4 Wounds are so badly injured that they are barely capable of moving. A character that has taken 5 Wounds counts as **blacked out** and is unconscious or writhing in agony.

RECOVERING INJURY

When attempting to recover their Injuries during battle or treat their Wounds naturally, characters should use a **Might + Reason** attribute test. Characters attempting to assist in the recovery of an ally should use **Empathy + Reason**.

Example: Kale Singh has been seriously hurt in battle. He is suffering from two Wound afflictions. Until his afflictions are healed, the difficulty of any actions involving Cunning or Might increase by two.

RECOVERING FROM STRESS AND AFFLICTIONS

Recovering from stress is as important as being able to inflict it.

A character recovers from all stress at the end of an action scene, and so all stress tracks are cleared. This is automatic, requiring only a brief rest. The only time this does not happen is if the next scene is set immediately after the first, where characters would have no time to catch their breath.

Stress is recovered from at a slower rate within an action scene. By spending 1 point of Momentum (repeatable) a character can remove 1 point of stress from any stress track. Alternately, characters can spend a conflict action to recover their own stress using the attribute test listed beside 'recover with' in the damage type heading. To assist an ally in recovering an affliction, see the damage type description for the relevant attribute test.

Recovering from afflictions is a trickier proposition. Removing afflictions cannot be done during an action scene.

To help an ally in recovering from an affliction you must attempt a Challenging (D2) attribute test using the 'relevant attributes' for the afflictions damage type. If successful, this test removes 1 affliction. You can recover additional afflictions of the same type by spending 2 Momentum for each additional affliction removed. A character may also remove an affliction of a different type for 4 Momentum.

Recovering from your own afflictions follows the same steps but the difficulty is increased by 1. Situational factors apply to these tests as normal.

Example: Jane Porter is trying to recover Kale Singh's Wound afflictions so he can get up and help her fend off an approaching horde of angry Warhoons. She must make an Empathy + Reason (D2) test. She succeeds and generates 2 Momentum. Her success removes one of Kale's afflictions and she spends 2 Momentum to remove the second.

OPTIONAL RULE: BLACKING OUT

Blacking out occurs in one of three ways. First, a character can suffer 5 of any one affliction. Second, a character can be blacked out by the narrator for narrative reasons. Third, a character can voluntarily black out.

If the narrator wishes to knock a character out for any reason they must pay the character a Luck point. This allows the narrator to capture the characters when normally it would require overwhelming opposition to knock them down. This ensures the narrative cliché of characters being captured is possible without the narrator causing multiple afflictions which might make escape impossible for the characters later on. The narrator is cautioned not to over-use this plot device, but when capture is desired it's better that the characters are out and out captured than subject to long drawn out conflicts they cannot win.

A character might look at the various threats in a scene and choose to voluntarily black out. Blacking out in this manner puts the character temporarily beyond harm's reach, but costs the character all their remaining Luck points and removes them from the scene — making it an excellent option when things look dire and a character is out of Luck. Whether the character is knocked out, swoons, has a panic attack, etc. is up to the player but the choice is made either when the scene begins or when they suffer an affliction. Characters who voluntarily black out awaken in the next scene with a sore head and 1 less affliction in each tracker but otherwise in any state that the narrator considers appropriate.

Example: After Kale Singh goes down during their battle with the Warhoons, Jane Porter realizes she is surrounded, has taken both a Wounds and Trauma affliction, and is out of Luck. She decides to voluntarily black out rather than take additional damage. The narrator describes a Warhoon warrior blindsiding Jane as she readies her rifle to shoot another of the attacking horde. Jane will wake up later with no afflictions but she'll be stuck in whatever situation her capture by the Warhoons has put her in.

NARRATOR CHARACTERS AND DAMAGE

Narrator characters s are split into three categories. **Villains**, **monsters**, and **minions**. Villains are full characters just like a PC. They have all the stress trackers that a PC has and work in exactly the same fashion. Villains include any important lieutenants who might recur throughout a campaign as well as particularly powerful beasts and any nemesis characters that might be defeated at the end of a campaign.

Monsters are weaker than villains but represent greater adversaries than standard creatures. They are usually formidable beasts and other non-human adversaries, but this need not always be the case. Monsters have only a single stress tracker which consists of the sum of their lowest and highest attributes. They also have a menace rating that reflects how many afflictions they can tolerate. A monster that fills its stress track or suffers more afflictions than its menace is dispatched but not necessarily dead. Usually the character taking out the monster chooses what happens, although some narrator characters may have a talent that dictates their final moments.

Minions are weaker and usually only show up in packs. Minion packs vary in size from two to five and any attack that deals damage will dispatch a minion. Extra Momentum can be used to dispatch additional minions with a single attack.

OPTIONAL RULE:
SIMPLIFIED STRESS

The *John Carter* stress and damage system is designed to emulate the stories of Burroughs and the pulp era of romantic adventure. Heroes were often hindered not only by physical damage but also guilt, doubt, and even madness. However, this system is a complex part of the 2d20 system and some groups may favor a simpler alternative.

This system makes the characters a bit more vulnerable in terms of raw stress they can take. However, it balances this by removing the vulnerability a character has from multiple stress tracks that can be targeted and exploited individually.

Heroes and villains and other major characters have a single stress track, like monsters. This track is equal to their lowest and highest attributes plus 10.

✶ Each time a player character or other major fills half their stress track they suffer an affliction. This affliction affects all tests and rolls.

✶ Afflictions are also suffered when a character takes 5 or more stress from a single attack.

✶ Stress and affliction recovery are much the same as the standard rules, with one key difference: All recovery tests for afflictions use the character's highest and lowest attributes for the test (though a character could have a talent that changes this rule).

✶ All combat dice effects that do additional damage of a particular type instead inflict additional stress.

Player characters have access to a special type of resource called **Luck** points. These points reflect the fact that the game's heroes have ambition and determination above and beyond most people — such individuals shape their own Luck by will alone. In play, Luck points are used to enable player characters to do incredible things, to the amazement of onlookers.

Luck points can be used to pull off exciting stunts, provide an edge during dramatic situations, or otherwise help to advance the story. In order to best take advantage of this system, however, there needs to be a steady stream of Luck points made available to the players. Narrators are encouraged to award Luck points to the players regularly, because it is a tangible way of supporting a swashbuckling style of play and increasing the involvement of the players. The more each player participates in making the game thrilling, keeps the plot twisting, and makes their characters memorable, the more chances they will get to do more of the same.

Each player character usually begins each session with Luck points equal to their weakest attribute (though some characters may begin each session with fewer), and cannot accumulate more Luck than this at any time.

Here are just a few of the ways Luck points can be spent during play:

✶ **Add a Bonus d20 to an Attribute Test.**
A player can add a bonus d20 to any attribute test for one Luck point. The extra die always rolls a result of 1, and automatically generates successes as if it were rolled normally as part of the attribute test. Bonus d20s gained by spending Luck still count towards the normal limit of three bonus d20s. If the use of Luck generates enough successes to pass an attribute test, the player need not roll any other dice, avoiding the possibility of complications.

✶ **Perform an Additional Conflict Action.**
During combat, a player character can usually only perform one Conflict action in a turn. By spending a Luck point, the player character can perform a second Conflict action, with no penalty. The player character may only gain one extra Conflict action in total.

✶ **Second Wind.** A player character can catch their breath and remove all the stress from one stress track by spending a Luck point.

✶ **Overcome a Weakness.** A player character may spend a Luck point to ignore the effects of all afflictions for a single Conflict action.

✶ **Influence the Story.** A player may spend a Luck point to introduce a fact or add a detail to the current scene. Such story declarations can have both narrative and mechanical effects. Story declarations should be plausible, and the narrator has the final say over whether a suggested fact or detail is valid. The narrator may also declare that particularly important additions to the story may cost more than one point of Luck.

Narrators are encouraged to come up with new ways Luck can be used in a campaign.

REGAINING LUCK POINTS

The narrator may sometimes award a Luck point to a single player in the group for a particularly noteworthy action — perhaps one player came up with the perfect plan to thwart the enemy, made a bold sacrifice for the benefit of the group, gave a memorable in-character speech, or perhaps uttered a funny quip that defused the tension and made everyone at the table laugh.

Other times, the narrator may choose to award Luck points to all the players based on their progress in a campaign, or during the transition between key scenes. Luck points make excellent rewards when characters reach narra-

Renown, Accolades, and Luck

Often a character's renown or accolades (*see Chapter 6: Growing Your Legend*) can create new opportunities or methods for fortune to intervene. A character who is a skilled dwar in Helium's navy might discover a fellow officer in an unlikely place who can render assistance, or a character's staunch First Born ally might end up captured by the same foes who hold the player characters, thus giving them extra help when they try to escape. These discoveries are paid for with Luck.

Using Luck in this fashion is nearly identical to Luck used in other ways. However, the presence of a relevant title or ally essentially "powers up" the Luck point, making it more effective. The exact bonus provided by this connection varies with each situation, but narrators will provide additional support, information, or opportunities when a character's Luck is directly related to the character's titles, allies, and general reputation and renown.

tive milestones, defeat an important villain, solve a mystery, or survive a tense encounter. They can also be spent immediately, and thus provide instant gratification.

As a general guideline, the narrator should award players with one to three Luck points per hour of gameplay, depending on the course of play and the rate they are being spent.

Beyond refreshing Luck points at the start of each session, there are a number of ways for player characters can gain Luck points during the course of play.

Awarding Luck

First and foremost, Luck points are given by the narrator during gameplay to reward players for good roleplaying, clever plans, successfully overcoming difficult challenges, using teamwork, or otherwise making the game more fun for all. Players may have other opportunities to gain Luck points by achieving certain goals within an encounter, reaching a milestone in the story, or choosing to be the one to suffer the complications of some dire event. As a general guideline, there should be two or three opportunities for players to gain Luck points per hour of play. In each case, the narrator should determine whether the point is warranted, and award a single point per instance.

Example: Richard's green Martian player character, Zem Zurros, tackles a pair of assassins intent on killing the royal family of Kadabra. His action sends both Zem and the assassins hurtling out of a window to the ground far below. As Zem's action was heroic, dramatic, and saved multiple important narrator characters, the narrator grants Zem a Luck point. He will likely need it…

It's generally useful for the narrator to ask the players to keep their Luck points visible, through the use of some tokens. This allows the narrator to judge how plentiful they are amongst the characters. If Luck points are being handed out too often and the players are all at the maximum, then the narrator can either hand them out less often, or can increase the challenges the player characters face. If the players are frequently low or out of Luck points, then it's a good time to evaluate if the

encounters are too challenging, or if the players are not accomplishing meaningful goals within the course of play, or even having a good time. Adjustments can then be made to improve that situation. A good rule of thumb would be that each player has, on average, about half of their Luck points at any given time.

Voluntary Failure

As described on page 51, characters may voluntarily fail attribute tests, at the narrator's discretion. This should only be invoked when a player character has something to gain or to lose when the attribute test is being made — generally, it's not that useful to have players roll when nothing is at stake. Voluntarily failing an attribute test provides the narrator with one point of Threat to be added to the Threat pool, and the player character immediately gains one point of Luck in return.

*Example: In a later adventure, Zem Zurros is accused of conspiring against Kadabra's royal family, the same people he saved from assassins! The accusations are preposterous and the narrator gives Zem a chance to appeal to reason and remind his accusers of his valor. However, Zem's player believes this accusation is part of a larger plot and hopes to uncover more information while playing the part of the fallen hero and wanted fugitive. Zem intentionally fails his **Passion + Reason** test to convince others of his innocence, adding a Threat to the narrator's Threat pool and gaining a Luck point he intends to use in unmasking the true culprits.*

CHAPTER 5: WEAPONS, TECHNOLOGY AND EQUIPMENT

> *I have ever been prone to seek adventure and to investigate and experiment where wiser men would have left well enough alone.*
> – John Carter, *A Princess of Mars*

Historically, Martian industry has concentrated on the requirements of warfare, survival, transport, and communication. Throughout the Dotar Sojat era, there are few advances in any of these areas. The products of Barsoomian science are considered perfect and technological development stagnates. Technical innovation only returns to Mars in the Jeddak of Jeddaks era with Carthoris of Helium's invention of the destination control compass. A new age of invention follows, particularly in airship design and navigation. It is an exciting period when research, discovery, prototyping, and espionage begin to redefine cultural, political, and martial relations on Barsoom.

Beyond developments made in the city-states or amongst the nomadic tribes of Mars, solitary masterminds and egotists experiment tirelessly. Driven by ambition, or jealousy, or an obsession with pure science, these eccentric geniuses transgress the borders of the sensible and the sane. Their creations rise unpredictably to threaten Barsoom's complex, antagonistic status quo and plunge the dying world into oblivion.

For heroes adventuring on Mars, the weapons, items, and technology of Barsoom form an integral part of their exploits. A finely balanced longsword might hold back a rising tide of savage Warhoons; a well-aimed shot from a radium rifle could bring down the scout-flyer of a fleeing spy; or the miraculous healing salves of the green Martian women might sustain a life long enough to learn some terrible secret from a mortally wounded warrior. Unspeakable vat-grown horrors can rise to threaten Barsoom itself, or an interplanetary ship can call down the attention of malevolent aliens.

New weapons, unforeseen technological advances, and experiments gone awry can invigorate any adventure, leading to unexpected twists with far-reaching implications for Barsoom and its peoples. Such encounters should quicken the blood, raise the stakes, and challenge the mettle of even the most intrepid heroes.

Accordingly, this section details the weapons, equipment, and technology found normally on Barsoom, and describes the unique items and devices conceived by the Red Planet's more eccentric inhabitants.

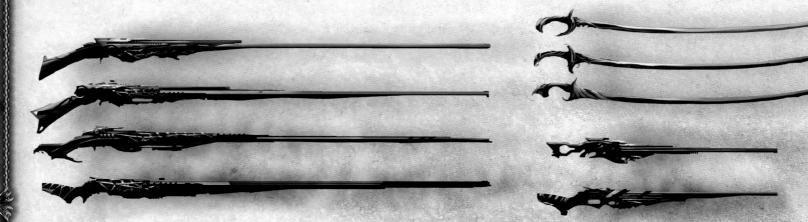

WEAPONS

For millennia, Barsoom's intelligent races have existed in a near-perpetual state of war. Countless weapons have been invented, employed, and rejected throughout this period until only the most effective remain in use. Although ancient, forgotten weapons may be discovered in Mars' ruined cities and dead sea bottoms, Barsoom's traditional armory is limited to straightforwardly produced, easily maintained melee weapons, firearms, and explosives.

MELEE WEAPONS

The sword is the most widely used weapon on Barsoom. There are various forms, but the most common is the straight, one-handed, needle-like longsword carried by the red and green Martians. These are single-edged, razor-sharp steel blades forged to retain keenness and flexibility during prolonged combat. In Earthly terms, they appear to be a hybrid of the European backsword and rapier.

Longswords are both mass-produced for military units and handcrafted for individuals. As a consequence, their designs can vary considerably, with many produced to individual specifications. They differ mainly in the pattern of the guard — which may be basket-, cup-, or ring-like. Their pommels are often ornate, bearing intricately jeweled designs indicating the bearer's rank and family.

Red Martian blades tend to be four sofads, or forty-seven inches, long. Green Martian longswords are slightly longer but given the green Martians' greater stature and their tendency to fence using their upper arms, any advantage gained against smaller opponents by this increased length is mitigated by height difference. Nevertheless, any hero from a race smaller than the green Martians must always fight with an awareness of when a mistimed lunge could leave shoulders and back exposed to a downward thrust.

Fencing with a longsword takes great skill, since the back of the blade is used to parry an opponent's blows and preserve the weapon's edge. This requires considerable dexterity and practice gained through harsh training and perfected in the field.

Most red and green Martian warriors complement their long blade with a single-handed, general-purpose short-sword. Double-edged, these are secondary weapons, usually drawn if the longsword is lost or damaged, or when fighting occurs on either crowded battlefields or in the confined spaces of Barsoom's cities, ruins,

WEAPON AND EQUIPMENT QUALITIES

DISHONORABLE
Dishonorable weapons impact the renown of the character. Using such a weapon can lead to serious consequences such as censure from allies, loss of rank, and sometimes imprisonment or death. Weapons that break the standard of Martian Honor usually have this quality.

EXPLOSIVE
For each effect rolled the weapon inflicts an additional 1 damage to the Fear and Injury stress trackers. If the target does not have these stress trackers, each icon rolled deals 2 damage.

The narrator can spend 1 Threat to force any character at Near range to the target to roll a (D2) test to evade the blast, or take 1 ⬟ damage.

Players using weapons with the Explosive quality can spend 1 Momentum to force a narrator character at a Near range to the blast to roll the same test.

FEARSOME
For each effect rolled the weapon inflicts an additional 1 damage to the Fear stress tracker. If the target does not have this stress tracker, it simply deals damage.

PSYCHIC
For each effect rolled the weapon inflicts an additional 1 damage to the Confusion stress tracker. If the target does not have this stress tracker, it simply deals damage.

QUIET
When you use a weapon with the Quiet quality, you gain 1 bonus Momentum to use on a test to keep your position hidden, providing you haven't already been spotted.

SHARP
For each effect rolled the weapon inflicts an additional 1 damage to the Injury stress tracker. If the target does not have this stress tracker, it simply deals damage.

POISON
If a weapon is coated in poison, such as the venom of a sith, it gains the Fearsome and Dishonorable qualities.

If poison is slipped into food or drink it does 2 ⬟ of damage with the Fearsome quality. If a character is discovered to have used or is caught using poison, they suffer the consequences of using a Dishonorable weapon.

or pits. Most short-swords are two sofads long with simple, unadorned hilts and a broad, thick blade for slashing and cutting. Amongst the red Martians, the short-sword lacks the cultural and hereditary importance of the longsword with its rank and familial embellishments.

The curved single-edged swords favored by the First Born are similarly plain, serviceable weapons. They are usually three sofads long with a heavy guard and a large pommel, which acts as a counterweight to the broad blade. Their shorter length places the wielder at a slight disadvantage in terms of reach when facing an opponent armed with a longsword, but the heavier blade enables the swordsman to swipe lighter weapons aside, leaving enemies exposed to attack.

More unusual are the hooked swords of the Okar. Single-edged, with a vicious hook at the tip, these blades are held in the left hand and used in conjunction with the yellow Martians' double-edged straight swords. Both are approximately three sofads long and form a formidable web of impenetrable steel in the hands of a skilled swordsman. The hooked sword is used to deflect, disarm, or snag the opponent, rendering him off-balance and vulnerable to a slash or thrust from the straight sword. To protect their left arm for this maneuver, Okarian warriors wear a buckler strapped to their wrist. In this, they are unique since they are the only troops on Barsoom to carry shields for anything other than ceremonial purposes. If an Okarian loses his hooked sword in combat, he usually reverts to a short-hafted axe, which has a sharply curved pick behind the main blade. The Okarians are the only race to use a military axe as the green Martians' hatchets serve more flexibly as both tool and combat weapon.

Daggers are carried in most Barsoomian cultures, though they differ greatly in size and design, ranging from the great knives of the green Martians to the long slender blades of the red nations. They are all designed as thrusting weapons, sharpened along the full length of both edges of the blade. Most often used for close combat, eliminating sentries, and extracting information from reticent prisoners, they are usually fitted with a broad cross-guard to protect the knifeman's hand and prevent the blade from snagging in the victim. Assassins tend to favor the red Martian design since it is an easily concealed and highly effective means of execution. By contrast, some panthans carry green Martian daggers in place of short-swords, preferring the shorter, heavier blade for close combat, or using them in combination with their longswords to slip inside their opponent's guard.

Equally varied is the Martian spear. The green Martian weapon is a forty sofad length of metal-shod wood terminating in a gleaming, elongated tip of steel two sofads long. They are carried into battle like lances by green Martian thoat-riders and are most effective when the opposing sides clash for the first time. Lacking a cross-guard, they can snag quickly and are usually abandoned in favor of longswords wielded from the backs of thoats or on foot. By contrast, red Martian cavalry and infantry both carry spears. The cavalry spear is ten to twelve sofads long with a cross-guard behind the tip to prevent it from catching in the bodies of the slain. Its infantry counterpart is rarely longer than ten sofads and is primarily a thrusting weapon used to break enemy cavalry charges or to engage similarly armed opponents. Both are hardwood shod with rings of metal and tipped with steel.

The Okar Nation's javelins are of similar construction, though they tend to be used by city guardsmen rather than by warriors deployed in the field. Seven sofads long, the Okar javelin is also used in hunting the apt and the orluk. The Kaolian sith spear is different again, being constructed entirely from a steel-aluminum alloy and measuring fifteen sofads from butt to tip. These are rarely used outside of Kaol, however, where they are employed exclusively for killing sith, the giant, venomous flying insects that plague the country's forests. The siths' venom is used to tip the spears since it is the only substance capable of killing the creatures quickly enough to save their victims.

BLADES AND MELEE COMBAT

Most blades, regardless of type, use identical statistics and, while an unusual blade might cause an increase in difficulty the first time it is used in combat, generally all blades conform to the following rules.

BLADES ARE SHARP

When an effect is rolled a blade inflicts 1 damage to the Injury stress tracker. If a creature doesn't have an Injury stress tracker it simply deals damage.

BLADES INFLICT DAMAGE

Rather than the usual 1 ⬛ damage inflicted by a successful attack, unless otherwise mentioned, blades other than daggers inflict 2 ⬛ damage. Daggers inflict the normal 1 ⬛ damage. In the rare instance that a club is used it does not gain the Sharp rule.

BLADES ARE EASILY AVAILABLE

It costs 5xp to carry any single type of blade as core equipment.

FIREARMS

In Martian culture, no warrior can engage another in single combat using a weapon greater than that with which he is attacked. If a soldier draws a longsword, no matter how superior the arms of his opponent might be, that opponent is compelled by custom and honor to engage him with a longsword or some lesser weapon. This tradition has almost certainly led to standardization in the array of weaponry carried by most Martians as no warrior would wish to face an assailant without an appropriate choice of arms. It is also perhaps one of the reasons why melee weapons still exist side by side on Barsoom with advanced firearms.

The radium rifle and the radium revolver are the only advanced projectile weapons used on Mars. Both fire small caliber rounds. Each bullet is composed of an opaque outer casing and an almost solid inner glass cylinder. At the tip of the cylinder is a minute particle of radium powder, which is highly explosive when exposed to even diffuse sunlight. When the bullet strikes its target, the opaque shell fragments, exposing the radium in the glass core. The radium then detonates with devastating consequences.

Explosive radium rounds are always manufactured by artificial light and are deployed largely in daytime conflicts, when they are most effective. If they are used at night, morning sends a tide of staccato explosions rolling across the landscape with the sun's terminator as unexploded rounds finally combust. Any warriors who are still on the field with exposed bullets lodged in wounds must act quickly to cover their injuries or face the possibility of a messy, eruptive death. For obvious reasons, field surgeons prefer to remove bullets at night or under artificial light. This often leads to patients' protracted suffering and difficult triage decisions.

Given their reduced effectiveness at night, and the greater complexity of their manufacture, radium rounds are regularly replaced with solid, flat-nosed bullets for nighttime warfare. These are usually cast or swaged from lead or zinc alloys. Before a battle, swaging is more common amongst the green Martians, who recognize that smoke from a bullet casting process could give away their presence.

Radium rifles and revolvers all use the same caliber rounds regardless of the culture manufacturing them. This standardization is not coincidental, nor did it occur simultaneously across Barsoom. Rather, it was the consequence of warring cultures developing and modifying weapons they could resupply in the field from the bodies of fallen comrades and enemies alike. The rifles hold magazines of 100 rounds; the revolvers are chambered for six cartridges. Reloads and spare magazines are packed in impact-resistant belt pouches to reduce the risk of accidental damage and a catastrophic explosion. Both pistol and rifle are fired using a raised button on the stock, which minimizes the potentially detrimental effect on accuracy of squeezing a trigger.

Most Martian firearms are constructed from comparable materials, and are exceptionally light and durable. The metal parts are usually fashioned from a white alloy of steel and aluminum, tempered to an extreme hardness. Stocks and grips are typically of a very light, intensely tough wood, though it is not uncommon for these to be made from bone or horn, depending on the materials available locally or through trade.

Despite this standardization of ammunition and construction, radium rifles and pistols often look very different, depending on the race or city-state producing them. Green Martian rifles display a barbaric splendor, being adorned with feathers, items of metal, or the teeth or dried fingers of vanquished opponents. Those of Helium are characterized by clean, graceful lines, and are often filigreed with rank or familial markings. Like the sword, the rifle in red Martian culture can also serve as a status symbol with particular armorers and gunsmiths enjoying greater prestige than others. The Therns are more practical, adding small shields to their utilitarian designs to protect the rifleman's face and upper body.

The range of the Martian radium rifle is misreported in Carter's first manuscript, presumably as a result of his unfamiliarity with the Martian language. He suggests that when equipped with wireless finders and sighters, the weapon has an effective range of approximately two hundred miles. Later accounts omit this range, though the descriptions of the rifle remain consistent. Martian rifles have an effective range of two haads, which Carter interprets incorrectly as two hundred miles rather than as the correct two miles. Radium revolvers have an effective range of considerably less. The best guns produced in Helium will kill at 100 ads or 0.5 of a haad.

With the perfection of such efficient radium weapons, there has been little change in their design or function for several millennia. This has not prevented individual inventors from developing alternate and more devastating firearms, however. In the Jeddak of Jeddaks era, Phor Tak, a scientist from the red Martian city of Jahar, developed a rifle capable of firing three kinds of invisible ray. Depending on the ammunition selected, the rifle could discharge rays that would disintegrate metal, wood, or human flesh by dissolving the molecular bonds holding the particular matter together. The range of these disintegrating rifles was less than a haad. Nevertheless, they threatened to destabilize the fine martial balance of Barsoom and render all of the Red Planet's armies and navies impotent. The threat was removed when Tan Hadron destroyed all stocks of the disintegrating rifle and ammunition at Phor Tak's estate in the dead city of Jhama. Rumors persist, however, that one or two of the weapons survived and are being actively sought by ambitious jeds and jeddaks eager to advance their power. In response, several red Martian city-states have laid in stocks of the blue substance manufactured by Phor Tak's assistant which provides some protection from the metal disintegrating ray when painted on the metal portions of ships, harnesses, and weaponry.

While pistols and rifles are the norm on Barsoom, some cultures — such as the Bowman of Lothar — do use the long bow. These weapons are effective, but require special training and most Martians will not be trained in their use as a matter of course.

FIREARM COMBAT

Most firearms, regardless of type, use identical statistics and, while an unusual weapon might cause an increase in difficulty the first time it is used in combat, generally all firearms conform to the following rules. Rarer and weirder weapons may have alternative damage ratings and rules.

FIREARMS ARE FEARSOME

When an effect is rolled a firearm inflicts 1 damage to the Fear stress tracker. If a creature doesn't have a Fear stress tracker it simply deals damage.

FIREARMS INFLICT DAMAGE

Rather than the usual 1 🎲 damage inflicted by a successful attack, unless otherwise mentioned, firearms inflict 2 🎲 damage.

FIREARMS ARE EASILY AVAILABLE

It costs 5xp to carry any single type of firearm as core equipment.

LONGBOWS

The most common ranged weapon other than the firearm is the longbow.

Longbows inflict the normal 1 🎲 damage but are Quiet. Weapons with the Quiet quality are not easily detected when used. A character attacking with a longbow gains 1 bonus Momentum on any test to conceal their location so long as they have not been spotted.

OPTIONAL RULE: RADIUM BULLET DETONATION

As noted in the description of Barsoomian firearms, radium bullets detonate when sunlight hits them. This makes them incredibly dangerous during the day and they must be removed from wounds inflicted at night or the later explosion can inflict grievous wounds. Narrators wishing to play up this effect can replace Firearms are Fearsome with the following effects for radium-based firearms:

RADIUM BULLETS ARE EXPLOSIVE

When an effect is rolled, a radium-based firearm inflicts 1 damage to the Fear and Injury stress trackers if the attack occurs in sunlight. If a creature doesn't have these stress trackers each effect rolled deals 2 damage. If this attack does not occur in sunlit areas, an effect rolled inflicts 1 damage to the Fear stress tracker instead.

In addition, if a target suffers an affliction from a radium-based firearm outside a sunlit area and has not had this injury treated before they are exposed to sunlight, the narrator can spend X Threat to inflict X 🎲 of damage to the target as the undetonated bullet explodes inside their wound! A narrator should avoid spending more than 5 Threat on this.

INCENDIARY COMBAT

Most incendiaries fall into one of two categories; hand-held or satchel. All incendiaries conform to the following rules.

INCENDIARIES ARE EXPLOSIVE

When an effect is rolled an incendiary inflicts 1 damage to the Fear and Injury stress trackers. If a creature doesn't have these stress trackers, each effect rolled deals 2 damage. The narrator can spend 1 Threat to force any character Near to the blast to roll a difficulty 2 test to evade damage from an incendiary. Players employing incendiaries can spend 1 Momentum on their attribute test to force an narrator character to make a similar test. Characters dodging the blast might roll **Daring + Reason**. Characters taking cover might roll **Cunning + Reason**, but the narrator could consider other combinations.

INCENDIARIES INFLICT DAMAGE

Handheld incendiaries inflict 3 🎲 damage. Satchel charges inflict 4 🎲.

INCENDIARIES CAN BE COMBINED TO DESTROY STRUCTURES

Every extra hand-held incendiary used to destroy an object adds 1 🎲 to the damage roll. Satchel charges count as two hand-sized charges.

INCENDIARIES ARE RARE

It costs 25xp to carry any single incendiary as core equipment. Tharks can pay 15xp to carry a hand-held incendiary.

INCENDIARIES ARE DISHONORABLE

Their use at all, by any character, will impact the renown of the character. Use against living opponents will lead to serious consequences including censure from allies, loss of rank, and sometimes imprisonment or death.

INCENDIARY DEVICES

Considered dishonorable weapons by most Martian cultures, battlefield incendiary devices are not unknown, though they are exceptionally rare. Only the green Martians use them and, even then, seldom employ them against living targets. Their use of radium incendiaries is ordinarily limited to the destruction of property, including downed airships that have been looted and set adrift, temporary fortifications erected around the camps of red Martians or other hordes, or fallen wood and other combustible materials blocking passageways through deserted Martian cities or their pits. In structure, the radium incendiary is a palm-sized version of the radium bullet with a greater amount of active material in its glass core. It is rare for radium incendiaries to be carried into battle given the customs defining Martian combat and the danger they pose to all sides involved in the conflict.

EQUIPMENT

The most important item of equipment for any Martian is the harness worn in place of clothing. Barsoomians dislike covering their bodies unless the temperature or climate require them to don robes of silk and fur to protect against the cold. In most circumstances, they find shirts, tunics, gowns and trousers restrictive and grotesque in their masking of an individual's natural health and vigor. Consequently, all Martians wear trappings that cover their modesty but little else.

Martian harnesses are usually of leather ornamented with precious stones, small metal plates, and badges of honor. Some green Martians harnesses bear the body parts of fallen rivals, or the feathers of extinct birds, passed from one defeated warrior to the next down the generations.

Harnesses play an important cultural role on Barsoom. Their jewels and enameled insignia depict the wearer's house or horde, rank, class and family. Awards, rewards and medals of service may also adorn a Martian's leather, providing a visual autobiography of the wearer's exploits. Even the civilian metal worn by non-combatants can be a complex accumulation of social and cultural information. Only common soldiers, panthans, or those who wish to conceal their identity wear harnesses of plain metal. As a consequence, the harness has become the single most important means of identifying individuals, their origins, and their disposition. It is also one of the chief means by which subterfuge and espionage is conducted as Martians often adopt the metal of families, factions, cities and cultures different from their own. It is one of Barsoom's great paradoxes that the harness is both trusted and abused as an indicator of identity.

Harness designs differ widely, but two predominate. The most common type features a broad belt from which a strap rises to the center of the sternum. This strap then splits at a small triangular metal plate, often bearing the wearer's rank or family insignia, before crossing over each shoulder and buckling to the main belt in the small of the back. A second popular version features two or three narrow belts around the waist. X- and Y-shaped straps cross the chest and back linked either by metal rings or stitched behind metal plates. Both forms sometimes feature leather pauldrons, the only piece of armor seen regularly on Barsoom.

The Martian harness serves a number of practical as well as cultural purposes. It has hangers and holsters for longsword, short-sword, dagger, and pistol. Hoops and ties accommodate the hand mirrors carried by many warriors for signaling and observing activity from behind cover. Its belt loops hold the long straps and boarding hooks used by air-sailors when effecting repairs to airships or boarding an enemy vessel. Cross-belts and pocket pouches provide storage for ammunition and the numerous other articles essential for life in the wilds of Barsoom.

MEDICINES AND COMMON ITEMS

Typical items include tiny folding jetan boards, concentrated food pellets made from preserved vegetable milk and the flesh of the Usa, or "Fighting Potato", and fire pistons and char cloths, the common Martian devices for producing flame. Most green Martians and red Martian soldiers, panthans, and explorers also equip themselves with a supply of healing salves, which are capable of curing all but the most grievous of wounds. The yellow, black and white races produce similar medicines, and it is rare for a Martian to die from injury unless they do so before medical care can be administered.

MEDICINES IN GAMES

Martian salves are miraculous in their ability to heal flesh and prevent death. Minor applications of salves are assumed to take place at the end of every combat as cuts and bruises are attended to. These applications don't need to be tracked, though not having salve might increase the difficulty of a healing test at the narrator's prerogative.

Entire jars of salves can be used to repair significant injuries. A small jar contains 1 dose of salve which can be used to instantly repair a single Wounds affliction. A large jar contains 2 doses and a medicine bag contains 4 doses. Up to 3 doses can be used in any 8-hour period but 1 dose is sufficient to prevent death most of the time.

Salve is reasonably common. A small jar of salve is available as core equipment for 5xp. Larger jars are less common, but a large jar is available for 20xp and a medicine bag is available for 45xp.

TORCHES AND ILLUMINATION DEVICES

Some red and black Martians carry radium flash torches, especially if they intend to explore Barsoom's subterranean realms or need to signal their presence to allies. These torches are compact devices six or seven sofs long. The duration of the light emitted is controlled by a button on the side of the torch. The button activates an iris that dilates between the torch's lens and its radium bulb, exposing or concealing the light source. The intensity of the light emitted is governed by a thumb-lever that raises and lowers the radium bulb's luminance. Such torches need no batteries since their radium bulbs will emit light for an inestimable period of time. A torch set on maximum intensity with a fully opened iris will provide a diffuse circular cone of light 100 sofads long with a target area 30 sofads wide. They can also be used to activate and deactivate locks keyed to particular sequences and intensities of light.

No new torches have been manufactured for millennia and the secret of their production has been lost. As a result, torches tend to be passed down through noble families or shared within military units. Purchasing a radium flash torch on the open market is an expensive undertaking and many dealers regularly commission panthans and explorers to scour the dead cities and sea bottoms for these ancient devices. In the Jeddak of Jeddaks era, rumors suggest that a considerable number might be found in the ruins abandoned by the Holy Therns in the Valley Dor. Few heroes have dared the area's white apes and plant men to uncover the truth of this speculation, however.

TORCHES IN GAMES

Torches remove all penalties for darkness and can be used to activate or pick some sophisticated locks.

Torches count as rare and can be purchased for 10Xp as core equipment.

FIELD GLASSES AND SIGHTS

Red Martian officers, nobles, merchants and more successful panthans are often equipped with a monocular field glass. Only the red Martians have the skill in lens and prism making to produce these items and the finest examples are manufactured in Helium and Ptarth. They are usually carried in leather cases suspended from their owner's harness.

The red Martians are reluctant to trade their field glasses since they recognize the military advantage obtained by restricting their availability. This has not prevented them from finding their way into the hands of other nations, however. It is not unusual, for example, to see them amongst the green Martians, who have procured many during their assaults on red Martian airships and settlements. In the Jeddak of Jeddaks era, many disgraced red Martians from Zodanga have sold glasses to the Okar and to the First Born.

High quality field glasses designed for locating individuals in a landscape have magnification ranges of 20x – 25x. Varieties magnifying in the 10x – 15x ranges are ideal for surveying the landscape, or large troop movements. Most models are expensive and beyond the means of regular soldiers, novice heroes, or unsuccessful panthans.

Weapons scopes can be manufactured using the same process that creates field glasses, but they are rare.

FIELD GLASSES IN GAMES

Field glasses provide 1 Momentum for the purposes of investigating an area at a distance. If mounted as a sight, they decrease any difficulty increase for range by 1 step. Possession of a field glass is a mark of rank and senior military figures without one may suffer increased difficulties in social settings.

Field glasses count as rare and can be purchased for 10Xp as core equipment.

CHRONOMETER

Cost prevents Martians of more humble status from affording a Barsoomian chronometer. These delicate instruments record and display the tals, xats and zodes of Martian time beneath a thick crystal carapace. They are usually worn on the wrist as part of a gold or leather bracelet. The finest are produced in Helium and Okar. Robust versions are standard issue to red and yellow Martian officers and few red Martian nobles would be seen without an elaborate time-piece amongst their courtly attire. By contrast, green Martians reject artificial chronometers, believing that true warriors are so in tune with their environment that they always possess an inherent sense of time.

CHRONOMETERS IN GAMES

Chronometers do not provide any obvious Momentum benefit, though few nobles wouldn't be seen without one. Failure to wear a chronometer marks the character as an outsider and may make some social tests more difficult.

Chronometers are a status symbol and cost 5xp as core equipment.

INVISIBILITY

The invisibility spheres manufactured by the warring cities of Invak and Onvak in the Forest of Lost Men are truly exotic Martian science. Within an hour, anyone consuming one of these large pills is rendered invisible for a full Martian day. This effect is also conferred onto objects coming in contact with the affected individual, though it passes quickly once contact is broken.

Although little is known regarding the composition of these pills, it seems probable that they are derived from glandular extracts from the chameleonic darseen. Most Martian scientists agree that true invisibility is impossible, implying that the pills make the skin of its user capable of mimicking its surroundings.

Several researchers have sent expeditions into the Forest of Lost Men in search of the secret of invisibility. None have returned. It would take a brave party of adventurers to solve the mystery. Similarly, many unscrupulous warlords and jeds wish to learn the formula of Phor Tak's invisibility compound. This substance has the quality of bending light rays, making any object coated in the material invisible. The answer to its mystery lies in ruined Jhama now.

INVISIBILITY IN GAMES

Invisibility is a game changer in a lot of ways. Attacking while invisible is dishonorable, but travelling while invisible is not. The invisibility compound allows a person to gain 2 Momentum on any attribute test to hide, sneak around, or evade pursuers reliant on sight.

A single pill is enough to hide a character and their carried equipment for a day. The effect cannot be controlled or extended except through eating a pill and starting the clock again. "Coating" an object is possible, but requires multiple pills or it will fade in much less time. An object coated in the invisibility serum maintains its effect for ¼ of a day for every pill used.

Invisibility pills are not available as core equipment.

GENERAL PREPAREDNESS

Any hero will begin with equipment appropriate to their nation, social standing, and profession. This is a permissive and fluid list in many cases, with characters being presumed to be sensible Barsoomians who have the things they need to prosper and survive unless circumstances dictate otherwise. Thus, a soldier is presumed to have a dagger, sword, pistol and battle harness with various tools and medicines. A scholar would have scientific instruments, writing materials for taking notes, field glasses, chronometers, and other high-tech tools. Pretty much every hero save a newly arrived Earthborn would have some form of weapon, though military and combat-focused characters carry more and deadlier weapons than others.

If there is some doubt that a character would have a particularly useful item with them at a given time, the narrator may require them to spend a Momentum to have it on hand. However, generally, characters should never be considered to be wholly unarmed or unprepared unless the situation dictates they have been ambushed, sabotaged, betrayed, or otherwise caught unawares.

TECHNOLOGY

Barsoom is a world of wonder, a curious fusion of barbaric splendor, magnificent cities, and startling, sometimes unexpected, technological brilliance. Its fabulous streets are illuminated by eternally bright lights that eliminate shadow; at night, its houses and farms rise for protection on pneumatic shafts; magnetic elevators convey passengers to the heights of lofty palaces; and intricate locks exchange crude metal keys for sophisticated melodies or sequences of light. Even the pits found beneath Martian cities have their wonders, not least the antique radium illuminator bulbs that seem destined to burn forever, or until some violence destroys them. Nevertheless, these achievements pale in comparison to what has been achieved through the eighth and ninth rays.

THE EIGHTH AND NINTH RAYS

In addition to the spectrum of seven colors known to those of Jasoom, Martian scientists have long recognized the existence of two additional rays, both indescribable to those who have not witnessed them for themselves.

The ninth ray is fundamental to life on Barsoom. In the vast and virtually impregnable atmosphere plant maintained by Helium, its energy is separated from the spectrum and transformed electrically into gas. This gas is then pumped to the five great air centers on Mars. When it is released into the air and comes into contact with the ether of space, it is transformed into the planet's breathable envelope, thus sustaining the planet's fragile atmospheric balance. Quantities of the gas sufficient to support Barsoom for years are stored in the atmosphere plant, which is safeguarded against failure by the redundancy of its engineering. A battery of twenty back-up radium pumps, any one of which can provide the power needed to circulate the ninth ray gas, ensure that the system will not experience a catastrophic failure.

A second atmosphere plant in Marentina in the Okar nation will sustain life at only Barsoom's northern pole should the primary plant fail.

The eighth ray, also known as the ray of propulsion, is an intrinsic property of light regardless of its source. The solar eighth ray propels the light of the sun to its orbiting planets. In turn, the individual eighth ray of each planet reflects the light received back into space once more. Barsoom and the other planetary bodies absorb the solar eighth ray, but their own eighth rays are constantly emanating outwards. On Barsoom at least, the emanations of the eighth ray provide a force counter to that of gravity. When the eighth ray is enclosed in tanks, it can be employed to raise huge weights from the ground.

For almost a thousand years, this technique has been used on Mars to develop and perfect aerial travel, transport, and combat.

MARTIAN FLIERS

Of all the wonders of Barsoom, few are as breathtaking as the majestic fliers that ply the azure skies of the dying world. From private and public pleasure craft to bulk cargo carriers to the mighty battleships of the red Martian navies, these fliers depend on their shipwrights' exploitation of the anti-gravitic properties of the mysterious eighth ray.

Airship design on Mars follows a set of standard principles. Tanks filled with the eighth ray and located below decks or lining the outside of the hull provide lift. This makes Barsoomian fliers vulnerable to being disabled by marksmen whose shots can rupture the tanks causing the eighth ray to vent into the atmosphere. Navigation controls are elementary and highly effective. A preset-altimeter ensures a vessel follows the uneven contours of the landscape, maintaining a fixed altitude. The air compass, when set for a particular destination, remains locked on that location. The pilot need only keep the vessel's prow in line with the directional indicator to reach the defined destination by the shortest route. In the Jeddak of Jeddaks era, Carthoris of Helium improved on the directional compass by adding an auxiliary device that steers the airship automatically on the selected course. On reaching the designated location, this destination control compass brings the vessel to a halt and lowers it to the ground.

Propellers powered by light radium motors drive Martian airships. Before the Jeddak of Jeddaks era, the fastest one-man flyer could attain speeds of approximately eleven hundred haads per zode, or one hundred and sixty-six miles per hour. After John Carter's ascension as Warlord of Mars, a padwar in Helium's navy designed a lighter, faster motor that doubled the speeds of almost all airships. These new motors are fuelless, drawing their energy from Barsoom's magnetic field, which is channeled through the accumulator to armature-like bearings surrounding the propeller shaft. By moving a simple lever to increase or reduce the number of armatures in series with the accumulator, the pilot controls a flyer's speed.

A flier's maximum speed is governed by the ratio of strength to weight in the vessel's hull. One-man flyers fitted with this fuel-less engine reach speeds in excess of two thousand haads per zode or three hundred miles per hour. Helium's scientists and aeronautical engineers are engaged in research to determine how to attain the greatest strength with the minimum of weight in the design of airship hulls. Their inquiries have seen numerous expeditions sent out across Barsoom in search of new materials for the construction of models and prototypes. Other red Martian cities regard Helium's air superiority with envy. Spies and infiltrators, especially from Toonol and Zodanga, constantly probe for weaknesses in the city's security to learn the secret of the new motors. On more than one occasion, Helium's forces have embarked on a frantic pursuit across the dead sea bottoms to reclaim stolen plans.

In addition to whatever decorative silks or flags they may bear, all ships carry identification lights, banners, or pennons, usually proclaiming their city of origin and the family of the ship's captain. It is not unusual, however, for ships to run under false colors to deceive enemies or pass unmolested through hostile territory. As a result, most red Martian city-states run air-patrols that will challenge approaching airships and seek clarification of their purpose and intent.

In structure, fliers vary considerably, though the majority of smaller vessels are built with skeel wood hulls and decks. Sorapus wood is used for cabins and upper works. Carborundum-aluminum, a light alloy, is used extensively in Martian fighting ships.

The smallest one-man air scouts are little more than a skeel wood deck over a thin metal hull containing the eighth ray. Sixteen sofads long, two wide, and three sofs thick, these delicate vessels are particularly vulnerable to ground fire. The pilot is either seated or lies on the deck behind a windshield.

Like the scouts, two- and three-man fliers have windshields rather than cockpits or cabins. Buoyancy tanks occupy all the below-deck space. For safety, the crew attach themselves to metal rings fixed to the deck using their harness hooks. Low metal handrails surmounting the gunwales provide further protection from falling overboard. The First Born favored such vessels until the destruction of their religion in the Prince of Helium era.

The patrol boats found in most red Martian cities follow the design of the ten-man cruisers operating in the navies of several city-states. Bulkier in structure, these vessels are equipped with a steel prow, rapid-fire radium guns in the bow, and cabins of sorapus constructed on their skeel decks. The patrol boats are all outfitted with horns and bulky searchlights.

Larger cruisers with crews of thirty to fifty men are also in service. These are fitted with radium guns fore and aft and three to four guns to port and starboard. Bomb traps (in bow and stern), the magazines, the galley, crew quarters, and storage areas occupy the hull space below deck.

Battleships are the largest aerial vessels seen over Barsoom. Rising in multiple decks, their upper works bristle with gun batteries set amongst observation platforms, firing positions, and command posts. Below decks, the magazines, bomb bays, crew and officers' quarters are built around the multiple propeller shafts, engines, and vast buoyancy tanks required to lift such massive airships. Most are armed with stern and bow guns, heavy batteries with wireless finding and sighting to port and starboard, and lighter weapons on the upper decks. Many have bomb batteries in their hulls, which are used not only to bombard ground troops, but also to devastate other airships targeted from above. Each battleship carries a complement of five ten-man cruisers, ten five-man scouts, and one hundred one-man scouts. Together with their fearsome firepower, this makes them the most formidable weapon on Barsoom.

Less massive are the giant freighters and passenger liners that trade and communicate between the docks and landing stages of friendly Martian cities. For heroes wishing to travel quickly and covertly, freighters and liners provide countless compartments, nooks, and hideaways where they can conceal themselves. Alternatively, they can book passage in the guise of travelling merchants or civilians and arrive at their destination concealed by the disembarking crowd.

EQUILIBRIMOTORS

Available in most red Martian cities for rent or purchase, the equilibrimotor is an individual aerial mode of transport. It consists of a broad belt lined with pouches containing sufficient amounts of the eighth ray to render the wearer's body weightless. The buoyancy of the belt can be reduced by venting some of the eighth ray through the belt's main valve, or increased by purchasing pressurized vials of the eighth ray from belt merchants or suppliers.

Attached to the front of the belt is a control panel linked to the small radium motor fixed at the back. Strong, light wings are connected to the upper rim of the belt and these can be repositioned using the hand levers that alter their position.

The silence and stealth afforded by equilibrimotors mean that assassins, thieves, spies, and kidnappers favor them as a means of infiltration and escape. As a result, they cause considerable work for the air patrols of most cities. They are also used to drop troops on cities from hovering fliers, though this strategy is only used when the besieging forces wish to occupy the settlement or capture its inhabitants.

GROUND FLIERS

Ground fliers are the most common means of private transportation in many Martian cities, including Helium, Ptarth, and Gathol. Most wealthy families have at least one ground flier and nobles may have several. Less wealthy Martians tend to hire public fliers. Servants and slaves always sit with the driver.

In Marentina, the Okarian ground fliers only travel along roads of ochre vegetation cultured from the dead sea bottoms. Powered by a small propeller at the stern, the vehicles move on rubber-like gasbags filled with enough of the eighth ray to raise the flier yet still allow it traction on the close-cropped sward. The rear wheels are geared to the engine for steering. These ground fliers are the only means of artificial transportation in the Okar nation until Talu becomes Jeddak of the Okar at the start of the Jeddak of Jeddaks era.

Elsewhere, ground fliers operate terrestrially and aerially. They have a ceiling of approximately one hundred sofads, with a top speed of sixty haads per hour. Vehicles travel either on the ochre roads, or rise to overtake slower transports or cross lanes. North-south traffic has right of way, with east-west traffic rising over it at intersections using the runways leading to each junction. All traffic moves in one direction along any given avenue. Parking areas are located at regular intervals in buildings sixty sofads above the pavement. Underpasses provide pedestrians with the means to cross major junctions safely.

Public and private ground fliers enable Martians to move quickly and discreetly around their cities. The anonymity of the public fliers makes them the transport of choice for spies and assassins wishing to avoid local air patrols.

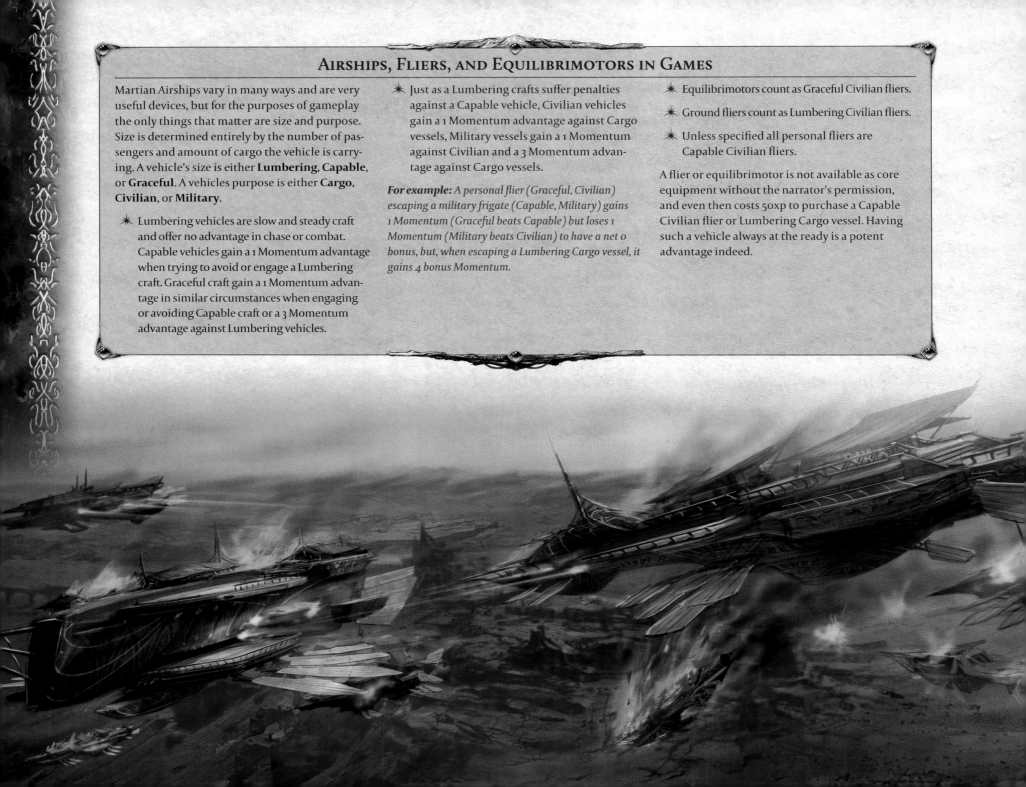

AIRSHIPS, FLIERS, AND EQUILIBRIMOTORS IN GAMES

Martian Airships vary in many ways and are very useful devices, but for the purposes of gameplay the only things that matter are size and purpose. Size is determined entirely by the number of passengers and amount of cargo the vehicle is carrying. A vehicle's size is either **Lumbering**, **Capable**, or **Graceful**. A vehicles purpose is either **Cargo**, **Civilian**, or **Military**.

* Lumbering vehicles are slow and steady craft and offer no advantage in chase or combat. Capable vehicles gain a 1 Momentum advantage when trying to avoid or engage a Lumbering craft. Graceful craft gain a 1 Momentum advantage in similar circumstances when engaging or avoiding Capable craft or a 3 Momentum advantage against Lumbering vehicles.

* Just as a Lumbering crafts suffer penalties against a Capable vehicle, Civilian vehicles gain a 1 Momentum advantage against Cargo vessels, Military vessels gain a 1 Momentum against Civilian and a 3 Momentum advantage against Cargo vessels.

For example: A personal flier (Graceful, Civilian) escaping a military frigate (Capable, Military) gains 1 Momentum (Graceful beats Capable) but loses 1 Momentum (Military beats Civilian) to have a net 0 bonus, but, when escaping a Lumbering Cargo vessel, it gains 4 bonus Momentum.

* Equilibrimotors count as Graceful Civilian fliers.

* Ground fliers count as Lumbering Civilian fliers.

* Unless specified all personal fliers are Capable Civilian fliers.

A flier or equilibrimotor is not available as core equipment without the narrator's permission, and even then costs 50xp to purchase a Capable Civilian flier or Lumbering Cargo vessel. Having such a vehicle always at the ready is a potent advantage indeed.

Experimental Vessels and Interplanetary Craft

Necessity and egocentricity often drive the incentive to produce unique and dangerous designs of airship, particularly in the Jeddak of Jeddaks era.

In an attempt to foil the schemes of the vengeful inventor Phor Tak, Tan Hadron of Hastor, and Nur An of Jahar designed the *Jhama*, a cylindrical vessel, pointed fore and aft, and fitted with a standard engine, making it no faster than a three-man flyer. Inside the *Jhama*'s outer hull is a cylindrical shell with the control cabin and quarters for four crew. The buoyancy tanks are located between the two hulls, and observation ports at the bow, stern, and along both sides pierce all three structural elements. These ports are shuttered on the outside and controlled from within. Hatches open onto a narrow walkway located along the upper surface of the cylinder. Disintegrating ray rifles are mounted fore and aft with a periscope giving the gunner an excellent view of anything coming within range of the guns. The ship is finished with a blue undercoat that protects it from the disintegrating ray rifles invented by Phor Tak and finished with a layer of the invisibility compound that bends light waves around the hull. Following Phor Tak's defeat, the *Jhama* was taken to Helium where it remains closely guarded.

In design, the *Jhama* is modeled on "The Flying Death", an aerial torpedo-like mine developed by Phor Tak to destroy the Jaharian fleet. The airships of Jahar were coated with the protective blue paint and equipped with the disintegrating ray rifles Phor Tak invented, originally for Jahar's ambitious jeddak, Tul Axtar. In an ironic twist, the torpedoes were attracted to the vibration frequency of the blue coating and target any ship it protects. The secret of the blue paint and The Flying Death may have gone to the grave with Phor Tak, but this is not certain. A servant may have taken the inventor's notes, or a hidden chamber may conceal the plans and formulae. The answers could lie in the ape-haunted corridors of *Jhama*, for anyone brave enough to risk the dangers.

Phor Tak's scientific eccentricity and egomania is not uncommon on Barsoom. During the Jeddak of Jeddaks era, Fal Sivas and Gar Nal, rival Zodangan inventors, exhibited similar traits in their competition to build Barsoom's first interplanetary craft and pillage the resources of Thuria.

In outward appearance and internal structure, both ships are almost indistinguishable as a result of the espionage conducted between their designers. Ellipsoidal in shape, with a bulbous bow tapering to a pointed stern, the ships are fifty sofads long and fifteen wide at the prow. A control room occupies the forward section of the ships and houses the complex mechanical and electrical systems for piloting the craft. From here, two crystal portholes provide views of the exterior world. Behind the control room are the crew cabins, more luxuriously appointed in Fal Sivas' craft. The storerooms, motors, oxygen- and water-generating systems, and temperature regulation controls are located in the stern. At full power, both ships can travel at speeds in excess of 3,250 haads per zode, or approximately 1,300 miles per hour.

These two craft differ in one important aspect: Fal Sivas' vessel is fitted with a mechanical brain, perfected through the vivisection of countless slaves. This brain is located above and between the view ports in the control room in a grapefruit-sized metal sphere. The brain has no capacity for independent thought, but governs the mechanical operations and autonomic functions of the ship's systems. Lenses in each of the two viewports relay visual information to the brain, which responds either automatically or as directed telepathically by the pilot. The brain also aims the ship's high-powered radium rifles when it enters combat.

The whereabouts of the two vessels is currently a subject of concern in Helium. After they returned from Thuria, both disappeared from Zodanga and have not been found. What new mischief might arise from Fal Sivas' ambition following the death of Gar Nal remains unclear.

Pneumatic Trains

The twin cities of Helium are unique on Barsoom, not least for their pneumatic train system. This remarkable feat of engineering uses conical-nosed, eight sofad long projectile-like caskets to transport passengers to their destinations at high speed along grooved tracks. Travelers purchase tickets from a station gatekeeper, locate their designated casket, and select their destination using the dial on its nose. They then lie down in the upholstered interior beneath the canopy where an attendant secures them in position. The casket accelerates slowly from the station before reaching supersonic speeds in the tunnels connecting each location. Most passengers are commercial or government commuters. The nobility and their servants and slaves rarely use the pneumatic system, which makes it useful for any aristocrat wishing to travel incognito.

Submarines

Until the Jeddak of Jeddaks era, submersible vessels are found only in the Omean Sea under the command of the First Born. These vessels are compact, torpedo-like oily-black objects containing little more than a command cabin, engine room, and stowage areas. With the fall of Issus and the collapse of the Martian religion centered on the Valley Dor, some of these vessels may have been piloted and taken overland into the red Martian irrigation system by disconsolate or resentful crews intent on piracy and revenge. Rumors are already beginning to circulate of strange, smooth-skinned beasts prowling the canals of Barsoom, and of shadowy figures haunting the margins of remote farmsteads. If such vessels are responsible, their crews could cause considerable panic and destruction along the Martian waterways. Brave heroes would earn considerable fame for exposing and ending such activities.

COMMUNICATION TECHNOLOGY

Although radio aerogram communication is possible between Barsoom's cities and ships, such technology is never used during wartime and only rarely employed in moments of peace. Martian code-breakers are so efficient in decrypting the newest and most elaborate cyphers that covert transmissions are almost impossible. Military commanders fear a loss of surprise, freighter captains dread air piracy, and the crews of passenger liners worry their airships will be victims of indiscriminate attacks. As a result, there is little electronic communication across Barsoom, leaving the airship as the major mode of personal and written interaction on the planet. The single exception is the use of photographic facsimile transmissions, which are employed within and between most Martian cities for recording and inspecting the identity of citizens and visitors. Photostatic devices are also publicly available in the Temple of Knowledge in most red Martian cities. These enable copies to be made of the temple's texts and scrolls.

Given the restrictions acting on wireless communication on Barsoom, it is perhaps unsurprising that Martians have turned their attention outwards to the other planets in the Solar System. Martian astronomical instruments, wireless photography, and wireless telephony have all been applied to monitor life on Jasoom and other worlds. Many Martians now speak Urdu, English, Russian and Chinese. However, it was not until Jason Gridley's discovery of the Gridley Wave in 1930 that two-way communication between Earth and Mars using Morse Code was possible. The precise social, cultural, and military effects on Barsoom of such monitoring and communication have yet to be felt.

BIOLOGICAL SCIENCES

In addition to airship design and communications, Martian expertise excels in the biosciences. The origins of that excellence lie in the ancient past when Barsoom's five vast oceans were the major means of trade across the planet. Among the Orovars of the city of Horz, Lee Um Lo distinguished himself as an embalmer of unparalleled renown. So great were his skills that those he embalmed still considered themselves among the living. Many of Lee Um Lo's subjects remained inert and undisturbed in the pits of Horz until the Jeddak of Jeddaks era, providing sustenance for Lum Tar O, a cowardly contemporary of Lee Um Lo whom he had embalmed. When John Carter killed Lum Tar O and woke the sleepers, they disintegrated on exposure to the realities of modern Barsoom.

It is possible that what the Orovars considered embalming was in fact a sophisticated form of suspended animation, administered in the moments before death to permit the subject's body an extended period of time to heal itself. Many of those interred beneath Horz were in their prime, untroubled by illness or injury, and were seemingly 'embalmed' for no other reason than to feed Lum Tar O.

Lee Um Lo's techniques remain a mystery, however, known in part to few modern Martians. Nevertheless, other caches of sleeping Orovars may exist elsewhere on Mars, either beneath the dead cities or in undiscovered rocky chambers in Barsoom's mountain ranges. They may hold the answer to Lee Um Lo's strange art. No doubt there are Martian factions eager to discover such groups for what they might also know of Mars' ancient history and of arcane knowledge lost in time and dust. Enterprising heroes will have little difficulty in being recruited for perilous expeditions in search of the secrets of the Orovars.

It is likely that Hin Abtol, the ambitious jed of Panar, knew something of Lee Um Lo's practices since he used a crude form of suspended animation to keep a standing army of a million men frozen in the ice around his capital. The true

successor to Lee Um Lo, however, is Ras Thavas, the arrogant, detached Mastermind of Mars. Ras Thavas advanced Martian biological science in two significant areas: longevity through transplant surgery — including brain transference — and the propagation of vat-grown synthetic life.

The transference of brains from one subject to another is an intricate process used to provide an aging or endangered brain with a young or undamaged body. The first stage involves the withdrawing of all blood from both subjects. This is replaced with a specially prepared embalming fluid that prevents decay without damaging the nerve or tissue structures of the body. The second stage is the removal and transfer of the brains, the reconnection of severed nerves and ganglia, and the sealing of the wounds with an anesthetic and antiseptic healing tape. The withdrawn blood is then treated with a revitalizing agent, rewarmed, and transferred to the body containing the corresponding brain. This revitalizing agent restores healthy function to all of the body's organs and systems. Should the surgeon wish not to reanimate one of the subjects, the embalming fluid will preserve the body and the withdrawn blood can be stored for later revivification.

Later in his career, Ras Thavas pioneered a technique for growing Synthetic Men — Hormads — in culture laboratories in the city of Morbus in the Toonolian Marshes. Although most of these deformed creatures were of low intelligence, some were as intelligent as most Martians. Following a coup by the Hormads and their almost complete destruction by John Carter and the air-fleet from Helium, Ras Thavas has taken residence in the Twin Cities and dedicated his genius to more benign research. However, his dispassionate nature and restless mind will lead him down dark and dangerous avenues. John Carter and Helium may yet regret pardoning Ras Thavas for his earlier experiments. Statistics for the Hormads appear in Chapter 13.

CHAPTER 6: GROWING YOUR LEGEND

> *It is strange how new and unexpected conditions bring out unguessed ability to meet them.*
> – John Carter, *The Warlord of Mars*

Player characters in *John Carter of Mars* gain power and influence in two ways: through experience and renown. Experience is how a character gains new talents, increases attributes, and generally becomes a stronger warrior, diplomat, hunter, or whatever their personal calling. Renown represents fame and influence gained during a character's adventures. It is used to acquire new allies, titles, and other social and political advantages.

Essentially, experience represents internal character growth and renown represents how the character grows as a part of the setting. At the end of each adventure, player characters will receive both experience and renown based on what they have learned and how their actions have impacted the world as a whole. These amounts are often tied to each other, with dangerous and dramatic adventures providing sizable experience and renown. However, it is possible an obscure adventure in the wilds of Barsoom may be great for experience but provide little renown. Conversely, a powerful player character might manage to conquer a foe relatively easily but in doing so gain a great amount of notoriety. Still, these rare adventures are outliers — generally the bigger the danger and obstacles, the greater the gains in both experience and renown.

EXPERIENCE

Experience is awarded by the narrator at the end of every adventure and represents how much a character has personally struggled and what potential they may unlock through adversity. Characters use experience to purchase new talents, change their flaws, gain core equipment, and improve attributes.

The costs for advancing your character through experience are provided on the following chart:

UPGRADE	XP COST
Add a talent	5xp per grade of talent
Change a flaw	10xp per change
Increase one of your attributes a first time	10xp
Increase one of your attributes a second time	20xp
Increase one of your attributes a third time	40xp*
Add a piece of core equipment (hand held)	5xp Per item

Every additional increase doubles this cost

Experience is generally awarded at the end of every session or adventure, depending on the preferences of the narrator. The methods of awarding experience vary with each narrator as well. Some prefer to give all player characters the same amount of experience. Others prefer to hand out awards for great roleplaying or particularly effective uses of talents and other abilities.

A good general guideline is to give players 1-3 experience per session. The end of an adventure or major campaign or story arc typically provides a bonus of additional experience, usually 3-5, though grand adventures and major campaigns may award even more.

Awarding additional experience causes characters to grow faster, which can be fun. It can also unbalance the game. Likewise, awarding too little experience can stagnate characters, making them feel like they never learn anything or improve. Narrators are cautioned to keep an eye on how quickly characters are developing and adjust experience awards as necessary. As a general guideline, it is usually better to give a bit too much than too little.

If periods of extended downtime occur during a game session, the narrator may award experience for an adventure so far and allow players to spend it at that time. This is a good way to represent periods of training and development. However, as characters in *John Carter* tend to change somewhat slowly and usually only through active and dramatic conflict, it is not required.

CHANGING YOUR FLAW

Over time a character may learn from mistakes or have a substantial change to their destiny or position that alters their character's flaw. An **Overconfident** character may finally learn he cannot handle every situation, or a character given to **Romantic Flights of Fancy** may adopt a more realistic outlook after some tragedy or other life-changing event.

Through their experience and by spending experience, a character can change their flaw. However, there are two conditions. First, they cannot remove a flaw, they can only exchange it for another. Second, there must be a valid and significant reason during play to motivate this change. The character does not one day suddenly wake up and decide to change their ways, this change must make sense based on how the character is played, their experiences, and events of past adventures.

Note that changing a character's flaw is fairly rare in the Carter stories, but it may be more frequent in *John Carter* campaigns. Also, a narrator may elect to let you change your flaw without charging experience if situations arising through play demand it, such as your character going through a serious loss or triumph that changes their outlook or destiny.

RENOWN

As noted earlier, renown represents the social impact, reputation, fame, and political power characters gain through their actions. In addition to providing a general guideline as to how famous a character and his exploits are on Barsoom, renown is also a character advancement resource that can be used to purchase allies, titles, and other useful representations of their fame and reputation collectively known in the game as accolades.

STARTING RENOWN

All player characters start with renown which they can spend during character generation. Even beginning characters in *John Carter of Mars* are usually socially well-connected or exceptional in some way. They may have a respected title or rank, or they may begin with several close allies, but they are not alone or unknown even in their earliest adventures on Barsoom. Earthborn characters are the exception; they start with no renown. No matter how famous they may be on Earth, on Barsoom no one knows or respects them until they prove themselves worthy through their actions.

By default, all player characters aside from Earthborn ones start with 10 renown.

GAINING RENOWN DURING PLAY

Renown is gained as a reward for great deeds witnessed by others. Even enemies who survive encounters with a character will one day relate tales which grow their renown. Saving large groups of people, rescuing important dignitaries, defeating fearsome enemies, or uncovering great secrets and lost treasures will gain a character renown.

Renown gains can be delayed by the narrator if no one other than the player characters witness a heroic or exceptional deed or exploit. However, eventually people will find out about the great things a character accomplished and they will receive renown for their actions.

Most adventures that make the player characters look good, skilled, or effective grant them 1 renown. If they do something truly exceptional or heroic, they gain an additional 1 renown. In some rare cases, such as saving a whole nation, ending or preventing a great war, or destroying an apocalyptic threat, they may gain even more renown. Acting dishonorably or villainously can often reduce or even eliminate renown rewards.

Note that until people are aware of their exceptional might and other abilities, Earthborn characters tend to gain a few extra renown as they leap and bound through their early adventures on Barsoom. This helps them mitigate some of the renown they lack in the beginning.

Example: After defeating a plot by a cabal of Holy Therns to replace a popular jeddak with a more devout and tractable ruler, the player characters each gain renown for their actions. Because discovering and defeating the Therns was both difficult and culminated in a high-profile battle in the jeddak's great hall, the narrator awards each character 2 renown. However, he grants the Earthborn characters, Jane Porter and Kale Singh, 1 additional renown as their exceptional strength and strange ways makes their heroism especially noteworthy. He also grants an additional renown to Haren Phel, who took a blow meant for the jeddak and nearly died doing so. Conversely, he reduces the award for Volan Von by 1 renown, as he refused an offer to duel a Holy Thern swordsman and shot the villain instead. While this action helped end the threat, it is in defiance of standard Martian codes of honor and thus, Volan's action hurts his overall reputation somewhat.

Unspent Renown

Unspent renown does not go away, it remains until a player uses it to purchase something for his character. In fact, characters and narrators will want to keep an eye on a character's total renown (spent and unspent) as it gives a general idea how famous a character is.

Characters trying to travel in disguise in areas where they are well-known find difficulties to do so raised by 1, more in places they frequent. Characters may also spend 1 Momentum in such areas to have an admirer recognize them. What they do with that recognition is up to them, but this individual is favorably disposed to being helpful in minor ways. For characters of lesser renown this means being recognized in your home district in a city or among a small tribe. For the most famous faces on Barsoom, this means there is nowhere they can go without a chance of being discovered! Such is the price of fame.

Unspent renown can also be used in place of Momentum to secure assistance temporarily during an adventure. Often a narrator allows characters to spend Momentum to gain additional insight or assistance in the form of useful information, the sudden appearance of an ally, or other types of "dramatic editing" to a scene. Unspent renown can be spent in place of Momentum to accomplish the same thing. Renown spent is returned at the end of the session it is used.

TOTAL RENOWN	REPUTATION AND EFFECTS
0-9	Obscure and unknown, reduce all difficulties to disguise yourself or travel unrecognized by 1.
10-20	Known in some circles or regions. No modifiers.
21-35	Known in your city or immediate region but generally unknown elsewhere.
36-50	Famous in your city or immediate region and known to your homeland's neighbors and rivals.
51-60	Famous in your entire nation and among its closest allies and enemies. Well-known in more remote lands with regular contact with these places.
61-75	Among the great heroes, jeddaks, and other champions of Barsoom. Known across most of the planet, save isolated enclaves and faraway lands.
76+	One of the most famous faces on Barsoom, like the great John Carter. Likely a jed or jeddak with many allies. Recognized by name or reputation everywhere on Barsoom.

OPTIONAL RULE: RENOWN USE DISCOUNTS

Narrators who want to encourage players to spend renown in play to secure aid can offer a discount on permanent renown purchases when renown is temporarily spent to achieve an in-play effect. A 1 renown discount is usually sufficient. This means that characters will more often make allies and friends of those they meet, or gain titles from those they already have excellent relations with during play, but it might require a bit of extra bookkeeping, so it is optional.

SHARING RENOWN

Player characters often only gain 1 renown at a time, but if they gain 2 renown or more for a particularly noteworthy deed, they can choose to grant one of their renown to another character. This represents the character humbly downplaying their own accomplishments and praising those of others. This altruistic act has no direct effect, but it can have long-term or significant effects during a campaign.

Sharing renown is meant to enable fun roleplaying situations and allow particular characters their unique moments and triumphs through play. If this leads to quibbling over renown, player conflicts, or other problems during play, feel free to ignore it.

Example: During an adventure where the player characters save a beloved jeddak from certain death, preventing a civil war, each of them is awarded 3 renown. However, realizing their friend Zala Zors wishes to marry the jeddak's son whom she fell in love with during the adventure, Kale, Volan, Haren, and Jane all downplay their own heroism and each grant Zala 1 of their earned renown. With 7 new renown (3 she earned and 1 each from four other player characters), Zala now has 7 additional renown and has greatly impressed the jeddak, his family, and the people of his nation. She uses this renown to help purchase a title within the jeddak's nation, representing the position she gains when she weds the prince at the beginning of the next session. The other player characters gain less renown because of their humility, but one of their own gains significant power and influence in exchange.

TRAVELING IN DISGUISE

Characters in the John Carter novels often protect themselves in strange lands by concealing their identity. This is useful when some villain has sworn to kill you when you meet, but makes it difficult to use the advantages your renown brings.

When traveling in disguise, characters cannot take advantage of their renown or any accolades they have purchased with it. They also cannot spend any of their existing renown.

However, they can still gain renown through their actions and may, if they desire, spend that for their false identity. This is how John Carter himself sometimes would earn a position or title in a foreign land while posing as a panthan or mundane traveler.

Of course, eventually a character's disguise will end and they will return to their real identity, revealing to all around the heroic adventurer they truly are. When this happens, renown purchases either transfer or are refunded, depending on what makes the most sense. Any unspent renown is added to the character's regular renown total.

Narrators and players alike should note these rules can be a bit fiddly, requiring the tracking of two different amounts of renown and accolades. Some groups may wish to avoid these rules, simply freezing all renown awards and uses until the disguise is revealed. In this case, narrators should still track renown gains to be awarded later once word gets around who the character really was.

ACCOLADES

Renown can generally be used to purchase accolades. Accolades are social or political advantages falling into two major categories: allies and titles. The following section details these accolades, what they do, and how much renown they generally cost. In addition, individual accolades distinct to certain groups or locations are found in various entries in the chapters describing the world of Barsoom.

ALLIES

Allies are groups or influential individuals the character can call on when they need assistance. Allies are often members of the same family or organization as the character, but this need not always be the case. After all, John Carter himself regularly makes allies of individuals from various races and cultures. Not all allies are even necessarily humanoid or sentient — an excessively talented and loyal beast may be an ally as well.

Allies are also how characters represent heroic or positive reputations within a particular group when they possess no particular position or title (for those, *see Titles*) with that group. Thus, a character who saves a fleet of Helium navy airships may take the Helium navy as allies, even if he holds no official naval rank. He also may take just the commanders and crews of those ships as allies, which would be less useful but also cost less renown to acquire.

Note that allies can be lost through death or if a character severely mistreats them or abuses their trust. Allies lost through misadventure and calamity are often eventually replaced with characters of similar backgrounds, history, or temperament; those lost by a character's own evil acts rarely are so replenished.

Generally, a group of allies will be no larger than a mercenary company, ship's crew, or similar band of half a dozen to fifty or so individuals. Having the favor of groups much larger is either significantly more expensive or involves purchasing titles instead (*see Titles*). Allies often have their own followers, titles, or resources they can bring to help a character. However, remember these things come to a player character indirectly through the ally and, because of this, may come with their own complications and limitations. After all, a jedwar may order some of his soldiers to aid a character, but that does not mean they will always follow the character unquestioningly or even enthusiastically.

In addition to seeking out allies for help, they may show up to aid a character if Momentum is spent. How much Momentum it takes for an ally to show up and help depends on how much aid they bring and how difficult or unlikely it would be for them to show up to offer assistance. It may only cost 1 Momentum for a jed to show up to render aid outside his city gates, but to have that same jed mount a rescue mission halfway across Barsoom would be much more expensive.

Example: John Carter has the First Born Dator Xodar as an ally and wishes his ally to assist him when his airship is shot down near Xodar's homeland in Omean. As Carter is near to Xodar's home base and the First Born has access to his own airships, the narrator says it will only cost 2 Momentum for Carter's ally to send a ship to pick him up. If Carter had been shot down in the arctic wastes of the north far from Xodar's realm or taken prisoner and locked away somewhere hard to reach, it would have been considerably more expensive.

Narrators can also decide certain allies are unable to assist a character at a particular time. This can be due to time, distance, or even some problem of which the characters are not yet aware. If your ally has been imprisoned by a rival or is seriously injured, he obviously cannot come to your aid. In fact, seeking out allies who previously failed to come to your assistance and finding them in peril is a great way to start a new adventure!

Cost: The exact cost of an ally depends on how skilled and connected they are. Allies that can regularly lend large numbers of troops or other resources to a character cost additional renown.

⁕ An ally that is either personally exceptional due to abilities and training or politically connected costs 2 renown.

⁕ An ally who is a powerful or otherwise exceptional beast costs 3 renown.

⁕ An ally that is politically connected and personally exceptional costs 4 renown.

⁕ An ally that has a band of soldiers, a single airship, or similar resources characters can make use of usually costs 1 additional renown.

⁕ An ally can have a company of soldiers, several airships, or similar resources for 2 more renown.

⁕ An ally can have an army, navy, or other vast resources for 4 renown.

Example: A heroic young officer or loyal gladiator a character meets on their adventures would be a fine 2 renown ally. If it turns out he is also a lost prince of a kingdom, he would be worth 4 renown. If it turns out he is the jed of a nearby nation and his father is the jeddak, giving him access to considerable resources? He is worth 6 or more renown.

Specific Versus General Allies

As noted earlier, allies can be defined as an individual of some importance or a whole group. Both are permissible and useful allies, though in practice they work a bit differently. Having an ally that is a single person, even one who brings other people and resources with them, provides the character with a person who will go to great lengths to assist them. However, this person may not always be available or in a position to assist the character. Such allies also require a more personal relationship be maintained and valued by the character lest they become alienated.

By contrast, an ally defined as a larger group has more diverse resources and availability but less focus. Their assistance usually takes longer to acquire and is often less enthusiastic and invested. A group may provide ample supplies, information, and even troops and transportation to a character they see as a great friend, but they will not spend months or even years seeking to save, aid, or otherwise assist their ally.

Example: An ally who is a loyal Thark chieftain will fight and even die for the character who is their friend. This ally costs 4 renown, as he is skilled and influential. If this ally can regularly lend the services of his

warband of Tharks he would cost 6 renown. However, when this chieftain is absent, wounded, or otherwise occupied, the character cannot gain as much aid as when his friend is present.

By contrast, an ally in the form of the whole Thark warband is also worth 4 renown, more if they are willing to lend the character Thark warriors or other potent resources on a regular basis. Any Thark of that band would see the character as a friend and give him some assistance, but none are pledged to follow, serve, or defend him as a personal ally like the Thark chieftain.

These differences tend to balance out in play, which is why there is no additional charge for specific or general allies, you simply pay for their capabilities and what extra resources they may provide the character, though doing so usually does make general allies; such as ruling families, armies, and other major groups, more expensive. It is allowable and even expected for characters to purchase allies of both general and specific types that overlap, though it may be more cost effective in some cases to purchase a title instead.

Allies Changing Power and Influence

Sometimes allies may increase or decrease in power. A jed may become a jeddak, a jeddak may abdicate in favor of his daughter or son, or the leader of a nation, army, or organization may see their group rise or fall in influence. If these changes happen in play as a direct result of player character action, there is no change in the renown cost of the ally. They are simply a natural consequence of play.

However, if these changes are a result of narrator fiat or a player wishing his ally to become more powerful without enabling their rise in station, then either the player is refunded the difference between the ally's old and new value (in the case of a decrease) or they must pay the difference between the old and new value (in the case of an increase). In other words, the cheapest way to make allies more powerful is to go out and help them rise in prominence and influence, but the quickest way is to just spend renown, meaning they have found their own avenues of advancement. The latter method is not necessary arbitrary; it simply represents how associating with daring heroes like the character has freed up time and opened opportunities for the ally to advance while off on their own.

Narrators, as a rule, should rarely decrease the value of an ally without giving player characters allied with them a chance to prevent this effect. However, sometimes a decrease is logical or necessary due to events in the campaign. When this occurs, player characters with such diminished allies get the renown spent returned to reinvest in a new accolade.

OPTIONAL RULE:
OUT OF YOUR ELEMENT

If a campaign begins with a character in a situation and location that would render an accolade largely ineffective or even a hindrance, the narrator may allow the character to purchase the renown for less than its normal cost. This allows a character to begin with an accolade they could not usually afford, such as the jeddak of a nation, or having both a respectable title and a very strong ally. However, this discount comes with a price. They cannot reach or access this accolade early on in any direct way until they repay the discount with renown earned during play. They may still benefit from the existence of the general accolade, but they cannot draw upon it directly in any meaningful way. With this option, you can even begin as a jeddak of a great nation with great potential power, but you are going to spend many adventures in exile, believed dead by most of your people or otherwise unable to take advantage of the prime benefits of your accolade.

This option is of most use when a character begins play as a captive, hostage, or is for some reason very far from home when a campaign starts.

TITLES

Titles are the most direct translation of renown into tangible benefit, providing a position of respect and access to the resources of a group or institution. Titles are earned ranks or hereditary positions that provide the character with both position and responsibility. Membership in the group that grants the title is implicit in gaining it; you are considered to be part of the nation, tribe, or organization that grants you rank and position among them. A title can give characters authority and access to groups with powerful resources. However, titles also come with the expectation of service or sworn allegiance. Betraying a group with whom you hold a title is a great way to lose it.

Titles may be official or unofficial, noble or professional, but they all work in essentially the same way. Every title conveys four things:

✴ A general rank in a group or society, such as dwar or jeddak.

✴ Membership in that group, such as the Helium Navy or the Kingdom of Okar.

✴ Resources that membership and rank grant the character access to, such as the ability to requisition troops, equipment, and secure sensitive information.

✴ Responsibility to the group to serve their interests loyally and faithfully, including protecting fellow members and commanding with integrity and skill when called to.

Most of the benefits of a title are common sense. However, there are also some direct mechanical benefits. When a character is dealing socially with a character in the same organization or group whom they outrank, they gain a bonus die in all social-based actions and conflicts. The same bonus applies when attempting to gain the respect or mercy of an enemy or rival. A jeddak of a rival nation may not help you, but they are less likely to kill you casually if they realize you are an important enemy, and thus a useful hostage or source of intelligence! In this case, any title equal to or above dwar (captain) will provide such a bonus, not simply a superior one.

Titles are also often impressive, lowering the difficulty of actions involving convincing someone of your importance or authority. In general, even if a title does not provide a bonus, it will have some effect on the difficulty of a social-based contest. Note that, at times, this may be an increase in difficulty, such as trying to convince a foe to release you when they know you are a valuable member of a rival's ruling class or military hierarchy. In some cases, a title might even grant a bonus die to your opponent in an opposed test, though these circumstances should be rare.

Example: Dejah Thoris, Princess of Helium, is trying to convince a Zodangan jedwar to release her after he has captured Thoris' airship in a raid. Dejah's title as Princess of Helium would provide her a bonus to convince the enemy jedwar to let her live or send word of her capture to her family. It might even reduce the difficulty for her to charm or seduce the jedwar into letting his guard down. However, attempting to demand her release from an enemy who stands to gain much fame and profit from her capture is highly unlikely, raising the difficulty of such tests and granting the jedwar a bonus die on any opposed test Dejah attempts to secure her release.

A character may also spend Momentum to immediately acquire the use of resources appropriate to their title. The exact cost depends on the circumstances. Getting a couple of guards to accompany a princess in her own palace is a 1 Momentum spend. Finding loyal cohorts in a rival city costs much more, and may, at the narrator's discretion, be impossible. The more resources a character wishes to use, the more Momentum they must spend.

Example: Dejah Thoris has escaped from her Zodangan captor and is hiding in a settlement on the Helium-Zodanga border. She wishes to find some loyal Heliumites to assist her in eluding her captors and getting back home. Given the distance from the capital and risk involved to any who aid her, the narrator charges her 3 Momentum to secure a few former Helium soldiers who remember their princess fondly and will hide her and defend her. If she wishes more citizens to assist her or seeks to borrow an airship to escape, it will cost her more Momentum. However, if she only desired a brief hiding place for a single night or a lone long-retired soldier to aid her, she might purchase that for 1 Momentum.

Cost: Title cost varies greatly based on what the title is and how large a group it covers. The cost of military rank in a kingdom's navy, for example, varies based on the size and power of the kingdom and the actual rank held. For the exact cost of a particular title, check the table to the right. These titles can also be used as a basis for unique titles created by narrators to honor and award characters during play.

The basic costs here assume that whatever group grants the title has modest resources, responsibilities, and reach: a small nation, a medium-sized army, a modest-sized guild or institution, or an active and large group of mercenaries or raiders. If a group that grants the title is particularly powerful or far-reaching, the title costs more. Generally, a title involving a large nation, powerful military force, or far reaching organization costs 1 and 5 extra renown from the base cost depending on just how influential and powerful the group or nation is. Likewise, if a group is exceptionally weak then the cost goes down between 1 and 5 renown. Thus, being a prince of Helium costs substantially more renown as it is more generally useful than being prince of a lost nation in a remote corner of Barsoom that has dwindled down to a few hundred subjects. Increased or decreased responsibilities from the normal for a position also affect the renown cost, such as a prince or princess who is far down the line of succession or a retired officer with no active duties or assignment.

Green Martian Titles

While green Martian tribes and hordes use major titles like jeddak and jedwar, they can sometimes be a bit looser with lower titles. However, green Martian characters can purchase most titles and define them as being an equivalent rank or position in their horde. Thus, even if a horde does not have teedwars, a green Martian character could still purchase the title defined as being a great sub-chieftain of the horde with many warriors under his command. Also, green Martians have no princes or princesses — their methods of childrearing prevent this.

Honorary and Former Titles

Honorary ranks in a command with few responsibilities usually cancel each other out in terms of benefits and disadvantages, costing the same as an active title. It is generally harder to secure real and effective aid, but little is expected of you. Likewise, being a retired member of a group is similarly balanced. You do not have much active power, but you are deeply respected, even by many of your superiors.

Promotions and Title Changes

Titles can be replaced as well as acquired. If characters impress their superiors or a ruler they are in line to replace abdicates or resigns, they may acquire a new, more expensive title by paying the difference between the two titles in renown.

In the rare instance that a character loses a title due to circumstances unrelated to their actions, they will receive the renown spent. This is usually part of some larger plot or adventure, and if this loss is intended to be temporary (such as a coup that the player characters are expected to put down in a coming adventure), a narrator does not need to refund the renown spent provided it still has some use.

COST/TITLE	DESCRIPTION
40: Jeddak / Jeddara	Leader of a nation, horde, or city state. Akin to an emperor or king. Have serious responsibilities of position and office.
20: Jed	Leader of a city or settlement that is part of a greater nation or horde. Akin to a lesser king, duke or baron. Numerous responsibilities.
10: Prince / Princess	Member of the royal or ruling family of a nation or city-state. Usually has fewer responsibilities but less defined authority than more formalized ranks.
8: Chieftain	Noble, equivalent to an Earth duke or baron. Part of an influential family or faction with holdings and responsibilities accordant to their station. Often used by the Tharks and other green Martians.
15: Jedwar	Great leader within a city-state or nation. Also known as lord-officer or marshal. Great responsibilities, but generally a fair amount of freedom.
12: Odwar	A general or commander of an army or armada. Serious responsibility to your troops as well as to your superiors, but high degree of personal discretion.

COST/TITLE	DESCRIPTION
8: Teedwar	A major, commands a battalion or a major warship with escorts. Responsible for your junior officers and troops, responsible to your superiors.
5: Dwar	A captain of a ship, company, or similar group. Very responsible for those under your command and must obey superiors, but some freedom of action.
2: Padwar	Lieutenant, commands a small group of soldiers or serves under a dwar of a ship as an officer. Moderate and well-defined responsibilities when on duty.
0: Than	Lowest rank of navy or army.
10: Dator	Prince of the First Born. Unique title to First Born nations.
5: Master / Mistress	Leader or high-ranking member of a guild, such as the assassin's guild.
2: Guildsman / Guildswoman	Member of a guild, such as the assassin's guild.

Example: The nation of Ptarth is overthrown by a rebellious jed. During this time, Thuvia, Princess of Ptarth, is not officially a princess of her homeland. However, as this development is part of an upcoming adventure and she still has the support of many loyalists among her nation during her time in temporary exile, she does not receive any renown spent on her title back. During this time she is still considered Princess of Helium, as she is currently married to Carthoris, Prince of Helium.

SPECIAL ITEMS AND RENOWN

Some readers may feel the ability to purchase special or unique items as character rewards with renown is missing from the accolades. This makes sense if you consider various stories or adventure set-ups where the daring heroes save the day and are rewarded with a magic sword or shiny medal, thanked profusely, and then they leave never to see those who heaped these rewards upon them again.

John Carter stories are different. Barsoomians are deeply honorable people, slow to trust and deeply committed to those they choose as their allies and companions. A jeddak may give a beautifully crafted sword to a warrior who served his people, but he will also *always* pledge some favor, offer some title, or arrange some other lasting and socially-oriented reward. A First Born ship's captain may give a red Martian princess who saves his ship a strange artifact he discovered and could never quite figure out the use for, but he will also consider her an ally or honorary member of his crew from that day forward.

Narrators should consider physical rewards for successful adventures or as gifts from allies or luminaries the player characters win over during their adventures. However, these treasures are not purchased with renown, they are side-effects of the heroism and bold actions that win the characters' respect, admiration, and advancement.

USING RENOWN TO CHANGE BARSOOM

Player characters can and should use renown and accolades to change life on Barsoom. Purchasing the right allies when holding certain titles creates lasting unions, alliances, and political shifts larger than the characters themselves. Allies linked by player characters may become friends and companions themselves, changing how whole groups and factions relate to each other. This is how John Carter unified much of Mars, through winning friends and influencing people.

Narrators should take note and keep track of the player characters' accolades for this reason, and so should the player characters. If allies are ignored and the responsibilities that come with titles neglected, things can go badly very quickly. On the other hand, if these things are nurtured and promoted, both the player characters and the characters, groups, and locales important to them will prosper and flourish. They may even unify or change in significant ways.

Example: Over time, Mark's player character Tormin has become a dwar of a famed panthan (mercenary) fleet and gained allies among various groups, including Jeddak Kulan Tith of the red Martian nation of Kaol and a roguish pirate known as Saja Min who commands several airships. After Tormin calls on Saja to transport his company on a mission to save Kaol from invasion, the pirate queen makes a positive impression on the jeddak. Sometime after the adventure, Tith makes an offer to Saja Min, offering her status as a privateer using Kaol as a home base, a move which bolsters Kaol's fledgling airship navy. When Tormin next visits his friend Kulan Tith, he finds Saja Min is now odwar of the nation's growing fleet of privateers. Without Tormin bringing these two forces together, this situation would have never developed.

This is also how the player characters take control of their own destinies on Barsoom. After a time, adventures and entire campaign arcs will center around the accolades they acquire through play. In this way, adventure begets more adventure, play enables more play.

SECTION 3

CHAPTER 7: HISTORY OF BARSOOM

As I gazed upon it I felt a spell of overpowering fascination – it was Mars, the god of war, and for me, the fighting man, it had always held the power of irresistible enchantment.
– John Carter, *A Princess of Mars*

Barsoom, called Mars by Earthborn humans, is the fourth planet. According to the Earthborn, it has a day which lasts 24 hours and 39 minutes (1 padan), and it completes a solar orbit in just over 685 Earth days (1 ord). Despite its distance from the sun, Barsoom is generally a hot planett. The temperature ranges from the low 100 degrees Fahrenheit during the day and plummets to 32 degrees Fahrenheit and below at night. Because of the thin atmosphere, Barsoom doesn't experience twilight as Earth does; dusk is more akin to switching off a light bulb, with day suddenly being plunged into night, and the reverse at dawn. Much of this information about the Red Planet is accurate, but, despite this, the denizens of Earth know so little of this world.

Barsoom was once largely covered with water, now the vast majority of those shallow oceans are dry, leaving huge expanses of lichen-covered basins stretching across the landscape. Low hills mark the boundary where the seas once met the land. In protected valleys there remains some standing water, taking the form of muddy marshes, swamps, and even forests.

Rain is completely unknown, making the air rather dry except within certain deep valleys and around the few remaining examples of standing water. Even here, the best precipitation one is likely to find is a light, low fog over the water, which quickly burns away in the harsh, unforgiving sunlight.

Ice can be found in the frozen polar caps, but these are much smaller than those found on Earth. Also in the south polar region can be found the Lost Sea of Korus, the only known large body of water on the surface of Barsoom. The Korus is one of the bodies of water that is drawn by pumping stations to be delivered by canals to the rest of the planet.

Barsoom has two moons. Thuria, the nearer moon, orbits the planet approximately every 5 zodes (11 hours), rising in the west and racing across the sky to set in the east approximately 2 zodes (4.5 hours) later. Cluros, the further moon, has a slower orbit that takes about 12 zodes (30 hours) to complete. Popular mythology refers to Thuria as female, and Cluros as her male partner.

ANCIENT BARSOOM

Eons ago, when Earth humans had yet to descend from the trees, civilization on Barsoom bloomed and flourished. The dominant races were similar to humans except for one major deviation; they were not mammals. Instead they were egg layers, and extremely long lived, with some living upwards of 2,000 ord (4,000 Earth years). The dominant races were of three major types; the white Martians known as Orovars who ruled the oceans, the yellow Martians known as Okarians from the north, and finally, the black Martians from the south who called themselves the First Born. A minor race, the green Martians, also existed, but only dwelt in the harsh areas of Barsoom that no other race found valuable.

Ancient Barsoom boasted five oceans, the greatest of which was the Throxus. Yet, despite the abundance of water, the climate on ancient Barsoom began to change; the oceans slowly withdrew and the atmosphere thinned. Three of the four original races, white, yellow, and black, came together and bred a new race, the red Martians, with the hopes that they would better withstand the new world that Barsoom was becoming. The green Martians found the new climate to their liking, and their numbers grew and spread faster than anyone had anticipated, proving to be a threat to all the other races.

As the climate became steadily worse, the First Born retreated to the south polar ice cap. There they created a new civilization for themselves on the sunken Omean Sea. Their leader, the Princess Issus, established herself as the Goddess of Life and Death, and began plans to spread her religion across the face of Barsoom.

The Okarians fled north, pursued by the green Martian hordes until they made their last stand in the Carrion Caves and crushed their pursuers in the narrow confines of the cave system. To deter any further pursuit, the Okarians piled the bodies of their green Martian adversaries in the caves and left them there to rot. With nowhere else to go, the yellow Martians built several domed cities in the frozen north pole.

Only the Orovars remained, and, in a desperate attempt to slow the death of their planet, developed a plan to replenish the air of Barsoom with a huge atmosphere plant, but before the construction was complete, all but a few of the Orovar had perished to the dwindling atmosphere. Their remaining numbers were quickly exterminated by the predations of the green hordes, leaving only the small hidden community of survivors in the Dead City of Horz.

Apart from the survivors in Horz, another group of white Martians built the city of Lothar in a hidden valley where they used their powerful mental ability to create life-like illusions to successfully fend off the green hordes.

Finally, a last group of white Martians, the Therns, fled south after the black Martians and settled in the fertile Valley Dor, where they propagated the worship of Issus instigated by the First Born through secret priesthoods around Barsoom. They taught that those who tired of life were to take the sacred pilgrimage on the River Iss to their reward in the paradise of the Valley Dor. But the Therns themselves never knew that they in turn were the victims of a ruse propagated by the First Born.

The First Born and the Lotharians persisted in their hidden cities, finding that, discounting death by accident or violence, they were effectively immortal. The Okarians, red, and green Martians, though, accepted the need spread by the religion of Issus to sail down the River Iss on their 1,000th year to the Valley Dor.

Under the constant harassment of the marauding green hordes, the red Martians survived and flourished, building great cities on the shores of the receding oceans. As the oceans continued to dry, they developed the canal system, an audacious plan to bring the life-giving waters from the poles to the farmlands and people of the cities. They also completed the construction of, and now maintain, the great atmosphere plant started by the white Martians that replenishes the thinning atmosphere of Barsoom, refusing to let their planet die without a fight.

Modern Barsoom

Thousands of years later, Barsoom is very different to the lush, green world it once was. The great oceans are all but gone, leaving nothing but dry sea beds overgrown with hardy, yellow lichen where the green hordes rule. Canals now stretch from pole to pole like great arteries, connecting isolated far-flung red Martian city-states, their banks lined with green and lush farmlands growing much needed crops for both people and animals.

Most of the red Martians city-states are powers unto themselves, though some have become small empires like Helium and Zodanga. War is a fact of life on Barsoom, as each nation and individual struggles to maintain what few dwindling resources remain.

Many more cities lie deserted and in ruin, scattered across the vast dead sea bottoms. These cities are now the temporary homes of nomadic green Martian hordes, rapacious white apes, and other monstrous creatures, making travel through these lands a dangerous endeavor at the best of times.

Of the other races of Barsoom, all that remains is legend at best. The yellow Martians are lost to history. The white Martians have faded from memory; the only indication of their existence are their murals found on the walls of many ruined cities. The black Martians have built for themselves a mythology that allows them to prey on many red Martian cites, but most particularly on the Thern priesthood they created. To the rest of Barsoom, the First Born are now known as the Black Pirates who hail from the nearer moon Thuria and travel to Barsoom to plunder.

There is reason to believe that Barsoom would have continued on with little to no change until the planet's resources were exhausted, had not the arrival of a Virginian gentleman changed everything.

Captain John Carter

The influence of Captain John Carter, formerly of Earth and Virginia, cannot be overstated. Carter's presence and actions change the face of Barsoom, redrawing borders and alliances. To understand Carter's history is to understand Barsoom, especially the three eras of play this game focuses on.

THE DOTAR SOJAT ERA

John Carter is a simple soldier and prospector who mysteriously finds himself stranded on a dead sea bottom of Barsoom. He is soon captured by the green Horde known as the Tharks, but quickly proves his mettle to them. He teaches the Thark Jed, Tars Tarkas, the value of friendship. While a captive of the Tharks, Carter meets a fellow captive, the incomparably beautiful Dejah Thoris, princess of the nation of Helium. Carter falls in love with the princess and, despite his ignorance of Barsoomian ways, eventually wins her heart. He assists in freeing her from the Tharks, and, after many adventures, successfully returns her to her father and city, where they marry.

THE PRINCE OF HELIUM ERA

Shortly after their marriage, Dejah Thoris produces an egg, but Carter's happiness is not to last. The atmosphere plant which produces the life-giving atmosphere of Barsoom, ceases to function, threatening all life on Barsoom with asphyxiation. In a brave effort, John Carter flies to the plant and succeeds in restarting the great engines, but the cost is almost too much for him to bear. Carter disappears from Barsoom and returns to Earth where he waits ten Earth years to return to his beloved Mars and the princess who waits for him.

On his return, Carter finds himself in the lost Valley Dor, hunted by plant men and white apes. He again meets with Tars Tarkas and learns that his beloved princess, distraught at the loss of her husband has, herself, sailed the River Iss. Together, Carter and Tars Tarkas discover the afterlife is far from the paradise Martians are led to believe. Carter discovers the Thern deception, frees the Princess Thuvia from her slavery, and learns of the piracy of the black Martians. Captured by the First Born, he is taken to their city on the shores of the underground Omean Sea. There he learns that the goddess Issus is nothing but an ancient cannibal crone, preying on the faith and lives of all who live on Barsoom. Carter also learns that his wife is enslaved by the black Martians and that he has a son, Carthoris.

Together, Carter and Carthoris lead a rebellion among the black Martians. He befriends the First Born Prince Xodar, and sees an end to the reign of terror of Issus. His beloved princess is once again kept from him, trapped in a prison that only opens once a year. Devastated by his loss, yet still a man of honor, he brings all he knows of the Thern deception and the cannibalistic nature of Issus to the rest of Barsoom, knowing his revelations will be perceived as blasphemy and see him sentenced to death.

Placed on trial, he is given a suspended sentence of one year, which he spends in the Mountains of Otz, waiting for the time when the prison that holds his princess captive will again open. But, once again, his princess slips his grasp as she is snatched away by the Holy Thern, Matai Shang.

After many more adventures, Carter catches up with Matai Shang in the arctic nation of the yellow Martians. He successfully leads a flotilla of red Martian fliers to free his princess from the clutches of the Jeddak of Kadabra, a feared and deadly tyrant. He earns the friendship of the yellow Martians and finally saves his beloved princess, Dejah Thoris. In honor of his brave deeds, and for uniting the warring races of Barsoom, Carter is granted the title of Jedwar of Barsoom; Warlord of Mars.

THE JEDDAK OF JEDDAKS ERA

Carter and Dejah Thoris live happily together in Helium. They have a daughter, Tara, and eventually a granddaughter, Llana. Carter spends much of his time working on destroying the assassin guilds of Barsoom and strengthening the bonds between the different nations and races. He and his family continue to have many adventures on Barsoom, but once again Dejah Thoris is threatened, this time kidnapped and taken to the planet Jupiter where she is held captive by the Morgors. Carter follows her captors, and frees her, but records of his adventures end there. Nothing is known of John Carter from that point on. Did he return to Barsoom, or did he meet his doom on Jupiter? No one knows, but his legacy remains on the Red Planet, and no doubt many other brave warriors will lift a sword in his name.

LIFE ON BARSOOM

Life is cheap for those who live on Barsoom. Warriors are rarely taken prisoner during war, rather, they are killed quickly and without mercy. Slavery is the main economic force, though slaves are often well treated and respected for the role they find themselves in. Red Martian city-states vie for control of what little resources remain and go to war at the slightest provocation to maintain whatever tenuous grip they may have on their sovereign lands.

BIOLOGY

Barsoomian life tends to be multi-limbed, with most animals possessing six, eight, or ten limbs. Only "humans" have the familiar physical pattern of two arms and two legs. Likewise, most life bears little fur, that which does tends to dwell in the far north and south where the freezing temperatures make fur essential. Despite their appearance, Barsoomian animals are not mammals; they lay eggs and do not produce milk. John Carter does refer to a single mammalian species but does not elaborate any further.

Reptiles are rare on Barsoom, but can be still be found in remote areas. They are described as repulsive, venomous, and those that have limbs tend to have six. They are often used in pit traps to disrupt unwary intruders.

The birds of Barsoom are gorgeously plumed as a rule, but all are silent. They can be found in a range of sizes from as small as an Earth hummingbird to as large as the assumed extinct malagor which is large enough to carry a green Martian in flight.

Insects are also common, and generally serve in the same ecological niche as insects on Earth do. They come in a large range of sizes with the largest of all being the highly endangered sith which grows to the size of a Herefordshire bull.

Among the intelligent races, an egg incubates for two and a half years before it hatches, releasing a child that is roughly equivalent to an Earth child of the same age. Barsoomian children grow quickly, reaching adulthood in approximately five years when they are ready to strike out on their own.

All animal life on Barsoom is telepathic to some degree. Most use this ability as a matter of survival, allowing them to detect prey or the approach of a predator. Others, like the predatory banth, use their telepathic ability combined with their roar to paralyze their victims with fear.

The intelligent races have honed their telepathy into a means of communication. A shared language is enjoyed across all Barsoom, though local dialects can occur. Some Barsoomians have honed their telepathy into more powerful abilities such as reading the minds of the dead, generating illusions, and even mind control. Any who apply themselves are able to learn these extended abilities, but it does take time.

The intelligent races of Barsoom also enjoy an extended lifespan. Barring accident or foul play, a Barsoomian can expect to live for a thousand years, at which point they are expected to make the pilgrimage on the River Iss to the fabled Valley Dor to live in an eternal paradise. Realistically though, most Barsoomians survive on average to their 350th year before they die in war, misadventure, or through assassination.

NAMING CONVENTIONS

Names on Barsoom tend to differ significantly from culture to culture. In many cultures, the second name of the father is normally incorporated into the first name of the son. Males tend to have one name consisting of one syllable and another name consisting of two syllables. Examples include Mors Kajak, son of Tardos Mors and Vas Sodat, father of Sodat Dav.

Females seem to have no such naming conventions except that their names often consist of two syllables, and they occasionally have two names. Examples include, Dejah Thoris, Llana, Thuvia, and Phaidor.

CLOTHING

The people of Barsoom do not wear clothes as a matter of modesty as they do on Earth. The harsh climate has led to a largely naked culture among both men and women. The only trapping normally worn is a leather harness to attach weapons to. Most Martians wear a number of different harnesses for different occasions, such as everyday wear, warfare, and even formal occasions.

Soldiers and adventurers tend to wear thick harnesses consisting of leather and metal which indicates the city or nation they hail from or to which they hold allegiance. Hooks and rings on the man's harness permit the attachment of weapons and gear, and when necessary ropes for hauling up the body — useful for rescues, boarding fliers, lashing down in a storm, etc. The straps of the harness, when combined, can make up a rope 10-12 feet long. The fully armed warrior's harness usually has depending from it: a long sword, a short sword, a dagger, a radium pistol, and pocket pouches for personal possessions.

Scholars and nobles on the other hand tend to wear harnesses with fewer straps, made of light leather or even delicate chains. This harness is often accompanied by, and decorated with, jewels, a sheer silk scarf, or a loincloth.

Short capes of silk or fur are frequently worn by both genders and most professions. For formal occasions, finely crafted harnesses decorated with precious metals and jewels to mark an individual's station are the norm, though some — often women — also include intricate and delicate jewelry. Wristbands and armbands are common among men while women often wear necklaces and fine head adornments as well.

Barsoomian nights are bitterly cold, and while the sparse fashions favored during the day are excellent for keeping cool, they do nothing to insulate the wearer during the night. Long robes, shawls, and capes of silk and fur are thus worn to ward off the cold night air and similar materials are used as bedding.

FOOD AND DRINK

Most Martian food is based on the milk provided by the mantalia plant, a bland tasteless liquid that is highly nutritious and can be made into substances resembling cheese, tofu, and porridge. Mantalia milk is the only food eaten by the green Martians, but red Martians supplement the milk with other

plants and nuts, fish caught in the canals, and thoat and rodent meat. Other foods include the fruit of the usa tree, which the armies and air navies of Barsoom use as rations. The usa tree is a plentiful and easily grown plant, but its fruit is tasteless despite its high nutritional value. By contrast, the fruit of the sompus tree has a sweet pulp and is a delicacy grown along the banks of the canals.

Food tablets, a form of concentrated energy that possesses the same nutrition as a full meal are available, though they are used only as emergency rations.

Water is by far the most common drink on Barsoom, either taken from the canals, or found in protected areas within dead cities. Mantalia milk is the next most common form of drink. While alcohol is known, its consumption is most often in moderation, with drunken behavior frowned upon heavily.

RELIGION

Although inhabited by a varied people, religion on Barsoom is remarkably similar, with common beliefs shared by almost every person.

Everyone on Barsoom participates in ancestor worship to a greater or lesser degree, a faith that requires neither great pomp nor ceremony, or indeed even temples. Barsoomians hold their ancestors in great esteem, particularly if they were famous or outstanding individuals. The most common form this faith takes is simply a request for the ancestors' help or oversight in an upcoming endeavor. Ancestors are also used in exclamations and when making oaths. Common phrases include:

> *"By my first ancestor!"*
> *"By the shell of my first ancestor!"*
> *"By the blood of my ancestors!"*
> *"In the name of my first ancestor!"*
> *"By my sacred ancestors!"*

Specific ancestors may also be called out. Such as *"By the blood of my father!"* or *"By the name of my mother!"* This is usually reserved for immediate family or very famous ancestors.

Barsoomians also believe that they originated from the Tree of Life, a primeval plant said to have grown in the Valley Dor twenty-three million years ago when the valley lay astride the equator. Within the fruit of the Tree of Life grew the first life: a multi-limbed worm, the hideous plant man, the ancestor of the white ape, and the first man from whom all the races of man originated. Although no scientific evidence has been found to substantiate the belief, it can be found in every nation on the planet, both civilized and savage. According to most accounts this "first man" was a black-skinned direct ancestor of the First Born, though not everyone necessarily agrees with this.

As the oceans on Barsoom began to dry up and disappear, a new faith appeared centered on the worship of Issus, the Goddess of Death and Life Eternal. The faith rapidly gained a following, and, with few exceptions, became the common belief among every nation and race on Barsoom. The faith teaches that, once a Barsoomian tires of life or reaches the advent of their 1,000th year, they are to set out on a pilgrimage along the sacred River Iss to the Valley Dor. There, an eternal paradise awaits them among their ancestors and loved ones, free of hate, blood, and warfare. Once the pilgrimage has begun, though, it is a grave sin to turn away from it. Any who do are doomed to live a lifetime of fear in hiding, or face execution at the hands of those who learn of their transgression.

The worship of Issus continues until it is revealed as a fraud perpetuated by the First Born and the Holy Therns thanks to John Carter and his son Carthoris. The belief is now only followed by the most isolated communities, or by those who refuse to accept the truth that is revealed to them by the Earthman.

Many other small cults have developed on Barsoom through the ages, but these are without exception restricted to a single city or small isolated nation. These cults generally only possess power equivalent to their membership and leaders, they lack the power of long-standing belief.

Society and Socializing

Civilized Barsoomians tend to be a gregarious and friendly people, despite their very warlike nature. The standard Barsoomian greeting is "Kaor!", while friends will place their right hands on each other's left shoulders at the same time. Placing both hands on both shoulders is an indication of very close friendship, or honored welcome.

Amongst red Martians and many other cultures, courtly refinement in manners is expected. Boors are not tolerated and sooner or later they will offend a better swordsman, and be disposed of in a duel. Women of all ranks and station are expected to be treated with the utmost chivalry at all times, and breaking this rule is a considered a grave error against the Martian code.

When courting, a lover lays his sword at her feet to pledge allegiance or state his admiration. If this is accepted, then a proposal is made by asking if the courter may refer to their lover as "my princess" or "my prince", depending on gender. One accepts this proposal by referring to the admirer as "my chieftain". The rules governing courtship are relatively simple from this point on except for one major exception; one may never marry the slayer of a former mate. This limitation is so closely adhered to, even killing a despised or villainous mate would likely result in the object of affection being forbidden to marry the killer, no matter how justified or heroic.

Social gatherings such as receptions and feasts are a common feature of social life; dancing by couples is a courtly tradition is maintained in nearly all Martian cities, and part of the education of any well-born Martian. Performers such as singers, musicians, and dancers are also a feature of these occasions.

As in many things on Barsoom, green Martian culture is an exception to these commonly held customs. They hold courtship to be mostly unnecessary beyond matings to continue their species. Only some rare green Martians have explored the idea of lasting love and courtship and they kept these relationships secret from their people.

Warrior Customs

More so than their social customs, Barsoomians take their warrior codes and customs very seriously, and to breach them relegates the offender to the status of a coward, or worse. Those who fail to abide by these customs are often ridiculed, scorned, or, in the most grievous cases, imprisoned or forced to fight for their lives in the Great Games, a frequent gladiatorial-style contest.

Possibly the most sacred of these customs is a form of combat etiquette where, if an individual is attacked, they are permitted to defend themselves only with an equal or lesser weapon; for example, if attacked with a long sword, a warrior may respond with a long sword, a short sword, or even a dagger — but not with a spear, pistol, or rifle. It is not only a grave breach of honor to disregard this custom, but also a show of cowardice, something most Barsoomians abhor. All Barsoomian cultures recognize this code. Note, this code applies to individual combat and small-scale conflicts more than open warfare — a soldier attacked by a hundred sword-wielding enemies is not necessarily considered a coward because he refused to throw down his pistol, though to face such numbers with his own sword is an act of great bravery!

A Barsoomian fighting man is expected to cultivate bravura. He never turns down a challenge, and always fights fairly. He observes the Barsoomian codes of chivalry towards women and non-combatants. Not only does he believe in his own fighting skills, but he will not hesitate to fight even against bad odds when duty or honor requires it. Quarter is never asked or given; to ask for it is cowardice, while to give it is a sign of weakness.

By laying his long sword at another's feet, a warrior signifies his pledge of loyalty and service

to that person, to the death. This offer is normally accorded only to someone who has great claim on one's allegiance or gratitude, or one greatly admired. When this gesture is offered to an ally, it is a pledge of fealty as a warrior. When offered to a prospective lover, it may also mean the beginning of courtship. In any case, the meaning of this gesture is so grave that it is considered shameful not to accept. If the offer is accepted, it is signified by picking up the sword, kissing it, and returning it hilt first, or buckling it onto the giver's harness. Rejection is signified by letting the sword lie. To return the sword point first is a grave insult, which is often cause for a challenge to a duel to the death.

Honors are often given to deserving warriors in the form of metal armbands clasped to the left bicep by their superior, or sometimes by the jed or jeddak if the recipient's actions are truly heroic. Exchanging such armbands is also a gesture of friendship.

Duels may be fought at any time with the warrior challenged selecting the weapon to be used. The duel may be to the death or to first blood only, which is normally determined at the same time as the challenge being issued.

Leaders are expected to lead by example and fight in the front lines with their men. It is shameful for an officer or noble to order his warriors to do something that he himself will not. Military leaders also act as commanding officers on fliers, and are expected to leap off the bow of the vessel if it is taken, shot down, or surrendered. Incompetent, and especially drunken, officers are sometimes disposed of by throwing them overboard from their fliers.

Most warriors owe their allegiance to a nation, city, or individual, but some are mercenary warriors without a country. These mercenaries, or panthans as they are called on Barsoom, are often criminals or fugitives, and many are loath to divulge their origin for fear of the price on their head. When not employed, a panthan strips his harness of all insignia and wears only the plain leather of an unallied warrior. This not only protects panthans from retaliation by former enemy soldiers, it also advertises they are currently for hire.

TITLES

Just like any other culture, Barsoomians have titles for members of their royalty, nobility, and military. Not all titles equate to those that are used on Earth, and those used for the upper ranks of society are rather small. A list is provided below.

TITLES OF ROYALTY
* **Dator:** a prince, used among the First Born
* **Jeddak:** an emperor, king of kings
* **Jeddara:** an empress, queen of queens
* **Jed:** a king
* **Prince:** the son of a jeddak, jeddara or jed
* **Princess:** the daughter of a jeddak, jeddara or jed
* **Chieftain:** a noble, equivalent to a baron or duke

TITLES OF MILITARY
* **Dwar:** a captain
* **Jedwar:** general of generals (a warlord)
* **Odwar:** general, commands 10,000 men.
* **Padwar:** a lieutenant, ranks of first and second class.
* **Panthan:** a mercenary without house or nation.
* **Than:** ordinary warrior or seaman

MILITARY ORGANIZATION
* **Utan:** 100 warriors commanded by a dwar.
* **Dar:** 1,000 warriors
* **Umak:** 10,000 warriors commanded by an odwar

Some cultures may be a bit less regimented with their military ranks, but the principle remains the same across Barsoom.

SLAVERY

On most of Barsoom, slavery is an openly accepted practice, and forms a firm basis for the economy. Slaves are generally well treated and respected, and are often placed in positions of high responsibility and power within households. Slaves are assigned to people based on their gender. Men are allowed to be personally served by both male and female slaves, though to take advantage of a female slave is seen to be both cowardly and dishonorable. Women are normally personally served by women, though if they possess personal male slaves, they are always eunuchs.

Slaves are procured in a number of ways. Primarily they are obtained through warfare, though some enter slavery though kidnapping. The children of slaves are also considered slaves, though the child of a free man and a slave is considered free. Criminals can be sentenced to slavery if their crime is not severe. Lastly, a free person can voluntarily enter into slavery, though this is normally an act of great gratitude offered to someone who has saved their life.

Slaves can be found in almost every stratum of Barsoomian life, ranging from pampered personal servants, to the major-domo of a palace, and even street sweepers who keep the broad avenues clean. Many slaves perform such mundane duties as cooking, cleaning, and maintaining a household while others utilize their specialist training in the repair and maintenance of machinery and buildings. Governments own a large number of slaves, which are put to work on public projects, while others work the government owned farms and mines scattered about the countryside.

Although it is not common, a slave can be freed. There are no hard rules concerning this action, though it is most often awarded as a sign of gratitude or reward by the owner. A slave, given this option, may refuse to accept their freedom if the offer is given in private, but if a witness is present they have no option but to accede to their former master's wishes.

ENTERTAINMENT

When not engaged in warfare or statecraft, Barsoomians enjoy relaxing with some form of game, often accompanied by setting a wager or two to make things a bit more interesting.

Jetan, a form of Martian chess, is a much-loved game among the red Martians. Much like chess, it is relatively easy to learn but difficult to master. The game represents the ancient war between the black and yellow Martians, and is played by two opponents. Game play involves alternating moves using twenty black pieces opposed by twenty orange. The first person to move is decided in any way agreeable to both players; after the first game, the winner of the preceding game moves first if he chooses, or may instruct his opponent to make the first move. The game is won when any piece takes the opponent's princess, or when a chief takes the opponent's chief.

Yano is a game of chance, which is believed to be as old as Barsoom itself. It is can be played by up to six players, and uses a court that is 15 sofads long. Each player has a tiny numbered sphere that he attempts to roll into a matching numbered hole at the end of the court. There are five rounds in the game, and the spheres are randomized at the beginning of each round.

The highlight of any city's calendar is the Great Games. These can feature a variety of sports, but concentrate primarily on combat — swordfights, wrestling matches, etc. A highly violent affair that glorifies the virtues of personal conflict, the Great Games can last many days and consistently draws large crowds who view the spectacle and lay bets on the combatants. Slaves and convicts are commonly featured combatants and are usually required to fight to the death, either against other captives, criminals, or savage beasts captured from the wild or bred specifically for the games. Free men and even nobles will often fight as well, but these combats are more often an open challenge over some dispute, with the rules of the engagement decided upon beforehand, ranging from the victor being the one who draws the first blood, all the way to and including a match to the death.

Lesser games, lasting a day at most, are held on a more frequent regular basis, and are identical to the Great Games in most respects. Dagger throwing is a common sport among warriors, and is a venue for wagering. Large sums of money can change hands in such contests. Races are also frequently enjoyed, either between riding thoats, or a very fast and low flying version of a flier known as a pod. Races are held in hippodromes and often draw as large a crowd as the Great Games do.

CRIME

Crime on Barsoom bears a close resemblance to crime on Earth, but it does have its peculiarities that are worth some mention. Theft for monetary gain is virtually unheard of, and an individual is able to leave their belongings in a public space assured that they will still be there when they return. Other property-related crimes are also generally unheard of and it is considered incredibly dishonorable to steal another's valued possessions.

Assassination, though a very common occurrence, is still illegal, and those found guilty are most commonly punished by a sentence of combat to the death in the arena. Despite this, skilled assassins often gain a remarkable amount of fame for their actions, especially if they are in the employ of powerful or influential individual. All Barsoomian cities host at least one assassin's guild which acts as a go-between for those seeking their services and the individuals that perform them. Still, it is not unusual to find brave, or some would say foolhardy, assassins not associated with any guild. The more powerful guilds ensure they maintain a monopoly on their vocation by making examples of those that flout their organization. Though not exactly legal in most cities, members of the assassin's guilds are often treated as heroes by many Barsoomians, and they hold a similar mystique and position as the gangsters of the 1920s did during Prohibition in the United States.

Kidnapping, either to be used or sold as slaves, or to be held for ransom is common. High-ranking or influential female nobles are often especially in danger of abduction. Considering the veneration that many nations have towards treating women well, most will stop at nothing to regain them, even resorting to open warfare between two nations when the victim is a noblewoman or princess.

TECHNOLOGY

The technology on Barsoom is an odd mix of the advanced, the primitive, and the fantastic. Although the red Martians have lost the secrets to making much of the technology from the past, they have also created wonders of their own. The greatest discovery by far is the substance the Barsoomians refer to as radium. This substance, which is different and far less radioactive than the one found on Earth, is used to power everything from the great atmosphere plant down to cities, individual buildings, and even vehicles. Radium is also used in ammunition which causes the bullets to explode when the radium is exposed to sunlight. Cold radium light bulbs are used in buildings and to light the streets at night.

The discovery of the eighth ray of anti-gravity was a major development for the red Martians. They have used this ray in the buoyancy tanks of their fliers, giving them aerial supremacy over the green hordes. Red Martian fliers are used in the air navy, to transport goods and people, and as private transport.

Along with the eighth ray is the ninth ray, which is used primarily in the atmosphere plant to produce the artificial atmosphere that sustains life on Barsoom. The ninth ray is separated from the other rays of the sun by means of a set of finely adjusted instruments on the sprawling roof of the plant, three-quarters of which is used for reservoirs in which the ninth ray is stored. Certain proportions of refined electric vibrations are combined with the ray, and the result is pumped to the five principal air centers of the planet,

where contact with the ether of space transforms it into atmosphere. There is sufficient reserve of the stored ninth ray to maintain the present atmosphere for a thousand years. The only danger is that some accident might befall the pumping apparatus, a battery of twenty radium pumps any one of which is equal to the task of furnishing all Mars with the atmosphere compound. Each pump is used for a day at a time.

Other technological wonders include holographic telescopes that are able to project images from any planet in the solar system, automaton food service, food tablets, and pneumatic transport systems. For more information about the science and technology of Barsoom, *see Chapter 5: Weapons and Technology.*

Yet, despite their advanced technology, Barsoomians still highly favor the use of hand-to-hand weapons in personal combat, primarily long and short swords.

In a similar vein, Barsoomians also rely heavily on beasts of burden, regardless of faster transportation. The green Martians in particular tend to ignore most technology except that of firearms and simple three-wheeled chariots. Green warriors ride huge savage mounts called thoats, while even larger elephantine beasts known as zitidars are used to pull their chariots. Wild carnivores the size of Earth lions, called calots, are trained as guard and fighting animals.

Among the red Martians, a smaller domesticated breed of thoat is used as a means of travel, a cavalry mount, and a source of meat and leather. Zitidars are also farmed for their meat and leather. A smaller domesticated breed of calot is used as a guard animal in many wealthy homes.

ARCHITECTURE

The majority of modern Barsoomian cities are walled to protect them from attack. The walls are periodically broken by gates that open onto wide avenues that lead into the heart of the city. Small, hidden doors are also constructed into the walls to allow clandestine entry to and exit from the city.

Inside the cities, closest to the walls, are the homes of the poorest of the city's residents, along with small business and industries. Moving deeper into the city, towards the center, one finds the dwellings of the middle classes, and then the estates of the wealthy. Finally, near the very center of the city are found the palaces and estates of the nobility and royalty, normally situated around a large open square or garden.

All dwellings within Barsoomian cities are designed to be raised upon a hydraulic shaft at nightfall, making it nearly impossible for the building to be entered from the ground and thus making assassination attempts difficult. Buildings that are too large to be completely raised into the air are designed so that the sleeping quarters can be raised on shafts.

Barsoomian architecture is highly ornate, featuring intricate bas-reliefs and sculpture on the outer walls. The bas-reliefs begin on the second or third floor to, once again, stop assassins from using the designs to aid them in gaining access to buildings through unlocked or unguarded windows on upper levels.

Larger buildings, palaces, and government offices all boast towers for fliers to land and moor. Every city will have at least one barracks for their airmen which boasts one of the highest towers in the city, normally located quite close to the jed or jeddak's palace.

All cities, both modern and ancient will boast at least one arena where combative games are held. They are built into the ground, so that the highest seats are at approximately ground level. The arena floor is dotted with gates which lead to tunnels where combatants and caged animals are kept ready for their time in the games. The tunnels will also connect with the larger tunnel system under the city.

Beneath every city can be found a series of tunnels and chambers utilized in a variety of manners. The most common use for the tunnels beneath a palace is as a prison, though other tunnels are used for storage or as secret passages to other parts of the city or even as means to leave the city unobserved.

RESOURCES

Martian cities need resources. Primarily food and water are the most essential, but also the most difficult to maintain. Water is brought to the cities via the vast canal networks which span the length and breadth of Barsoom. The majority of water is drawn from the North Pole, where huge automated pumping stations located along the great ice barrier melt the glacial ice using geothermal taps and then pump it into the canals. The canals are enormous underground conduits that were built as straight as possible so that additional energy isn't expended to maintain the flow through curves and bends. Water is pumped through the canals to various populated centers. Running over the top of the canals are broad white turnpikes, used primarily to transport cargo but along which travelers can also be found.

Along either side of the canals are high-walled, well-guarded farms. Networks of underground pipes irrigate the fields in a manner that preserves as much water as possible from evaporation. Farming techniques perfected over the millennia assure a steady supply of food, though it is never exactly plentiful. Produce from the farms are stored in immense warehouses where they await shipment to the cities. Unfortunately, these stockpiles attract raiders, and the cities on the borders of green Martian territories, or those that do not maintain good relations with their neighbors, often face attack.

Cities built along the canals are designed with a distribution network of underground tunnels and pipes which draw water directly from the nearby canals to supply wells, fountains and buildings. Water is held in very high regard by the people of Barsoom, and any waste or excessive use of the precious resource is frowned upon very harshly.

The Empire of Helium is unusual in that its canals draw their water from the Lost Sea of Korus, located at the South Pole. Huge automated underground pumping stations beneath the coast of the Korus desalinate the water, and then pump the fresh water into massive submerged pipes that travel beneath the Valley Dor and the Otz Mountains, and then onto the surface and into canals that then supply the nation.

Some cities are lucky enough be have been built in valleys where enough water remains below the surface to provide sustenance for fields and forests.

Martian civilization also relies heavily on mining, though not nearly as much as farming. Mines tend to focus on metals, especially those needed to maintain advanced and delicate technology or to build and repair fliers, or on radium which is the source of all power on Mars. Radium is consumed in prodigious amounts by power plants and weapons, and needs to be constantly replaced. By its very nature, radium cannot be stored in bulk, so the mines are constantly in use. Red Martians venture deep into the dead sea bottoms looking for new sources of this vital mineral, and radium mines can be the source of brutal and sometimes genocidal wars as cities fight desperately over this dwindling resource.

CHAPTER 8: THE GREEN HORDES

> *Leave to a Thark his head and one hand and he may yet prevail.*
>
> – Ancient Thark Proverb, *The Gods of Mars*

The green Martian hordes rule the wilds of Barsoom. Historically antagonistic to all the other races, they are known for their violent ways and martial skill. Nomadic in nature, they were the raging death of the Orovar white race and smaller communities of red Martians who sought to settle in the dead sea bottoms, where they now dominate. Organized into numerous hordes, the green Martians fight among themselves as often as they battle others, and few can travel their territory safely.

The martial prowess and ferocity of the green Martians is legendary throughout the many cultures which call Barsoom home. It has been speculated that, should the green Martians ever be able to put aside their feuds, all Barsoom might be theirs. Instead, the green Martians fragment into smaller communities, of which the largest are the four great hordes — the Tharks, the Warhoons, the Torquas, and the Thurd. Each of these great assemblages of Martian life is thousands strong and ruled over by a jeddak whose name is enough to cause the smaller, more fragile race of red Martians to tremble with fear.

The number of green Martians is estimated at around 5 million, though that number is imprecise and fluctuates wildly, given the daily activities of most green Martians involve the shedding of blood — an enemy's, for preference, but, if one is unavailable, a fellow horde-member serves just as well. While the four great hordes comprise the largest concentrations of green Martians to be found on the plains, these still only account for a tiny proportion of the whole. There are many smaller groups prowling the spaces between the dead cities, though many of these owe some form of fealty to one of the great hordes and will gladly follow them to battle and plunder. Elsewhere, there are more substantial convocations, typically called tribes for want of a better name, though even these savage marauders are incapable of challenging a true horde.

Long rumors, in the corridors of Zodanga, say out in the vast wilderness of the Martian steppes, a fifth and greatest horde is nascent and growing. It is for this reason the red men of Zodanga wage their unrelenting war of extirpation on the green Martians: a raw terror of what might, one day, emerge from the plains. In the end, appropriately enough, it is a mighty confederacy of the green Martians, led by Tars Tarkas, which lays the Zodangans low. Scattered survivors of the great slaughter still maintain that all green Martians, even Tars Tarkas will, one day, be forced to join the hidden horde of the unknown jeddak and bring war to all the peoples of Barsoom.

PHYSIOLOGY

Green Martian males reach a height between approximately 1 ad 2 sofads and 1 ad 5 sofads (twelve and fifteen feet), with tusks protruding from their mouths, green skin, and a double torso with two sets of arms, perhaps their most distinctive trait. The lower set of arms are often used as legs if they are needed, providing extra stability and speed. Their eyes are set at the extreme sides of their heads, a trifle above the center, and protrude in such a manner that they may be directed either forward or back independently of each other, thus permitting these remarkable creatures to look in any direction, or in two directions at once, without the necessity of turning their heads. The irises of the eyes are typically blood red, while the pupil is dark. The eyeball itself is very white, as are the teeth. It is this latter feature which adds a most ferocious appearance to an otherwise fearsome and terrible countenance, as the lower tusks curve upward to sharp points which end about where the eyes of earthly human beings are located. The whiteness of the teeth is not that of ivory, but the snowiest and most gleaming of china. Males and females of the species are nearly identical, but females are typically lighter in coloration and stand 1 ad to 1 ad and 2 sofads (10 to 12 feet) tall. All members of the race are completely hairless.

The green Martian's combination of towering height, green skin, multiple long limbs, red eyes, and gleaming white tusks present a singularly formidable appearance. They wear very little to no clothing, usually only a harness and/or some types of ornaments to depict clan and rank. While the skin of the young is lighter and darkens into adulthood, it is almost impossible to tell a green Martian's exact age from their physical appearance.

Green Martians can exist for long periods without food or drink. When the green Martians do eat, they exist almost exclusively on the mantalia, a plant found in the desert which makes a liquid similar to milk — up to eight to ten quarts a day — which also provides a cheese-like food. Because of this diet, when a green Martian goes on the hunt, the prey is generally taken for hides and other resources, rather than as a source of meat.

Culture and Traditions

To outsiders, green Martian culture is as fearsome and aggressive as their appearance. Theirs is a culture that is defined by conflict, expressions of dominance, and the strength of the horde against rivals, fearsome beasts, and the harsh climate.

For the Horde

The basic social division of the green Martians is the horde and its origin stems from the first great horde of green Martians to conquer the ancient cities of the Orovar, long ago. Even though this great horde is long disbanded, its remnants and successors form the basis of green Martian culture today.

The exact origin of the green Martians is unknown. What is known is that they were once separated from the white-skinned Orovar race by vast oceans. In the waning days of old Barsoom, when the oceans began to recede, they came across the drying seas in a vast horde and began raiding the once-great Orovar civilizations, forcing them into the remote regions.

The green horde took over the Orovar's abandoned city states and occupied the great plazas and buildings in the center of these settlements. Unable or unwilling to use the Orovar's abandoned technology or maintain these once-great settlements, the green-occupied cities largely fell to ruin or were reclaimed by the wild. However, the green hordes themselves held their new homes with their size, brute strength and skill at arms. Eventually the green hordes ran out of enemies to fight and turned on each other. The great horde began to fracture and split into smaller hordes based on the city-states they occupied.

Green Martians are referred to by the name of their horde, which in turn takes its name from the ruined city it inhabits. Thus, the horde that occupies the ancient city of Thark is known by that name. The horde that controls Warhoon are known as the Warhoons, the horde that controls the ancient Martian city of Torquas are called the Torquas, and so on. New rivalries between the hordes cause them to stagnate, and, while they fight among themselves, the red people of Mars thrive. Now that the red kingdoms of Barsoom dominate much of the planet, the green hordes dwindle — though they are still a potent and deadly threat wherever they dwell.

Children of the Horde

The green Martian birthing process and childhood experience is a huge factor in understanding their culture. They make the average green Martian a being of cruel amusements and grim outlook. During their development, green Martian youths know no mother, father, or siblings. Their training is focused on promoting ferocity and competition among them. They have no home or family aside from the horde, and quickly learn they can only claim what they can take by force and defend with might. However, it ensures the survival of the race even in the harsh environments where the green Martian hordes live. The lack of weak hatchlings and strict population control helps ensure the horde structure is seen as necessary and not as cruelty or harsh treatment for its own sake.

After a pair of male and female green Martians mate, the female lays eggs which are collected by the horde. A typical Martian female brings forth about thirteen eggs each Martian year, or ord. Each egg typically measures about four inches from top to bottom and weighs about six ounces when laid. Eggs which meet the size, weight, and specific gravity tests are hidden in the recesses of a subterranean vault where the temperature is too low for incubation. Every year these eggs are carefully examined by a council of chieftains and all but about one hundred of the most perfect are destroyed out of each yearly supply. After five years, about five hundred eggs have been chosen and these are placed in air-tight incubators to be hatched by the sun's rays after a period of another five years. Upon hatching, the infants are collected and transported to a gathering of the horde. Those eggs that did not hatch at the scheduled collection time are presumed flawed or weak and destroyed.

Upon arrival in a horde gathering, the young are all released. Disoriented and frightened by their experience, they scatter. The green Martian females collect them, often fighting amongst themselves to earn the right to care for the strongest or healthiest hatchlings. After the hatchlings are again collected, they are once more examined for any defects or problems, cleaned, and taken to various large caverns to be raised. Any child that is deformed or defective in any way is killed on the spot, without sadness or fanfare from any member of the community.

The green Martian young are miniature replicas of their parents when they emerge from the egg, standing about three to four feet tall with a yellowish-green skin color that darkens as they age. Their childhood training consists solely of learning to talk, using the weapons of warfare, learning to hunt, and other practical survival skills. They are the common children of the community, with no particular connection to anyone, save the females who chance to capture them as they leave the incubator. These females are a youth's caretaker and educator until they are grown, though they are taught to hold these surrogate mothers in no special regard upon reaching adulthood.

A Harsh Existence

The women and children of a green Martian male's retinue may be likened to a military unit for which he is responsible in various ways. Women are in no sense wives. Children are responsibilities, not offspring. The green Martians spare no words or consideration for familial love and devotion. Their mating is a matter of community interest and instinct. The council of chieftains of each community control the matter, often directing certain pairings believed to create strong spawn for the hordes.

In a typical horde, the males are responsible for hunting and war while females oversee manufacturing things such as weapons and healing salves, caring for children, and other duties. Given the competition and constant dueling among the horde, protecting their own charges and holdings is a full-time job for most males, especially chieftains, jeddaks, and other leaders. Likewise, females are never idle — life is hard and there is always something that needs doing.

The average life expectancy of a green Martian after the age of maturity is about three hundred ords, but would be nearer the one-thousand mark were it not for the various means leading to violent death. Only about one green Martian in a thousand dies of sickness or disease, and in hordes that adhere to the belief in the afterlife provided by the River Iss, perhaps two in a thousand take this journey. The other nine hundred and ninety-seven die violent deaths in duels, in hunting, and in war. The greatest risk during the age of childhood comes from the white apes of Barsoom, who claim the lives of numerous careless or unfortunate youths.

Green Martians dispose of their dead by using a funeral pyre. Little ceremony or sentiment is spared for most deaths, though the passing of great chieftains and champions stirs some dormant sentiment and emotions in the hearts of many horde members.

By the time John Carter creates his grand alliance, including the great Tars Tarkas, many hordes are slowly changing to embrace warmer emotions and sentiment. Aging green Martians no longer take the journey down the Iss in most cases, instead finding some other way to seek their death or give their lives new meaning. These changes to green Martian culture are strongest among the Tharks and their allies, and weakest among their enemies such as the Warhoons.

A Warlike Race

There are other natural causes tending toward a diminution of the population, but nothing contributes so greatly to this end as the fact that no male or female Martian is ever voluntarily without a weapon of destruction. The weapons of the green Martian include long sword, short sword, spear, dagger, pistol, hatchet, and rifle. All are deadly in the hands of a trained warrior, but it is not for the use of these weapons the hordes are most feared.

The typical green Martian rifle has a range of three miles, and can fire one hundred rounds before reloading. Although practically, even with wireless finders and sights, it is accurate to only two miles, the green Martians are acknowledged as the best marksmen on Barsoom with this paticular weapon.

The rifle is made of a white metal stocked with wood. The wood is made from a highly prized source, while the metal is an alloy of aluminum and steel, an exceedingly hard temper. Just like other matters of production, the females generally oversee making the powder, cartridges and firearms. In time of actual warfare, women often form reserves, and, when the necessity arises, fight with even greater intelligence and ferocity than the men. However, as even the greatest marksman cannot fire without working rifles and ammunition, the hordes are reluctant to deploy their most skilled female arms crafters to the front lines.

The green Martians spears also deserve special mention. The spear is forty feet in length, metal tipped and shod. They use it from the back of a thoat, similar to the way knights in medieval times on Earth used lances. They hold the weapon in two arms of the same side and lean the opposite direction to maintain balance while charging their foes.

The training of the young is conducted solely by the women, who attend to the education of the young in the arts of individual defense and offense.

Green Martian warriors and chieftans are trained in the higher branches of the art of war, in strategy and the maneuvering of large bodies of troops. They will never run from battle, as retreat is an alien concept to them. They face death with a proud determination.

LAWS, LANGUAGE, AND TRADITIONS

Green Martians make laws as they are needed – a new law for each emergency. They are unfettered by precedent in the administration of justice. Customs are handed down verbally through ages of repetition, but the punishment for ignoring a custom is a matter for individual treatment by a jury of the culprit's peers. All property among the green Martians is owned in common by the community, except personal weapons, ornaments, and the sleeping silks and furs of the individuals. These alone one can claim undisputed right to, though he may not accumulate more of these than required for his actual needs. The surplus he holds merely as custodian, and it is passed on to the younger members of the community as necessity demands.

Green Martians speak the universal language of Barsoom, and, like all other races of Mars, exhibit some telepathic powers, which they employ to control their domestic animals, directing their thoats mentally rather than with a bridle and bit.

PRISONERS

Prisoners of varied importance are routinely captured. Prestigious captives are taken before the tribal leader. It is the responsibility of the war-party leader to ensure that this happens. This prisoner is not allowed to be killed except in the cases of self-defense or attempted escape. If the prisoner escapes, the captor is required to forfeit his rank.

Captives, even non-green Martians, are often allowed reasonable freedom of action and can even gain rank and status with the horde provided they do not attempt to escape. Of course, they are also expected to live by the rules of the horde, a fact which often leads to the death of these outsiders in duels or through misadventure.

Green Martians often find humor in the suffering of others, and will roll about the ground in fits of mirth upon witnessing death, maiming, and torture. Their lifestyle and culture creates an ever-present sort of "gallows humor" in them that overcomes all gentler mirth. They are a cruel and taciturn race, generally lacking outward expressions of love, sympathy, or pity. However, these limitations are cultural, not genetic. Over time, some green Martians have developed warm and sophisticated positive relationships with others. Though seemingly impossible to some, once earned, the devotion and friendship of a green Martian is as unyielding as the lives they live.

RELATIONSHIPS WITH OTHERS

Most green Martians have a tenuous relationship at best with other creatures of Barsoom. They are at constant odds with various red Martian kingdoms, in addition to the other green Martian tribes. They hold no love for the First Born raiders they encounter and give little thought to the Okar in their distant arctic lands.

The green Martians are an equestrian race, rarely walking other than to move about their camps. One of the more notable aspects of the green culture is their domestication of many of the various beasts that are found in the wilds of Barsoom. There are three such creatures found among them used for mounts: thoats, zitidars, and calots. Green Martian thoats (*see page 177*) are of superior size and strength to better carry their large riders. Mammoth-like zitidars (*see page 182*) are used to pull the greens' great three-wheeled chariots. Finally, the fierce calots (*see page 164*) are trained to be caravan guards, usually placed at the rear of the caravan to protect from sneak attacks by rival tribes.

With the arrival of John Carter, some green Martians are starting to see the value in kinder treatment towards their animals, especially among the Thark horde. Carter's animals during his time with the Tharks are utterly devoted to him in ways rarely seen among the green Martians. The reason for this is simple: Carter treats his pets and mounts as respected and valued companions. They repay his kindness with fanatic loyalty. Perceptive and thoughtful green Martians such as Tars Tarkas copy this treatment, increasing the efficiency and loyalty of green Martian animals in some camps. The advantage this gives the Tharks in conflicts with their enemies is discussed shortly.

THE GREAT HORDES

The four great hordes of the green Martians each take their name from the dead city which they have claimed as their own and made their fortress. To whom these cities once belonged, few now care to speculate; a testament to the completeness with which green Martians occupy any environment they own, becoming ultimately synonymous with it. The great hordes each have their similarities and, to an outsider, can appear indistinguishable. However, each horde has its own identity which immediately identifies a member of one horde to their comrades, although, to one unlearned in green Martian customs, it often seems to be no more than an inclination of the head.

THARKS

The most populous and prosperous of the four great hordes, the Tharks, are also the green Martians most unlike their kin. The appearance of John Carter and his alliance, then friendship, with the jeddak of the horde — Tars Tarkas — quickly changes the nature and bearing of the Tharks. While still a ferocious martial presence on the plains, emotional bonds with both red and other green Martians become more common; new technologies and new philosophies begin to influence the ways Tharks interact with each other and with the world through which they stalk. As the Tharks flourish, with more hatchlings to rear and more resources to share, the horde is now preeminent amongst the green Martians of the plains and its close ties of friendship with Helium ensure that this preeminence is unlikely to fail in the near future. It was not always thus.

Prior to the ascent of Tars Tarkas, the Tharks were ruled by Tal Hajus. Tal Hajus was a savage, wicked creature, possessed entirely by his basest, most carnal appetites. During his reign, the bloodshed between the Tharks and their deadly rivals, the Warhoon, reached its highest point — at least according to the collective memory of both hordes. The peculiar standards of the green Martians mean that, while Tal Hajus' depredations were known,

they are not deemed sufficient to invoke the Right of Challenge. While warfare was plentiful and looting was good, few openly criticized Tal Hajus, even for those acts which the green Martian typically eschews. The area over which the horde spread itself means that many Tharks were unaware of Tal Hajus' many crimes. Only the five largest of the individual communities comprising the Thark horde occupied the city from which they derived their name. The rest resided in the deserts nearby, foraging and fighting with other green raiders who roamed the area.

These circumstances have changed a little since Tars Tarkas made himself the ruler of the horde at the edge of his blade. Now, the dead city the Tharks claim is closer in use to a human settlement, such as Helium. Red Martian traders visit to sell and bargain with green Martians on occasion, and the living spaces are not apportioned, any longer, at the point of a sword.

Recent changes in Thark culture should not be taken to mean that they are weak or decadent, though the Warhoon claim otherwise. The Tharks retain their fierce love of battle, now tempered with a greater willingness to utilize the subtle tactics of combat which Tars Tarkas and John Carter spread through the ranks. This extends even to the treatment of the beasts with whom the Tharks go to war: their thoats and calots. Where once these creatures were treated harshly, controlled through the exertion of brawn and brutality, now there is kindness and consideration. This enables the Tharks to rely on their mounts, and on the calots who accompany them when hunting or riding to war, in a fashion that other hordes cannot. In the past, the truculent thoats, infuriated by ill treatment, would often unseat riders or refuse to heed the orders, even riding off in the wrong direction

or deliberately trampling nearby warriors. Now, these dangers imperil only the Tharks' enemies.

There is one traditional aspect of Thark life which has not changed. The constant threat of the enormous white apes which still occupy the region in which the Tharks make their home. The white apes dominated the dead city of Thark before the arrival of the green Martians and there are still large numbers of the ferocious creatures to be found in the vicinity. This enables the Tharks to retain their natural, warrior instincts, despite the relative stability of their community. All young Tharks are taught to fear the white ape and to respect it as a foe, just as the mature Thark is taught to hunt it and kill it. White apes form a strange part of Thark lore and ritual, their pelts are prized and sometimes worn as a symbol of rank by jeds who have just attained the title.

Tharks are the most advanced of the many hordes of green Martians who occupy the Barsoomian plains, and their dominance draws many envious glances from those who would take what the Tharks possess without understanding the means by which it has been earned. Fortunately, under the wise leadership of Tars Tarkas and his successors, the Tharks endure.

NOTABLE THARKS

TARS TARKAS

Eventual Jeddak of the Tharks, best friend of John Carter, and valiant hero of the green Martians. Tars is one of the most well-known green Martians in history, especially outside of his own people.

TAL HAJUS

Jeddak of the Tharks. Cruel and decadent. Killed by Tars Tarkas.

SOLA

Troubled young Thark woman. Daughter of Tars Tarkas and friend to Dejah Thoris and John Carter.

SARKOJA

Elderly Thark woman. Respected but rarely trusted. Eventually draws the ire of Sola and Tars Tarkas and flees the horde.

Tharks in Your Campaign

Tharks make for an excellent default for any green Martian character. They are well-defined in the Barsoom novels and possess strong connections to Helium, John Carter, and other important elements of the setting. When ruled by Tars Tarkas, Tharks are keen and valuable allies. Under Tal Hajus, they are more disorganized and brutish. In both instances, they are clever and dangerous.

Warhoon

Long renowned for their savagery and lust for carnage, the Warhoon form the brutal antithesis to the Tharks. Battle and warfare inform each and every aspect of Warhoon society, from the tattered ruins of the ancient city in which they live — its walls a ravaged reminder of feuds fought out to a bloody conclusion — to the gladiatorial pits in which the captives and slaves of the horde are forced to fight to survive, or preferably die as spectacularly as possible. Led by the grizzled Dak Kova, the Warhoons are now more vicious and dedicated to the pursuit of battle than ever before. Under the previous jeddak, the young and callow Bar Comas, the horde was fragmented. The apparent weakness of the horde's leader led to a period of relentless feuding and internecine warfare as the jeds settled their grudges with each other and awaited the moment to seize the title of jeddak for themselves. In the end, it was Dak Kova who issued the challenge which Bar Comas could no longer avoid. Under Dak Kova, those internal struggles are turned outwards, as the Warhoons conduct more raids than ever before, loot villages and communities throughout the expanse of the Barsoomian hinterlands, and leave behind a swath of handless and headless corpses. The Warhoon adorn themselves in the severed hands of their vanquished foes. Their enemies' skulls, once divested of flesh, are used as drinking receptacles or boundary markers. It is impossible to mistake the moment one arrives at Warhoon territory — while there are almost no signs of living quarters at all, there are ranks of skulls, mounted on spears, turned to the color of rust by the red sand.

There is, it is said, a second Warhoon jeddak, whose horde occupies the southern half of the Warhoon territory. This green Martian is usually dubbed Kab Kadja but there is very little known of him beyond this. There are some among the anthropologists and ethnographers of Helium who speculate that Kab Kadja may be only a myth, a figure of legend who will one day return to lead the purest warriors of the green Martian horde to the end of the River Iss. Others, among them men like Kantos Kan who have been the recipients of the Warhoons' hospitality, maintain that such a view is ludicrous. The Warhoon have no interest in grand narratives. Uniquely among the green Martians, the Warhoon consider any of their number who have survived long enough to venture along the length of the River Iss a failure. Not dying in the swirling chaos of blades and yelling is to avoid the blade of your appointed killer — the most heinous example of cowardice. Many of the duels which the Warhoons engage in frequently — John Carter witnessed as many as eight such battles to the death in a single day — are between those green Martians who feel themselves grow too old and fear for their reputations as warriors. It is said that, upon winning a duel against a younger opponent, an elderly Warhoon is seen to weep at the notion he will not perish in battle. This concern does not usually last for long, however, as there is always another battle to be fought and another feud to be resolved. The Warhoon are perhaps the most warlike examples of a warlike race. Dedicated to the clash of metal and the report of radium pistols, there is a good reason that their flesh is more scar than skin, even with the very young. The Warhoon are a formidable foe and any who encounter them must be wary.

Notable Warhoons

BAR COMAS

Warhoon jeddak. A fierce but relatively young ruler who misjudges the capabilities of those who covet his position. Killed by Dak Kova, who replaces him as jeddak.

DAK KOVA

Jeddak of the Warhoon who wins his position after killing Bar Comas. Cruel and convinced that the Warhoons must be even more ruthless to gain respect and power.

WARHOONS IN YOUR CAMPAIGN

Due to their status as the enemies of the Tharks, Warhoons are often "bad guy" green Martians. They aren't evil, but they are savage and dangerous. Warhoon player characters could reject their people's violent ways or they could refine them, depending on the exact set up in the campaign.

TORQUAS

The green Martians can be found in almost every corner of Barsoom, hardy enough to survive and prosper in even the most inhospitable areas of the planet. So, when Carthoris, Prince of Helium, pursues his kidnapped beloved, Thuvia of Ptarth, it is not surprising that he should find her amongst them. Torquas, the city which this horde of green Martians has claimed as their own, was once among the most famed cities on Barsoom — a monument of architectural achievement, of culture, sophistication, and elegance. It is scarcely recognized as such any longer. The domestic ministrations of the Torquasian horde have not been kind. Anything of worth which the city possessed was long ago claimed by Hortan Gur, the formidable Jeddak of the Torquas, though rumors still maintain that some great secret treasure from Barsoom's ancient past waits to be found, sealed away beneath the city. There are many who dismiss this story as something less than folklore, but, as those who believe murmur, it is not as though the green Martians are known for their interest in anything they can't use as a weapon.

Notable Torquas

HORTAN GUR

Jeddak of the Torquas. Loses to the Lotharian's illusory forces, but considered a fierce and skilled leader prior to his defeat.

TORQUAS IN YOUR CAMPAIGN

Torquas are largely open to interpretation by players and narrators. During earlier eras, they are led by a jeddak respected for his vision and ability. By the time the Jeddak of Jeddaks era comes, Hortun Gur's reputation and the overall leadership structure of the Torquas are in flux. Especially during this period, the Torquas may become allies of a dangerous civilization, fall apart into chaos, or undergo some other deep cultural change.

Hortan Gur's position is far from certain. Since the Torquasian's defeat at the illusory point of Lotharian arrows, he has faced two challenges from ambitious jeds. While he has triumphed in both of these duels, this has not reified his position. Instead, it has revealed the cunning of the older jeds, who merely wait for him to become wearier and wounded before striking. Prior to his failure against the Lotharians, in which so many of his finest warriors were slaughtered by an enemy they were unable to truly fight, Hortan Gur was considered a jeddak of vision. It is perhaps well for the red Martians and others who prefer peace to warfare that his reign appears likely to fail imminently.

THURD

Almost nothing is known of the Thurd, save that the city they inhabit was thought lost forever, consumed by a vast storm which left nothing it touched alive. What had been, before the arrival of the storm, a thriving city was left a deserted labyrinth of stone. The green Martians who claim Thurd as their home and remain within its walls to this day are whispered to be different from their kin. While their brutality and love of combat remains as steadfast as ever, it is said they no longer speak with one another but can, instead, communicate via some form of telepathy, voicelessly transmitting their thoughts to each other. Others assert that the Thurd have no jeddak and no jeds, instead carrying out strange rituals in which each green Martian speaks their mind and a consensus is reached before any action is undertaken by the horde. It is also said, however, that several neighboring communities of green Martians, eager to add warriors to their ranks, mistook these rumors of peculiar behavior as signs of weakness. The few, badly wounded, survivors who returned from these raids are eloquent testimony to the wrongheadedness of such a belief. Whatever is true of the Thurd, whether they are afflicted with mysterious conditions unique among the green Martians, or whether their relative isolation from their kin has resulted in some minor differences of culture, is currently impossible to know. It would take adventurers with the bold spirits of a John Carter or a Tars Tarkas to make the journey and determine the veracity of these tall tales. Of course, on Barsoom, anything may be possible, and wherever strange possibilities wait to be discovered, so too does great danger.

THURD IN YOUR CAMPAIGN

Even more than the Torquas, the Thurd serve as a cipher and mostly blank slate for narrators and players to develop. Player characters from the Thurd hordes have great flexibility in how they present their characters and narrators can define them according to the needs of whatever campaign or adventure involves them.

CHAPTER 9: THE RED KINGDOMS

Epochs ago, when the seas of Mars first began to dry and its air first began to thin, the three original races of Barsoom set aside their differences and worked together to save their world. Millennia of effort and technological exploration could not slow the death of their world, but it did produce a genesis of a different kind. The bloodlines of the three races mixed, diluting the hereditary traits of each race and combining to create something new: the red Martians.

When it became clear their battle against the death of Barsoom would be lost, the ancestral nations of the Holy Therns, First Born, and Okar retreated to remote holds, leaving their great cities abandoned. The red Martians made their homes in these empty spaces, and expanded across the face of the planet. They became Barsoom's dominant race, forming a more diverse society across a greater breadth of territory than any other nation.

Red Martians are shaped much like the humans of Earth, though most tend towards beautiful features and bodies of more athletic proportions. Their skin is reddish-copper. They wear their black hair long, but rarely grow hair on their faces or bodies. Like most Martians, they wear little in the way of clothing except in extremely cold weather. Instead, many decorate their bodies to represent accomplishments, rank, or key personal events. They use body paint, metallic ornaments, jewelry, and other substances for this purpose. Some red cultures may even use tattoos and body modification. The exact nature of these ornaments varies between kingdoms and sometimes denotes special deeds or significance, especially those claimed by a victor in battle.

RED KINGDOM CULTURE

All Martian races are warlike, and red Martians are no exception. All red Martians received basic training from childhood in their traditional weapons: pistol, sword, hatchet, dagger, and closed fist. This is true of every tradesman, farmer, statesman, and scientist, while soldiers and warriors receive additional training (and much experience) as part of their professions.

Their armies and navies are paragons of military discipline, efficiency and might, allowing them to historically take what they wanted even from the ancient and powerful ancestral races, and to keep it in the face of the larger and more ferocious green Martians.

Despite this, the red Martians are more civilized (by Jasoomian standards) than the other races, even those far more ancient and developed. Unlike those other peoples, they understand the emotion of love, and form emotional bonds with spouses and children. They have mastered several forms of art, most notably mural painting and marble statuary, as well as music and dance. Red Martian cities are dotted with gardens which, though not as lush as those on the wetter and more verdant Earth, are beautifully arranged and carefully kept. While mercy to enemies is largely unknown, they are not unnecessarily cruel towards captives and opponents.

OF CAPITALS AND KINGDOMS

Red Martian society is feudal. A given kingdom is held by a jeddak, who rules from the capital city and holds any other cities he can intimidate by force or entice through commerce. Each of those smaller cities is ruled by a jed. Jeds hold absolute power in their personal realms, but owe absolute fealty to their jeddak. Districts within the city, as well as outlying settlements and farms, are administrated by chieftains who hold the same relationship with their territory and jed as the jed does with his city and jeddak.

Violence is at the heart of red Martian society. Combat is a perfectly acceptable and even preferred method for handling slights, affronts, and grievances — to the point it is said violence between red Martians is the only force keeping the population of these otherwise long-lived beings in check. A jeddak holds sway by being the most powerful warrior and cunning politician among the jeds of his nation. A jed rules his territory by overpowering all rivals there. Becoming jed of a city is simply a matter of besting the jed in honorable combat, or of having the jed assassinated, then defeating rival aspirants to the throne. It's a warlike organizational system, held (barely) in check by three traditions dear to the hearts of all red Martians: rule of law, personal honor, and courtly love.

RULE OF LAW

Despite the feudal organization of red Martian society, even the jeddaks are bound by the rule of law. These traditions date back millennia, and fill a place in red Martian hearts more akin to how Jasoomians feel about religion. They are broken only in the most extreme circumstances, and, even in extremis, some red Martians prefer death or the destruction of an entire nation to breaking the bonds of law.

Each nation has its own set of codes. When they are broken, the criminal is brought to judgment either by the jed or jeddak, or by a council of rulers and nobles. Punishments are harsh — almost always death, slavery, or exile — as befits a race so comfortable with violence.

Even vying for a throne requires rigid adherence to the law. Though any jed or jeddak may be challenged to combat for his title, the circumstances under which this may take place are specifically defined and often bewilderingly complex. One who slays a ruler under other circumstances is deemed unfit for the throne.

Rule of law among the red Martians extends even to assassination. Unlike on Jasoom, where an assassin waits in the shadows to strike a victim from hiding, the act on Barsoom is carried out in plain sight. An assassin of the red Martians is a skilled fighter hired to challenge a lesser warrior in single combat. Though the justification for the challenge is often vanishingly thin, this murder is carried out according to law and custom.

Law extends to alliances and marriage, owing in large part to how the red Martians adore their nobles much like a twentieth century Jasoomian adores a celebrity. Because of this, political marriages are a common tool for cementing alliances between cities, or between powerful clans within a nation. Some are not above abducting a noble in order to force the hand of an influential royal, family, or even an entire kingdom.

PERSONAL HONOR

Honor is more important to a red Martian than life itself. No red Martian willingly lies, or shows cowardice of any sort. This is so central to the being of even non-warrior red Martians that potential mates are less swayed by overt shows of bravery. They consider such bravado commonplace, and probable masks for cowardice, preferring the quiet instances of courage denoting a stronger personality or more seasoned warrior.

The race's rules of personal combat are an example of this honor in action. Although they are rarely found without several traditional weapons close to hand, if attacked, a red Martian will only defend himself with the same weapon his attacker bears, or with a lesser weapon. A warrior attacked with a dagger might draw a dagger in his defense, or face his opponent unarmed. He would never draw a sword, pistol, or other weapon to create an unfair advantage. To do so risks such dishonor that death is the preferable fate. Though this is true of nearly all the races of Barsoom, it is observed with unusual fervor among the red Martians.

When a red Martian gives his word, all but the basest villain keeps his promise or dies in the attempt. Nowhere is this facet of honor more sacred or demonstrative than an oath of fealty to a ruler or of loyalty to a friend. Such oaths are taken so seriously most red nations have a ritual surrounding their giving and taking, not dissimilar to wedding vows. For example, the throwing down of a sword at another's feet symbolizes a sacred oath:

"My sword, my body, my life, my soul are yours to do with as you wish. Until death and after death I look to you alone for authority for my every act. Be you right or wrong, your word shall be my only truth. Whoso raises his hand against you must answer to my sword."

COURTLY LOVE

Red Martians love and revere romance. Those in love cannot abide to see the subject of their desire injured or humiliated, and are ideally expected to risk their lives to prevent such a thing from taking place. Rescuing a lover in peril is so common that all red Martian cities observe a custom by which the rescued party can offer their hand in marriage. This traditionally involves a male rescuer and a female captive. The woman addresses the man as "my chieftain," and the man responds by saying "my princess." This betrothal ceremony is taken quite seriously, more seriously than the wedding itself by many.

Of course, the wedding ceremony itself is cause for gravity and celebration as it combines the themes of personal honor and courtly love. The specifics vary from city to city, but most include the clamping of golden collars around the throats of husband and wife alike to symbolize their eternal service to one another. Such ceremonies are attended by as many friends and allies as both families have, and are invariably held in beautiful places to symbolize the importance of love in general and the ideal of courtly love.

Though not as overtly discussed, love between comrades-at-arms is an equally powerful force. At times, the love of one warrior for another has moved thousands of red Martian ships to war, and changed the fates of cities, races, and nations. This bond is hard-won, and found usually only under the most dire of circumstances, but, once established, can be severed only in death.

CONFLICTS OF INTEREST

Many of the most interesting stories among the red Martians take place when two of these fundamental characteristics come into conflict. What happens when the legal duty of a red warrior to his jed contradicts his personal honor, or an oath to a friend? Or when the passions of courtly love run contrary to the law? What is a warrior to do when the one who rules his heart asks him to betray the jeddak who rules his land?

For example, the pride and lust of a red Martian has been known to cause one to forget personal honor in the name of a twisted form of courtly love. More than one war, coup, or conflict was started by a powerful red Martian desiring a comely member of the opposite sex, then abducting the object of desire in an attempt to force marriage. Without a family member or lover to rescue the victim, this too often ends in slavery or suicide. When a powerful and courageous lover or family member is on hand… those become the tales red Martians sing and talk of for generations to come.

RELIGION

The religious beliefs of the red Martians can be clearly divided between those held prior to John Carter's second arrival on Barsoom, and those held after his arrival and subsequent campaigns against the Holy Therns and First Born.

Prior to John Carter's arrival, nearly all red Martian kingdoms worship Issus, Goddess of Life Eternal and of Death, along with a form of ancestor worship not dissimilar to many Asian cultures on Jasoom. Though this worship rarely impacts daily life — red Martians are a pragmatic people focused almost exclusively on the here and now — any red Martian who lives to reach 1,000 years of age undertakes a pilgrimage to the Valley Dor. The pilgrim boards one of many boats found on the banks of the River Iss and follows its flow through a cavern complex to the Valley Dor to enter a second life of bliss in paradise. None return from this pilgrimage, and those who claim to are universally put to death as heretics.

RELIGION IN THE JEDDAK OF JEDDAKS ERA

John Carter's return to Barsoom gives him first-hand experience with the Valley Dor and exposes the promise of paradise as a deadly lie. He ultimately exposes the Holy Therns' pernicious role in that deceit, and discovers the true identity of Issus herself. He then dethrones the mortal imposter to godhood. This news is neither quickly nor universally well received, but some years after his crowning as Jeddak of Jeddaks, most red Martians accept the truth. They no longer take the pilgrimage to the Valley Dor, or worship in Issus' name. They still hold dear to their reverence for ancestors, and many spend their lives living up to the example of a revered and long-passed forebear.

TECHNOLOGIES

As befits any science fiction adventure, time spent among the red Martians is time spent surrounded by amazing (if sometimes far-fetched) technologies. Interacting with the capabilities of these devices, and circumventing their limitations, is at the heart of much of what happens while traveling among their people and through their cities.

Many aspects of red technology are incredibly advanced to the eyes of a Jasoomian. Flying machines zoom at high speeds, thousands of ads above the ground. Towers soar to heights no human architecture can rival. Healing salves save wounded soldiers from apparently certain death. A single facility can alter the atmosphere of the entire planet. Mad science defies what we think we understand about physiology, psychology, and physics. In the context of these wonders, however, two things must be understood.

ANACHRONISTIC WEAPONS

Though green Martians have rifles with awesome stopping power and astonishing range, and red Martians have vast dreadnought warships, both prefer to fight with sword and dagger. Long-distance communication technology is all but unheard-of, and surface transportation between cities relies on livestock-drawn carts while the airships soar overhead. Technologically, red cities are a study in contrast between high technologies and classical-age techniques.

THIS IS BUT A SHADOW

The histories of Barsoom say the primal races possessed technologies far beyond those now used even by the Holy Therns. Many devices used in day-to-day red Martian life are things the people know how to use, but could never build, repair, or replace. The tradition-bound culture of the red Martians has stifled creativity and technological development in most nations, leading them to rely instead on the creations of those who came before.

At least, this was so before John Carter arrived. For various reasons including but not limited to

Carter's disruption of religious tradition and the scientific exploration of his son Carthoris, new experimentation and development has begun even in some of the more conservative circles. For example, Carthoris invented a new autopilot for airships, which directs a craft directly toward a set destination without need for a pilot.

Further, the events surrounding John Carter's later exploits call some of the histories into doubt. In military conflicts with the Holy Therns, First Born, and Okarians, the red Martians emerged victorious. Had the original races possessed the fabled technologies of old, one would expect a vastly different outcome. No evidence of advanced technologies were found during the battles for, and the sacking of, those races' strongholds. It is possible (though certainly not an agreed-upon fact) the fabled technologies of old were not as advanced as has been assumed through the ages.

THE GREAT RED MILITARY

The "Great Red Military" is something of a misnomer since neither the red people nor any red nation has a united military of the sort found among modern Jasoomians. Instead, the soldiery of the red cities is organized much like their people as a whole.

THE RED ARMIES

Any given chieftain, jed, or jeddak has a personal guard of fighting men loyal to him. If he needs more troops for anything from a raid to a full-scale war, he calls for the aid of allied leaders. The size of an army any given red Martian can muster is directly related to the loyalty he has earned. Thus, a jeddak can assemble much larger forces than a chieftain, but a popular and beloved chieftain could form a force large enough to challenge the troops fielded by a disliked or craven jed.

Red armies rarely last longer than the threat or adventure for which they were assembled, soon after falling to raiding or simply returning home to their lives. Even so, an assembled mass of red soldiers is a disciplined and enthusiastic force, fearing nothing and giving no mercy to whatever stands in its path.

There are exceptions to this rule. The frozen armies of Pankor, for example, are organized as a cohesive whole under the rule of that city's jed, and wealthy Gathol maintains a standing army via a system of required public service. Each jeddak keeps a personal bodyguard with a degree of authority more like a modern, Jasoomian army or police force. Still, there is no tenet of red Martian culture to support the structure or authority of an army beyond loyalty to the jeddak and the tradition of personal honor. More than one jed or even jeddak has fallen when his poor treatment of troops and subjects put their loyalty in the hands of a rival.

AIR SUPERIORITY

The airship navy of the red Martians is their key to military dominance over the larger and fiercer mounted cavalry of their green rivals. Each city (with some exceptions) has a fleet of military airships, along with thousands of trade barges and personal vehicles. Travel and communication between the far-flung red cities of Barsoom is possible solely because of these fast transports. They connect communities many hundreds of karads apart and allow reasonably safe passage over the hordes of green Martians on the surface. When brought to war, they carry thousands of soldiers to battle and give them the advantages of position and visibility over ground-based foes.

Airships range in size from a one-man craft to great battleships crewed by 10,000 men. The larger craft often host a small fleet of service vehicles. For example, the 10,000-man dreadnaughts of Helium each carry five ten-man cruisers, ten five-man scouts, and 100 one-man light vehicles for use in small formations or as escape vessels.

Red airships use captured light waves for buoyancy. Each contains a reservoir of light from the eighth ray, a wavelength responsible for propelling the light of the sun from its source and for all reflection of light from planets and moons. The repulsion of this reservoir keeps the vessel above the Barsoomian surface. A reservoir ruptured by accident or violence causes these rays to leak, potentially scuttling the airship or sending it plummeting to the ground 100 haads or more below.

Propulsion for these craft works via tapping into the magnetic field of Barsoom, a technique which gives each vessel essentially unlimited traveling range. Earlier vessels can travel at up to forty karads per hour (166 mph), but after the Helium navy developed a lighter, more powerful motor during the Jeddak of Jeddaks era, the maximum speed increased to nearly 100 karads per hour (300 mph).

Each red airship of any size is equipped with a compass-like device with a needle which fixes on a journey's destination rather than on magnetic north. Once set to its target, the needle points toward the goal and a navigator need only keep the ship's prow pointed in the indicated direction (assuming, of course, no enemies have tampered with the compass in a plot to lead the ship astray).

The airship navies of the red Martians are outfitted with a diverse array of weapons. Some smaller craft go unarmed, relying on the marksmanship of individual crew members to pick off targets with personal weapons. Such ships usually have grappling harpoons, allowing for boarding actions common to Barsoomian naval combat. Other ships, especially the larger dreadnaughts, carry large batteries of cannons and guns. Despite this, Barsoomian codes of honorable combat often see naval officers eschewing larger weapons in favor of bringing equivalent, and therefore honorable, arms to bear on their foes. Large cannons, bombs, and other munitions are reserved for mass battles against equivalent forces–to use them against smaller or inferior forces is seen as a sign of weakness and villainy.

AIRSHIP DESIGN

Regardless of kingdom, most red Martian airships run to similar design. Most consist of one or more decks built on a frame of buoyancy tanks. Personal fliers have a single deck large enough for a single Martian and possibly a passenger or two. The largest battleships keep the same basic shape, but are as wide as buildings and boast dozens of decks capable of transporting thousands.

Though red Martians are rarely innovative with their technologies, new features of the airships are one of the few places where they do occasionally produce something new. Creating a new kind of vessel — whether it's an improved design or a new kind of airship altogether — is well within the ability of red Martians. This means adventures based around a threat from a superior warship, an expedition in a prototype, or stealing a new and dangerous technology, are an excellent fit for adventures involving red Martian kingdoms.

As a general rule, red Martians are as unsentimental about their vessels as they are about everything else. Airships are rarely named, and few craft develop a reputation beyond those of her crew and officers. Stories of the *Revenge* or *HMS Ulysses* and other infamous ships, so common on Jasoom, are not part of general red storytelling or military tradition. Were a ship to be given a name and develop a reputation for war, or exploration, or even peace, it would be a truly noteworthy (and adventure-worthy) occurrence.

JOHN CARTER AND THE RED MARTIANS

Although John Carter's arrival and influence do not change the fundamental nature of red Martian culture and organization, he has a strong impact on the balance of power and helps to shape the "modern" history of much of Barsoom. How much influence varies, depending on which era of play a campaign is set in.

DOTAR SOJAT

When John Carter first arrives on Mars, the cities of Helium and Zodanga are locked in a centuries-long war. Though neither has fully gained the upper hand, Zodanga is poised to win because of their abduction of Dejah Thoris. Inspired by his love for Thoris and his fierce friendship with the Heliumite Prince Kantos Kan, he enlists the help of the green Martian Tars Tarkas. Carter forges an alliance leading to the sack of Zodanga, and it becomes a vassal state to Helium. With the nation's strength no longer sapped by the long, expensive war, Helium rises to become the predominant power among the red Martians of Barsoom.

PRINCE OF HELIUM

John Carter's influence is felt largely by his absence for most of this period, which includes the growing renown of his son, speculation as to Carter's whereabouts, and the growing influence of Helium as Barsoom's first superpower.

Near the end of this ten-year period, John Carter lands in the Valley Dor where he discovers the deceit of the Holy Therns and the madness of the First Born. He gathers an unprecedented army and navy (a feat made possible by the growth in Helium's power since his absence) to raid both races and make both elder peoples become peers to the red Martians rather than their rulers and gods.

From that start, he overthrows the ruling regime of the Okar almost by accident — the Okarian ruler stood between Carter and his beloved Dejah Thoris — and unites green Tharks, red Heliumites, First Born and some Okarians in a single alliance. As a reward, he is named "Jeddak of Jeddaks," warlord of the combined peoples.

JEDDAK OF JEDDAKS

In this later era, the alliance under John Carter rules and faces challenges within and without. This newfound unity does not completely stop scheming and warring between the member states (it doesn't even stop such striving against Carter himself!), but it does add a new layer to the feudal structure of the red cities.

THE RED NATIONS OF MARS

The red Martians live in vast, partially ruined cities once ruled by the ancestral races whose blood intermingled to create them. Such metropolises, if they can truly be called such, are sprawling affairs ringed with high and easily defensible walls, boasting buildings 100 ad (1,000 feet) high and higher. Broad avenues lead from wide gates to a central district, housing the buildings of government. Individuals have their pick of palatial, abandoned homes. Those with higher status may choose to live close to the home of the city's jed, while those of lower status live closer to the edge. All the gardens, apartments, shops, and buildings of state are repurposed by their current occupants, but bear signs of the beautiful and more accomplished original owners.

Each city's influence extends outward along adjacent canals, the only source of fresh water over most of Barsoom. Small settlements and individual farms provide crops for the population. Because of the warlike nature of life on Barsoom, even these smaller communities are built defensively. Many have homes that rise on stilts at night to prevent attack, or at least make approach noisy and arduous as to prevent taking sleeping occupants unawares.

Though all Martians (regardless of race) speak the same tongue, each red city has its own written language so inhabitants can communicate with some degree of secrecy. In larger cities, individual districts, or even families, may have their own written tongue.

The surface of Mars is more wilderness than civilization, but its storied surface is still dotted with the nations of red Martians. What follows is a description of the most notable and unusual of the red nations, along with adventure ideas for each.

Helium

The greatest of the red kingdoms, the Twin Cities of Greater and Lesser Helium are at the center of the events surrounding John Carter and his offspring. Because of this, they are at the center of red Martian life during the Prince of Helium and Jeddak of Jeddaks eras. Even during the Dotar Sojat era, its conflict with Zodanga becomes the pivotal battle of the time and is responsible for much of what follows. These facts give us a more complete picture of life in Helium, and a wider sampling of the city's important occupants.

Greater Helium is the home of the Jeddak of Helium and center of the empire. One of the most populous cities on Barsoom, it boasts a standing military of 100,000 between its army and naval crewmen. Just over two karads (seventy-five miles) away, Lesser Helium is a thriving trade port and lesser brother to the capital. Both cities host towers more than one mile high: the Yellow Tower in Lesser Helium, and the mighty Red Tower in Greater Helium.

Helium's flag is blue, and its citizens wear blue, in remembrance of the long-dead oceans of their once thriving planet.

Greater Helium

The Jeddak of the Helium Empire rules from this, the greatest red city of Barsoom. It is a sprawling metropolis of extensive palaces and broad avenues, with a single entrance in its massive and ancient walls. The Gate of Jeddaks opens onto the broad, moss-covered Avenue of Ancestors. The Avenue, in turn, runs thirteen and a half haads (five miles) to an enormous plaza at the center of the city, sitting in front of the renowned Temple of Reward.

The Temple of Reward is a vast complex of rooms, apartments, offices, and chambers. All are centered around an enormous colosseum where all members of Heliumite society can observe as their jeddak passes judgment on criminals or bestows reward upon heroes. When an individual is to be judged, he is led up the Aisle of Hope, a passageway within the Temple leading under the eyes of the assembled jeds, and to the Pedestal of Truth. There, the accused or accoladed stands before the Jeddak of Helium who sits at the Throne of Righteousness. Though it is within the power of the jeddak to pronounce sentence unilaterally, the votes and opinions of all assembled jeds and chieftains carry weight, and the person at the pedestal is always permitted to state his case to the body.

Lesser Helium

If Greater Helium is the political and military hub of the empire, Lesser Helium is its commercial center. The city is fabulously wealthy with slaves, silks, furs, and jewelry, and the sky overhead teems with freighters and passenger liners. The city hosts a system of public transportation which fires eight-foot-long, conical capsules along a grooved track at impressive speeds and connects the various neighborhoods of the widespread metropolis.

At the center of Lesser Helium lies the great market: a plaza of over one haad on each side where a Martian (a red Martian, at least), can buy anything at all. The great slave market of Helium stands at its center. Here, great crowds surround a central block where bidders vie to purchase slaves captured from nearby cities and on long-range expeditions. On any given day, one can find a laborer for any given task — if one can bid well enough and afford to make good on the bid.

Though wealth is more obvious in Lesser Helium, security is laxer here than in the capital. More than one adventurer with no desire to be discovered has entered the Twin Cities via Lesser Helium because air and foot patrols are less intense there. Once inside the secure perimeter, travel to Greater Helium is easy and relatively unmonitored.

The Atmosphere Plant

When the air began to fail on Barsoom, one of the ancestor races (or a collaboration of two or all three) built the atmosphere plant. The complex covers eleven square haads (four square miles) and is protected with outer walls fifteen ads (150 feet) thick. Its glass ceiling is one-half ad (five feet) thick. The facility is designed to repulse all attempts at invasion or sabotage, and for good reason.

The plant pumps out life-giving air at a rate roughly equivalent to how quickly breathable atmosphere depletes on Barsoom. Were it to fail (as it did near the end of the Dotar Sojat era), life on the Red Planet would become extinct for lack of air in a matter of months. Though all Martians understand the importance of the atmosphere plant, many Martians are willing to risk death to further a cause or keep an oath. Attempted raids and sabotage have happened before, and will almost certainly happen again.

All red Martians learn the principles of atmosphere manufacturing as children. The plant harnesses the ninth ray of light, which the glass roof of the facility collects. It is then converted into pure energy and stored in enormous reservoirs within the plant. The plant then turns the energy into a gas, which further transforms upon contact with the ether of space, ultimately becoming the breathable atmosphere life on Barsoom requires.

At any given time, only two red Martians know how to enter and exit the facility, a technique requiring the mental visualization of a series of sounds: essentially a telepathic combination lock. The keeper, as well as his assistant, live a monastic life while taking care of the complex. The two divide the watch between them, each spending five teeans (about half a Martian year) alone tending to the facility and protecting it from harm. They are ultimately responsible for training their replacements at the end of their tenure. Near the end of the Dotar Sojat era, the keeper of the atmosphere plant and his assistant both die before they can train replacements. The plant breaks down in a catastrophe threatening the death of every being on Barsoom (except for a population of Okar near the North Pole, who have built a similar plant designed to maintain an atmosphere bubble around their own immediate domain). Only the quick actions of

John Carter prevent this disaster, but, in doing so, he triggers his return to Earth. He is not seen again on Mars for ten years.

Notable Heliumites

Helium is both the most influential city of the red kingdoms, and the home of John Carter and his family. For both reasons, it has a wider array of influential and important citizens than other red nations. A complete list would be far beyond the scope of this gazette, but some of the most important include:

JOHN CARTER

A Jasoomian and adventuring hero, Carter is extremely strong in comparison to Barsoomians due to the greater gravity and air density on Earth. Carter becomes renowned in Helium after leading a successful assault on their rival Zodanga, and is later elevated to the status of Jeddak of Jeddaks by a multi-racial council of Martians. Afterward, he continues to have many adventures across the planet and becomes one of the driving forces of Barsoomian politics, society, and history.

DEJAH THORIS

The beloved Princess of Helium and daughter of Lesser Helium's Jed Mors Kajak, this woman would have led an interesting and influential life even had she never met John Carter. As his wife, she is arguably the most famed and beloved individual of all red Martians. Besides her place in the political and social weave of Helium's nobles, she is also strangely susceptible to abduction by enemies. This trait led directly to many of John Carter's world-changing campaigns.

CARTHORIS

Son of John Carter and Dejah Thoris, he has almost the full strength of his Jasoomian father. He is captured by slavers of the First Born, and his rescue by his father begins the campaign which overthrows their false god-queen Issus. Later, his marriage to Thuvia of Ptarth cements an alliance between Helium and that nation. A natural inventor and adventurer, his exploits will eventually rival his father's, and his innovations make small but significant changes to daily life on Barsoom.

TARA

Daughter of John Carter and Dejah Thoris, she possesses both her mother's royal bearing and her father's tenacity, making her a formidable individual. She is one of few Martian women to have slaughtered men in self-defense. She marries Gahan, Jeddak of Gathol, in a union allying the smaller but wealthy nation to Helium.

MORS KAJAK

Jed of Lesser Helium and father of Dejah Thoris, Mors Kajak is far from being an "also ran" in feats of daring and military might among the red Martians. When his grandson Carthoris disappears (captured and enslaved by a First Born raiding party), he organizes an enormous fleet of exploration and conquest to find him. They are brought down by the Okar of the north, and Mors himself is enslaved. Freed from this fate by John Carter, he is instrumental in the Jasoomian's elevation to the rank of Jeddak of Jeddaks.

TARDOS MORS.

The mighty and long-lived Jeddak of Helium, he is the grandfather of Dejah Thoris and father of Mors Kajak. He rules over the Heliumite Empire during its heyday, and is the first red Martian to ever forge an alliance with the green Martians.

KANTOS KAN

An airman of Helium, Kantos Kan is captured by green Martians of the savage Warhoon clan. In their dungeons, he meets John Carter. They escape from the Warhoon gladiatorial games by fighting such a long battle against one another the bored spectators do not notice Kantos Kan's killing of Carter is merely a sword slipped into the Jasoomian's armpit. They are separated during the escape, and later meet in Zodanga. He remains friends with John Carter throughout both their lives, nearly marrying his son Djor Kantos to Carter's daughter Tara.

HOR VASTUS

An officer in Helium's great airship navy, Hor Vastus joins the stage of world-shaking events when he encounters John Carter escaping the Valley Dor. He is one of the first red Martians to believe the horrible truth about the Valley and the Holy Therns who rule it, and risks execution for supporting Carter's blasphemous claims. In time, he assembles the largest navy ever seen by red Martians to aid John Carter's raid on the First Born's subterranean stronghold.

Helium in Your Campaign

Helium serves as the center for most of the action in Burroughs's novels, and is a presence in even those stories which do not focus on John Carter and his family. It would be easy to let it serve the same purpose in your campaign: a thriving, homogeneous empire at the center of Barsoomian society.

You could opt to make Helium an opponent. Not all Barsoomians are happy in the shadow of Helium and its interloper Jeddak of Jeddaks.

ZODANGA

For thousands of years, the city of Zodanga ruled a vast and mighty empire, held together via force of arms and a strict, brutal system of laws and punishments. Much of its power was aimed at eradicating the green Martians, against whom the entire nation held the most bitter of enmities. Such was their hatred of the green men of Barsoom, their armies did not hesitate to destroy that race's incubators and slaughter children by the hundreds as they lay gestating in their eggs.

The remainder of Zodanga's power spent over a century focused on a fierce war with the Twin Cities of Helium. They were poised to prevail through a combination of treachery, abduction and political marriage, which would make them the most powerful red nation of Barsoom. John Carter's arrival, and his coincidental love for the imprisoned Dejah Thoris, tips the balance of power when he unites green Tharks and red Heliumites against Zodanga.

Zodanga, its central and capital city, is a vast urban sprawl surrounded by carborundum blocks seven and a half ads high and five ads thick (approximately seventy-five feet by fifty feet). Were these walls not perforated at regular intervals by poorly guarded gates, it is possible even Carter's great combined army of Tharks and Heliumite warriors could not have penetrated them. The central plaza of Zodanga occupies a full square mile, and many of its buildings exceed 100 ads (1,000 feet) in height. Though not as ornately beautiful as Greater Helium, or as ostentatiously wealthy as Lesser Helium, the city's avenues and edifices are clean and impressive.

Zodangans wear red colors and fly a red flag, symbols of the blood shed by their warriors over many centuries of conflict.

NOTABLE ZODANGANS

Though the history of Zodanga is filled with stories of individuals famed for impressive exploits in their own right, Zodanga's people of the Dotar Sojat, Prince of Helium, and Jeddak of Jeddak eras are almost exclusively defined by their relationship with Zodanga's conquering state of Helium.

THAN KOSIS

Jeddak of Zodanga during the city's heyday and its centuries-long war against Helium, Kosis is a harsh but honorable ruler. He was killed during the sack of Zodanga.

ZAT ARRAS

After Helium invaded Zodanga with the help of the green Tharks, Zat Arras was appointed its jed under the condition he swear allegiance to Helium, its jed, and its empire. In later years, the temptation to raise himself to the station of Jeddak of Helium proves too great. He secretly imprisons John Carter and openly lobbies for his execution for blasphemy. When Carter escapes, Arras's fate is predictable.

SAB THAN

A Prince of Zodanga, Sab Than has the misfortune of falling in love with Dejah Thoris after she is captured and brought to the palace as a prisoner. He demands she give him her hand in marriage to prevent immense bloodshed in a successful siege and sack of Greater Helium. She agrees despite having already fallen in love with John Carter. Since only death can stop a red Martian betrothal, this engagement greatly reduces the lifespan of this prince.

UR JAN

The leader of the Zodangan Assassin's Guild, and a Martian with little to no honor. When circumstances conspire to put him in direct conflict with the mighty John Carter, he conspires to kidnap Dejah Thoris rather than face his opponent honorably. He is a skilled fighter who will go to any length to achieve his goals, and would make an excellent long-term antagonist in many campaigns.

GAL NAR AND FAL SIVAS

These rival scientists hail from Zodanga and work primarily on vehicles and controls for vehicles. For example, Fal Sivas has developed a mechanical brain to control ships so they can fly without direction from a living pilot. A microcosm of the strife and scheming within all levels of the city's society, they spy on one another, attempt to sabotage the other's reputation, and steal ideas in an ongoing feud. Both are willing to perform cruel experiments on slaves to further their scientific explorations, but neither will risk his own life to test a new idea. It is rumored one may soon unveil a flying machine capable of true interplanetary travel.

ZODANGA IN YOUR CAMPAIGN

Crime and punishment are key themes for adventures set in Barsoom's second-greatest city. While political power in Helium is largely unified, the many factions of Zodanga continue to vie for what power leaks from the Twin Cities' clenched fist.

Zodanga could also be the center of a rebellion plot against Helium. Instead of adventurers running in the shadow of the mighty John Carter, the players could be working to free the neck of Zodanga from its ancient rival's boot.

INSPIRATIONS FROM JASOOM

Although he never said so publicly, it is largely believed that Edgar Rice Burroughs based Zodanga on the earthly city of Chicago of the 1920s: a massive metropolis full of gangsters, corruption, and architectural wonders. Similarly, the Twin Cities of Greater and Lesser Helium are inspired by the cleaner and separated cities of Minneapolis and St. Paul.

Other cities on Barsoom have far less clear Earthly inspirations, and were most likely created to forward one plot device or another.

KAOL

Kaol existed in isolation for thousands of years, located many hundreds of haads from the nearest other red nations. It sits on a rare region of marshy ground, which gives rise to one of the few remaining forested areas on Barsoom. Its walls and towers are nestled in a thick jungle, invisible from the air but for spires here and there set to watch the sky for airships and other threats from above. Their isolation has led to a variety of cultural differences between Kaol and other red nations.

Although they are aware of the existence of airships, Kaolians got along without them for most of their existence and instead travelled solely by land. (They would later begin purchasing airships from other cities and using them in both commerce and warfare.) They are the only red Martians to use the huge zitidar as pack animals (others deem them undignified beasts of burden fit only for the "lesser" green Martians), which they hitch to enormous wagons for travel along a network of well-maintained roads. Squads of soldiers patrol these roads bearing weapons coated with the poison of a sith, a vicious and venomous animal native to the jungle there.

The nation's capital, Kaol, is much like other red cities except for its great outer wall. This wall is seven and a half ads high (seventy-five feet), and totally encircles the city with a barrier of stone polished smooth as glass and completely unscalable. Its remote location has made the nation more backward than other red cities. For example, the Kaolians do not hear of John Carter's campaign against the Holy Therns and First Born, and still worship Issus even as Carter pursues Phaidor to the city walls.

NOTABLE KAOLIANS

Few Kaolians become "named characters" in the canon of Burroughs's works, with Kulan Tith being the only worth particular mention. This leaves much room for a narrator to create families, plots, heroes, and villains without altering any of what's been written before.

KULAN TITH
Jeddak of Kaol and a devout worshiper of Issus. Immediately upon being told of Issus' fraud, he accuses John Carter of blasphemy rather than believe the evidence before his eyes. It is only after personally witnessing the simultaneous treachery of a Holy Thern and a First Born exile that he comes to accept the truth. He later becomes a staunch ally of Helium and boon companion of Carter's son, Carthoris.

DUSAR

All red Martians value honor, but not all Martians are as honorable as others. Perhaps the citizens of Dusar resent the larger and wealthier nations nearby, and work against them as a jealous younger brother might scheme against his sibling. Perhaps the Holy Therns are at work behind the scenes, poisoning the minds of jeds and chieftains who would otherwise be more fair, honest, and just. Whatever the cause, the men and women of Dusar seem more willing to lie, scheme, and betray than other red Martians. They have a history of conflict and rivalry with both Helium and Ptarth, but are unwilling to enter into open war against either as they would be almost effortlessly destroyed.

Dusar is famed for its honey, and for a mead-like honey wine it produces from same.

NOTABLE DUSARIANS

ASTOK
This prince of Dusar is a prime example of the Dusarian's penchant for subterfuge and deceit. When refused as a suitor by Thuvia of Ptarth, he kidnaps her with the intent of forcing her to comply with his proposal. In addition to this unspeakable act of barbarity, he sets in motion a series of nefarious deceptions aimed at framing Carthoris of Helium for the crime. Had it been successful, it might have triggered a war between Helium and Ptarth which would have left Dusar in a position to profit from the weakening of both nations. When his plan fails, he lacks the courage even to die in honorable combat.

DUSAR IN YOUR CAMPAIGN

Although some of its people play a large role in one of the more central Barsoom novels, Dusar is something of a blank slate. Adventures set in Dusar (or among Dusarians) can be of broader scope or with more specific details without abandoning the canon of the setting.

PTARTH

Ptarth is a red Martian kingdom ruled by Thuvan Dihn, a jeddak of renown. If there is a "typical" red Martian city, this is the example. Her people have the warcraft for which all reds are respected, but are no more conquest-driven or puissant than the other kingdoms. Their art is as beautiful, but no more bautiful, than those of other cities. Their kingdom is neither the richest nor poorest, nor the largest or smallest.

Ptarth's greatest claim to notoriety is nearly going to suicidal war against Helium over the fate of Thuvan Dihn's daughter, Thuvia. Thuvia has many adventures with John Carter, and attracts the love of his son Carthoris. Shortly after her betrothal to Kulan Tith of Kaol, she is abducted by a prince of Dusar but Carthoris is accused of the offense. If not for Carthoris' rescue of Thuvia, war might well have been inevitable.

NOTABLE PTARTHIANS

True to the nature of their kingdom, few Ptarthians stand out in the annals of Barsoomian history. Those who do were swept into greater events by the actions of more outstanding men and women from other nations and races.

THUVAN DIHN

Jeddak of Ptarth and father of Thuvia, Thuvan Dihn is to red Martians as Ptarth is to red cities. He is a proud, powerful and cunning leader of a nation of proud, powerful and cunning men. Though his daughter gets caught up in greater events, Thuvan Dihn stands out neither as a particularly great nor particularly poor example of red Martiandom.

THUVIA

This Princess of Ptarth departs her family and home city earlier than is customary and takes the final pilgrimage to the Valley Dor. There, she is captured by the Holy Therns and kept as a slave for fifteen years. Rescued by John Carter, she guides him out of their stronghold and helps him escape, only to be captured by the First Born and trapped in their Tower of the Sun. Later freed, she is betrothed to Kulan Tith, Jeddak of Kaol. She is kidnapped yet again by Astok, another suitor, and rescued by Carthoris in a coup that both stops war between Ptarth and Helium, and sees to the marriage of Thuvia to Carthoris. Thuvia is the only known Martian able to control the ferocious banth, which she does by speaking in a specific tone of voice only she can produce.

HOVAN DU

A victim of experiments by Ras Thavas of Toonol, Hovan Du was as typical a red Martian as any of his countrymen. While in the mad scientist's clutches, half of his brain is exchanged with half the brain of a white ape. Ras Thavas keeps both hybrid bodies operating long enough to make observations and notes, then he re-exchanges the halves to return both subjects to normal. Once restored, Hovan Du is released and returned to normal life in the city of Phundahl.

PTARTH IN YOUR CAMPAIGN

With the possible exceptions of Zodanga and Helium, Ptarth undergoes the most fundamental changes between the different eras of play on Barsoom. These changes beg the question of how different Ptarthians feel about what has come to pass. Revenge, rebellion, and religious orthodoxy could all play a role both in adventures set here, or in the makeup of characters hailing from Ptarth.

Manator is distant from other red Martian nations, and made even more remote by the treacherous ground surrounding the city. Haads upon haads of rocky badlands make ground travel nearly impossible, and the air about the nation is swept by treacherous winds that all but stop any approach via airship. The nation consists of three major cities: Manataj, Manatos, and Manator.

The cities are even more technologically backward than Kaol and Toonol, with walls and defenses built to withstand attack from archaic weapons only. They have no landing stages or spires for flying craft. Their warriors carry swords, spears, and bows, never firearms. They ride a smaller species of thoat into battle while wearing feathered headdresses. It can be fairly said Manatorians are as warlike and ferocious compared to other red Martians as red Martians are warlike and ferocious compared to Jasoomians. If a jed or jeddak of Manator's courage is ever questioned, he is required to prove his bravery on the spot or lose his rank to whoever questioned him. Manator's backwardness also shows itself in a greater degree of superstition than held by other nations. Most Manatorians believe in witches and ghosts, and avoid previously important buildings and portions of their cities said to be haunted.

Like many Martian cities, Manataj, Manatos and Manator all feature wide expanses of empty manors, abandoned apartments and disused parks once thriving when Barsoom was still a living planet. Though the Manatorian population is not significantly larger than other cities', the nation holds nearly one million slaves. Most of the slaves are descendants of captives taken from Gathol during past wars, and the nation relies on the existence and labor of those slaves even more than other red nations. It has been speculated the available work of Manator's slaves is responsible for the nation's backward ways. They have provided the aristocracy with a lifestyle so comfortable none are motivated to foster change or growth.

Taxidermy is a fine and respected art in Manator. The wealthy of the nation often decorate their homes with the preserved corpses of beloved relatives or defeated enemies. In the great hall of the capital, the corpses of deceased jeddaks are beautifully preserved and mounted on their thoats, lining the walls of a room which only the living jeddak may enter. He does so to ask these predecessors counsel and they are rumored to answer.

The wealthy of Manator often play a chess-like game called Jetan, played on a ten-by-ten grid of yellow and black squares. The game is said to be a re-enactment of an epic historical battle between the Okar and the First Born, and in Manator is played using pieces made from the taxidermic bodies of dead slaves. Elaborate games are also played using slaves as living pieces, in which the slaves must duel to the death when a capture is made possible by an aristocrat's choice of move. These grim contests are played in gladiatorial arenas, and draw thousands to the spectacle.

Notable Manatorians

A-KOR
Jeddak of Manator, and former keeper of the Towers of Jetan, he is the illegitimate son of O-Tar and a slave woman. As a prince, he is beloved by the people of his city—enough so his father becomes jealous and plots his death. He is at the center of a plot to expose O-Tar's cowardice resulting in that Martian's undoing and his own ascendancy to the throne.

O-TAR.
A previous jeddak of Manator, he is a perfect physical specimen and a warrior paralleled in ability only by John Carter himself. An inveterate bully who relies on his strength in any battle he knows he can win, he is in fact cowardly even by Jasoomian standards. When confronted publicly with the truth of his cowardice in a misadventure involving the rumored ghost of O-Mai, he commits suicide to make way for a braver jeddak.

O-MAI.
A near-legendary Manatorian jeddak of old, O-Mai was so vicious he earned the nickname "The Cruel" even among the horrific jeddaks of Manator. He is said to have died of fright during some haunting or vision, and was so feared the people of Manator left him in his chambers where his body was left undisturbed. None would brave seeing his corpse for fear of provoking the wrath of his ghost. He lay in his sealed apartments for five thousand years before the drama of O-Tar and A-Kor ended with a scheme involving his body and his legend.

Manator in Your Campaign

The savage nature of Manator permeates every aspect of its culture, and should permeate any adventure set within the empire. Any campaign with more than a smidgen of the supernatural would fit here better than anywhere else on Barsoom, as would a game centering even more on matters of courage and honor than other stories told on Mars. The Jetan games make for a unique twist on the classic gladiator trope found in many tabletop campaigns.

AMHOR

Amhor lies far to the north of Helium. It is a smaller kingdom, with only one city truly rating the designation. Other urban areas within its boundaries are nearer to what a Heliumite would call a settlement or estate. Their chief industry centers around the raising of thoats and zitidars. They raise both for export both as pack or saddle animals, and as butchered meats and crafted hides.

The Zoo of Amhor is infamous throughout Barsoom, in large part because of the jed's habit of capturing live and sentient beings to be part of the exhibits here. The collection also includes specimens of the most vicious and bloodthirsty animals from across the planet. This fact caused considerable mayhem when Vor Daj escaped from his own display cell, setting free the other imprisoned creatures in the process.

NOTABLE AMHORIANS

The most notable Amhorian is its horrific jed. Most Amhorians who amass a degree of fame do so through their interactions with this infamous madman.

JAL HAD

The terrible Jed of Amhor, his reputation is vile even among other despotic rulers of backwater red kingdoms. He thinks nothing of murder and deceit to keep himself in power, and his sexual tastes are nothing short of disgusting. At least two women have chosen death over marriage to this ruler.

JAD-HAN

While still a young (by Barsoomian standards) man, Jad-Han was captured by the First Born and enslaved in their capital city of Kamtol. While imprisoned there, he meets and is later freed by John Carter. Jad-Han is brother to Janai.

JANA

This noblewoman of Amhor seriously considered suicide when Jal Had tries to claim her as his wife. She instead flees her home, and, after several adventures, marries Vor Daj of Helium. She lives the rest of her days there in safety, free of Jal Had's reach and amorous advances.

AMHOR IN YOUR CAMPAIGN

Amhor's key trait is the presence of its villainous jed, who can make for a great campaign villain himself, or make the city a looming threat as he amasses further power and insanity. Alternatively, the adventurers could all be members of Jal Had's court, struggling to keep their heads on their shoulders while protecting the populace as best they can

Phundahl

A small kingdom on the edge of the Toonolian marshes, Phundahl is wildly different from most red Martian nations. It spans but one city and a few islands. It has reasonable access to water, and makes less use of red technologies than most other civilizations of its kind. Her citizens do not follow the goddess Issus. Instead, they worship the god Tur, whom they claim created Barsoom and all of the beings who live there.

Phundahl is an extremist society whose members respect only the knowledge found in the Turgan (the Bible of their religion). The book is said to have been written by Tur himself, and no Phundahlian ever reads words found elsewhere. Similarly, they neither travel nor permit the use of telescopes, since what either might show directly contradicts the word of Tur.

Tur, they say, lives on the sun and created everything on Barsoom for his own amusement. His followers are oppressive and paranoid, viewing any but the most obsessive orthodoxy toward their faith as suspicious and tantamount to heresy.

Notable Phundahlians

DAR TARUS

The Jeddak and High Priest of Phundahl, he rose to power in a series of events bizarre even by the standards of that city (which is a society bizarre even by the standards of Barsoom). He begins life as a warrior in the court of Xaxa, becoming renowned for his physical beauty and vigor. A higher noble in the court desires his body for a brain transplant, so he is assassinated and his brain removed for storage in Ras Thavas' archives. Eventually, John Carter frees the warrior's consciousness and returns his brain to his body. The particulars of this adventure also deposed Phundahl's reining jeddara, whom Dar Tarus succeeds to the throne.

XAXA

One of the few jeddara (female jeds) among the red Martians, Xaxa was High Priestess of Phundahl for many centuries. She is described as ignorant, arrogant, selfish, and stupid, and uses the strict draconian tenets of her religion to keep her subjects mentally enslaved. She demands high taxes to feed her opulent lifestyle, and takes what she wants from her subjects, even unto their lives and minds.

HORA SAN

Nearly 400 years before the reign of Dar Tarus, it was said the god Tur would speak directly to the people of Phundahl. Hora San, Jeddak and High Priest of the time, disappeared one night never to be seen again. On that same night, Tur ceased speaking to his worshippers. Near the end of Xaxa's reign, Hora San's skeleton is discovered in a hollowed-out statue of Tur, suggesting a simultaneous answer to both mysteries.

Phundahl in Your Campaign

Much like Toonol, Phundahl is a risky place for outsiders who do not at least pay lip service to the worship of Almighty Tur. Because of its backward nature, it lacks much to offer anybody inclined to visit. By contrast, a campaign featuring one or more Phundahlians out in the rest of Barsoom meeting challenges to their worldview could go far beyond the initial and obvious comic relief.

Duhor

Lying far to the north of Helium, Duhor is an enemy of that nation until the Prince of Amhor attacks their unprotected flank to raid the palace for attractive slaves and potential mates. Thus, begins an enmity which still runs hot even by the standards of the fighting-blooded men of Barsoom.

Notable Duhorians

VALLA DIA

Daughter of Jeddak Kor San, her beauty wins from afar the attention of Jal Had of Amhor. He abducts her in the action that begins war between Duhor and Amhor. She avoids becoming his plaything by disguising herself as a servant girl, and is ultimately sold to the mad scientist Ras Thavas. She is later rescued and wed to the Jasoomian Vad Varo.

KOR SAN

The Jeddak of Duhor, his hatred of Helium is surpassed only by his love for his daughter Valla Dia. He plans to marry her to a Duhorian noble to keep rule of his nation within those of Duhorian blood, and he goes screaming into war against Amhor when he hears of her abduction.

VAD VARO

A Jasoomian adventurer who served in Earth's First World War under the name Ulysses Paxton, he is transported to Mars as he lay dying in a trench in Europe. Much like John Carter before him, his exploits on Barsoom begin in earnest when he meets and falls in love with Martian Princess Valla Dia of Durhor

Duhor in Your Campaign

Unless they occur in the time before his arrival, any adventure in Duhor would have to account for the influence and presence of Vad Varo/Ulysses Paxton. His shadow in this city rivals John Carter's over Barsoom in general. Though far from a villain, he could make for an excellent antagonist or boon patron (or both).

Toonol

Toonol is an expansive city of glistening minarets sitting on the eastern edge of the monster-haunted Toonolian Marshes. It stands in stark contrast with many other red cities in that they trade far less frequently, possess no flying vehicles, and neither worship Issus nor believe in the pilgrimages to the Valley Dor at life's end.

Instead, the aristocracy of Toonol practice an intellectual philosophy based on science and mental rigor. This worldview is practiced with all the vigor of a religion, but has neither priests nor holy book. It has four core tenets:

* There is no creator god, nor any living god to guide or judge Martian behavior.

* All life came from the Tree of Life, but nothing created the Tree.

* Good deeds do not exist. There are only selfish deeds with good outcomes.

* The only sin is to fail.

Toonolians are enthusiastic practitioners of what Jasoomians often call "mad science" — especially experimentation on living, often unwilling, subjects. Successful experiments, or even a reputation for pursuing a potentially successful or important discovery, is as easy an upward social path in Toonol as feats of arms among other red Martians.

Though Toonol lags behind other red nations in most technologies, their embracing of scientific exploration does occasionally lead to advancements unseen elsewhere on Barsoom. One such advancement is the equilibrimotor, a belt allowing individuals to fly without an airship. It is about the size and thickness of the life belts used by nineteenth and twentieth century Jasoomian passenger liners, with the padded cells filled with the eighth ray just as the buoyancy reservoirs of red airships are. The belt also contains a radium motor for propulsion and a set of levers for controlling height and direction of travel.

Toonolians look down on other red Martian kingdoms because they view their religion as backward and anti-intellectual. They are the hereditary enemies of the nation of Phundahl, which sits nearby.

Notable Toonolians

VOBIS KAN

Jeddak of Toonol, and patriarch of the aristocratic House of Kan. Vobis is an unpopular ruler with a reputation for flights of insanity and cruel treatment of enemies both real and imagined. His favor is as much a curse as a blessing, since falling out of it can be deadly.

MU TEL

Nephew of Vobis Kan and heir to the throne should his uncle pass. He is immensely popular among the Toonolian people due to his more reasonable outlook and reputation for kindness. It is an open secret in Toonol that he would like to usurp the jeddak's throne with or without violence, but fears the consequences of open revolt. He has more than once conspired with Toonolians and outsiders to bring a more subtle (or at least plausibly deniable) end to his uncle. Thus far, he has been unsuccessful.

GOR HAJUS

A great assassin, Hajus would defeat his victims in fair combat through vastly superior skill at arms. He was also known to refuse to kill anybody he considered worthy of life. When he refuses an assignment from Vobis Kan, he is executed and his body sold to Ras Thavas. He is preserved in that scientist's vaults until his revival by Vad Varo. This apparent resurrection leads to Thavas' exile. Hajus himself escapes and settles into a position of power in Phundahl.

Toonol in Your Campaign

Adventuring Barsoomians in Toonol find themselves in a sticky predicament, especially if they do not know enough about Toonol's religion to effectively pose as followers. The disdain and paranoia felt by Toonolians for outsiders makes for a hazardous environment. Of course, rumors of powerful technology invented in the city might make the journey worth the risk.

Adventurers from Toonol are likely to be interested in scientific exploration or the religious aristocracy. Both can drive interesting scenarios — especially when combined and in conflict.

GATHOL

Gathol is widely considered the oldest city of Barsoom, a designation which means it is staggeringly ancient. It also has the designation of being the only city not part of an empire or kingdom. It sits on a mountain in the middle of a wide salt marsh, and its people still speak of the times it sat on an island shore in the middle of Barsoom's mightiest ocean. The mountain is home to rich veins of diamond, so rich the millennia of mining have yet to play them out, making Gathol the wealthiest of red nations.

Because of this wealth, Gatholians are a vain lot. You can always tell a soldier is from Gathol by the gold and diamond ornaments worked into their harness. The city itself obsesses with keeping what they have, combining its defensible position and large standing army to prevent even attempts at invasion.

Each citizen of Gathol is required to give one hour of service each day to the city, though most capture a slave to perform this hour. Because many masters only require their slaves to perform this single task, slaves in Gathol are generally better off than their counterparts in other kingdoms.

NOTABLE GATHOLIANS

GAHAN
Jeddak of Gathol and husband to Tara of Helium, this famed swordsman meets his future wife in John Carter's palace during the Jeddak of Jeddaks era. In the days that follow, both he and Tara are captured by the Kaldanes of Bantoom. His heroic rescue in Bantoom (and later in Manator, owing to the usual run of bad luck that befalls lovelorn heroes on Barsoom) wins Tara's love and hand.

LLANA
Princess of Gathol and daughter of Tara and Gahan, Llana is as skilled at fighting as any warrior in her city. She has a reputation for flirtatiousness and making extreme demands of suitors to prove their loyalty and worth. Though this causes consternation among her parents and grandparents, she has yet to become enmeshed in a situation from which she couldn't extricate herself.

HAJA
Aunt of Gahan, this princess of Gathol is captured by Manatorian slavers and forced to join the harem of Jeddak O-Tar. In time, she gives birth to A-Kor, O-Tar's son and the man who would eventually cause the jeddak's suicide. She eventually marries Jed U-Thor, a comrade of her cousin and Jeddak of Manatos.

GATHOL IN YOUR CAMPAIGN

The wealth of Gathol makes it ripe for adventures to or in the city, either to find wealthy patronage or steal treasure. The nation needs guards for caravans, as does any nation trading for the diamonds responsible for her wealth. The age of Gathol might provide other hooks for character, color, and peril. Who knows how many secret places have lain buried undisturbed, and what dangers lurk within?

MORBUS

When Ras Thavas found the dead and empty city, he populated it with his Hormads. These Synthetic Men are the product of his experiments into the nature of life and death, and become a population ruled by seven Hormad jeds of equal power. They prove too like the life forms on which they were based, and one conspires to betray and overcome the others. Shortly after that event, one of Thavas' other experiments goes bad and a mass of flesh grows to absorb the city, its island, and most of the Hormads. A fleet from Helium commanded by John Carter destroys the hideous growth before it can expand to threaten the entire world.

NOTABLE MEN OF MORBUS

RAS THAVAS
Originally of Toonol, Thavas is one of the most disturbed and brilliant scientists of a nation of disturbed and brilliant scientists. Born a noble, this famed "Mastermind of Mars" conducts a long series of terrifying and horrific experiments producing results both beneficial and malign for life on Barsoom. This includes ground-breaking work in limb, organ, and brain transplants, as well as reviving the dead. It isn't until Vobis Kan drives him from Toonol for imagined treachery that this mad genius gets truly out of hand. He relocates to Morbus and sets about creating life itself. The result is the Hormads, who slip from his control and nearly destroy him. Were it not for the intervention of John Carter, who needs his brilliance to rescue the terribly injured Dejah Thoris, he would have died. After the event, he is given asylum in Helium. How free he is to practice his experiments and continue his work in that more enlightened nation is not a matter of public knowledge.

MORBUS IN YOUR CAMPAIGN

In all three stages of history, Morbus makes an excellent "lost city" for adventures: a perilous place to visit for contact with Ras Thavas' esoteric knowledge or to quest for a long-forgotten clue or piece of technology.

PANAR

Even more remote than Kaol, Panar sits at the north pole of Barsoom. Its capital, Pankor, is in most ways like other red cities in its architecture and emptiness (though it is practically unique in that its name doesn't match the name of the empire). However, it lays beneath an enormous glass dome like the cities of the Okar. Because of its distant location, surrounded by barren ice and cold, the city spent millennia stagnating with neither trade nor contact with other nations of any race.

Outside the protective glass of Pankor is a grisly sight: the bodies of one million soldiers. These dead sentinels are frozen in suspended animation, kept ready for restoration via ancient technologies. At one time, the Jeddak Hin Abtol had them all reanimated to march and go to war. Unlike the armies of other red cities, the frozen soldiers of Panar have low morale and can even be described as cowardly. They are motivated chiefly by fear of being frozen again should their service prove unsatisfactory. Still, in their numbers they are a serious threat. Were it not for the actions of Helium's air navy led by John Carter, they might have succeeded.

NOTABLE PANARIANS

HIN ABTOL

A vainglorious jeddak made arrogant and proud by centuries of absolute power, Hin Abtol begins his own end when he visits the city of Gathol and falls in lust with its princess Llana. Denied her hand, he animates his million troops to make war.

PANAR IN YOUR CAMPAIGN

Because its only claim to fame is the threat of its army, Panar is best suited as an adversary in most Barsoom campaigns (or as a location adventurers must infiltrate). Alternatively, a campaign consisting of soldiers in the Panarian army could make for a tense, dark game as the player characters attempt to please their ruler and remain unfrozen, despite increasingly impossible orders.

CHAPTER 10: OKAR AND BEYOND

> *The ancient chronicles of the first historians of Barsoom – so ancient that we have for ages considered them mythology – record the passing of the yellow men from the ravages of the green hordes that overran Barsoom as the drying up of the great oceans drove the dominant races from their strongholds . . . They tell of the wanderings of the remnants of this once powerful race, harassed at every step, until at last they found a way through the ice-barrier of the north to a fertile valley at the pole.*
>
> – Thuvan Dihn, *The Warlord of Mars*

Ancient by the standards of Jasoom, Barsoom is filled with terrible wonders, mysteries that only the most forthright dare challenge. Beyond Helium, the other red Martian kingdoms and the dead sea barrens of the green Martian hordes, the history of Barsoom is manifest on sands and moss that no being of the civilized lands has tread for a thousand thousand years. Obscure cities, isolated cultures, forgotten technologies, and horrifying dangers are half-lost to the tides of time, lying side by side with the oldest traditions of Barsoom.

NORTHERN POLAR REGION

Barsoom's northern polar region is cold, desolate, and snow-covered, removed from the rest of the world by desolate granite foothills and a massive barrier of solid ice that prevent any traffic other than by air, with two exceptions.

The Carrion Caves are a former riverbed that breaches the cliffs of ice and rock and leads to the land of the Okar. When Talu becomes Jeddak of the Okar he determines to cleanse the caves of the filth that has accumulated within it so that the green Martians may find an easy way to the land of the Okar. While a second exists, a narrow corridor that carves a passage through blocks of ice, fallen rocks, and deep snow — the gateway to Panar — little is known of it. Beyond the barriers lie Okar, the home of the yellow Martians, and Panar, a nation of red men living within their hothouse city of Pankor. Okar and Pankor engage in no contact, each dwelling within their hothouse metropolises. Given Okar's penchant for taking red Martian slaves, this is likely the best situation for both nations.

Of course, simply reaching the north is only the beginning of the troubles heroes will face.

MATTERS OF SURVIVAL

Warmth is a precious commodity in the northern regions, with frozen death kept at bay only by the glass domes of the yellow and red Barsoomians. Should someone wish to venture forth onto the ice, the only survivable period is the northern arctic 'summer,' when Barsoom is at perihelion from the sun, barring approaching by air in a sealed craft or some other technological means. Wearing the appropriate protective clothing, such as the yellow-and-black furs of the orluk or the pure white skin of an apt helps for a time, but Martians cannot live in the polar north outside protective structures for more than brief periods.

The frozen environment of the north serves as an additional protection for those who dwell there. No army could survive trekking across the frozen wastes and arctic storms make air travel difficult. Those challenging the northern polar region are well-advised to remember why it is called 'the forbidden land'. Heroes traversing these regions will face difficult terrain, the predatory apt and other, lesser-known, creatures adapted to the chilling temperatures, violent winds, and worse. Overland travel on foot or by sledge in this region is at least a (D2) difficulty danger doing 1 🎲 of damage from falls, frost, or other dangers. These dangers increase substantially as travelers encounter seracs (ice cliffs), sudden, explosive pressure ridges, hidden crevasses, and katabatic winds roaring forth from the great ice and granite barrier surrounding the pole.

Exposure to ice and snow in the northern polar regions is considered a danger, especially if someone isn't properly attired. Characters moving around outside a heated environment (a vehicle, building, or covered city, for example) during the winter suffer the effects of extreme cold, typically below −30 degrees Celsius. For every 5 minutes of exposure to this intense chill, the character must face a Challenging (D2) danger using their **Might + Cunning** which does 3 🎲 of damage. Increase the difficulty of this danger by one step for each test after the first. Failure on this test inflicts an immediate 3 🎲 of damage. This biting cold has the Sharp quality, inflicting an additional point of stress to the Injury stress track for each effect rolled.

Wearing the appropriate protective clothing, such as the yellow-and-black furs of the orluk or the pure white skin of an apt reduces the difficulty of the danger by 1 step and requires tests to be made every 30 minutes instead. If the character is wearing wet clothing, the difficulty of these dangers increases by two steps; sodden clothing in freezing conditions is extremely dangerous. More advanced cold-weather gear may provide greater benefits and, conversely, being closer to the poles or traveling at night may increase the difficulty or damage of the danger.

Traveling outside during the brief summer period is somewhat more forgiving. Those without protective clothing must make a test every hour (instead of every 5 minutes) and those with protective clothing need not make a test to resist the cold more than once every four hours.

Another risk is snow-blindness. This condition occurs when bright sunlight — uncommon on Barsoom — reflects off the pale snow. The light burns the eyes, which can cause temporary blindness. The narrator may spend 3 Threat on any character moving around in the northern polar summer without adequate eye protection (dark glasses or goggles) during the day. This imposes a special danger requiring a Challenging (D2) **Daring + Might** test to avoid. Failure results in temporary blindness, increasing the difficulty of all actions that require sight by 2 for the rest of the scene.

Vehicles and other machines may freeze up if left unused for long periods of time; if the machine has been left unattended and unused while exposed to cold conditions for eight hours or more, it requires a **Reason + Cunning** test to get a frozen vehicle started again. This difficulty starts at Average (D1) and increases by 1 every day the vehicle has been left unused in the cold, to a maximum of Epic (D5) difficulty.

POLAR STORMS

Those braving the intense cold face another danger: the unpredictable ice and snowstorms that occur even during the polar 'summer' and make the northern region all but impassible any other time of year. Spotting the signs of a storm requires a Challenging (D2) **Daring + Reason** test. A Daunting (D3) test can then be made to find suitable shelter, such as a cave or crevasse. Momentum from the test made to spot the impending storm is useful in lowering the difficulty of the danger it presents or granting bonus dice to tests. Use the following effects for a polar storm should a character fail to avoid it.

Even if a character cannot find total shelter from a storm, narrators are encouraged to allow clever characters to find partial shelter or perform heroic actions to lessen the dangerous effects. A rock outcropping or a makeshift shelter might not allow a traveler to survive a storm completely unscathed, but it could save their life. Narrators are encouraged to throw obstacles, complications, and use Threat generously to make the journey more interesting rather than punitive.

DANGER 1: LIGHT STORM

Light snowstorms storms inflict 1 🎲 of Confusion damage for every 30 minutes of exposure. All sense related tests suffer +1 difficulty penalty.

DANGER 2: SNOWSTORM

A full snowstorm inflicts 2 🎲 of Confusion damage for every 30 minutes of exposure. All sense related tests suffer a +2 difficulty penalty. Complications from failed rolls take the form of blinding headaches, temporary blindness, and minor frostbite. Tests involving keeping one's balance or footing are +1 difficulty.

DANGER 3: BLIZZARD

Blizzards inflict 3 🎲 Confusion damage for every 15 minutes of exposure. All sense related tests suffer a +3 difficulty penalty. Complications are more severe than snowstorms — lingering blindness, crippling headaches requiring rest, and severe frostbite. Tests involving keeping one's balance or footing are +2 difficulty.

DANGER 4: WHITEOUT

Whiteout conditions make visual sense tests impossible; all other sense related tests suffer +3 difficulty penalty. Whiteouts inflict 4 🎲 Confusion damage for every 15 minutes of exposure. Complications from failed rolls include being lost in the storm, severe hypothermia, and frostbite. Tests involving keeping one's balance or footing are +3 difficulty.

DANGER 5: KATABATIC STORM

Katabatic storms are among the deadliest weather hazards on Barsoom. While sandstorms strip the flesh from the unprepared, katabatic storms are far more insidious. Movement and sensory based actions are essentially impossible and being caught out in this storm causes 5 🎲 of Confusion based damage per 5 minutes and can result in madness or death. Narrators are encouraged to use these only for dramatic purposes.

A History of the Okar

Beyond the vast heights of the great ice barrier lies the first of the two civilizations that dwell there, the hothouse cities of the nation of the Okar, home and final redoubt of the nearly-mythical yellow Martians. The Okar Nation and others have not always resided at the pole, and there was a time in eons past where the yellow Men lived alongside Barsoom's other races.

The long, torturous exodus of the yellow Martians begins in the Valley Dor (*see Chapter 14: Secrets of Barsoom*) during the long decline of Barsoom into the arid world of the modern day. As the axis of the planet shifted and the sun cooled, the Valley Dor shifted southward over the millennia, and the once-verdant lands spawned by the Tree of Life withered and perished under the assault of the encroaching cold. Even the Tree itself perished, its task completed, the cold sinking icy claws into its very heartwood.

The bipedal races and other creatures underwent diaspora and for a time, the white-skinned Orovars became the dominant race of men on Barsoom. During the continuing cosmic decline of Barsoom half a million years ago, the yellow Martians, who had long held their own counsel, left the civilized lands and peace behind, seeking a new home.

Before their final departure and long exodus north, the future Okarians acquired the secrets of the atmosphere processors, the alteration of their women to become oviparous, and, given the existence of technologies like their hothouse cities and the Guardian of the North, other mighty sciences long lost to the mists of time and degeneracy.

As Barsoom's seas and rivers began their long descent into red dust, the green Martians became more numerous, spreading across Barsoom as a barbarian horde. In a genocidal campaign, they drove the yellows even further north, hounding their every step, slaughtering the yellow Men by first the score, then hundreds, then thousands. Finally, the survivors reached the foot of the great ice barrier. It was there the yellow Martians set their backs to the great cliffs of ice and stone and prepared to face the enemy that had pursued them for centuries.

The yellows made a last-ditch effort against their green-skinned tormentors in the 27 caves forming the only major passage beyond the mountains and into the future lands of Okar. Each stood their ground in the caves, forcing the larger greens into tight quarters where the last of the yellow Martians held the advantage. Though casualties were great on both sides of the battle, the yellows ultimately prevailed.

Okarian Sword-Fighting

Okarians have, in their millennia of isolation, developed fighting techniques unseen by any other men beyond the great northern barrier. These sword-fighting forms reflect the Okarian national character — brutal, efficient, and, most of all, deceptive. The Warlord of Mars himself reflected that he was nearly bested by a master of these techniques and only fortune saved him.

Okarian sword-fighting relies on three unusual items to complement the style itself — a cup-shaped buckler no bigger than a dinner plate strapped to the left wrist, an arming sword which ends in a brutal hook, and a second, straight sword much like a Jasoomian gladius.

The hook sword is largely defensive, able to bind, disarm, and otherwise trap and manipulate an enemy's weapon. The hook sword's edge means it cannot be grabbed out of the way, but it is hard for an inexpert wielder to land a blow with the edge. Okarians typically hold the hook sword out front, presenting the shield, with the blade either straight up or parallel to the ground. This allows blocks with it while punching with the hilt and rotating, hoping to get a bind on an opponent's blade or strike an unaware foe with the blade.

The straight sword is held in the right hand, and is the primary weapon of attack. It is used primarily for stabbing, but it can cut as well. With the strong defenses of the hook-sword and shield, Okarian swordsmen use the straight sword to dart into openings to deliver wounds to their foes. To keep the straight sword out of reach of an opponent's defense, it is either held back over the shoulder if one wishes to slash, or low on their hip threatening an opponent's off-hand, but not out front, where it might be swept.

When Okarians get the measure of an opponent and sweep or bind their blade, the common tactic is to step in with the straight sword and stab. If the stab misses, the swordsman performs a draw-cut as they pull back to defend themselves. If the stab misses, but the Okarian has achieved a decent bind, they step past them at an angle, slashing or cutting as they do.

Those who haven't encountered the Okarian fighting style before may face + 1 difficulty to rolls related to battling such a foe. A skilled Okarian swordfighter may develop talents that aid in trapping and disarming an opponent, reflecting their mastery of this style.

Having already encountered the massive, savage apts of the polar north, the yellow Martians left the dead in great, rotting piles, the stench of such so great that not even the bitter cold could quash it. The act was not merely one of repaying like for like, but a strategic one — with the dead decaying within the warmer caves, the apts native to the region arrived to feed upon the carrion left behind. It took little time for the passage to Okar to fill with the vicious beasts, eager to feed on the remains. With the single passageway through the ice-shrouded mountains all but impassable, the Okar, the last of the yellow Martians, were free to settle the valley within the barrier peaks.

It is unknown to any living Barsoomian what span of time the yellow Martians required to construct their great hothouse cities, but however long such vast feats of engineering took, the Okar passed into the mists of myth and legend until rediscovered by the Warlord of Mars, John Carter, and his boon companion, Thuvan Dihn, Jeddak of Ptarth. It is an encounter none will soon forget, fraught with intrigue, betrayal, and ultimately, bloody-handed revolution.

THE CARRION CAVES

Until the time of the Warlord of Mars, the Carrion Caves are considered a legend, an exaggeration to frighten the gullible. The truth is far more horrible. The Carrion Caves are quite real, and if there is a Barsoomian equivalent to the Jasoomian concept of Hell, surely, they qualify.

While the apts are a perennial hazard to those traversing the distant north, the creatures tend toward solitude, each with their own hunting territory or, rarely, in small packs. With the decision to use the bodies of the dead as a lure to the apts, a deterrent is provided should anyone come across the caves. As more of the dead accumulate and the waste of the Okar Nation is dumped in the caves, the yellow Martians begin a cycle of horror that ends only with the defeat of Salensus Oll, the tyrannical and cruel Jeddak of the Okar Nation.

Those wishing to reach Okar before the caves have been cleared following the fall of Salensus Oll have two options, both time-dependent — attempt the infiltration during the majority of the month where the apts are scattered throughout the labyrinthine chambers, or do so during the time when the vile creatures are concentrated in only a few caves.

Beyond the caves lies apparent desolation. Bare rock and ice confront those few who emerge, with a well-trod path leading north. Travelers are well-advised to not be deceived by the existence of the path — the journey is filled with switchbacks, terrifically difficult terrain, and is described by Carter, an experienced outdoorsman, as 'some of the worst traveling I have ever seen.'

Following what is, under ideal circumstances, an hours-long hike, the great labyrinth of rock and ice gives way to slowly-descending paths. It is from the very apex of these paths that the traveler can see Marentina, the first of the incredible hothouse cities of the Okar Nation. While it is another hour or two by Barsoomian reckoning to reach even the closest outpost of the Okar, the way into the Valley of the Okar is bliss compared to what came before.

It is a huge, white-furred creature with six limbs, four of which, short and heavy, carry it swiftly over the snow and ice; while the other two, growing forward from its shoulders on either side of its long, powerful neck, terminate in white, hairless hands, with which it seizes and holds its prey.

Its head and mouth are more similar in appearance to those of a hippopotamus than to any other earthly animal, except that from the sides of the lower jawbone two mighty horns curve slightly downward toward the front.

"Its two huge eyes inspired my greatest curiosity. They extend in two vast, oval patches from the center of the top of the cranium down either side of the head to below the roots of the horns, so that these weapons really grow out from the lower part of the eyes, which are composed of several thousand ocelli each.

"This eye structure seemed remarkable in a beast whose haunts were upon a glaring field of ice and snow, and though I found upon minute examination of several that we killed that each ocellus is furnished with its own lid, and that the animal can at will close as many of the facets of his huge eyes as he chooses, yet I was positive that nature had thus equipped him because much of his life was to be spent in dark, subterranean recesses.

– The Warlord of Mars

Those brave or foolhardy souls that dare the Carrion Caves prior to the death of Salensus Oll at the hands of John Carter will inevitably encounter apts, and in numbers. Only the extremely clever, resourceful, or lucky can expect to pass through 27 caves filled with the reek of filth, decay, and corpses reduced to bones, saponified fat, and rotten meat. This is considered difficult terrain, adding a +1 to the difficulty of any tests that must be accomplished speedily.

If approaching the caves during the apts' active period, the difficulty will be at a *minimum* a Dire (D4) **Daring** + **Reason** test, with failure resulting in the likelihood of the heroes being overwhelmed by a flood of angry, vicious apts. If the characters can approach the caves during the appropriate time, a period lasting a few days each month, their chances of survival improve substantially. The difficulty of the test drops to Challenging (D2) as the sated apts are sleeping.

Along with the threat of the apts, the Carrion Caves present an omnipresent but far more subtle menace — disease. Despite the frigid temperatures, the effluvium of the Okar Nation has been dumped in the caves for centuries, resulting in a miasmic, filthy, plague-infested hellscape. For every hour heroes spend in the caves, they face a Challenging (D2) **Daring** + **Reason** test to avoid catching some form of illness. Should they suffer a failure, they acquire some unpleasant illness (affliction: Wounds) increasing the difficulty of all tests by 1 step. If a complication ensues, narrators are encouraged to be creative with the outcome.

More information on the apts can be found in *Chapter 13: Beasts of Barsoom*.

THE OKARIAN KINGDOM

The cities of the Okar lay in deep valleys and every street, plaza, and open space are roofed with glass. The domed coverings keep the snow and ice at bay and further creates a hothouse effect that makes the interiors of these domed cities warm and comfortable. This design and splendor holds true for each of the cities of the Okar Nation. Each is encased in shimmering panes of crystal, geodesic domes that rise like jewels from the barren ice-covered valleys.

The yellow Martians, as Carter points out, live in a virtually-unparalleled luxury and security — their valley is hidden behind the great ice barrier, their cities enclosed by the great domes, sky-lights, and other glassworks that are art, science, and engineering laid side by side. Their technology is found nowhere else on Barsoom. Yet theirs is a disquieted kingdom, filled with political maneuvering, harsh betrayal, even murder and assassination.

Much of this can be laid at the feet of a single man and his band of cronies — the tyrant Salensus Oll, worshipper of the apts and ally to the Therns, whose rule is based on deception, cruelty, kidnapping, and base slavery. Thanks to his control of the Guardian of the North, Oll has a never-ending supply of red Martian slaves to slake the base labor needs of the Okar Nation, to fight in brutal gladiatorial competitions, and, when they are spent or must be punished for some arbitrary infraction, fed to the half-tamed apts popular among Oll's followers. With such methods of torture and terror at his disposal, those who dissent the Jeddak of Jeddaks' rule must move cautiously lest they become his next victims.

TECHNOLOGY

Unlike much of the planet, the Okar retain, and have even improved upon, the sciences originally developed by the ancient Barsoomians. Beginning with their mysterious hothouse cities, which function much like conventional greenhouses on Jasoom, to their improved atmosphere plant, to the terrifying magnetic weapon called The Guardian of the North, the yellow Martians are rivaled by few other natives of Barsoom. But such achievements come at a heavy cost — for some of the citizens and elites of Okar, a life of unparalleled luxury has given rise to a vicious, callous, and bloodthirsty culture urged on by the false religion of the Therns and the Jeddak Salensus Oll.

The three known hothouse cities of the yellow Martians — Illall, Kadabra, and Marentina — are wonders at odds with the savage character of many of the Okarians. Within their crystalline domes lie lush avenues wrought of sod and long-forgotten sea plants serving as roads for both foot traffic and the peculiar ground fliers of the yellow Martians. Glittering crystal buildings stand side-by-side with forbidding basalt structures.

The massive gardens provide food and aesthetic pleasures for the citizenry, kept at peak growth throughout the year by the summer-like heat gradually released from captured sunlight. As Solan, the operator of the Guardian of the North in Kadabra points out, the trapped heat is kept in great tanks beneath each city, and if it were released too quickly, would ignite an inferno that none would survive.

> Through the actions of John Carter and his allies, Salensus Oll is finally overthrown and replaced with Talu, valiant young former Jed of Marentina. During this period Okar becomes a fierce ally of Carter and Helium. Hin Abtol, the Jed of Panar, claims to have deposed Talu later in the period and conquered all the cities of Okar.
>
> However, even if this boast is true, when Hin Abtol is defeated, the Okar likely once again control their own nation.

Guardian of the North

Given the difficulty of reaching the northern regions without technological assistance, it seems hardly surprising that the devious ruler of the Okar Nation, at least until the arrival of the John Carter, utilizes a means by which the hothouse cities will not only remain hidden, but the Okar are supplied with a bloody bounty of red Martian slaves. These dual purposes of slaves and continued secrecy require the Guardian of the North.

Resting directly above Barsoom's northern magnetic pole, the Guardian is a massive obelisk of black stone or metal, and the source of the disappearances over the centuries of every expedition to the region. The Guardian emits a powerful magnetic field upon command from the control room at its base, and affects the eighth ray as well, making resistance by aircraft utterly futile. Fliers that smash into the device fall slowly to the ground, much to the misfortune of their respective crews.

Those not killed by impact with the irresistible attraction of the Guardian face a more terrible fate still — the wounded are disposed of by the Okarian guards or torn to bloody offal by trained apts. Those that survive have nothing to look forward to beyond a life of slavery at the hands of the followers of Oll. The red Barsoomians pressed into foul servitude remained so until freed by John Carter himself.

The operation of the Guardian is deceptively simple — a single lever in the central control room at its base activates or disables the device. Prior to its presumed destruction at the hands of Talu, Prince of Marentina, the Guardian's sole controller was the yellow Barsoomian Solan. In times following the ousting of Salensus Oll and the death of the treacherous Solan, it is logical to assume that the Guardian is either destroyed or left unattended. Despite his advanced age, nearing one thousand, Solan is a formidable opponent, capable of besting even the Warlord of Mars in combat, and his mind is as sharp and deadly as the hook-shaped blades he wields with a master's flourish. Narrators setting adventures in Kadabra before Solan fell in battle to John Carter should create the old man as a duelist and a villain who is a match for the best swordsman in the group despite his age.

Those attempting to breach the great ice barrier by flyer will face the power of the Guardian — and likely their destruction. **John Carter** narrators are discouraged from making an encounter with the Guardian too deadly for heroes despite its irresistible power as presented in *Warlord of Mars*. To that end, we suggest the utter destruction of whatever craft the heroes arrive in, a substantial amount of physical harm, and their capture by the legions of apt-riding Oll loyalists. This provides ample drama and opportunity for the heroes to formulate an escape later, after they've witnessed the horrors that the Oll regime inflicts on both slaves and opposition.

Kadabra: City of the Apts

The capital city of Okar, Kadabra is a jewel of incredible splendor even among the other cities of the yellow Martians. Fully one hundred miles (271 *haads*) across, it is the largest of the domed cities in the valley beyond the great barrier. It is also, until the time of John Carter, ruled by the mad tyrant Salensus Oll.

Under Oll, Kadabran life even for the common Martian is luxurious, even decadent. As the largest domed city of Okar, Oll demands nothing but the best for his people, so long as they remain loyal. His footpads are everywhere, and viciously enforce the dictator's rule. Those who resist are, at best, stripped of status and enslaved; many are slain out of hand to maintain the rule of fear. For the worst offenders, Oll provides a unique torture — the devilish Pit of Plenty.

Those willing — or forced — to make the journey to the capitol of Okar will first encounter the mighty gates sealing the city and, if they are particularly unfortunate, witness the Guardian in operation. Any who do not pass the scrutiny of Oll's city militia aren't merely denied entry; they are immediately captured or killed, considered enemies of the state. For those who do enter, though, accommodations are as grandiose as the dictator's ego, if not as poisonous.

The Okarians of Kadabra rely, or so the citizenry believes, on the backbreaking labor of captured slaves, primarily unfortunate red Martians kidnapped during expeditions to the north. Slaves suffer, at best,

wretched indignities, and at worst execution for even the smallest infractions. Those who inflict such horrors on the slaves find nothing wrong with such behavior; the savage nature of Barsoom has overtaken their very souls.

Such sentiments are far from universal — Talu, Prince of Marentina being the prime example — but few possess the will to enact revolution instead of living in unparalleled luxury, even if the cost for such is visible to any within sight of the Guardian.

Accommodations follow the peculiar traditions of the yellow Martians — public houses, for example, vary only slightly, with no privacy save for married couples. Given that the houses are constructed of the same clear glass and crystal as the cities' domes, such amenities are not possible. The lack of privacy serves a dual purpose — such an environment makes it difficult to conspire against the Jeddak Oll.

Rooms for the men without wives are of white marble or heavy glass, with raised sleeping platforms. If a guest does not have their own sleeping furs, they are provided them at a nominal charge. Once a guest's belongings have been deposited upon one of these platforms they are a guest of the house, and that platform is their own until they leave. No one will disturb or molest their belongings; there are no thieves upon Mars.

As assassination is something to be feared and the proprietors of the hostelries furnish armed guards, who patrol the sleeping-rooms day and night. The number of guards and gorgeousness of their trappings usually denote the status of the hotel.

No meals are served in these houses, but generally a public eating place adjoins them. Baths are connected with the sleeping chambers, and each guest is required to bathe daily or depart from the hotel.

Women are given rooms on the second or third floors, though their accommodations vary little from the men's. The guards who watch the women remain in the corridor outside the sleeping chamber, while female slaves move among the sleepers within, ready to notify the warriors should their presence be required while attending to the female guests. Any disturbances are dealt with swiftly and harshly, as is the Martian way.

THE PALACE OF TERROR

Given the decadent lifestyle that the Okarians enjoy, it comes as no surprise that the palace of the tyrant Salensus Orr, Jeddak of Jeddaks of the Okar Nation, should be an exercise in excess. Without, walls of dark, hard Martian basalt quarried from the mountains surrounding the Valley and its hothouse cities provide a nigh-impenetrable bulwark against attackers and an imposing reminder of Oll's rule.

Within the palace's walls, lush gardens vie with labyrinthine corridors, apartments, and countless other chambers within the palace to produce a maze as twisted as the intrigues that infest the house of Salensus Oll. Those unfamiliar with the bewildering interior of the palace find themselves lost without a guide; this is by design.

Those wishing to serve Oll may apply to become members of the palace guard at the recruiting center directly across from the palace with the captain of the guard. After having their vital statistics recorded and sent to the appropriate government offices in Kadabra, aspirant recruits are sent through the palace gates to the barracks.

The barracks of the palace guard are divided in twain — one wing where new recruits are held and another where the fully-vetted and seasoned guards are housed. New recruits are told this separation is to prevent a testing of their mettle by Oll's loyal soldiers, but the truth is more sinister — troops are sequestered and monitored for any hints of disloyalty or treasonous behavior against the Jeddak of Jeddaks. Those that are caught are usually executed out of hand, though a few unlucky souls are brought before Oll himself for a mock 'trial'. For those few unfortunates, Oll's most wicked punishment awaits – the Pit of Plenty.

THE PIT OF PLENTY

Whoever the originator of this vile method of torture was or is, few torments on Barsoom rival it. A wide, circular pit one hundred feet deep, its sides are glassy and nearly impossible to climb without some form of external assistance. A prisoner left alone in utter darkness would soon go mad from such conditions alone, but the torment of the Pit does not end in mere isolation with no apparent hope of escape.

The material comprising the pit is a variation of the same crystal used in common Okarian buildings, specially polarized to give the appearance of dull opaqueness. Oll prefers to leave prisoners alone in the absolute darkness for a day before the true torture begins. Once they are accustomed to and unnerved by the isolation, the tyrant's minions illuminate the smooth crystal walls, creating an illusion that all manner of delectable food and quenching drink are within easy reach.

Aside from the mouth of the pit, invisible to any within it, one means of escape exists — a hidden tunnel, halfway up the side, big enough for a man (and a tight fit for a green Martian) that leads to the chambers beneath the Guardian of the North. Anyone wishing to utilize it must have some assistance in the form of rope or other climbing gear; it is otherwise inaccessible.

Most prisoners of this devilish torment go mad long before they die of privation. Salensus Oll has been known to lower apts into the pit to dispose of obstreperous foes like John Carter.

With the fall of Salensus Oll, the palace has become a more open and welcoming place. Talu's guard serve him out of love and loyalty, instead of fear and greed. Also, the various red Martian slaves taken by Oll over the years are gone, returned to their kingdoms and families. While intrigue is still common and even the beloved Talu must fear his rivals and enemies, the dark days of Salensus Oll are fading into memory.

NOTABLE KADABRANS

SALENSUS OLL
Jeddak of Kadabra and ally of the Holy Thern, Matai Shang. Oll is a vile, lustful tyrant who rules his people with fear.

SOLAN
Switchmaster of the Guardian and expert swordsman. Solan is a greedy old man whose skill with a blade is equal to nearly any on Barsoom, even the fabled John Carter himself!

KADABRA IN YOUR CAMPAIGN

As the capital of the Okar, Kadabra will likely feature prominently in any adventure or campaign that involves Okar, its people, intrigues, or history. Early in the time periods covered by John Carter, Okar is a dangerous if isolationist city-state run by a cruel tyrant. Later it is a remote stronghold of potential allies and hidden dangers. In either event, traveling to and from the city is treacherous, especially during the Dotar Sojat and Prince of Helium periods when the Guardian will destroy any airship that dares venture too close.

Marentina

Marentina is somewhat a mystery. While it shares the crystal domes and vast gardens of the capitol at Kadabra, it is largely represented as a lesser city with similar technology but fewer inhabitants. Beyond this, little is known, though it is notable for being the home of Talu, who eventually comes to rule the Okar.

Marentina is the closest city to the Carrion Caves, and thus the first that travelers braving such are likely to encounter. Its city guards, under Prince Talu, nephew of the villainous Salensus Oll, while fierce, are far less brutal than those found at the capitol. Unshakably loyal to the Okar destined to become the Jeddak of Jeddaks of Okar, they are the day to the hellish night of Oll's own loyalists. Marentina also maintains the Okarian atmosphere plant, a site of vital importance should the primary Barsoomian plant fail as it once nearly did. Talu's city can be reasonably presumed to disdain the trade of slavery, unlike Kadabra, given its prince's burning hunger to free Okar from the yoke of his uncle.

At the end of the Prince of Helium era, Talu raises his forces in rebellion against his villainous uncle and aids John Carter and the forces of Helium in overthrowing the tyrant. For his courage and due to Carter's firm belief that a people should govern themselves, he suggests Talu for the new Okarian jeddak. The Okar cheerfully accept the young man, and since that day the Okar have become strong allies of Helium and its allies.

Notable Marentinans

TALU

Nephew of Salensus Oll, Jed of Marentina, and eventual Jeddak of the Okar. Talu is brave, charming, and honorable — all the things his uncle is not.

Marentina in Your Campaign

As the most accessible of the Okarian cities, Marentina is likely to be the first Okarian settlement many characters encounter. If visiting during the time Talu is Jed, they may find the young man's charm and nobility a sharp contrast to his uncle and those who favor Salensus Oll's attitudes and demeanor. Marentina likely has a bit of a "bustling frontier city" feel mixed with a "stronghold on the border of hostile territory". The exact mix of these two extremes likely varies greatly with the era during which the player characters visit — the earlier eras being noticeably more paranoid and unfriendly than the Jeddak of Jeddaks era.

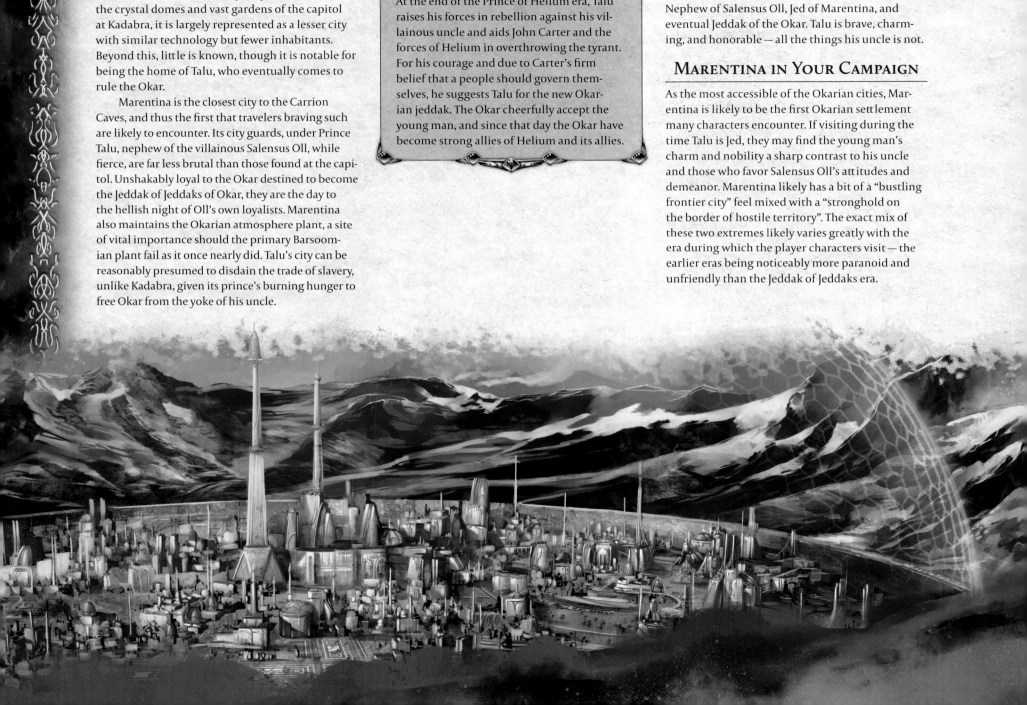

ILLALL

Of the city of Illall, little is spoken, save that it maintains little commerce with the other cities of the Okar. Some have posited that, in addition to the great distance one must travel to reach Marentina or Kadabra without access to fliers, that Illall does not have access to the mighty orluk and thus makes a poor trading partner.

ILLALL IN YOUR CAMPAIGN

Narrators are encouraged to adapt and customize this mysterious location for the needs of their own campaign. While Burroughs' information on it is perhaps frustratingly vague, this lack of information creates a glorious canvas for narrators to paint their own version of the city. Perhaps it is home to a secret cabal of assassins? Or maybe some grand device is hidden beneath it capable of wondrous feats? Given the technology and history of the ancient Okar, there are numerous possibilities.

THE THREAT OF PANAR

Panar is a red Martian nation at the north pole of Barsoom, virtually unknown until it attempts to take over the world, ruled by the Jeddak Hin Abtol. Panar is described in more detail in *Chapter 9: The Red Kingdoms*, but is mentioned here due to its proximity to Okar and out of the possibility that, prior to his defeat by John Carter and the forces of Helium, Panar's army may invade or occupy the Okarian cities for a time.

BARSOOM'S FURTHEST REACHES

Outside the polar regions and far from Barsoom's known nations, there are numerous hidden lands and locales. These are unknown to most of the denizens of Barsoom, as such, they are described later in *Chapter 14*. However, there are a few places that deserve mention here.

THE BLACK RAIDERS

The First Born, or black Martians as they are sometimes called, are known to be raiders and pirates. They are physically imposing specimens and every First Born encountered is deadly and capable whether at the helm of an airship or wielding sword and pistol.

First Born, their secrets, and their connection to the history and beliefs of Barsoom are detailed in *Chapter 14: Secrets of Barsoom*. First Born players should check out this section, as should any who spent an extended time as their slave or captive. Narrators should let a First Born player character in particular examine the section on the First Born.

Many Barsoomians believe the Black Raiders hail from Thuria, the closest of Barsoom's moons. None outside of their own people call them First Born for much of their history, instead calling them the black Martians, Black Raiders, or, in the case of those who have been attacked by them, less charitable epithets.

Once John Carter and his allies confront the Black Raiders and reveal their secrets to the world, their secrets described later in this book become common knowledge. In place of their veil of mystery, the First Born become a small but mighty ally for Helium, led by famed raider turned Jeddak, Xodar and possessing technological marvels known only to them, such as submersible technology. Why does a barren planet with one remaining river need submarines? That is one of the First Born's many secrets!

THE HOLY THERNS

The Holy Therns are known, if at all, across Barsoom for being holy men and representatives of the great goddess Issus, who is central to the Barsoomian beliefs of the afterlife. In truth, the Therns, like the Black Raiders, are not what they seem. First Born player characters would know something of the Therns' true nature, as would any characters who spent time as their slaves or captives.

The Therns, their secrets, and their connection to the history and beliefs of Barsoom are detailed in *Chapter 14: Secrets of Barsoom*. First Born players should check out this section, as should any who spent an extended time as a slave or captive of the Therns. If the narrator allows, there are also rules for playing Therns or other white Martians.

IT'S OKAY NOT KNOWING

There are more cultures and places alive on Barsoom than the detailed so far. Many show up in one story of the Barsoom novels, sometimes to never be mentioned again, hidden away in enclaves, distant places, and the like. From the Goolians of the Toonolian Marshes to the Kaldanes of Bantoom, there are many dangerous and strange hidden cities, cultures, and lands on the planet.

Which is why they are not detailed here, but instead in the narrator's section of this book. Not because players shouldn't know about them, or that it will be terrible if they skip ahead and read about them, it's simply just in case a group has players who aren't intimately familiar with the Barsoom novels and the narrator wants to reveal the secrets of these places and groups to them. So, while some secrets have been leaked or hinted at earlier in the book out of necessity, many more have been saved for future chapters and books.

CHAPTER 11: BEYOND BARSOOM

While the main focus of **John Carter of Mars** is the planet Barsoom, there are places of interest on nearby planets as well. This chapter gives a very brief overview of these locations to help place Barsoom in its proper context compared to Earth and other planets in the Solar system. Future supplements may detail locations and cultures from these worlds, especially those which appear in the Barsoom novels.

Note that this section presumes that stories, places, and books written by Burroughs about other realms, heroes, and adventures exist in the same general world as Barsoom as Burroughs himself regularly alluded to them. However, as this is **John Carter of Mars** and not *The Many Worlds of Edgar Rice Burroughs*, the details of such stories and the people and places they describe are kept deliberately brief.

EARTH TIMELINES AND CHARACTERS

Time, as it is understood on Earth, is a fairly fluid concept on Barsoom. With various races living centuries and Earthborn visitors from both the late 19th century and World War I coming to the planet at various points, the exact Earth year a Mars-based campaign takes place is subject to some debate and ample creative license. Years may pass on Jasoom between some adventures on Mars, with the player characters barely changing during these periods of downtime. This means that narrators and players can mingle characters and Earth cultures from a moderately wide historical range without breaking the general feel and tone established in the John Carter novels. Fictional characters from other works can also be presumed to exist if desired. After all, Burroughs himself often referenced his other works in the John Carter novels, though usually only briefly.

However, a good rule of thumb is to set most events involving the main periods of play between the late 1800s and mid-1900s. This allows for a wide variety of Earthborn characters or plot elements if desired, but keeps the pulpy feel of the original novels generally intact. While it is far from canonically accurate, fictional or historical personalities from these periods may find themselves on Barsoom as well. Sure, you'll never read a Burroughs tale of how Percy Fawcett and Professor George E. Challenger once traveled to the Red Planet through a mysterious cave located deep in the Amazon, but maybe Amelia Earhart or Percy Fawcett didn't simply vanish on one of their respective journeys, instead finding themselves on a Red Planet far from home. That such tales and ideas aren't official canon in no way prevents them from happening at your gaming table.

EARTH

Also known as Jasoom, Earth is well-known to Barsoomian scientists, who use long-distance sensors to study the world from afar. While many on Barsoom know and care little about the third planet from the sun, it is generally known and accepted that sentient life exists there by educated Barsoomians. Most Barsoomian scholars and nobles are generally aware of the major events and upheavals occurring on Earth at any given time, such as large-scale wars and major industrial developments. However, as interplanetary communication is unheard of until the Jeddak of Jeddaks period — and even then, quite rare — few on Mars concern themselves with Jasoom beyond casual observation.

Earthborn characters who find their way to Barsoom are another matter noteworthy for their unusual skin tones, strange language, and superior physical might. But even in these rare cases, it is the immediate individual who concerns most Martians, not their far away home planet.

Still, there are wonders on Jasoom worth noting. In addition to Earth history and events well-known and recorded in historical texts and newspapers, the Earth of *John Carter of Mars* is home to lost cities, remote islands filled with monstrous man-things, lost islands where dinosaurs and other prehistoric creatures still roam, orphaned aristocrats raised by animals to become masters of the wilderness, and countless intrigues and plots in small kingdoms and nations across the world. There are even rumors Jasoom is hollow and home to a strange world known as Pellucidar, filled with strange creatures and animals and cultures thought long gone from the surface world. These wonders have little to no effect on Barsoom, save that living in such a strange and wondrous version of Earth tends to make any Earthborn individuals who come to Mars a bit more accepting of strange circumstances, odd creatures, and alien cultures.

When Earthman Jason Gridley discovers the Gridley Wave, he and others are able to use the wave and devices calibrated to employ it to communicate with far off locations, including Barsoom and the aforementioned inner earth of Pellucidar. Gridley Wave communications increase the ability of interested Barsoomians to study Earth culture and languages. In truth, few possess the inclination and opportunity to do so, but as John Carter becomes more important to the destiny of Barsoom, there are definitely those who seek information about the world of his birth.

LUNA

Earth's moon is believed by most to be uninhabited. However, there are rumors of hidden inhabitants on Jasoom's nearest celestial neighbor, totalitarian regimes seeking to rule the moon, and other threats. Whether these are true is unknown, but perhaps some future exploration from Jasoom or Barsoom may reveal the truth of the matter.

VENUS

Covered in clouds largely impenetrable to outsiders, Venus is a mystery to both Earthborn humans and Martians alike. Rumors persist of a solo astronaut who ventured to Venus while attempting to travel to Barsoom and there discovered many wonders and various thriving cultures on the world. But these rumors are unconfirmed. The explorer, Carson Napier, claimed the world was known as Amtor by the natives, though the veracity of this and his other claims is unknown. On Barsoom, Venus is known as Cosoom.

MERCURY

Little is known of the nearest planet to the sun, known to Martians as Rasoom, only great scientists such as Ras Thavas have managed to conduct any studies of the world. The extreme heat and distance from Barsoom fouls scientific instruments and makes observation difficult. It is believed people dwell there of great power with a highly refined and sophisticated culture. However, what powers they possess or the exact details of this culture are unknown. Rasoomians are also supposed to have exceptional "flexibility", but it is uncertain if this describes a physical, emotional, social, or ethical malleability.

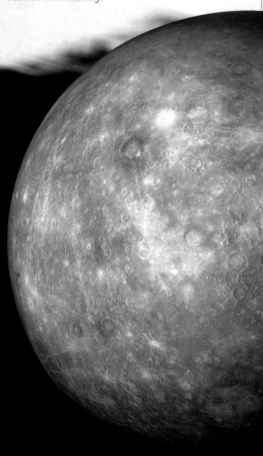

JUPITER

In contrast to Venus, Barsoomians know more of Jupiter and its moons. Also known as Sasoom, the planet is ruled by the Morgors, also known as the Skeleton Men due to their skeletal appearance. Other races are also found on the planet, including a race of blue-skinned human-like beings called the Savators.

The Morgors often send spies to Barsoom — which they call Garobus — sometimes even abducting people to interrogate for information. Their ships escape notice through use of a special sand-like substance that renders their ships functionally invisible to various methods of detection, including normal sight.

After the nation of Zor was conquered by Helium, the Morgors kidnapped a former prince of Zor. This Prince, Multis Par, gave the Morgors the idea of invading Barsoom by securing the assistance and cooperation of influential leaders through coercion. The Morgor emperor, Bandolian, attempted to implement this plot by kidnapping first John Carter and then Dejah Thoris. This plan ultimately failed, resulting in Carter and Dejah escaping with the help of several allies, including members of the Savator and Morgor races.

MOONS OF BARSOOM

The two Martian moons, Thuria and Cluros, hang in the night sky over the Red Planet. Thuria is by far the closer of the two moons, orbiting at roughly 15,700 hads (5800 miles) to Cluros' 39,280 (14,500 miles). Thuria travels around Barsoom in roughly 3 zode (7.5 hours) while Cluros takes roughly 12 zode (30 hours) to do so.

Thuria is populated by various beasts and two humanoid races, the Tarids and Masena. Tarids resemble red Martians in features and form, but they have white skin and blue hair. They tend to show their age more dramatically than, and lack the general vigor of, the Martian races. However, unlike the red Martians and similar races, Tarids developed the ability to hypnotize others to ignore their presence as a form of self-defense. The Tarids once ruled Thuria, but their empire fell long ago, leaving only a few isolated citadels. Tarids worship a fire god that is a personification of Sol, the solar system's sun.

The Masena are two mouthed, one-eyed, tree-dwellers who have yellowish manes and can change color to blend into their environment. They will devour their prey alive if necessary, and have no reservations about preying on other humanoids for sustenance.

In stark contrast to Thuria, little is known of Cluros due to its distance from Barsoom, though scholars claim some form of humanoid life exists on the planet. However, the exact form this life takes is unknown.

SECTION 4

CHAPTER 12: NARRATORS OF MARS

> *Now, at last, I saw the grim humor of the method they had adopted to do me this great honor, but that there was any hoax in the reality of the title they had conferred upon me was readily disproved by the sincerity of the congratulations that were heaped upon me by the judges first and then the nobles…*
>
> – John Carter, *The Warlord of Mars*

This chapter and all subsequent chapters deal with the job of the narrator in **John Carter**. In many ways, narrators are simply other players there to play and have fun alongside everyone else. Nevertheless, they have special authority and responsibilities. Where the other players only portray a single character in the world of Barsoom, the narrator portrays all other characters and controls the environment in which the game occurs. A wild banth doesn't attack or a band of raiders doesn't descend upon a group of player characters unless the narrator wills it. This gives narrators a lot of power during the game, but it is power that needs to be used well and effectively or the game doesn't work.

It's an Adventure!

Note that in **John Carter** published materials, sometimes the catch-all term of "adventure" will be used in place of "episode" or "serial." In such cases, this is because the length and importance a particular adventure may have in a narrator's games is unknown — one group's episode can grow into another group's serial. This is true of the adventure seeds in the back of this book, as well as *Mind Merchants of Mars*, the adventure included in *Chapter 16*.

How to Narrate

There are multiple methods to narrating **John Carter**, but they fall into three main classifications: the episode, the serial, and the campaign.

Episodes

Sometimes called "one shot adventures" or "chapters", episodes are "one and done" scenarios where the players play out one scenario or series of encounters and that is it. Episodes are great for pick-up games and conventions, though, unless part of a larger series of game sessions, they do not use various elements of **John Carter**, particularly experience and renown advancement.

Running an episode is pretty straightforward: pick a few scenarios that relate to each other and play out the events, adjusting as the players come up with unique and interesting solutions to the problems they face. Unless an episode features characters who will be used in multiple episodes or a regular campaign, it is usually a good idea to have pregenerated characters for players to use in order to save time and get everyone playing sooner.

Example: Jack wants to run an episode to introduce his gaming group to **John Carter**. He creates player character versions of John Carter, Dejah Thoris, Carthoris, Thuvia, and Tars Tarkas using the statistics provided in Chapter 15: Champions of Barsoom as a model. He then concocts a series of connected scenarios involving an airship ride to a royal wedding in Kadabra and a pirate attack to kidnap the royal family of Helium. Jack and his players will play through the pirate raid and

related scenarios based on how the player characters handle the events of his episode, John Carter and the Pirates of Kadabra.

Serials

Often called "adventures" or "seasons", serials are a number of interconnected episodes that cover a single plot or story. Serials link these episodes and the scenes they contain together to create a single cohesive whole. Serials are akin to a single novel or short story in terms of plot and focus, though they are driven by player action, roleplaying, and dice mechanics instead of an author's imagination and craft.

Serials usually follow a three or five act structure, with introductory encounters leading to a climactic central battle or other major scene and a brief aftermath followed by a period of downtime that may or may not be dealt with during play. However, there are numerous variations on this model and most narrative tricks such as flashbacks, beginning a serial *in medias res* (in the middle of the action), and other tactics can spice up the basic serial format. The sessions of each serial often end on a cliffhanger to keep the players excited to come back next time, but this isn't strictly necessary — though it is a lot of fun!

Running serials can be challenging, but they are mostly a matter of preparation and improvisation. A narrator should have numerous scenes planned, yet be willing to adapt to what the players and their characters do. A serial that is too brittle or inflexible in its format can break, resulting in narrators floundering without any idea of what to do next, or players getting frustrated when they are channeled into a handful of options or results no matter what they do.

*Example: Jason wants to run a **John Carter** serial for his local gaming group. He drafts a plot involving a renegade Okar jeddak with a massive magnetically powered floating fortress. He then designs a series of interrelated episodes introducing the player characters to this threat, giving them ample opportunities to fight and roleplay with the antagonist and other important characters, and then a chance to finally defeat the jeddak, destroying or disabling his fortress. With the structure of his serial ready, Jason has his players create characters and his serial, Sky Castles of Mars, is ready to begin!*

CAMPAIGNS

Sometimes called a "series", campaigns are the main method of playing *John Carter*. Campaigns consist of a linked serials and occasional solo episodes that feature the same characters dealing with ongoing developments, challenges, themes, and other elements of an evolving setting. A campaign is where the character advancement mechanics really shine, especially renown. Over a campaign, player characters can grow from relatively unknown adventurers to heroes, warlords, nobles, and leaders of great alliances of various important nations and individuals. While the events of a single serial can occasionally change the world, a campaign features numerous such changes, allowing players and narrators to create their own dynamic and unique version of Burroughs' Barsoom through play.

Campaigns are both easy and challenging. They're easy because they are basically just a framework for serials and episodes. They're challenging because the best campaigns have dramatic arcs, recurring plotlines, interesting factions and regular narrator characters, and other recurring elements. Campaigns can be narrow or broad in scope, with player characters taking the role of everything from world-traveling heroes to the members of a single, small group. This chapter will discuss some of the regular challenges of campaign design later.

FIVE RULES FOR AN EFFECTIVE NARRATOR

While there are numerous guidelines and bits of useful guidance that can be given to narrators in *John Carter*, there are five major pieces of advice that most fall under. Keeping these in mind when reading this chapter, planning game sessions, and running the game will help narrators navigate many challenges.

1. BE FAIR

The rules are there for a reason; they put all the characters on the same playing field. A narrator character might be stronger or better with a sword than a player hero, but they both should use the same general rules to do battle. Foes should not be unbeatable or be given abilities so beyond what a player can achieve with their characters that conflicts seem to be exercises in frustration and constant defeat. Especially when you begin narrating *John Carter*, feel free to err of the side of the players and their heroes. A few easy successes while you find the right balance to best challenge a group is preferable to killing them off early by throwing too many terrible or overpowered threats at them.

2. BE EXCITING

Burroughs and his contemporaries rarely let heroes rest on their laurels or get complacent. You shouldn't either. When long stretches of inactivity make sense in an adventure or during a campaign between adventures, do not tarry on those moments. Instead move on to when things are happening, throw new and interesting challenges at players and their heroes regularly. If they are lost in a jungle, give them strange beasts or dangerous natives to fight. If they are exploring a ruin, present them with a mystery, hazard, or adversary to challenge them.

3. BE CONSISTENT

Whatever you do for or to one player or their hero, be prepared to do to another. If all the character's drink the same poisoned wine, they should all have to resist its effects. Of course, some might weather these dangers differently or have an easier time of it due to special preparations or abilities, but don't be arbitrary in your administration of the rules.

Also, present the world consistently. Consistency is especially important if you break from the canonical world of Burroughs and Barsoom. If you change what the players know from the stories, you are the source of these differences. If you make changes haphazardly or inconsistently, it will cause confusion and reduce enjoyment during play. It is fine if you want to introduce a new custom to Barsoomian culture or add a historical event, but do not suddenly remove or change those elements once your players learn and begin to rely upon them.

4. BE UNPREDICTABLE

Consistent does not mean boring. You should regularly present unknown or surprising situations for player heroes to deal with. Burroughs' tales are filled with surprising developments, strange technologies, and new revelations. Even whole new cultures or world-shaking secrets are open to introduction into a *John Carter* campaign.

5. BE COOPERATIVE

Narrating a game is not a contest. You are not there to beat the other players or show them up. You are there to help them play their characters in fun and interesting ways. This often means throwing hostile characters and dangerous adversaries in the way of player heroes or challenging them with dangerous obstacles or tense situations. However, the goal of this should be mutual enjoyment, drama, and fun. Frustrating or opposing a player's character is fine, and often expected, but, if your adventures, challenges, and situations are frustrating your fellow players, you're doing it wrong and should adjust.

*Example: Jack's episode was such a hit with his group they decided to start a new regular **John Carter** campaign. After some discussion, the group decides they want a campaign focused around action and intrigue during the Prince of Helium era right after John Carter "dies" restarting the atmosphere plant. The players will create new characters for this campaign and Jack crafts a short serial to begin his new campaign and his campaign. Blades of Mars, is ready to begin.*

NARRATING SCENES

John Carter uses a scene structure. A scene isn't a set unit of time, but rather a snapshot of events and time where significant action occurs. A scene might last minutes, hours, or even longer. Setting the scene is one of the chief tasks a narrator has during play. They establish various details, which characters are present, what dangers and immediate problems occur, and essentially play the role of "director" in the scene — though one having limited control over their stars, the player characters.

When narrating a scene, it is important to be engaging but also to provide relevant information. A long droning information dump isn't any fun, but, if it is important the player characters know they are in a cave with two exits and you never mention it, that will only cause confusion later. Keeping record of important details in a scene is often helpful.

When setting a scene try to stick to simple basics and then expand as needed: **Where** are you? **Who** is there? **What** is going on? **When** is it? In many cases these questions only need simple answers such as "You are alone in the courtyard of the ruined city at night." Other times, certain details require expansion either for dramatic effect or to further some important plot point or detail.

If there are any obvious tests or dangerous characters present in a scene, narrators should have those ready to use. It saves time and lets them respond quickly when a player character immediately leaps to attack the white ape you just described or tries to scale that dangerous cliff

CAMPAIGN FOCUS

Narrators and players might occasionally find it useful to give their campaign a narrow focus, with players agreeing to create and play characters who fit into a certain number of concepts or archetypes. There are numerous possibilities for a campaign. Some include:

PANTHAN MERCENARIES

The players are a band of panthan mercenaries. They travel from city to city and often between nations, fighting for whoever can afford their services. Will they eventually become part of an established army or will they remain sellswords and mercenaries?

FORCES OF HELIUM

The players are officers and soldiers in the armies and navies of Helium, or some other nation. They undertake dangerous missions and engage in thrilling battles on behalf of their leaders, perhaps one day rising to the high command themselves.

A ROYAL FAMILY

The players are members of a royal family of Barsoom and their allies and aides. This option usually involves most player characters being members of the same race, but this need not always be the case — after all, the Helium Royal family includes Earthborn, red Martian, and Mixed Heritage characters. Courtly intrigue and politics based action are commonplace in such campaigns.

EXPLORERS

Barsoom is filled with mysteries, lost technology, and secret locations. In this campaign, the players take the role of characters driven or tasked with exploring these far-off places. Travel is commonplace in this campaign, and player characters are often a mix of scouts, scientists, and other knowledgeable but rugged adventurers.

WARRIORS OF THE HORDE

In this campaign, the player characters are green Martians and other characters adopted into a horde. The focus here is on the culture and survival of the green Martians in a world where the red Martians are currently ascendant and hostile environments and creatures are a constant threat. Similar campaigns could focus on First Born raiding parties or an Okar outpost.

SPIES LIKE US

In this campaign focus, the characters are spies, assassins, or other covert operatives. This focus usually means that all the characters come from the same race and nation, but this need not necessarily be the case, especially in the Jeddak of Jeddaks era. In fact, perhaps Carter and his allies form a multicultural task force of spies and covert operatives to keep Barsoom safe from insidious plots and hidden threats.

CARTER AND COMPANY

Here the player characters are close associates of Carter and his allies. They may even play some or all of the heroes of the Barsoom novels themselves. This campaign focus can feel constrained by canonical portrayals and events, but it can also be great fun as the player characters take the role of Barsoom's most famous champions.

without pause, as player characters so often do.

In fact, if a player interrupts you setting a scene with an impulsive and half informed action, it is usually a good idea to let them jump in and fill out any other important details as you go. There are two reasons for this. One, the player is telling you they are ready to get things moving again and it is a good idea to let them. Two, if they truly did act too rashly and missed out on crucial information, there is no better way to represent this than letting them dive into a fray before you had a chance to tell them about those other two apes nearby.

DRAMATIC TRICKS

Narrating is not exactly like writing or filmmaking. It's much less predetermined, and the players are more involved in decision making than actors or an audience would be. However, there are some classic dramatic tricks that can be used when setting scenes that work well in roleplaying games.

THE FLASHBACK

Sometimes instead of saying "you remember when…" it is useful to craft a scene that is temporally removed from the current action. The characters can play out the events of the flashback, or perhaps simply witness them for short scenes. The dangers of the flashback are overuse and continuity errors, but they can be fun if used occasionally.

THE FLASH FORWARD

Less common than the flashback, the flash forward is useful if you want to establish that a particular scene or part of an episode took place earlier and will eventually lead to the scene in the future. This can be tricky as it requires predetermined action from various characters, including the player characters. If used, narrators should take care to flash forward to scenes that could easily happen and unfold in a variety of ways.

THE CUT AWAY

If you want to portray an event or conversation the players should know of but which they did not witness, you can cut away to that scene and describe it. The same guidelines for establishing this scene apply, including asking the players for input. The risk of the cut away is that it often takes the players out of scenes where they can affect outcomes and act directly.

A variation of the cut away is the "quick cut", where action suddenly shifts to another place and character doing something important or significant. This is extremely useful for conflicts where the player characters are in different locations, it keeps everyone engaged and active — though it can get confusing if players or narrators lose track of who is where.

THE DREAM SEQUENCE

This is included as a warning, not a suggestion. Dream sequences almost never work. You might have some fun narrating a brief dream sequence that hints at prophetic events, but do not take whole scenes, or worse, episodes and say "and it was all a dream." Just do not do it.

ASK THE PLAYERS

When narrating scenes, it is often useful to have help. Fortunately, the players are there too, and they can be called on for embellishments, suggestions, and additional details as needed. Sometimes this will occur when a player spends Momentum to add a detail useful to their character to the scene. Other times, narrators can simply ask a player whose character would have a good idea about the scene questions like "So you've been here before, describe the throne room of Ptarth."

Players are also useful to answer an additional question beyond the standard **Where**, **Who**, **What**, and **When** important to setting most scenes: **How**? If something involves their characters or would be in their realm of knowledge, ask them. How did they arrive on a scene? How long have they been there? In many cases, the "hows" of a scene are, in part, due to player character action; let the players fill in the details for you whenever possible.

Remember that scene additions suggested by the players are not set until you confirm them, but you should try to confirm more often than deny or your players will rarely make interesting suggestions going forward. A good model of confirming and adding detail to scenes is to use "Yes, and (additional details)" and "Not exactly, but (similar details you're more comfortable with)" This might not always be possible, but the more cooperative tone and approach leads to a better group dynamic in most cases.

In the single episode or throughout a whole campaign, narrators are arbiters of the 2d20 rules system in *John Carter* campaigns. They set difficulties, decide when narrator characters use talents and Threat, and otherwise use the game's mechanics to make play fun, challenging, and engaging. Using the system effectively means the game plays faster, smoother, and in a more engaging way. Without this part of the narrator's role, the game can quickly devolve into unenjoyable chaos.

There are multiple considerations to using *John Carter* effectively in play. For new narrators especially, this may seem daunting. However, it mostly comes down to three broad categories to consider.

SETTING DIFFICULTIES AND CREATING DANGERS

Setting difficulties for tests and creating dangers for player characters to face is one of two ways narrators primarily interact with the player characters. These not only serve as obstacles for the player characters, but also serve as pacing mechanisms for adventures.

Many tests are Average (D1) or Challenging (D2). More difficult tests are less common, though given the heroic nature and focus on high action in *John Carter*, it will not be unusual to see multiple tests per session that are Daunting (D3) or greater. Likewise, most dangers will be rated 1 or 2, doing small amounts of damage that make things harder, but do not incapacitate the characters outright.

Note, with ample Momentum or applicable talents, characters will succeed often even at difficult tests. This is not an accident. Much of the action in *John Carter* is about interesting degrees of success punctuated by periodic instances of significant failure. Narrators should keep this in mind when setting difficulties — better to aim a bit low and let characters succeed in interesting ways than to torment them with constant and frustrating failure.

If things seem too easy, increase the number of enemies or dangers, but if the player characters seem to be doing well based on skillful play and good fortune, let them triumph.

Of course, since tests are there to create obstacles and model interesting occurrences, they do not need to be used all the time. If the results of a test are interesting, or the cost and benefit of success and failure are significant, then, by all means, pick up the dice and call for a test. If they are not, do not worry about it. Even actions that normally call for tests, such as combat, can be quickly narrated if there is no true danger or threat.

JUST DO IT

Unlike many roleplaying games, *John Carter* does not have skills or aptitudes. Competency is assumed in most cases and talents reflect exceptional skills and aptitudes only. Between their race, archetype, and experiences in play, most characters are familiar with numerous actions from airship piloting to swordplay to surviving in harsh environments.

If a character would realistically, or even somewhat plausibly, know how to do something, they can do it. Only if it is interesting for them to fail, or the scope of success is important, are tests called for. Otherwise, describe what is happening and keep things moving. Get to the next dramatic fight, tearful romantic reunion, or other dramatic and interesting event. Even technically difficult actions can often be handwaved away if time or precise success are not required. Hours, days, or even years can be, at times, done away with in a few moments, provided nothing notable occurs. In fact, this happens in the Barsoom novels all the time.

MANY PATHS FORWARD

Tests should determine the results of important actions, and failure can occur as well as success. However, no single result of a test should choke the progress of a scene. If a character fails to climb a wall to reach a kidnapped lover, that should not be their only chance to reach them. If a character is captured by the enemy, they should not be locked up in an escape proof cell forever. One failure should not lock characters into a singular result any more than one success should mean they never lose at anything again.

When calling for tests, and creating scenes and obstacles that require tests, narrators should consider the consequences of success and failure as well as where these results lead. If a test seems to have only one outcome, it is unnecessary or unfair and should be re-examined.

STRESS AND AFFLICTIONS

While *John Carter* is fairly "rules light", the method by which damage is tracked is robust. Characters can succumb to mental, emotional, or physical stress during play and even great heroes can experience bouts of impairment from crushing doubt, madness, or terrible wounds. While much of the damage taken is determined by which attributes a player uses to defend themselves, the narrator can control the focus of various scenes by the tests they call for and the attributes they allow to be used in defense. If a narrator desires a scene to be more about existential dread and peril, they will call for tests that cause Fear or Confusion. If they wish to allow heroes to remain stalwart in the face of deadly physical peril, most damage should be Injury based.

Selecting damage is important since afflictions impair further actions of certain types. If you envision a scene making combat more difficult, it should cause Injury stress and Wound afflictions. If it will make characters more fearful and reticent, it will cause Fear and Trauma. If it tears at a character's judgment, it will cause Confusion and Madness. Talents may affect this, but this is generally the case.

Portraying Characters

The other way narrators commonly interact with player characters is through playing narrator characters. From hungry banths to villainous masterminds to engaging love interests, various characters' actions create drama and challenging scenarios for player characters. Opposed tests, conflicts, and other actions involving narrator characters challenge and endanger the player characters.

Minions, Monsters, and Pacing

Encounters with villain-class characters are always significant affairs, but those involving minions are often more about pacing than serious and lasting threats to the player character's life and limb. A horde of minions is more useful to slow player characters down in many cases, than trying to seriously harm or defeat them. There are two reasons for this. One, minions are not that tough and it is often folly to expect them to defeat a battle-tested and heroic player character. Two, if the minions get lucky and bring down a player character it is usually not that interesting. What is more likely and effective, is for the narrator to use minions to harass, weaken, and otherwise slow down player characters so that their encounters with more significant adversaries and obstacles later are more challenging.

Monsters, especially those with low menace, are used similar to minions, though they can take more punishment and thus are more of a threat. Monsters of sufficient ability might even defeat a player character outright, though often such threats can be quickly done away with when other characters rally to their fallen comrade's aid. This makes monsters useful to remind player characters of the dangers of Barsoom without risking slaughtering them all in every combat.

Narrator Characters Actions

When an action doesn't directly involve a player character, narrators should just determine what happens and describe it. If it makes sense for an ally to skewer a villain's henchmen as the player characters deal with their boss, make it happen. If it seems like now is the right time for that wounded guardsman to heroically sacrifice himself to buy the player characters time, they do so. You do not need to roll or spend anything, just do it. Only when an action directly impacts a player character do tests need to be considered. Whole battles can be narrated and described while player characters perform their own actions.

Using Threat

Threat is one of the narrator's greatest resources. Its abilities make narrator characters more effective while its limitations help structure scenes and game sessions. When Threat is high, the narrator can — and should — throw more troubles and turmoil at the player characters. When Threat is low, things slow for a time and the pace relaxes. As Threat only lowers through use and player actions, this ebb and flow develops a natural pace for games.

The Threat Pool

Perhaps the narrator's greatest tool during play is their Threat pool. The Threat pool provides an ample but finite resource to assist narrator characters in opposing and challenging the players and their characters. It grows and shrinks mostly through player choice and action, making it easy to manage.

As discussed in *Chapter Four: Adventuring in Barsoom*, Threat is mostly spent as Momentum used on behalf of narrator characters. It has some additional abilities described there as well, chiefly breaking ties and allowing narrator characters to act before player characters in a turn. However, there are three special uses for Threat not mentioned in the general rules. These are covered here, and represent three potent powers a narrator can draw from.

Gaining and Using Threat

Threat begins each game session equal to the total of all the player character's Luck points. It grows:

* Each time a player character uses Threat in place of Momentum. The pool grows by the same amount used by the player.

* When a narrator character generates additional Momentum with success. The narrator can place Threat into the pool instead of enhancing the result. Minions can add 1 Threat in per test, monsters can add Threat equal to their menace rating, and villains can add Threat equal to their lowest attribute.

* When a test generates a complication (*see Chapter 4: Adventuring in Barsoom, page 48*). The narrator may add 2 Threat to the pool instead of creating the complication.

* If a player character is allowed to succeed at a cost (*see Chapter 4: Adventuring in Barsoom, page 51*). The narrator can elect to have some or all of the cost of that success be paid in the form of increasing the Threat pool. For every complication worth of cost a player character pays for success, the narrator can instead increase the Threat pool by 2.

Threat ebbs and flows based on both player and narrator character actions. The more player characters succeed without needing to draw Threat to amplify their own dice rolls, the more quickly Threat reduces. The more they need the extra push increasing Threat provides, the more complex things get later. Essentially, Threat allows player characters to buy temporary success with problems later while giving narrators a guided resource to use to make things more challenging for the player characters, eliminating some of the guesswork of creating new problems and obstacles during play.

Example: *During a turn, two player characters take actions that increase the Threat pool. One takes 2 Threat to spend as Momentum for a test. This increases the Threat pool by 2, one for each Threat used by the player character. Another generates a complication with an* *action, but the narrator elects to increase the Threat pool instead, adding 2 Threat for the complication. The Threat pool grows 4 Threat this turn, minus whatever Threat the narrator may have spent.*

COMPLICATIONS

Narrators can generate complications by spending Threat. Typically spending 2 Threat creates a standard complication. Particularly minor or serious complications may be worth more or less Threat, but 2 is the standard.

Complications are an inconvenient change of circumstances. A complication can present an obstacle to further progress, requiring a new approach (like a route of escape being blocked), a loss of personal resources (such as using up ammunition or medical supplies), or something that hinders the character temporarily (a dropped weapon, a social faux pas, or a stuck door). It does not represent an injury to the character, and is merely a temporary setback.

The important thing to remember is that a complication is an inconvenience, not a benefit nor a catastrophe. They make things more difficult, more interesting, but they do not seriously harm important characters or eliminate important opportunities. Complications are independent of success or failure, and it is entirely possible to succeed at an attribute test while simultaneously generating a complication. The complication should only take effect immediately after the attribute test's results have been applied. A character may become vulnerable when fighting but, if the attribute test succeeded, the attack still connects before the character suffers the complication.

Example: As red Martian noble, Zala Zors, and her bodyguard, swordsman Haran Phel, face down a group of assassins intending to end Zor's noble line and silence her bodyguard, the narrator decides to make things a bit more interesting. As Zala draws her pistol and takes aim, the narrator spends 2 Threat to introduce a complication: her pistol was damaged in the airship crash that brought them to their current situation. With a curse, Zala throws down her pistol and draws her sword!

CREATING DANGERS

Narrators can create or reveal previously undiscovered dangers in a scene by spending Threat. Perhaps the floor on a ruined building begins to give way, or a sudden storm surfaces. Dangers cost 1 Threat per die of damage they inflict on those who fail to avoid them. They also cost additional Threat for each difficulty above 2 they possess in tests to avoid them.

Example: After Earthborn adventuress Jane Porter shoots a charging white ape dead with her rifle, the beast's heavy body falls to the floor in the ruins where Jane and the beast fought. The narrator spends 2 Threat and tells Jane she feels the floor begin to shudder and then collapse under the impact of the dead ape hitting the old, crumbling masonry. If Jane doesn't avoid this new danger with a Challenging (D2) test, she will take 2 ⬡ from the fall as the floor gives way!

REINFORCEMENTS

Often a villain can call additional minions to help them. Or perhaps the wilderness will yield up a sudden new threat in a scene to make things more exciting and dangerous. To reflect these sudden additional adversaries, narrators can spend Threat to have new minions or monsters join the current scene. These characters will act at the end of the current turn after all already present narrator characters have gone.

For each Threat spent, the narrator can add 1 additional minion to the scene. To add a monster, the narrator can pay Threat equal to the monster's menace rating.

Example: As the red Martian duelist, Haran Phel, closes on Jamak Hun, a vile Thern priest who has kidnapped his lover, the narrator describes Jamak drawing a golden whistle to his lips and blowing a single shrill note. Suddenly a panel in a nearby wall opens and two fierce banths are released to attack the swordsman. From down a nearby hall, three Thern guardsman also appear to protect their superior. These banths are considered monsters with a menace rating of 2 each. The guards are minions. The narrator pays 7 Threat to add these characters to the scene, 2 for each banth and 1 for each guard.

DRAMATIC ENVIRONMENTS

In addition to dangers or calling in reinforcements, sometimes narrators want to make a sudden but significant change to the environment of a scene. Normally they can simply describe this new change. However, if this change creates a new series of problems or challenges for player characters, they should pay Threat to introduce this new change.

A minor change to the environment, enough to cause a minor delay or raise a narrow set of tests by 1 difficulty, costs 1 Threat. These include changes in lighting, footing, or other shifts that make things a bit more interesting but are easily dealt with by most characters. Moderate and major changes, which either raise difficulties more or affect more types of action, cost additional Threat. A fog that makes all vision based tests 1 additional difficulty higher would cost 2 Threat, 1 for the difficulty, and 1 because it's a broad effect. If the fog was also mildly toxic, making exertion difficult, it would cost more Threat.

Example: As Okar spy, Volan Von, and his comrade, the green Martian, Zem Zurros, reach the lost valley where a mad scientist has imprisoned their companions, a strange yellow mist rises from the mutated ochre. The mist has a mildly hallucinogenic and sedative effect, making tests involving perception and exertion difficult as the mist warps senses and slows respiration. The narrator spends 3 Threat to create this change to the environment: one each for increasing difficulties on exertion and perception based tests by 1 and one more because the mist coats the whole valley entrance, making it almost impossible to avoid.

Changes to the environment usually last for a scene or until done away with. If an environment sticks around, it is usually appropriate to spend an additional Threat to continue its effect for another scene, but only if it remains a hindrance.

Dividing the Group

While "do not split the party" is common wisdom from other roleplaying games, it is worth noting that, if the Barsoom novels were played out using the rules of this game, the narrator would be regularly spending Threat to exercise this option. On Barsoom, it seems characters are regularly separated from each other and their allies. Entire episodes might pass with characters mostly operating in totally different locations. While sometimes this is voluntary, the narrator can force the issue by spending Threat. By spending Threat equal to the largest groups of characters, a narrator can create and describe an event that divides the group into smaller groups. The narrator also decides which characters end up with each group. Unless the narrator spends additional Threat each scene, the characters will find a way to regroup after the current scene ends.

Example: While exploring a ruined city, Zala Zors, Jane Porter, and Kale Singh end up in an ancient laboratory. As they are looking around for a light source, the narrator decides Jane accidentally hits a switch that triggers an energy field that traps her on the opposite side of her companions. The narrator pays 2 Threat to accomplish this, equal to the size of the larger group of player characters. At the end of the current scene, Jane will find her way back to her friends unless the narrator pays additional Threat.

Note that dividing the group creates more work for the narrator, who now must track the actions of two or more groups and work to keep them engaged. Thus, this option is not for everyone, and narrators who are not comfortable with splitting their groups should do so sparingly.

Seizing Initiative

At the start of the round before anyone has acted, or at any time immediately after a player character has finished acting (and before another player character has begun to act this turn), the narrator can spend 1 point of Threat to interrupt the player characters' turns and allow a narrator character to immediately take a turn.

The narrator character's actions are resolved normally and, once finished, the turn order passes back to the player characters, unless the narrator spends additional points of Threat to allow additional narrator characters to take their actions before the player characters. Any narrator character acting out of order like this does not get to act again that round.

Example: As Kale Singh turns to face a trio of orluks stalking towards him, the narrator describes the alpha of the orluk pack surging forward in a great rush to attack him. The narrator spends 1 Threat and the orluk alpha gets to go immediately, before Singh. However, the alpha will not go again until next turn.

Narrators should also note, since Threat can be spent as Momentum on behalf of narrator characters, they can also spend Threat to deliver a Counterstrike during a conflict. This costs a hefty 3 Threat, but it can allow a villain or beast to deliver a serious blow to a character at a dramatic moment.

Luck for Villains

Villains don't gain Luck like PCs but are able to use all the effects of a Luck point. Using such an effect costs 3 Threat. The abilities of Luck can be found in *Chapter 4: Adventuring in Barsoom, page 68.*

Advancement Rewards

Narrators determine the renown and experience player characters receive. The pace at which these rewards are provided alters the pace of a campaign. If characters receive experience and renown quickly, they rapidly become powerful and important figures in the setting. If they receive these rewards more slowly, they spend more time rising in prominence. Neither option is superior to the other, though it is often easier to give smaller amounts of experience and renown early in a game and adjust it upwards than the reverse.

Renown is important since the accolades it buys are the chief way that player characters change the setting in significant ways. By gaining titles and allies, the characters grow in power and inspire great change based on their adventures. Their allies often unite or join forces, and the armies or nations with which they hold title become more important in the setting.

Challenging but Fair

As the narrator controls the adjudication and application of most of the rules, there is always a temptation to simply "have your way." If you decide a particular encounter should have a particular outcome, you can make that happen. If you decide a certain character should die or be removed from play, you can do that.

The problem here is twofold. First, arbitrary decisions like this tend to hurt player-narrator relations. Players justifiably do not like it when narrators undermine or eliminate their accomplishments or rob their characters of agency. Second, it is simply not fun for most groups. Players are there to play their characters and have fun, not act out a narrator's whims and plans.

Instead, narrators should use the rules to craft and implement challenging scenarios, present dangerous but manageable foes, and otherwise present a balanced and entertaining experience. When a difficulty for a test is overwhelmingly high, it should be because that task involved is nigh-impossible, not because the narrator does not like the idea of it happening. If a player character is ambushed and beaten down by overwhelming odds, it should be because they alerted an enemy to their presence or charged in recklessly, and such situations should usually result in capture or other temporary setbacks, not death.

Remember, you are not the other players' enemies. You are just playing them at the table.

OPTIONAL RULE:
ACHIEVEMENTS

In addition to standard accolades, narrators might decide to allow player characters to purchase special achievements with renown. These advancements take a group, location, or event that is important to the player characters and cause it to grow in power and prominence. A horde of green Martians might expand and conquer a larger territory, or a small red Martian city-state might annex a neighbor. Typically, a minor but significant change costs between 3 and 5 renown, while major changes cost 8 or more renown. Achievements can also represent scientific advancements such as Carthoris' developments in airship design or other ideological developments, such as John Carter teaching the Tharks to treat their beasts of burden with increased care and affection.

Achievements differ from developments brought about purely by roleplaying in that they are considered part of the character and thus cannot be truly and permanently destroyed. A new nation formed during a campaign but not purchased as an achievement might be crushed or disbanded, but one bought as an achievement will endure, though not necessarily in the exact way it was originally conceived.

Achievements are optional because they require additional bookkeeping, usually by both the players and narrator. Also, they are not as easily codified as an ally or title, and, as such, may not be suitable for groups who prefer clearly defined renown advancements.

CAMPAIGN TONE AND THEME

To understand the tone and themes at play in *John Carter*, it helps to understand two types of stories that combine to make up the Barsoom tales: planetary romance and rationalist pulp.

WHAT IS PLANETARY ROMANCE?

Romance, in the literary sense of the word, refers to a work that focuses on the extraordinary exploits of heroes. Romance hearkens back to the medieval cycles of Arthur, Charlemagne, and the Greco-Roman epics; indeed, the word itself ultimately derives from "Roman". "Planetary Romance", then, is a specific genre of romance that takes place on an exotic alien world, in which the plot is partially or completely reliant on the nature of that world. Planetary romance is a direct descendant of the adventure novels of the late 1800s (such as the works of H. Rider Haggard). In part, it is an evolution of the "lost world" genre, substituting alien worlds for the real-life "lost worlds" of Asia, Africa, and South America. Planetary romance also has commonalities with space opera, which developed at the same time (and by some of the same authors).

Like lost world stories, planetary romance protagonists usually come from a more civilized world (often Earth), and are forced to contend with hostile lifeforms, extreme landscapes, and decadent empires. In many cases the protagonist was a misfit on his home planet, and is much more suited to the barbarity of his new world. Like space opera, in planetary romance, the mode of travel is irrelevant; the action is firmly focused on what the protagonists do when they reach their destination. Like pulp adventure, protagonists are always getting into trouble, and they usually have to get out of it through their own wit, skills, and strength of character. Even when a character is rescued by others, it is usually due to their inherent nobility and ability to make strong allies.

Barsoom is an early example of planetary romance; while not the first, it was one of the first to achieve popular acclaim. In the Barsoom novels, Burroughs harnessed the wholesale collision of the futuristic and the medieval: soldiers bear swords alongside ray-guns; classical and feudal empires support modern technological armies; great flying machines are powered by strange alien energies while the barbarian hordes below wrestle their fractious mounts into submission. Medicine is described only briefly; it is a mere plot device to allow the protagonist to recover quickly, alchemical in its potency. There is no magic; the closest Barsoom comes is telepathy, which is common yet limited, and bizarre science, which is powerful yet the province of only certain groups and individuals. In practical terms for the narrator, Barsoom is a world with social structures common to low fantasy (tribal barbarians, feudal empires, etc.), with magic replaced by technological trappings.

WHAT IS RATIONALIST PULP?

At their heart, the Barsoom tales are rationalist pulp. Heroes fight enemies born of lust, ignorance, and tyranny to save their friends, loved ones, and those cultures and places they call home. False gods, lying priests, deceitful nobles, treacherous assassins, and many other cruel adversaries are the biggest threats. These themes are also romantic, of course, but they are steeped in a rational view of the universe. Heroes fight evil because evil is irrational, selfish, and oppressive to everyone but a select few — the villains and their ilk. Villains commit evil acts because it benefits them. Evil and selfish people exist, and will prosper unless stopped. These people can come in any size, shape, or color. So can heroes and their allies.

By contrast, while the people of Barsoom can be almost heartlessly pragmatic and even a bit emotionally stunted at times, it is all temporary and fixable. There are no "evil" races on Mars. Some beliefs are shocking to Earthling sensibilities, and cultural differences can certainly lead to comedic or tragic misunderstandings (a common Burroughsian theme), but there are no orcs or what have you. Even largely "evil" races like the Therns have individuals who start to see that oppression and cruelty are a hollow and ultimately poor substitute for love and loyalty. Remember all this when narrating the game and portraying the different races and cultures of Barsoom.

The beasts and nature of Barsoom pretty much echo all the above. There aren't really "evil" animals or beasts on the planet. Just hungry, territorial, or savage ones. Even the plant-men are just acting on instinct. So, when using beasts and the environment in the campaign, focus on the challenges and feral dangers of the world instead. It helps make the truly evil individuals stand out from all the other numerous challenges characters face.

In the case of weird or quasi-mystical phenomena? It is *always* science. The explanation may be strange or even a bit nonsensical to modern standards, but there is always a rational explanation for every strange occurrence or bizarre event. It is just that, in the rationalist pulp adventure of *John Carter*, that explanation is also often utterly fantastic.

COMBINING THE TWO

If you combine the swashbuckling glory of planetary romance with the grounded but dramatic action of rationalist pulp, you find *John Carter*. No magic, but plenty of monsters and strange happenings. No evil races or irredeemable cultures, but plenty of dangerous groups and individuals for bold adventurers to defeat. Everything is amazing, challenging, and glorious, but it all makes a sort of sense — albeit sense that usually requires strange alien rays, telepathy, and other such phenomena as explanations.

With these two genres in mind, narrators can craft countless scenarios for their campaigns. Strange scientific cabals, political intrigues, dangerous beasts, and countless mysteries lurk in the intersection between the two-fisted emotional action of planetary romance and the inquisitive and contemplative adventures of rationalist pulp.

USING BARSOOM

While the rules and mechanics of this game are suitable for a variety of pulp-based action games, this is *John Carter*. Players take the roles of adventurers on the planet Barsoom and face perils similar to those seen in Burroughs' novels. This means that narrators should take care to concentrate on what makes Barsoom unique and interesting. New additions to the setting should not overwrite or undo what has been established, rather it should complement and enhance it.

Barsoom has its own ecology and logic. Creatures are many limbed and strangely hued. Technology is old yet powerful. The world is dying but everywhere life is fighting hard to survive and prosper. Religions and tradition are based in ancient observances and even deceptions, but these things make sense to those who believe in them. People are terrible, wonderful, kind, cruel, and many other things; often dramatically so.

Barsoom is a glorious and exciting place and there is nowhere else like it, which is why it is so much fun to play in. Of course, it is also at times familiar, with teeming jungles and vast deserts and beasts that are strange but also resemble animals and myths from our Earth. These elements mix to create a world of familiar wonder, and narrators can use this to craft their own version of Barsoom for their players to enjoy.

This book is filled with information and advice on how to present characters, creatures, and phenomena that feel appropriate to Burroughs' Barsoom. Use them as you see fit to enhance your gaming experiences.

BUILDING CHARACTERS

You cannot have a game without narrator created and run characters. From faceless minions to romantic foils and villainous masterminds, characters are at the heart of most conflicts narrators will present for player characters.

Nearly all Martians are warlike, honorable and loyal — three characteristics capable of making somebody either an asset or a liability. Characters who are deficient in these categories are unpredictable and often dangerous. Even the savage green Martian who openly mocks many displays of love and friendship serve their horde and its leaders faithfully to help the horde thrive and survive. While not every character is a fighter, note that nearly everyone on Barsoom knows the basics of self-defense and it is a rare Barsoomian who will not fight in their own defense or for those they hold dear.

Skill at, and enthusiasm for, war make for excellent soldiers and terrifying rebellions. A sense of honor means a man can be trusted, but also demands trustworthy leadership. Loyalty can cut both ways, since a debt owed to a rival can spell disaster to a jed or a former friend. Martians are passionate and determined generally, and even random encounters can lead to interesting relationships.

Beyond those personal traits, their role in society is a vital part of any character's identity. Knowing where he fits in the feudal hierarchy, to whom he is allied, and what threats or opportunities lie in their current social context, is as important to a Barsoomian as a mother and father are to a man from Jasoom.

Personal loyalties are the lynchpins of any Martian's personal story and place in the world. When building any named character (as opposed to unnamed "extras" who exist solely to pursue player characters or be mowed down by them), consider who he or she loves, hates, and owes loyalty to. These details will help you understand the motivations, conflicts, and pressures integral to who that character is.

CRAFTING VILLAINS

A good villain is central to most pulp-style planetary romance adventures. Without a good antagonist, the plot can sometimes slow or even stop. Attacking beasts and marauding pirates can get the action fairly far along, but a solid villainous antagonist is required to bring things to a satisfying climactic conflict and summary conclusion.

The following section discusses some key tips to making a good villain.

EVIL, NOT VILE

Villains are evil, but they usually do not engage in overly graphic or disturbing acts. The average **John Carter** antagonist is driven by unsavory impulses, somewhat dishonorable, and perhaps a bit of a coward. They are not a crazed serial killer or similarly disturbing threat.

Example: Jack needs a villain for his next serial. As the players are getting a bit tired of fighting raiders and pirates, he decides to make the next major villain an evil and corrupt jeddak of a small remote nation. The jeddak is cruel and overly ambitious, but mostly honorable and courageous enough to command loyalty among his army.

Also, sometimes antagonists are misunderstood or capable of reform. Even Tars Tarkas starts out taking John Carter prisoner and Xodar is an enemy of Carter until he switches sides. Not every villain should be a potential ally, but it is a recurring theme in Burroughs' work that compassion and friendship can recruit at least some of your enemies to your cause.

OKAY, MAYBE A LITTLE VILE

Many antagonists in the Barsoom stories have flaws and deeply disturbing behaviors that make them a stark contrast to the heroes they face. These behaviors are rarely graphic and more often than not are implied, but they are typically unsettling. For example, more than one villain in the Barsoom stories is a cannibal. Several are racist. Many delight in torture and torment. These are not nice people and the average **John Carter** antagonist who doesn't end up being a misunderstood later ally often possesses at least one onerous trait that helps alleviate any lingering guilt the protagonists might feel about throwing them off a high cliff or skewering them with a sword.

Example: Jack realizes if his evil jeddak is a bit more despicable it will motivate the player characters to oppose and perhaps depose him. He decides that while the jeddak is honorable, he hates non-red Martians with an irrational and sadistic vigor, especially green Martians. He is likely to gleefully torture any green Martians who come into his clutches, and will treat his fellow red Martians who count greens as friends as fools and traitors to their own kind.

Narrators should take care to not give villains traits that upset or disturb their players, though they should totally give them traits that upset or disturb the players characters. When in doubt, narrators should discuss any borderline cases with their group and if necessary make alterations to their villains to make them more fun and less disruptive.

THROUGH THE MIRROR DARKLY

Most good villains reflect something about the heroes who fight them. Usually this is some twisted variation of a hero's nobility or abilities. A master swordsman may have a villain who is similarly skilled, but dishonorable or cowardly. A skilled and noble hunter might be opposed by a wild beast or a heartless killer who hunts humans for sport.

Example: Jack considers the characters in his group while designing his evil jeddak. One of the players is playing a green Martian hunter. He thinks it would be interesting if his hateful jeddak villain likes to hunt green Martians for sport, releasing them into his own private hunting preserve to track and kill them. This draws an interesting but twisted parallel between the villain and the player character hunter who may be his next target.

This tendency to reflect a hero's abilities goes for game statistics as well. An evil jeddak will have abilities similar to their heroic counterpart. A deadly warrior should be a match for the hero he opposes in battle. Characters do not need to be identical, but they should have attributes and talents that allow them to engage with each other in dramatic ways.

NOT TOO MANY AFFECTATIONS

A few affectations or distinguishing features makes a villain memorable. However, too many makes an otherwise memorable villain comical. After three or four noticeable traits, villains begin to resemble campy parodies more than distinguished threats. Look at famous villains in literature and film for inspiration: most have a few noticeable quirks and major traits that are well defined and interesting.

Example: Jack decides the jeddak is almost ready, but he needs a few quirks or affectations to help him stand out. Going with the theme of a green-hating sadistic hunter, Jack decides the jeddak has a nasty scar on his face from a green Martian blade — perhaps hinting at why he hates the greens. He also decides the jeddak wears a cloak of tanned green Martian hide, a ghoulish affectation that broadcasts his contempt and obsessive hatred.

Affectations are also a great way to give a lesser antagonist a bit of style. Minions that wear special colors or items, or a monster or henchman with a distinct scar can easily provide a bit of memorable color to a scene.

THEY ARE SUPPOSED TO LOSE

Villains might not always lose but that is typically their lot. They are there to challenge, but ultimately be defeated by, the heroes. In **John Carter**, this means Villains are there to lose to the player characters more often than not.

Example: Jack designs his jeddak, giving him attributes and talents on par with the player characters. However, he also makes sure to play the character as arrogant and hateful, providing numerous opportunities for clever and motivated characters to get the better of him.

Villains should not have overwhelming attributes and talents which prevent their defeat. When in doubt, it is better to keep these abilities a bit low and use Threat to boost them when needed. If the villains return and survive they can always be boosted with additional attribute ranks and talents if necessary.

BUT THEY ARE NOT STUPID

Unless a villain is actually supposed to be stupid or foolish, they should adapt and react to situations with intelligence and personality. If player characters foil their schemes, they may seek revenge, but they will also likely try to correct past mistakes. Clever villains may seek to seduce or harass a character's friends and allies, undermine their reputations, or otherwise weaken them.

A motivated and skilled villain can do a lot of damage. Even when they eventually fall, the effect of their actions may have lasting repercussions.

WATCH YOUR PLAYERS

When trying to figure out which narrator characters to focus on during play, watch your players and their characters. In many cases, players will make it clear which villains they really despise and want to defeat, which romantic interests they wish to explore, and who they want as allies and regular members of the game's cast of characters.

It is also fine to craft characters with certain reactions in mind. You may design a particular character as a romantic interest for a character based on what you know of their player. A villain might be selected to offend the sensibilities of a particular character above all others, prompting them to select them as a personal nemesis. However, do not lock your decisions in so firmly you cannot adapt. Sometimes the character you suspect would appeal to someone is better suited as a foil, rival, or enemy for another character entirely.

If watching your players doesn't work, just ask them. It is a bit less organic, but it gets to the same result: giving the players the experiences and interactions they want at the table. This is especially useful when designing romantic interests, as it is often difficult to determine exactly what a player and their character want in a love story.

SELECTING ERA

John Carter is designed to be set in three time periods, each following the other and mapping to the life of Carter and the events of the Barsoom novels. The era an episode, serial, or campaign occurs during affects much of the political situation and history of Barsoom. There are advantages and disadvantages to each era.

As Martians are extremely long-lived, campaigns can easily span all three eras. Player characters who begin in the Dotar Sojat era might rise to prominence alongside heroes like Carter, Tars, Dejah, and others. They may even match or exceed their accomplishments.

DOTAR SOJAT

Set during a time when Carter was a captive of the Tharks and an unknown newcomer, this period allows player characters to operate on equal footing with Carter and his companions. However, this is a period of great strife. There are no lasting alliances and most races and cultures are hostile to each other. First Born, green Martian, and Okar characters in particular would be unusual and distrusted outside their own lands and groups. Narrators wishing to closely follow the canonical events of the Barsoom novels may find this period somewhat limiting, as certain events must unfold.

PRINCE OF HELIUM

This era provides several years where Carter and his allies are important, but not spread across the whole of the planet. In fact, for several years during this period, Carter himself is presumed dead and many of his allies are imprisoned, missing, or otherwise occupied with their own affairs. This provides player characters with immense freedom, though again narrators wishing to preserve precise canon of the Barsoom tales must take care to preserve certain events, such as the defeat of Issus or the return of Thuvia of Ptarth to her father. Many of the challenges of the Dotar Sojat period remain, though playing green Martians and red Martians together in the same group is easier, especially if characters are Tharks and Heliumites.

JEDDAK OF JEDDAKS

The era is both the most open and limiting at the same time. Due to the actions of Carter and his allies, there are numerous alliances making it easier to mix groups of different races and cultures. However, the shadow of Carter hangs heavy over this time. He is a great warrior and statesman famous across Barsoom and his adopted home of Helium possesses many allies and great power. Player characters may find it hard to carve out their own place in such a time.

This era tends to be a time of science gone awry and corrupt jeddaks with mad schemes of global domination. Such threats *always* need heroes to oppose them.

CONVENTIONS OF THE GENRE

Burroughsian adventure stories, planetary romance, rationalist pulp, and pulp adventure all have certain, and often complimentary, genre conventions. When crafting episodes, serials, and campaigns, narrators should employ these conventions to help their games feel appropriate to the source material.

OUT OF THE FRYING PAN

In many cases, victory is sweet but short-lived. This is especially true before the climactic resolution of a particular scene, episode, or serial. A defeated beast's death cry calls others of its kind, a downed foe reveals he is part of a larger force nearby, or an airship crash narrowly survived causes an avalanche. Many of the better action films provide great examples of how to throw new complications and dangers at player characters to keep things moving.

Often an episode or serial will end on a cliffhanger that sets up a new problem. This is a genre convention it is highly recommended narrators try at least once or twice in their games — it really keeps players coming back for more and helps remind everyone easily where you left off; people tend to remember their characters hanging by their fingertips more than sitting in the middle of trade talks.

YOU DO NOT UNDERSTAND

These are a Burroughs staple. It really is not a classic Burroughs romance or lifelong friendship if the characters do not deeply misunderstand each other at least once. A red Martian noble might think an Earthborn character being polite is proposing marriage, a green Martian might puzzle at a new comrade's compassionate treatment of a foe and think them weak or mad, and so on. These misunderstandings are often easy to clear up once the characters get a chance to talk, which is why narrators wanting to set up such situations should throw ample problems at characters to draw out their eventual reconciliation. Again, there is no better example of this method than Burroughs' work.

CURSE YOUR INEVITABLE BETRAYAL!

In many Barsoom novels and other stories of the period, it is not all that hard to spot the character who will eventually betray the heroes. That is because those tales perfected the "wait, the native warrior who I butted heads with has returned to kidnap my loved ones!" plot twist. Depending on the group, narrators may need to hide these twists and reveals more when they use them. Some groups love to spot the bad guy and then play along until things develop, others refuse to play along.

Remember, unless treated terribly by a player character, allies *never* betray the player characters. *Ever*. That is why they are bought with renown and considered part of the player characters. However, cultural misunderstanding and temporary circumstances may lead characters to believing a trusted comrade has turned against them.

HEY, A NEW… LOOK OUT!

Introducing new places, beasts, characters, technology, and other elements to the setting or scene are often accompanied by a new problem or crisis. The easiest way to introduce a new beast is to have it attack. The best way to meet many characters is in the middle of some peril. This allows the players to see something in action, which answers a lot of questions right away. Is that beast dangerous? (Yes). Do we need to worry about that gun-shaped thing that guy is pointing at us? (Also, Yes). Are those armed soldiers friendly? (Not right now).

AND… RAIDERS ATTACK!

Author Raymond Chandler once described his method of keeping action moving in his stories as "If things get slow, have someone kick in the door brandishing a gun." While there are not that many doors on Barsoom, this advice holds in spirit. If things are slow, have a new threat appear. You can figure out why the threat appears later if necessary. Whatever the reason, it serves to get things moving again.

The Barsoomian equivalent of this idea may be "If things get slow, have someone kidnap the heroes' loved ones." Again, take care to not always menace the same characters with this trick.

DANGEROUS WONDERS

The world of Barsoom is filled with dangerous and amazing things. There is rarely a place, creature, or event that is merely "something we saw once." Ancient ruins hide strange technology and bizarre monsters. New cultures are fascinating but also usually encountered at some tipping point.

Even when filling in background details, narrators should track the things they introduce into the setting, even in passing, and consider how to later implement them in more dramatic and significant ways. To use an example from *A Princess of Mars*, Carter visits the atmosphere plant before it fails years later. This brief tour places him uniquely in a position to save the day later.

THREAT, PACING AND PULP ACTION

Using Threat to create regular "Okay, but…" or "Sorry, however…" additions to scenes is a great way to mimic the pulp action of the Barsoom novels and similar tales. Many of the genre conventions discussed in this chapter can be enabled by spending Threat and well-timed uses of such methods help keep action moving. Not every fight needs to lead to a new problem and sometimes players characters should be given an attempt to rest and recover, but generally, John Carter is about fast action and high heroics — keep it moving!

EXPANDING THE WORLD

This section focuses on advice for narrators seeking to customize and add their own kingdoms, cities, important landmarks, cultural events, and other elements to the world of Barsoom.

CRAFTING NEW KINGDOMS

It is completely within the power of the narrator to create his own kingdoms and nations of the various races of Barsoom. Such creations are keeping completely within the example set by Edgar Rice Burroughs, who regularly crafted new cities, settlements, and kingdoms whenever a narrative demanded one. In addition, players may create new kingdoms through the actions of their characters, either by splintering existing nations or even settling or creating new ones through their deeds. Each of these new creations will be informed greatly by the dominant race and culture of this new kingdom or settlement.

As they are the dominant race of Barsoom, most new kingdoms or city states will be red Martian kingdoms, but the same basic guidelines presented in this section work for Okar and First Born settlements as well. Even the white Martians have their citadels and settlements, ranging from oppressive slave states to isolationist enclaves.

In most new cities, nations and individuals will be important because of how they *differ* from others of their race. The process begins with embracing the themes and factors making Martians who they are. If a new city or nation differs too much from a red Martian or other race's settlements, it runs the risk of feeling too different to fit into Burroughs' world.

GREEN MARTIAN HORDES

Green Martian settlements are different in their construction, being often temporary and connected to a race of nomadic warriors, wanderers, and raiders. They keep mobile and constantly challenge the wilderness, preferring regular conflict and tribal structures that claim many lives but keep their race strong. Thus, a new green Martian settlement usually takes the form of an ancient ruin or lost city serving as a temporary base of operations for a group of green Martians, either an established horde or a new one of the narrator's creation.

BUILDING CITIES

Most known cities are built on the bones of a dead civilization. The few exceptions are the ancient strongholds of isolated groups of First Born, Okar, and white Martians. However, in most places, people occupy structures and locations constructed long ago by civilizations long since passed.

Barsoomian architecture is vast and filled with wide gardens, sweeping plazas, towering buildings and mighty walls. Commerce and security are of paramount importance, as the cities require trade to thrive and defenses to survive. Even hidden cities and strongholds need methods of bringing in food, weapons, and other supplies.

In most Barsoom novels, new cities and the kingdoms that surrounded them were most clearly defined by a specific way in which they differed from the norm presented by Helium. One had a deceitful or cowardly jeddak. Another worshipped strange gods. Yet another was positioned in a lush jungle, and another on a harsh polar cap. When defining a new city or nation for your Barsoom campaign, begin with how it differs and expand on the implications and consequences of that difference to make the city truly unique and interesting among the existing cultures of Mars. This line of thought and questioning will help you populate your nation with interesting characters, bizarre landmarks, and interesting plots.

New cities can be placed wherever the narrator desires and wherever there is territory to flesh out. When doing so, take notice of this new creation's neighbors and environment. Hidden citadels may be found in a lost valley near an established kingdom, but it is unlikely a large active city-state at the center of a large kingdom would be located too close to other nations without this disrupting local politics, travel, and trade.

BUILDING SETTLEMENTS

Martian settlements are small communities lying outside the walls of their ruling cities. In the case of the green Martians, these may be small tribes or clan groups that owe allegiance to a larger horde. These settlements consist of a few buildings inhabited by those working and protecting the surrounding territory. Many settlements are built in Mars' canals, next to waters pumped to the surface by the enormous waterworks of the First Born. The remote nature and small size of most settlements makes them less strategically important than cities and often, those who live there are less concerned with politics and intrigue than defense and survival.

Two questions are paramount when creating a new settlement: to whom is the settlement loyal, and how does it survive? Few settlements are allowed to exist without declaring allegiance to a more powerful city or kingdom. Which nation a settlement serves impacts everything from what resources they extract to how they build and maintain their homes. In terms of survival, most settlements exist without walls or armies in the war-ravaged Barsoomian wilderness. Many have their sleeping huts built on extendable stilts for safety. Others rely on the threat of vengeance from their patron nation or the protection of hired mercenaries.

Obviously, the answers to who a settlement serves and how it survives are closely tied. How they are answered can help give the settlement color, personality, and a firmer place in your world. Threats to either answer are the sort of things of which high adventure is made!

A MIX OF NEW AND OLD

The races of Barsoom follow different paths, but they all, in their way, protect themselves and seek to thrive on their increasingly barren and hostile world. Each race sees itself as the best equipped to survive in the harsh world of Barsoom, though each approaches this role differently. When introducing new cultures, kingdoms, or other groups consider this reality.

The reds took on a role as custodians of their dying planet. They inhabited and cared for the great, empty cities and tried to restore something of their former glory. They maintain the great atmosphere plant to keep all Martians alive. In observing their courtly manners and codes of honor, they attempt to recreate the great cultures and to imitate the revered individuals of history. The red love tradition, and work to keep it alive — even if keeping it alive means dying themselves.

The green Martians embrace the deaths of the old cities and kingdoms, preferring instead to be unapologetically mobile, ruthless, and focused on the survival of their horde over any individual morals or sentiments. They seem cruel to outsiders, but their methods ensure their survival and make them deadly foes to their enemies.

Meanwhile the Firstborn and Okar, once much more powerful and widespread, dominate their own secluded spaces. They cling to their old ways and traditions as proof of their superiority or as a testament to their past glory. Possessing might and knowledge, they nevertheless cannot compete with red or green Martians for raw numbers or territory. This means they prize secrets, especially those which can weaken enemies or protect their territory. These hidden strengths come in many forms, from elaborate disinformation campaigns to strange technology. White Martians also embraced such tactics, but tend to focus on one or two concepts to the exclusion of all else, such as the Holy Therns' devotion to using false religion and slavery to dominate the "lesser" races.

Any new Martian elements will be most powerful if they either serve or challenge these racial and cultural traditions. An unnecessarily savage red Martian kingdom is memorable, so is an excessively honorable one. Likewise, a settlement of valiant and altruistic First Born resonates as an anomaly and a ruthless cadre of raiders presents as a grave threat. In many cases a culture or kingdom mixes strong traditional elements with revolutionary ones. As seen in Burroughs' works, some of the most sweeping adventures on Barsoom began when one tradition clashes with another.

CULTURAL EVENTS AND CUSTOMS

Each kingdom will have their own significant happening and customs. Events within Barsoomian cultures are usually tied to political, economic, or military necessity. A kingdom may keep slaves to fuel its labor force and then force the strongest of them to fight in gladiatorial combats to entertain the elites and keep the number of skilled fighters among their slaves under control. A nation may go to war for resources or to avenge some slight. Jeds and jeddaks rise and fall. Great families unite or fracture. Victories are celebrated, and defeats are mourned. In many cases, these events should be directly tied to player characters and their actions, but at times, narrators may find it useful to craft an event that affects a city, kingdom, culture, or group caused by other sources.

Creating cultural events and new customs is tricky because you must strike a tight balance. Events must be large and noteworthy enough to warrant the attention of adventurers, and to meaningfully impact some aspect of the game. Customs must be interesting, but not alter things so much that the setting no longer feels familiar. A hundred little cultural variations or conflicts between kingdoms may be realistic from an anthropological point of view, but during play these little differences often lead to confusion and distraction. Because of this, it is usually best to focus on a handful of significant and memorable events and customs.

BUILDING NEW LANDMARKS

New landmarks may be introduced as part of a new kingdom, city, or settlement, but this need not be the case. An established nation may have an important location the player characters never before encountered, or a lost ruin may be home to a wondrous structure. Landmarks can be grand active affairs like the Guardian of the North, or forgotten half-buried ruins whose secrets are known to no living Barsoomian.

As a rule, Martians do not build their own landmarks, but rather create landmarks by either occupying an already important or impressive edifice, or by converting a normal abandoned building into a structure fit for another use. Actual construction of new buildings is nearly unheard of. Even active landmarks with powerful abilities are often powered by ancient science.

Ironically, the first rule of creating a new landmark for a campaign is the building must *not* be new. It will likely be millennia old. Its original purpose may be greatly different from how it is used today. For example, an ancient complex of luxury apartments may serve as a modern-day palace or a temple may be home to modern scientists conducting various research projects.

PAST AND PRESENT PURPOSES

When crafting a landmark, think about who built it. Was this the work of the united races as Barsoom began to die? Or did one of the original races build it alone before or after the alliance lived and died? Was it built by a mysterious, as-yet unknown race? These details determine the shape, style, size, location and other physical characteristics of the landmark.

Once that is decided, choose what the current owners are doing with it *now*. This determines the social context of the location, the décor, how many guards are likely to be present, and similar details important in any adventure which takes the PCs to the site. Also consider whether the site has secrets unknown to its owners and inhabitants — even great palaces or fortresses of modern Barsoom may contain secret chambers and devices unknown to current residents.

All this said, any new construction is an event worthy of investigation, and could be the basis of an adventure or entire campaign. Such an endeavor would only occur when the purpose of this new facility, base, device, or other construction could not be served by an existing structure.

CRAFTING COURTLY LOVE AND INTRIGUE

Given that John Carter is a game of planetary romance, themes of love and courtly intrigue are commonplace. Each culture treats this differently and in these differences tension thrives.

Honor and tradition are part of Martian heritage, but so is aggression, aspiration, and a desire to take what you believe to be (or wish to be) yours. The laws make outright rebellion within a kingdom an uncertain means for climbing to the top. As a result, various societies on Barsoom are full of courtly intrigue, star-crossed lovers, plots within plans, and wheels within wheels. Few Jasoomians would call Martians subtle, but the waters of their society run deep. Any new population would have a rich history and context of political intrigue including alliances forged, favors made, secrets kept, and grudges nursed.

Even the green Martians have their occasional variations of these themes, as seen with Tars Tarkas, the warrior who loved his mate and knew the identity of, and protected, his daughter despite tradition.

MAKERS OF WAR

Most new Martian kingdoms, locations, and cultures will enter into the campaign as part of some violent action. Raiding parties or invading armies are often among the first contact point for a new group in Barsoom. Martians are quick to anger, quick to go to war, and quick to risk their lives in defense of a friend. Violence is as much a part of Martian life as social media is part of the lives of twenty-first century Jasoomians. The obvious application of this is the introduction of a new war, enemy, or conflict, but the most interesting new Martian elements will be those where the conflict *within* a war band or army is as dangerous as that against which they fight.

STANDARD DEVIATIONS

Of course, it's your game. If you want a Martian city where personal honor is unimportant or a green Martian kingdom where family ties are valued, you should go right ahead. Exceptions make the most interesting stories. But think about why this difference exists. What makes this city, nation, or individual stand out? How did that happen? Coming up with this reason improves play in two different ways.

Within a campaign setting, explaining why a given culture has diverged maintains verisimilitude and immersion. Does the nation have a remote location like Manator? A different religion like Phundahl? Does it rest in a unique environment like Kaol or Toonol? Some combination of all three such as Kadabra? Giving adventurers the details to explain these differences keeps the world consistent, and can give clues as to how to solve some of the mysteries stemming from those differences.

Outside of the campaign setting, understanding the reason for the difference provides creative springboards for other aspects of the new nation you have created. Imagine you want a nation with no tradition of slavery or indentured servitude. Why would that happen? You decide this came from a jeddak who rose to his position after being captured and made a slave some two thousand years ago. Upon rising to his position, he forbade slavery and made all existing slaves full citizens of his nation. This explains the difference for any players in the game, and also suggests many avenues for adventure.

Certainly, many great families lost fortunes when they lost their slaves. Some must be plotting revenge. Perhaps the city has highly advanced automation to make up for the labor lost when the slaves were freed. How are relations with nearby nations? Are they cordial, since this city never raids their caravans for slaves? Or are they strained, with the new city's policy meaning their own slaves frequently attempt escape toward freedom? As you can see, answering the first question inspires so many other questions the entire nation almost writes itself.

SOURCES OF INSPIRATION

While much inspiration for **John Carter** adventures can be found in the works of Burroughs, it is not the only place narrators can mine for a source of ideas. This section points to various places a narrator can look when in need of inspiration for their episodes, serials, and campaigns. Ideas of plots, characters, locations, and other elements of a campaign can be borrowed from such sources.

The fusion of the medieval and the futuristic that is typical of planetary romance in general, and Barsoom in particular, provides the narrator with a source of inspiration *beyond* the usual pulp adventure and space opera influences — everything from the epics of Homer to the *Bhagavad Gita* becomes fair game. (Leigh Brackett famously based *The Enchantress of Venus* on *I, Claudius*.) John Carter's Earthborn might makes him a veritable Hercules among Barsoomians; his superiority in warfare is reminiscent of Alexander. Carthoris' pursuit of Thuvia echoes Tristan and Isolde. The savage gladiatorial contests of the green Martians would not be out of place in ancient Rome, while French troubadours could sing *chansons* of valiant Heliumites set to receive a massed Warhoon cavalry charge.

While Burroughs' Barsoom tales are relatively straightforward sword-and-planet stories, narrators may also gain inspiration from other notable works of planetary romance. Cosmic horror enthusiasts can turn to the works of Clark Ashton Smith, particularly the Captain Volmar and Xiccarph stories. Narrators that prefer their planetary romance to include a dash of psychological horror may find C. L. Moore's *Northwest Smith* stories (1933-1947) to their taste; *Shambleau* is a particularly excellent example. Narrators seeking a more complex hero can turn to Leigh Brackett's Eric John Stark (1949-1951) stories. Frank Herbert's *Dune* (1965), of course, is a masterwork in exploring the politics of power in a planetary romance setting. Anthropologists can turn to Ursula K. Le Guin's *The Left Hand of Darkness* and *The Dispossessed*. Finally, in terms of pure adventure, narrators could do worse than to turn to the works of Jack Vance, especially *The Dying Earth* (1950).

BURROUGHS' WORKS

The first place a narrator should look is the Barsoom series itself. Narrators are not advised to copy the style of the books, which are largely travelogues interrupted by periods of intense action. That said, the books are packed with setting details, rich, evocative descriptions, and characters both major and minor that can provide a springboard for adventure.

Example: Mark has been asked to run a pick-up episode to introduce some players to the world of Barsoom. All his players have decided to play red Martians, which allows Mark to set the introductory game in one of Barsoom's more civilized lands. After some thought, he chooses to set it in Zodanga, in the time of the Warlord. Zodanga is part of the great Empire of Helium, but is, in John Carter's own words, a "hotbed of sedition," as well as the home of the most powerful assassin's guild in all of Barsoom. Mark decides that a Zodangan plot against the Warlord of Mars and his consort will make a fine introductory episode.

MYTHS AND LEGENDS

Barsoomian heroes are larger-than-life, extraordinary people. Thus, myth and legend is a natural source of inspiration for an enterprising narrator. Quest and adventure legends especially lend themselves to such use, such as the labors of Hercules, the travels of Rustam, and the tales of Susanoo. Deities, demigods, and heroes alike make excellent archetypes for narrator characters. The ongoing conflict between Athena and Poseidon could be the inspiration for a city ruled by a wise, powerful Jeddara, surrounded by a sea of barbaric green Martians. The tales of Robin Hood suggests a campaign in which the adventurers are exiles, unjustly outlawed by a cruel jeddak, who now lurk in the forests and hills surrounding the city, preying on the jeddak's lackeys and bringing hope to the people.

Example: Jennifer is designing the outline of her upcoming campaign. For logistical reasons, the campaign must be structured in a picaresque fashion, allowing players to drop in and out. Considering various possibilities, she realizes that the Odyssey's structure meets her needs. She develops a campaign in which the adventurers have been abandoned in the lost reaches of Barsoom in the wake of a great war; tumbling from disaster to disaster, they seek their way home.

LITERATURE

Literature is a rich and varied source of ideas for an imaginative narrator. Pulp and adventure stories are obvious sources, and can be quite fruitful. Narrators who want to focus on the medieval aspects of Barsoom have a wide range of possibilities. The Arthurian cycle alone, beginning with the pseudo-historical History of the Kings of Britain, all the way through modern re-interpretations, could provide structure and material for an entire campaign: Ar Thurah is jeddak of a great Barsoomian city, and the adventurers are his loyal padwars, fighting on behalf of their prince to keep order in the empire.

From the other side of the world, the Chinese classic novels *Water Margin* and *The Romance of* the Three Kingdoms offer a multitude of ideas. *The Romance of the Three Kingdoms* describes two opposing warlords and their followers during the fall of the Han dynasty, and their efforts to replace or restore the ailing empire. *Water Margin* is the tale of a band of outlaws who, after years of fighting the Imperial Army, are granted amnesty by the emperor and organized into a military unit to battle invaders and rebels.

Example: Jack needs a villain for an upcoming adventure. He's always loved "The Three Musketeers", and takes inspiration from the fictional Cardinal Richelieu. He creates a Holy Thern patterned on the Cardinal, whose constant attempts to control a mostly-red Martian empire with a weak jeddak threaten to throw the empire into disarray, and must be countered by the adventurers.

CINEMA

Movies, too, can be a great source of inspiration. The works of Georges Méliès, especially *A Trip to the Moon* and *The Impossible Voyage* have fantastic storylines and vivid visuals that could easily be re-imagined in a Barsoomian context. *Metropolis* suggests an adventure in which a cruel jeddak uses a Hormad in female form to disrupt a popular uprising. An adventure derived from *The Seven Samurai* has a group of panthans, unaffiliated with any prince, choosing to fight for honor rather than pay to protect a poor farming village from Warhoon pillagers. *Star Wars* inspires a campaign centered around the adventures of a farm boy (who is actually the heir to a jeddak of a lost city), a smuggler with a heart of gold, and a warrior princess.

Example: Mel likes the idea of using the Hormads as villains for her upcoming adventure. Taking inspiration from Blade Runner, she decides that a small group of intelligent Hormads escaped the Helium navy's fire-bombs, and has made their way to Amhor. There, they plan to lure Ras Thavas back to Amhor so that they can take their revenge. The adventurers are dispatched to kill the remaining Hormads, but one of them might be a Hormad themselves...

PREMADE ADVENTURES AND ADVENTURE SEEDS

Modiphius also puts out premade adventures for **John Carter** and there is both a short premade adventure and a list of adventure seeds in the final chapter of this book that provide ideas for various episodes and serials. In some cases, adventures for other role-playing games can be adapted to **John Carter** with minimal trouble, though the rules and various details would need to be changed.

CHAPTER 13: BEASTS OF BARSOOM

There will be deep little ravines where moisture lingers and things grow which we can eat; but there may be green men, and there will certainly be banths and other beasts of prey. Are you afraid, Pan Dan Chee?

– John Carter, *Llana of Gathol*

Barsoom is a dying world. The creatures that survived its decline did so by being resilient and adaptable. Some, like the apt and the sith, occupy niche environments. Others, like the banth or the white ape, are found across Mars. Most are dangerous. Several are ferocious. All add color to the Red Planet.

Encountering strange and antagonistic brutes is an occupational hazard of adventuring on Barsoom. Whether the heroes are engaged in rescuing a princess, exploring forgotten ruins, or racing against time to prevent a war, they will confront hideous or malevolent creatures bent on their destruction. In most cases, such life forms are in their natural habitat, or acting as guardians or servants, or emerge as the products of bizarre experiments. With a little thought, however, the Beasts of Barsoom can be the focus of many engaging and challenging scenarios in their own right.

The following entries detail all the named Martian species. They provide a physical description, summarize the creature's behavior, explain where it is most likely to be encountered, and suggest how it might form the basis of an adventure.

Included in each entry are the statistics for a standard specimen of each beast or creature type. Also included is the menace rating of each creature if they are a monster. As discussed in *Chapter 4: Adventuring in Barsoom*, menace denotes how many afflictions a monster can take before being taken

out of a conflict. In many cases this number is a range, representing that members of this species may be more or less dangerous depending on their size, ferocity, and the needs of the narrator during an encounter. The most common menace rating for such a beast is also included in brackets.

In addition, some beasts have attacks which are Fearsome or Sharp. These effects are described in *Chapter 5: Weapons and Technology*, but they are repeated here for convenience:

FEARSOME

When an effect is rolled, the attack inflicts 1 damage to the Fear stress tracker. If a target doesn't have a Fear stress tracker it simply deals damage.

SHARP

When an effect is rolled, the attack inflicts 1 damage to the Injury stress tracker. If a target doesn't have an Injury stress tracker it simply deals damage.

USING BEASTS IN GAMES

When any of the life forms described in this chapter are employed, the emphasis should always be on thrilling, high-risk exploits requiring the players' courage, fortitude, and intelligence. They can quicken the action, provide unexpected reversals, and launch the heroes into pulse-pounding exploits.

BEASTLY MEASUREMENTS

Like other parts of this text, all measurements of size, distance, and time are given in Barsoomian terms. While these can be found elsewhere in this book, as this chapter makes frequent use of certain measurements those conversions are recreated here:

* One **haad** is 1949 feet

* One **sofad**, or 'Martian foot', is 11.694 inches

* A **zode** is 2 hours and 28 minutes

* One **padan** is the 24.5-hour Martian day

* 67 padans is a **teean**, or Martian month.

* Ten teeans make an **ord**, or Martian year.

Note that in cases where an Earth term for a unit of time such as day, month, or year is used, it refers to the Martian version of this unit.

Apt (MONSTER)

SAVAGE CARNIVORE OF THE NORTHERN POLE

Fierce, fur-bearing creatures attacked us by daylight and by dark. Never for a moment were we safe from the sudden charge of some huge demon of the north. The apt was our most consistent and dangerous foe.

– John Carter, *The Warlord of Mars*

ATTRIBUTES

DARING	CUNNING	EMPATHY
5	5	3

MIGHT	PASSION	REASON
7	4	3

STRESS	MENACE
10	2–4 (3)

TALENTS

PREDATOR
Apts deal 3 🎲 basic damage with the Fearsome quality.

RESILIENT
Apts gain a bonus d20 to avoid environmental dangers and traps.

UNIQUE EYES
Apts suffer no penalties from bright light or darkness.

PHYSICAL DESCRIPTION

The apt is a ferocious, white-furred predator standing six to eight sofads at the shoulder. Unlike many Barsoomian creatures it is quadrupedal and its four short legs carry it easily over the difficult northern terrain. From its thickset body, a long, broad neck rises to a nightmarish head. Its wide mouth contains a palisade of chisel-like incisors and canine tusks that tear flesh and shear bone. The lower jaw supports two massive down-curving horns the apt uses to gore its prey. On either side of the stout neck, its powerful arms terminate in hairless hands used for seizing prey or grappling rivals.

The apt's most distinctive feature is its enormous ovoid eyes. These cover almost half the creature's head from the top of its skull to beneath its horns. Each eye is composed of thousands of ocelli, simple single-lens structures individually lidded with a flexible membrane. The apt can open and close these membranes in any combination. In this way, it can hunt in a range of light levels and protect itself against snow-blindness.

BEHAVIOR

In contrast to most Martian species, apts kill for pleasure as well as food. Whether roaming singly or in pairs, they are always hostile and attack small groups without provocation. Hunting pairs are bolder, charging even large or well-organized forces with little regard for their own safety.

Apts eat both fresh meat and carrion. Their lairs, typically made in caves, are rank with the putrefaction of their kills. Valuable equipment is sometimes scattered amongst the carnage, though obtaining such items is a risky enterprise.

Sleeping for one padan in every teen, apts are tireless and vigilant, habitually prowling their dens in search of carrion or a mate. Rutting amongst apts is a violent business with males wrestling for fertile females. Deaths are rare, but many male apts bear the scars of severe goring on their bodies and eyes. After mating, apts lay 2–3 eggs per ord, which take four teaan to hatch. The females come into season every second ord.

SPECIES RANGE

Apts are found exclusively in Barsoom's northern polar region. The majority are wild, ranging across the snowfields and glaciers in search of prey or a mate.

During the Prince of Helium era, Salensus Oll, Jeddak of Jeddaks and Ruler of Okar, the country of the yellow Martians, reveres the apt. He trains the creatures to guard the Carrion Caves, the only route into Okar, and to devour those Barsoomians whose airships are destroyed by the huge magnetic needle outside the Okars' capital city, Kadabra.

Following Salensus Oll's death, Talu, the new Jeddak of Jeddaks of the North, clears the Carrion Caves of apts and begins to cull the creatures. Apts are therefore increasingly rare in the Jeddak of Jeddaks era, though they remain a danger to unwary travelers exploring Barsoom's icy northern wastes.

PLOT SEED

Kan Tor, a Martian official transporting an item of incalculable importance, disappears in Okar's frozen wilderness. Rumors suggest apts attacked his caravan and bore the dead away to who knows where. The adventurers must seek out and recover the item, which may be lying somewhere in the creatures' horrid and lightless caverns.

ARBOK (MONSTER)

DEADLY ARBOREAL REPTILE OF BARSOOM'S FORESTS

The earthman's first thrust sliced harmlessly through the beast's outer skin. A huge claw knocked him off balance, and he found himself lying on the ground with the great fangs at his throat.

– Narrator, *John Carter of Mars*

ATTRIBUTES

DARING	CUNNING	EMPATHY
5	4	3

MIGHT	PASSION	REASON
6	3	3

STRESS	MENACE
9	2–4 (3)

TALENTS

ARBOREAL

May move through trees as if they are on the ground. Any difficulties for climbing based actions are reduced by 2.

AMBUSH PREDATOR

Gains a 2d20 bonus on its first attack.

DOUBLE SKIN

Reduces all damage taken by 1.

HALLUCINOGENIC BLOOD

When an arbok is injured for the first time, its subdermal fluid is often sprayed onto the skin of its attacker. Any character Near to the arbok suffers 4 🎲 Confusion damage. A Simple (D0) **Might + Reason** test can be made to avoid some of this damage. Every point of Momentum spent will reduce this damage by 1 🎲.

PHYSICAL DESCRIPTION

Reaching lengths of six to eight sofads, arboks are aggressive arboreal reptiles. They are unique amongst Barsoom's indigenous species for having a double skin. The scaled outer membrane, which is regularly sloughed, is patterned to mimic the patterns of light and shade found in their forest habitats. Some red Martian lumber cutters hunt the arbok for its hide, which, when tanned, makes durable harnesses and footwear. The arbok's inner skin is tough and leathery. Smooth, bony plates along flanks and belly protect its vital organs. Between the skins is a fluid-filled space thought to help the arbok regulate its temperature, enabling it to remain active in the chill Barsoomian night.

With its six limbs bearing short, sickle-shaped claws, the arbok is a natural climber. It is able to scale trunks and move through the tree canopy at startling speed. Its forefeet are armed with two scythe-like talons it uses to snag branches or rake open prey. These hooks are no less deadly than the creature's heavy jaws with their array of serrated fangs.

BEHAVIOR

Arboks are exceptionally dangerous. With an instinctive hatred of all humanoids, they attack on sight. They seldom withdraw from combat unless they are protecting the shallow scrape where they lay their eggs. By nature, they are excellent trackers, pursuing their ground-dwelling prey by sight from the forest canopy. They usually attack by dropping on their victims from above.

SPECIES RANGE

Arboks are found only in forests. They are most common in the Helium Forest where they represent a recurrent threat to Martian foresters and loggers. Smaller populations are found in other areas across Barsoom, though their precise numbers are unknown.

PLOT SEED

When a group of foresters report seeing visions of Martian sailing ships plying restless oceans, the player characters are sent to investigate. Are the men mad, possessed, or the victims of some elaborate plot? Latan Quey, the scientist accompanying the adventurers, forms another theory: the foresters have discovered the hallucinogenic effects of the arbok's subdermal fluid. Quey sees an opportunity to make a fortune — until the foresters succumb to murderous psychosis.

BANTH (MONSTER OR MINION)

PITILESS STALKER OF BARSOOM'S DEAD SEA BOTTOMS

And so it launched its great bulk toward me, but its mighty voice had held no paralyzing terrors
for me, and it met cold steel instead of the tender flesh its cruel jaws gaped so widely to engulf.

—John Carter, *The Gods of Mars*

ATTRIBUTES

DARING **7**	CUNNING **7**	EMPATHY **4**
MIGHT **8**	PASSION **4**	REASON **4**
STRESS **12**	MENACE **1–4 (3)**	

TALENTS

APEX PREDATOR

The banth can use its **Cunning + Might** for any attack or defense. If successful on an attack, it deals 3 ☗ basic damage with the Sharp quality.

FLURRY OF CLAWS

If successful on a defense, the banth automatically Counterstrikes (no skill test is required) and deals 2 ☗ damage.

TERRIFYING ROAR

The banth precedes combat with an ungodly roar. The banth makes a **Cunning + Daring test** inflicting 3 ☗ Fear damage on any target who can hear it and fails to defend. **Cunning + Reason** is a common test used to defend against this roar.

PHYSICAL DESCRIPTION

The banth is a savage beast of prey feared by all Barsoomians. Sinuous and sleek, its long, tawny body is hairless except for a coarse, thick mane that covers its mighty neck. The presence of this mane has led Jasoomians on Barsoom to nickname it 'the Martian lion', but the creature shares little else with the African carnivore. Its ten powerful legs make it much swifter. Over short distances, it can propel itself across the Martian hinterlands at speeds in excess of 110–130 haads per zode. Its flexible spine, long, supple tail, and broad, clawed feet make it a highly maneuverable, sure-footed opponent. Although its talons are terrible, it is the banth's colossal jaws that pose the foremost danger. Its mouth, which divides its

head almost in half, is lined with rows of sharp, narrow fangs capable of mortally wounding anything smaller than a zitidar.

Of all Barsoom's predators, the banth has the most highly developed binocular vision. Cold and cruel, its radiant green eyes not only strike terror into the hearts of its prey but also enable it to see clearly for two to three haads.

Banths are outstanding trackers and can follow a two-day old spoor with ease. Despite their small ears, they also have acute hearing making them difficult animals to surprise.

Most adult banths grow six to eight sofads in length and four sofads high, though observers have reported larger specimens. They are oviparous, like most Barsoomian vertebrates, laying two to three eggs every other ord. These incubate in caves or deserted ruins located at the center of a breeding pair's territory. Once the young hatch, they spend their first three teeans learning to hunt with either parent. Banths usually make their lairs in caverns or amongst the suburban ruins of Barsoom's ancient cities.

BEHAVIOR

Banths roam singly, in pairs, and sometimes in packs. They are both hunter and scavenger, subsisting on either fresh kills or carrion, though they prefer the flesh of red Martians above all else. Banths are drawn to any accumulation of corpses — the site of a battle or a downed airship, for example — where they pose a considerable threat to survivors.

The banth is the canniest of hunters. It does not risk attacking large groups unless they are weakened by injury or fatigue, and banths have been known to pursue well-armed groups for many days until hunger, thirst, and exhaustion take their toll on potential prey. When a banth commits to an attack, it charges headlong, issuing a terrifying roar that paralyses its target temporarily. In that moment, the banth leaps upon its victim, usually with fatal consequences.

About one in ten thousand red Martians has a natural affinity with banths, though this rapport is not apparent until he or she encounters the creature for the first time. The precise explanation for such kinship is unknown, but, in Helium, Ras Thavas maintains it is the product of an exceptional combination of pheromones associated with dominance. Whatever the reason, these fortunate individuals are always safe from banth attack and can control up to six of the creatures at any time. Controlled banths respond to simple verbal and telepathic instructions without concern for their own safety. They will not harass any adventurers accompanying such gifted individuals unless instructed to do so.

If banths are captured when young, it is possible to train them as guardians. During the Dotar Sojat era, the Therns of the Valley Dor employ banths to patrol the tunnels honeycombing the Golden Cliffs. The beasts dispense with intruders and any dead slaves.

Banths are also used in war by the Lotharians who, until the end of the Prince of Helium era, revered Komal, an unusually large specimen, as their god.

SPECIES RANGE

The banth's natural habitat is the low arid hills surrounding the dead sea bottoms. They also hunt white apes in the ancient cities beside Barsoom's vanished oceans.

Across Mars, Banths are used as beasts of war, to draw ceremonial and war-chariots, and for guarding subterranean complexes, including the pits lying below many Martian cities. Most of these banths have either been stolen as eggs or captured young and raised in captivity.

BANTH COMPANIONS

Being able to have banths as pets or companions requires at least a grade 2 talent relating to taming banths, animal empathy, or a special rapport with wildlife. A pet banth costs 15xp for a banth considered a minion, or 30xp for one considered a monster. Characters who satisfy the talent prerequisite for having a banth companion may take a banth minion instead of their starting piece of core equipment.

In addition to its formidable combat and tracking skills, the banth's fearsome presence gives its master an extra d20 to roll when attempting to frighten or intimidate someone so long as the banth is active. Characters can upgrade a minion banth to monster status by spending an additional 15xp.

Banth minions have 1 less Cunning and Daring than normal. Banths and other animal companions are considered core equipment for purposes of replacing them or in instances where a narrator removes them from a scene.

PLOT SEED

While crossing one of the agricultural strips that border Barsoom's canals, the heroes are waylaid by Devan Pel, a red Martian farmer whose livestock is being preyed on by an abnormally large banth. Devan Pel is not a rich man, but he promises eternal gratitude to anyone who slays the beast and explains why it only attacks thoats, leaving the herdsmen unharmed. Could someone be controlling the banth for some unknown purpose? And why did his beautiful daughter reject the gallant Zodangan Teedwar, Lon Saran?

CALOT (MONSTER OR MINION)
FEARLESS AND LOYAL MARTIAN WATCH-DOG

He wheeled instantly and charged me with the most appalling speed I had ever beheld. I had thought his short legs a bar to swiftness, but had he been coursing with greyhounds the latter would have appeared as though asleep on a door mat.

– John Carter, *A Princess of Mars*

ATTRIBUTES

DARING	**CUNNING**	**EMPATHY**
4	7	5
MIGHT	**PASSION**	**REASON**
6	4	4
STRESS	**MENACE**	
11	1–3 (2)	

TALENTS

UNBEATEN SPEED
The calot can move faster than any other Martian beast. If in a direct race with another animal, it will win that race unless tricked in some fashion.

TRACKER
Reduce difficulties of all tests to follow and detect prey by 1. All such tests also receive a bonus d20.

VICIOUS BITE
Calots deal 2 🎲 basic damage when they bite.

SHAKE IT OFF
If a calot is dispatched it can roll 1 🎲, on an effect it isn't harmed and spends a Conflict action shaking off the damage.

PHYSICAL DESCRIPTION

Three to four sofads in height, the wild calot is an ugly, lumpish thing. With a waddling gait, bristle mane, ten short legs, and large batrachian head, it has a mismatched, hybrid look. A wide mouth with three ranks of razor-sharp tusks further exaggerates its ill-favored appearance. Narrow, yellow eyes make the creature seem permanently suspicious and few civilized Martians can hold its stare for long.

Despite its ungainly body, the calot is the fastest animal on Barsoom. It can run at 170–200 haads per zode for a thousand haads or more. A highly efficient metabolism gives the calot unparalleled stamina and most mature specimens can sustain a speed of 130–150 haads per zode for an entire padan without rest. The animal's piston-like legs and short, robust claws make it remarkably agile on both rock and the soft silt of the dead sea bottoms.

BEHAVIOR

Calots are courageous beasts. Being highly intelligent, with keen instincts and good memories, they are easily trained. Within a short time, they can follow complex verbal and telepathic commands. They respond well both to the cruel instruction of the green Martians and to the kindlier techniques introduced by John Carter during his advent on Mars. However, those calots raised empathetically show greater loyalty than those subjected to the green Martians' regime. They protect their masters and mistresses steadfastly, often traveling vast distances in their service.

The omnivorous calot is extremely vocal. Warnings are given through guttural growls or snarls; understanding is voiced in rumbling purrs; and attention is sought through a coughing bark. Any intention to attack is announced with a protracted howl and a stiffening of their bristly mane.

SPECIES RANGE

Wild calots are found in packs in most Barsoomian hinterlands. They are dangerous if threatened or hungry, but avoid well-armed parties or trade caravans unless antagonized. In combat, they are formidable opponents, seizing foes in their broad mouths and shaking the unfortunate victim to death. They have no fear of the banth or the white ape.

The green Martians have domesticated calots for use as war hounds, to guard their prisoners and caravans, and for gladiatorial combat against other animals, captives, or slaves in the arenas of Mars' dead cities. Historically, other Martian races have shunned the creature, considering it a primitive brute, and used 'calot' as a term of abuse. However, in the Jeddak of Jeddaks era, several red Martian families follow John Carter's example and employ tamed calots as guardians. Carter's own calot, Woola, is a near constant companion of the Warlord and is of invaluable service to him on several of his wild escapades. Although originally employed by the Tharks to guard Carter during his imprisonment, Woola is won over to the Earthman's cause by kindness and affection and accompanies him during his escape with Dejah Thoris.

The beast's devotion to its master and a strong desire amongst red Martian nobles to emulate the Warlord means that calot ownership has become fashionable in several cities, including Helium, Ptarth, and Dusar. Consequently, a small trade in calot eggs has grown up across Barsoom. Experienced green Martian wranglers are sometimes employed to train the hatchlings after their eight teean incubation period.

CALOT LOYALTY

A pet calot costs 15xp for a calot considered a minion, or 30xp for one considered a monster. If desired, starting characters can take a calot companion instead of a piece of core equipment. The calot will support its master in combat granting 1 bonus Momentum to attack rolls so long as the calot stands. Characters can upgrade a minion calot to monster status by spending an additional 15xp.

Calots and other animal companions are considered core equipment for purposes of replacing them or in instances where a narrator removes them from a scene.

PLOT SEED

When Teedwar Oma Lor's faithful calot, Morda, returns to Helium without his master, an expedition is mounted to discover what happened to Lor's diplomatic mission to Kobol. The adventurers find themselves following the animal into some of Barsoom's most inhospitable terrain where they uncover a plot to drive Helium towards civil war.

DARSEEN (MINION)

MISCHIEVOUS AND OPPORTUNISTIC THIEF

On Barsoom there is a little reptile called a darseen which changes its colors to harmonize with its background, just as do our earthly chameleons

– John Carter, *Swords of Mars*

ATTRIBUTES

DARING	CUNNING	EMPATHY
3	7	5

MIGHT	PASSION	REASON
1	2	3

TALENTS

LIGHTNING QUICK CHAMELEON

A darseen is practically invisible most of the time. Any attack against it is at a +3 difficulty.

PHYSICAL DESCRIPTION

The diminutive darseen is one of the smallest and least threatening of Barsoom's many vertebrates. Feeding exclusively on vegetation, including Mars' ochre moss and red sward, these little lizards measure less than two sofads from the tip of their pointed snouts to the end of their whip-like tails. Many metropolitan authorities view them as pests, but their chameleonic skin and remarkable speed make these ten-legged opportunists hard to catch.

BEHAVIOR

Inquisitive and acquisitive, darseen are drawn to most shiny objects and often steal trinkets, pieces of harness, jewelry, and even small bottles. It is not uncommon to see such items suddenly begin moving, apparently unaided, across floors, up walls, and over ceilings, borne away by near-invisible thieves. The darseen's remarkable ability to climb depends on innumerable tiny hooks formed from the curved tips of the skin cells on its feet. Its forelegs lack such cells and have evolved into supple 'hands', which the darseen uses for carrying away fruit and pilfered items. Adventurers and urban workers sometimes discover 'darseen hoards', caches of stolen articles tucked away in obscure places.

SPECIES RANGE

With the exception of the poles, darseen are found in most areas of Barsoom. All Martian cities have thriving populations that feed on palace lawns, in public gardens, and on refuse. Efforts to limit darseen numbers have proved unsuccessful, though the presence of a sorak in the household tends to prevent intrusions by the bold little lizards.

PLOT SEED

Ven Forna, statesman, diplomat, and decorated Heliumite naval officer, is dead, killed in front of his family by an invisible assassin. The only clue to the nature of his killer is a faintly iridescent scrap of lizard skin. With the official investigation stalled, the grieving family employs the adventurers to solve a mystery that leads them from the ransacked apartments of a murdered scientist, through the abandoned studio of an acclaimed taxidermist, to the heart of the assassin's guild and a conspiracy to overthrow the Jeddak of Jeddaks. Has someone really discovered the means to tan darseen hide without it losing its chameleonic property?

MALAGOR (MINION)

PRIMEVAL GIANTS OF THE AIR RESTORED BY OTHERWORLDLY SCIENCE

About twenty birds were winging toward us. That in itself was sufficiently astonishing, since they were easily identifiable as malagors, a species long presumed to be extinct; but to add to the incredibility of the sight that met our eyes, a warrior bestrode each of the giant birds.

– Vor Daj, *Synthetic Men of Mars*

ATTRIBUTES

DARING	CUNNING	EMPATHY
3	4	4

MIGHT	PASSION	REASON
7	2	2

TALENTS

MOUNT

Malagors can carry a character with no increase in difficulty to any action.

PROTECT THE NEST

Becomes a monster with 9 stress and menace 2 when protecting a nest.

FLY

Malagors are immune to falling and can fly.

ARMORED BEAST

Attacks with ranged weapons are at +3 difficulty outside Near range.

PHYSICAL DESCRIPTION

Once extinct on Barsoom, the mighty malagor is recreated by Ras Thavas, the Mastermind of Mars, during the Jeddak of Jeddaks era. The restored malagors are striking creatures with a wingspan of almost twenty-five sofads. Their elongate, crested heads rise on long, supple necks to an imposing fifteen sofads, and most measure eight to ten sofads high at the base of the wing. Although the malagor's wings and body are feathered, its legs, neck, head, and tail are covered in large, flat scales thick enough to deflect any missiles not fired from close range. Nevertheless, they are vulnerable to gunfire from the ground or the decks of airships.

BEHAVIOR

Malagors reared in captivity, or bred for transport, are rather stupid and easily controlled through simple telepathic commands. When directed telepathically, they are swift aerial steeds capable of covering four hundred haads per zode. A well-fed adult can carry a single rider for twelve hundred haads without pause. Birds loaded with heavier burdens — two persons or cargo — must rest more frequently.

The wild malagors reaching maturity in several new colonies across Barsoom are not easily subdued. Most are antagonistic, particularly if they are protecting nesting grounds or young, and attack any who approach. In flight, they attack with a serrated beak and taloned feet, snapping and slashing at their targets. On the ground, the malagor uses its thick, supple tail to strike down enemies before tearing at them with claws and beak.

In recent times, malagors are reported harrying airships and seizing crewmembers, perhaps in response to growing numbers and shortages of food. Malagors are not strict carnivores but favor flesh over vegetation for its higher energy value.

SPECIES RANGE

Originally bred in the dead Toonolian city of Morbus in the Jeddak of Jeddaks era, the malagor has since spread to many areas of Barsoom. Greater numbers are still found in the Toonolian marshes, but small colonies have been reported in the salt marshes around Gathol, on the hills around Dusar, and as far south as Ghasta. It is certain their numbers are increasing. Airships now log any encounters with malagors since they can pose a hazard to vessels and crews should they chose to attack. Any use of malagors as steeds is always investigated.

PLOT SEED

The abandoned hulk of the great Heliumite airship Vildenrar is found drifting over the hinterlands east of Zodanga, its buoyancy tanks damaged, its log missing, and its guns removed. The only clues to its fate are the claw marks scarring its deck. The adventurers are among the first to discover the ship and attempt to solve the riddle. What attacked the Vildenrar, and what is more valuable than the airship itself?

ORLUK (MONSTER)

FLEET-FOOTED KILLER OF THE NORTHERN WASTES

All were clothed in magnificent furs — the six in the black and yellow striped hide of the orluk, while he who approached alone was resplendent in the pure white skin of an apt.

– John Carter, *The Warlord of Mars*

ATTRIBUTES

DARING	CUNNING	EMPATHY
5	5	2

MIGHT	PASSION	REASON
6	3	2

STRESS	MENACE
8	1–2 (1)

TALENTS

ICE WALKER

Orluk's move on ice and snow as if it were normal terrain. They reduce the difficulty of navigating or avoiding any snow or ice based dangers by 1.

BONY PROTUBERANCES

The Orluk attacks with a basic damage of 2 ⬡.

PHYSICAL DESCRIPTION

The orluk is a heavily built carnivore that grows fifteen to eighteen sofads high. Like many Barsoomian animals, it is a hexapod. Its six long legs spread the creature's weight across a wide area, allowing it to cross weak ice with little risk. Its long neck is covered in armored plates that rise to form a low ridge along its spine. This ridge runs to the tip of a thick tail tufted with a riot of yellow hair. The tail is used in combat and for balance when the beast negotiates treacherous or uncertain ground.

Orluks are hideous brutes. Their heads are adorned with large bony protuberances on the cranium, cheeks, muzzle, and jaws. These are covered in dark skin that is often torn during mating contests or combat. As a result, orluks frequently appear battered and scarred. Even their gaping jaws, lined with a double row of pyramidal teeth, sometimes display canines split or broken from hunting and competition for mates.

For all its repulsiveness, the orluk's most striking feature is the splendid and highly prized yellow and black striped fur that covers its legs and flanks.

BEHAVIOR

Orluks hunt in small packs, often feeding on the apt. The contests between these two predators are fearsome exchanges of raw violence that occasionally result in the deaths of both hunter and hunted. Orluks attack by circling their targets, running swiftly in decreasing rings until they can strike inward, seizing a victim in their mighty jaws and dragging it away from its companions. This strategy leads some Martian scientists to conjecture that the orluks' vibrant coloration may be a means of confusing their prey as they surround it.

SPECIES RANGE

Orluks are found only in Barsoom's northern polar region where the yellow Martians of Okar hunt them for their fur. The Okarians use the luxurious pelts to make cold weather clothing and for export, since Orluk hide is valued across Barsoom as an indicator of status on formal, military, and ceremonial attire.

PLOT SEED

The Okarians manage the population of orluks carefully to maintain their lucrative fur supplies. It is source of great concern to the jeddak, therefore, when Okarian air patrols report seeing large numbers of the creature dead and skinned in the icefields. Fearing a greedy Okarian faction within his own government, the jeddak asks the players to investigate. Is this a simple case of poaching, or is a wider agenda being served?

PLANT MAN (MONSTER OR MINION)

BARSOOM'S FRIGHTFUL CYCLOPEAN HORROR

The plant man charged to within a dozen feet of the party and then, with a bound, rose as though to pass directly above their heads. His powerful tail was raised high to one side, and as he passed close above them he brought it down in one terrific sweep that crushed a green warrior's skull as though it had been an eggshell.

– John Carter, *The Gods of Mars*

ATTRIBUTES

DARING	CUNNING	EMPATHY
5	6	2

MIGHT	PASSION	REASON
6	4	2

STRESS	MENACE
8	1–3 (2)

TALENTS

LEAPING

A plant man can leap from one range to the next closest, avoiding any obstacles and difficulty increases that do not wholly stop their movement. They may do this for free as part of an attack or other action.

TAIL WHIP

Tail whips deal 2 🎲 basic damage to characters and 4 🎲 basic damage to inanimate objects.

PHYSICAL DESCRIPTION

The plant men of Barsoom are perhaps the most peculiar-looking creatures found anywhere on the planet. Blue-skinned, hairless and bipedal, they have long, flexible tails growing from a round root to a thin blade-like tip. They use these tails for balance and in combat. Their torsos and legs are human-like though massively enlarged. They stand ten to twelve sofads high on wide, flat feet two to three sofads long. By contrast, their seemingly boneless, prehensile arms are abnormally small and terminate in short-fingered, taloned hands. At the center of each palm is a lipless mouth rimmed with many small, pointed teeth.

Plant men have a single white eye protruding from a ring of pallid skin at the center of their faces. The iris and pupil are undistinguished, making the creature appear blind. Below the eye, the nose is a raw round hole, wet and ragged. The chin, which lacks a mouth, curves smoothly into the neck. Much of the head is covered by a welter of black, snake-like hairs slightly shorter than a sofad, which wriggle and writhe about the face like a mass of ropey worms. These strange growths are actually the plant man's ears which, when stimulated, rise on the head and move independently to locate the origin of any particular sound.

BEHAVIOR

The plant men's behavior is as unusual as their appearance. They feed either by using their clawed hands to suck blood from fallen victims or to crop Barsoom's red sward. The mouths in the creature's palms consume the blood and vegetation before it is swallowed along the arms. These mouths are also the source of the plant men's purring speech.

Plant men live in large herds and reproduce asexually. Tubers form in the creature's armpits, swelling quickly to become miniatures of the adult. These replicas are rooted to the parent by stems attached to the top of their heads. As the young plant men reach maturity, the stem withers and the offspring detach, becoming independent entities.

When the plant men are not grazing they move in huge bounds, covering twenty to thirty sofads with each leap. In this way, they approach their enemies at great speed, vaulting over their foeman's heads and striking down with their mighty tails. Few can withstand a blow from a plant man's tail, which has the power to break necks and shatter skulls. Since a plant man's brain is scarcely larger than a fingertip, it has no sense of self-preservation. It fights without fear and, as such, it is remorseless in combat. Plant men are far from invulnerable, though, and bleed a syrupy green sap when wounded.

Both the Therns and the First Born domesticated the plant men and trained them to respond to certain sound stimuli. Precisely how they achieved this is not known and after the destruction of the religion of Issus it is possible that the secret has been lost forever.

SPECIES RANGE

During the Dotar Sojat era, the plant men are found only in the Valley Dor. Here they prey on those Martians who have taken the long pilgrimage down the River Iss to what they believe is the afterlife. For reasons not understood entirely, the plant men coexist harmoniously with a large population of white apes.

PLOT SEED

A trading caravan travelling the long and dangerous route from Kobol to Gathol is attacked and plundered. The sole surviving merchant returns to Kobol fatally wounded. Dying on his silks and furs, he tells an improbable story of wild blue creatures bounding over the wagons and cracking skulls. He insists that his assailants were guided by a strange howling cry. Before the risks any further caravans, he asks for volunteers to investigate the truth of the dead man's claims. He refuses to jeopardize Kobol's small army or navy, which is only now being rebuilt after Helium sacked the city. He fears that Kobol may be besieged once more and its tentative recovery collapse. If the adventurers oblige, they will earn the gratitude of an ambitious and honorable jed.

SILIAN (MINION)

RELENTLESS PREDATOR OF LOST AND LIGHTLESS SEAS

[T]he slimy and fearsome silian whose wriggling thousands seethe the silent sea beneath the hurtling moons…"

– John Carter, *The Gods of Mars*

ATTRIBUTES

DARING	CUNNING	EMPATHY
4	4	3

MIGHT	PASSION	REASON
3	3	2

TALENTS

MASSIVE BITE
The silian's base damage in physical conflicts is 2 💀.

SLIPPERY
Gains a bonus d20 to defend against melee attacks.

POWERFUL SENSES
Gain a bonus d20 to detect prey in the water

PHYSICAL DESCRIPTION

Limbless and thick as a red Martian warrior's thigh, the silian is a sinuous aquatic reptile that grows to lengths of between six and ten sofads. They have a long, narrow body and a mouth lined with strong, glass-like teeth. The silian's ability to disarticulate its jaws allows it to seize and swallow prey much larger than its tapered, streamlined head would first suggest. Cartilaginous plates, much desired as trophies by the First Born, protect the eyes and upper jaw.

Silians secrete a thick slime from glands beneath their scales. This slime helps streamline the silian as it powers through the water and makes them difficult to wrestle in unarmed combat. Silian slime, like its blood, is toxic.

BEHAVIOR

Silians are bloodthirsty predators with sensitive sensory pits just above their eyes. These pits can detect prey moving in the water up to a hundred ads away. As a result, any creature entering silian-infested water will be attacked. Silians hunt singly and in shoals, driving through the water with powerful strokes of their long tails. They feed by darting at their prey, snapping pieces from it, and withdrawing for another strike. When the target is sufficiently weakened, the silian bites off and swallows the head or limbs of its victim.

SPECIES RANGE

Silians are most widespread in the Omean Sea and the Sea of Korus. Smaller populations are known in the River Iss and some red Martian canals.

PLOT SEED

During a barge journey along one of Barsoom's canals, a shoal of silians leap from the water to beset the adventurers. The creatures' uncharacteristic behavior is partly explained by the peculiar devices bonded to each silian's sensory pit, but these devices pose a wider mystery. Who is controlling the silians — and why?

SITH (MONSTER)

VENOMOUS FLYING KILLER OF KAOL'S FORESTS

Even my powerful and ferocious Woola was as helpless as a kitten before that frightful thing. But to flee were useless, even had it ever been to my liking to turn my back upon danger, so I stood my ground, Woola snarling at my side, my only hope to die as I had always lived — fighting.

— John Carter, *The Warlord of Mars*

ATTRIBUTES

DARING	CUNNING	EMPATHY
6	6	3

MIGHT	PASSION	REASON
5	4	2

STRESS	MENACE
8	1–3 (2)

TALENTS

FLY

Creature is immune to falling and can fly.

TAIL STING.

Tail sting deal 4 🎲 basic damage to characters and the target must make an immediate **Might + Reason** (D3) test or suffer an immediate Injury impairment.

HORRIFIC BUZZING

In the first round of combat the sith gets a Free action to make an **Empathy + Passion** conflict test against all opponents close enough to hear their buzzing (usually Near range or better). This attack inflicts 3 🎲 Fear damage.

PHYSICAL DESCRIPTION

Siths are monstrous flying insects eight to ten sofads long whose armored bodies are great darts of chitin and cartilage. They ride the air lightning-fast on four thickly veined membranous wings that hum to a rising shriek when they attack.

The sith is a doubly dangerous foe. At its head, fearsome mandibles wait to crush the armor and bones of any hapless warrior daunted by its bewildering speed. At the tip of its segmented tail, a poisoned sting the length of a short sword is set to spear any incautious opponent with lethal accuracy. The beast's massive, multifaceted eyes give the sith all round vision, making it impossible to outflank. Its only blind spot lies directly behind the wicked tail, a position few would chose for themselves. Along its armored thorax, each of its six jointed legs is strong enough to fell an adult Martian. The legs terminate in hook-like structures which the sith uses to carry off its prey.

BEHAVIOR

Hostile, vicious, and tenacious, siths attack without mercy, biting and stinging their opponents to death. Occasionally, they bear Martians aloft, taking them to some remote spot before killing them and filling the corpses with eggs. These eggs hatch in less than a teean, emerging as thick, white larvae that consume the putrefying flesh. The larvae pupate slowly before hatching and it takes a full ord for the juveniles to reach maturity.

SPECIES RANGE

Siths are found only in the forest of Kaol where red Martian warriors armed with long sith spears have hunted them almost to extinction. The spears are tipped with the siths' own venom, harvested from the two large poison sacs located in the abdomen. An adult sith can yield two gallons of venom, unless the sacs are depleted from stinging. It is certain that the siths would have been exterminated if their venom was not a secret ingredient in several lucrative commercial products exported from Kaol across Barsoom.

PLOT SEED

Jonan Lath is one of Kaol's celebrated perfumers. Red Martian women from Helium to Gathol wear his scents and their effects on red Martian men are legendary. Few realize that the key ingredient is sith venom. In the last ord, Lath grew tired of financing costly hunting expeditions and decided to raise a colony of sith secretly in Kaol's pits. His stouthearted agents gathered a quantity of larvae but, when fed on thoat meat, they sickened and died. It was then Lath realized what was necessary. After obtaining more larvae, he drugged, kidnapped, and murdered a succession of slaves. Few nobles bothered with the fate of their missing servants until one compassionate prince enlisted the adventurers' aid. Now the heroes find themselves in a race against time to solve the mystery and prevent a herd of deadly sith escaping into the city.

SORAK (MINION)

SOFT-SKINNED COMPANION TO MARTIAN MAIDS

'Calot!' he hissed. 'Ever did I think you carried the heart of a sorak in your putrid breast.'

– Thurid, *The Gods of Mars*

ATTRIBUTES

DARING	CUNNING	EMPATHY
3	3	7

MIGHT	PASSION	REASON
2	2	2

TALENTS

THERAPEUTIC

Spending any lengthy amount of time with a sorak can restore Fear or Confusion afflictions. No test is needed for this so long as the character is able to relax. The sorak can remove 1 of each type of affliction.

DARSEEN HUNTER

The sorak is not affected by the darseen's Lightning Quick talent.

COWARDLY

The sorak instinctively flees from any combat with larger creatures, gaining a bonus d20 on any test to run away from a fight.

PHYSICAL DESCRIPTION

The six-legged sorak is a domestic animal often kept as a pet by unmarried or widowed red Martian women. They are also popular with children and families. Rarely growing larger than a sofad from nose to tail, most soraks are pale-colored or lightly patterned. Stroking the silky skin of a sorak calms the nerves, creating a deep sense of emotional wellbeing. The creatures can be temperamental, though, and often scratch over-affectionate owners with their retractable needle-like claws.

BEHAVIOR

Soraks are notoriously lazy, cowardly, and distrustful of strangers. They only rise from their habitual torpor when they sense the presence of a darseen. Any sorak scenting one of the chameleonic lizards stiffens, rouses itself, and begins a meticulous search of its territory. The sorak's brilliant, faceted eyes — usually yellow, amethyst, or emerald in color — are acute, and few darseen escape the creatures' little fangs.

SPECIES RANGE

Soraks are found in most Martian cities, though they are favored in the red Martian nations' metropolises and farmsteads. They are rare in Barsoom's northern and southern climes as they have an intense dislike of the cold. Few green Martians tolerate them.

PLOT SEED

Marah Tesh, the stern, plain-speaking widow of one of Hastor's most decorated teedwars, adores her soraks. Her palace is filled with the indolent little creatures. She indulges them endlessly with tidbits from her own plate and sips from her glass. When seven of them die immediately after being fed from her dinner table, Marah Tesh is both aggrieved and frightened. Someone is clearly trying to poison her. Can the adventurers unravel the mystery of the attempted assassination and discover who might wish Marah Tesh dead before another attempt is made?

SPIDER, MARTIAN (MINION)

SHRIEKING INSECTS OF THE VALLEY HOHR

It opened its hideous mouth and emitted a terrific scream so out of proportion to its size and to the nature of such insects with which I was familiar that it had a most appalling effect on my nerves.

– Tan Hadron, *A Fighting Man of Mars*

ATTRIBUTES

DARING	CUNNING	EMPATHY
5	6	3

MIGHT	PASSION	REASON
4	3	3

TALENTS

WEB WALKER
In any location where as spider has slung its webs, reduce any difficulty for movement the creature makes by 2.

SCREAMING DEATH
Spiders gain Fearsome and Sharp and attack with 3 🎲 damage whether screaming or biting.

IMMOBILE
If for any reason the spider's webs are destroyed, the spider cannot attack or move and must spend every available action reconstructing a rudimentary web. The web is rebuilt by spending Momentum and is complete once 30 Momentum is spent over the course of several Simple (D0) tests.

PHYSICAL DESCRIPTION

Bloated and black, the venomous Martian spider is an entirely arboreal twelve-legged horror. Since their legs grow upward from their backs, they find terrestrial movement impossible. They travel instead through the shrouds of their gossamer webs by clinging to the main strands. In this way, they hunt for prey trapped in the sticky threads. Moving with surprising speed, they often mass around their larger victims, delivering countless bites with their shockingly large mouths and needle fangs.

BEHAVIOR

Martian spiders are bold and aggressive. They often attack in packs, attracting other spiders to prey with deafening, high-pitched screams. Although they breed prodigiously, young spiders are a staple part of the adults' diet and only the most agile survive to maturity.

SPECIES RANGE

Martian spiders are found only in the Valley Hohr on the outskirts of the cursed city of Ghasta where their webs festoon the trees and bushes for many haads.

PLOT SEED

When Tan Hadron of Hastor and Nur An escaped Ghron, the insane and oppressive Jed of Ghasta in the Jeddak of Jeddaks era, they vowed one day to return and liberate the city. Their plans are now underway, but they need a group of resolute adventurers to infiltrate the city and gather intelligence on the disposition of Ghron's forces. Unfortunately, the only way into the city is through the Valley Hohr.

SYNTHETIC MEN / HORMADS (MONSTERS)

UNNATURAL, VAT-GROWN FIENDS

I tell you, it was a gruesome sight. The thing kept on fighting, and its head lay on the ground screaming and cursing. John Carter had to disarm it, and then it lunged forward and struck him with the weight of its headless torso just below the knees, throwing him off balance.'

– Vor Daj, *Synthetic Men of Mars*

ATTRIBUTES

DARING	CUNNING	EMPATHY
5	4	3

MIGHT	PASSION	REASON
6	3	3

STRESS	MENACE
9	1–3 (2)

TALENTS

DISTURBING MUTATIONS
Hormads gain the Fearsome quality on all attacks.

FEARLESS ABOMINATIONS
Hormads are immune to any damage dealt by Fear based attacks. This also means they take no additional Fear damage from Fearsome weapons.

RESISTANT BEYOND BELIEF
Hormads can, when they suffer an affliction, roll a single combat die. If the result is an effect the affliction is ignored.

PHYSICAL DESCRIPTION

The Synthetic Men, or Hormads, are artificial creatures first produced in the Jeddak of Jeddaks era by Ras Thavas, the Mastermind of Mars, in the dead city of Morbus in the Toonolian Marshes. When Ras Thavas loses control of his experiment to a group of intelligent, ambitious Hormads, he is forced to produce millions of the creatures for an attempted conquest of Barsoom. John Carter subsequently destroys the Hormad threat and Morbus itself with Helium's enormous navy.

Hormads are misshapen things grown in vats from tissue cultures. They lack the symmetry of natural creatures. Their bodies are agglomerations of misplaced features, disproportionate limbs, and twisted torsos. Eyes and ears might be too small, or too large; noses could be elongate proboscises or snub buttons; a mouth might be a raw slash or a puckered ring of teeth. None will be in its proper place. A forehead might smile, eyes blink from a chin or cheek, ears hang down from an outsized, lumpish jaw. Their mismatched legs give them a rolling gait, and their arms can reach to the ground or be withered at the shoulder. All have at least one good, weapon-bearing arm, however, and each makes a formidable foe.

BEHAVIOR

Most Hormads are of low intelligence. The brighter Synthetic Men quickly assume positions of authority over their fellows and become self-styled jeds or jeddaks, though such authority means little to other Martians. On Barsoom, Hormads are considered vermin and few nations tolerate them in their cities. Their reputation for strength and fearlessness, however, has discouraged most jeddaks from eradicating them entirely.

Synthetic Men fight with disregard for their own safety, lacking any sense of self-preservation. They feel neither pain nor shock, nor do they experience self-doubt. They always advance resolutely, armed with swords, meshes and nets, and seldom flee from battle. Injuries that would kill a Martian make no impression on a Hormad, which can withstand multiple wounds without faltering. Beheading prevents a Synthetic Man from making a coordinated attack, but its body continues fighting blindly, posing a threat to enemies and allies alike. Only decapitation and dismemberment render a Hormad harmless.

SPECIES RANGE

Unknown numbers of Synthetic Men escaped the destruction of Morbus and fled into the Toonolian Marshes. From there, they spread across Barsoom, establishing small colonies in abandoned towns and caves. Some turned to piracy after luring down passing airships. Many of the less disfigured became solitary panthans or formed mercenary companies fighting for any who would pay them in food or coin. Others banded together to raid red Martian farms and homesteads. All are distrusted generally, and only the most ignoble Martians hire Hormad mercenaries.

PLOT SEED

Heliumite spies in Zodanga have observed agents loyal to the dead Prince, Sab Than, traveling into the hinterlands and dead towns for secret meetings with various groups of Synthetic Men. Fearing a new conflict between Zodanga and Helium, the spies report their findings to their jeddak. Within hours Ras Thavas, now resident of the Twin Cities, has disappeared. The adventurers are part of Helium's efforts to track the scientist down before he is forced to begin his experiments anew.

THOAT (MINION)

HULKING TEMPERAMENTAL STEEDS AND DRAFT ANIMALS

They are constantly fighting amongst themselves, and woe betide the rider who loses control of his terrible mount.

– John Carter, *Llana of Gathol*

ATTRIBUTES

DARING	CUNNING	EMPATHY
3	5	2

MIGHT	PASSION	REASON
8	4	2

TALENTS

TAIL SWIPE

A thoat without rider can attack with its tail dealing 2 💀 basic damage.

MOUNT

A thoat can carry 1-3 riders depending on its size. These riders do not impede the animal in any way.

CAVALRY

A thoat rider gains a bonus d20 when making melee attacks against dismounted characters. Making more than one such attack is considered dishonorable in most cultures across Barsoom.

PHYSICAL DESCRIPTION

There are two species of thoat on Barsoom. The red Martians ride the smaller type using it for civil and military purposes and as a draft animal. They also raise thoats commercially for meat, hides, and thoat oil, a secretion used widely as a lubricant and cleanser. Most red Martian armies use the thoat as a cavalry mount in the manner of the green Martians, who favor the larger variety. Unlike their smaller cousins, which rarely grow higher than six sofads, the thoats of the green Martians stand ten sofads high and weigh almost twice as much.

Apart from their size difference, both species are similar in appearance, with ridged, bony faces and wide, gaping mouths full of square teeth. They are eight-legged, with long, heavy necks balanced by a wide, flat tail. These tails, held out straight to aid balance and maneuverability when the creature runs, are wider at the tip than the root. In combat, the thoat can use this tail to unseat or fell opponents.

A thoat's glossy, hairless skin serves as light armor, protecting them from injury. They are mainly dark grey in color. This gradually turns to a vibrant yellow at the broad feet of their columnar legs. Their bellies are pure white. Occasionally an albino thoat is hatched and, if it survives to maturity, it is highly sought after by the jeddaks of both red and green nations as a symbol of status.

BEHAVIOR

Where the small, domestic thoat of the red Martians is gentle by nature, the grunting, squealing, cantankerous wild thoats of the green Martians are aggressive, malicious, and habitually volatile. Since both species breed quickly, it is probable that, without the husbandry of the green and red Martians, thoat populations would explode, then crash, all across Barsoom.

The green Martians tame their beasts with violence and cruelty, impressing their will on the creatures with regular beatings. Once a thoat is trained, its rider controls it telepathically without reins or bridle. Nevertheless, no matter how subdued the beasts appear to be, they often rebel and kill their riders and handlers without provocation.

Both species live in herds, feeding on the yellow moss-like vegetation growing across Barsoom. From this they obtain all the nutrition and most of the moisture they require to survive for long periods. Their metabolism is extremely efficient, enabling them to run at speed for great distances. An adult bull thoat can cover fifty haads in three hours. Its padded, nailless feet and the muscular shock absorbers of its legs allow it to move comparatively quietly, even when charging.

Experiments conducted by both red and green Martians following John Carter's example during and after the Prince of Helium era have proved that both species respond with greater alacrity and loyalty to kindness rather than brutality. Of the green Martians, only the Tharks under Tars Tarkas are known to have put this practice into effect. The hordes of Warhoons, Thurd, and Torquas continue to treat their thoats brutishly.

SPECIES RANGE

Thoats are found everywhere except for the polar regions. The smaller variety is normally bred for meat on the red Martian farms bordering the irrigation canals. Its larger counterparts wander the dead sea bottoms in territorial herds. It is from these that the green Martians take their mounts and stock.

PLOT SEED

A rare white thoat has been seen in green Martian territory and an aspiring red Martian jed wishes to gift it to his jeddak. He asks the adventurers to capture the beast, not realizing that there are other nobles planning their own expeditions, or that the green Martian jeddak would very much like a white thoat of his own.

THOAT MOUNTS

A thoat mount is considered a 15xp piece of core equipment. The mount will not revolt except under the most trying circumstances.

ULSIO (MINION)

REPULSIVE BURROWER THROUGH DARK AND FORGOTTEN PLACES

It was quite a battle. That ulsio was the most ferocious and most determined beast I had ever seen, and it gave Pan Dan Chee the fight of his life.

– John Carter, *Llana of Gathol*

ATTRIBUTES

DARING	CUNNING	EMPATHY
5	4	3
MIGHT	PASSION	REASON
2	2	4

TALENTS

VICIOUS VERMIN
All attacks are Sharp.

DISEASED
If Injury damage is inflicted, the target must make a **Daring + Might (D1)** test to avoid an immediate affliction.

SWARMING BURROWERS
At any time, a Threat point can be spent by the narrator to have 3 🎲 additional ulsio join any fight where ulsio are present.

PHYSICAL DESCRIPTION

The six-legged ulsio is the ugliest creature on Barsoom. Pinkish-grey and hairless, this rat-like creature has thick, coarse skin often scarred from infighting in nests and burrows. Its short, robust legs terminate in splayed feet equipped with broad, blunt talons for digging through earth and soft stone.

The ulsio's close-set eyes are small, sunken chips of malice, black as the holes the beast routinely excavates. Its most repellant feature is its skinless, bony jaws. These gaunt mandibles project from the ulsio's fleshy jowls making it seem like the creature's face is rotting away. Both upper and lower jaws contain five sharp, chisel-like teeth used to gnaw through wood, stone, bone, and soft tissue. The average ulsio grows to three sofads in length, yet is agile enough to leap for the throat of any humanoid it encounters.

BEHAVIOR

Although they often nest in subterranean rooms and corridors, ulsios are burrowing creatures known to excavate vast warrens under most of the dead cities. Their tunnels can run for several haads, doubling and redoubling on themselves to form complex, labyrinthine networks dug by successive generations. Such mazes are punctuated with dens, nests, and larders where the ulsios store food in times of plenty. The burrows are filthy places, littered with decaying scraps, putrid gobs of animal fat, and feces. Living amidst such filth, the ulsios are remarkably resistant to infection but are active carriers of a score of virulent diseases. A bite from an ulsio can sometimes result in sepsis or worse if not treated with appropriate salves, though the Martians' natural resilience gives them some immunity.

Ulsios are ill tempered, often squabbling amongst themselves for food or a mate. They attack any who encroach on their territory and prey on those incarcerated in a city's pits. Prisoners often lose fingers or toes to cunning individuals using their extensive tunnels to conduct lightning raids on cells and holding pens. If a group of adventurers strays close to ulsio warrens, the creatures can attack in large numbers.

SPECIES RANGE

Ulsios are found across Barsoom. Their greatest numbers occur in the pits beneath the ancient Martian cities. Sizeable populations are known to exist at Horz, Korad, Jhama, and Xanator. Less advanced red Martian cities, like Ghasta, Manator, and Raxar are also home to hordes of the creatures. Helium and other sophisticated metropolises, including Zodanga and Gathol, keep their ulsio populations under control by various means but they are impossible to eradicate entirely.

PLOT SEED

Kobol is suddenly over run by a plague of ulsios pouring from the city's pits. The creatures are terrified and enraged. People are attacked in the street. Homes are invaded. The army is impotent to stem the rodent tide. In despair, the jeddak calls for outside aid, offering a substantial reward to anyone who can restore order to the city. Are the heroes brave enough to venture into Jhama's ancient pits and discover what is driving the ulsios from their lairs?

WHITE APE (MONSTER)

THE EMBODIMENT OF TERROR ON BARSOOM

I may say that of all the fearsome and terrible, weird and grotesque inhabitants of that strange world, it is the white apes that come nearest to familiarizing me with the sensation of fear.

– John Carter, *The Gods of Mars*

ATTRIBUTES

DARING **7**	CUNNING **5**	EMPATHY **4**
MIGHT **10**	PASSION **4**	REASON **4**
STRESS **14**	MENACE **2–4 (3)**	

TALENTS

FEARSOME BEAST.
All attacks made by a white ape are Fearsome.

MIGHTY BEAST
A white ape can always use Might to attack targets in melee, or through intimidation.

HARD TO KILL
A white ape can spend 3 Momentum to remove an affliction without the need of rest or healing.

PREDATORY INSTINCTS
White apes gain a bonus d20 when seeking to smell or otherwise sense prey or food.

DRAMATIC RETURN
During combat with the apes the narrator can spend 5 Threat to have an otherwise dispatched ape return and attack a character. This ape is considered to have 2 impairments but gains 1 bonus d20 on this attack. This can only be done once per scene.

MASSIVE ROCKS
If an ape throws a rock at a character it will usually miss, but when it hits the weight and power of the throw makes for a dangerous weapon. All thrown attacks are at +2 difficulty but do 3 additional damage ⬢ if they hit. Throwing rocks is usually a **Daring + Reason** test for the apes.

PHYSICAL DESCRIPTION

The deathly pallor of the white ape gives it a spectral quality and provides some camouflage when it moves through the bleached marble ruins of Mars' dead cities. It is entirely bald but for a mass of coarse hair that rises on its head like a crest. Standing ten to fifteen feet high, the white ape is an agile biped, which, like the green Martian, has an intermediary pair of limbs halfway between the legs and upper arms. These limbs are used for running and for grasping prey or improvised weapons. The paws of the white ape are massive and capable of completely enclosing the throats or limbs of any Martian it encounters.

Above its barrel chest, its square head sits on a corded neck. The eyes are small and close set. The ears are positioned high on the skull, but lower than those of the green Martians. With twenty different muscles controlling each cup-like ear, the white ape can pinpoint and distinguish sounds with remarkable precision. In this way, it can locate its prey easily in the mazy streets and plazas of dead cities like Horz, Jhama, Thark, and Warhoon. Its teeth and muzzle recall those of the African gorilla, though they are both many times larger. The two canines that protrude from the upper jaw are formidable piercing weapons and its flat, broad incisors are efficient in shearing bone and stripping flesh.

With its keen senses, formidable physical strength, and the ability to use stone clubs, the white ape should be treated with great caution.

BEHAVIOR

White apes are brutal, ravenous creatures that attack intruders in their territory. If they are armed, they favor bludgeons fashioned from broken masonry. They hunt singly or in breeding pairs. Sometimes small groups of immature apes band together, though this is not common.

White apes are not stupid. They are shrewd hunters and track their quarry carefully until they find an appropriate position from which to attack. They usually prey on green Martians, taking a heavy toll on hatchlings, young females, and any warrior foolish enough to pit himself alone against their ferocity. However, they prefer the taste of red Martians, and risk much to obtain a morsel of their tender flesh.

The white apes' intelligence makes it possible to train. As a result, they are found in the care of panthans and wandering entertainers who use the creatures to earn money with displays of strength or daring. Nevertheless, the white ape can never be entirely trusted. Their aggressive nature often reasserts itself, sometimes with fatal consequences for their handlers and members of the audience.

During the Dotar Sojat era, the First Born domesticated white apes and they were a common sight in their city. How this was achieved remains a mystery. Some years later, in the Jeddak of Jeddaks era, a tribe of sophisticated white apes dwelled in the derelict city of Aaanthor. Mimicking the green Martians, these apes wore harnesses of banth hide and showed signs of evolving beyond their typical savage nature.

SPECIES RANGE

White apes are found in Barsoom's deserted cities, in the Valley Dor, and in the Toonolian Marshes, though captive apes are rare in Toonol.

PLOT SEED

Movan Deu, Helium's eminent entertainer, is aggrieved. Rorkar, his magnificent white ape, the great crowd-pleaser, is dead. Without him, Movan Deu faces financial ruin. Not wishing to lose his wealth or his status, he approaches the heroes with a proposition: search Barsoom for the finest white ape egg imaginable, bring it to him, and enjoy a lavish reward. Unfortunately, for both Movan Deu and the adventurers, Rorkar's death was no simple tragedy. Pel Nar, a rival, poisoned the ape and will do anything to destroy Movan Deu for once dishonoring his sister — including eliminating the players.

ZITIDAR (MONSTER)

COLOSSAL BEAST OF BURDEN

These brutes are huge mastodonian animals that tower to an immense height even beside the giant green man and their giant thoats; but when compared to the relatively small red man and his breed of thoats they assume Brobdingnagian proportions that are truly appalling.

— John Carter, *The Warlord of Mars*

ATTRIBUTES

DARING	CUNNING	EMPATHY
3	5	2

MIGHT	PASSION	REASON
11	4	2

STRESS	MENACE
13	4–5 (4)

TALENTS

MASSIVE BEAST
The zitidar reduces any damage taken by 2. Also, if a target attempts to parry or otherwise block a blow from the zitidar instead of dodging or evading it, the zitidar may use its **Might** for that attack.

MOUNT
A zitidar can carry 3-10 riders depending on its size. These riders do not impede the animal in any way. A zitidar can also pull a wagon with a sizable number of riders (10-30)

BROAD RIDGED HORNS
A zitidar may reduce the difficulty to land a blow by 2, to a minimum of 1. Upon successfully landing a blow, they may deal 6 🎲 damage that is Fearsome.

LUMBERING BEAST
A zitidar is truly massive and incapable of traversing narrow streets or even entering most cities.

PHYSICAL DESCRIPTION
Zitidars are the largest animals on Barsoom, with mature males growing to heights of twenty-five to thirty sofads. They stand on four broad padded feet that allow them to move surprisingly quietly across Mars' dead sea bottoms. Grey or dark green in color, their hide is thick enough to withstand even radium bullets approaching the end of their trajectory. Their heads are massive; their thick, prehensile trunks as agile at seizing an incautious Martian as they are at cropping lichen.

A great, bony frill protects the creature's thick neck. This frill grows higher and more elaborate as the creature matures. In some specimens, it becomes so massive that it provides a rider with an immense natural shield. Two broad, ridged horns curve out from the creature's forehead and two enormous tusks turn down and out from the upper jaw before curling up to a point close to the zitidar's small, angry eyes. The frill, horns and tusks, much larger in the male than the female, are used in the animals' thunderous trials of strength. The sounds of these cacophonous battles, which often end in serious injury, echo across the Martian landscape, the squeals of the vanquished mixing with the wild trumpeting of the victor.

BEHAVIOR
Zitidars are notoriously bad tempered and require intelligence and determination to control. Once broken by an experienced herdsman or wrangler, the zitidar will usually obey the rider's goad. They are unpredictable, however, and sometimes seize the rider and dash him to the ground. Despite the zitidars' fickle nature, the green Martians make widespread use of them to draw their chariots and wagons. Such creatures are often splendidly adorned with the symbols and tokens of the horde.

SPECIES RANGE
Except for the poles, zitidars are found throughout Barsoom. Herds roam wild across the dead sea bottoms and they are common amongst the green Martian hordes. Several red Martian nations, including Gathol, Manator, and Kaol, raise them for their meat and hide, which is cured to make harnesses and footwear.

PLOT SEED
Dawn breaks over a herd of zitidars lying dead in the salt marshes of Gathol. Every animal died from a single wound to its forehead. No sound was heard in the night, no growling, or stampeding. A single, coordinated attack exterminated the group — but why were they killed, and with what weapon? The heroes are either sent to investigate by the Gatholians or the bewildered and angry farmer enlists their aid. Is he the victim of rivalry, or is the massacre of his animals simply a test for something far more sinister?

FURTHER BEASTS

Ancient yet timeless, Barsoom's mysteries run deep, and for every species described in the stories, others remain tantalizingly enigmatic. The sources of the silks and furs common to every Martian bedchamber and camp are never revealed but something must be spinning the silk and the fur must be from beasts more common than either the apt or the orluk.

Brightly plumed birds, venomous snakes, monstrous subterranean lizards, and unseen horrors of the lowest stygian pits are all known on Mars. The Toonolian Marshes are a place of rodents, reptiles, and insects more gigantic than even the deadly sith. Elsewhere, there is at least one rare marsupial reptile and one unique mammal. These unnamed, obscure creatures are an invitation to be creative in building a more varied and vivid Barsoom.

For any narrator wishing to develop new creatures, it is important to bear in mind the creation myth recounted by the First Born. According to legend, all species on Mars evolved from the Tree of Life, which grew in the Valley Dor twenty-three million years ago. Many life forms blossomed and grew, withered and died on the great Tree. Eventually, large buds formed. Each bud was divided into four compartments and each compartment contained a particular organism. The ancestors of the plant men grew in one cell; a sixteen-legged worm occupied another; in the third was the predecessor of the white ape; and in the fourth the forefather of the black Martians. When these buds burst, the plant men remained attached to the parent Tree. The other creatures, now trapped in separate shells, struggled to escape, and in their struggles, they scattered their shells across Barsoom. When the first black Martian finally broke free, he cracked open the other pods and released the archetypes that populated Mars.

Most Martians accept this myth as true, though they may dispute the details of the version recounted by the First Born, given its probable bias. Whatever the precise truth, the legend does define the four commonest types of Barsoomian: humanoids (the red, black, yellow, and white Martians), the largely bipedal, six-limbed species (like the green Martians and the white apes), the multipede descendants of the sixteen-legged worm (the banth, the calot, and others), and the plant men, which have evolved very little, except for growing larger.

The design of any new species should acknowledge this evolutionary history and follow the templates it establishes. Equally, physical characteristics often associated with one type of animal on Jasoom — scales or fur, for example — are not always discrete on Mars. The calot has a mane yet demonstrates reptile-like qualities. Some organisms bear the thick skins and tusks of pachyderms; none have hoofs; and all — with the exception of Mars' solitary mammal — are oviparous.

The following tables are intended to help narrators design basic forms for authentic-seeming Barsoomian species. They need not be followed rigidly and any improbable or incredible combinations can be rejected or rerolled.

BODY TYPE

Many Barsoomian creatures are vaguely analogous to animals on Jasoom. The banth is lion-like, the ulsio is the Martian rat, and the calot a faithful hound. Accordingly, the body types in the table below are suggestive rather than definitive, providing a range of general animal forms.

d20 Roll	Result
01–06	Mammalian
07–13	Reptilian
14–16	Avian
17–19	Insectoid
20	Aquatic

SIZE

Most of the beasts encountered on Mars are medium to large in size and this is reflected in the size table. It is worth noting that Mars' lower gravity allows insects like the sith to reach truly colossal proportions.

d20 Roll	Result
01–02	Diminutive (less than 1 sofad)
03–05	Small (1–2 sofads)
06–11	Medium (3–5 sofads)
12–17	Large (6–10 sofads)
18–19	Massive (10–25 sofads)
20	Gargantuan (25+ sofads)

FEATURES

Many of the dangers posed by Barsoom's animals depend on unique or dominant features: the plant man's tail, or the banth's fearsome jaws. The features table draws together some of the potentially deadly attributes of Mars' wildlife. Roll twice on the following table, re-rolling duplicate results.

d20 Roll	Result
01–02	Tail
03–04	Prehensile tail
05–06	Tail club/sting
07–08	Mane (hair, fur, or spines)
09–13	Talons or claws
14–16	Large teeth (canines and/or incisors)
17	Horns and/or tusks
18	Compound eyes
19	Venom sacs
20	Poison glands

NUMBER OF LIMBS

One of the defining features of Barsoomian fauna is the dominance of multiple legs. Most species have 6–8 limbs in various configurations. The next table lists the prevailing types.

d20 Roll	Result
01–02	2 (biped)
03–06	4 (quadruped)
07–08	6 (centaur-like)
09–13	6 (hexaped)
14–15	8
16–17	10
18	12
19	Multipede
20	Limbless

SKIN TYPE

The beasts of Barsoom display a variety of different body coverings ranging from the fur of the apt to the chitinous segmented body of the sith. The table below gives the nine commonest types and emulates their general frequency.

d20 Roll	Result
01–03	Scaly
04–09	Smooth
10–12	Furred
13–15	Hairy
16	Feathered
17	Thick hide
18	Armor plates
19	Chitin/Carapace
20	Chameleonic

FINISHING TOUCHES

Once a creature's basic appearance is generated, the narrator is encouraged to develop details of the creature's behavior and habitat. The emphasis should always be on how the organism can contribute to the action-adventure feel of the game and how it can evoke the key theme of the Martian stories: bravery, honor, and romance pitted against power, greed, and lust.

Once all these elements are determined, Narrators should assign attributes and talents to a beast if they expect the creature will enter into conflict with the player characters or other important characters in the campaign. The most effective way to set a beast's statistics is to do what the Barsoomians themselves would do: compare them to established beasts. Make your new creation "as Daring as a banth (Daring 7), nearly as powerful as a white ape (Might 9 compared to the white ape's 10), but with the brain of a thoat (Reason 2)" and so on. If you are stuck for a particular attribute rating, give the beast a score between 3 and 5, this is typical for most creatures' attributes that seem neither prominent nor deficient.

CHAPTER 14: SECRETS OF BARSOOM

The scene that met my eyes was so un-Martian that my heart sprang to my throat as the sudden fear swept through me that I had been aimlessly tossed upon some strange planet by a cruel fate.
– John Carter, *The Gods of Mars*

While Barsoom has enjoyed civilization far longer than Earth, it is still a planet of mystery. Hidden valleys and canyons conceal forgotten civilizations. Strange, unheard-of creatures lay hidden in isolated fortress cities, and unbalanced masterminds craft extraordinary inventions. Legends abound of these mysteries, but Barsoomians are pragmatic, far too concerned with day-to-day survival to entertain exploration for its own sake. The arrival of John Carter, whose curiosity and travels to save his imperiled princess revealed many wonders, still left many secrets to be discovered.

The River Iss and the Valley Dor

Also known as the River of Death and the River of Mystery, the River Iss flows the length of Barsoom, and is the last of the Red Planet's great rivers. Finding its source far in the north polar region along the great ice barrier, the river works its way through and drains the Toonol Marsh in the east, without which the marsh would fill and return to being a large lake. The Iss turns south to follow the ancient seabeds until it enters the Koalian Forest to add precious water to the forest soil. Emerging from the forest, the Iss wanders ever southwards, entering valleys and craters, creating small lakes, marshes, and even fertile croplands, until it enters the snowfields of the Barsoomian arctic. Here the river flows below ground until it returns to the surface in the Otz Valley.

The Otz Valley, also known as the Land of Lost Souls, is a tremendous depression taking in almost the entire south polar region. The valley has a temperate climate, and is suspected to be warmed by some subterranean heat source. The River Iss cuts a deep canyon across this valley, creating a narrow band of well-watered and fertile land at the outer base of the Otz Mountains. Here dwell many pathetic Barsoomians, either forsaking their journey to the Valley Dor or escaping the clutches of the Therns. Forbidden to return to their homes on pain of execution, they eke out what rude existence they can. These people band together into small tribes and constantly wage war against each other. Often insane and cannibalistic by nature, they offer a fearful sight and dire warning to all who consider abandoning their pilgrimage.

Some 271 haads from the Otz Valley's outer edge rises the Otz Mountains, an imposing mountain range that encircles the Valley Dor and the Lost Sea of Korus. The valley slopes upwards into foothills and then mountains proper. The River Iss forces its way through the mountains in deep, narrow canyons.

The inner border of the Otz Mountains, known as the Golden Cliffs, rises vertically from the floor of the Valley Dor, towering in places to a height of over two-and-a-half haads. The face of the Golden Cliffs is covered completely with veins of gold ore studded with rich tracks of ruby, emerald, and diamond. The foot of the cliffs is strangely uncluttered, with only the occasional half-buried boulder of precious stone to mar the smooth and abrupt cliff wall.

The Golden Cliffs and Otz Mountains are strongly fortified by the Holy Therns, who live both on the mountain summits and within a maze of subterranean caves and tunnels. The palaces and temples of the Therns are a beautiful sight to behold, festooned with colonnades, courtyards, and gardens. The tunnels that riddle the Golden Cliffs are busy thoroughfares for slaves and Therns during daylight hours, and at night are guarded by ferocious banths.

Encircled by the Otz Mountains is the Valley Dor, a fertile depression located at the Barsoomian South Pole. The Valley Dor is an enormous crater-like basin which has a tropical climate with the summer lasting 240 days. During this season, due to the tilt of the planet's axis, the sun is almost directly overhead.

The valley is covered with manicured crimson grass-like vegetation and contains groves of magnificent trees, some growing upwards for a thousand sofads or more and with trunks a hundred sofads in diameter. The trees are remarkable in their coloration, with smoothly polished trunks of scarlet, white, ebony, yellow, or the deepest purple. The leaves are similarly colored. Strangest of all though, is the way the lower branches are pruned to a uniform height of fifteen sofads, giving the forest floor an almost cathedral-like appearance. Brightly colored voiceless birds make these forests their home.

For those who complete their pilgrimage, the Valley Dor is a welcome sight, a paradise that they are taught to revere from the moment of hatching. Some are even lucky enough to enjoy this paradise for a few short moments before the true nature of the Valley Dor is thrust upon them.

High on the Golden Cliffs, well within sight of the cleft through which the River Iss enters the valley, is a balcony on which a Holy Thern sentry stands watch. On his command — a shrill whistle that can be heard across the valley — he summons the other inhabitants of Dor. Blood-sucking plant men and ferocious white apes kill and feast upon the hapless victims. Those that are not devoured by the white apes have their bloodless bodies collected at night to be prepared and served as food for the Holy Therns.

Not all pilgrims face this gruesome fate. Some manage to elude slaughter, or, those considered of exceptional beauty in face and form, are captured and enslaved by the Therns to serve their every whim. In Thern culture, an avoidance of physical labor and exertion through use of slaves is considered proof of the race's superiority. When the slaves have outlived their usefulness, they are drained of blood by the plant men and consumed by the Holy Therns. Many forced to serve the Therns would say those slaughtered on arrival were indeed the fortunate ones.

The River Iss meanders through the Valley Dor until it finally empties into the Lost Sea of Korus in the center of the valley. The Korus is the only existing ocean on the surface of Barsoom, and is inhabited by aggressive aquatic reptiles known as silians.

Located on the shores of the Lost Sea of Korus and surrounded by forests, far from the where the River Iss empties, lies the Golden Temple of Issus, a magnificent palace of hand-wrought burnished gold where winding walkways paved with crushed rubies, emeralds, turquoise, and diamonds pass through scarlet swards and between ivory-stemmed trees decked with brilliant purple blooms. This is the fabled home of Issus, Goddess of Death and Life, Daughter of the Lesser Moon.

THE RIVER ISS IN THE JEDDAK OF JEDDAKS ERA

Before the Martian Valhalla was revealed as a falsehood by John Carter, the Therns maintain a network of access points and safe houses along the River Iss where boats are maintained for those wishing to take the final pilgrimage. Now that the cult of Issus is no longer followed, these way stations are steadily falling into disrepair.

THE HOLY THERNS

The Holy Therns reside in the Valley Dor near the Lost Sea of Korus where they perpetuate the religion of Issus. Living in great temples on the summits of the Otz Mountains, the Therns promote the pilgrimage that all Martians are expected to take along the River Iss when they reach their 1,000th year. Through their secret temples found in every known city of Barsoom, disguised Therns proselytize their false religion. The very same disguised Therns act as informants, passing information back to their fellow white Martians in the Valley Dor to keep them abreast of current world events, secrets, and wars. Nothing, it is said, escapes the notice of the Therns.

Martians are taught the religion of Issus from the moment they hatch. They believe that the River Iss will bear them to the Valley Dor, which will be their ultimate resting place, a paradise where their loved ones who have made the pilgrimage before them will be waiting to greet them. They also believe that once the pilgrimage has begun it must be concluded, and those that turn back, or somehow return from the Valley Dor are to be put to death for their act of blasphemy. This means those who follow the Thern's false faith are doomed once they begin, either killed as heretics or consumed when they arrive at the Valley Dor by monstrous plant men, great white apes, or the Therns themselves.

The Therns in many ways resemble red Martians, though their skin is fair and their eyes range through blue, green, hazel, and yellow. The men strike strong vital figures, and the women are statuesque and beautiful. All Therns though, are completely bald due to ages of inbreeding. They cover their baldness with blonde wigs, which have become such a part of their attire and culture that to be caught without a wig is a grave social embarrassment.

Therns view themselves as superior forms of life, as far above the other races of Barsoom as they are above the animals they eat. They are proud, arrogant, and aloof, viewing the rest of

WHITE MARTIAN PLAYER CHARACTERS

White Martians aren't available as a default player character race. In *John Carter* stories, they tend to be too involved in some antagonistic plot or isolated in some insular conclave to really fit in with the other races. Even during the Jeddak of Jeddaks era, where Carter leads an alliance of red, green, Okar, and First Born Martians. There aren't really any white Martian allies and the general attitude towards such groups as the Holy Therns is very negative.

However, narrators can allow white Martian player characters if they feel it fits their campaign. In such cases, use the following race template. In addition, many white Martians have talents that represent strange powers or abilities particular groups have developed over the centuries.

ATTRIBUTE BONUSES
Subtract 1 from Empathy. Add +2 to two of the following attributes: Cunning, Daring, or Reason.

WHAT YOU KNOW
* The secrets and schemes of your people.

* How to use myths and deception to manipulate others.

* The basic cultures and history of most of the races of Barsoom.

* The general theories behind most advanced technology on Barsoom.

* The location and purpose of the secret bases, enclaves, and settlements of your people.

WHAT YOU DON'T KNOW
* How to easily relate to others as equals

WHAT YOU CAN DO
* You know the basics of personal combat.

* You can direct and lead others, especially your slaves and subordinates.

* You can operate most machines, vehicles, and technology.

This basic race option can also be used to represent Holy Therns, Orovars, and Lotharians. While Orovars are more honorable and scrupulous than the Therns, they are also very reclusive and rare, again making them not particularly suited for most campaigns. Lotharians PCs are also exceedingly rare and would likely possess talents relating to their ability to generate hypnosis based illusions, though the incredible power of these abilities may overshadow other characters if not handled with care.

When the religion of Issus is revealed as a falsehood by John Carter, most Therns find themselves at a loss. Many remain in the Valley Dor where they are ruled over by the First Born. Others travel the face of Barsoom as panthans, selling their swords to the highest bidder. Small groups of Holy Therns still remain in hiding, maintaining hope and plotting the ways that they may revive the worship of Issus.

the population of Barsoom as their commodity, property, and sustenance to be harvested and used as they will. Cannibalistic as they are, the act of consuming human flesh adheres to strict rituals. Holy Therns will not consume the flesh of other Barsoomians until it has been drained of blood by the plant men, believing that the taint of life would thus be removed and the flesh made suitable for consumption.

Thern culture is also significantly different to the other cultures of Barsoom. Therns do not adhere to the common warrior customs of Barsoom, seeing no issue in using superior weapons against their opponents. Whether they adhere to the established warrior customs when fighting other Therns is unknown, but it is likely they behave more honorably towards their own kind than the other races they belittle, despise, and consume.

Thern culture is broken into 10 tiers or cycles. The lower cycles consist of the Lesser Therns while the upper cycles consist of the Holy Therns. The Lesser Therns serve the Holy Therns as vassals, acting as guards, soldiers, slave masters, and beast callers. The Holy Therns are the priests of Issus, and are led by the Holy Hekkador of the Tenth Cycle.

The Therns themselves believe that they are the Chosen of Issus. Their religion is complex and shares many similarities with the primary faith of Barsoom mixed with those of the First Born. When a Thern reaches their 1000th year, they make a holy pilgrimage to the Temple of Issus, believing this the true way to Heaven. There they believe they live eternally basking in the Issus' glory. Souls of those dying before their 1000th year instead pass into a plant man. If the plant man dies before the appointed 1000th year mark, their soul then passes to a white ape. If the white ape dies before end of the one thousand years, the soul passes to a silian and is forever lost.

For all their superiority and arrogance, Therns are completely unaware their own religion is a ruse perpetuated upon them by the black Martians. Those traveling to the Temple of Issus are themselves captured and enslaved or killed.

THE OMEAN SEA

The Omean Sea is a subterranean ocean some five or six haads beneath a large portion of the south polar region. The main source of its water is the Lost Sea of Korus, which lies in part above it. The Omean is the primary sanctuary of the First Born and harbors their entire fleet with ease. The entrance to this underground sea is through a five-haad diameter funnel of a long extinct volcano, deep within the polar ice field. There are also man-made passages from the shores of the Omean to the Temple of Issus. The sea contains many islands, one of which is the Isle of Shador which serves as a prison. The cavern that houses the sea is lit by a phosphorescent substance in the rock.

BLACK MARTIANS

Referring to themselves as the "First Born" but referred to by other Barsoomians as Black Pirates, black Martians see themselves as superior to all other Martians, and treat them accordingly, considering them as little better than animals. This contempt even extends to cannibalistic practices amongst some First Born against the other Barsoomian races, especially their goddess-queen Issus.

Originally believed by other Martians to come from Thuria, the lesser moon, they are later discovered to dwell on Barsoom. In fact, the First Born are the earliest form of human life on the Red Planet.

Black Martians are a technologically advanced people, with access to everything from radium pistols and rifles to some of the most advanced fliers found on Barsoom. Unlike other races, they use submarines and other marine technologies lost to the surface world while traveling the Omean Sea.

In appearance, black Martians are similar to red Martians, except for the color of their skin which is like polished ebony. They are, on average, slightly taller than red Martians, and all are strongly built. They are without exception an extremely handsome race with black eyes and thick black hair, though some shave their heads. Male black Martians have no facial hair, while the skin of both males and females is smooth and flawless.

Black Martians are totally averse to performing menial physical labor, though the arts of raiding and combat are well respected. They often raid surface civilizations of Barsoom (primarily the Therns in the Valley Dor or the southerly red Martian city-states). To aid in these endeavors, their great fliers are stolen and modified by slaves to operate both in air and on water.

KAMTOL

Kamtol is a city of black Martians located in the Valley of the First Born; a beautiful valley located at the bottom of a deep hidden rift. The city boasts a population of some 200,000, many of whom are captured red Martian slaves. Elaborately carved, pure white walls, broad avenues, and graceful, lofty towers mark the gorgeous city.

The inhabitants of Kamtol settled the valley in preference to accompanying the rest of the First Born who chose to follow the River Iss and settle below the South Pole. Doxus, the Jeddak of Kamtol, keeps the population under strict control through the use of a paralytic-stroke-inducing machine which records his every subject's nerve index.

The black Martians of Kamtol are in contact with, and receive frequent guests from, the city of the First Born on the Omean. The two nations of black Martians occasionally organize raids on red Martian cities together.

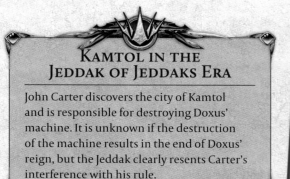

KAMTOL IN THE JEDDAK OF JEDDAKS ERA

John Carter discovers the city of Kamtol and is responsible for destroying Doxus' machine. It is unknown if the destruction of the machine results in the end of Doxus' reign, but the Jeddak clearly resents Carter's interference with his rule.

Issus

The black Martians were originally ruled by the Eternal Issus. A beautiful princess when the First Born first retreated to the Omean, she maintained her life by unknown means far beyond the norm. Functionally immortal, she becomes the perpetrator of the Religion of Issus, styling herself a goddess of death and eternal life. Through her machinations this false religion is taken to the Therns and spread across the planet, manipulating all with messages delivered through the Therns' Holy Hekkador through secret tunnels and passageways. The Therns have no idea the Black Pirates, whom they believe hail from the Nearer Moon, are sent by the very goddess they worshipped to raid and rob them.

Grown impossibly old and hideously ugly by the time John Carter arrives on Barsoom, Issus is served unfailingly by her subjects. She is personally served by a number of hand-picked female attendants selected from the slaves. The lives of her attendants are neither pleasant nor long, as they are permitted to live for only one year after laying eyes on the 'holy vision of her radiant face' before being killed and eaten.

Issus assigns officers from among her most competent people. Called dators, they are the equivalent of princes among the other Barsoomian civilizations. They are expected to follow Issus' orders precisely, lead by example, and are seen as paragons of the First Born. Dators command the great warships that make the raids on the surface world as well as forming an advisory council for Issus herself.

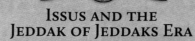

ISSUS AND THE JEDDAK OF JEDDAKS ERA

This is all brought to an end by John Carter when he opposes the First Born after they kidnap his wife, the incomparable Dejah Thoris. In his battle to free her, he reveals Issus' deception to the First Born, the Therns, and finally to the rest of Barsoom. The disillusioned First Born tear Issus' still living body to pieces in retaliation. Dator Xodar is raised to the station of jeddak for his part in the unveiling of Issus' lies. Now members of the great alliance of peoples brought together by Carter's efforts, the First Born of Issus behave more peacefully towards their neighbors under Xodar's guidance, though some factions among them still partake in piracy.

THE DEAD CITY OF HORZ

Formerly the capital city of ancient Barsoom's greatest nation, Horz lies 3,000 haads north of Gathol. The city was once the capital of Barsoom's greatest empire and the seat of learning and culture of the dominant white-skinned Orovars. It is also the point from which the longitude and latitude of Barsoom is calculated. The Orovars, thought to be long extinct, maintain a small colony of survivors in a walled and underground refuge within the ruins of their ancient city.

THE OROVARS

The Orovars are the original white men of Barsoom, existing over 500,000 years ago before Barsoomian oceans began to dry up. They ruled most of the land and created a peaceful civilization. The Orovars conquered illness and perfected their medical sciences until their lifespan exceeded 1,000 years. Great fleets of Orovar ships sailed the five oceans of ancient Barsoom, exchanging goods between the continents and throughout countless islands.

This golden age of plenty came to an end when the oceans of Barsoom began to recede and rain ceased to fall. Lakes and rivers vanished, and in a desperate bid to save their cities, the Orovars extended their wharves and built new cities time and time again in pursuit of the retreating seas. Yet, despite their greatest efforts, shipping eventually ceased and the Orovar cities were over-run and pillaged by the land-roving green hordes, scattering the original inhabitants across the face of Barsoom.

A band of Orovars from Horz eventually returned to their sacked city and rebuilt their civilization in secret, masking their home as an abandoned and crumbling shell. Horz now stands as the last outpost of this nearly extinct race, with only a few thousand of the ancient Orovars left.

Orovars resemble Caucasian Earth humans. Their pale features, which tan easily, are complemented with blue, green, or violet eyes, and their hair is normally a pale blonde or white, though auburn hair can be found among them very rarely. Orovar men are unable to grow beards, and they are completely free of body hair.

The Orovars of Horz are an exceptionally secretive people, owing their very survival to this trait and the strange abilities they have developed. They are fortunately just and scrupulously fair people. Crime is almost unknown among them. They have a strong sense of honor and will tolerate no act of cruelty. Despite their exile they are a happy and carefree people.

In all other respects, Orovars are very similar to the other Barsoomian races. They have a tendency to wear ornamental headdresses decorated with jewels and precious metals; an affectation which is unusual amongst the other races.

LOTHAR

Lothar is a secluded city in a valley surrounded by mountains in the Gulf of Torquas. The valley is lush with many trees and scarlet grass. Lothar is frequently attacked and besieged by the savage green hordes of Torquas.

The city is home to the Lotharians, a small group of survivors of the ancient white Martians. Numbering only 1,000 men with no women, they are the last remaining survivors of the once great city of Lothar, a formidable world power before the drying of Barsoom's oceans.

LOTHARIANS

The most distinguishing feature of the Lotharians is their powerful telepathic abilities. Over the centuries they have strengthened and perfected their natural Martian telepathy into a weapon to assist them in their defense, developing the ability to create illusions that can affect the real world as if they were flesh. The Lotharians are one of the few cultures on Barsoom that do not use radium weaponry, instead arming their illusionary warriors with bows and hand axes. The illusionary warriors are also used to populate the city. These phantom warriors, along with illusionary banths, defend the city against the marauding green Martian hordes threatening to over-run the once great civilization. As part of a complex and ancient code involving the use of their powers, it is forbidden for a Lotharian to use his powers to create the likenesses of women or children.

The Lotharians are an ancient race, with some of the oldest among them remembering Barsoom before the oceans disappeared. Their long lives have caused them to suffer some mental imbalances though, and they become more and more disturbed with each passing aeon.

The Lotharians are divided into two philosophical factions. One group advocates the creation of food and drink with the powers of their minds to sustain their bodies, while the other faction advocates life without the intake of food, illusionary or not. Philosophical argument and debate between these two factions can continue for days at a time, and has occasionally broken out into open conflict.

The Lotharians are unusual in that they never fell under the sway of the Therns and the religion of Issus. The only religion followed in Lothar is that of the god Komal, a huge banth that is fed living sacrifices to keep him appeased. When the Jeddak of Lothar tried to feed Thuvia, Princess of Ptarth, to Komal, she befriended the banth with her unusual ability to tame the great beasts. He then followed her out of the city where he was killed in the melee between red Martians of Dusar and the green horde of Torquas, thus bringing an end to the "god" of the Lotharians. What their race will do now for spirituality, if anything, is unknown.

BANTOOM

Bantoom is the land of the Kaldanes, a series of fertile valleys and low hills populated by roaming banths. Open streams, an exceedingly rare sight on Barsoom, meander through the valleys. The Kaldanes live in individual walled hives that consist of a single tower above a warren of underground tunnels. Bantoom lies south of the equator and several thousand haads to the west of Gathol.

KALDANES

The Kaldanes are creatures who are all head and no body. Ninety percent of the Kaldane volume is brain, making them highly intellectual with a strong racial memory but possessing practically no emotions. Their vast intellect also allows them to telepathically instill their will in others for as long as they maintain eye contact. They have six short spider-like legs which allow them to walk up walls and along ceilings, and two lobster-like chelae with which to manipulate their environment. Their heads are rather loathsome in appearance; the face being grotesque with protruding wide-set eyes and a round puckered hole that serves as a mouth. Lacking lungs, they have no need to breathe. Kaldanes often ornately decorate their heads with jewels and precious metals.

Through selective breeding, Kaldanes have been able to raise what would be called instinct into a racial hereditary memory. Every Kaldane hatches with the full knowledge and memories of all its ancestors.

Kaldanes live in different clans, each ruled by its own "king". The kings differ from other Kaldanes by being larger and having a slightly bluish hue. The king is able to produce eggs with no need for a mate, from which all Kaldanes in the clan are hatched. Every thousand or so eggs produced is a king egg from which a king Kaldane will hatch. Most king eggs are destroyed but some are stored in the case of the demise of the current king. At which point, a king egg is allowed to hatch, and the new king takes the name of the previous king and life in the clan continues as if nothing had happened.

While Kaldanes do not have a religion, they have a philosophy and goals that they follow zealously. Their main goal is to become the perfect brain, believing that their physical bodies are worthless except what is needed to support cerebral function. Kaldanes believe that they are all identical and that if one Kaldane likes something, they all do. Similarly, if one Kaldane dislikes something, they all do. Kaldanes believe that they are superior to all other life forms on Barsoom, and all other life may be exploited as they will if useful and destroyed if not.

The Kaldanes have bred the headless creatures called Rykors to fight and work for them. They control the Rykors by crawling on top of their bodies and settling into leather collars on the Rykor's necks. From this position, they become the Rykor's brains and direct their movements by manipulating the Rykor's spinal column with their legs. Despite the Rykor's humanoid appearance, Kaldanes have no compunction in consuming their flesh.

RYKOR

The Rykors are a race of headless humans. They seem to be a kind of red Barsoomian with the perfectly proportioned and beautiful bodies of men and women. Rykors have no brain, eyes, or ears, only a mouth located directly on the neck. These headless creatures are ruled by the Kaldanes. Without the direction of a Kaldane, a Rykor normally remains in the same place as it was left, barely moving or eating. Kaldanes can be rather vain regarding some Rykors, decorating their favorites with jeweled harnesses and other adornments.

OTHER SIGNIFICANT RUINS AND HIDDEN KINGDOMS

Hidden in rifts and valleys, or secreted in the few thick remaining forests, huddle hidden kingdoms, often ignorant of all that has occurred outside of their limited borders. Some are the remnants of mighty empires which once sailed the seas before the oceans receded, now living in decline and isolation. Others use their hidden status to raid surrounding nations and cities, content that their own city is safe from retribution.

The ancient dead cities of Barsoom are all built along similar designs, and can be very large. Great avenues lead to huge quays and wharf areas show where the vanished oceans once lay. Gigantic central plazas are surrounded by the crumbling remains of palaces while courtyards and concealed cul-de-sacs provide ample room to remain unseen. Though the dead cities are deserted by human occupants, these areas are frequently used by green Martian nomads and the fierce white apes. Water can also be found in these ruins along with the yellow moss that provides fodder for thoats and other creatures due to the superior soil located in the crumbling ruins as opposed to that upon the vast dead sea bottoms. Other plants and occasional forgotten orchards can sometimes be found that also provide sustenance.

Under every ruined city is a maze of tunnels and chambers, previously used to store food and riches and to act as prisons and dungeons. These tunnels now host a number of different vermin including ulsios, lizards, and serpents. It is quite possible other strange creatures live in these dark places underneath Mars — bizarre subterranean beasts who prey on any foolish or brave enough to enter their lairs. There are even legends of strange humanoids known as the "pit dwellers" who prey on any who venture into their subterranean territories beneath the dead cities of Barsoom, though little is known of these creatures.

GHASTA

A tropical valley not too far from the city of Tjanath, the Valley Hohr was formed by the River Syl flowing across the crater of a gigantic and long extinct volcano. Hemmed in by mighty cliffs and located in a rocky and barren part of Barsoom, this remnant of an ancient era is a haven of trees, flowers, shrubs, and birds and insects of both a prehistoric and modern world. Much of the jungle is covered in the webs of the deadly Spider of Ghasta, protecting the small, totally isolated walled city of Ghasta located in the center of the valley.

The population of Ghasta, is quite small, consisting of only the 100 male members of the court who are served by 600 slaves. Known as the Spider Martians, these lords of Ghasta are powerfully-built hairy men who have utterly subjugated the city's population. Their Jed, Ghron, is a sadistic maniac who lures travelers into captivity with his beautiful slave girls and riches. Ghron's grotesque appearance is described as more closely resembling a hairy ape than a typical red Martian male.

Those captured by the Spider Martians of Ghasta are bribed or threatened into serving the mad jed. They are promised wealth and power if they support his tyranny over the people of Ghasta and aid him in his hideous amusement in the torture chamber. Those who do not support him are consigned to his torture chamber where he burns his victims alive or has them twisted into deformed conditions for the sheer enjoyment of inflicting pain. While some valiant heroes have escaped Ghron's clutches, he still rules in Ghasta.

INVAK AND ONVAK

Invak is a city hidden deep in the Forest of Lost Men, a jungle located on the Barsoomian Equator. Invak has a long-standing rival and enemy city in Onvak, also hidden in the forest. The buildings and walls of both cities are covered in vegetation, making it almost impossible to distinguish them from the forest around them. The inhabitants of both cities are red Martians and they have created a pill that allows them to become invisible for 24 hours. Special lights in the city render the inhabitants visible to each other. Both Invak and Onvak have been at war for some considerable time, the logistics of which are difficult due to the enemies being unable to see each other.

The inhabitants utilize a naming convention which is notably different from that used by other red Martians. All male noble names end in US, while all female noble names end in AS. Royalty follows the same convention but their names always begin with two consonants.

THINGS PCs WERE NOT MEANT TO KNOW

While this chapter has focused on the secrets of Barsoom, some game masters may find that their players have read all the John Carter series and none of these revelations are secrets to them. This may cause an issue with some groups. The best way of overcoming this is by creating your own secrets to be revealed in time to the players.

Barsoom is large enough to still hold many secrets, even in those areas that appear, at first glance, to be thoroughly explored. The Toonolian Marshes are a prime example of an area that has been described but hardly explored in full. We know that the Kangaroo Martians live there, along with what Hormads remain, and there are savage primitive tribes. But what else? An entire series adventure could be designed around discovering what hidden and lost civilizations can be found in the marshes.

On the floor of the dead seas are uncountable ruins, each holding their own secrets, all waiting to be discovered by the player characters. Are there new races to be found among them? Perhaps a secret cabal of Therns has taken control of a green horde and is plotting to release a new religious ruse upon Barsoom. Or perhaps a forgotten race hidden for thousands of years is newly discovered.

Even the novels introduce some mysteries that are never fully explained. Perhaps the characters will have the chance to discover exactly who the Pit Dwellers are. Are they degenerated white Martians? Do they have a decaying civilization located deep below the surface of Barsoom? And what of the keeper's diadem found on the person of the Holy Thern Sator Throg? How did he come by it, and what were his intentions?

Finally, there is the greatest mystery of all. What happened to John Carter and Dejah Thoris on Sasoom? We know that they escaped from the Morgors but little else. Are they still alive? What are they doing? Do they need help in returning home? And what of the Morgors' planned invasion?

As you can see, Barsoom still has many secrets to give up, and it's up to you and your players to reveal them.

STRANGE LOCALES AND WONDERS

Apart from inhabited and abandoned cities, Barsoom also possesses a veritable treasure of exotic locations to draw the interest of any curious hero. Although the majority of the landscape is dominated by the broad, shallow dry sea beds covered with hardy ochre lichen, there are also lows hills hunted by ferocious banths, rugged and impassable mountains soaring high into the air, and deep valleys that shelter small pockets of Barsoom's lush past.

ARTOLIAN HILLS

The Artolian Hills are an extensive range of hills surrounding the city of Duhor. Though generally a low range, some of its peaks are snow-covered. It lies between 2,000 and 3,000 haads north of Ptarth and the same distance west of Phundahl.

TOONOLIAN MARSHES

A great remnant of the mighty oceans that covered much of the surface of Barsoom, the Toonolian Marshes stretch east and west for 500 haads, across the northern part of the globe, with a maximum width of 800 haads. The land is marshy, with the occasional rocky island supporting jungle growth. Narrow water channels and small lakes are scattered throughout the area. Strange beasts and water-dwelling reptiles inhabit the swamps along with degenerate tribes isolated from the rest of the world.

Along the marshes' eastern extremity can be found the red Martian city-state of Toonol, and at its western extreme is the red Martian city-state of Phundahl. About midway along its northern shore is the destroyed city of Morbus, and on the island of Ompt within the swamp is the village of Gooli, home of the kangaroo Martians.

GOOLIANS

The Kangaroo Martians are a small population of two hundred inhabitants of kangaroo-like people that are capable of extraordinary leaps. They are a primitive tribal race of oviparous marsupials. From the waist down they resemble long-tailed kangaroos. They carry a short sword, dagger, and spear as weapons. They live in primitive huts on their island and rather foolishly pride themselves on being great warriors; foolishly because they are actually little more than boastful cowards and thieves that are often preyed upon by cannibalistic savages who live on the nearby islands in the marshes.

HORMADS

The Hormads, or Synthetic Martians, are the inhabitants of the ancient island city of Morbus. Originally, the Hormads were simply the by-products of the bizarre experiments of Ras Thavas, the Mastermind of Mars, who was using Morbus as the center for his laboratory. As time went on and the Hormads become greater in number and intelligence, they overthrew Ras Thavas and enslaved him, forcing him to produce millions of Synthetic Martians like themselves from his laboratory vats, with the intention of conquering all Barsoom.

Most of these creatures are hideously deformed, of extremely low intelligence, and have no central brain. Consequently, they cannot be fully destroyed except by complete incineration. Every part of the body tissue is alive in its own right. A head severed from the body may still talk and the body may run about. This renders them a formidable enemy, as they have no fear of destruction. Even if limbs are severed or decapitation occurs, they are easily repaired. However, decapitation renders them inefficient and maniacally unmanageable. Fortunately, they are poorly coordinated and bad swordsmen.

The more powerful Hormads forced Ras Thavas to transplant their brains from their hideous bodies into more handsome bodies, often those of captured red Martians. It became a mark of great honor and even greater envy to have a handsome body.

The majority of Hormads are destroyed by John Carter, but some may still thrive in the marshes.

SYL RIVER

The Syl River is a great underground stream flowing far beneath the cities of Tjanath and Manator, through the Valley Hohr and then on to join the River Iss. The underground banks of the Syl are home to the enormous white lizards that search the subterranean caverns for food.

Strange Powers and Secrets

The strange powers that have been displayed by the inhabitants of Barsoom are a varied lot but most appear to be some form of telepathy. They are generally displayed by individual groups of people as a type of racial ability. Despite this, as has been proven by John Carter, with the assistance of a teacher and dedicated practice, it would not be out of the question for any Barsoomian to expand their abilities to include new applications.

The following section details some of strange powers and secret abilities displayed in the *John Carter* stories. Example talents calling upon these powers have been included with each. These talents can be used as presented or as inspiration for narrator created talents. These abilities may also show up in player characters as well, though this is far less common and often requires an appropriate combination of race, archetype, and background to justify.

Banth Empathy

This is certainly a rare power, barely understood by those who possess it let alone those who witness it. It has been stated that Banth Empathy is not an aspect of telepathy, nor does one who possesses the power realize that they have it until they are confronted by a banth; an overall dangerous proposition at the best of times.

With a simple sound or whispered word, the possessor of this power is able to exert their control over a banth or group of banths, rendering the creatures docile and placid servants. The banths are willing to obey the commands of the possessor of this power, even if those commands place the creatures in some danger.

It could be theorized that this power could extend to other animal species on Barsoom, though the only person to have been seen exhibiting this power in any form is Thuvia of Ptarth, and that only with banths. Possessing Banth Empathy allows a character to have one or more banths as regular companions if desired (see *Chapter 13: Beasts of Barsoom*).

TALENT
BANTH EMPATHY (GRADE 3)
Banth's see you as kin more than prey. They may even follow your commands.

- **Circumstance:** When encountering banths

- **Effect:** Banths do not attack you unless they are first attacked, starving, or otherwise aggravated. You may attempt to persuade, tame, or coerce banths into assisting you or following simple commands. This is usually a (D3) test, possibly more for complex or difficult requests. If successful, 1 Momentum can be spent to make another command to the same banth.

Characters can create more potent versions of the talent presented here to lower difficulties in making commands or provide additional d20s when making such rolls.

Illusion Generation

Illusion generation is the ability to create images through the power of telepathy. This power is exhibited primarily by the Lotharians who use it in the defense of their city. These illusions are so powerful that those who see them will believe that they are real, so real in fact, that any damage done to them by the illusion will cause psychosomatic damage to the victim and can lead to death.

Lotharians can use their abilities to affect a large group of people, or a single individual. Their illusions encompass the entire spectrum of sensory input and require a strong force of will to disbelieve.

While Lotharian illusions are not real, they have been sometimes known to affect the physical world. Illusionary food can be used to provide sustenance, while on at least one occasion an illusionary warrior has developed a life and existence independent of the Lotharian who created him.

TALENT
MINOR ILLUSIONIST (GRADE 3)
You can create small illusory items that are so convincing they behave as the real thing.

- **Circumstance:** Making illusory items

- **Effect:** You can create any small item which has a function and form you are familiar with. Though illusory, this item seems so real it operates exactly as a real object. You can maintain one such item at a time.

This talent allows for creation of standard core equipment style items. To create multiple items or for items that require multiple uses of core equipment to possess, add 3 grades to this talent for each additional item or rank.

TALENT
MASTER ILLUSIONIST (GRADE 6)
Your mastery of illusion is so great you can mimic living things so accurately they seem real. Your creations can interact with the environment as if real, and can even kill others if directed.

✳ **Circumstance:** Making illusory creatures

✳ **Effect:** You can create creatures that function as real. Though illusory, these creatures seem so real they operate exactly as a real creature. You can maintain one creature at a time. These creatures operate as a minion version of the real creature it copies.

This talent allows the character to craft an illusory minion roughly equal to a guardsman, raider, or a moderately dangerous beast like a calot. Being able to craft more creatures or more dangerous ones increases the grade of this talent: 1 grade for an additional minion or 3 grades for a significant increase in the power of your creations.

TALENT
PROJECTION (GRADE 10)
You now realize much of reality is an illusion and can place illusionary versions of yourself across time and space.

✳ **Circumstance:** When joining a scene

✳ **Effect:** You can spend 2 Momentum to enter a scene you are aware of regardless of distance or location. You function as if you have joined this scene normally, though you in fact controlling a hyper-realistic illusion of yourself. Any damage done to you during this scene disappears at the end of the scene.

MIND CONTROL

A power exhibited primarily by Kaldane kings, mind control allows them to take control of another's actions. Those who are subjected to this power are aware that they are no longer in control of their actions. They can, with an extreme expression of will, reassert control of their bodies, though it is an exhausting process. This power requires eye contact from the Kaldane to be fully successful.

Drone Kaldanes are sometimes able to express this power over lesser beasts, including Rykors.

TALENT
MIND CONTROL (GRADE 3)
You can assault a target's mind, breaking their will and eventually taking control of their actions. This requires eye contact to initiate.

✳ **Circumstance:** When making eye contact

✳ **Effect:** You can make a Conflict action using **Daring + Reason** that does 1 🎲 of Confusion damage. Effects rolled on this attack inflict 1 additional Confusion damage. If your Mind Control attack creates an affliction in a target, you can then attempt to control the target's actions with a **Cunning + Reason** test to take control of them. Once in control, they may command the character to act as they see fit. If the character wishes to oppose the controller's commands they can take 1 🎲 Confusion damage and make another test.

Mind Control costs an additional 1 grade for every extra die of Confusion damage the initial attack does. Also, characters adept at Mind Control often have additional talents or a more advanced version of the Mind Control talent that gives them bonus d20s or other advantages when attacking others.

"GET OUT OF MY MIND!"

Mind Control is a useful narrator device, but it can be very frustrating for many players. Generally, it's safer to use such mental domination-based abilities on a character's allies, friends, companions, foils, and even innocent bystanders while leaving the player heroes free to act. However, sometimes it makes sense for a villain to use his Mind Control on a player character. If done sparingly, this can lead to interesting role-playing opportunities.

However, if a player is not having fun being the subject of mental control or simply finds themselves under a protracted period of control due to bad dice rolls, remind them they can spend a Luck point to ignore the effects of any afflictions for a Conflict action. As this talent requires an affliction to work, this also breaks the control for this action. This allows characters to exert their will and seek to disable or otherwise end their mental servitude while still making Mind Control appropriately dangerous.

MIND READING

While all Barsoomians are telepathic to some extent and able to read each other's surface thoughts, only those that are especially trained can probe deeper into the minds of others. This ability is not fool proof, and those with a strong will and superb training can resist the mental examination.

An extension of this power, one that has only been exhibited by royal psychologists, is the ability to read the minds of the dead. This power is difficult to use, and becomes more difficult the longer a corpse has been dead until the memories are lost forever.

TALENT
MIND SCAN (GRADE 2)
* **Circumstance:** When making mental contact

* **Effect:** When in conversation with another character you can make an opposed (D1) **Empathy + Reason** test to scan the surface thoughts of the character you're speaking with. Success means the character will answer one "yes or no" question so long as the question has bearing of the character's current knowledge or emotions. Additional questions can be asked for each Momentum spent. Mind Scan requires the character to be at Near range and every step of distance increases the difficulty of the test by 1.

More advanced versions of this talent increase the grade by 2 to allow for answers that are full sentences or short phrases rather than "yes or no" or which provide bonus d20s or lower difficulties on the Mind Scan test.

TAXIDERMY

This craft is practiced by the morticians of Horz whose skill is so profound that the corpses maintain the semblance of life. In some cases, their technique is so deft that the corpses themselves do not realize they are dead, continuing about their business as they had in life. If and when it is revealed to the corpses that they are indeed dead, they crumble into dust.

TALENT
TAXIDERMY (GRADE 8)
You can craft the dead so expertly they reanimate and believe themselves to be alive.
* **Circumstance:** Reanimating the dead

* **Effect:** You can reanimate the dead by crafting a creature from dead flesh and bringing it back to life. These creatures function as normal characters as long as they do not realize they are not truly alive. If they discover this, they instantly crumble to dust.

Characters possessing this talent may take loyal minions they have raised from the dead as core equipment or allies. However, these individuals are destroyed if they discover their true nature and will need to be replaced with new subjects.

TRANSLOCATION

This exceedingly rare power has only been exhibited by one person –John Carter – which he uses to travel to Earth and back. He claims to have learned how to use this power voluntarily after studying the abilities of illusion possessed by the Lotharians.

When using this power, a physical copy of the user's body and everything worn at the time, are transmitted to the location visualized. The original body remains in a death-like sleep while the new body acts and interacts with others as normal. This power has the ability to bridge interstellar distances, though the exact range is unknown.

Translocation is more of a plot device than a power suitable for a talent. If it indeed exists outside its limited usage by Carter, it is mostly present only to explain moving between worlds.

STRANGE AND LOST TECHNOLOGY

Ambitious, avaricious, resentful, cowardly, or coldly rational, many of Barsoom's jeds, jeddaks and scientists aspire to extend their influence or gain favor with the powerful. They sometimes turn their attention to the possibilities of science and the mysteries of the past to achieve their aims. From artificial monster men to flying weapon-laden spacecraft, there are countless instances of science serving the domineering, the corrupt, or the mad.

While many of these devices and scientific discoveries are detailed in *Chapter 5: Weapons and Technology*, there are still many examples of powerful and strange devices used to terrorize, control, and dominate throughout Barsoom. In Kadabra, Salensus Oll, Jeddak of the yellow Men of Okar, used the vast black shaft known as the Guardian of the North to draw countless airships electromagnetically to their doom. Its destruction by John Carter at the end of the Prince of Helium era ushered in a new age for the Okarians and freed countless red Martian slaves. In the First Born city of Kamtol, the Jeddak Doxus recorded his every

subject's nerve index, and used a machine capable of inducing remote paralytic stokes to control the population. Again, John Carter destroyed the device, this time during the Jeddak of Jeddaks era, leaving Doxus dispossessed and eager for revenge.

For narrators, such devices can ensure that a hero's life on Barsoom is never predictable. Furthermore, those examples are just a few of the numerous possibilities of such science-spawned threats. Dangers and challenges from new inventions, rediscovered technology, or the products of experimental science are always emerging. No warrior or adventurer can ever be certain when a ruthless ruler or a single-minded scientist might unleash some unpredictable horror on the Red Planet. On Mars life, and death, are capricious things.

The following two tables are designed to help narrators deploy authentic-seeming Barsoomian technologies and weird sciences to generate immersive plots.

To determine the general scientific field to which a device or process belongs roll on the following table:

Once the general scientific field is determined, roll on the New Technology and Arcane Science Plot table in the appropriate section to establish what the new technology/arcane science is and what its effect(s) might be.

Inventions like these can provide a variety of plot lines, and narrators are encouraged to develop new and extraordinary items in keeping with Barsoom's history and cultures. Whatever weird or esoteric chemicals, materials, or mechanisms are created, they should encourage the heroes to explore dangerous paths and plunge themselves into unpredictable, high-stakes adventures.

D20	RESULT
01-06	Electrical
07–13	Chemical
14-16	Mechanical
17–19	Biological
20	Interplanetary

ELECTRICAL (01–06)	CHEMICAL (07–13)	MECHANICAL (14–16)	BIOLOGICAL (17–19)	INTERPLANETARY (20)
01-05 A scientist discovers a means of projecting the eighth ray as a focused beam, enabling him to move huge loads with ease. His invention is stolen and within a week a weapon that sends airships and warriors tumbling into space has attacked a Martian city.	Gol Phan, an apprentice to Ras Thavas, secretly discovers a narcotic means of transferring a subject's consciousness into another's body. Over the next few days there are reports of young Martian women being seduced by previously respectable nobles and officers. Family feuds erupt, duels are fought, and Helium's upper classes reel from a series of scandals. Enlisted as independent adjudicators, the heroes are called in to investigate.	A red Martian expedition to a dead city unearths an immense armored juggernaut half-buried in a sand-filled dock. The machine resorts to its original programming to harvest any biological matter found in Mars' ancient oceans. It thunders over the dead sea bottoms, consuming all in its way. Helium's scholars suggest that only the technical knowledge in Orovar can stop it.	A scientist working for an enemy jed or jeddak discovers a way of growing duplicates from the biological patterns of living beings. He kidnaps members of Helium's court and replaces them with changelings loyal only to him.	Kor San, an exiled Gatholian scientist, has tapped the vast potential of the ninth ray to open a portal to Sasoom. The Skeleton Men of Jupiter seize the opportunity to establish a beachhead on Mars. If Barsoom is to survive, the portal must be sealed at any cost.
06-10 Vanthek, a noble red Martian scientist stricken by grief at the loss his princess, develops a machine that gives physical form to powerful memories. Not all the embodied memories are welcome, however, and when the eidolons created rampage through his palace, they take the machine for themselves. Can the heroes stop the eidolon insurgency before old scores are settled and old hatreds rekindled?	Whilst working on a potion to help cure sleeplessness, Arran Tel, a young scientist, stumbles on a compound that allows modern day Martians to 'dream' their way into the past and inhabit the bodies of those who live there. Arran Tel is betrothed to a princess, so, when he is found comatose, the heroes are requested to find the cause. They must swallow the formula and follow the young man through the gates of dream and into the labyrinth of the past.	Scientists working for the Guild of Assassins have secretly perfected a 'cloak of silence', a mechanically generated field that deadens all sound. When nobles are tortured and murdered without anyone hearing their screams, the heroes are asked to investigate.	A group of panthans in plain armor open fire on a red Martian patrol. Initially, they experience no ill effects beyond temporary paralysis. Later, their bodies begin to decay. The dreadful canker spreads quickly beyond the initial victims. Faced with the possibility of a widespread plague, the local jed or jeddak dispatches the heroes to discover the dark secret of what is dubbed 'the canker rifle'.	The radium pumps of the great atmosphere plant are failing as their power is syphoned wirelessly by an unknown force. While Barsoom faces extinction, the heroes must race to discover the truth and expose Kalak, a yellow Martian scientist drawing Barsoom's energy into a vast accumulator to power an interplanetary ship capable of travelling to Cosoom (Venus).
11-15 When a red Martian military flier is discovered shattered on one of Barsoom's dead sea bottoms, there seems no obvious answer to the mystery. Then, when the survivor of a second vessel reports how his ship was frozen out of the sky, the hunt begins for an unmarked airship bearing what becomes known as an 'ice cannon'. Who wields the dreadful weapon? And what is their purpose?	Martian warriors pride themselves on their courage, so, when a small party of skirmishers routs a superior force, the heroes are sent to investigate. The only clue to the warriors' ignominious defeat is that they are all suffering from an unknown fever contracted from contaminated water. It seems that an enemy scientist has discovered a virus capable of inducing cowardice. Where might he strike next? And at what magnitude?	Mon Tar, a Zodangan engineer working on amplifying Martian telepathy, constructs a helmet through which he can manipulate the minds of those around him. He decides that it is time for Zodanga to reap its revenge on conceited Helium.	Someone has recovered part of the ancient wisdom of Lee Um Lo and raised an army of the dead. They shamble across Barsoom: red, green, yellow, and black Martians marching side by side, upheld and driven on by an unknown power. Any military contact only swells their numbers. The heroes must discover who is controlling the dead, and why.	Fal Sivas has constructed new interplanetary vessels to return to Thuria. He is recruiting brave panthans to form a legion of shock troops to vanquish the Tarids and Masenas and take the wealth of Barsoom's largest moon for himself. John Carter wants him found and stopped.
16-20 A red Martian scientist researching the untapped potential of the eighth ray discovers a means of generating a body-shield that will deflect a blade and repel a radium bullet. Realizing he has discovered a means of revolutionizing warfare on Barsoom, he seeks out the highest bidder. Helium's spies learn of the secret auction and the heroes are sent to abduct the scientist and secure his invention. Events do not go according to plan.	Polan Gee, the shadowy vivisectionist of Toonol, has distilled a chemical capable of simulating death. He has used it to feign the passing of Alara Nia, a Ptarthian princess, whom he desires. When Alara Nia's body vanishes, her parents ask the heroes for help, voicing their suspicions about Polan Gee. After tracing the wily vivisectionist to Toonol, they find him dead, and no sign of Alara Nia. Hours later, Polan Gee's body also disappears.	'The Long Ear' is a miraculous listening device invented by Sonal Tey. It enables the operator to eavesdrop on conversations conducted at whatever planetary coordinates are inputted into the machine. When Sonal Tey overhears a plot to kill the warlord, he informs John Carter, who sends the heroes to uncover the conspiracy and expose the plotters.	A red Martian scientist researching the untapped potential of the eighth ray discovers a means of generating a body-shield that will deflect a blade and repel a radium bullet. Realizing he has discovered a means of revolutionizing warfare on Barsoom, he seeks out the highest bidder. Helium's spies learn of the secret auction and the heroes are sent to abduct the scientist and secure his invention. Events do not go according to plan.	When Barsoom's first great airship left Helium, it was hailed as a triumph of Martian ingenuity. Tragedy struck almost immediately, however, as the vessel's over-charged ray tanks carried it into space with the loss of all hands. For nine centuries, the Lansor has orbited Barsoom, its crew held in the cold fist of space. No longer. Pandar Lorn, Ptarth's accomplished aeronautical engineer, has constructed a space vessel capable of reaching the Lansor and returning the bodies of the dead to their families. All he requires is a crew brave enough to risk everything for the rewards of the bereaved, but there are some who wish the dead to remain undisturbed, especially those few crewmen who avoided the disaster and have lived 900 years under false identities.

CHAPTER 15: CHAMPIONS OF BARSOOM

> *I do not believe that I am made of the stuff which constitutes heroes, because, in all of the hundreds of instances that my voluntary acts have placed me face to face with death, I cannot recall a single one where any alternative step to that I took occurred to me until many hours later.*
>
> – John Carter, *A Princess of Mars*

John Carter features a number of powerful or influential individuals that were featured in numerous stories and tales from around Barsoom; some of which helped shape the fate of the planet itself. When roleplaying in their world, characters will occasionally come into contact with these icons and have a chance to interact with them.

The characters presented in this chapter are portrayed in their adventuring prime. Narrators wishing to represent more, or less, experienced versions of these characters may wish to alter their talents or attributes. Aside from a few exceptions, no core equipment or accolades are provided — these are generally player character mechanics. Narrator characters instead typically possess the equipment and resources demanded by circumstance and plot

The characters are broken down into the three different eras of play.

* **Dotar Sojat era:** These are the characters from when John Carter has just arrived upon Barsoom through to when he becomes a prince of Helium and husband to Dejah Thoris.

* **Prince of Helium era:** These are the characters that stem from the "Prince of Helium" era of play. They will either not be present in the Dotar Sojat era or less experienced than presented in this chapter.

* **Jeddaks of Jeddaks era:** These are the characters that stem from the "Jeddak of Jeddaks" era of play.

CUSTOMIZING CHAMPIONS

The characters here may seem light on the number of talents they possess compared to player characters. Many powerful or influential characters possess only one or two talents, though in some cases these individual talents are very potent. Still, many characters in this chapter lack the multiple talents common to many starting player characters.

This isn't an accident.

John Carter of Mars is about the heroism and adventures of the player heroes, not narrator characters. Narrator characters are important and must be able to challenge player characters and meet expectations based on their backgrounds and history, but they are not the starts of a campaign. That spotlight belongs to the player characters.

Thus, the statistics for the characters in this chapter, especially their talents, are designed to represent abilities that help them match the actions they perform in the Barsoom novels. They have considerable power but will not be overwhelming narrators with numerous talents to track or roll over player characters whenever they show up. Despite the title of this game, this even holds for Carter himself—he is a valiant champion and famous hero, but the focus of play in most campaigns will not be about him.

If your game involves Carter, Tars, and other narrator characters charging in and showing up the player heroes, consider scaling back their abilities and involvement.

Likewise, if you feel these characters need additional talents or higher attributes to properly reflect their abilities in the novels or so they can properly challenge experienced or powerful player characters, feel free to make any changes you see fit to the entries provided here.

If the players would like to use John Carter and other characters as their own, narrators and players should use the statistics here as a guide, but should feel free to alter and customize their abilities, especially their talent list. They will also need flaws, renown, accolades, and core equipment. In many cases these are obvious: Dejah Thoris is a princess of Helium with strong allies among her family and clearly has some sort of flaw that causes her to often be separated from her companions or targeted for abduction, while Carthoris has strong connections to his parents and grandparents, is a prince of Helium, and is rarely without his sword or personal flier.

DOTAR SOJAT ERA

DEJAH THORIS

A PRINCESS OF MARS

"Nothing that can harm me outside my pride. They know that I am the daughter of ten thousand jeddaks, that I trace my ancestry straight back without a break to the builder of the first great waterway…"

ATTRIBUTES

DARING	CUNNING	EMPATHY
4	5	8

MIGHT	PASSION	REASON
4	9	6

TALENTS

INSPIRES GREATNESS (GRADE 5)

You inspire others to greatness and will be a great leader of your people if given the opportunity.

✴ **Circumstance:** Must have completed a great feat of bravery, daring or passion.

✴ **Effect:** Once per scene, you can spend 1 Momentum per individual to mark a character as her follower or champion. This must be a character who loves or respects her. These characters gain a bonus d20 when following your commands or acting to defend you. They may also take one affliction meant for you.

PROACTIVE ORATOR (GRADE 2)

When you speak, others are inspired to action.

✴ **Circumstance:** If allowed to speak before a conflict.

✴ **Effect:** You can always go first in a conflict where you are allowed to speak before it begins. You may pass this ability to go first to an ally instead by spending 1 Momentum.

PROUD DAUGHTER OF MARS (GRADE 3)

A daughter of great rulers and possessing great passion and fierce pride, you can move with certainty and purpose when necessary.

✴ **Circumstance:** Her first action in a conflict.

✴ **Effect:** Your first action in a conflict, regardless of its nature, can be performed using **Empathy + Passion** and gains a bonus d20.

KNOWN ACROSS BARSOOM (GRADE 2)

Your travels far and wide, and your grace, beauty, and status as Princess of Helium, are well known across the Red Planet.

✴ **Circumstance:** When dealing with a new group or individual.

✴ **Effect:** Make a **Reason + Passion** (D2) test. With a success and for every 2 Momentum, you can declare a fact that they have heard about you or your companions. You also gain a bonus Momentum when seeking to gain information about the new group or individual you meet.

BACKGROUND

Dejah Thoris. Noble of Helium. Princess of Mars. Few figures in the history of Barsoom are as important or dynamic as the granddaughter of Tardos Mors and daughter of Mors Kajak. A skilled scientist and stateswoman, Dejah is extremely active in diplomatic and scientific missions for her kingdom before fate brings her into the life, and eventually the arms, of her husband, John Carter.

Dejah met Carter while both are captives of the Tharks. Carter's ignorance of Barsoomian culture causes early rifts and misunderstandings between the two, but eventually the Virginian's passion and Dejah's empathy for the outsider win out and a romance blossoms between them. Carter and Dejah's relationship is one of constant challenge and struggle, as the two are regularly separated by duty and calamity alike. However, through it all, theirs remains one of the great love stories of Barsoom and beyond.

Dejah Thoris in the Prince of Helium Era

By the time Dejah and Carter are married, she has joined him on numerous adventures. When she believes Carter dead for a time, she mourns him deeply and concentrates on her noble duties and raising their son, Carthoris. When Carthoris is thought dead as well, she seeks the Valley Dor and land of Iss, instead becoming a slave of the crone-goddess Issus. Eventually she finds freedom with the help of her loved ones and family and is reunited with her beloved Carter, returning to her noble station.

Dejah Thoris in the Jeddak of Jeddaks Era

In later years, Dejah's time is split between her family and duties as Princess of Helium. Due to her value as a political captive and hostage, Dejah is often the subject of various plots to abduct her so that her would-be captors can use her to exert influence on the great state of Helium. These plots are in addition to the challenges of normal matters of state on Barsoom, which includes fragile alliances and constant threat of war.

Dejah is a keen stateswoman and experienced scientist who is beloved by the people of Helium for her personal charisma and strength of character. Latest in a line of great warlords and leaders, she is fiercely independent and possesses an indomitable spirit. Though she favored scientific and political training over military arts, like all red Martians Dejah learned from birth to fight for survival and in self-defense.

John Carter

WARLORD OF MARS

"Possibly I am a hundred, possibly more; but I cannot tell because I have never aged as other men, nor do I remember any childhood. So far as I can recollect I have always been a man, a man of about thirty."

ATTRIBUTES

DARING	CUNNING	EMPATHY
7	7	4

MIGHT	PASSION	REASON
9	6	4

TALENTS

LEGENDARY HERO (GRADE 5)
You faced countless challenges on Barsoom and triumphed through courage, will, and force of arms.
- ✳ **Circumstance:** In a duel or when facing six or more opponents.
- ✳ **Effect:** You can instantly fill your Momentum pool to its limit as your first Conflict action.

EARTHBORN STRENGTH (GRADE 3)
You are tenacious and your Earthborn strength and years of experience give you a substantial edge in battle.
- ✳ **Circumstance:** In melee combat.
- ✳ **Effect:** You can always use Might for attack and defense and it does an additional 1 🎲 of damage with attacks.

GENTLEMAN OF VIRGINIA (GRADE 3)
Despite sometimes missing social cues and misreading the emotions of others, your compassion and honesty eventually win you many friends and allies.
- ✳ **Circumstance:** When dealing fairly and openly with others.
- ✳ **Effect:** Roll 2 bonus d20s on tests to gain the trust of others by being open, honest, compassionate, and helpful. This works on beasts as well, provided you have treated them kindly.

LEAPS AND BOUNDS (GRADE 2)
Your Earthborn muscles allow you leap great distances and perform great feats of strength.
- ✳ **Circumstance:** When moving on Barsoom and planets with similar gravity.
- ✳ **Effect:** You may close one range category automatically, ignoring any obstacles or intervening terrain as long as you have clearance and space to leap between your starting point and destination. You may spend 1 Momentum to move an additional range category.

BATTLE VALOR (GRADE 1)
You are a true warrior and steadfast soldier at home in the chaos and carnage of war, always willing to meet your fate with sword and pistol in hand.
- ✳ **Circumstance:** When suffering Fear damage in combat.
- ✳ **Effect:** You may ignore the first 2 points of damage to your Fear stress track taken during combat. You suffer Fear damage after this during a combat scene or from other situations normally.

BACKGROUND

Captain Jack Carter of Virginia, the first Earthman to reach Mars, is the single most legendary hero and, arguably, the most successful warlord Barsoom ever knows. He was a successful soldier in the American Civil War for the state of Virginia. While on a gold-hunting expedition in the desert with his friend Powell, they are attacked by Apache warriors. In spite of a brave defense, Powell is gravely wounded and the pair take shelter in a mysterious cave. Powell dies from his injuries, but Carter finds himself completely paralyzed by an unknown means and unable to move. By force of will he breaks free, but finds that he has left his body behind. He emerges from the strange cavern and gazes into the desert night sky. His eye falls upon a single red dot – the planet Mars. Mars draws him forward, pulling him from Earth, and swallows him up. In mere moments, he is there, standing in the Barsoomian desert, as alive and vital as he had been on Earth before entering the cave.

After arriving, John Carter discovers the difference in Martian gravity grants him increased strength and agility unlike any other on the planet. He finds his way to a small construct, which he later learns is an incubator for hatching the eggs of the green Martian people. Soon, he is captured by a patrol of green Martians sent to check on the eggs. The Tharks, as this tribe is called, are impressed with his physical abilities and take him back to their camp. Among the green Martian Tharks he learns the collective language of the planet, develops Martian telepathic abilities, and gains the trust of Sola, his minder, and Tars Tarkas, a fierce green Martian warrior. Woola, a multi-legged, dog-like beast, imprints upon John Carter, and Woola's insurmountable speed and loyalty will save Carter many times over. During his time with the green Martians, a fleet of passing airships is attacked, and John Carter's future bride, the red Martian Princess Dejah Thoris of Helium, is captured. Along with his new love and his close green Martian friend Sola, Carter leaves his first Barsoomian family and begins a long and sordid career of adventure, excitement, and world-changing events.

During a stretch of time under the thumbs of the Warhoon, a rival green Martian tribe, John meets and battles both against and with his soon to be lifelong friend, Kantos Kan. The two of them share many adventures together, crossing blades with Martians of all colors and metals.

John helps to see the coronation of his green Martian ally Tars Tarkas to Jeddak of Thark, interrupts the forced nuptials of his love and the savage Sab Than of Zodanga, and elevates the city-state of Helium to the highest esteem of Barsoom. He becomes the Dotar Sojat, a warlord amongst green Martians and a recognized Barsoom hero.

SOLA

UNIQUE AMONGST GREEN MARTIANS

"My fair companion was about eight feet tall, having just arrived at maturity, but not yet to her full height. She was of a light olive-green color, with a smooth, glossy hide. Her name, as I afterward learned, was Sola, and she belonged to the retinue of Tars Tarkas."

ATTRIBUTES

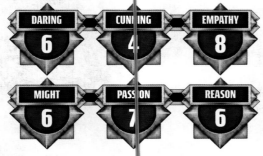

DARING	CUNNING	EMPATHY
6	4	8

MIGHT	PASSION	REASON
6	7	6

TALENTS

FOUR-ARMED FOR WAR (GRADE 1)

Your warlike, combative culture and four arms give you an edge in combat, allowing you to attack with multiple weapons or steady your rifle with ease.

✳ **Circumstance:** When attacking with melee weapons or using a rifle.

✳ **Effect:** When you generate Momentum while attacking with a melee weapon or rifle, gain an extra Momentum.

STRENGTH OF COMPASSION (GRADE 3)

When acting to protect someone in your charge, your heart guides you.

✳ **Circumstance:** Protecting someone else.

✳ **Effect:** When acting to protect or help a loved one or someone in your charge, you gain a bonus d20 on all relevant actions and you can always use Passion and/or Empathy as part of the test. This talent doesn't allow for attacks, but can be used if defending on behalf of another.

WOMAN OF THARK (GRADE 1)

You are trained to maintain and make weapons, forage food, and otherwise see to the survival of yourself and any in your charge.

✳ **Circumstance:** Using survival skills.

✳ **Effect:** You gain on additional Momentum from any successful test that involves survival skills (creating weapons, finding food, etc.).

SOLA IN THE PRINCE OF HELIUM ERA

Sola maintains a devoted friendship with Dejah Thoris and goes with her on the penultimate pilgrimage to Dor. They are both captured by First Born, but her green Martian size and power proves to be problematic for the pirates, who throw her overboard. She survives the fall through luck and tenacity, but it is one of the last times she decides to adventure away from Thark.

BACKGROUND

John Carter's first real "friend" amongst the green Martians of Thark, Sola is different than all other green Martians and has been so since the first moments of her life. Unlike most green Martians, her mother Gozava kept her egg and hatched her personally, in secret, instead of taking her to the tribal leaders for judgment and group incubation. Once hatched, her mother mixed her in with the newly hatched children recently arrived from incubation. A rival named Sarkoja sees her buck against green Martian tradition and tries to have her punished by the jeddak at the time, but Gozava convinces the leaders that she has destroyed her egg and that Sarkoja is mistaken.

Even though she was only in maternal contact with Gozava for a few days before being deposited in the incubated hatchlings, Sola soaks up something that nearly all green Martians go their lifetime without feeling — honest emotions toward friends and family. This connective empathy with others is what links her to John Carter.

Sola is assigned to the Earthman after Tars Tarkas brings him back from the wastes, helping him learn the language of Mars, survive the harsh conditions of his early captivity, and eventually aiding him and his future bride Dejah Thoris time and time again. Her unique ability to care about others and feel for their plights, combined with her green Martian strength, size and ferocity, makes Sola a fantastic ally to have in the commonplace Barsoomian conflicts.

It is revealed that Sola is the blood daughter of Tars Tarkas himself, and their relationship comes to mean a great deal to both father and daughter afterwards. Sola becomes the first "Princess of Thark", and her father, the Jeddak, becomes known as the first green Martian patriarch to actually care for its offspring.

MORS KAJAK

FAMED JED OF HELIUM

"I look out upon these people and see my brothers, sons, sisters and daughters.
I see the future of Helium in their faces, and the future of Barsoom."

ATTRIBUTES

DARING 5	**CUNNING** 6	**EMPATHY** 6
MIGHT 5	**PASSION** 7	**REASON** 7

TALENTS

LEADER'S EYE (GRADE 1)
You are a keen judge of character and ability.

✳ **Circumstance:** When analyzing individuals and groups for their capabilities.

✳ **Effect:** When using Momentum to gain information about a group or individuals skills, capabilities, and battle prowess you gain an additional Momentum to use.

LOYAL BODYGUARDS (GRADE 1)
You inspire fanatic loyalty in your guards and subordinates.

✳ **Circumstance:** When an attack inflicts an affliction.

✳ **Effect:** As long as a bodyguard or loyal subordinate is within Near range of you, you may pass an affliction you just took onto them as they sacrifice themselves to save you. This must be a time tested companion and not just an narrator character aligned to your cause.

PASSIONATE COMMANDER (GRADE 2)
You lead from the front and let your heart guide your troops and your sword.

✳ **Circumstance:** When leading troops or other followers.

✳ **Effect:** You may always use Passion with actions relating to fighting at the front of your troops or commanding them in battle. You may reroll any one d20 on such tests, taking whichever result you prefer.

BACKGROUND

The father of Dejah Thoris and the titled Jed of Helium (Lesser), Mors Kajak is a strong link in what becomes the Carter family chain on Barsoom. His father, Jeddak Tardos Mors, is the first listed patriarch of their line and the topmost ruler of Helium throughout the early history of the territory and passes that right on to the son. Mors is a qualified and well-liked leader of his people, and a good example of even-headed red Martian nobility.

MORS KAJAK IN THE PRINCE OF HELIUM ERA

Mors Kajak is happy that his daughter married John Carter and spends much of his later years supporting not only their union, but also his spreading family tree when they have children, and eventually grandchildren. So involved Mors becomes in the success of his family line, that he personally takes out his fleet to search for his missing grandson, Carthoris, and is captured by the yellow Martians of Okar — only to be rescued and freed by John Carter soon after. If ever he questioned his daughter's reasoning for marrying the Earthman, those thoughts are dispelled.

SALENSUS OLL
VILLAINOUS JEDDAK OF OKAR

"The only thing more dangerous than the great apes of Barsoom is that yellow Man that controls them."

ATTRIBUTES

DARING	CUNNING	EMPATHY
6	7	3

MIGHT	PASSION	REASON
7	6	6

TALENTS

RUTHLESS FEROCITY (GRADE 7)
You were born to cause pain and suffering and do it better than most anyone else.

* **Circumstance:** When inflicting your first affliction in a scene.

* **Effect:** Instantly cause a second affliction of the same type to the same target.

TAKE WHAT IS YOURS (GRADE 4)
While your men fight off your opponents, you are best at running off with the prize.

* **Circumstance:** When you have seized what you consider a worthy prize.

* **Effect:** Once per session at the end of a round you can choose to leave a scene immediately with your prize — a captured princess, a rare artefact, an enemy's prized possession, etc. If your opponents manage to find a way to locate or pursue you, this begins a new scene.

BRING THEM TO THEIR KNEES (GRADE 2)
Few things in life give you pleasure more than causing suffering.

* **Circumstance:** With actions that will cause someone or something harm.

* **Effect:** You can always use Might for actions that will cause harm. Note that harm doesn't necessarily mean causing damage, though such actions would qualify for this talent.

BACKGROUND

Salensus Oll is the great Jeddak of the yellow Martian territory of Okar, a massive and savage creature that dominates his subordinates with raw power, machinations, and fear. He manages a prolific fighting arena, keeps beasts of all types, and is known for his successful handling of Barsoomian apes. He is a mighty warrior, but only gets his own hands dirty in special instances that require a personal touch.

SALENSUS OLL IN THE PRINCE OF HELIUM ERA

Always covetous of Dejah Thoris, Salensus Oll captures the princess of Helium and brings her to Okar. As airship cavalry come to rescue her, he activates a powerful electromagnet weapon that brings the vessels crashing to the ground where the yellow Men and his beasts can easily overtake them. Among these captives is John Carter's own father-in-law, Mors Kajak. John then takes it upon himself to rescue them. He rounds up his close allies and goes to Okar to provide succor to the people of Helium. In the end, Salensus dies unceremoniously upon John Carter's blade never having learned not to meddle in the affairs of the Dotar Sojat.

TARDOS MORS

LEGENDARY JEDDAK OF HELIUM

"Never before has there been a more powerful Jeddak amongst reds, and his name will go down in history."

ATTRIBUTES

DARING	CUNNING	EMPATHY
7	6	5

MIGHT	PASSION	REASON
6	7	6

TALENTS

BORN LEADER (GRADE 3)

There is little than can get you down and you are considered one of the most respected rulers on Barsoom.

✳ **Circumstance:** In social interactions and conflicts.

✳ **Effect:** When commanding your troops or leading them into conflict, you may always use Passion for any attacks or other related non-defend actions. In addition, you gain 1 bonus Momentum on any social interaction with red Martians.

THE POWER THAT MADE THE THRONE (GRADE 4)

Helium did not rise to its strength on the back of a weak leader.

✳ **Circumstance:** When facing personal or political enemies.

✳ **Effect:** Increase Momentum gains from actions involving facing down enemies or rivals, personal or political, by 1. This talent covers both social and physical conflicts.

BONDS STRONGER THAN IRON (GRADE 2)

Your loyalty to your family and friends is unwavering.

✳ **Circumstance:** When defending family members and close allies.

✳ **Effect:** When taking an action in defense of your family or close allies, you may reroll any failed die in a test, keeping the better result. You may only reroll the dice once and cannot reroll dice that generated any successes, only those which failed completely.

BACKGROUND

The Jeddak of Helium when John Carter came to Mars, Tardos Mors is the father of Jed Mors Kajak and grandfather of Dejah Thoris. Under his rule, Helium rises to become a Barsoomian power to rival any other, and red Martians all over the planet know of his name and accomplishments. Somewhat of a traditionalist, Tardos learns flexibility and acceptance of others from the successes of the Earthman John Carter. If it were not for the presence and actions of his eventual grandson-in-law, Helium might not have ascended quite like it has.

Tardos Mors is among the most jovial of celebrants during the victory gala after the defeat of Zodanga, which shows his patriotism for Helium to be honest and true. Proving to be a true hero for Helium, Tardos gladly appears at his granddaughter's wedding to John Carter and shows his support of the union. In a unique instance of Barsoomian solidarity, it is Tardos that sees past centuries of violence to extend an alliance to the green Martians of Thark — the first of its kind in history.

TARS TARKAS

JEDDAK OF THARK

"He sat his mount as we sit a horse, grasping the animal's barrel with his lower limbs, while the hands of his two right arms held his immense spear low at the side of his mount,"

ATTRIBUTES

DARING	CUNNING	EMPATHY
6	8	4

MIGHT	PASSION	REASON
8	6	5

TALENTS

SUFFER THE COWARDS (GRADE 5)

You do not tolerate cowardice and happily deliver punishment to those who act without bravery or integrity.

✴ **Circumstance:** When attacking a fleeing or cowardly foe.

✴ **Effect:** When an enemy displays great cowardice and you attack them, any 🎲 from this attack are doubled.

LEADS WITH STRENGTH (GRADE 3)

When leading Tharks or other green Martians, your strength and unwavering resolve guides them.

✴ **Circumstance:** When leading green Martians

✴ **Effect:** You may always use Might and Daring in tests involving leading or directing green Martian characters. You also gain a bonus d20 to roll on any such tests. This includes challenges to your leadership.

TRUE FRIENDSHIP (GRADE 1)

Long standing friends know each other well, so well that fighting side by side comes naturally and makes you both more effective.

✴ **Circumstance:** When fighting alongside others.

✴ **Effect:** When fighting alongside someone you consider a close friend, you are always considered to be helping them, granting them 1 bonus d20 to all actions in conflict.

FOUR-ARMED FOR WAR (GRADE 1)

Your warlike, combative culture and four arms give you an edge in combat, allowing you to attack with multiple weapons or steady your rifle with ease.

✴ **Circumstance:** When attacking with melee weapons or using a rifle.

✴ **Effect:** When you generate Momentum while attacking with a melee weapon or rifle, gain an extra Momentum.

BACKGROUND

Tars Tarkas is the powerful green Martian warlord, would-be Jeddak of Thark, egg-proven father of Sola, and brother-in-arms with the Dotar Sojat, John Carter. His life makes him cruel and savage, but he has a spark of inspiration within him that makes the green Martians of Thark into more than just tribal brutes.

Although he grew up as a bloodthirsty warrior under the harsh rule of Jeddak Tal Hajus, Tars Tarkas softens inside when he meets a female green Martian named Gozava. This Thark woman teaches him through conversation, and physical and telepathic contact, that their society can be more than it is; the heartless cruelty of their people can be set aside to find strength in caring for one another instead. Tars Tarkas is never the same after her influence upon him, he falls in love with Gozava and maintains a secret relationship with her without his jeddak knowing. They even manage to have an egg together long enough for the hatchling, Sola, to have their empathy imprinted upon her as well. Their love is secret, but within it they find great strength — and tragedy. After Gozava places their hatchling with the others, a rival female named Sarkoja turns her in to Tal Hajus, who has her imprisoned, tortured, and eventually killed. Her death sets Tars Tarkas on a hate-filled quest to see

Tal Hajus dead on his metal to avenge his beloved.

Tars Tarkas is the first green Martian John Carter ever interacts with. He first learns about the Earthman's ability to leap, his impressive agility, and eventually his soldier's instinct and powerful strength. While they first travel together, Tars and John capture the beautiful Dejah Thoris from a fallen airship; thus begins their long adventurous life together.

From John Carter's inspirational speech within the arena of Thark, the green Martians are convinced that Tars Tarkas will be a greater jeddak than Tal Hajus and incite the two mighty warriors to battle for the role. Tars Tarkas, fueled by the love for his fallen wife and recently revealed daughter Sola, defeats him easily and takes the mantle of Jeddak of Thark.

Once in power of Thark, Tars Tarkas joins Carter in marching on Zodanga to help him rescue Dejah Thoris. He gathers several tribes of green Martians under his metal and helps bring about the fall of the rogue red Martian territory, turning then to help Helium with the army sieging their walls. It is Tars Tarkas' help in this historic time that helps forge the first alliance between Helium and Thark ever known on Barsoom.

TARS TARKAS IN THE PRINCE OF HELIUM ERA

For nearly ten years Tars Tarkas maintains his side of the peace between Thark and Helium, with visits from John Carter and his new bride Dejah Thoris keeping their friendship strong. When the Barsoomian atmosphere plant generator stops functioning and Martians everywhere began to succumb to unconsciousness, Tars Tarkas is among the last to fall and first to awake after the threat passes — finding his Earthman friend missing from Barsoom. The chaos that follows makes the alliance harder to maintain, and by the time John returns many years later, old tensions are high again.

THE JEDDAK OF JEDDAKS ERA

Spending much of his time keeping his leadership among the Tharks and maintaining their relations with Helium and other allied states, Tars still spends a portion of his time beside his best friend and companion, John Carter. It is the unwavering support of Tars and his people that helps cement Carter's elevated status among the alliance they helped build and the friendship between the transplanted Virginian gentleman and green Martian warlord is the stuff of modern legend on contemporary Barsoom.

Tars Tarkas, like all green Martians, is a mighty warrior skilled with gun, sword, and spear who can fell his foes with ease. The ability to set aside hate and the instinct to kill in order to make friends and understand the need for allies helps make him the most famous and successful Jeddak of Thark ever known to Barsoom.

CARTHORIS

PRINCE OF HELIUM; SON OF LEGENDS

"There was much of his mother's incomparable beauty in his clear-cut features, but it was strongly masculine beauty, and his grey eyes and the expression of them were mine."

ATTRIBUTES

DARING	CUNNING	EMPATHY
6	7	5

MIGHT	PASSION	REASON
7	6	6

TALENTS

LEGENDARY HERO (GRADE 5)
You inherited your father's ferocity in battle.

✴ **Circumstance:** In a duel or when facing six or more opponents.

✴ **Effect:** You can instantly fill your Momentum pool to its limit as your first Conflict action.

LEAPS AND BOUNDS (GRADE 2)
Your Earthborn heritage allow you leap great distances and perform amazing feats on Barsoom.

✴ **Circumstance:** When moving on Barsoom and planets with similar gravity.

✴ **Effect:** You may close one range category automatically, ignoring any obstacles or intervening terrain as long as you have clearance and space to leap between your starting point and destination. You may spend 1 Momentum to move an additional range category.

ADVENTURE'S CALL (GRADE 2)
Your heart calls you to adventure.

✴ **Circumstance:** When avoiding dangers in a new location.

✴ **Effect:** When exploring an unknown place or making a new discovery, you may always use Daring in tests to avoid dangers and can reduce all difficulties by 1 (to a minimum of 1).

BACKGROUND

Born from Dejah Thoris' egg fertilized by John Carter himself, Carthoris — whose singular name comes from both parents' surnames — grows up in Martian society without the influence of his true father until well into adulthood. He is gifted with John's Earth-spawned agility, some of his strength, and all the greatest parts of being a red Martian. A skilled swordsman and pilot, Carthoris sets out on an expedition into the Omean Sea early in life — and was captured by the malicious First Born.

Imprisoned since his capture, Carthoris is allowed out of his bonds to do battle for the First Borns' amusement. It is during this long pattern of arena battle after arena battle that Carthoris is first introduced to his father, John Carter. With the help of the First Born pirate Xodar, the trio escape and return to Helium.

CARTHORIS IN THE PRINCE OF HELIUM ERA

Shortly after, Carthoris and his father embark on several adventures together. They mount rescues, engage in daring assaults on enemy territories, and put many enemies of peace on Barsoom to the blade. Despite such a rocky childhood without him, Carthoris' adult life becomes just as much of a legend as his father's, once they were reunited. During this time, Carthoris falls in love with Thuvia of Ptarth and undergoes a great adventure to win her love and free her from a despised political marriage.

HIN ABTOL

JED OF PANAR

"Hin Abtol laughed. 'Hin Abtol,' he said, 'chooses his wives — they have nothing to say about it."

ATTRIBUTES

DARING	CUNNING	EMPATHY
5	6	5

MIGHT	PASSION	REASON
4	9	8

TALENTS

BLOODY-MINDED LEADER (GRADE 5)

You have spent years commanding your armies to serve your fanatic desires and violent whims.

- ✳ **Circumstance:** When commanding or leading your troops.

- ✳ **Effect:** When commanding your troops or leading them into conflict, you may always use Passion for any attacks or other related non-defend actions. In addition, you may sacrifice any guard or troop loyal to you within Near range to avoid taking an affliction. Your follower blacks out and is likely dead or dying if a minion, but you avoid the affliction.

EYES ON THE PRIZE (GRADE 8)

When you give a command or set a goal, you will see it done no matter the costs.

- ✳ **Circumstance:** When choosing a goal or target.

- ✳ **Effect:** When you first appear in a session, set a target to be captured or taken over. This may be a character or a location. Any action that turn, by you or your followers, that directly advances this goal gains 1 additional Momentum on any successful action.

BACKGROUND

The self-styled Jeddak of Jeddaks in the North, Hin Abtol is a power-hungry would be conqueror from the Panar territory. Over the many years of his rule, this red Martian warlord accumulates a massive army of more than a million soldiers, but his state is so poor and lacking in resources that he keeps the majority of them in a cryogenic frozen state until he needs to make a show of force.

From within his capitol city of Pankor, Hin Abtol mounts several offensives against the other people of Barsoom. His most noted campaign sees him capture his desired Llana, a declaration of war on the city-state of Gathol, and one that sets him directly against John Carter. The result of warring against Carter ends in much the same way as the attempts of others — with Hin Abtol in chains and his army in disarray.

HOR VASTUS

TRUSTED NAVAL OFFICER OF HELIUM

"'That you are back is sufficient, and let Hor Vastus' sword have the high honor of being first at thy feet.'"

ATTRIBUTES

DARING	CUNNING	EMPATHY
7	7	5

MIGHT	PASSION	REASON
5	6	6

TALENTS

DARING STRATEGIST (GRADE 3)

You are a skilled strategist who knows the capabilities of your crew and ships like your own arm.

- ✳ **Circumstance:** When commanding troops or making battle plans.

- ✳ **Effect:** You may always use Daring when making battle plans or strategies. Any difficulties for such tests are reduced by 1

CUNNING COMPANION (GRADE 2)

Your support of your friends and superiors often helps carry the day.

- ✳ **Circumstance:** When acting to support an ally.

- ✳ **Effect:** When performing actions involving understanding, convincing, or aiding your friends or superiors you may always use Cunning. Further, once per scene you may take an action to make a **Cunning** + **Daring** Challenging (D2) test. If successful, give a friend or superior a Momentum. You may give additional Momentum earned in this test to your friends and superiors as well, or you may spend 2 Momentum from this roll to reduce the Threat pool by 1.

BACKGROUND

Padwar in the great navy of Helium, Hor Vastus is a trusted friend to Dejah Thoris, Xodar, and John Carter. He is the honored pilot and commander of an airship sent to fetch the royal cadre from their wanderings of the Valley Dor, and pledges his metal to Carter (and his son, Carthoris) for the battles to come.

When the battle is brought to the First Born, Hor Vastus and his incredible martial prowess are integral. Knowing how military warships function inside and out, he knows the best crews to choose and the finest vessels to appoint them to. Although Carter and his inner circle of heroes are in the limelight in the conflict, Hor Vastus' naval force make sure they have the room and ability to do so.

ISSUS

DAUGHTER OF THE LESSER MOON, MOTHER OF THE NEARER MOON, GODDESS OF DEATH

"Not a hair remained upon her wrinkled skull. With the exception of two yellow fangs she was entirely toothless. On either side of a thin, hawk-like nose her eyes burned from the depths of horribly sunken sockets. The skin of her face was seamed and creased with a million deep cut furrows. Her body was as wrinkled as her face, and as repulsive."

ATTRIBUTES

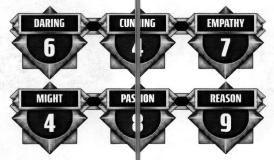

DARING	CUNNING	EMPATHY
6	4	7

MIGHT	PASSION	REASON
4	8	9

TALENTS

MASTER MANIPULATOR (GRADE 2)
You are ancient, evil, and brilliant. Manipulating others is like breathing to you.

✳ **Circumstance:** When manipulating others.

✳ **Effect:** When manipulating, threatening, or otherwise coercing them to action, you may always use Reason and Passion.

LIVING GODDESS (GRADE 4)
You are a goddess in the flesh, a source of awe.

✳ **Circumstance:** In nonphysical conflicts.

✳ **Effect:** In nonphysical conflicts with others, you do 2 additional ⚅ of damage. Also, any effects rolled on your combat dice do an additional point of Fear damage.

I STILL LIVE (GRADE 5)
You are eternal and you will never be brought down by mere mortals.

✳ **Circumstance:** In nonphysical conflicts.

✳ **Effect:** Spend 3 Momentum. You escape the scene through some secret passage, the sacrifice of loyal followers, or some other intervention. If you cannot spend this Momentum, you are finally left to your fate.

BACKGROUND

The grand manipulator of an entire religion, Issus — or Vil-lissus — is an extremely ancient black Martian who manages to place the Therns and First Born in her schemes long enough to become the center of their entire faith structure. From within her Grand Temple inside the Omean Sea she plucks all the strands of her web like a master puppeteer. Though centuries old and incredibly powerful, it is only during her final days when she encounters Carter and his allies that her existence is known to Barsoom generally. Prior to this time, she is believed to be a figure of myth.

Issus' machinations are that of total and unequivocal control of Barsoom through faith and superstition. Many journey far to her temple to witness her "greatness", and her dominance of the faithful lasts generations. Jeds hear her and lay waste to entire villages in her name. Thern priests spread her manipulative message like gospel. Green Martians shiver in fear to think that the great Goddess of Life Eternal has turned a baleful eye their way. It is tradition to worship her, and Issus' power base has a foundation of fear, mystery, and spiritual dependence.

It is not until John Carter crosses paths with the horrible old crone that her rule is questioned — and torn apart in shambles. Carter adventures to the Omean Sea with troops, ships, and soldiers lent to him by Tars Tarkas. His sacrilegious presence is quickly challenged by the Therns and the First Born. Cleverly, he causes the Therns and First Born to fight one another while Carter deals with his foes flying under a Zodangan banner. It is during this final conflict that Issus is revealed as a sham through finding fallacy in her rule; her devoted followers fall upon her. Although she is bodily torn to pieces by those loyal to her ancient theocracy, the echoes of her manipulation and what she taught the Therns about controlling Barsoom continues to be a trouble for generations to come.

MATAI SHANG

HOLY HEKKADOR OF THE HOLY THERNS

"Through the power of Iss — our power — all can be accomplished in time. It is fortunate that all we have is time, my friend."

ATTRIBUTES

DARING	CUNNING	EMPATHY
7	5	6

MIGHT	PASSION	REASON
5	6	7

TALENTS

BELOVED THEOCRAT (GRADE 4)
To the faithful, you are a trusted confidant and advisor.

* **Circumstance:** When dealing with faithful Barsoomians.

* **Effect:** In interactions with Barsoomians who believe in the afterlife, the paradise at the end of the River Iss, and your false faith's other edicts, you may always use Reason and Cunning on any tests to coerce, intimidate, or deceive them. You also gain a bonus 2d20 on such tests.

TREACHEROUS (GRADE 2)
You bear few loyalties to anyone.

* **Circumstance:** When betraying another.

* **Effect:** If you betray or abandon another, you may use Cunning for any action directly related to this betrayal, such as ambushing them or escaping a scene by leaving them to die or be captured. Any Momentum generated by such successful actions is increased by 1.

BACKGROUND

The last great Holy Hekkador, or religious leader, of the mighty Therns, Matai Shang is the head of the false religion of Issus. He is a direct foe, and arguably a nemesis, to John Carter for many different campaigns, even after his religious cult is exposed for the fraud that it is. When Matai Shang loses his power base following the dissolution of his religious foundation, the Thern is so consumed with anger that he turns to an ambitious leader amongst the First Born — a dator named Thurid.

Once allied with the conniving First Born, Matai Shang and Thurid kidnap the Princesses Dejah Thoris of Helium and Thuvia of Ptarth in an attempt to bring Carter to them and eventually to his knees. Their captives are brought to the far north territory of Kadabra and held by the insidious Jeddak Salensus Oll, but, when Carter and his friends come to the rescue it is not enough. During the final moments of the battle on board an airship high above the ground, Matai Shang is betrayed by Thurid and flung over the side to his death. He is avenged a moment later by his daughter Phaidor, who uses her rage and leverage to hurl the First Born into the air to follow her father plummeting to the ground below.

THUVAN DIHN

JEDDAK OF PTARTH
"I will keep my eyes on my young son-in-law, as he is going to surprise us all."

ATTRIBUTES

DARING	CUNNING	EMPATHY
6	6	6

MIGHT	PASSION	REASON
5	7	6

TALENTS

BONDS STRONGER THEN IRON (GRADE 2)
Your loyalty to your family and closest friends is unwavering.

✳ **Circumstance:** When defending family members and close allies.

✳ **Effect:** When taking an action in defense of your family or close allies, you may reroll any failed die in a test, keeping the better result. You may only reroll the dice once and cannot reroll dice that generated any successes, only those who failed completely.

LEADS FROM THE FRONT (GRADE 3)
You will not ask your followers to do anything you would not do yourself.

✳ **Circumstance:** When leading troops or other followers.

✳ **Effect:** When undertaking a task or mission you could have left to your followers and subordinates, you gain 1 additional Momentum on successful actions directly related to completing this task. Furthermore, when interacting with your subordinates and followers you may always use Passion for actions to lead, convince, or guide them.

BACKGROUND

Once a loyal and devout follower of the false religion of Issus and the Holy Therns, Thuvan Dihn quickly sees the light and switches allegiance when it is revealed that Matai Shang has kidnapped and enslaved his beloved daughter, Thuvia. Joining Carter on a quest to free her and Dejah Thoris from captivity, he becomes a great ally for the Earthborn Martian Warlord.

THUVAN DIHN IN THE JEDDAK OF JEDDAKS ERA

Since the early days of their alliance, Thuvan has become an even greater ally to John Carter through the mingling of their families. Red Martian territories are never known for longstanding alliances between one another, but when Carthoris marries Thuvan Dihn's daughter it seals good relations between Ptarth and Helium for a long time to come. This alliance is looked upon as even more unique considering it is nearly replaced with Thuvan Dihn declaring war on Helium outright. His daughter is kidnapped — a common theme in Barsoomian politics — by a vessel that disguised to look as though it is from Helium. Thuvan Dihn is enraged and nearly sends forces marching on the distant city, but it is revealed to be a plot by Astok, Prince of Dusar. Bloodshed is averted and the subsequent marriage between the Prince of Helium and his daughter instead makes history.

THUVIA OF PTARTH

PRINCESS WIFE OF CARTHORIS
"Her heart begs her to one path, her duty another. Which road she walks will determine the fate of Ptarth itself."

ATTRIBUTES

DARING	CUNNING	EMPATHY
7	4	8

MIGHT	PASSION	REASON
4	7	6

TALENTS

BANTH EMPATHY (GRADE 3)
Banth's see you as kin more than prey. They may even follow your commands.

✳ **Circumstance:** When encountering banths.

✳ **Effect:** Banths do not attack you unless they are first attacked, starving, or otherwise aggravated. You may attempt to persuade, tame, or coerce banths into assisting you or following simple commands. This is usually a Daunting (D3) test, possibly more for complex or difficult requests. If successful, 1 Momentum can be spent to make another command to the same banth.

BANTH MASTERY (GRADE 3)
For some reason, Banths warm to you like few others. You are surprisingly safe even in the claws of such fearsome beasts.

✳ **Circumstance:** When encountering the banths of Barsoom.

✳ **Effect:** When making a test with your Banth Empathy or a similar action to coax or coerce such a creature, you gain a bonus 2d20. You also gain this bonus if you are attacked by banths.

VALIANT DAUGHTER OF PTARTH (GRADE 3)

You are capable of incredible moments of self-sacrifice, courage, and, when justified, vengeance.

* **Circumstance:** When aiding others.

* **Effect:** When you take damage while acting to aid another, you reduce the overall damage taken by 1. Also, you may use your Passion when attacking or defending against those who have personally wronged you or your loved ones.

BACKGROUND

Princess Thuvia, daughter to the Jeddak of Ptarth, finds the pressure to soon marry, for political reasons, distasteful. She never sees most suitors at court as anything other than a burden to her later life. Many theorize that it is her depressing view of her future life that causes her to set out on an early pilgrimage to the finality of the Valley Dor.

Upon reaching what should be paradise, Thuvia instead finds fear and capture at the hands of the religious Therns. She is rescued by the unlikely duo of John Carter and Tars Tarkas, who she helps through the Otz Mountains to potential freedom. They are set upon by the First Born, but John fights them off while Thuvia and Tars Tarkas reach an airship to escape. She is later captured again (and again) and finds herself in a prison with Dejah Thoris. The two beautiful red princesses become good friends in this time, in spite of the fact that both women have deep feelings for the Earthman Carter. They are eventually rescued from their captor, the insidious Matai Shang, by Xodar, John, and his son, Carthoris.

THUVIA OF PTARTH IN THE JEDDAK OF JEDDAKS ERA

Once returned to Ptarth, Thuvia becomes the target of multiple suitors — Carthoris, Prince Astok of Dusar, and the Jeddak Kulan Tith of Kaol. Carthoris is not well spoken enough for her, and Astok is little more than a cur, so she reluctantly accepts Kulan Tith as her betrothed. Astok feels wronged and refuses to accept the outcome. Instead he disguises an airship to look as though it comes from Helium and Carthoris in order to kidnap Thuvia for himself. This nearly brings the two red Martian city-states into bloody war, but is thankfully undone before any permanent damage occurs.

The ploy is uncovered when Prince Carthoris successfully rescues Thuvia from Astok, which changes her opinion of Carter's son dramatically. It is not long after her rescue that she chooses him as her husband after all, sealing a longstanding blood alliance between Ptarth and Helium for many long years to come.

Loyal, intelligent, and possessing a rare gift to soothe and control savage beasts such as the Barsoomian banth, Thuvia is a true noble of Barsoom. Like her friend Dejah Thoris, she is beloved by her people and possesses great reserves of willpower and resolve sometimes disregarded by those who see her as simply a political pawn or prize to win. Such individuals create a strong contempt in Thuvia, especially since her days as Matai Shang's slave and captive of Issus.

XODAR

DATOR OF THE FIRST BORN

"Xodar, Dator of the First Born of Barsoom, is accustomed to give commands, not to receive them."

ATTRIBUTES

DARING	CUNNING	EMPATHY
6	7	5

MIGHT	PASSION	REASON
6	5	7

TALENTS

AIRSHIP PIRATE (GRADE 3)

You are a master of pursuit and boarding actions.

* **Circumstance:** When chasing or boarding an airship.

* **Effect:** Gain 2d20 bonus dice on any action directly related to chasing down and boarding an airship. Your first attack when boarding a vessel also receives this bonus.

BATTLE-TESTED LEADER (GRADE 2)

Your crew and other subordinates follow you because they see your ferocity and success in battle. Any under you who would betray you are swiftly dealt with.

* **Circumstance:** When chasing or boarding an airship.

* **Effect:** You may always use Daring to command, coerce, or intimidate your crew and other subordinates and should any crew member or subordinate betray you, you gain a bonus d20 on all actions to discover, defeat, and punish them for their disloyalty.

BATTLE VALOR (GRADE 1)

You are a true warrior and steadfast soldier at home in the chaos and carnage of war, always willing to meet your fate with sword and pistol in hand.

* **Circumstance:** When suffering Fear damage in combat.

* **Effect:** You may ignore the first 2 points of damage to your Fear stress track taken during combat. You suffer Fear damage after this during a combat scene or from other situations normally.

RUTHLESS WARRIOR (GRADE 3)

You are a deadly warrior against whom few can stand in battle.

* **Circumstance:** In physical conflict.

* **Effect:** Your attacks with both ranged and melee attacks do an additional 1 🎲 of damage. If the target suffers at least one affliction, you do an additional 1 🎲 of damage.

BACKGROUND

This First Born pirate once worshipped the ancient goddess Issus and fought against John Carter in her service. However, after enslavement and imprisonment by Issus for failing to stop Carter from defeating him and his raiders, he comes to recognize the evil and rot inherent in the First Born society under Issus. After Xodar ends up in the same prison cell as Carter, he quickly realizes they are on the same side of the conflict. Already impressed at John Carter's fighting prowess and physical abilities, Xodar chooses to serve him as a loyal lieutenant and brother-in-arms, eventually becoming leader of the First Born under the great alliance of kingdoms and races which recognize John Carter as Jeddak of Jeddaks.

During his time imprisoned with Carter, Xodar helped teach Carter and his inner circle about black Martians, the First Born, and some of the oldest parts of Barsoomian culture and tradition. He is also a tremendously capable warrior skilled with sword, spear, firearm, and airship. Xodar might be subordinate to Carter in skill, but he is a prime example of a strong Martian warrior that quickly adapts to the world around him no matter the reason. He never gives up in the face of adversity, sees the world with the tactics of a lifetime soldier, and has the strength of character within him to see his plans through to fruition each and every time. Xodar becomes one of John's most trusted friends and fellow soldiers for a reason.

JEDDAK OF JEDDAKS ERA

GAHAN OF GATHOL

JEDDAK OF GATHOL, HUSBAND TO TARA
*"She has come to love Turan, and through that sell sword,
she has unknowingly come to love me as well."*

ATTRIBUTES

DARING	CUNNING	EMPATHY
6	8	5

MIGHT	PASSION	REASON
5	7	5

TALENTS

ACE FLIER (GRADE 2)
You have taken the art of flight to a new level.

✳ **Circumstance:** When piloting an airship.

✳ **Effect:** Reduce any difficulties for navigating or avoiding airborne dangers by 1. Also, whenever you succeed at a test involving piloting, gain an additional Momentum.

CONVENIENT DISGUISE (GRADE 1)
You are adept at taking the role of another to find the proper moment to act, usually a common panthan or some other oft-overlooked soldier of fortune.

✳ **Circumstance:** When entering a scene.

✳ **Effect:** Spend 1 Momentum and adopt an alias or false identity. You may join a scene as that character later on during the adventure regardless of obstacles or circumstance, but only if you reveal to at least one other character your true identity during that scene. For you first action after revealing your identity, gain a bonus d20 to that action. If you elect to not reveal yourself, you lose 2 Momentum.

VALIANT SWORDSMAN (GRADE 3)
For you, more numbers just means more targets.

✳ **Circumstance:** When facing multiple opponents in melee combat.

✳ **Effect:** When facing multiple opponents, you can reduce the cost of a Counterstrike by 1 Momentum for every 2 opponents (minimum 0).

BACKGROUND

Gahan is the Jeddak of the territory of Gathol who marries the daughter of John Carter and Dejah Thoris, Tara. A strong leader and skilled warrior, Gahan is at home in charge of naval forces from the helm of his personal flier, Vanator. During a nasty storm that knocks Vanator adrift into the wastes, Gahan eventually finds the land of Bantoom. During his unexpected stay in Bantoom he helps mount a rescue that saves Tara from captivity.

TARA

DAUGHTER OF JOHN CARTER, PRINCESS OF HELIUM
"She is her father's daughter, the way she defies fate. The beauty of her mother as well, which combines for a worrisome sum."

ATTRIBUTES

DARING	CUNNING	EMPATHY
6	5	6

MIGHT	PASSION	REASON
5	8	6

TALENTS

SURPRISING FEROCITY (GRADE 2)
Those who take Tara for granted soon become aware of her fierce temperament and proud upbringing.

✴ **Circumstance:** When succeeding in a conflict.

✴ **Effect:** When in conflict with a character who believes Tara to be frail, timid, or otherwise incompetent, she rolls one extra d20 for the conflict and, if Momentum is generated on this roll, she gains 1 bonus Momentum. This bonus lasts for the rest of the current conflict or as long as her opponent underestimates her, whichever is longer.

PASSIONATE RETRIBUTION (GRADE 3)
The blood of John Carter runs in Tara's veins, and, though she lacks her father's purebred Earth strength, she can bring alarming power to bear when necessary.

✴ **Circumstance:** When you Counterstrike in physical conflict.

✴ **Effect:** When you Counterstrike after being physically attacked, you may always use Passion for your Counterstrike. Also, you do an additional 2 🎲 of damage if you succeed.

SHE PERSISTED (GRADE 3)
As a proud daughter of Helium and child of the great John Carter and Dejah Thoris, Tara does not submit easily.

✴ **Circumstance:** When resisting seduction, coercion, or mind control.

✴ **Effect:** When making a test to resist seduction, coercion, or mind control, gain 2 bonus Momentum to spend on the test.

BACKGROUND

Tara is the younger sister of Carthoris, the daughter of John Carter and Dejah Thoris. She has the noble air of a princess about her, much like her mother always has, but her father's resourcefulness and tenacity have always shined brightly. These inheritances come in handy when she is swallowed up by an air storm and became lost in Bantoom.

She is a fiery and obstinate girl, always ready to defend her beliefs and, on several occasions, her body. She has been forced to kill would be rapists, kidnappers and enemies of Helium by her own hand — another trait she seemed to pick up from her father. Tara does not bend knee unless she chooses to. She waves off the advances and gifts of the noble Gahan of Gathol when he tries to court her unsuccessfully, but later on, when he disguises himself as a panthan named Turan and fights bravely in her presence, she accepts him as a suitor and eventual husband.

ULYSSES PAXTON

EARTHBORN SOLDIER

"When I awoke I knew that Carter's tale was no mere legend. I was on Mars, his strange Barsoom, and I was somehow whole again."

ATTRIBUTES

TALENTS

SCIENTIFIC ASSISTANT (GRADE 1)
You apprenticed under the great Ras Thavas and learned much of Barsoomian science.

* **Circumstance:** When dealing with Barsoomian science.

* **Effect:** When analyzing, researching, or working with Barsoomian science and technology, you may always use Reason and roll a bonus d20 on all tests.

EARTHBORN STRENGTH (GRADE 3)
You are tenacious and your Earthborn strength and years of experience gives you a substantial edge in battle.

* **Circumstance:** In melee combat.

* **Effect:** You can always use Might for attack and defense and does an additional 1 🎲 of damage with such attacks.

LEAPS AND BOUNDS (GRADE 2)
Your Earthborn muscles allow you to leap great distances and perform great feats of strength while on Barsoom.

* **Circumstance:** When moving on Barsoom and planets with similar gravity.

* **Effect:** You may close one range category automatically, ignoring any obstacles or intervening terrain as long as you have clearance and space to leap between your starting point and destination. You may spend 1 Momentum to move an additional range category.

SOLDIER OF JASOOM (GRADE 3)
Your experiences in combat and career as a soldier on Earth help you in battles, allowing you to fend off both physical and psychic assault and strike back at those who would harm you.

* **Circumstance:** When attacked physically or psychically.

* **Effect:** You can ignore the first 2 stress you take in a conflict. Also, you may Counterstrike against any physical attack for 1 Momentum instead of the usual cost of 3.

BACKGROUND

Ulysses Paxton is from a much later time than when John Carter was active on Earth, the era of World War I. He is a studious reader of Burroughs' chronicles of Carter's tales from Barsoom. So much so that, when his legs are blown off in the war and he lies there dying, he finds himself looking up at the red speck in the sky thinking about faraway lands, hoping with all his will that Burroughs' tales are true.

He awakes on Mars, whole and full of life. Pleased to be alive and part of this amazing world he has read so much about, Ulysses begins to journal everything happening to him during his time on Mars. These notes end up eventually sent to Burroughs for publication, adding Ulysses' stories to the collective Barsoomian chronicles.

In his first few minutes of being on Mars, before he even has a chance to try out his increased strength and agility, the scientist Ras Thavas and a small entourage come upon Ulysses and attack him as a possible threat. Paxton shoots up high into the air to safety, the sight of which shocks Thavas into staggering aside. This momentary stunning gives one of his patient/prisoners, Dar Tarus, the opening he feels he needs to attack the scientist. Ulysses sees the misunderstanding for what it is and does not want the scientist to fall victim to it. He moves to stop Tarus — unfortunately killing him in the process. For saving his life, Ras Thavas makes Ulysses his new assistant and renames him Vad Varo.

Ulysses/Vad Varo's time with Ras Thavas shows him a remarkable array of things that even John Carter has never laid eyes upon during his time on Barsoom. One of the most interesting — and horrifying — things that Ulysses witnesses is Ras Thavas' ability to perform actual brain transplantation from one body to the next. This scientist can actually put a person's mind in a new body, even in the body of the recently deceased!

In one instance, Ras Thavas puts the mind of a horrible jeddara named Xaxa in the beautiful body of a young woman called Valla Dia. Ulysses feels so badly for the young girl forced to live such a nightmarish existence that he promises to undo this horrific mind swap, and manages to eventually do so. Ras Thavas, who is old and getting more infirm with each week, has plans to steal Ulysses' powerful Earthman body with this transplantation technique. Gaining the aid needed to stop him, Ulysses frees several other brain-swapped beings; among these are the warriors Gor Hajus, Dar Tarus, and a powerful white ape with the mind of a Martian named Hovan Du. There is much conflict and body-swapping to put Valla Dia in her proper place, but at the end Ulysses — still going by the name Vad Varo, marries the beautiful young princess and becomes the Jed of Phundahl. At his wedding, Vad Varo/Ulysses is greeted by a man that he has only ever before read about in tales on Earth, John Carter himself. Happy to see that Vad Varo has already ended the mind-swapping threat to Barsoom, he gives Helium's gratitude and makes an alliance with the only other wayward Earthman on Mars.

Because he clearly seems to be a hero of his own story who joins the cast of Carter's tales as an ally and fellow adventurer, Paxton makes excellent inspiration for Earthborn PC heroes in a campaign. He is a prime example of how a player character can interact with great heroes such as Carter, Dejah Thoris, and others and still be their own character with unique, individual goals, triumphs, and challenges.

LLANA OF GATHOL

GRANDDAUGHTER OF JOHN CARTER AND DEJAH THORIS
"She is as beautiful as her grandmother ever was, but it is what she inherited from her grandfather that should worry you."

ATTRIBUTES

DARING	CUNNING	EMPATHY
5	8	6

MIGHT	PASSION	REASON
8	7	5

TALENTS
SKILLED SWORDSWOMAN (GRADE 2)
You have the training and natural aptitude to wield a blade effectively.

* **Circumstance:** When using a sword.

* **Effect:** Add a bonus d20 when attacking or defending with a sword.

I WILL NOT (GRADE 4)
You are almost epically stubborn and will never surrender yourself or your values without a fight.

* **Circumstance:** When resisting mind control or coercion.

* **Effect:** When someone tries to control, seduce, or otherwise convince you of an action you do not wish to undertake, you gain 4 bonus Momentum to spend on any tests to defend or resist these efforts.

BACKGROUND
Llana of Gathol is the very attractive and adventure-prone daughter of Gahan of Gathol and Tara of Helium. This puts the blood of both Dejah Thoris and John Carter into her veins along with the ancestry of some of the great jeds and jeddaks of Helium. She has the beauty of her mother and grandmother, but her father and grandfather's spirit has turned her into a plucky, exciting girl quite capable of using a sword in her own or another's defense. Llana has taught herself to be goodhearted and always ready to lend her influence — or her blade — to the aid of those less fortunate than she.

There is a lot of her grandfather's spirited view of the world within her as well. She speaks her mind when she wants to, she chooses her own companionship, and when she makes up her mind it would take a tremendous amount of persuasion to change it. This is particularly evident when she chooses to enact a seductive dance in front of many nobles to woo her lover Pan Dee Chee. It is not a skill she is well versed in, but she wants to show her affection nonetheless. Chee becomes her husband despite the scandalous display, a fact that never does sit too well with her grandfather.

Narrator Character Archetypes

Barsoom is a huge and varied world with a cast of characters just as wide and kaleidoscopic as our own. For every hero upon which legends are built, there are hundreds of those who make the bricks of their foundation.

The following character templates cover many archetypal, typical, narrator characters for use in your games. Exemplars of these archetypes from the novels are also included and, in the case of characters who do not already have their own statistics and entries, these archetypes can serve as mechanics for those characters with minimal or no alteration. If a character might have two archetypes, simply combine the talents of the two and adjust attributes as you see fit. Narrators may also add additional talents to flesh out these archetypes as they see fit.

The statistics provided in this section do not include stress or Threat ratings by design. Depending on the exact character these archetypes are used for, they may be adjusted accordingly to the needs of the narrator.

Assassin

"My metal is pledged to the one jeddak before whom we all shall bow one day. My hand is death, the blade that sees all laid low."

Exemplars: Gatun Got, Head of the Assassin's Guild of Amhor; Gor Hadrus, famed Toonolian assassin, Ur Jan, Head of the Assassins' Guild of Zodanga.

ATTRIBUTES

DARING	CUNNING	EMPATHY
6	7	4

MIGHT	PASSION	REASON
5	4	5

TALENT
EASY TARGET (GRADE 1)
Lesser targets are no challenge to your skills as a master assassin.

✳ **Circumstance:** Targeting a minion.

✳ **Effect:** You can automatically kill a target minion through typical assassination methods (melee, strangulation, poison, etc.).

Barsoom is a planet of conflict. Its nations and peoples seem destined to be put at odds, sometimes escalating to wide scale violence. Battles between war bands or nations can be vicious, bloody and terribly destructive. While the rush of going to war with their enemies is sometimes second to none, there are times that a far more subtle act is required — assassination.

Powerful Barsoomian people hire assassins when a precision strike is needed. Most often used to target a single specific person, or occasionally a small group in one place, assassins are specialized agents of death-dealing. A good assassin prides him or herself on not only their lethality, but also their ability to end their targets' lives without getting caught. There are assassins that specialize in killing from afar with firearms, but the best assassins to be hired are those who are masters of stealth and up-close murder.

BENEVOLENT LEADER

"I love my people. It is my responsibility to make the hardest of decisions on their behalf, some of which could have lasting repercussions on their very lives. For as long as I draw breath, I will continue to make them."

Exemplars: Tardos Mors, Jeddak of Helium, Mors Kajak, Jed of Lesser Helium, Talu, Jeddak of Marentina, Dejah Thoris, Princess of Helium.

ATTRIBUTES

TALENT
BELOVED RULER (GRADE 4)
The people of the nation love the ruler with all their heart and the ruler has never given them reason to falter in this affection. When making requests of his people, even the hardest of heart will usually acquiesce.

 ✳ **Circumstance:** When commanding their people.

 ✳ **Effect:** Characters under the command of a beloved ruler must obey their orders or suffer 2 🎲 Confusion damage. This damage can be resisted with a **Passion + Reason** Daunting (D2) test with Momentum reducing damage by 1 🎲 per point spent.

Barsoom's tribes and nations might seem random and anarchic to outside observation, but, with the right leader in place, they can become powerful entities. Historically, when a jeddak, chieftain or boss has the honest support of their people, they have managed true greatness. The greatest achievements and advancements in Barsoomian socio-political structure have notably been under the watch of a beloved leader.

These leaders are trusted to make the right decisions for their people, by their people. They rarely have to dedicate resources to watching their own populace for unrest or internal sabotage; their reputations and high approval rates make them a desired asset. While a benevolent head strengthens the relationship between leadership and the masses, it does make them a prime target for external threats looking to strike a blow against the peoples' morale.

CORRUPT WARLORD

"Through strength, manipulation, and fear I took control, and the wake of my rise to power shall force the weak to their knees. My subjects shall hear my name and tremble, for I will be their terrible, wonderful lord."

Exemplars: Salensus Oll, Okarian Jeddak of Jeddaks, O-Tar, Jeddak of Manator; Tul Axtar, Jeddak of Jaha; Zat Arras

ATTRIBUTES

TALENT
BEND TO THE LASH (GRADE 6)
Those who do not obey a warlord find their families punished with vicious tortures. Disobey at your peril!

 ✳ **Circumstance:** When commanding their people.

 ✳ **Effect:** Characters who are under the command of a corrupt warlord must obey their orders or suffer 4 🎲 Fear damage. This damage can be resisted with a **Daring + Passion** Daunting (D2) test with Momentum reducing damage by 1 🎲 per point spent.

Barsoom can be a treacherous planet to survive upon, and most of its population gathers into civilizations in order to live. Sometimes these civilizations are in the command of caring leaders who look out for their people; far too often this is not the case. For every good-natured leader that rises to power, being pushed upward by the helpful and loving people they come to rule over, there is the opposite — a dark despot who climbs to a position of control by crushing the oppressed and walking upon their broken backs.

Unscrupulous jeddaks and other warlords that seize control through less-than-magnanimous means maintain their vicelike grip of power with fear and domination. They will use any means to keep their underlings in line, forcing those they defeat to pledge their metal to them, serve on bended knee, or suffer the lash. Despotic rulers like these must keep their people in line at all times lest they soon be targeted by the next cunning soul looking to topple them from their sometimes proverbial throne.

DUELIST

"I have been honing my fighting skills ever since I could hold a weapon in these hands. I am like a dancer, an artiste, and so much more. When I stand ready against a foe, they are one mistake away from certain death. That mistake is often as simple as not surrendering before our metal even touches."

Exemplars: Ptang, warrior of the First Born; Solan, Switchmaster of the Guardian of the North.

ATTRIBUTES

DARING	CUNNING	EMPATHY
6	7	5

MIGHT	PASSION	REASON
5	4	4

TALENT

QUICK DISARM (GRADE 3)

As a duelist, you'd rather not make work for yourself and favor disarming a foe over killing them.

✳ **Circumstance:** When parrying an attack.

✳ **Effect:** On a parry, the duelist can make a free Counterstrike but **must** use this action to attempt to disarm their opponent. If their opponent has no weapon, they can make a regular Counterstrike instead.

Battle and martial prowess is important to the warrior peoples of Barsoom. Over the generations it has seeped into many facets of their culture. Honor, respect, positions of power; on occasion, these are directly linked to how good a duelist someone is. They stand proudly out in the open against their opponents, putting their lives in danger to defeat a foe. Whether granting their enemy quarter or quick release, the best duelists are among the greatest close-in fighters the world has ever seen.

Duelists tend to focus upon one particular style or methodology to their martial abilities. Fencing and other swordplay is commonplace. The occasional pure hand-to-hand pugilist shows how brutal the right application of force can be, but masters of more exotic weapons like spiked chains or bone-crushing mauls have risen to fame as well. No matter their choice of weapon or fighting styles, a good duelist will be famed for one thing — victory.

GLADIATOR

"I long for the roar of the crowd, the adoration of the people, and the splash of warm gore upon my face! There is no greater rush than ending a foe in front of thousands of frenzied admirers."

Exemplars: Floran, Gatholian gladiator of Manator; Carthoris of Helium (while imprisoned by Issus).

ATTRIBUTES

DARING	CUNNING	EMPATHY
5	6	5

MIGHT	PASSION	REASON
7	4	4

TALENT

BLOODY BLOWS (GRADE 3)

When you strike an opponent, it is a brutal symphony to stir the crowds.

✳ **Circumstance:** When striking a foe in melee.

✳ **Effect:** Your melee attacks gain the Sharp and Fearsome quality.

With powerful martial prowess and skilled warriors found throughout Barsoomian culture, brutal combat and gory deaths are commonplace. The masses are so used to violence and battle that they are not only desensitized to it, they find themselves longing for it. The result has been the rise of fighting pits and gladiatorial arenas in many population centers across the world, especially in places where the green Martians thrive.

Unlike soldiers dedicating their lives to ending threats quickly and efficiently, gladiators devote their whole existence to the entertainment of the masses through bloodshed. They focus their skills upon deadly, close quarters weaponry in order to give the people what they want. Fighting unchecked beasts like Martian white apes or leonine banths can bring hand blistering applause from thousands of onlookers, but every gladiator knows there will come a day when another trained gladiator will stand across the pit from them. The call of the mob to the jeddak or chieftain in charge of the fights may spare a fallen gladiator — or they could call for their head. Gladiators fight, kill and possibly die for the crowd; everything else is secondary.

Green Martian Warrior

"By my tusks and my green skin, I am a finger on the clenched fist of my jeddak. My metal is his to wield or waste as he sees fit, and all my hands will carry the weight placed upon me until the River Iss."

Exemplars: Tars Tarkas, Jeddak of Tharks, Zad, Thark warrior; Dak Kova, Jeddak of the Warhoons, Tal Hajus, Jeddak of Tharks.

ATTRIBUTES

DARING	CUNNING	EMPATHY
6	5	4

MIGHT	PASSION	REASON
7	4	3

TALENTS

MERCILESS ASSAULT (GRADE 3)
While even the least warlike of the Tharks is a challenge in combat, warriors are demons dealing blow after blow even when their enemy is dead!

✳ **Circumstance:** When attacking with melee weapons or using a rifle.

✳ **Effect:** When you generate Momentum when attacking with a melee weapon or rifle, you deal and additional 2 🎲 damage.

FOUR-ARMED FOR WAR (GRADE 1)
Your warlike, combative culture and four arms give you an edge in combat, allowing you to attack with multiple weapons or steady your rifle with ease.

✳ **Circumstance:** When attacking with melee weapons or using a rifle.

✳ **Effect:** When you generate Momentum while attacking with a melee weapon or rifle, gain an extra Momentum.

Unrelenting, savage, and martially focused to the point of being seen as primitive, green Martian warriors are biological killing machines. All green Martians forego clothing in favor of leather harnesses dotted with jewelry and small trinkets. Warriors fill their harnesses with clan baubles to mark their allegiance, trophies from their notable kills, and the weapons with which it will surely and shortly put to good use.

Guardsman / Soldier

"I am one of many; a single piece of the whole. My sword and shield are all that stands between my brethren in arms and death, as his do the same for me. We can be bricks in the wall or hornets in the swarm, as the jeddak commands."

Exemplars: Gor-don, Padwar of Pankor; Man-Lat of the First Born

ATTRIBUTES

DARING	CUNNING	EMPATHY
5	6	6

MIGHT	PASSION	REASON
5	4	5

TALENT

I HAVE EYES (GRADE 1)
While you might seem to fade into the background you see everything

✳ **Circumstance:** When watching for trouble

✳ **Effect:** The character can roll 1 bonus d20 when attempting to spot a hidden character or ambush of any sort.

Barsoom cannot seem to avoid conflict long, and where its people gather together it soon becomes evident how much they need a structured and loyal martial force. Members of a local militia or guardsmen corps can stand up for their people. Often called Thans, they are soldiers that come together under the banner of their chieftains and jeddaks to march out to battle. These are the people who make it their role in society to fight and die for their friends and neighbors.

Soldiers and guardsmen are trained with arms and armor that can be easily manufactured, acquired, and repaired by their local populations. The purpose of a standing martial force is to help maintain the peace, or enforce their leaders' will. Both roles can take their toll on standing numbers, requiring the training and replacement of fallen members to be as easy as possible. Should their numbers fall too far, the populace is left with weakened defenses — something a good leader will never allow to happen.

HOLY THERN PRIEST

"By the waters of the holy River Iss, I am an echo of the voice of Barsoom itself. Its creatures are mine to mold and shape like the clay of Her basin. Aside from those black demons that hound our doors, the people of Barsoom dance on the ends of my strings."

Exemplars: Matai Sheng, Holy Hekkador of the Holy Therns; Sator Throg, Priest of the Holy Therns.

ATTRIBUTES

DARING	CUNNING	EMPATHY
5	4	6

MIGHT	PASSION	REASON
4	4	7

TALENT

DECEITFUL LOGIC (GRADE 2)

They've spun so many truths into lies that the two sound as one when they speak.

✷ **Circumstance:** When attempting to convince another character

✷ **Effect:** When trying to persuade a character, the Thern priest can always use Reason to aid in convincing the character. In addition to this they can roll 1 bonus d20 on the test.

Arguably the most powerful Barsoomian people, the Therns are the direct descendants of the Orovar white Martians. They inherited their predecessors' penchant for high technology, their Caucasian-white skin, and their desire to control the whole of Barsoom. From within their cliffs and cave complexes above the Valley Dor, the Therns do their best to manipulate everything around them to their own ends.

Therns that hold elevated positions within the priesthood have the power and ability to become a magnanimous benefactor or a treacherous antagonist toward any and all. They influence so-called "lesser" Martians to do their bidding as well as take direct control over a menagerie of Barsoomian predators — all of which they can use to aid or hinder those they feel are beneath them. Of course, for most Therns, this is everyone.

OFFICER

"I serve the jedwar, as he serves the jeddak, as my teedwar serve me. All the way down to the thans, there are orders to be followed and services to be done in the chain of command. It is my job to be the strongest link I can be."

Exemplars: Tan Hadron of Hastor, protagonist of *Fighting Man of Mars*, Tokar Bar, Dwar of the Kaolian Road.

ATTRIBUTES

DARING	CUNNING	EMPATHY
5	6	5

MIGHT	PASSION	REASON
5	4	6

TALENT

RANK AND FILE (GRADE 2)

An officer is never without his aides. Unless ambushed in personal quarters, he is attended by at least 2 bodyguards who fight with great valor.

✷ **Circumstance:** When attended by bodyguards.

✷ **Effect:** The bodyguards may add 1 bonus d20 to any attack and the officer can add 1 bonus d20 on any defense.

Starting with the first rank of authority and working up the ladder of officers, the padwar earn their twin-feathered headdress when they begin command of a small team of thans. The dwar may add a third feather and an utan of one hundred soldiers or a small naval vessel. Granted a large warship or a full thousand-man dar of foot soldiers, the teedwar rank comes with yet another headdress feather and a great amount of respect amongst red Martians. Odwar officers have an entire umak at their disposal; ten-thousand soldiers or several warships are in their hands. The final line between officers and Martian royalty is the jedwar, who answer only to the jeddak and his inner circle — they are the top of the military and command all loyal soldiers.

PANTHAN

"I am a soldier. My sword will keep my family fed, and my current loyalty is based upon who will stretch the seams on my purse the most. Call me a mercenary, call me a sell sword, but do not question my skills."

Exemplars: Fo-nar, Panthan from Jahar; John Carter (in the guise of Dotar Sojat).

ATTRIBUTES

TALENT

WITH BLADE OR BULLET (GRADE 2)

Panthans are deadly, not due to any particular training or technique, but because they will take risks that conventional soldiers might not. Often this daring pays off!

* **Circumstance:** When attacking with a standard melee or ranged weapon.

* **Effect:** The panthan can always use Daring when attacking with a standard weapon. Note this includes sword, pistols, and rifles, but not bows or clubs.

Panthans are professional soldiers who join the ranks of structured military units as paid weapons and little more. Many of these men at arms are devoted to their roles, possibly looking to rise in rank and responsibility with a proper unit, or they might be happy enough swinging a blade for a survivable wage.

Although panthans are not heavily influential in the overall scheme of martial culture individually, they make up tremendous numbers on the battlefield. They are omnipresent in some cultures' militaries and are far leaner in others, but the role of paid, grunt forces are commonly filled by the single-feathered headdresses of the mercenary panthans.

PIRATE / RAIDER

"I am a predator, same as any other on the wasted stretches. I fill my belly the same as the banth does, but my fangs are my metal and the flesh is your goods and wealth."

Exemplars: Ban-Tor of the First Born, Zithad of the First Born

ATTRIBUTES

TALENT

BOARDING ACTION (GRADE 2)

Air pirates are notorious for leaping aboard airships and kicking the pilots to their deaths. Often the action of a raid is over before the pirates can decide what to do once they have landed.

* **Circumstance:** When attempting to board an airship.

* **Effect:** When attempting to get aboard an airship, the character can reduce any danger by 1 🎲 and automatically dispatch 1 minion.

In a world filled with battle, soldiers, and warlords, it should come as no surprise that raiders and pirates exist. Trade and supply caravans often travel between established civilizations, and those who are not protected well enough will eventually find themselves targeted by predatory warriors. Raiders and pirates survive and thrive by preying upon those who cannot defend themselves. Many First Born are raiders and pirates, as are numerous renegades from various red Martian kingdoms.

Raiders are equipped with weapons and armor they have put together from past loot, making up for their disrepair or ill-fittedness with personal skill and greed. They do their best to keep casualties to a minimum, as survivors are more likely to give the locations or schedules of more and better loot. This is not to say that pirates and raiders are not brutal killers, especially when dealing with capable defenders. A caravan that puts up a good fight could force otherwise loot-minded raiders into the role of bloodthirsty killers — sending a message to anyone else that might stand up to them in the future.

ROYAL ADVISOR

"I am the voice that whispers in the ears of the jeddaks. I am the conscience that may stay the warlord's blade. I can only hope that when I speak the truth of the matter, my words will be heard and taken to heart."

Exemplars: E-Thas, Major-domo of Mantor; Hamas, Zondangan advisor.

ATTRIBUTES

DARING	CUNNING	EMPATHY
4	4	6

MIGHT	PASSION	REASON
4	6	7

TALENT
EAR OF THE JEDDAK (GRADE 1)
While not powerful in their own right, royal advisors are experts in getting rulers to listen to sound advice.

✷ **Circumstance:** When attempting to convince their jeddak of a fact or course of action.

✷ **Effect:** The royal advisor can roll 1 bonus d20, though each dice that fails will cost 1 Momentum.

Wherever can be found a powerful person in charge of a population, whether it be a chieftain, jed, jeddak, or warlord, there will oftentimes be someone special by their side. This trusted person or persons serve as the advisory chorus to the leader; providing the necessary information to them when it is most needed. Barsoomian leadership roles can function without proper advisors, but they are rarely successful or long-lived due to the tumultuous nature of Martian cultures.

A good royal advisor adds a missing element to their patron leader. A battle-hardened warlord might require a soft, socialite's voice whispering how to deal with the times between conflicts. A foppish jed who talked his way into his position may need a skillful warrior's tactical advice by his side, and any leader who deals with cross-cultural boundaries often should think about having an advisor that knows their neighbors quite well. In effect, a good royal advisor needs to be capable of telling or showing their leader what he needs at exactly the right time.

SCIENTIST / ENGINEER

"I am found wherever knowledge is being put to good use without a weapon in hand or tactics in mind. The application of learning to adapt beyond shortcomings in technology, academia, and more. We are the brains within the Barsoomian body."

Exemplars: Fal Sivas, mad scientist of Zodanga, Phor Tak, villainous scientist of Jahar

ATTRIBUTES

DARING	CUNNING	EMPATHY
5	4	5

MIGHT	PASSION	REASON
4	5	8

MAD INVENTION (SPECIAL)

Many scientists are obsessives with weird and wonderful devices of which they have exclusive use. The narrator should look at Chapter 14: Secrets of Barsoom *and* Chapter 5: Weapons and Technology *to determine which weird devices they have access to.*

Despite its somewhat barbaric appearance from the outside, Barsoom can be quite technologically advanced. Airships fly with magnetically-charged wings or air-buffeting coil generators. The Therns perform feats so advanced that some might call it magic. Even the arguably primitive green Martians use centuries-old alchemy and industrial methods, but the results prove the science behind them is sound.

No matter the field of learning being discussed, there are those who are the teachers, inventors, and testers within them. Scientists and engineers are very important to Barsoomian cultures, more so the more "advanced" a civilization has become. They are both what feed the minds of Martian academics, and the source of the food itself. Without hosts of qualified scientists and engineers working to make their world flourish, Barsoom would very well stagnate, sicken and die between conflicts.

YOUNG NOBLE

"It will one day fall upon my shoulders to be someone to look up to in the family, but for now I learn what that means and how to survive this life long enough to do so. I was born to do this, you will see."

Exemplars: Phaidor, Princess of the Holy Therns; Sab Than, Prince of Zondanga, Thuvia of Ptarth.

ATTRIBUTES

DARING	CUNNING	EMPATHY
5	6	5

MIGHT	PASSION	REASON
4	5	5

TALENT

RISING STAR (GRADE 1)
While not yet the head of their house, the young noble carries a lot of potential influence. Politically savvy characters will realize that it is in their interests to offer minor favors now to gain greater favors later.

* **Circumstance:** When performing a **Daring** + action.

* **Effect:** The rising star will receive 1 additional item of equipment when they have convinced a character to aid or support them. Alternatively, the equipment requested could be of higher quality (a nicer flier, a better-quality sword, etc.).

From the mighty warlord broods of the green Martians to the long-reaching dynasties of the reds, nobility is omnipresent. Nobles do not simply appear in the world; they grow up from youthful beginnings like everyone else. They just don't have the same childhoods everyone else does. Nobles are often encountered while be held as hostages by their nations' enemies.

Nobles are groomed from a very young age to exemplify the ideals and goals of their family. A young Thern noble is going to spend time learning Barsoomian history and social manipulation, a decorated young princess of a red Martian city will learn etiquette, dancing, and honorable fencing styles. Every green Martian who might one day wear the mantle of jed must be a consummate warrior to defend his position and role. Young nobles are the future of their bloodlines, and those around them who know it take extra care to keep them safe.

ADJUSTMENTS FOR RACE

In cases of archetypes that could be applied to members of multiple races, the statistics reflect a character of the red Martian race as they are the most commonly encountered. To reflect an individual of another race, narrators can make minor adjustments as follows:

* **Earthborn:** +3 Might.

* **Green Martian:** -1 from Empathy, +2 to Might.

* **Holy Thern/White Martian:** +1 Reason, +1 Cunning, -1 Daring.

* **First Born:** -1 Empathy, +1 Cunning

* **Okar:** +1 Cunning, -1 Passion

Be sure and add any racial talents to the final character.

BACKER CHARACTERS

BO BAI

SAVAGE ZODANGAN ASSASSIN

"War is the butchery of men less innocent and less intelligent than the thoats of the green hordes. Assassination, by contrast, is Barsoom's highest art, achieved with a palette of blood."

ATTRIBUTES

DARING	CUNNING	EMPATHY
6	10	4

MIGHT	PASSION	REASON
8	6	6

STRESS TRACKERS

CONFUSION	FEAR	INJURY
4	6	10

TALENTS

EASY TARGET (GRADE 1)

Lesser targets are no challenge to your deadly skills as an assassin.

✷ **Circumstance:** Targeting a minion.

✷ **Effect:** You can automatically kill a target minion with typical assassination methods (melee, strangulation, poison, etc.)

NEVER UNARMED (GRADE 2)

Your retractable banth talons are formidable weapons, and your preferred means of execution.

✷ **Circumstance:** Whenever you wish to set aside your weapons and launch an unarmed attack.

✷ **Effect:** The thrill of exposing your claws gives you an additional 2 Momentum.

PAIN DOES NOT HURT (GRADE 4)

You are remarkably resistant to injury and possess superior focus and force of will. You can ignore injuries that would disable lesser individuals.

✷ **Circumstance:** When taking an affliction.

✷ **Effect:** Use a Conflict action to remove any one affliction. You cannot remove more than three afflictions in a single scene and must take a Conflict action to remove each one.

YOU WILL REGRET THAT (GRADE 4)

Injury often doesn't slow or discourage you, it only spurs your desire for retribution. If a foe injures you, you push past the pain and unleash your vengeance upon then.

✷ **Circumstance:** After being wounded by another.

✷ **Effect:** Ignore the effects of an affliction for the rest of the scene. Also, for the rest of the scene gain a bonus d20 to attack and roll an extra 1 🎲 of damage against the person or creature who caused this affliction. You can only use this for one affliction and one target at a time.

FLAW

NIGHTMARE RECOLLECTIONS

After your years of agony at the hands of an insane scientist, you despise anyone engaged in scientific research. When faced with anyone undertaking biological investigations, especially vivisection, you lose 3 Momentum as you are overcome with traumatic flashbacks to your suffering. If you cannot loose 3 Momentum, take the excess in Fear damage.

BACKGROUND

Abducted as an egg from a Zodangan noble family by agents of Ras Thavas, Bo Bai spent the first ords of his life as a captive of the vain Mastermind of Mars. In Ras Thavas' Toonolian laboratories Bo Bai was one of several subjects in the scientist's early experiments with transplant surgery. Long before he was fascinated by longevity and brain transfer, Ras Thavas was occupied with hybridizing the physical properties of different Barsoomian species. He was sponsored in this endeavor by Vobis Kan, Jeddak of Toonol, who was eager to increase the lethality of his warriors. The jeddak reasoned that all Martian fighting men were vulnerable as long as they carried weapons separate from themselves. He charged Ras Thavas with finding ways to overcome this weakness.

Most of the Mastermind's grotesque experiments died on the operating table or else went mad at the sight of what they had become. Only Bo Bai survived, a near-feral red Martian ignorant of both his past and his situation, whose scarred hands bore the retractable talons of the awesome banth. Knowing Bo Bai had no loyalty to Toonol, nor any love for Ras Thavas, Vobis Kan considered the Zodangan too dangerous to live. He ordered Ras Thavas to kill him. Ras Thavas could not

bring himself to destroy so perfect an example of his art, however, and faked Bo Bai's destruction. Anaesthetizing and spiriting him away aboard his flyer, he gave the boy to Ur Jan, then a master of the Zodangan assassin's guild.

Under Ur Jan, Bo Bai learned his art with an enthusiasm the master had never seen in an apprentice before. Bo Bai had a talent for murder: cold, calculated and efficient. He was merciless and indefatigable, a skilled poisoner, knifeman, and strangler. His signature mode of execution, however, was to open the throat of his victims with a single, four-clawed slash of his Banthian talons. It was not long before his successes earned him significant notoriety.

After the sack of Zodanga and during John Carter's campaign against the assassins' guild, Bo Bai inscribed his reputation in blood across Barsoom, claiming kills in Phundahl, Duhor, Dusar, and even Helium itself.

Although pathologically vicious, Bo Bai follows a strict code. He refuses all contracts on those he considers innocent while actively seeking those offered on scientists, slavers and nobility. In this way, he hopes to kill his way back to the unknown men or women who disfigured him and exact a poetic revenge.

MAYHEW CROSSKEY

SARDONIC EARTHBORN WITH A LOVE OF HISTORY
"It's plain to me that madmen designed the curriculum for the lessons of history."

ATTRIBUTES

STRESS TRACKERS

TALENTS

STUDENT OF BARSOOMIAN HISTORY (GRADE 1)
You have studied under Telo Urdat, from whom you have learned much of Barsoomian history.

- ✳ **Circumstance:** When encountering situations involving ancient Barsoomian peoples, artifacts, locations and customs.

- ✳ **Effect:** When analyzing, researching or observing the relics of Barsoom's past, you may always use Reason and roll a bonus d20 on all related tests.

EXPERT RIFLEMAN (GRADE 1)
With a long gun in your hand, there are few who can match your ability to place a shot where it will do the most damage.

- ✳ **Circumstance:** When you hit with a rifle.

- ✳ **Effect:** Roll an extra 1 🎲 of damage on a successful attack.

KEEN MARKSMAN (GRADE 1)
You are a careful and discerning shooter whose ability to think clearly and calculate a target's distance and speed improves your shooting.

- ✳ **Circumstance:** When using firearms.

- ✳ **Effect:** You may always use Reason when shooting a firearm.

LEAPS AND BOUNDS (GRADE 2)
Your Earthborn muscles allow you leap great distances and perform great feats of strength while on Barsoom.

- ✳ **Circumstance:** When moving on Barsoom and planets with similar gravity.

- ✳ **Effect:** You may close one range category automatically, ignoring any obstacles or intervening terrain as long as you have clearance and space to leap between your starting point and destination. You may spend 1 Momentum to move an additional range category.

EARTHBORN STRENGTH (GRADE 3)
You are tenacious, and your Earthborn strength and years of experience gives you a substantial edge in battle.

- ✳ **Circumstance:** In melee combat.

- ✳ **Effect:** You can always use Might for attack and defense and does an additional 1 🎲 of damage with such attacks.

MILITARY MIND (GRADE 3)
With considerable knowledge of Earth's history and warfare in the classical world, and an accomplished teaching record, you are a skilled military educator and strategist.

- ✳ **Circumstance:** When assessing battlefield terrain, troop positions and dispositions, and likely enemy weak points.

- ✳ **Effect:** When using Momentum to gain information about the battlefield and allied and enemy troop capabilities you gain 2 additional Momentum.

FLAW

CYNICAL OUTLOOK
Your honorable nature is tempered by an abiding cynicism towards others. When you are subject to or attempt a self-less act, lose 2 Momentum from your pool. If you cannot lose 2 Momentum, take the excess in Confusion damage for having your worldview shaken.

BACKGROUND

An Englishman by birth, Mayhew Crosskey is the only child of a wealthy Anglo-French family with an estate on the Sussex Downs. Born in 1888, he was bookish by nature, showing little of the adventurous spirit that defined his father's expeditions to Arabia and the Hindu Kush twenty years earlier. His appetite for history was voracious, however, and he consumed his father's journals with a passion.

Eager to ensure his son gained the masculine vitality befitting a Crosskey heir, his father sent him to study history under Howard Beale at Yale University. Beale had accompanied the older Crosskey on his Arabian adventures and was also notorious for plundering a number of sites in Egypt, Palestine and Peru. Between 1906 and 1909, Mayhew learned much more than history from Beale. By the time he graduated, he was a skilled outdoorsman, a crack-shot, a gifted field archaeologist, and a talented horseman. The wan, scholarly child had grown into a muscular athlete of considerable intellect.

As studious as ever, Mayhew accepted a junior post at the university where he taught classics and ancient history. Influenced by the work of Oswald Spengler, he developed a pessimistic view of humanity's future. His growing cynicism and sarcastic nature endeared him to his students, who valued his acerbic insights into human nature, but brought him into conflict with his faculty peers.

Sensing Mayhew's discontent, Beale recommended him for Hiram Bingham's expedition to Peru in 1911. When the expedition was attacked by bandits along the Urubamba River, Mayhew was fatally wounded and lost. Dying on the riverbank, he found himself transported to Barsoom.

His advent on Mars saw him captured by Jal Had, the repulsive, tyrannical Jed of Amhor, and exhibited mistakenly as an Orovar in the city's zoo. Learning the Barsoomian language and traditions from fellow captives, he eventually escaped Amhor by subtly manipulating his jailer. Once free of Jal Had, he travelled extensively in the guise of red Martian scholar Matath Croy, learning as much as he could of Barsoomian history and culture. Most often he accompanied trading caravans, paying for passage by serving as a guard. His physical prowess and skill with a radium rifle and pistol earned him the sobriquet "the fighting scholar". Recently, he settled in Lesser Helium to teach the military application of historical principles. He has also involved himself in the exploits of Telo Urdat, the acclaimed Heliumite archaeologist to whom he is both student and bodyguard.

MOR GANZEL

OBSESSIVE HOLY THERN
"Faith is the lever at the fulcrum of power."

ATTRIBUTES

DARING	CUNNING	EMPATHY
6	8	4

MIGHT	PASSION	REASON
6	9	7

STRESS TRACKERS

CONFUSION	FEAR	INJURY
7	9	8

TALENTS

MASTER OF DISGUISE (GRADE 1)
You are a master of disguise, transforming yourself completely and effectively. It is possible even your closest friends have never seen your real face.

✴ **Circumstance:** When disguising yourself.

✴ **Effect:** Spend 1 Momentum to leave a scene. Then spend 1 Momentum to replace any minion-class character in a scene, revealing you were actually in disguise all along.

DECEITFUL LOGIC (GRADE 2)
Therns have spun so many truths into lies that the two sound as one when they speak.

✴ **Circumstance:** When attempting to convince another character

✴ **Effect:** When trying to persuade a character, you can always use Reason to aid in convincing the character. In addition to this you can roll 1 bonus d20 on the test.

HORRIBLY PLAUSIBLE (GRADE 2)
You are a skilled manipulator, capable of recruiting others to whatever twisted cause you follow with deviously eloquent rhetoric.

✴ **Circumstance:** When attempting to persuade others of the rightness of your viewpoint.

✴ **Effects:** When acting to persuade others, you can reroll one failed die in any Passion-based test.

SPEAK OR DIE (GRADE 2)
You have an innate talent, and an impressive array of implements, for extracting information from your captives.

✴ **Circumstance:** When questioning captives as to their identity and purpose.

✴ **Effect:** You may always use Cunning and Passion when interrogating others to reveal information about themselves or coercing them into following your instructions.

A KNIFE IN THE DARK (GRADE 2)
Murder is best committed beyond the prying eyes of others, unless you wish to make a point.

✴ **Circumstance:** When attacking with a knife in darkened environments.

✴ **Effect:** You may roll 1 bonus d20 on attack rolls and gain a 1 🎲 bonus to damage rolls when attacking with a knife in low light conditions.

FLAW

ARROGANT CONCEIT
Holy Therns are, by nature, conceited and you are little different. If you are bested in combat by a red Martian, you lose 2 Momentum. If you cannot lose 2 Momentum, take the excess in Fear damage.

BACKGROUND

Before John Carter exposed the false religion of Issus, Mor Ganzel was a Holy Thern of the Eighth Cycle. He resided in an exquisite palace at the summit of the Otz Mountains, served by a multitude of slaves forced to endure his proclivity for cruelty and excess. When Carter broke the power of the Therns, Mor Ganzel rejected the rule of the First Born and left the Valley Dor to plot revenge.

Adopting the guise of a red Martian panthan, he travelled from city to city using a network of secret Thern temples. At each, he re-affirmed the faith of his shaken brotherhood. Gradually, his inflammatory rhetoric transformed many of the surviving Therns from a beaten, aimless cult into an underground movement dedicated to the destruction of the red nations. Mor Ganzel's message was simple: the 'paradise' myth of the Valley Dor could only be restored by laying waste to the history, knowledge, and culture of the red Martians. With their society in ruins, the red nations would look to their old beliefs for certainty, and Mor Ganzel and his brethren would answer their prayers. The Therns would return in triumph to the Valley Dor, cast out the First Born, and expunge all memory of the false Issus. They would rebuild and re-occupy their shattered palaces and temples, remaster their great banths, and once more bend the plant men and white apes to their will.

A hypnotic orator, Mor Ganzel has all the arrogance of his race but none of its indolence. In planning the destruction of the red Martians, he is a dynamo. He sits like a pale, bald spider at the center of a web of intrigue, spinning lies and deceit in response to the intelligence gathered by his network of spies in Helium, Gathol, Ptarth, and other cities.

In the teeans since Carter's destruction of Thern society, Mor Ganzel has grown into his role as chief tactician for a clandestine sect of Thern terrorists. Many of his adherents now perceive him as a new Holy Hekkator in waiting, destined to restore them to their rightful position at the apex of Barsoomian culture.

Not content to remain in the shadows, Mor Ganzel has adopted the persona of San Tal, a red Martian trader in precious minerals. These are supplied to him clandestinely by agents in the Valley Dor. Having earned the respect of wealthy patrons, military officers and other merchants, he now spreads rumors and lies throughout the red nations, fostering distrust and subtly edging each city state towards war.

RAZ OMASC

BRILLIANT RED MARTIAN SCIENTIST

"On Barsoom, scientific endeavor is simply another form of combat. We scientists engage our rivals in intellectual duels, broadcasting every scholarly feint to disguise the one triumphant riposte. And when intellect fails us, many turn unashamedly to espionage, larceny, and assassination. New discoveries on Barsoom are almost always born of blood."

ATTRIBUTES

DARING	CUNNING	EMPATHY
9	6	6

MIGHT	PASSION	REASON
7	6	5

STRESS TRACKERS

CONFUSION	FEAR	INJURY
5	9	7

TALENTS

RATIONAL MIND (GRADE 1)
You see through any attempt control your mind using drugs or telepathy.

* **Circumstance:** When suffering Confusion damage in combat.

* **Effect:** You may ignore the first 2 points of damage on to your Confusion stress track during combat. You suffer Confusion damage after this during a combat scene or from other situations normally.

WEALTH OF KNOWLEDGE (GRADE 1)
You possess a wealth of scientific knowledge, both theoretical and practical.

* **Circumstance:** When researching a scientific phenomenon or device.

* **Effect:** You may reroll any single failed die in a science-related Reason test.

PERCEPTIVE SCIENTIST (GRADE 2)
Your scientific analysis is so keen you even glean insight from failure and your successes are even more impressive.

* **Circumstance:** When analyzing a scientific device or theory.

* **Effect:** Roll a bonus d20 when analyzing scientific devices and theories. The narrator must answer one "yes or no" question about the device or theory regardless of the result of this roll.

ORIGINAL THINKER (GRADE 2)
You have a remarkably imaginative, creative mind capable of thinking your way out of the most challenging situations.

* **Circumstance:** When faced with intellectual challenges or puzzles.

* **Effect:** You gain an additional 1 Momentum.

FIXED (GRADE 3)
You can fix even the most damaged of equipment, often with minimal tools and in record time. Unlike simple jury rigs and patches, your repairs are permanent — at least until you break it again.

* **Circumstance:** When repairing a device.

* **Effect:** Take a Conflict action and automatically repair one device or piece of equipment. This repair is permanent, lasting until the device is damaged again.

FLAW

DANGEROUSLY CURIOUS
When encountering unfamiliar technology for the first time, you become distracted and must investigate, even in life-threatening situations. If you ignore the unfamiliar technology or otherwise choose not to investigate it you lose 3 Momentum.

BACKGROUND

During the renaissance in Barsoomian science and innovation that followed Carthoris' invention of the destination control compass, Raz Omasc became one of Helium's most mysterious scientists. Secretive yet benevolent, he had distinguished himself formerly with enhancements to the Twin Cities' pneumatic train system, some minor advances in airship design, and several esoteric papers on the untapped possibilities of the eighth ray. Latterly, he has passed into a quiet semi-retirement on his estate outside Lesser Helium.

Carthoris' discovery, and its catalytic effect on Martian technology, drew Raz Omasc from his intellectual lethargy. He returned to his abandoned laboratory complex in Lesser Helium and began an unprecedented period of research and experimentation. No field of enquiry was beyond his interest.

In the biological sciences, he sought to reconstitute the dust of the dead, reanimating ancient Martians who might bestow their knowledge upon him. His expedition to Horz, and what befell the party of adventurers who accompanied him, was the talk of Helium for many teeans. Even now, the results of this mission are a matter of speculation, since he has closely guarded the results of his experiments. Nevertheless, members of Helium's scientific community have noted the increase in security at Raz Omasc's laboratory and the appearance of hardened panthans on its walls. Unconfirmed reports of pale-skinned apparitions at the windows have set Helium alight with speculation.

In metallurgy and chemistry, Raz Omasc's successes have been both public and publicly beneficial. He developed a new means of tempering steel, making Heliumite blades the envy of Barsoom. His epidermal aerosol delivers a layer of synthetic skin to radium bullet wounds, preventing the rounds from exploding until they can be surgically removed; and his advanced equilibrimotor delivers more precise aerial control than those of other cities. His recent experiments in optics promise field glasses of greater range than those currently available.

Raz Omasc's greatest breakthrough, however, is in the temporal possibilities arising from the manipulation of the eighth ray. From research conducted in the dusty, forgotten archives of Barsoom's dead cities, Raz Omasc has learned to accelerate the Eight Ray using powerful magnetic fields. The resulting vortex opens gateways to Barsoom's near-mythic past, enabling temporal explorers to wander its ancient avenues and sail its vast, shallow seas. Retrieving these explorers has thus far eluded Raz Omasc, but he remains optimistic that this setback can be overcome.

Now, just as Raz Omasc is recruiting adventurous, discreet warriors for his temporal experiments, curious rivals are turning to espionage to learn his secrets.

SOLUS REIL

RESOURCEFUL RED MARTIAN HERO

"Never trust a man with dust on his sword. He is likely a politician, a coward, or both."

ATTRIBUTES

DARING	CUNNING	EMPATHY
7	5	6

MIGHT	PASSION	REASON
4	8	10

STRESS TRACKERS

CONFUSION	FEAR	INJURY
10	7	5

TALENTS

FEARSOME FENCER (GRADE 1)

Your reputation and talent with a blade unnerves and even terrifies many opponents, making it easier for you to disarm and dispatch them.

※ **Circumstance:** When holding a sword or other melee weapon.

※ **Effect:** When fighting in accordance with Martian honor, you can disarm a character for 1 Momentum less than normal.

LIVE OFF THE LAND (GRADE 1)

The wilderness opens up to you like an old friend, revealing bounties and secrets.

※ **Circumstance:** When surviving in the wild.

※ **Effect:** You may automatically forage or scrounge enough to eat and drink and can locate or construct basic shelter. For each Momentum spent you may also locate enough sustenance and shelter for a number of extra people equal to your Reason.

MASTER OF DISGUISE (GRADE 1)

You are a master of disguise, transforming yourself completely and effectively. It is possible even your closest friends have never seen your real face.

※ **Circumstance:** When disguising yourself.

※ **Effect:** Spend 1 Momentum to leave a scene. Then spend 1 Momentum to replace any minion-class character in a scene, revealing you were actually in disguise all along.

CUNNING STRATEGIST (GRADE 3)

You are a skilled strategist who knows the capabilities of your men like your own arm.

※ **Circumstance:** When commanding troops or making battle plans.

※ **Effect:** You may always use Cunning when making battle plans or strategies. Any difficulties for such tests are reduced by 1.

RUTHLESS EFFICIENCY (GRADE 3)

You are unquestioningly loyal to your jed and carry out your orders with unflinching precision, no matter what is required.

※ **Circumstance:** When given a specific mission by a superior officer, jed, jeddak, or jeddara.

※ **Effect:** Until you complete your mission, you may add a bonus d20 to all tests related directly to the accomplishment of your task. The narrator is the arbiter of whether or not a test is connected explicitly to your assignment.

FLAW

IN THE COMPANY OF STRANGERS

Your naturally distrustful nature means that if for any reason you cooperate with non-Gatholians that you do not trust or who do not align with your motives you loose 3 Momentum.

BACKGROUND

Barsoomian political relations, even amongst allies, are often exercises in intrigue. Between enemies, plots circulate within plots, sweeping spies, assassins, and agitators into a maelstrom of subterfuge and deceit. Few Martians have the perspicacity, diligence, or tenacity to expose these schemes, or the guile to entrap spies and spymasters, poisoners and fifth columnists. Of those with such aptitude, Solus Reil of Gathol is unmatched in the arts of counterespionage, reconnaissance, and guerilla tactics. He has led his Jed, Gahan's, intelligence network for almost fifty ords.

His accomplishments include thwarting a Zodangan plan to collapse the galleries of Gathol's largest diamond mine, exposing a conspiracy masterminded by Nutus of Dusar to poison the city's great herds of thoats and zitidars, and preventing an assassination attempt on Gahan's life by agents of Phundahl. In response, Gahan dispatched Solus Reil to Phundahl to learn the reason behind the Phundahlian plot. Already skilled in deception, Solus Reil adopted the guise of a priest of Tur. He penetrated the inner sanctum of the city's Jeddara and high priestess, Xaxa, and learned of her intention to eliminate the jeds and jeddaks of other red Martian nations. This mass assassination would

form the prelude to a Phundahlian crusade that would spread the worship of Tur across Barsoom. Unlikely as the scheme appeared, Solus Reil understood Xaxa's commitment and her ability to place agents close to even the most well protected rulers. He alerted Gahan and left the city, but not before he had introduced a subtle, slow-acting poison into Xaxa's food. In time, she would lose her mind, and no one would suspect the role he or Gathol played in her demise. Over the next few padans, a series of arrests rippled across the red nations as Phundahlian agents were seized.

Returning to Gathol, Solus Reil resumed his duties. More impressed than ever by his wily spymaster's performance in the field, Gahan set Solus Reil a new task: to investigate rumors of the green horde of Torquas massing for war. Leading a cadre of Gatholian guerilla fighters, Solus Reil ventured south – and disappeared. His final message to Gahan suggested a new alliance between the Torquasians and the mysterious city of Thurd, where an unknown species of green Martians make their home. Eager for news of his resourceful spymaster, Gahan has sent several missions into the wilderness, but the dead sea bottoms are vast and nameless forces seem arrayed against him.

TELO URDAT

BOLD RED MARTIAN ARCHAEOLOGIST

"Barsoom is a splendid artifact: a world of ruins and mysteries and unfathomed history. Who could resist venturing into its deserted cities and forgotten depths in search of ancient technology and fabulous possibilities?"

ATTRIBUTES

DARING	CUNNING	EMPATHY
7	9	4

MIGHT	PASSION	REASON
6	6	6

STRESS TRACKERS

CONFUSION	FEAR	INJURY
6	7	9

TALENTS

FIND THE WAY (GRADE 1)
You can find safe paths and hidden places with ease. You are also more likely to bypass and survive hazards like dangerous terrain, ancient traps, and other deadly obstacles.

✳ **Circumstance:** When travelling in wastes, ruins, and wilderness areas.

✳ **Effect:** When facing an environmental danger (falls, traps, etc.), you roll 1 less combat die than normal.

ARCHAEOLOGICAL MASTERY (GRADE 2)
You have spent much of your life in the ruins of ancient Barsoom and few have greater knowledge than you of the Red Planet's forgotten past.

✳ **Circumstance:** When exploring the ruins and dead sea bottoms of Mars.

✳ **Effect:** When analyzing, researching or observing the relics of Barsoom's past, you may always use Reason and roll 2 bonus d20s on all related tests.

KEENLY DARING (GRADE 2)
You instinctively take cover or move to defend yourself when needed.

✳ **Circumstance:** When defending against physical attacks.

✳ **Effect:** You may always use Daring and/or Reason to defend against physical attacks.

INTELLIGENCE OPERATIVE (GRADE 2)
You are a keen listener, always attentive to any conversations occurring around you, and especially conscious of whispered exchanges, surreptitious gestures, and rumors with a ring of truth.

✳ **Circumstance:** When travelling through crowded marketplaces, assembly rooms, or other places where Barsoomians gather and converse.

✳ **Effect:** When attempting to listen in on, or observe, the behavior of others, you may always use Cunning and roll 1 bonus d20 on all tests related to these activities.

FLAW

FORTUNE AND GLORY
If you are exploring an ancient city or subterranean region and encounter an interesting artifact, you cannot leave it behind. You loose 3 Momentum if you do not attempt to recover it or spend time making plans to do so in the future.

BACKGROUND

Among the otherwise undistinguished inhabitants of the red Martian city of Ptarth, the resourceful and daring Telo Urdat is a notable exception. A warrior of considerable prowess, his interests nevertheless lay not in martial achievements but in the ruins and relics of Barsoom's rich and vibrant history. After long ords of distinguished service to Thuvan Dihn, Jed of Ptarth, Telo Urdat left the navy to pursue his fascination with Barsoomian archaeology.

At first, he learned all he could from the libraries of Ptarth, Helium, Zodanga, and other red cities, studying under a succession of scholars, conversing with experts, and making himself known to influential jeds amongst the red nations. Afterwards, he began a series of audacious excavations across Mars. At first, he ranged in the relative safety of the Artolian Hills surrounding Duhor, uncovering evidence of a lost Okarian colony and retrieving a cache of ancient technology, including radium flash torches and exquisite monocular field glasses. Through the sale of these items, Telo Urdat funded further enterprises.

His subsequent expeditions quickly became the source of campfire stories as he survived one extraordinary venture after another. In Aaanthor he narrowly avoided capture by white apes while retrieving a lost idol of Issus for a wealthy collector in Phundahl; in the Carrion Caves on the borders of Okar, he fought savage apts to plunder countless artifacts lying amongst the accumulated dead; in Horz, he recovered scientific instruments and records belonging to the Orovars, selling many to Raz Omasc ahead of the scientist's own excursion into the city. He was a prisoner for a time in Invak, escaping with his life and a quantity of invisibility pills that enabled him to undertake increasingly daring exploits. At Korad, he walked unseen amongst a green horde to document the city's murals and mosaics, and record the stories etched in its wind-honed marble; he lived undetected amongst the Lotharians for almost a teean, chronicling tales of ancient Barsoom; and in the wastes between Manator and Gathol he uncovered the wreck of an interplanetary craft of unknown design. What he found within remains the subject of considerable speculation, as does his connection to a certain fugitive Zodangan inventor.

Telo Urdat's exploits have made him the darling of red Martian society, and he moves freely across Barsoom amongst the wealthy and the influential. None have guessed that he is Thuvan Dihn's most accomplished spy.

TYROK DOV

"It is a humbling thing to look on Barsoom and know that without our care its peoples are naught but the final layer of dust on a dying world."

ATTRIBUTES

DARING 7 — CUNNING 9 — EMPATHY 4

MIGHT 5 — PASSION 5 — REASON 9

STRESS TRACKERS

CONFUSION 9 — FEAR 7 — INJURY 9

TALENTS

PASSIONATE ORATOR (GRADE 1)

Your unwavering loyalty and love for your people moves others to aid you. Even when dealing with the sworn enemies of your nation, culture, or group, you can often gain concessions or create opportunities with your words.

* **Circumstance:** When speaking to convince an audience.

* **Effect:** You may reroll the result of any failed die roll in a Passion-based attempt to convince or charm others.

WITTY REPARTEE (GRADE 2)

Your tongue is as quick and lithe as your blade! You are always able to slip in a comment or call out important information to your allies even during the tensest situations.

* **Circumstance:** When performing an action.

* **Effect:** You may always take an additional Spoken action as part of an attack, defense, or other action.

MAD INVENTION (GRADE 3)

You are a brilliant engineer, with all manner of weird and wonderful designs pouring from your fertile imagination.

* **Circumstance:** Once per ord after the party at which you first announce a design idea.

* **Effect:** A major piece of new technology is produced, (an interplanetary craft, subterranean explorer, or item devised by the narrator) which will function as planned following an appropriate number of successful Reason tests (narrators decision). Failed Reason tests will generate unexpected consequences (determined by the narrator).

CUNNING LOTHARIO (GRADE 4)

You are a master of seduction not out of any romantic inclination but simply as a means to an end.

* **Circumstance:** When using seduction to gain access to riches or equipment.

* **Effect:** You can always use Cunning to make seduction tests for the purposes of gaining property. After a successful test, you automatically gain 2 Momentum and can use 2 Momentum (repeatable) to gain any 1 piece of equipment that could normally be purchased as core equipment.

FLAW

MISPLACED CONFIDENCE

Sometimes, your popularity and success go to your head. Every time you fail a test employing Reason, you lose 1 Momentum.

BACKGROUND

Tyrok Dov is one of the two most important men on Barsoom. Entrusted with the telepathic harmony needed to access the atmosphere plant, he and his fellow guardian ensure the facility's vast radium pumps continue to replenish the planet's air supply. For five teeans – half a Martian year – a single guardian lives isolated inside the factory. His companion, meanwhile, enjoys unfettered freedom in the outside world and a personal safety known only to those who are truly essential.

How each guardian passes his period of isolation is a matter of personal choice. Tyrok Dov, once a Heliumite engineer of considerable standing, divides his time between designing sophisticated and extraordinary machines and planning extravagant parties. Known across Barsoom as a daredevil, hedonistic genius, he enjoys considerable celebrity status. His return from the atmosphere plant is always cause for celebration amongst the nobles and dignitaries of Helium.

Tyrok Dov's social gatherings are near-legendary affairs with spectacular firework displays, eclectic culinary fare, and colorful guests drawn from Barsoom's many nations. In the spirit of cooperation defining the Jeddak of Jeddaks Era, red Martians rub shoulders with Okarians, green Martians, and First Born. The central attraction of Tyrok Dov's parties, however, is always the Great Unveiling, the presentation of the guardian's latest engineering design. This is achieved with the greatest amount of pomp to attract the maximum amount of sponsorship. Tyrok Dov is a showman at heart, and he works the crowd tirelessly, his teeans of isolation invigorating his charisma as much as they do his engineer's imagination. Work commences on his designs at his extensive workshops in Lesser Helium as soon as the necessary sponsorship is secured. Many of his projects take several ord to complete, but when they are finished Tyrok Dov's adventurous spirit rises to the fore. To cheering crowds he has completed the fastest circumnavigation of Barsoom in a streamlined flyer of his own design; he has explored the waters of the River Iss and the Sea of Korus in a submersible crewed by First Born scientists theorizing the existence of a vast inner Barsoomian sea; and he has scaled the heights of the great polar barrier aboard an airship to reveal lost cities entombed in ice.

Two additional projects are nearing completion: an interplanetary craft intended to reach the great Heliumite battleship lost in space for almost a millennium when its buoyancy tanks were overfilled, and a great drilling machine designed to burrow beneath the dead sea bottoms and reveal the secrets of Barsoom's subterranean worlds. When Tyrok Dov returns from his latest sojourn in the atmosphere plant he will be looking for brave adventurers to accompany him. Barsoom holds its breath in anticipation.

Par Stalus

STALWART RED MARTIAN NOBLE

"A warrior may change his metal – but he would feel the edge of my blade if he was under my command."

ATTRIBUTES

STRESS TRACKERS

TALENTS

BATTLE VALOR (GRADE 1)
You are a true warrior and steadfast soldier at home in the chaos and carnage of war, always willing to meet your fate with sword and pistol in hand.

* **Circumstance:** When suffering Fear damage in combat.

* **Effect:** You may ignore the first 2 points of damage to your Fear stress track taken during combat. You suffer Fear damage after this during a combat scene or from other situations normally.

FEARSOME FENCER (GRADE 1)
Your reputation and talent with a blade unnerves and even terrifies many opponents, making it easier for you to disarm and dispatch them.

* **Circumstance:** When holding a sword or other melee weapon.

* **Effect:** When fighting in accordance with Martian honor, you can disarm a character for 1 Momentum less than normal.

WHO DARES WINS (GRADE 1)
Striking swiftly and fiercely will often compensate for small numbers or other tactical disadvantages. You learned long ago to hit hard, fast, and put foes down without hesitation.

* **Circumstance:** When using a particular type of weapon.

* **Effect:** Pick a category of weapon (sword, pistol, spear, etc.), You inflict an additional 1 🎲 of damage and add 1 to the total damage rolled on successful attacks with that weapon.

Note: You can use additional grades of this talent to apply this effect to other weapons (one per grade).

NOBLE REPUTATION (GRADE 2)
Honor, loyalty, and an outstanding dedication to duty ensure you stand out among panthans.

* **Circumstance:** When interacting with Heliumites and other red nations.

* **Effect:** You may always use Daring when interacting with other Heliumites and their allies and gain a bonus d20 for all such tests.

NO ONE SHOULD SUFFER THIS WAY (GRADE 2)
The pain of seeing your closest friend in distress means that you endeavor to provide aid to those who in need of it, so that no one suffers the same pain.

* **Circumstance:** Whenever you meet someone in distress over a lost or missing friend, family member or loved one.

* **Effect:** You gain 1 bonus Momentum on successful tests relating to finding, recovering or rescuing a missing person you have agreed to search for. The narrator has the final decision on which tests are relevant to your cause.

FLAW

FEAR OF FAILURE
If you fail to find the person you were charged with searching for, discover them dead or your actions cause their death, or for any reason give up the search, lose 2, 3 or 5 Momentum points respectively. If you have insufficient Momentum points, take the excess in Confusion damage.

BACKGROUND

A childhood friend to Dejah Thoris, Prince Par Stalus became one of the princess's most trusted confidants after John Carter disappeared from the atmosphere plant. At the time, he was an odwar in Helium's army and Tardos Mors' special envoy to Ptarth. Many red Martian cities honored him, and he was renowned as an astute tactician and shrewd battlefield commander. In Ptarth he had planned, with typical efficiency, the defeat of the Landless Revolt, a ragtag army that had risen in Morbus under Nal Tan, the self-styled 'Jeddak of the Wastes'.

When Carter vanished, Dejah was inconsolable. Tardos Mors recalled Par Stalus in the hope that her old friend might console his grieving granddaughter. On his arrival, Dejah begged Tardos Mors to release him from all duties save one: finding Carter. Moved by Dejah's plea, he agreed.

Thus began the greatest adventure in Par Stalus' distinguished career. Starting at the atmosphere plant, he scoured Barsoom for any clues to Carter's whereabouts. His investigation led him from the ruins of Zodanga into conflict with the assassins' guild and eventual safety amongst the Hordes of Thark. Here, he and Tars Tarkas agreed to coordinate their search for the missing Earthborn. Leaving Thark, he combed the red kingdoms, becoming embroiled in thwarting coups, assassination plots, and the insane schemes of Barsoom's most degenerate scientists. Everywhere he was celebrated as a brilliant military mind, yet in his heart he knew defeat. Always he returned to Helium with intelligence for its jeddak and sorrow for its heartbroken princess.

Dejah's despair moved Par Stalus and he fell in love with her. Steadfastly honorable, he knew he could only express that love by finding Carter and reuniting him with his wife and son. He resumed his quest with greater resolve, journeying ever further: to Okar, Tjanath and the Toonolian Marshes, through haunted cities, darkened pits, and lightless caverns. All to no avail.

When he finally returned to Helium, he learned Dejah had taken her final pilgrimage down the river Iss. Carthoris was also absent from the palace. Shaken by the news and overcome with regret, he exiled himself, becoming one of Barsoom's most esteemed panthans. When he learned of Carter's return to Mars, his heart rejoiced at the thought of the family reunited, but his abiding love for Dejah, and his conviction he had failed her, kept him from ever returning home. He now roams Barsoom, a noble, heroic warrior for hire.

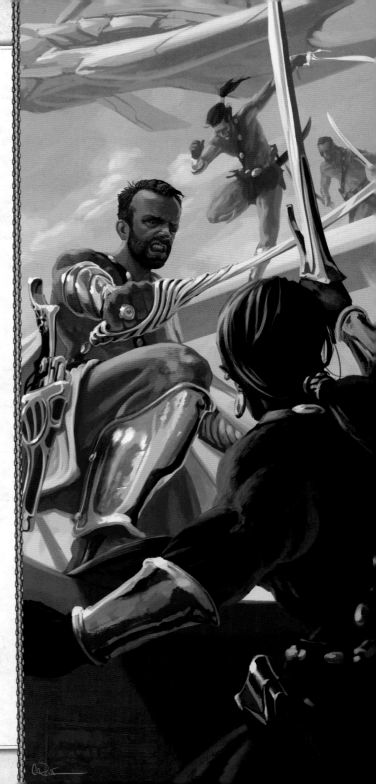

CHAPTER 16: MIND MERCHANTS OF MARS

> *I have ever been prone to seek adventure and to investigate and experiment where wiser men would have left well enough alone.*
>
> – John Carter, *A Princess of Mars*

The following introductory adventure is designed for three to six new player characters for ***John Carter***. This adventure works for any era of play or player characters races with minimal adaptation.

OUT OF THE ARENA

Barsoom its dying. Howsoever the peoples of that planet struggle, their world hurtles inexorably toward its terminus. Such conditions breed harsh weather and harsher men and women. Yet, unlike the desperate nations of our Earth (Jasoom), in those circumstances most dire and testing, a majority of Barsoomians cleave to honor rather than raw savagery.

Ah, but there is savagery — wide gulfs exist between those living in the towering spindles of Helium and those eking out an existence in oppressive slums and dangerous wastes, where the wise go heavily armed, and slavery is routine. It is in these deplorable, latter conditions the player characters begin their first venture into this beautiful but deadly landscape.

As we begin our adventure, the fearsome green Martians known as the Warhoon capture the player character heroes and force them to fight for sport and amusement in their legendary pits. There is not a moment's breath to worry over death, for, even now, the characters are pushed out of their pens into the stark Barsoomian sun.

RARER EARTHBORN

This adventure assumes that Earthborn characters are rare on Barsoom but not completely unheard of. In addition to any player character Earthborn, the adventure introduces another Earthborn character who is neither of the canonical Jasoomian expatriates from Burroughs', John Carter and Ulysses Paxton. Another Earthborn is also mentioned and features into the later plot of the adventure.

Narrators wishing to keep Earthborn characters very rare should consider removing the Earthborn character of Patterson from this adventure, either by having him expire early in the adventure after relaying any relevant information to the heroes, or by replacing him with a helpful Barsoomian.

EPISODE ONE:
IN MEDIA RES

Literally, in Latin, *in media res* means "in the middle of things." This adventure throws the player characters in at the deep end. As the adventure begins, the player characters are thrust into a large Warhoon arena where they must fight for the sport of their captors and their own survival. It is recommended the adventure begins the instant the characters are dragged from their underground cells and thrust into the glaring light of Barsoom's day to immediately face a host of experienced gladiators. This opening showcases how Barsoom works best, with constant adventure and danger thrusting characters into situations where heroic action and cooperation are often the key to victory and survival.

Narrators should briefly describe the vast area with screaming and taunting Warhoons far above them. The gladiatorial arena is at least some seventy feet deep, sheer and unclimbable without inviting attacks from the Warhoons above. In addition, a dome made from the bones of some great, unnamed beast form a cage atop the pit. This is unusual for such Warhoon pits, which are unusually uncovered to afford a better view of their captives' demise, a fact that any Barsoomian native with experience with the green horde would know.

However, there is no time for speculation, as a group of gladiators advance. Among them are four capable warriors — two red Martians and two Tharks. They charge without mercy.

The player characters find weapons near where they are pushed from the pens. These are a collection of swords, daggers, and polearms. Each player character has time to grab one weapon of their choice. Any core equipment a character possesses is either found here as well, or was somehow secreted on their person. If having a par-

ticular piece of core equipment flies in the face of logic, the character gains 2 bonus Momentum to start with instead and the narrator should inform them they will recover their core equipment later, during, or shortly after, this scene.

Narrators should jump right into this combat. If the player characters wonder at how they were captured or seek to explain the circumstances of their incarceration through roleplaying that is great, but don't slow down the action. There will be time enough for introductions and explanations once the immediate threat is dealt with.

While combat is routinely to the death, it serves little purpose to kill the player characters at the outset of the adventure. This encounter serves two purposes — setting a brutal tone for the adventure and, obliquely introducing the plot, see page 49 for "What is Going On?" For now, the characters are aware they are captives and must immediately defend themselves.

Their opponents are not new to these pits, as their many scars evidences. The combat with such foes is fierce and fast-paced. The gladiators attack, threaten, and perhaps even taunt a wounded or shaken foe, but they never stop. Narrators should only slow down to explain rules. Otherwise, keep the dice rolling and the Momentum building. Let the players get into the action right away. John Carter is a game of planetary romance, and that genre has lots of action. Hook the players like Burroughs hooked his readers — from the very start.

While the pace is quick and the combat frenetic, the narrator need not lord victory over the player characters. Their opponents appear much tougher than they really are mechanically. A victory up front — at least for some of the characters — serves to boost enthusiasm and help along the plot.

WARHOON GLADIATOR (MONSTER)

ATTRIBUTES

DARING	CUNNING	EMPATHY
5	5	4

MIGHT	PASSION	REASON
6	4	3

STRESS	MENACE
9	2*

TALENTS
FOUR-ARMED FOR WAR
Your warlike, combative culture and four arms give you an edge in combat, allowing you to attack with multiple weapons or steady your rifle with ease.

✷ **Circumstance:** When attacking with melee weapons or using a rifle.

✷ **Effect:** When you generate Momentum when attacking with a melee weapon or rifle, gain an extra Momentum.

RED MARTIAN GLADIATOR (MONSTER)

ATTRIBUTES

DARING	CUNNING	EMPATHY
6	6	5

MIGHT	PASSION	REASON
4	4	5

STRESS	MENACE
10	2*

The total menace rating of the gladiators should be roughly equal to that of twice the number of players. If necessary add 1 extra red Martian, or 1 extra red Martian and 1 extra green Martian, or reduce the menace rating of some of the gladiators.

IF THE CHARACTERS WIN

If the player characters win the battle, the War-hoons whoop and cheer their violent victory. Then they are ordered to return to their cages. If they refuse, several Warhoons take aim at them from above with deadly green Martian rifles. The message is clear: the Warhoons are grateful for the entertainment, but won't hesitate the shoot the characters if they disobey.

If necessary, the narrator can prod the characters gently to bide their time. Now is not a good time to escape and any warrior or adventurer such as the player characters would know this.

IF THE CHARACTERS LOSE

The player characters will likely win this fight, but it is not a sure thing. The characters lose the fight due to black out, either by taking too many afflictions or voluntarily doing so. If this occurs, they are beaten, knocked unconscious, and thrown back into their cells. Their wounds are roughly but effectively treated by Warhoon healing salves while they are out and they will return to fight in the arena the next day. They will continue to do so until they win.

If the characters lose, allow them to explain and define the circumstances of their incarceration and capture after the first battle and interact with each other. Earthborn characters in particular will likely be quite confused and need many answers.

WHO ARE YOU, AND HOW DID YOU GET HERE?

Since we began with action — and no time to detail the whys and wherefores of the circumstances — immediately following the combat, have each player narrate how their character came to be a slave.

Were they captured during an ambush, sold as part of a debt, born into slavery, or spirited from the mortal coil on Earth to wake in shackles? Encourage the players to fill in some details, but they needn't flesh out their backstories. Of course, it's fine if they do, but you can literally jump right in after learning the rules, making some characters, and worry about backstory details later.

STICKING TOGETHER

The player characters are not necessarily alone when thrust into the area. A Thark named Tal Ptomj and a human named Patterson Brood may both be present (see 'In the Pens'), if the characters could use some combat backup in this scene.

Narrators should especially consider including Tal if there are no green Martian player characters. Similarly, they can include Patterson if there are no Earthborn player characters. If such characters exist, these characters are optional. They may be fun additions to the adventure at this point, but they may also bog things down or make the players feel their characters are less important and unique.

If either of these characters is present, the narrator may use them during the opening combat when the tide turns against a player character. For the cost of 2 Momentum, Patterson or Tal Ptomj intervene to help at an opportune time, distracting or wounding a foe to give the player characters time to rally or recover. Remember a character shy on Momentum can accept Threat to gain it for this purpose!

While something of a deus ex machina, the intervention can save a character's life and indebt them to their fellow traveler. This debt becomes important later on. Also, remember that for Barsoomians, aiding another in combat creates a bond of honor.

What is Going On?

While the heroes of this tale have no knowledge of broader events at this point, the narrator should. As an introductory adventure, the plot is largely linear, though sidebars offer points upon which an enterprising narrator might expand.

The basics are simple. At some point in recent days the player characters were beset by Warhoon slavers and captured, at least if they are native to Barsoom. If not, they simply woke in the slave pens, their bodies perhaps left bleeding out in the mud of Gettysburg, Flanders Field, or wherever else you wish. Unlike John Carter's arrival, though, these green Martians, the Warhoon took no chances with strange outworlders — hence the cage.

Prior to any of the characters' involvement, the Warhoon struck a deal with one of the criminal gangs that run the underbelly of the city of Zodanga. Slave trade is a booming business in this blighted land, and the Zodanga slavers want strong stock for unknown purposes. Moreover, they will pay handsomely for Jasoomians. Why they are so interested in alien slaves is unknown.

Any group victorious in the pit is sold to a Zodanga slaver the next morning. This Barsoomian, Isalia Ang, buys the player characters after they win or, if they do not win, simply buys them because humans are among them. If the group contains no Jasoomians, use the narrator character, Patterson Brood, included. For the purposes of the adventure, he is tossed in the pit with the heroes at the adventure's beginning.

> For adventures set during the Prince of Helium era and beyond, Zodanga is less an earnest enemy of Helium and instead an oft resentful part of it. This doesn't change the antagonists in this adventure much; the slavers simply are a bit less open about their activities and dealings with the Warhoons. However, it suggests a grander conspiracy or underworld operation to hide such activities within Helium's borders.

A Brief Outline

After the fight in the pit, the characters have about one day to heal and possibly attempt escape. The adventure itself presumes that escape is not currently feasible, though individual narrators may allow an inventive plan to work. From there, Isalia the slaver buys the characters, among others, in the morning and they are loaded into a wagon pulled by the larger variety of thoat.

The players may escape from the wagon on their own or may find freedom during a Thark attack. Either way, they have made friends with two narrator characters who have reason to travel to Zodanga. Whether for pay, out of honor, or for vengeance, the group tracks the slavers to the slums of Zodanga where a reckoning is had and some questions answered while others remain elusive.

While Earthborn player characters will no doubt struggle with the culture, language, and traditions of the strange and savage world they now inhabit, narrators shouldn't overdo this. Carter picks up the basics of language and learns to function at least as a bumbling outsider quickly, and the same should be the case with any Earthborn characters. At least by the end of this adventure, they should know much of the basics of life on Barsoom.

In the Pens

Tossed back in the pens after the fight, the player characters have time to discuss, recover, and interact. If they attempt to engage other slaves kept in the pens, they find only two friendly slaves among the largely cowed herd. The first is the aforementioned Patterson Brood, a human. The other is one Tal Ptomj, a Thark, whose people are bitter enemies of the Warhoon. Indeed, the latter finds cruel aspersions cast his way whenever the guards see fit to rain slop down upon the slaves from a cage above.

Patterson is a male Jasoomian of approximately twenty-five to thirty years of age. His last memory of Earth was dying on some battlefield as the enemy splashed their boots in the mud around him and they sky turned a color he swears he had never seen before. He held the rank of major in whatever army

he died serving. He's been here a bit longer than the player characters and, via telepathy and an affinity with languages, can serve to translate Barsoomian. Narrators should feel free to change Patterson's name, gender, or ethnicity to fit their group.

Tal Ptomj was captured scouting the edge of Warhoon territory. He had heard talk of Tharks going missing recently, but, until he was enslaved, he gave it little thought, presuming they had fallen prey to beasts. Tal is young, but capable.

> ### Removing Patterson and Tal
>
> There is serious danger when including an Earthborn and Thark character as narrator characters in this adventure. If the narrator isn't careful, it is very easy for players of Thark or Earthborn characters to feel decidedly less special for their inclusion.
>
> If this is the case, consider either killing off Patterson and Tal, replacing them with more commonly encountered red Martian captives of similar ability and attitudes, or removing them entirely. This is especially useful if narrators and players wish for Earthborn characters to be near-unique in their campaign.

Escape

It is the natural goal of almost any gamer, when imprisoned, to attempt escape. We expect your players, and their characters, to act no differently. However, it serves the adventure better if the player characters remain in bondage for some small while. As noted in "A Brief Outline", the adventure contains a failsafe mechanism by which the group can affect escape — the Thark raid in Episode Two, (see page 251).

Like the cage above the pit, the pen in which the player characters find themselves is designed to withstand the unnatural strength of an Earth native. This might cause the players to raise eyebrows but, depending on the era and specifics of your campaign, there may be no reason for their characters to consider this out of the ordinary.

The only direct interaction with guards occurs when groups are pushed out of the pens into the area and when they are broken into lots for purchase. The Warhoon guards are tough and numerous. The narrator may choose to allow escape at this point. If so, the characters escape the pens, fight their way through many Warhoon, and flee into the unforgiving landscape. Simply move and alter the adventure so that the characters run into the Thark raid or its immediate aftermath.

EVENTS

The life of a slave is one of oppressive routine. It isn't fun, and you should only highlight things that are out of the ordinary. These include the following:

✳ Feeding — Guards pour a milky-colored gruel from above.

✳ Herding — Guards either push slaves out to fight, or round up those they wish to sell.

✳ Fighting — A fight breaks out between slaves.

✳ Conversation with Patterson — The characters speak with Patterson and learn something of him and his background. See Patterson below.

✳ Conversation with Tal Ptomj — The characters speak with Ptomj and learn something of him and his people.

✳ Spotting Isalia — One of the other slaves, perhaps one of the above-named characters, watches a beautiful red Martian in the stands. She stands out, as most of the crowd is understandably comprised of Warhoon. Slaves who have been in the pens for some while, who are not warriors or humans, attest that the woman comes weekly to buy slaves. Her painted body reflects allegiance to one of the gangs in Zodanga.

✳ Isalia Leaves — A small airship arrives and takes Isalia off in the direction of Zodanga. For non-natives of Barsoom, it is quite a sight.

PATTERSON BROOD
HUMAN OF JASOOM (VILLAIN)

ATTRIBUTES

DARING	CUNNING	EMPATHY
4	5	5

MIGHT	PASSION	REASON
7	4	4

STRESS TRACKERS

CONFUSION	FEAR	INJURY
5	5	7

Brood is a strange fellow. Whether that is due to current circumstance or hidden motive is left to the narrator in this adventure. A soldier, Patterson fought in the Spanish-American War and was wounded during the Battle of Las Guasimas in 1898.

In any event, Patterson was shot or otherwise wounded by the enemy, he believes gravely so, and seems convinced he "died" and was transported here. He claims to have no additional memories of who he was on Earth or why he now finds himself here.

Patterson was here for about one week prior to the arrival of the player characters. Jasoomians were flung into the pen unconscious, he says, while the others were prodded inside at spear point. He is no more aware of the how and why of such travel than they.

Patterson claims another human was penned with him for a day and taken by caravan to Zodanga. He wants to go there to find out just what is going on.

TAL PTOMJ
THARK WARRIOR (MONSTER)

ATTRIBUTES

DARING	CUNNING	EMPATHY
5	6	4

MIGHT	PASSION	REASON
6	6	3

STRESS	MENACE
9	3

Tal is young, though perhaps only other green Martians recognize this. He is currently surly. In his usual circumstances with his people, he's boastful and impetuous. It was a combination of these qualities which caused him to venture too far into Warhoon territory and be captured.

Angry and desiring revenge for his enslavement, Tal Ptomj would love little more than to kill all the Warhoon around him. He respects the player characters' skill in the arena and is friendly with Patterson, at least as friendly as two such newly introduced species may be.

Later in the adventure, Tal Ptomj's respect for the player characters goes some way toward other Tharks tolerating any non-Tharks in the group.

Assuming the narrator did not opt to allow early escape, the adventure proceeds when Isalia arrives near the gate to the pen in which the characters are imprisoned. Getting a closer look at her proves valuable as they try to identify and find her later in the adventure.

For now, she points at the group and uses the word "Jasoomian" when her finger lands on a human. These are of particular interest to her, though no one can say why. After the sale, she gives a large, scarred Warhoon a coin and then leaves. That evening, under a red-streamed dusk, a small airship arrives and takes her away. This is one of the events noted above.

The next morning, the player characters, along with Tal Ptomj and Patterson if they are present, are split from the rest of slaves in this pen and herded into a giant covered wagon drawn by two pairs of huge thoats, see page 177.

EPISODE TWO:
COUNTING PADANS TO ZODANGA

This episode finds the player characters moving by caravan toward the city of Zodanga. For more on Zodanga, see page 117. At about the halfway point, Tharks attack the caravan and, in the ensuing chaos, the slaves may escape.

THE CARAVAN

The covered wagon is a hot, huge affair with multiple cages for slaves on one of three levels, allowing for the transport of many slaves. Sweat, body odor, oppressive heat, and general despair mark the passage between the Warhoons and Zodanga as the distance slides by under the giant wheels of this massive vehicle. Many hundreds of slaves, along with a good deal more cargo, might fit into this beast of a transport, suggesting the slave trade in Zodanga is active and robust.

Red Martians slavers run the caravan, traders who move between the last great cities making a living off a variety of cargo including sentient beings. As before, the group is put in a cell fit to withstand human strength. Trying to break out due to raw force would be a Dire (D4) **Might + Cunning** test and would invite immediate attack from the guards. Trying to pick or break the lock requires a Daunting (D3) **Cunning + Reason** test and will invite similar hostility unless someone distracts the guards or 4 Momentum is spent for fortune to provide such a distraction in the form of an equipment malfunction, minor argument, temperamental thoat, or some other incident.

Characters can speak more with Patterson and Tal Ptomj. The latter claims this trade route is frequently targeted by raiders from his tribe. Smart characters certainly note that a raid from the outside may be their best means to escape, especially if they possess archetypes who would easily know such things, such as Fugitive, Spy, or Soldier.

A few smaller wagons and thoat steeds travel with the main vehicle, serving as guards. These wagons hold guards, supplies, spare weapons and ammo. Any important core equipment taken from a character will either be found in one of these wagons or will be carried by a guard who secured the item from the Warhoons as part of the characters' sale.

THARK RAID

Thark raiders pick the trade routes between cities for sport, spoil, and desire for honor earned only in combat. They strike quickly and viciously. On the third or fourth day heading toward Zodanga, a group of Tharks attack.

They are mostly indifferent to the plight of the slaves and take only as many slaves as they can easily carry back to their own territory. In fact, killing Warhoons is much more of a priority than worrying about the "loot" itself. Any slaves freed in such raids are often either killed for sport or left to the dangers of the wild.

IMPORTANT CHARACTERS AND THE THARKS

Tharks, however, are given deference; a fact that gives the player characters a chance to secure aid. Tal Ptomj actually knows one of the raiders, as his clan is allied with them. The same may be true of any green Martian player characters who are either Tharks or their allies. Also, if this adventure is set during the Prince of Helium or Jeddak of Jeddaks eras, then red Martians from Helium and natives of allies of Helium gain some consideration, though not much unless they possess impressive titles and position.

Narrators should not neglect characters' allies here as well. If any character spent starting renown for a Thark ally or title, they will find their accidental rescuers much more accommodating. If there is any reason for the Tharks to aid the player characters, they will at least free and resupply them after the raid, though additional assistance is harder to come by and the product of accolades or exceptional uses of talents or Passion-based tests.

DURING THE ATTACK

The attack itself gives players the chance to grab a guard, or for a Thark to open their cell. Better to allow them their own method of escape, and use the Thark as a last resort. The exact method of their escape from the cell might involve lifting the key from a distracted guard, choking one to death through the cage, or organizing the entire group to force their way through the bars. Specifics are not as important as agency, here.

Once free of the cage, characters must fight their way out of the giant wagon. The vehicle is nearly three Jasoomian stories high. Each level has ladders between them, but these are only present on the outside. For every level they must descend, beginning with the top, the player characters encounter four Red Martian Guards.

As with the arena fighting previously, if the player characters struggle too much, ease off and allow some Tharks to arrive to take on some of the guards or reduce the guards to minion status. This adventure, while full of combat and some intrigue, is also about learning the rules and easing players into the setting.

To up the tension, the Tharks set fire to the wagon while slaves are still inside. Player characters must make Might tests each turn or be overcome with smoke. Their allies must then carry them out.

GREEN MARTIAN CHIEFTAIN (MONSTER)

ATTRIBUTES

DARING	CUNNING	EMPATHY
5	5	4

MIGHT	PASSION	REASON
6	4	3

STRESS	MENACE
9	1

TALENTS

FOUR-ARMED FOR WAR (GRADE 1)
Your warlike, combative culture and four arms give you an edge in combat, allowing you to attack with multiple weapons or steady your rifle with ease.

✷ **Circumstance:** When attacking with melee weapons or using a rifle.

✷ **Effect:** When you generate Momentum when attacking with a melee weapon or rifle, gain an extra Momentum.

For a Green Martian Raider (mentioned on page 255), remove the menace rating, stress track and the Four-Armed For War talent.

RED MARTIAN GUARDS (MONSTER)

ATTRIBUTES

DARING	CUNNING	EMPATHY
6	6	5

MIGHT	PASSION	REASON
4	4	5

STRESS	MENACE
11	1

TALENTS

DARING DEFENDER (GRADE 1)
Your daring nature and ability to defend your-self serves you well in battle.

✷ **Circumstance:** When defending against any opponent you can clearly observe.

✷ **Effect:** You may always use Daring to defend against an attack by an opponent you can cleary observe.

Outside the Wagon

Destruction, in the form of a trail of broken, dying red Martians, sketches out the Thark fury. One smaller wagon belches forth dark smoke to the sky while, even now, the rolling citadel from which they escaped sparks and flares in angry flame.

As noted, Tal Ptomj knows one of the Tharks, an adult male who thinks the younger Thark foolish and overly impulsive. Still, he agrees to take Tal Ptomj and his four-limbed friends back to his camp.

The rest of the Tharks think little of the group but don't object to bringing them along. Any slaves not with Tal Ptomj are either shackled anew or left behind. The Tharks are eager to hunt Warhoon, but dispatch some of their number to return to the tribe with slaves and other spoils.

Thark Camp

This is not a permanent residence by any means. Tharks live on the move and this war party camp is even more temporary than most, consisting of sleeping furs and supplies cast under rock outcroppings and shallow caves. Most of the Tharks have thoat mounts. Any surviving thoats from the caravan are also brought to the camp. If this adventure is set during the Prince of Helium period or later, the Tharks noticeably treat their animals well and the animals are very well behaved and obedient — a lesson learned by the Tharks from their dealings with John Carter. To the player characters, these green Martians are more antagonistic, playing the role of unimpressed, gruff warriors and bravos who wish to show they are stronger than any player characters who displayed great martial prowess in the earlier battle. These Tharks won't start a fight — unless a narrator thinks it will be interesting or a player character insults them — but they are not particularly friendly.

However, while the Tharks are not gentle, they are in no way as cruel as the Warhoon before them. They shove the heroes out of the way and laugh at their misfortune, but they do not otherwise abuse or attempt to injure them unless attacked.

Camp offers an opportunity for needed rest, nourishment, and the dressing of wounds. Tal Ptomj, if present, can help secure any assistance the party needs within reason. Patterson and any other humans in the group may commiserate during the night. He speaks again of the captives taken to Zodanga.

The player characters are free to break from their new comrades though, having fought side-by-side on more than one occasion, Barsoomian characters feel a bond of honor — the cause of one is the cause of the other until the blood debt is paid. This is one reason why the adventure suggests opening with Patterson and/or Tal Ptomj aiding the player characters. For Jasoomians, such loyalties may not apply, but the world of John Carter is one of codes and chivalric rules. It is not a free-for-all riot of self-interest, save for the worst of villains.

If the player characters trek out for parts unknown, use the adventure seeds in *Chapter 13: Beasts of Barsoom* to fuel your imagination. Threads might lead back to Zodanga and, if all else fails, players themselves are often roused to fury by a chance at vengeance, and no player likes to see their character in chains. Still, player agency is largely paramount, and if the group wants to venture off the adventure's path, let them.

The Tharks agree to outfit the group with supplies, second hand weapons, and possibly thoat mounts. With many slavers dead from the raid, supplies are plentiful, though narrators may require tests to secure or scavenge unusual or rare equipment.

ALONE IN THE BADLANDS

This episode may be as brief or as drawn out as the narrator wishes. The player characters are in open desert and badlands heading for the nearest major settlement, Zodanga. A road does lead to the city, of course, but Warhoon find slaves on that route. Perhaps, that is how some of the player characters found themselves in bondage to begin with.

If the player characters decide to take the road, they encounter Warhoon raiders in search of slaves and spoils. Unlike the Tharks, they give no quarter and kill anyone they do not take. The narrator can spend Threat to have Warhoons ambush the party during this trip with the following cost: 2 Threat per monster-class Green Martian Chieftain and 1 Threat per minion-class Green Martian Raider (*see the Green Martian Chieftain stat block*).

The badlands are harsh and very sparsely vegetated. Survival skills come into play as travelers are forced to ration water where none can be found. Where the topography is relatively unforgiving, the beasts which stalk it are more so.

Twice each padan (day) roll a combat die 🎲. If an effect is rolled (a 5 or 6), an encounter occurs. The following table offers random encounters the narrator can use as is, select manually, or simply discard. For encounter specifics, see the entries following the table.

D6 ROLL	BADLANDS ENCOUNTER
1	Banth
2	Thoats
3	White Apes
4	Wild Calot
5	Dead Leavings
6	Downed Airship

1. BANTH

Killer banth prowl the area, and two lair nearby. They attempt to approach when the light is in their favor near dusk, when sentient eyes have more trouble. One attacks first, retreats, and attempts to divide the group for the second to attack.

If defeated or tracked, their trail leads to a low cave littered with the bones of green and red Martians. Amongst the calcified detritus is a working radium gun and a fine sword. In a leather satchel among the bones is a map showing an entrance to an old Zodanga sewer system the gangs now use for smuggling.

2. THOATS

From a distance, this group of thoats appears wild. Upon closer inspection, however, they have saddles. Their riders are not present. By following the eight-legged marks, player characters can track the creatures back to their former owners, a pair of dead Warhoon shot through with radium bullets. Who killed them? Whoever it was didn't bother to strip the bodies. Even more mysterious.

If the characters don't have mounts they can attempt to capture and ride these thoats with a Challenging (D2) **Empathy** + **Daring** test.

3. WHITE APES

This scarred and wounded white ape doesn't immediately attack but is clearly half-mad from the pain of infected wounds. This is a much-abused guard-beast that slipped away from an earlier slave caravan not unlike that which the player characters found themselves in. Any characters who have dealt with white apes before know this creature is acting strangely.

This encounter unfolds based on how the characters act. The ape is suspicious of, but conditioned to fear and obey red Martians. That said, like the characters themselves, a taste of freedom goes some way toward the rejection of future shackles. Any tests to get the ape to react in any way towards the group that isn't cautious retreat is a Dire (D4) test and failure likely results in the wounded and confused beast attacking.

This white ape uses the statistics of the White Ape Enforcers found in Episode 4, but it has only 2 menace rating due to its injuries.

4. WILD CALOT

In the slums of Zodanga, wild calots run the streets looking for scraps, vermin, and perhaps even the odd small child. While most are hunted down, some make it out of the city and into these inhospitable wilderlands. A pair of them, emaciated and weaker than others of their kind, is desperate enough to attack anything they can eat. Characters who recognize the animals' desperate state and are willing to feed or care for the beasts may find a loyal companion, but these animals are feral and used to viewing most as either prey or threat, making such a relationship very difficult to establish — increase any difficulties in tests to calm or control these calots by 2.

Use the statistics for calots found in *Chapter 13: Beasts of Barsoom* for these two, reducing their Might and Cunning by 1 for their poor condition.

5. DEAD LEAVINGS

The characters come across a dead body, discarded equipment, or some other reminder that life is hard and death comes easy on Barsoom. Narrators can use this encounter to hint at some future mystery or adventure, or it may simply be a curiosity.

6. DOWNED AIRSHIP

This red Martian airship was downed in combat, evidence of that is apparent to anyone with Barsoomian combat experience. Like a giant, broken dragonfly, the craft is spread over a largish area.

The ship was shot down some time ago. Bodies have been stripped by scavengers and many supplies are gone. However, the parties who made salvage of this wreck were not thorough and observant, or merely tenacious, player characters can still find items of use. Succeeding in a Challenging (D2) **Reason** + **Cunning** test can reveal some extra ammunition, basic melee weapons, and supplies. Greater success may lead to locating a more exceptional item such as a functioning firearm or a stash of medicines.

Episode Four:
ZODANGA

This final episode finds the characters entering the city in secret then seeking Isalia and the slaves she holds.

THE GATES OF ZODANGA

This mighty city, or once mighty depending on era, boasts huge walls of impossibly strong and thick carborundum. One can scarcely see the tops of the walls from the rough desert basin at the edge of the dead sea upon which the city sits. Perhaps, in days long forgotten these parapets looked out over crashing waves.

Gates lead inside but are well guarded. Sneaking in is possible by a variety of means. Four feature below, but any plan — reasonable or outlandish — might succeed if the narrator so decides.

* Using an ancient sewer system, one can access the city. The player characters may have previously found the map to this entrance on page 254 or one among them may have enough of a larcenous bent to think of such a thing. It is not uncommon for goods to be smuggled in such fashion. The sewer is old and narrow, however, and escapes being sealed either by virtue of its size, or the corruption of officials inside.

* Human cargo doesn't simply come in the slave variety. There are other gangs besides the one sought which are willing smuggle people into and out of Zodanga. Should the player characters watch the goings on at one of the gates long enough, certain less-than-noble persons become apparent. The cost of any such transaction is left to the narrator but we suggest the smuggler and their gang demand a favour in return, to be specified later.

* Slavers come and go from the city. It is not unreasonable that the characters might impersonate a small group of freelance slavers or even bounty hunters. This allows plausible explanations for why such a motley crew seeks entrance to Zodanga. Those characters hailing from Helium may need to pose as slaves.

* Posing as panthans (mercenaries) looking to hire on with Zodanga or some organization within the city may gain the heroes access.

However the characters decide to get into the city, narrators are encouraged to allow them to do so relatively easily. They have struggled hard to get here and frustrating them at this point doesn't gain much in the way of drama or adventurous opportunities. Any tests required to secure a way in are likely Challenging (D2), but resourceful characters should succeed with little problem. Any complications that arise from such attempts to infiltrate or enter the city can take the form of increased scrutiny by the Zodangan guards, gangs, or other interested parties.

ZODANGA IN BRIEF

Like any Barsoomian city, Zodanga possesses many traits. While known for its corruption, gangs, and crime, it has (or had) strength to match the Empire of Helium, its mortal foe. It is the underbelly, that skein of illicit desires and those who fulfill them, that preoccupies the Zodanga visited in this scenario.

Zodangan gangs are organized, similar to the gangsters of Earths 1930s-era Chicago. They war over territory, bribe officials, and keep a thriving black market supplied. Some of these outfits deal in slaves as well. Isalia works for such an outfit, which in somewhat grandiose fashion calls itself the Thuria Cartel. Isalia does not represent her the cartel in this affair but player characters, of course, do not yet know this and characters connected to the guards of any major city may well have heard of this group. It is up to the narrator whether the cartel is a small or serious power and whether the cartel features in future adventures.

Their first order of business is finding the red Martian woman. It is possible they caught her name while in the slave pens or in one of the guards' crude remarks aboard the wagon. If not, her singular beauty and painted body mark her. For the right price, information about Isalia is available.

Players often come up with ideas that no scenario could possibly cover. Perhaps your group will do the same here. If not, here are some likely means of finding Isalia.

* The Bar Crawl — It is rather a staple of role-playing games that information is obtainable in less reputable bars and their like. This truism applies here, though it carries some risk. Asking around about a member of one of the gangs rouses suspicion, and the narrator may decide the curious receive a visit from some of the gang and their white ape enforcers. However, they might find people pointing to a man called Carth Val-ab.

* Posing as Slavers Looking to Buy — This works best if humans are in the group, as most Barsoomians cannot effectively lie to one another. A human might be best able to pretend they are a slaver in search of product. Isalia clearly deals in the slave trade, so asking for her raises few suspicions. As before, the group receives the name Carth Val-ab.

* Interrogation — The gang helped enslave the player characters and had further designs on them. Honor demands satisfaction. Capturing a member of the outfit and "leaning" on them is justifiable in such a circumstance. Again, they receive the name Carth Val-ab.

Other methods of securing this information exist and the narrator should allow the player characters to explore them. The important thing is that whatever their methods, they will eventually discover that Carth Val-ab is an important figure in the slaver syndicate they seek and might be willing to help them for the right price. All receptive informants say that Carth frequents a restaurant in a specific sector of the city where he holds court with his "crew."

Carth Val-ab
(Villain)

ATTRIBUTES

DARING	CUNNING	EMPATHY
7	6	6

MIGHT	PASSION	REASON
4	4	5

STRESS TRACKERS

CONFUSION	FEAR	INJURY
6	6	7

TALENTS

LIAR

When lying to fellow Barsoomians, Carth gains 1 bonus Momentum.

BACKSTABBER

When attacking a foe that is not aware of his presence or his hostile intent, he gains 2 bonus d20 on his first attack.

EQUIPMENT

* Short Sword (2 ❂ base damage, Sharp)
* Dagger (Sharp)
* Pistol (2 ❂ base damage, Fearsome)

Carth is a stoat-faced red Martian whose slim, weasely features are offset by ample charm. Unlike the vast majority of his fellow Barsoomians, Carth is practiced in the art of deception, making him a dangerously manipulative enemy if crossed. He is no slouch with a blade or pistol.

Carth Val-ab is a member of the same gang as Isalia. Both rank in the outfit, but are not in a position to lead, should the chance arise — at least not yet. Both would like to be.

He and Isalia were partners and, once, much more, or so he claims. That relationship soured, and Carth now believes Isalia has a profitable side venture of her own outside the outfit. Carth wants in on it, but Isalia knows all his usual thugs. No one, though, knows these newcomers.

Carth wants to know what his onetime partner is up to, and these outlanders provide the means. So long as they agree not to kill Isalia — for there is still love between them — Carth tells them where to find her quarters in the city. He recommends following her to where she buys, utilizes, or sells the slaves. He is certain she does not move them through any public slave market. He offers the one clue he knows — Isalia deals with a group she calls "The Mind Merchants."

ISALIA'S STORY

The outfit she works for is among the most prominent in the city, but Isalia's ambition exceeds her patience. She therefore entered into a deal to acquire strong slaves for a mysterious patron. These slaves are not sold nor utilized in the normal fashion and a high price is paid for any unusual specimens, such as Earthborn, First Born, etc.

She keeps the slaves drugged and asleep in a disused warehouse. There, a "white-skinned woman" visits them periodically, performing what she calls "experiments." The woman gives no name or information about herself, but the money is good, so she asks no questions. Sometimes there are bodies to remove, slaves dead with no visible marks save a slight hollow, withered look that seems more psychic than physical in nature.

FINDING THE SLAVES

The player characters can follow Isalia from her apartment to the warehouse if they employ some guile and stealth, defeating her **Empathy + Reason** with their **Daring + Cunning**. Isalia always has three members of her crew and two White Ape Enforcers with her when traveling or expecting trouble. Their stats are found on page 258.

They can also ambush Isalia at her apartment and force her to tell them where the slaves are. If they are clever, they can catch the gang leader with only a guard of two of her crew. However, if she gets a chance to call for help using her Gang Captain talent, additional help will come from guards she has living nearby and stationed near her as additional security, including, possibly, a white ape enforcer, Isalia's favored pet.

Finally, if the heroes break in and kill Isalia during an altercation, they will find documents pointing to the location of the warehouse. However, if they kill Isalia after making a deal with Carth not to, they have made a grave enemy of both him and the rest of their gang.

At the Warehouse

This ancient structure once served as a repair bay for some long-forgotten craft and has since been repurposed to serve as a storehouse for slaves and illicit goods. Nothing appears notable about this warehouse unless one watches it for some while. Then, white forms may be spotted along the canted roof — a pair of white apes. Across the thoroughfare from the warehouse, perceptive player characters may also note red Martians paying close attention to the front door of the warehouse and some patrolling the area, members of Isalia's crew. This is the place.

Stealth or raw force are likely means of accessing the warehouse. The player characters might elect to attack Isalia earlier and press her for the information, in which case she accedes to their demands. In any event, they must either fight or sneak past the guards to gain entry.

If the heroes provoke a fight or draw attention to themselves, they will face two White Ape Enforcers (total) plus two of Isalia's Crew for each of their number. If Isalia herself is present, she may call for additional assistance using her Gang Captain talent.

Inside the Warehouse

The outer areas of the warehouse store various goods, mostly low-end merchandise the gang traffics in from time to time. However, once further in, past these storage containers the true purpose of this place is revealed. At the center of the warehouse is revealed the ultimate fate of the slaves brought to this place.

Concentric circles of bunks are arranged around a strange central device. Upon most of these, in quiet repose, is a sentient being. In addition to various red Martians are the occasional Okar and green Martian.

Each being has wires attached to their head. These wires spread like ganglia across the floor and junction at a crystal as tall as a man. A device plated in chrome contains the crystal and taps into the minds of those in coma-like states in the beds.

Isalia Ang
Outfit Captain (Villain)

ATTRIBUTES

DARING	CUNNING	EMPATHY
6	6	7

MIGHT	PASSION	REASON
4	4	6

STRESS TRACKERS

CONFUSION	FEAR	INJURY
7	6	6

TALENTS

FOR THE RIGHT PRICE
Gain a bonus Momentum when performing a violent or underhanded task for great profit.

GANG CAPTAIN
Take a **Daring + Empathy** action to call for assistance. You may then spend Momentum to summon Isalia's Crew minions (1 Momentum per minion) or trained White Ape Enforcers (3 Momentum per beast). These characters arrive on the scene at the beginning of the next turn.

EQUIPMENT

✴ Sword (2 🎲 base damage, Sharp)

✴ Dagger (Sharp)

✴ Pistol (2 🎲 base damage, Fearsome)

Beautiful even for a red Martian woman, Isalia is outright stunning to any those of similar genetic stock and appearance. A lithe body covered in naught but scant ornaments and painted sigils marks her as a member of her outfit. She has an aura of cruelty that shines in her eyes.

As a captain, she controls a section of the outfit's territory and commands a crew. She once loved Carth and perhaps does so still. However, since their falling out over business and advancement in the gang, she cannot afford to look weak by giving him any consideration she would deny another rival.

Removing the wires carefully from a particular subject will cause them to slowly awaken, though they will remain extremely disoriented and groggy for at least another half hour. Destroying the machine directly causes a terrible feedback that damages the subjects, killing some and traumatizing others. A Challenging (D2) **Cunning + Reason** test will alert anyone thinking to destroy the machine to free the subjects — let any player character about to destroy the machine make this test, don't have them inadvertently kill over a dozen slaves with one rash action without giving them a chance to stop. Additional success on this test will alert the character that this device seems to be some sort of mental transference or siphoning device, but its exact operation and function requires further study to determine.

Near this array of bodies and strange science are rows of bodies covered in tarps — the remains of whatever slaves have expired while connected to this machine. Among them is an older Jasoomian, roughly fifty to sixty years of age. The exact cause of death of this person and others is unknown, but it seems most likely the machine took something from them that they could not survive without.

Another four of Isalia's crew are posted here at all times. If the heroes want to free the captives, they must somehow do away with these gangsters. If interrogated, Isalia's crew does not know what the device does, nor how to operate it; they simply hook up the slaves and then remove the bodies of those who don't make it. If questioned, they will confess sometimes living slaves are taken from here by "that white-skinned woman." They cannot say why some slaves are taken from the machine by the woman and others are left to waste away here.

WHITE APE ENFORCERS (MONSTER)

ATTRIBUTES

DARING	CUNNING	EMPATHY
7	5	4

MIGHT	PASSION	REASON
10	4	4

STRESS	MENACE
14	3

TALENTS

MIGHTY BEAST

You can always use Might to attack targets in melee, or through intimidation.

HARD TO KILL

You can spend 3 Momentum to remove an affliction without the need of rest or healing.

PREDATORY INSTINCTS

You gain a bonus die when seeking to smell or otherwise sense prey or food.

DRAMATIC RETURN

During combat with the apes, the narrator can spend 5 Threat once to have an otherwise dispatched ape return and attack a character. This ape is considered to have 2 afflictions but gains 1 bonus d20 on this attack.

MASSIVE ROCKS

If an ape throws a rock at a character it will usually miss, but, when it hits the weight and power of the throw makes for a dangerous weapon. All thrown attacks are at +2 difficulty but gain 3 Momentum for damage if they hit. Rocks count as technology for the apes making this a **Daring + Reason** test.

ISALIA'S CREW (MINIONS)

ATTRIBUTES

DARING	CUNNING	EMPATHY
5	5	5

MIGHT	PASSION	REASON
4	4	4

MAKING THE END EPIC

As befits a Burroughs-inspired tale, weirdness and science fantasy give way to frantic melee in the end. The warehouse's chief defense is its obscurity but, once people begin fighting, it is likely authorities arrive. While Zodanga is a corrupt city, it does not allow chaos on the streets.

The action here should be dramatic and over the top. Daring infiltrations, horrifying reveals, white apes plunging through skylights into the room, gangsters shooting off radium guns, and dueling rapiers are all in the player characters' futures. As the adventure began with action, so too, should it end.

If the scene begins to drag, narrators can consider having the authorities show up. Otherwise, let them handle things themselves. After all, they're the heroes.

While the adventure concludes with the successful rescue of the captives and an end to the slaver's operation, much is purposely left unresolved. Some ideas for follow up adventures and larger plots follow.

WHERE TO GO NEXT

Various clues to the goings on at the warehouse might make their way into the player characters' hands. For example, this may be one of many such warehouses in this city and others. Isalia might have a map of such locations, as she is nothing if not curious and enterprising.

The device is not regular Martian science, suggesting the involvement of some mad genius or secret cabal of villainous scientists who seek to exploit the minds of their captives for some nefarious purpose. These "Mind Merchants" likely have some connection to the Thern, or some force from Jasoom or even another world, hence the "white skinned woman."

Questioning any rescued captives about their experiences may give some clue to the device and its use. Perhaps a captive remembers being in another body, possibly on Earth or somewhere farther? Perhaps their minds were even transported to another era? Perhaps they felt their consciousness seep into the body of another and vice versa, not unlike the way in which humans seem to travel to Barsoom.

Alternatively, perhaps the weakening and disorientation felt by the captives is because the device drains a subject's mind to provide some potent resource. Perhaps the crystal is a great container that contains the minds and souls of numerous victims.

Narrators should select a purpose and effect for the machine that meets their needs. If they plan to make their campaign a sprawling exploration of Barsoom and beyond, in this era and others, the device likely transfers minds and pushes consciousness to strange, distant places. If they have other plans for their heroes, then it is likely a disturbing and dangerous power source whose architects may rise to threaten the heroes again, but whose ambitions are more material and immediate.

In either event, it seems these mysterious "Mind Merchants" sought to harness the minds of their victims for some vile end and, at least for now, the heroes have stopped them. These villains may now either become a more important part of the ongoing campaign or they may fade into the background. Burroughs' work is filled with examples of both; plot seeds that later bore great fruit and interesting diversions that were resolved and rarely mentioned.

ENDING REWARDS

The heroes should receive both renown and experience for their part in this adventure. In addition to 1-3 experience per session this adventure takes, reaching Zodanga, shutting down the slavers, and learning the fate of the captives is worth an additional 3 experience. As a guideline, this adventure likely grants around 4 to 7 experience if resolved successfully.

Completing the adventure also gains the characters 2 renown, plus possible bonuses for great deeds and exceptional displays of skill or power.

CHAPTER 17: FURTHER ADVENTURES

> *It is strange how new and unexpected conditions bring out unguessed ability to meet them.*
> – John Carter, *The Warlord of Mars*

As we reach the end of this book, we leave the narrator with a series of additional plots and adventure frameworks to explore. These are not full adventures, but a mix of plots, ideas, and advice that can be easily turned into adventures for *John Carter of Mars* campaigns.

Several ideas in this chapter go well beyond canonical Burroughs, but in each case, they are inspired by similar tales of adventure, romance, and daring. Also, given the strange and wonderful worlds Burroughs created, many plots and ideas from other films, novels, television, and literature can be easily adapted for use in *John Carter* campaigns.

SHORT ADVENTURE IDEAS

Each adventure contains an adventure seed, which is the core conflict of the adventure. Possible characters that would be involved are also listed, usually by their archetypes in **bold text** (*see Champions of Barsoom*). It then discusses possible variations upon the core idea, including example sources from which to draw inspiration.

In most cases the characters in these adventure seeds are highly mutable. They can be of various races, a different gender, and may come from various locations across Barsoom. Also, in every case, the characters presented can be swapped out for similar and established characters in a campaign. If a campaign already has a collector of rare artifacts, vile scheming nobleman, or similar character who would serve as an antagonist, ally, or foil, use them instead of those described here.

METEOR MYSTERY

I have ever been prone to seek adventure and to investigate and experiment where wiser men would have left well enough alone.

– John Carter, *A Princess of Mars*

ADVENTURE SEED

A meteor strikes in a far-off corner of the principality the adventurers serve (either as panthans or sworn followers). After the initial reports of the strike, communities in the area begin to fall out of contact with the capital, including any guard outposts in the area. The adventurers are dispatched to investigate.

Upon discovery, the meteorite is found to emit a strange radiation or is made of a rare substance that has powerful and possibly dangerous properties. It could be used to craft a dangerous weapon or might have dangerous mind-altering or mutagenic properties on the local flora and fauna.

CHARACTERS

* **A Corrupt Warlord** seeking to harness the meteor's strange abilities.

* A **Scientist** who wishes to study the meteor.

* A **Holy Thern Priest** that believes the meteorite can be used to control or dominate parts of Barsoom.

VARIATIONS

* The meteor is a weapon sent by an unknown race from space. Perhaps this is just an initial test of the native reaction; perhaps it is the opening skirmish of an all-out war.

* For an ironic twist, this plot seed could play as an inversion of *War of the Worlds* — steampunk Jasoomian war machines, using a science unknown to Mars (whose technology is based on the nine rays of light). In this case, the initial meteor strike becomes the equivalent of the landing at Horsell Common, and the adventurers' actions are critical to preventing a world-wide disaster.

* Narrators that want to add a dash of atomic horror might instead run this as a body-snatcher, one-mind, control-based invasion. This variant explores the Martian character, pitting their ferocious individuality and passion against the emotionless collective of a life form that wishes to dominate their will. For additional complexity, perhaps the Kaldanes of Bantoom discover the invasion first — and decide to allow it to continue in pursuit of their own goal of intellectualizing Barsoom.

* The meteor is the result of Martian experimentation. Barsoom, particularly in the post-John Carter era, is positively littered with scientists, sane and otherwise. The "meteor" could be a new weapon developed by a remote city, in tests to determine its reach and effectiveness before being unleashed. It could be the result of an accident — experimentation with new effects of the known rays of light, or an attempt to derive or identify a new ray of light. It could also be a failed attempt to dispose of an accident by lofting it safely into space.

* This variation pays homage to *Them!* The meteor releases some agent that affects the native Barsoomian wildlife, making it even more dangerous than usual. Banths grow to the size of thoats, calot trees pull up their roots and move to seek their prey. The agent could be biological, or, as suggested above, it could be the work of some lost or never-discovered ray. This variant is especially suited to adventuring groups that include one or more scientist heroes, as the goal in this case is to find a scientific solution before either the mutating agent or its victims reach civilization.

STAR-CROSSED LOVERS

Yes, I was a fool, but I was in love, and though I was suffering the greatest misery I had ever known I would not have had it otherwise for all the riches of Barsoom. Such is love, and such are lovers wherever love is known.

– John Carter, *A Princess of Mars*

ADVENTURE SEED

One of the adventurers receives a message from an old friend, Haj Matah: he has fallen deeply in love with Solora Parthis, daughter of a rival city's jeddak. Haj Matah is certain that Solora's father will not allow the two to wed. Thus, Haj plans to follow the age-old Martian custom of abducting his future bride. By Haj's account, Solora is willing to be 'abducted', however, she is well-guarded by her father's men. Haj Matah requests the help of his old friend to stage the abduction.

CHARACTERS

* A dashing young **Officer** also in love with Solora.

* A rival **Young Noble** seeking to sabotage Haj's efforts to embarrass him.

* A traitorous **Royal Advisor** seeking to remove Solora or Haj (or both) to spark a war for his true masters.

VARIATIONS

* Solora is in league with her father; the entire situation has been staged to capture the adventurers, and Haj Matah is the unwitting tool. The adventurers have caused Sol Partha significant trouble during some past adventure, and he intends to exact his revenge.

* Haj is not telling the exact truth. Solora never agreed to the abduction, and her panic when she is captured is quite real. Once Solora is in Haj's possession, he strands the adventurers at the rendezvous point and escapes with his prize. The adventures must then find and rescue Solora before her angry father demands their heads.

* Solora has not told Haj that she is betrothed to a man of her father's choosing, purely for political gain. The adventurers must face the forces of both Solora's father and her betrothed. Further, they have a difficult choice: help her follow her love, or return her to her duty.

* Haj and Solora are madly in love, but their families have been enemies since the waterways of Barsoom were first raised. The cause of the feud is lost to the depths of time, but the mutual hatred is still fresh. The adventurers must find a way to bring peace to the two families, or Haj and Solora's love will be drowned in Martian blood.

FINALLY, VENGEANCE!

"Wreak your vengeance to the utmost," was my message to the green allies, "for by night there will be none left to avenge your wrongs."

– John Carter, *The Gods of Mars*

ADVENTURE SEED

Pand Rojark is the sworn enemy of one of the adventurers, having committed some great offense against their family. Pand lives in an expensive, well-fortified estate within the adventurers' home city; he never ventures out without at least two well-paid panthans for bodyguards. Lan Xaxab, an ally of the adventurer, has discovered a way to evade Pand's defenses, so that they can finally erase the stain on their reputation and honor.

Pand's status and weakness should be tailored to the adventurers, as should the nature of the offense. He is most likely a **Corrupt Warlord**, skilled **Assassin**, eccentric but talented **Scientist**, or other dangerous and powerful foe. Pand may also have various dangerous beasts trained to guard him.

CHARACTERS

✴ A skilled **Duelist** Pand hired to protect him.

✴ A former **Gladiator** who serves as Pand's chief enforcer.

✴ A native **Young Noble** who has been turned against the adventurers by Pand's lies.

VARIATIONS

✴ One obvious source of inspiration for this adventure is *The Princess Bride*. Pand killed the adventurer's father, but is protected by a powerful patron. The adventurers must somehow remove or evade the patron's protection in order to bring justice to Pand. In doing so, however, they risk making an enemy of the patron.

✴ Pand is not truly responsible for the offense committed against the adventurer's family; Lan is. Pand has discovered that Lan framed him, and Lan needs the adventurers to silence Pand before Pand can expose his treachery.

✴ Pand did commit the offense; however, the offense was a reaction to a greater insult dealt him by one of the adventurer's family members. (Lan is not aware of this.) Pand is aware of the weakness Lan has discovered, and waits for the adventurer in order to offer them a choice: they can either reveal their relative's perfidy, or they can kill Pand without cause. To choose the first option means the reputation of their entire house will be stained (but their own honor will be intact); to choose the second ruins their own reputation.

✴ Lan has been working for Pand all along. Lan may simply have provided information about the adventurer to Pand, or he might have taken a more active role, causing difficulties in the adventurer's life. The "weakness" is a trap, and Pand intends to capture the adventurers and sell them into slavery in a distant land.

✴ Pand is a powerful man from a city that is a traditional rival of the adventurers' home. Killing or embarrassing him has the potential to start a war their city may not have the wherewithal to win. The adventurer must choose between honor and the welfare of the city.

BARSOOMIAN CRUSOE

It must have been several hours before I regained consciousness and I well remember the feeling of surprise which swept over me as I realized that I was not dead.

– John Carter, *A Princess of Mars*

ADVENTURE SEED

Sol Tared, a padwar on friendly terms with one or more of the adventurers, has a younger brother, Thur Tared, who has long sought his life. Thur has finally managed to execute a plan to ensure his brother's death, without suspicion falling on him. Sol has been assigned to escort a small but valuable cargo to a far city via airship — the same ship that the adventurers are travelling on. Thur has sabotaged the automatic compass and buoyancy tanks, ensuring that the airship will crash well off course, in the wilds of Barsoom. The adventurers must find a way to return to civilization and bring proof of the crime with them.

Sol is likely an **Officer** or **Young Noble**, as is his brother. The two's rivalry can be deep and logical or ridiculous and petty. The exact nature of Thur's hatred will likely say much about his personality and character.

CHARACTERS

✳ An **Assassin** hidden on the ship tasked with ensuring Sol dies.

✳ A **Green Martian Warrior** and their band who seeks to capture the stranded adventurers.

✳ A band of **Raiders** seeking to prey on the survivors of the crash.

VARIATIONS

✳ One potential source of inspiration to flesh out this adventure is *Flight of the Phoenix*. The crew and passengers include Martians from several rival cities, and tempers run high. Worse, the site of the crash is barren, even by Barsoomian standards. The only food and water are the ship's stores, which were intended only for a single trip. Moreover, the local fauna views the stranded travelers as an unexpected feast. The travelers are fortunate, however — one of the other passengers, an older Martian from a rival city, claims to be an airship designer; he states that the survivors could build a smaller airship from the wreckage, and salvage enough of the eighth ray from the crashed ship's buoyancy tanks to limp back to a safe port. Complications include disagreements among the passengers, wild animal attacks, unexploded bombs, and the need to salvage the evidence of sabotage while also cannibalizing the ship's wreck. Oh, and the airship designer? He's just a hobbyist — but the mathematics, he says, should scale up….

✳ This seed could also begin a story arc, rather than forming a self-contained adventure. A narrator might use this storyline as an opportunity to reveal the secrets of a hidden corner of Barsoom: lost valleys, ruins long abandoned to white apes and green Martians, strange and deadly creatures, and isolated cities ruled by cruel despots or madmen. *Battlestar Galactica* is an excellent template for this type of story arc, including the probability that at least one assassin survived the crash.

✳ The airship crashed in an area contested by two tribes of green Martians. The survivors find themselves embroiled in the peculiarly violent form of politics and diplomacy practiced by the green tribes. One of the tribes is willing to ransom them, but the ransom demand alerts Thur that his brother survived the crash.

STOLEN TREASURE

*It was quite evident from his very mannerism that Thurid had keenly guessed the man's weakness
— even the clawlike, clutching movement of the fingers betokened the avariciousness of the miser.*

– John Carter, *The Warlord of Mars*

ADVENTURE SEED

Yerst Ganxax, one of the adventurers' enemies, accuses their friend Ptor Nastam of stealing an artifact from his personal collection. Although there is little evidence that Ptor was responsible for the theft, he has fled the city in the direction of a dangerous ruin, and his flight is considered evidence of guilt. The heroes are also implicated in the theft, due to their friendship with Ptor and their enmity with Yerst. To regain their honor, the adventurers must follow their friend's trail, recover the artifact, and discover the truth behind the theft.

The artifact is intended to be a standard "MacGuffin", more important for the plots it generates than any abilities it may possess. However, it is possible the artifact is an important ancient machine or holds some secret valuable to those who study Barsoom's past. Yerst and Ptor can be customized to fit the adventurers and their relationship.

CHARACTERS

* A group of **Panthans** hired to retrieve the artifact and dispose of the thief.

* A **Benevolent Leader** whose people are the original owners of the artifact and wants it back.

* A **Green Martian Warrior** who leads the horde who lives in the ruins Ptor fled towards.

VARIATIONS

* No one knows what it is, but everyone wants it; its passage is marked by a trail of blood and bodies. For those who wish to add a dose of hard-boiled detective to their planetary romance, *The Maltese Falcon* remains a classic of the genre, in both literary and cinematic format. This is particularly well-suited to a group that includes one or more assassins, thieves, or other members of the underworld. Shifting alliances and betrayals, both expected and unexpected, leave the adventurers unsure of whose side they're really on, and nobody comes out clean.

* Ptor stole the artifact. A relic of long-deserted Aaanthor, Ptor believes it is the key to a hidden vault of Orovarian technology. He plans to use the contents of the vault to restore the city to its former glory, with himself as its jeddak. First, however, both he and his pursuers must contend with the great white apes and roving green Martians that are the city's only inhabitants. Should the adventurers win through to the center of the city, they find that the artifact is indeed a key. The contents of the vault depend on the campaign, but should range from the useless to the interesting-but-not-valuable: a library long-since disintegrated to dust; a box of water chips for a primitive atmosphere plant.

* Ptor didn't steal the artifact; the artifact stole him. Half a million years ago, during the fall of the Orovars, Val Dar Kom, a brilliant but deranged scientist, developed a means of transferring a full Martian mind into an artificial envelope. He tested his creation upon himself; although his body died, his mind remained, trapped in the artifact. Over the millennia, the artifact has drifted from one owner to another. It took half the intervening years for Val Dar Kom to project his thoughts beyond the shell of the artifact, and the rest to develop the strength and techniques to overcome a moderately-trained Martian mind. Val Dar Kom wants to reach his laboratory so that he can permanently replace Ptor's mind with his own, not realizing that his laboratory is now the haunt of monsters.

MANNERS AND MARTIANS

I verily believe that a man's way with women is in inverse ratio to his prowess among men.

– John Carter, *A Princess of Mars*

ADVENTURE SEED

The Festival of the Air is upon Helium — the anniversary of the day John Carter restored air and life to the dying planet. The doors of the Warlord's palace have been thrown wide, and for this one day, all Barsoomians walk as equals as they offer tribute to the planet's savior. On this day, duels to the death are forbidden; even assassins stay their hands during the festival. It is a time of celebration; yet for the noble families of Helium and its allies, it is also a time to find suitable mates for their unwedded children. The maneuvers and machinations involved in matchmaking make Barsoomian wars look like children's games.

For campaigns set in earlier eras, another important festival day can be used. The main focus here is on romance and intrigue over violence and action. Given the realities of life on Barsoom, this will likely be a definite change of pace from regular adventurers. Narrators should design potential romantic rivals, foils, and love interests for any players who desire their characters engage in such pastimes.

CHARACTERS

✳ Various **Young Nobles** and **Officers** seeking romance.

✳ **Benevolent Leaders** and **Corrupt Warlords** alike seeking alliances through marriage.

✳ Hot-blooded **Duelists** seeking to circumvent the festival's ban on dueling.

VARIATIONS

✳ It is a truth acknowledged across all Barsoom, that a single padwar in possession of a good name, should be in want of a wife… and one of the adventurers is the padwar in question. The adventurer might be flattered by the attentions of several lovely Martian ladies, but they're all of rival houses. Choosing one of them might make enemies of those not chosen; choosing none of them might make enemies of them all. This variation is best played with a light touch, as a comedy of manners. The hero in question may be of either gender, although a female hero faces the additional complication of a potential abduction attempt.

✳ One of the adventurer's friends, Taran Dar, is hopelessly in love with the beautiful Kandelia, and she with him. The blight upon their feelings is Hamul Lek, Kandelia's husband. Hamul is the scion of a noble family, but he spends his days drinking and gambling like a mere panthan, and there is no love between him and Kandelia. Red Martian custom forbids a woman to wed the man who kills her husband, so Taran cannot remove the obstacle to their love. Therefore, he asks the adventurers to contrive some point of honor upon which to duel Hamul… to the death.

✳ Another of the heroes keeps being accosted by angry young women and offended young men; before the day is half over, he's been challenged to no fewer than three duels by irate suitors. It turns out that another of the celebrants is a panthan of particularly uncouth nature, who bears a remarkable resemblance to the hero in question. The hero and his friends must track down the boorish panthan in order to clear his name before blood is shed.

✳ While most involved agree to abide by the customs of temporary non-violence, pirates and raiders make no such promises. A gang of villainous raiders could easily attack a gathering of young men and women, seeking to kidnap them as slaves or intending to ransom them back to their families.

RED REBELLION

I am ready to cast off the ties that have bound me. I am ready to defy Issus herself; but what will it avail us?

—Xodar, *The Gods of Mars.*

ADVENTURE SEED

The heroes are trapped in Dusar during a slave uprising. Nutus, Jeddak of Dusar, has been sinking further into madness after the aborted war with Helium (as recounted in *Thuvia, Maid of Mars*.) His son Astok is a brute. Between the two of them they have driven most of the warriors of honor out of the city, leaving only the dregs. The slave revolt is well-organized, and somehow the slaves have acquired weapons.

Nutus' madness and Astok's brutality render them both **Corrupt Warlords**, though Astok may be more of an angry **Young Noble**. They will not willingly end the conditions that led to the rebellion.

CHARACTERS

* A **Young Noble** sympathetic to ending slavery and aiding the rebels.

* A **Gladiator** who has risen to become a battle-tested leader of the uprising.

* A **Royal Advisor** with information on how the rebellion began and valuable insight into how to stop it.

VARIATIONS

* The heroes may be slaves themselves, and involved with, or leaders of, the slave uprising. *Spartacus* provides inspiration here, as the slaves attempt to escape the city and find a place of safety, while fighting off the army of Dusar. Infighting among the leaders of the revolt may doom the uprising before it's truly begin, however.

* The heroes are here to investigate rumors spread through several cities about an organized slave rebellion. They were not expecting to be caught in the uproar, as it was a random act of cruelty on the part of a Dusarian jed that set the revolt off. Now the heroes must decide whether to side with the jeddak of the city, or with the rebels — a decision which will have potentially far-reaching consequences.

* The slave revolt is a complication arising from the true trouble at the heart of Dusar: a remnant of the cult of Issus, led by a Holy Thern, has been manipulating the increasingly-unstable Nutus. The Thern has almost convinced Nutus that he is meant to be the replacement for Issus; that just as hot Thuria gives way to cool Cluros in the night, so it is time for the Goddess of Death to give way to a God. The Thern knows better, of course; he's simply creating a power base for himself in Dusar, with the intention to take his vengeance on Helium. The rebellion was triggered by Nutus' demand for slaves to be sacrificed in his "holy" name.

PRISON BREAK

I must escape, but now, as my eyes became accustomed to the dim light, I saw strewn about the floor, that which snatched away my last hope and filled me with horror.

– Hadron of Hastor, *A Fighting Man of Mars*

ADVENTURE SEED

The adventurers have been imprisoned in a city of a distant nation. Unlike the walls of most Martian cities, the walls of this city are meant to keep the inhabitants in, as the city itself is the prison. The city may be guarded and patrolled by soldiers on thoats and fliers, or it may be protected by its remoteness and surrounded by a vicious tribe of green Martians.

This is a good way to introduce new characters to the campaign as fellow prisoners. It's also a fine way to introduce new locations and threats, with the adventurers first as prisoners, then escapees, then liberators and rivals of the villains in power.

CHARACTERS

✳ A **Corrupt Warlord** ruling this distant nation.

✳ A scheming **Royal Advisor** running the prison.

✳ An imprisoned **Green Martian Warrior** captured from the local horde.

VARIATIONS

✳ The heroes have been framed for (or, possibly, actually committed) a crime in the nation's capital city. One of the city's jeds summons them to an audience, during which he informs them that they have been poisoned. It is a slow poison with a single antidote, which he will give them upon their return from a dangerous mission. The prison city is a haunted place, full of outcasts, criminals, and the mad — and their jeddak's airship has crashed inside. The heroes must bring him, and a critical peace treaty, back to the capital, before they succumb to the poison.

✳ The heroes have infiltrated the prison to find a specific inmate, who holds information critical to the security of their city. He won't give up the information unless they break him out, but he is dangerous and cruel; set free, he will be a threat for years to come. Furthermore, if their escape plans come to the notice of other inmates, they will either be betrayed to the guards, or forced to help even more criminals escape.

✳ The adventurers are prisoners of war, captured by the soldiers of a cruel regime, and sent to the prison city, which they claim to be escape-proof. The prison commander has a standing order that for every escape attempt, the would-be escapee and two other random inhabitants are to be killed, as a deterrent. Escaping singly, then, is not an option; the heroes must band together with the other war captives and work together in secret to pull off… *The Great Escape.*

ALL CONTACT LOST

For five days of cold and suffering and privation we traversed the rough and frozen way which lies at the foot of the ice-barrier. Fierce, fur-bearing creatures attacked us by daylight and by dark. Never for a moment were we safe from the sudden charge of some huge demon of the north.

– John Carter, *The Warlord of Mars.*

ADVENTURE SEED

The adventurers are dispatched to an outpost in one of the distant reaches of Barsoom. The outpost is surrounded by harsh terrain and savage creatures. Communication with them has never been reliable, but now it has ceased completely. The heroes are ordered to discover what happened, resolve the problem, and return to report.

The outpost has been attacked by white apes, apts, or some other savage creature and the survivors need rescue. The apes were driven to attack by some unknown foe, either an enemy of the adventurers and their allies or some new threat.

CHARACTERS

✳ A surviving **Officer** who is barely holding out against the assault.

✳ An **Assassin** working for the true architect of this threat.

✳ **Pirates** or **Raiders** using the beasts to weaken the outpost before they attack.

VARIATIONS

✳ The heroes are guided by the sole survivor of a previous expedition to a similar outpost. The survivor, who may not be entirely sane, states that her supply caravan was attacked by a previously-unknown beast of savage mien and fearsome capability. It killed all the other escorts before the survivor trapped the beast inside the caravan and set it ablaze. She believes it is responsible for the outpost's silence. Upon arrival, something knocks the heroes' flier out of the sky, and it becomes apparent that the outpost's residents have become food for more of the beasts. Worse yet, the outpost was performing some scientific experiment that has become unstable without skilled oversight, and is counting down toward a catastrophic failure that will kill them all unless they can escape.

✳ The outpost is far to the north, founded as a waypoint to Okar and a facility to study the ice wall as a potential source of water. When the heroes arrive, they find the outpost entirely abandoned, save for one lone calot, who greets them with happiness. The outpost's final log entry notes that the researchers discovered a bizarre creature in the ice; they cut it free and were thawing it out for study. When the heroes attempt to leave, however, they find their flier has been sabotaged. Meanwhile, members of the expedition begin to disappear, and others seem to behave oddly.

✳ The outpost belongs to a rival nation, one with whom the adventurers' nation has an uneasy truce. The adventurers are ostensibly dispatched to lend assistance, in order to relieve some of the tension between the nations. In reality, the adventurers have been tasked to recover something important from the outpost. Examples include a significantly advanced flier, developed in secret; surveillance photographs showing the dispositions of enemy troops (or their own); or a captured spy for their own nation.

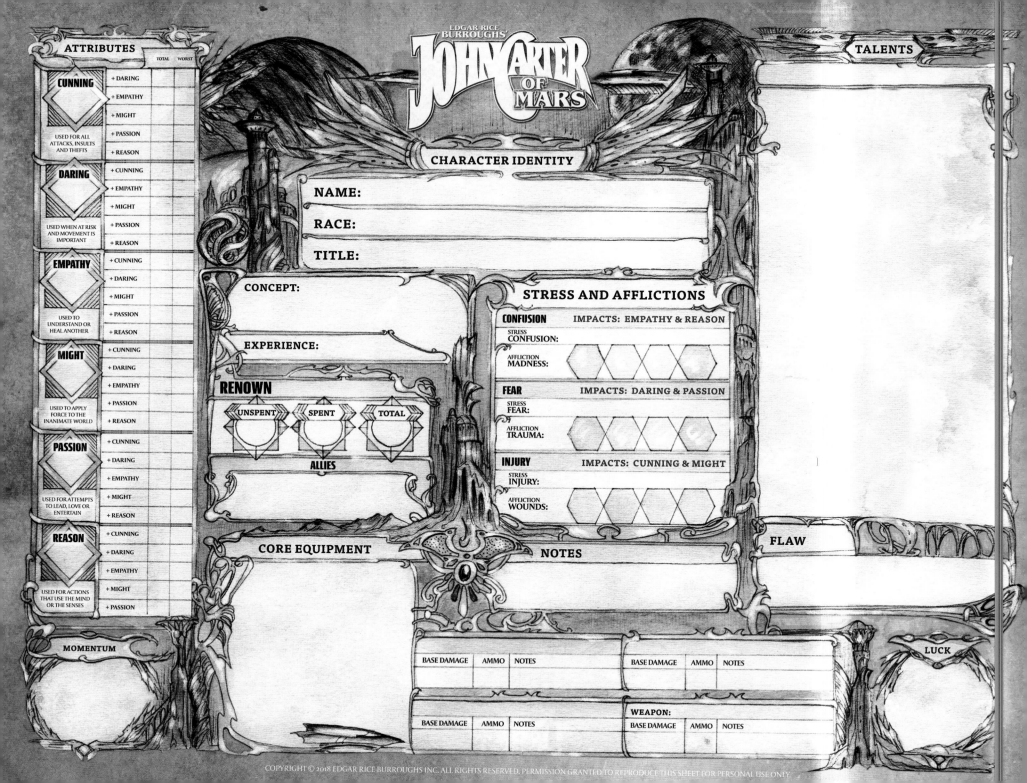

ATTRIBUTES

		TOTAL	WORST

CUNNING
+ DARING
+ EMPATHY
+ MIGHT
+ PASSION
+ REASON
USED FOR ALL ATTACKS, INSULTS AND THEFTS

DARING
+ CUNNING
+ EMPATHY
+ MIGHT
+ PASSION
+ REASON
USED WHEN AT RISK AND MOVEMENT IS IMPORTANT

EMPATHY
+ CUNNING
+ DARING
+ MIGHT
+ PASSION
+ REASON
USED TO UNDERSTAND OR HEAL ANOTHER

MIGHT
+ CUNNING
+ DARING
+ EMPATHY
+ PASSION
+ REASON
USED TO APPLY FORCE TO THE INANIMATE WORLD

PASSION
+ CUNNING
+ DARING
+ EMPATHY
+ MIGHT
+ REASON
USED FOR ATTEMPTS TO LEAD, LOVE OR ENTERTAIN

REASON
+ CUNNING
+ DARING
+ EMPATHY
+ MIGHT
+ PASSION
USED FOR ACTIONS THAT USE THE MIND OR THE SENSES

MOMENTUM

EDGAR RICE BURROUGHS' JOHN CARTER OF MARS

CHARACTER IDENTITY

NAME:

RACE:

TITLE:

CONCEPT:

EXPERIENCE:

RENOWN

UNSPENT	SPENT	TOTAL

ALLIES

STRESS AND AFFLICTIONS

CONFUSION   IMPACTS: EMPATHY & REASON
STRESS CONFUSION:
AFFLICTION MADNESS:

FEAR   IMPACTS: DARING & PASSION
STRESS FEAR:
AFFLICTION TRAUMA:

INJURY   IMPACTS: CUNNING & MIGHT
STRESS INJURY:
AFFLICTION WOUNDS:

CORE EQUIPMENT

NOTES

TALENTS

FLAW

LUCK

BASE DAMAGE	AMMO	NOTES		BASE DAMAGE	AMMO	NOTES

BASE DAMAGE	AMMO	NOTES		**WEAPON:**		
				BASE DAMAGE	AMMO	NOTES

RENOWN - TITLES AND ALLIES

TALENTS

NOTES

WHAT YOU KNOW

WHAT YOU DON'T KNOW

WHAT YOU CAN DO

KICKSTARTER BACKERS

A. Eklind, A. R. Baumann, A.Stoddard, Aaron "Ebony" Johnson, Aaron Doherty, Aaron Rucker, Abe Sargent, Adam Brunton, Adam Clark, Adam Clayton, Adam Doochin, Adam Dork, Adam Longley, Adam M. Coleman, Adam McAteer, Adam Sparshott, Adam Thornton, Adam Toulmin, Adoka Tarkis, Adrian MW Smith, Adrian Tchaikovsky, Adumbratus, Agis Neugebauer, Al Billings, Al Rosales, Alan Brzozowski, Alan D Kohler, Alan Le Couteur, Alan Sinder, Albert Archer, Alberto "Mythantar" Carpena, Albertorius, Alex Bell, Alex De Quintana, Alex J Pepper, Alexander "Stainlezz" la Motte, Alexander Flach, Alexander Geib, Alexander Gent, Alexander Kluding, Alexandre Boisgard, Alexandre Deynes, Alexei McDonald, Alexis Díaz-Pérez ¡De Yasún!, Alexis, Jeremy, & Orpheus, Alison L Settle, Allen R. White, Amaran DeReis, Ambika Kirkland, Amra of Helium, The Black Banth, Anders Stafberg, André "Hoargald" Kleilein, André "Sunwolfe" Powell, André Roy, André Valle, Andrea Migone, Andreas Hötzel, Andreas Löckher, Andres Zanzani, Andrew "Doc" Cowie, Andrew and Monica Marlowe, Andrew Baird, Andrew Bethell, Andrew C. Cole, Andrew Carrick, Andrew DeLorenzo, Andrew Edwards, Andrew Gillespie, Andrew Hales, Andrew J. Luther, Andrew James McDole, Andrew Lawton, Andrew Lotton, Andrew Wilson, AndrewO in San Jose, Calif, Andrey Mabinguari, Andrija Popovic, Andy Brown, Andy Fones, Andy Gibson, Andy Rennard, Andy Ross, Andy Schwartz, Ángel Salas Martínez, Angelo de Stephano, Angelo Pileggi, Anglico, Angry Gnome Productions, Anita "Neeters" Twitchell, Anthony "Runeslinger" Boyd, Anthony J Proudlove, Anthony Pawlikowski, Antoine Boegli, Antti Kuusela, Anuriad, April & Chip Moore, Aramis, Armin Sykes, Arnaldo (Che) Lefebre Piñeiro, Arran Dickson, Artem Slobodyan, Arthur "ShadowHawk" Lewis, Arthur Clingenpeel, Arthur L Settle, Arthur William Etchells III, Arzilia ERB, Asen R. Georgiev, Ashley Phillips, Atillâ Çatırtav, Audun Løvlie, Aurelio Juan Bueno Alvarez, Austin & Kiara Diaz, Aziyadé Koudrine

B.A. Umberger, Balazs 'Glowface' Foldes, Bandelier David, Bart, Bartek Ewertowski, Bartlomiej Zarzycki, Bascu, Bashuk Tror Silentshield, Batro, Bear Weiter, Becky Boyer, Ben Drake, Ben Woerner, Benedek Bulcsú, Benedikt Simon, Benjamin A Hoyt, Benjamin Koch, Benjamin Lecrone, Benjamin Powell, Benjamin W Royal, Bentley Burnham, Bethany Hekatean Heramia, Bettina Gunn, Bil Corry, Bill Carter of Mars, Bill Charleroy, Bill Henderson, Bill Martin, Bill Walsh, Bill, Sonja, Tristan & Bowler Shoemaker, Billy B. Raby, Birragum, Bish (Ireland), Bissy, Black Bunny, BlindGeek, Bob Gilkeson, Bob Huss, Bob Keller, Bob McGeeney, Bob, Jedwar of the White Apes, Bobby Jennings, Bobster Miller, Boring Sid, Brad Bell, Brad D. Kane, Brad Elledge, Panthan, Brad Katz, Brad Younie, Breaze, Brendan Sharples, Brennan Taylor, Brent Collins, Brent Woodside, Bret & Wendy Neeld, Brett Bozeman, Brett-Mad Abbott, Brian "Commodore Startgazer" Whitcraft, Brian "Fitz" Fitzpatrick, Brian "Zabaoth" Kulesza, Brian BMAN Babendererde, Brian Bremer, Brian Butler, Brian Dean, Brian Goudie, Brian Griesbach, Brian Holder, Brian Hubel, Brian Isikoff, Brian J. Caldwell, Brian Koonce, Brian M. Chumney, Brian Marsh, Brian Norquist, Brian P. Kurtz, Brian Roy, Brian W McLain, Brian Young, Brian Zuber, Brother Tom, Bruce Baugh, Bruce E Coulson, Bruce Gray, Bruce R. Cordell, Bruce Turner, Bryan Beyer, Bryan Considine, Bryan Scoggins, Bryan young, Bryant Durrell, Bryce Leland Carlson, Burt Smith, Bwaomega, Byron D. Molix

C J Hunter, C. Ian Avery, C. Michael Hall, Cabe Packard, Caleb Louie, Caleb Segers, Calmujo, Cameron Haigh, Cameron Manski, Cameron Paine, Cameron Taylor, Cameron Youngs, Camille Cauvet, Camlain, Captain David J. Parks Q.N.S., Carl Herzog, Carl L Gilchrist, Carl Pabst, Carl Rigney, Carl Zahrt, Carlo Tietz, Carlos E Restrepo, Carnwulf, Chad Drummond, Chant Macleod, Charles "Dreamstreamer" Alston, Charles Coleman, Charles D. Fitzpatrick, Charles Fodel, Charles Hammond, Charles Lister, Charles Mitchell, Charles O'Hara Lowe III, Charles Q. Choi, Charles Rivers, Charlie Vetters, Chase M Walker, Chris "Cluck Amok" Cluckey, Chris & Brigid Hirst, Chris "Ace" Hendrix, Chris A Challacombe, Chris Beck, Chris Bekofske, Chris Blanchard, Chris Bowling, Chris Bruscas, Chris Collins, Chris Cooper, Chris Dalgety, Chris DiNote, Chris Edwards, Chris Gardiner, Chris Halliday, Chris Hartford, Chris Heath, Chris Herschel, Chris Hladik, Chris Moore, Chris Newell, Chris Parson, Chris Patient, Chris Quin, Chris Sleep, Chris Sternheimer, Chris Tutt, Chris Vogler, Chris VonPickles, Chris Welsh, Chris White, Christian A. Nord, Christian Lacerte, Christian Lindke, Christian Toft Madsen, Christine Morgan, Christoph Balles, Christophe Van Rossom, Christopher A. Bell, Christopher and Connie Kelly, Christopher Dubuque, Christopher E. Harkleroad, Christopher Gray, Christopher Hill, Christopher James Cary, Christopher Joyner, Christopher Kearney, Christopher Laginja, Christopher M. Bower, Christopher P. Crossley, Christopher Peregrin Stilson, Christopher Pickens, Christopher Pitts, Christopher Robichaud, Christopher S Bonni, Christopher Thomas, Christopher W. Dentel, Col., Christopher Western, Christopher Weuve, Christopher Wilson, Chub, Chuck Couch, Chuck Thornton, Ciaran Harper, Cindy Williams, Cirk R. Bejnar, Claude Féry, Claudio Andres Poblete Palma, Claymore Nash, Clifton R. Maxwell, Clint Williams, Clyde Lee Graham, CM Morgado, Cody J. F. Robinson, Colin Chapman, Colin Jessup, Colin Matter, Colin Nesbitt, Comedy, Comfort & Adam, Commodore Longbeard the Cruel, Conan McKegg, Corey Bass, Corey Elliott, Cornelius Milertens, Corsic'Anar, Corto the Calot, Count von Kulmbacher, Courtenay W Parham, Coyotekin, Craig Bishell, Craig Gaddis, Craig Hackl, Craig Johnson, Craig McRoberts, Craig Mitchell, Craig Robertson, Craig S, Craig T., Crazy Rhino, Cris M., Curt Meyer, Curt Wiederhoeft

D. Shaffer, D.Forrest, Dalton Cernach de Andrade, Damian A. Bruniany, Damian J. McCarthy, Damon Richardson, Dan "MaxHavic" Thacker, Dan Doolittle, Dan Kramer, Dan Perrine, Dan Wells, Dane Dueck, Daniel C. Barton, Daniel Doodeman, Daniel Dunlap, Daniel Engström, Daniel Gray, Daniel J Scheppard, Daniel J. Lee, M.D., Daniel Jacobs, Daniel Lander, Daniel Markwig, Daniel P. Colbert, Daniel T. Kulhanek, Daniel W Black, Daniel Zielke, Danilo Bernocchi, Darko Cvijanovic, Darkspi, Darrel D. Miller, Darren Buckley, Darren Bulmer, Darren Cobb, Darren E.M. Shimasaki Ph.D., Darren Hansen, Darren Omoth, Darren Stevens, Darrin Conant, Darryl Brazee, Darryl Harvey, Darth Mauno, Daryl Pruett, Dave "Wintergreen" Harrison, Dave Bardy, Dave Holets, Dave Perry, Dave The Nerd, David, David A. Ullery, David A. Zecchini, David Anderson, Jr., David B. Semmes, David Bent, David Chayet, David Crowe, David Crowell, David Dennis, David E. Dalton, David Edelstein, David Futterrer, David Garbowski, David Hallett, David Harrison, David Homola, David Jones, David L Pinnick, David Laine, David Mandeville, David Morgans, David P. Karcher III, David Paul, David Paul Guzmán, David Penney, David Peterson, David R Howard, David R Miller, David Rache, David S. Robinson, David Scott, David Seley, David Speakman, David Stephenson, David Weir, David Yellope, Dawid "Dievas" Wojcieszynski, Dean Schallhammer, Dear Tony Blair, Declan Feeney, Dennis M, Deon V Beswick, Derek Dunlavy, Deron Dorna, Devilman9050, Devin Croak, Devrim Turak, Dick Boardman, Dicky Miller, Diego Jose Medina, Dietmar Bloech, Dietmar Böhmer, Dimitri Achminov, Dimitris - Jimoebius - Giannakis, Dimuscul, Diogo Lugarinho, Dirk Cjelli, Dirk Redemann, Dmjalund, Doc-T, Dog Might Games, Dokkalfar, Domenic Iannello, Dominic Hladek, Dominique Locatelli, Don Arnold, Don Porter, Donald F. Harrington, Donna Montgomery, Dorlisa McCracken, Doug Atkinson, Doug Ellis & Deb Fulton, Doug Harmon, Douglas Jessup, Douglas M. Walls, Douglas Shute, Dr Bob, Dr. Donald A. Turner, Dr. Gavin T.D. Greig, Dr. Gerd Hauser, Dr. Jim Gerlach, Drew (Andrew) South, Drew A. Calderone, Drew Hodgson, Drew Taylor, Drew Wendorf, DT "Sketch" Butchino, Duamuteffe, Duke Proteus, Dustin Evermore, Dustin Hawk, Dustin Keckta, Dylan Craig, Dylan Stotts

E J SAVIDGE, E S, E.W. Childers, Eamon Fawcett, Ebatbuok, Ed Kowalczewski, Ed Youngstrom, Edgar Burke, Edgar Flaathen, Edo Carter, Edward Chusid, Edward Gough, Edward Gray, Edward Hobbs, Edward MacGregor, Edward Shupp, Edward Sturges, Edward Unger, Ehedei Guzmán Quesada, EJ Adams, Eliseo Romero, Elizabeth Ellis, Elliot Williams, Eloy Lasanta, Elyezer Costa, Emmanuel "Cartomancie" Delva, Eoin Burke, Eric "Cult Classic" Staggs, Eric Blaine, Eric Blair, Eric Braun, Eric Brenders, Eric C. Magnuson, Eric Coates, Eric D. Anderson, Eric J. Lawrence, Eric Larsen, Eric M. Rupert, Eric McCommon, Eric POUPARDIN, Eric Sergeant, Eric Staeheli, Eric 'Thalsion' Durand, Eric Torraca, Eric Zylstra, Erik C. Jordan, Erik Deissler, Ermes Cellot, Etienne Olieu, Eva & Fiona Denehy, Evan Riley, Even Nelson, Evil Ernie Givens, Ewan Spence

Fabio Zanelli, Fabrice Breau, Fabrice Canepa, Farkas Tivadar, Fearchar Battlechaser, Federico, Felipe "PePe" Nogueira, Felipe "fierce tiger" Morales, Felix Le Rouzes, Felix Shafir, Fer Hoyos, Fermin Serena Hortas, Fernando De la Guardia, Fernando Segismundo Alonso Garzón, Fiddleback, Fletch Bruno, Florian Hübner, Florian Merx, Forrest McDonald, Franc Gabusi, Francesco A Bambina, Francis Flammang, Francis Helie, Francis J. Ascunce Mook, Francois R, Francois Valente, Frank C. Carr, Frank Falkenberg, Frank Hart, Frank J. Williams, Frank Kadi, Frank Reding, Frank Serio, frankf70, Frankie Mundens, Franklin DeWayne Dutcher III of Wisconsin, Franklin E. Powers, Jr., Franz Georg Rösel, Fred Bittick, Fred Faulkner, Fred Lang, Fred Monroe, Frédéri "Volk Kommissar Friedrich" POCHARD, Frédéric VALLAT, Freya Sessrúmnir, Frits Kuijlman, Fritz W Charles

G Murray, Gábor Ráski, Gabriel Glachant, Gaiska Gómez, Galen Pejeau, Game King Comics & Collectibles, Gareth Crees, Gareth Hodges, Garett Smith, Garvin W Anders, Gary McBride, Gary Stishan, Gary Stratmann, Gav Fuller, Ged Trias of Mars, Gene Reddick, Geoff Blakey, Geoffrey (Jetstream) Walter, Geoffrey A. Rosen, Geoffrey Davis, Geoffrey H Wathen, Geoffrey M. Combs, George Alan Johnson, George R Paulishak, George Strayton, George Vasilakos, George Wilson, Gerald J Smith, Gérard Kraus, Gerard van Druten, Gero Burgard, Gert-Jan van der Krogt, Gian Domenico Facchini a.k.a. J.D. Porters, GildedKoi, Giles Timms, Gilles Cherrier, Gina Ricker, Ginger Stampley & Michael Croft, Gisleburt, Giulio Cesare Giorgini, Glen "Autobahn" Bucher, Glen R. Taylor, Glyn Owen, GM Rich, GMD Online, Gnarish Peregrinus, Gnome Archivist, GooB, Göran O. Bergström, Gordon William McLennan, Gorham Palmer, Gorka Luis Martinez Mezo, Graeme Rigg, Graeme Smith and M'liss Garber, Graham Lee, Graham Robinson, Grant E Moulton, Grant Erswell, Greg Banks, Greg Frank, Greg Maroda, Greg Morrow, Gregory D. Mele, Gregory Faber, Gregory Sharp, GrimJack21502, GrimMariner, Gruntfuttock, Grzegorz Zawadka, Guerin Payne, Guillaume Hervouët, Gulyás Attila, Gunnar Pétursson, Gustavo Rocha, Guy Davis, Guy Hoyle, Guy McLimore, Gyynineer

H. M. 'Dain' Lybarger, Hank "Burger Buns" Cappa, Hans & Maria Cummings, Harbadix, Harlan Frerking, Harry, Heather Tucker, Heber, Helmut Grillenberger, Henning O. Geisler, Henrik Eriksson, Henrik Sturesson, Henrique C L Jucá, Henry "PandaDad" de Veuve, Henry and Constane Jedynak, Henry Lopez, Henry Vogel, Herb Mallette, Hermann Agis, Highlord Tamburlaine, HIntFishy, Hirod Silverblade, Holger R. Hansch, Hope Rohlin, Howard Brody, Hugh Casey, Hugh Thompson, Hunter Allen, Hunter Crawford & Margarete Strawn, Hyperborean Heretic

Iain McLean, Ian, Ian Kaufman, Ian Lee, Ian S Cunningham, Ian Sundwall of Jupiter, Ian Waller, Ian Webber, Iblis Riote Crinsame, Ignatius Montenegro, Imredave, In Memory of Bob Alvarez, In memory of Bruce Hoover, Ingolf Schäfer, Ington, item_note, Iván de Neymet Franco, Ivan Finch, Ivan Jalencas, Ivan Orsi, Ivan Torres

J. D. Mankowski, J. Donald Hobart, Jr., J. Patrick Walker, J.C. Connors, J.J. DiBenedetto, Jack Kessler, Jack Defevers of Kentucky, Jack Fletcher, Jack Gulick, Jack J. Ward, Jacob Kemp, Jacob Mauch, Jacob R, Jacob Spadt, Jaih Wilks, Jaime Unson, James "pandaman" Forest, James Burton, James Culshaw, James Dawsey, James Dezomits, James Dillane, James Estes, James F tillman, James Folkerth, James G. Jordan, James 'Grim' Desborough, James Groesbeck, James Hamel, James Ladd, James Morrison, James Nagle, James Patrick Parks, James Robert Heller, James 'The Great Old One' Burke, James Wallace, James Weaver, jamie, Jamie Revell, Jamie Wheeler, Jan Harding, Jan Mäkinen, Jan Vetter, Jared Espley, Jared L. Cooley, Jared Nathan Garrett, Jars Tharkus, Jason "Xiao Houzi" Sharp, Jason "JiB" Tryon, Jason B Smith, Jason Coleman (binaryx), Jason Dickerson, Jason Durall, Jason E. Roberts, Jason MacDougall, Jason March, Jason Neff, Jason Pasch, Jason Pruitt, Jason Rosales, Jason Southworth, Jason Stewart, jason storey, Jaume Fabregat, Javier Bermejo Marigomez, Javier Monserrat Rodriguez, Jay Barnson, Jay Mac Bride, Jay Peters, Jay Trask, Jay Watson, Jayson Wehrend, JD DeMotte, Jean Durupt, Jean-Marc "Popidus" Danty, Jed Cook, Jeddara Tanza Dejohn (Katherine Vallotton), Jedediah Scott, Jef Wilkins, Jeff "Kragen" Williams, Jeff Estep, Jeff Iverson, Jeff Lee, Jeff Messina, Jeff Robinson, Jeff Scifert, Jeff Sinclair and Stewart Skeel, Jeff Tyler, Jeff W, Jeff Zitomer, Jeffery Williams, Jeffrey Beckham, Jeffrey Harlan, Jeffrey P. Hosmer, Jeffrey S. James, Jennifer E. Hennin, Jeremy Coffey, Jeremy Epp, Jeremy Faust Bednarski, Jeremy Glover-Drolet, Jeremy Hendrix, Jeremy Lambros, Jeremy Mettler, Jeremy R Ewing, Jeremy Seeley, Jérôme "Elkoran" SINTES, Jerome Chenu, Jerry "LordJerith" Prochazka, Jerry Hamlet, Jerry Weiler, Jerry Williams of San Diego, Jesse Allison, Jesse Roberge, Jesse Rosen, Jim Hart, Jim Karlsson, Jim O'Sullivan, Jim Roots, Jim Spivey, JKW, JM Maanon Montana, João Mariano, Jodi Porteous, Jody Kline, Jody Wintringham, Joe Bowman, Joe Kontor, Joe Malouff, Joe Monti, Joe Mullahey, Joerg Sterner, JoeViturbo, Joey Mordecae Dimmock, John "Millionwordman" Dodd, John & Andrew Port, John A W Phillips, John Andrew Rossi, John Anthony, John Beck,

John Bellando, John Bonavita, John Brent Macek, John Carter McKnight, John Carter o Earth, John D. Burnham, John D. Kennedy, Jo Davies, John Desmarais, John Graham, John Griffis, John Gustafson, John H. Bookwalter J John 'johnkzin' Rudd, John Kraemer, John L DeSalvo, John Lambert, John M. Kahane, Joh Portley, John Matta, John Moore, John Potts, Prichard, John R. Trapasso, John Sneeden, Jo Vikør Green, John W. Thompson, John Wals John Willoughby, Johnathan Greene, Johnn Urquidi, Johnny Redactor, JohnnyVoodoo, Jo Zeigler, Jon Leitheusser, Jon Woodall, Jonas K son, Jonathan A. Cohen, Jonathan Buchanan Jonathan D. Harter, Jonathan E Daigle, Jonat Harmon, Jonathan R. Craton, Joran aus den Schatten, Jordan Block, Jordan Boyd, Jordan ters, Jordan Sanderson, JORDAN SHIVELEY, Jo Cas, Jorge Carrero Roig, Joris Evers, Jory Black lock, José Antonio Ávila Herrero, Jose Antoni Vera Majail, José Ignacio Macaya Sanz, Jose L Gray, Jose M. Nieto, Jose 'speedknob' Fitchett, Joseph "Ofletar the Old" Hepler, Joseph "Che Lockett, Joseph A. Higgins, Joseph B. Prozinsk Joseph Boeke, Joseph Evenson, Joseph Grube Joseph Hoopman, Joseph Jackson, Joseph Kosiek, Joseph Lloyd Pack, Joseph Provenzan Joseph Stone Studio, Josh Cifrian, Josh Jackso Josh Medin, Josh Whitten, Joshua Ayakatubb Joshua Edwards, Joshua Gopal-Boyd, Joshua Hearn, Joshua K Reardon, Joshua Klingerma Joshua Lew, Joshua Rose, Joshua SAJK Kanapk Joshua Thrasher, Josselin Caron, J-P Spore, JPD Juan Carlos Manchado Torres, Juan Tron, Julia Chan, Julien Cordry, Junaydi Bin Baharudin, J Myllyluoma, justchris, Justin Buell Smith, Jus Giuliani, Justin Ruscoe, JWR

K K, Kacy Green, Karamu Phoenix, Karl David Brown, Karl Kreutzer, Karl Rodriguez, Karl Troxell, KButsch, Keil Hubert, Keith Armour, Keith Bieberly, Keith E Cripe, Keith J Scherer, Keith Johnson, Keith Jurgens, Keith Savage, Kelly Fergason, Kelvin Fong, Ken Foster, Kennedy Williams, Kenneth Tedrick, Kent Shuford, Ketil Perstrup, Kevin "TheLawfulGeek" Kutlesa, Kevin B. Madison, Kevin Bender, Kevin Cook, Kevin Curow, Kevi Grubb, Kevin J. "Womzilla" Maroney, Kevin Jandreau, Kevin Kenan, Kevin Martin, Kevin Moody, Kevin P. Harris, Kevin PulpGM McHal Kevin R. Fox, Kevin Schreur, Khanada Taylor, khoshmar, Kieran Dolan, Kirk J. Westbeld, Kir Thompson, Kit Kindred, KJ miller, KJW, Koltor Chase, Krellic, Kremlin K.O.A., Kristen "KEG" Golding, Kristopher Volter, Krzysztof Fabjańsk Kurt Blanco, Kurt Dreflak, Kurt McMahon, Ku B Franks, Kye Norman, Kyle A. Gibson, LA

L Lachie Hayes, laresgod, Lars Idar Hagen, Lars Thomsen, Leandra Christine Schnei Lebby, Lee Chalker, Lee Hughes, Lee Kolb, Lenurd the Joke Gnome, Leo Byrne Jenicek of Jasoom, Leó Páll Hrafnsson, Leon Powell, Leon ard A. Pimentel, Leonard Chuah, Lester Ward, Lex & Lee, Lex Benedict, Liam Elliott, Liam Kel Linda Martelle, Lindhrive, Liryel, Lisa Padol, Lobo, Logan Laren Liuzzo, Lord Alexander & K Bohdi, Lord Chumley, Lou Bajuk, Louis Count Louis Downs, Louis Richards, Luc Teunen, Luc Beltrami, Lucas Sokolowski, Lucho Castro, Luc Heyhoe, Lucy Jefferies, Luis "Trolles" Rodrigue Luis Andrade Rios, Luis M. Brunner, Luke Cunningham, Luke Huitt, Luke La Batlus, Luk McLaughlin, Luke Patterson, Luke Spry of Ear Luke W Cozad, LynnMarie Panzarino

M M, M. Scott Reynolds, M. Travis White, M3rauer, Maarten Nivo, Mad Gav, MadBeardMan, Maghinat, Magnus Bergqvist, Majdi Badri, Major McCroskey, Malcolm Serabian, Malcolm Smith, Manikhon, Manuel Castellano, Marc Oliver Schneeberger, Marc Pantel, Marc Stehle, Marco Oreste Migliori, Marco Pisoni, Marcus and Leslie Arena, Marcus Anderson, Marek Jurko, Mario N. Bonassin, Mark A. Weems, Mark Buckley, Mark Carter, Mark Chapple Baumann, Mark Cockerham, Mark Crew, Mark Edwards, Mark Fitzpatrick, Mark Gamble, Mark Hanna, Mark Haughey, Mark Humphries, Mark J. Featherston, Mark L Ward, Mark Lewis, Mark Leymaster of Grammarye, Mark Malone, Mark Mekkes, Mark R Blake, Mark Read, Mark Roylance, Mark Solino, Marko Soikkeli, Markus Haydn, Markus Raab, Martin Bailey, Martin E Stein & Scott A Saxon, Martin Ellermeier, Martin Gallo, Martin Goodson, Martin Helsdon, Martin Trudeau, Marve Nelson, Mary McMurtrey, Mason Todd, Mathieu de Rôliste TV, Matias N. Caruso, Matt "Iskevosi" Bell, Matt Downer, Matt Hayward, Matt Ladage, Matt Ramsey, Matt Ryan, Matt Shursen, Matt Stafford, Matt Trepal, Matt Wester, Matteo Signorini, Matthew "Hazmatt" Callison, Matthew "J Wall" Wallace, Matthew "Matt-Man" Endicott, Matthew "Thundermonk" Orwig, Matthew and Kimberly Herman, Matthew Bates, Matthew Broome, Matthew C. Goodman, Matthew D. Wechsler (Carrier), Matthew Dean Reynolds, Matthew Drought, Matthew E Hayes, Matthew E. Yeoman, Matthew Jones, Matthew Kiel, Matthew Miller, Matthew Moorman, Matthew R Martinez, Matthew Rees, Matthew S. Robertson, Matthew T Newby, Matthew Truong, Matthew V Howell, Matthew Wasiak, Matthew Wellens, Matthew Wray, Matthew X. Gomez, Matthias Brauer, Matthias Weeks, Matti Rintala, Mattia Giardini, Mattia Norando, Matty Maple, Matz Rohde, Max Moraes, Max Potts, Max Wright, Melanie Ratzeburg, Mervi Hamalainen, MG, Micchan e Nanchan, Michael "Stargazer" Wolf, Michael "Wolfheart", Michael "Scotty" Scott, Michael Beck, Michael Bowman, Michael Chellew, Michael Conran, Michael Cyrion Kirschbaum, Michael D'Auben, Michael David Pereira, Michael Dinos, Michael Feldhusen, Michael Fredholm, Michael G. Palmer, Michael G. Potter, Michael Gallagher, Michael Harley Dawson, Michael Hayes, Michael Hill, Michael Holcomb, Michael J Maley, Michael J. Schuler, Michael Lanzinger, Michael M. Brislawn, Michael Ma, Michael Machado, Michael Miller, Michael Morales, Michael P Wilson, Michael Patrick Thomas Hartwell, Michael S. Lyons, Jr., Michael Sausaman, Michael Schwartz, Michael Sprague, Michael Surbrook, Michael Taylor, Michael Thompson, Michael Tisdel, Michael Vito Costanzo, Michael W. Mattei, Michael Waters, Michael Wright, Miguel Ângelo Ribeiro, Mike "Laz" MacMartin, Mike "CthulhuPunk" Williams, Mike A. Weber, Mike B, Mike Burgess, Mike Coleman, Mike Davis, Mike Everest, Mike Herrington, Mike McMullan, Mike Mihina, Mike Montgomery, Mike Olson of Earth, Mike Robilotti, Mike Stewart, Mike Taylor, Mike Tristano, Mike Welker/Soundchaser, Mike Wightman, Mikhael Karas, Mikko Hyökki, Mikko Kauppinen, Mikmo, Morgan Hazel, Morgan Weeks, Mortaneus, Moxou of Terra

N Nacho Toris, Nate Combs and Mike Cline, Nate Ng, Nathan (Froggy) Phillips, Nathan Heironimus, Nathan J Phillips "Froggy", Nathan Mezel, Nathan Nolan, Nathan Reetz, Nathanael Eddy, Nathaniel B. Krinsky, ND Schultz, Ned Appenzeller, Ned Leffingwell, Neil Coles, Neil Ferguson, Neil Mahoney, Nesox Kalim, Newton E. Grant, Niall Boyd, Niall Gordon, Nicholas D Johnson, Nicholas Gibson III, Nicholas Impey, Nicholas Kricos, Nicholas Taylor Joan Cardarelli, Nick Bate, Nick Clements, Nick Keyuravong, Nick Middleton, Nick Riggs, Nick Roach, Nick, Julia, Issy & Theo Lowson, Nickolas Hartunian, Nicolas Tasia, Nicole Goodchild, Nigel Price, Nigel Rich, Niklas Grundstrom, Nikolaus Bartunek, Nina Blain, Norbert Franz, Norm The First Born Albert, Núria Casellas

O Occam's Spork, Olav Müller, Oliver "DerKastellan" Korpilla, Oliver Crosbie Higgs, Oliver Kasteleiner, Oliver von Spreckelsen, omphaloskepsis, Orko the Jeddak, Otis E. Sykes, Oubliette, Outlaw and Princess of Tor, Owen Clarke, Ozzy Beck

P Pablo "Fenris" Gimenez, Pablo Blanco, Paintybeard, Paladin von Korff, Paradox Girl, Pascal BEHEM, Pat Cohn, Patrice Mermoud, Patrick "Scarabus" Hanna, Patrick & Sarah Pilgrim, Patrick Antouly, Patrick Bergin, Patrick Camp, Patrick Healey, Patrick Mastrobuono, Patrick Mathews, Patrick O'Shea, Patrick Vaughan, Patrick W. Huval, Paul B Martin, Paul Browning, Paul C. Grimaldi, Paul D., Paul D. Azhocar, Paul Dexter, Paul Diaz Truman, Paul Edward Cooper, Paul Forsythe, Paul Harris, Paul Hayes, Paul Hudson, Paul J Mendoza, Paul J. Appel, Paul Kidd, Paul Mallinson, Paul O'Neal, Paul 'Rabbit' Bulpin, Paul Rossi, Paul Sebastian Liistro, Paul Sheppard, Paul Tassell, Paul Thompson, Paul Umbers, Paul 'Walrus' Warwick, Paul Watson, Paul Weimer, Pedro Duque Fabregas, Pedro Rafael Martínez Pérez, Pedro(Te), Pekka Mäkelä, Per Stalby, Pete Griffith, Pete Neale, Pete Tracy, Peter Allen, Peter Baldwin, Peter D Engebos, Peter Holland, Peter Metcalfe, Peter Michael Hart, Peter Peretti, Peter Petrovich, Peter Thomas Guiglio Maccheroni, Peter Trajdos, Peter Wright, Petri Wessman, Phantomoftruth, Phil Lucas, Phil Stepp, Phil Wolf, Phil Wright, Philip Barnes, Philip Hodder, Philip Rice, Philip Skinner, Philip W Rogers Jr, Philipp Jung, Philippe Bouchard, Philippe Deville, Philippe Sallerin, Phillip Avery, Phillip Bailey, Phillip Pontious, Phillip Robinson, Pierre Chaloux, Pierre Leboisselier, Pieta Delaney, Piotr Adamiak of Warsaw, Poland, Piotr Zbierski, Pj & Becky Foxhoven, Prime, PrometheusUB, Protoklaun, Puiheng Steve Tse

QR Quentin Hidalgo, R. Whitehead, R.R. Hunsinger, Rabbit Burner, Ralph Mazza, Ralph Pizarro, Ralph Schonemann, Ralph W. Middaugh, Jr., Rami Rautkorpi, Raminagrobis, Randall S Trussell, Randall Wright, Randolph Brühl, Randy Andrews of the Reno Dungeon Crawler's Guild, Raneul O'Hairt, Raphael Bressel, Raven Daegmorgan, Raven Knighte and Conrad Serge, Ray "MetricTon" Olan, Ray D. Arrastia, Raymond Hale, Raymond Rangel, Rayston, Raziel86, Rebecca Scott, Red Dice Diaries, Remi Fayomi a.k.a. Negromaestro, Rémi Foulon, Remi Letourneau, Remington Riddle, René Schultze, 'Reseru' Sansone, Rhea Shelley, Ric Bretschneider, Rich "Red Martian" Palij, Rich Fleider, Rich Phares, Rich Scrase, Rich Warren, Richard & Sandra Acero, Richard A. Spake, Richard Auffrey, Richard August, Richard C Plemons, Richard Harrison, Richard Hickman, Richard Ing, Richard L. Skinner III, Richard Low, Richard McGraw, Richard Rossi, Richard Scott, Richard Smeeton, Richard Steinfeldt, Richard 'Vidiian' Greene, Richard W. Rohlin, Richard Wagener/Darkeldar, Richard Whitney, Rick Jones, Rick Neal, Rob Briggs, Rob Dean, Rob Kalbach, Rob Lusk, Rob McCray, Rob Williams, Robert "Ayslyn" Van Natter, Robert A Lang II, Robert and Amanda Daley, Robert Block, Robert Day, Robert G. Male, Robert Gagnon, Robert H Hudson Jr, Robert H. Mitchell Jr., Robert J Schwalb, Robert L. Flowers Jr., Robert L. Maple, Robert Linton, Robert M. Everson, Robert Manio, Robert Mills, Robert Najorka, Robert P. V. Davis, Robert Pettigrew, Robert Saint John, Robert Slaughter, Robert Small, Robert Smith, Robert Strickland, Robert Weebe, Roberto Hoyle, Robin K Paul, Rockett-Man, Rockyglenn, Rodger Moore, Rodgher De Steele, Rodney Leary, Roger Awhimate, Roger L Harvell Jr, Roland Schruff, Rolf Böhm, Roman Emin, Ron Kehir, Ron Beck, Ron James, Ron Silva, Ron the " Lone Wolf" Smay, Ronald D. Meyer, Sr., Ronald K. Janik, Ronald Kent, Ronald L. Johnson, Ronald Olexsak, Ronald Watkins, Ross Jackson, Roy Sachleben, RPG Crunch, Ruben Caparros Perez, Ruben van der Zee, Rui Abreu, Runebeard, Russ Williams, Russell Norman Headridge, Rustin Holmes, RVH, Ryan A. Pelkey, Ryan Chaddick, Ryan Dukacz, Ryan Goossens, Ryan Kent, Ryan S. Szesny, Ryan Wymer, Ryan Young

S S J Jennings, S. Klay Sheddan, Sabrina Klevenow, Sadhbh Duffy, Sam Curry, Sam Wong, Samantha & Travis Bryant, Sammo, Sandler L. Bryson, Sandro Cipiccia, Sandy Herbig, Sára Zoltán, Sarah Newton, Sarah R. Phillis, Sayamol Chankajorn, Schlendryan, Scott A. Koch, Scott Aldrich, Scott Barnes, Scott Bennie, Scott C., Scott Cambers, Scott E. Robinson, Scott Forward, Scott Heyden, Scott Hornbuckle, Scott Kehl, Scott Kelley Ernest, Scott Kunian, Scott Marchand Davis, Scott Maynard, Scott McMillin, Scott Mcsloy, Scott Montgomery, Scott Paquette, Scott Skene, Scott Spieker, Scott Tanner, Scott Templeman, Scott Turns, Séamus Paterson, Sean Dunlap, Sean Eugene Amadeus Harvey, Sean K Blake, Sean M Smith, Sean Marius Mahan, Sean Mulhern, Sean Nicolson, Sean P. "Loki" Reilly, Sean P. Phelan, Sean Richmond, Sean Sherman, Sean Silva-Miramon, Sean W Cravens, Seb K., Sebastian Diehl, Serge Billarant, Serge Dubrova, Seth A Gilbert, Seth Hartley, Seth Klein, Seth Tupper, Shahazadei Blackthorne, Shane C. Bradley, Shane Kirby, Shane Lacy Hensley, Shannon "Izagrah Kahn" Lewis, Shannon Mac, Shari L. Armstrong, Shaun Bruner, Shaun D. Burton, Shaun Parry, Shawn Campbell, Shawn Carpenter, Shawn Lamb, Shawn P, Shawn Polka, Shawn Walters, Sheila Davis, Shen Hung-Yang, Shenzoar, Sigve Solvaag, Silvio Herrera Gea, Simon Brunning, Simon Cotterill, Simon L. Vlahovic, Simon Morgan, Simon Stroud, Simon 'Ugavine' Holden, Simon Ward, Simone Giuliani, Sir Phalanx, Skylar Simmons, Slawick Charlier, Slipperboy, Sonny and Morgan Stjernstrom - Barbarianbrothers, Soulsorcerer, Spence Sanders, Spry Sam, Stacy Forsythe, Star Eagle, Stefan Anundi, Stefan Scott Huddleston, Stefan Wertheimer, Stefano Monachesi, Stephan Szabo, Stéphane Sabourin, Stephen A Turner, Stephen Birks, Stephen Bourne, Stephen Esdale, Stephen Graham Jones, Stephen Harris, Stephen Hattey, Stephen Jackman, Stephen James Rehm, Stephen Lewis Silverwood, Stephen Margrison, Stephen Marks, Stephen Milligan, Stephen Newman, Stephen Reuille, Stephen Schleicher, Stephen Schuck, Steve (Erekose) Edwards, Steve A Pontious, Steve Albany, Steve Austin, Steve Baker, Steve Brashear, Steve Braun, Steve Hanson, Steve Hill, Steve Lord, Steve Mollman, Steve Wallace, Steven Carr, Steven D Warble, Steven Ellis, Steven G. Elder, Steven Grove Johnson, Steven Humphries, Steven K. Watkins, Steven Lum, Steven M. Smith, Steven Thesken, Steven Vest, Steven Ward, Stewart Thain, Stoo, Stuart N. Bonham, Stuart Whitehouse, Sven Siefert, Sven Swenson, Sven Wiese

T T.S. Luikart, Tadd McDaniel, Tadgh (Lyon) Pound, Tal Meta, Tamas Malindovszky, Tanith Korravai, Tara Cameron, Ted Cooper, Ted Woods, Tejon Blalock, Teófilo Hurtado, Terri the Terrible, Terry Anschutz II, Terry J Deibler Jr, Terry L Pike, TGabor, Thaddeus Ryker, Thalji, Thayne Blake, The Eisenberg, The Hoeksema's, The Illustrious Sean Connolly, The Masseys, The Naris Lords, The Rangdo of Arg, the Raymond Clan, TheElectricDragon, Theodore Jay Miller, Theron Bretz, Theron Teter, Thibault Wyrsch, Thimo Wilke, Thom Shartle, Thomas "8th Ray" Affinito, Thomas Burke, Thomas Claude Zink, Thomas Dowd, Thomas Fassnacht, Thomas Fleming, Thomas Frank, Thomas James, Thomas Marsh, Thomas Martin, Thomas P. Kurilla, Thomas R, Thomas R., Thomas W. Phinney, Tifany A. Oslin, Tiffany Korta, Tim "Alamias" Cox, Tim "Thoth" Cooke, Tim Brookes, Tim Crothers, Tim Derkoningen, Tim Ellis, Tim Rasely, Tim Rudloff, Tim Rudolph, Tim Stroup, Tim W Brown, Timothy Baker, Timothy Carroll, Tina Engström, Tina Perkins, Tobias Sechelmann, Tobias Southworth-Barlow, Todd Kes, Todd McCorkle, Todd Stephens, Todd Waggoner, Tom "The Monster" Hoefle, Tom Ladegard, Tom Leaf, Tom McCarthy, Tom Mechler, Tomas Burgos-Caez, Tomas Syrstad Ruud, Tomasz "Sting" Chmielik, Tommi Putkonen, Tony Evans, Torbjörn "Major Darwin" Johnson, Tory Cristancho, Tracy S. Landrum, Travis Armstrong, Travis Foster, Travis Pritchett, Trenton Vartabedian, Trev Harmon, Trevor A. Ramirez, Trip Space-Parasite, Troy Brooks, Troy C. Giersdorf, Tucker Rumm, Tuomas H, Tyler Shelton

UV Uwe Peter, Uwe Schreiber, Uwe Schumacher, Vadis, vehrka, Vénuat Sébastien, Verkath Herkais, Vicente Gutierrez, Vicente Sampedro Burgos, Vicki Vicster Lalonde, Vico Montomoli, Victor "Ezzerharden" Diaz, Victor E. Serrano, Vincent Arebalo, Vincent DiCello, Vincent E. Hoffman, Vincent J. Stella, Vincent W. Rospond, Viral, Vitas Varnas, Viveka Nylund, Vladimír "Oblud" Pospíšil, Vojtech Pribyl

W W. David Lewis, W. David Pattison, Wade A. Wilcox, Wade Geer, Wade Rockett, waelcyrge, Wajanai Snidvongs, Walter Anfang, Walter Randolph, Warren P Nelson, Warren 'Sejkel' Seychell, Wayne Weddle, Wes Rist, Wesley E. Marshall, Wiley Marooney, Wilfred Helling, Wilhelm Fitzpatrick, Will Cassey, William Cauthron, William D. Smith Jr., William E. Burns III, William Frost, William G. Edmunds Jr., William J Hearne, William Schaeffer Tolliver, Witt Sullivan, Wolf Larrysson, WolfDawg, Woodrow B Olson, Woodrow Hill, Woola's Best Friend Timmy, Woz, WP, Wrathamon

XYZ Xathrus Nelson, Xavier Spinat, Xerxes, Xthulu, Yancy Evans, Yuna Ulc, Z Stein, Zachary S. Maloney, Zack Nelson, ZahanMara, Zeph G. Ponos, Zephier, 장일환 (Dani Jang)

GLOSSARY OF CORE GAME TERMS

Accolade (page 86)
Character advancements bought with renown, in the form of allies or titles.

Actions (page 63)

✳ **Movement action**
A character takes this action during an action scene. A character can move to any point within away range.

✳ **Spoken action**
With this action, a character can use simple speech that requires little to no effort. Spoken actions never include attribute tests.

✳ **Free action**
A Free action is used to accomplish a minor activity within a turn that does not warrant the use of a Conflict, Spoken or Movement action, such as moving anywhere within Near range (as long as there is no obstruction to your movement) or picking up an object. A Free action never involves an attribute test.

✳ **Counterstrike**
After a character has defended during an opposed test they may spend 3 Momentum to gain an immediate Conflict action. They may only use this action against the character that initiated the opposed test but cannot save any Momentum generated. You may not Counterstrike against a Counterstrike.

✳ **Conflict action**
The focus in an action scene. Conflict actions are normally used to make attacks, normally require attribute tests. Characters may only have one Conflict action per turn.

Advancement rewards (page 147)
The collective name for the rewards players receive in the form of experience points (xp) and renown.

Affliction (page 65)
A long-term effect of damage that is harder to recover from. Each affliction received puts a penalty on certain attribute tests depending on the type of affliction. If a character suffers 5 or more afflictions, they are no longer able to continue in the scene and are blacked out. See below for they types of affliction.

✳ **Madness**
When a sufficient amount of the Confusion damage type is inflicted, characters suffer the Madness affliction. Madness increases the difficulty of attribute tests using Empathy or Reason.

✳ **Trauma**
When a sufficient amount of the Fear damage type is inflicted, characters suffer the Trauma affliction. Trauma increases the difficulty of attribute tests using Daring or Passion.

✳ **Wounds**
When a sufficient amount of the Injury damage type is inflicted, characters suffer the Wounds affliction. Wounds increases the difficulty of attribute tests using Might or Cunning.

Ally/allies (page 86)
Allies are groups or influential individuals that characters can call on when they need assistance. Allies are bought as part of character advancement using renown.

Assistance (page 52)
When a character makes an attribute test, other characters can help to achieve successes in order to pass the test. The character making the attribute test is the leader and the other characters are assistants. The leader makes the test as normal and the assisting characters all roll 1d20 making a test using their own attributes. As long as the leader scores at least 1 success, any successes the assistants make also count towards succeeding on the task. Assistants may not use bonus dice, Momentum or spend Threat when they assist.

Attribute challenge (page 51)
These are used when multiple attribute tests are needed to complete a task. Each attribute challenge has a difficulty and a threshold. The threshold is the number of Momentum that must be generated over multiple attribute tests in order to succeed on the attribute challenge.

Attribute test (page 47)
Whenever the outcome or success of a character's actions is in doubt they must make an attribute test. The narrator will state the difficulty of the test and which attributes to use to get the target number. Then the player rolls 2d20 and any other bonus dice they have for the test. Each dice roll under the target number they generate 1 success. If successes are generated equal to or over the difficulty the character passes the attribute test. Any extra successes become Momentum.

Attributes (page 47)
The six attributes represent the capabilities of a character. Attributes are rated from 4 (average) to 12 (legendary) and these scores represent how competent your character is in each attribute. See below for individual attribute descriptions.

✳ **Daring**
Comes into play whenever a character is at risk and movement is important. Daring covers movement, piloting, and defense actions of all sorts.

✳ **Passion**
Governs any attempt to lead, love, or entertain. It is used whenever another character needs to be convinced to attempt an action.

✳ **Cunning**
Used whenever a character wants to weaken another. Cunning is used for all attacks, insults, and thefts.

✳ **Reason**
Supports any action that applies the mind or senses to work out a problem.

✳ **Empathy**
Used whenever a character seeks to understand or heal another. Empathy is used to heal all types of afflictions and to understand what your senses might be telling you about a person.

✳ **Might**
Used to apply force to inanimate objects. It is used outside of combat to lift, bend, and break items.

Black out (page 67)

Blacking out occurs in one of three ways. First, a character can suffer 5 of any one affliction. Second, a character can be blacked out by the narrator for narrative reasons. Third, a character can voluntarily black out. If a character blacks out they are unable to take any action at all and is no longer a viable character.

Character advancement (page 83)

Collective term for when characters spend experience or renown to improve their characters.

Complication (page 48)

Complications occur when a 20 is rolled during an attribute test. Complications occur regardless of the success or failure of a test. A complication can present an obstacle to further progress, requiring a new approach (like a route of escape being blocked), a loss of personal resources (such as using up ammunition), or something that hinders the character temporarily (a dropped weapon or a stuck door). It does not represent an injury to the character, and is a temporary setback.

D20 (page 46)

A twenty-sided dice that is used for all attribute tests. Xd20 represents how many dice should be rolled with x being the number of dice. 2d20 (two twenty-sided dice) is the default for all attribute tests before any bonus dice are added.

D6 (page 46)

*A six-sided dice used to roll for damage. These are called combat dice and are represented as x ⬡, where x is the number of dice rolled. Special **John Carter of Mars** dice have icons on the faces to represent damage and effects. The table on page 46 describes what each number or icon (for specialized **John Carter** dice) represent.*

Damage (page 65)

When an attack is successful or a danger is not overcome characters have damage inflicted on them. Damage is inflicted by rolling the appropriate number of d6's, known as combat dice or ⬡. This is a damage roll. Every point of damage inflicted on a character increases the stress by 1 on that characters stress track.

Damage type (page 66)

Damage has three types, Confusion, Fear and Injury. Each damage type has a stress track. When a character or creature suffers damage, it will be one of those three types. See below for descriptions of each type of damage.

✳ **Confusion**

Confusion is damaged inflicted on the mind. Things such as complex tasks or the fog of war can inflict Confusion.

✳ **Fear**

Fear is damage inflicted on the will. Things such as a terrifying creature can inflict Fear.

✳ **Injury**

Injury is damage inflicted on the body. Things such as being struck with a sword or falling from a height can inflict Injury.

Difficulty (page 49)

Difficulty determines how easy or hard an attribute test is and how many successes must be achieved in order to pass that test. Difficulty is measured from 0 to 5, with 0 being so easy that no test is needed and 5 being almost impossible. The difficulty number is how many successes are needed to pass an attribute test and are represented in the text as (Dx), where x is the difficulty number. See page 49 for descriptions of each difficulty.

Difficulty modifiers (page 50)

Difficulty modifiers are circumstances that increase or decrease the standard difficulty of a test. These are things such as lighting conditions, noise, distance and even things such as characters understanding (or not understanding) the language being spoken to them or dealing with a narrator character who is distrusting of you.

Experience (page 83)

Experience is awarded by the narrator at the end of each adventure, representing the characters overcoming struggle. Experience, or xp, is used to buy core equipment, talents, flaws or spent to increase attributes. Narrators will usually award 1 to 3 experience per session.

Flaw (page 27)

Flaws represent psychological flaws, social constraints, or just plain bad luck. Flaws work by costing the player Momentum or inflicting damage on them if they take part (or don't take part) in certain situations or actions. Flaws can be changed by spending experience.

Luck (page 68)

Characters usually begin each session with Luck points equal to their lowest attribute and can never accumulate more Luck than this value. Luck represents the characters heroic abilities and allows them to pull off exciting stunts. Luck points can be spent to do things such as purchase bonus dice, take an extra Conflict action or over come an affliction. Players can regain Luck when it is awarded to them by the narrator or by voluntarily failing an attribute test at a key moment.

Menace rating (page 65)

A menace rating is used for monster-class narrator characters or creatures to determine how many afflictions they can withstand before they are dispatched. The menace rating is equal to the number of afflictions the character or creature can tolerate.

Momentum (page 53)

When the number of successes on an attribute test exceeds the difficulty, Momentum is generated. Momentum can be spent to improve the outcome of tests, to gain more information, inflict extra damage as well as a number of other options. Momentum can be spent as soon as it is generated or it can be saved in the Momentum pool for later use. Characters can donate generated Momentum to another players Momentum pool with the narrator's permission.

Momentum pool (page 53)

The Momentum pool is where Momentum that is not spent immediately is stored for later use. Players can spend Momentum from their pool on a successful attribute test in the same way as Momentum generated on the test is spent. The Momentum pool can never have more Momentum than the characters lowest attribute.

Momentum spend (page 54)

A Momentum spend is the term used to describe specific uses of Momentum.

Multiple effects talents (page 43)

Multiple effect talents are made by combining two or more low-grade talents into a higher-grade talent. The grade of a multiple effect talent is equal to the combined grades of each effect of the talent.

Narrator (page 140)

The narrator is the person who runs and prepares the game. They control all the characters (except the player characters) and decide how they act and what they do. They are responsible for setting scenes, establishing the environment and determining the unfolding events. They must interpret how the rules apply to a given situation and decide on the difficulty of tasks and rule on the outcome of unusual situations or disagreements. The narrator is not playing against the players.

Narrator character (page 67)

Narrator characters are any character or creature under the narrator's control. This is all of the characters and creatures aside from the player characters

Opposed test (page 49)

An opposed test happens when one player resists the actions of another. An example of this would be during combat. Both characters make an attribute test. To decide who wins the opposed test the amount of Momentum generated on each test is compared. The character that generated the most Momentum wins the opposed test.

Player characters (page 6)

Player characters are the characters that the player controls. They are the player's representation or avatar in the game. Player characters are also called player heroes,

Players (page 6)

*Players are the people who are taking part in a game of **John Carter of Mars**.*

Qualities (page 71)

Some weapons or attacks within the game have qualities. These are ways of dealing extra damage in combat. They come into play when an effect is rolled on the combat dice and some attacks always have qualities. The qualities are Dishonorable, Explosive, Fearsome, Psychic, Quiet and Sharp.

Range (page 59)

Range is how distance is described for the purposes of movement and combat. Ranges are not measured by specific distances but by four categories and one state. See below for descriptions of each.

✳ **Immediate**

The state of Immediate is when an object or character is within arm's length of the acting character. Immediate is something that the player can declare when the character is moving.

✳ **Near**

Not immediately adjacent to but close enough to reach a target fairly easily. Characters can shoot at, speak with, and generally interact with anyone Near.

✳ **Away**

Away distances place a target apart from others. This includes places that can only be reached by dramatic actions such as leaping and climbing.

✳ **Far**

Reachable only by the most long-distance attacks or methods of interaction. Most firearms have a range of Far, and this generally covers the furthest a character can see.

✳ **Too far**

Targets that are Too Far may be visible or otherwise detectable, but they are beyond the ability to interact with physically. Communication requires special technology.

Recovery (page 67)

Recovery refers to the way in which a character recovers from stress or treats or recovers an affliction. All stress is lost at the end of a scene. During a scene a character can spend 1 Momentum to remove one point of stress. Characters can also attempt to remove the stress of another character or ally by using the attribute test listed under each damage type. To recover or treat an affliction, a character must make the appropriate attribute test listed under each affliction, following the guidelines on page 67.

Renown (page 84)

Renown is awarded to a character when they do heroic feats. It represents their fame throughout Barsoom. Renown can be used to purchase allies and titles as part of character advancement. Renown does not have to be spent immediately and can be saved for later use.

Reputation (page 85)

Reputation is how well known you are and how you are perceived by the people of Barsoom. Your total renown (spent and unspent) determines your reputation according to the table on page 85.

Round (page 57)

A round is the period of time it takes all characters in a scene to take one turn each.

Stress (page 65)

Stress is how characters are affected by damage. Each point of damage a character receives adds one point of stress to the stress track related to the type of damage inflicted.

Stress track (page 65)

Each time a character suffers damage, stress is added equal to the damage to the stress track of the type damage type inflicted. Fear damage adds stress to the Fear stress track, Confusion damage adds stress to the Confusion stress track and Injury damage adds stress to the Injury stress track.

Talents (page 38)

Talents represent skill or mastery of certain abilities and allow characters to boost their chances of success on certain actions. Talents have a circumstance that determines when the talent can come into play, and an effect that happens when the circumstance is met. Talents are graded according to how powerful, broad or narrow of an effect they have.

Target number (page 47)

The target number is the number that must be rolled under on an attribute test in order to succeed. The target number is calculated by adding together the values of the two attributes used for the test.

Threat (page 145)

Threat is used by narrators to increase the tension and drama in a scene. Narrators can spend it in the same way players use Momentum, players can pay in Threat instead of using Momentum and narrators can use it for other effects such as bringing in reinforcements or to alter the scene.

Threat pool (page 145)

The Threat pool is the collection of Threat that a narrator has, similar to how players have a Momentum pool. When narrator characters generate Momentum on rolls, they can convert this to Threat and add it to the Threat pool.

Title (page 89)

A type of accolade that can be purchased with renown to advance a player character.

Turn order (page 57)

The turn order is the order in which player characters and narrator characters take their turns in an action scene. This can be determined in a few ways as described on page 57.

Voluntary black out (page 67)

A player can decide to voluntarily black out, this costs them any remaining Luck points they have and removes them from the scene. The character can take no further damage and awakes in the next scene with 1 less affliction, but may be in any situation the narrator decides is appropriate.

Voluntary failure (page 51)

A choice that a character can take with the narrator's permission when they are asked to make an attribute test where they stand to gain or loose something significant. A character can choose to fail the test, giving the narrator 1 point of Threat and gaining 1 Luck point for themselves.

INDEX

FURTHER ADVENTURES

TALENTS INDEX

BEAST TALENT INDEX

FLAW INDEX

PLAYER CHARACTERS ARCHETYPES

NARRATOR CHARACTERS ARCHETYPES

TABLES AND IMPORTANT SIDEBARS INDEX

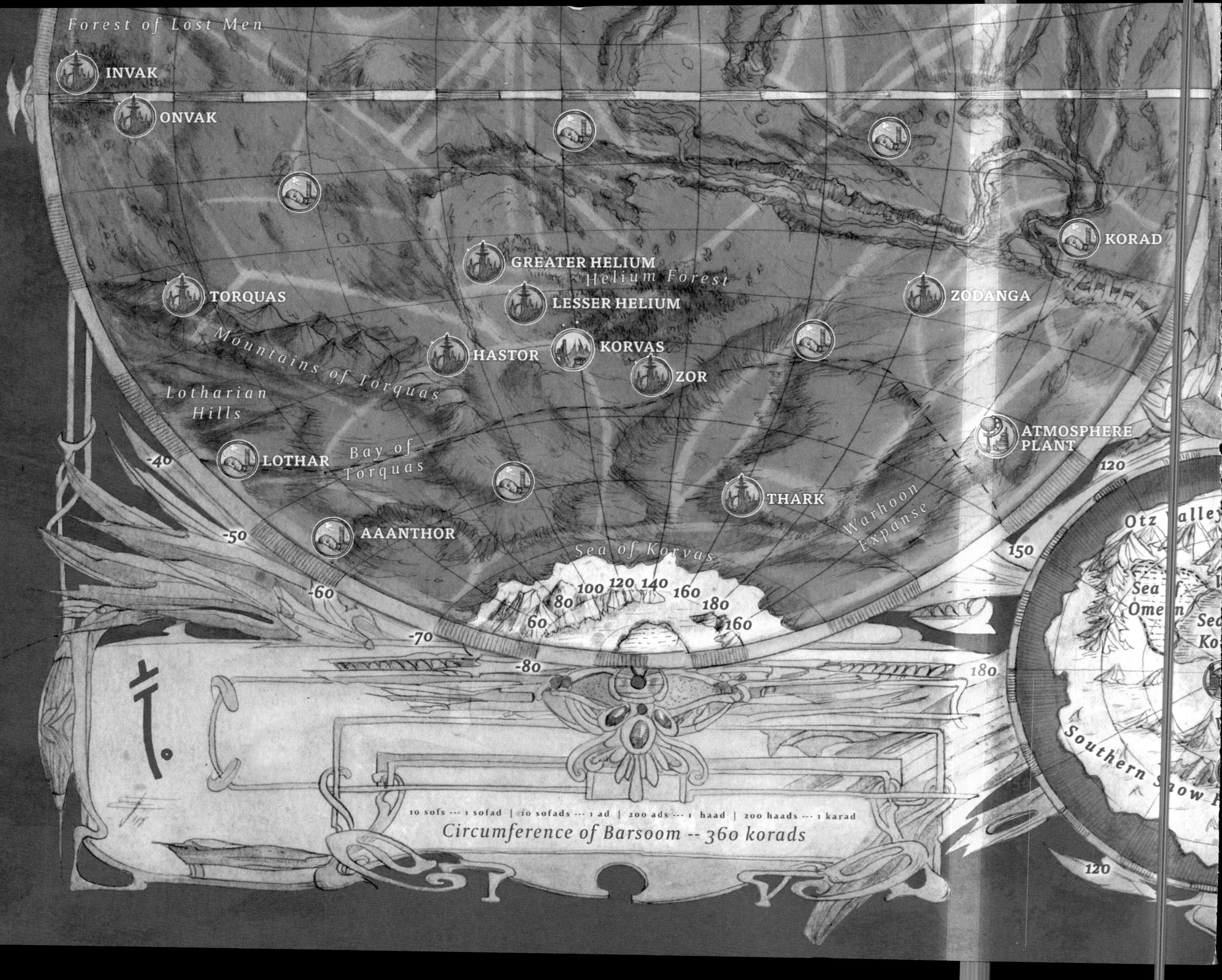

Forest of Lost Men

INVAK

ONVAK

KORAD

GREATER HELIUM

Helium Forest

TORQUAS

LESSER HELIUM

ZODANGA

Mountains of Torquas

HASTOR

KORVAS

ZOR

Lotharian Hills

ATMOSPHERE PLANT

-40

LOTHAR

Bay of Torquas

120

THARK

Warhoon Expanse

-50

AAANTHOR

150

Sea of Korvas

100 120 140

-60

160

80

180

60

160

-70

180

-80

Otz Valley

Sea of Omean

Sea of Korus

Southern Snow

120

10 sofs --- 1 sofad | 10 sofads --- 1 ad | 200 ads --- 1 haad | 200 haads --- 1 karad

Circumference of Barsoom -- 360 korads